Alfred M. Fuller

GENEALOGICAL AND

PERSONAL HISTORY

OF

FAYETTE COUNTY,

PENNSYLVANIA

UNDER THE EDITORIAL SUPERVISION OF

JOHN W. JORDAN, LL.D.

Librarian of Pennsylvania Historical Society, Philadelphia

AND

JAMES HADDEN,

of Uniontown, Pennsylvania; author of "Washington and Braddock's Expeditions Through Fayette County," and the reproductions of Judge James Veech's work entitled "The Monongahela of Old, or Historical Sketches of Southwestern Pennsylvania to the Year 1800"

ILLUSTRATED

Volume II.

NEW YORK
LEWIS HISTORICAL PUBLISHING COMPANY
1912

1233379

GENEALOGICAL

AND

BIOGRAPHICAL

West Virginia He owned a large estate, but was not a slave holder He married Lyda Travitt, also born in Virginia, where both died leaving issue 1 Anna, married Joseph Young, a gunsmith, and resides in West Virginia 2 Aaron, now residing in Fayette county, he married a Miss Workman 3 Mary, married John Allen, a farmer of Fayette county 4 Martin, a miner of Fayette county, married and has issue 5 William, of whom further

(II) William, son of Aaron F and Lyda (Travitt) Haney, was born in Marshall county, West Virginia February 2 1839, died in Putnam county, Virginia, February 2, 1889 He grew to manhood in Marshall county, receiving his education in the school of his neighborhood He was a coal miner until his enlistment in a West Virginia regiment, serving two years in the Union army, during the war between the states After the war he came to Fayette county, Pennsylvania, locating at Dawson He worked in the Brown and Cochran coal mines until 1887, then moved to Putnam county Virginia, on the Big Kanawha river, where he died two years later Both William Haney and wife were members of the Methodist Episcopal church

He married Harriet Workman, born in Marshall county West Virginia, in September, 1842, who survives him She is a daughter of Joshua and Rebecca Workman, born in Virginia, who lived on a farm in that state until death Their children 1 Robert, deceased, was a miner of Fayette county, married Jane Norris 2 Ebenezer, a miner, now living in Charleroi, Pennsylvania; married Mary Norris 3 Harriet of previous mention, widow of William Haney 4 A son died young 5 A daughter died young Children of William and Harriet Haney 1 Henry, died aged two years 2 Rebecca, married Henry Huffini, a miner, now residing at Vanderbilt, Pennsylvania 3 Aaron, died aged twelve years 4 John W of whom further 5 Lyda, married Wesley Goe, a fire boss in the employ of the W J Rainey Company at their mines near Vanderbilt 6 Sarah, residing with her aged mother 7 Job, unmarried, a railroad employee in Ohio

(III) John W, son of William and Har-

riet (Workman) Haney, was born in East Liberty, Fayette county, Pennsylvania, July 22, 1866 He attended the public schools in Lower Tyrone township, Fayette county, Pennsylvania, having previously attended in Putnam county, Virginia He returned to the latter county in 1887 with his parents, remaining until his father's death in 1889 In 1890 he came to Jimtown, Fayette county, Pennsylvania, where for seven years he worked in the coal mines in different capacities He was a clerk in hotels at Dawson and Brownsville, continuing in that business for three years He then entered the employ of the Pittsburgh & Lake Erie railroad as brakeman and after four years service was promoted to the position of conductor After five years service as conductor he was appointed yard master at Dickerson Run which position he now holds He is a Republican in politics a member of the United Brotherhood of Trainmen and of the Knights of Malta He married January 11, 1899, Ida M Ramsey, born near Harrisburg, Pennsylvania, daughter of John and Mary Ramsey, both deceased John Ramsey was a contracting stone mason, moved to Dawson, Fayette county, where he died Children of John W Haney Charles born June 10, 1900, Donald April 23, 1902, Gladys, March 7, 1904, Margaret, December 27, 1907 Mildred, twin of Margaret The family home is in Liberty, Pennsylvania, where Mr Haney built a residence in 1906

Five generations of this family have resided in America RANDOL The first of these generations emigrated from Ireland, and nothing much is known of that and the succeeding generation in America The third generation was represented by George Randol who married Mary Kennedy, and both were natives of what is now northern West Virginia He was a farmer and later in life removed to Brownsville, Pennsylvania, where he died George Randol and wife were the parents of seven children, as follows 1 Samuel, who lived in Allegheny county, Pennsylvania he served in the Federal army in time of the civil war 2 William, also served in the Union cause in the civil war after which he resided in Pittsburgh, Pennsylvania 3 Alexander, served in the Confederate army 4 F——, was a well-to-do farmer 5 Robert, was a farmer 6 Jane, married and lived near Pittsburgh, Pennsylvania 7 Joseph, of whom further The above family were all reared and lived on the old home farm until after the civil war when they became much scattered, most of them going to Allegheny county, Pennsylvania

(IV) Joseph, son of George and Mary (Kennedy) Randol, was born near Fairmont, West Virginia, in July, 1832, died in September, 1904 He was reared on a farm where he remained with his father until the breaking out of the civil war, when he engaged as a deck hand on a river boat Later he returned to farm life where he spent the remainder of his days Politically he was a Democrat, and in his church faith was a Methodist Episcopalian He married Hannah Elizabeth Rodabaugh, born in Preston county Virginia, near the north line of the state, in August, 1825 She was of German descent, the family coming from the Fatherland, she being of the fourth generation in America The parents were sturdy farmers, and both natives of West Virginia Joseph and Hannah Elizabeth (Rodabaugh) Randol had five children as follows 1 Maggie married John Shaffer, a farmer now living in Monongahela county, West Virginia 2 George A, of whom further 3 and 4 (twins) William, deceased married Almeda Hostetler and was the father of four children, he was a railroad man Frances, married Will Mollison, she is now deceased 5 Sarah, married Robert Dean and they reside in Monongahela county, West Virginia, on a farm

(V) George A, son of Joseph and Hannah Elizabeth (Rodabaugh) Randol, was born February 19, 1858, near Morgantown, West Virginia He was educated in the common schools of West Virginia, and at the age of twenty-one years commenced to mine coal at the old White mines in Fayette county, Pennsylvania He gave all of his time up to the years of his majority to his father, then started in life for himself Many years he dug coal, drew coke and was variously engaged in the mines of the Rainey Coal Company In 1886 he went to the Fort Hill works above Dawson, where he has generally been engaged ever since in mining operations In 1900 he was promoted to yard boss at Fort Hill and still holds this position He is thoroughly posted in most of the details in coal mining and shipping He votes the Democratic ticket, nationally, but locally chooses the best man, regardless of party lines He belongs to the Independent Order of Odd Fellows, the Modern Woodmen and keeps abreast with the workings of these two orders He married, March 15, 1884 Mary Jacobs, born near Laurel Hill Church, Fayette county, Pennsylvania, May 1, 1856 daughter of John and Jane (Hainey) Jacobs, both natives of Fayette county Her father is a farmer by occupation

DULIERE The Duliere family of Point Marion, Fayette county, Pennsylvania, were originally from Belgium, Europe, where Henry Duliere was born, a son of Leopold Duliere, of Ransart, Belgium, a contractor of mason work, and his wife, Marie Oome (Quinet) Duliere Their children were Fannie, Onoline, Joseph, Henry, Pierre, Louis, Paul, Lucien, Fortune

(II) Henry, son of Leopold Duliere was born in the town of Jumet Belgium August 16, 1838, died in Meadville, Pennsylvania, July 21, 1886 He was a window glass worker and until 1882 worked at his trade in his native land In March of that year he emigrated to the United States, locating in Meadville, Pennsylvania In the summer of the same year he sent for his family and on September 15 1882, his wife and five children sailed from Antwerp Belgium landing in New York, September 30. reaching Meadville, October 4, following The family kept together until 1886 when Henry Duliere, the father, died He had become a naturalized citizen, voted with the Republican party and was a Catholic in religion He married Olphonsine Dufour born in Jumet, Belgium October 11 1844 who survives him She is a daughter of Nicholas Joseph and Henriette (Lechien) Dufour, both native Belgians Children of Henry and Olphonsine Duliere 1 Angele, born at Jumet, Belgium, September 2, 1864 2 Florise, born in Jemappes, Belgium, (also the birth place of all the following children) 3 Estel, born March 6, 1869 died January 26, 1870 4 Este Zoe, June 9, 1871 5 Olphonsine Blanche September 18, 1873 . 6 Gaston George, April 12 1876 These five children all accompanied their mother to the United States and joined their father in Meadville

(III) Florise, eldest son of Henry and Olphonsine (Dufour) Duliere, was born May 25, 1867, at Jemappes, Province of Hainant, Belgium He was educated in the public schools, and was fifteen years of age when the family came over to the United States

He began his residence in Meadville, Pennsylvania, October 4, 1882, continuing there seven years He learned the glass blower's trade and worked at window glass making until 1907 His father died in 1886 and in 1889 he moved to Findlay Ohio working at his trade in that city four years In 1893 he moved to Dunkirk, Indiana, remaining there seven years In 1900 he located in Point Marion, Fayette county Pennsylvania, where he established in business as a manufacturer of window glass In 1902 he was elected secretary of the Jeannette Window Glass Company, and since 1908 has been manager of the company He has been very successful as a glass manufacturer and is the capable efficient manager of a prosperous enterprise He was one of the organizers and since August 9, 1909, a director of the People's National Bank of Point Marion

He is a Republican in politics and in 1908 was elected a member of the borough council He is a communicant of the Methodist Episcopal church, and a member of the Benevolent and Protective Order of Elks

He married June 10 1892, at New Brighton Beaver county, Pennsylvania, Orlena Sherwood, born there December 21, 1874, daughter of William Sherwood, a pottery manufacturer, and his wife, Esther E (Couch) Sherwood She has a brother John Snellingburg Sherwood and a sister, Mae Olive, married George Cable Children of Mr and Mrs Duliere born at Point Marion, Pennsylvania Sherwood Florise, born August 20, 1903, William Henry, January 21, 1908

McSHANE The present representative of this family in South Union township, Fayette county, Pennsylvania, although born in the state of Iowa, descends from an early Fayette county settler, Daniel McShane, born in Ireland, who accompanied by his wife, Jane (McDonald) McShane, came from the north of Ireland to America in 1780, settling in New Jersey later coming to Fayette county, Pennsylvania He had two sons John, Barney, of whom further

(II) Barney, son of Daniel and Jane (McDonald) McShane was born in Fayette county, Pennsylvania, in 1799, died in Linn county, Iowa in 1879 Accompanied by his family, he removed to Iowa in 1852 He married Betsy Romine, a native of Virginia, whose death occurred in 1880 Children, all of whom are deceased but John Frank, Luther, Jacob William, of whom further, David, Eliza, John, Porter

(III) William, son of Barney and Betsy (Romine) McShane was born in Woodbridgetown, Fayette county, Pennsylvania, February 20, 1829, died October 29, 1898, in German township He was his father's assistant on the farm and in his stock dealings He attended the public schools, receiving a fair education He accompanied his father to Iowa remaining until 1865, then returned to Fayette county, settling in North Union, later in German township, where he became a farmer also engaged in the buying and shipping of live stock He was a good judge of cattle and made his business a profitable one He was a Democrat in politics, and a member of the Baptist church He married, in 1852, Elizabeth Hurst, born in Georges township, Fayette county, Pennsylvania, daughter of Nathaniel Hurst, a farmer and miller at what is now Ruble's Mills near Smithfield He died in Uniontown in 1875, aged eighty years He married Mary Eliza Wells Children of Mr and Mrs Hurst 1 Sarah, married Thomas Batton 2 Elizabeth of previous mention died April 15 1875, aged forty-five years 3 Julia, married Lee Tate 4 Isaac, married Catherine Griffin 5 Rebecca, married Joseph Baker 6 Martha, married William Rankin 7 Porter, killed when a boy, while hauling logs 8 Frances, married Stephen Hankins

Children of Mr and Mrs McShane 1 Mary, married Hugh Cameron and lives in Linn county, Iowa 2 Elizabeth, lives in Uniontown 3 Anna, deceased married George Strouble, now a farmer of German township 4 William of whom further 5 Julia, married Edward Porter now assistant superintendent of the Union Supply Company at Uniontown 6 John died 1878 aged thirteen years 7 Martha married William Grove a farmer of German township 8 Porter, married Annie Mosier

(IV) William (2) son of William (1) and Elizabeth (Hurst) McShane, was born near Cedar Rapids, Iowa, March 11 1861 He was four years of age when his father returned to Fayette county, Pennsylvania, settling first in North Union township later lived in other parts of the county, William attending different public schools After growing to man's estate he spent seven years in Iowa and Colorado farming and working in the gold mines He then returned to Fayette county spending three years in German township, then was five years in Uniontown He then located on a farm in South Union township where he is now living He is a stockholder and for three years was a director of the Buchanan Coal & Coke Company of West Virginia He has served as school director, the present being the fifth year in that office He is a Democrat in politics and with his wife belongs to the Baptist church is a Master Mason of Mahaska Lodge New Sharon Iowa

He married, December 10 1890, Anna Vail, born in Menallen township, Fayette county Pennsylvania daughter of Abraham Vail of Welsh descent a farmer of Menallen township later of Iowa where he died August 18 1887 aged fifty-six years He married Ellen Dixon, also born in Menallen township who survives him now living at New Sherwood Iowa, aged seventy-two years Children of Mr and Mrs McShane 1 Elizabeth born November 9, 1892 a student at Vassar College, where she recently won signal honor in a discussion of the now vital question, Initiative, Referendum and Recall 2 Edward born August 2, 1894 student at Uniontown high school 3 Ruth,

born May 27, 1896, student in Uniontown high school

McHUGH This family is of Irish descent, the first record being of Bernard McHugh born at Yellow Creek, Bedford county, Pennsylvania He became interested in canal transportation and owned several boats He died when comparatively a young man, and when his children were quite small, consequently little record can be obtained of him He has a brother Edward living in Cambria county Pennsylvania Bernard McHugh married Elizabeth Sweeny born in Huntington county, now Blair county, Pennsylvania Children Edward, Albert and William A the latter the only survivor of his family

(II) William A, son of Bernard and Elizabeth (Sweeny) McHugh was born at Hollidaysburg, Blair county Pennsylvania, December 7, 1850 He was educated in the public schools of Blair and Huntington counties, adding to his knowledge by much study outside of his early years in school His youth after his father's death was spent in Huntington county and Pittsburgh, Pennsylvania His early employment was with a butcher and later he became a coal miner in Huntington county In 1868 he came to Fayette county locating in Connellsville working in the mines and at coke burning for several years In 1873 he opened a meat market in Connellsville continuing successfully until 1883, when he disposed of his business From 1884 until 1891 he was engaged in the hotel business in Connellsville In 1893 he purchased the Central Hotel in Uniontown Pennsylvania In 1894 became proprietor of the McClelland House in Uniontown continuing until 1898 In 1900 he organized the Fayette Brewing Company of which he is vice-president and manager He is also interested in the development of coal lands and other business investments He is a Democrat in politics and in Connellsville served on the school board He is a member of the Roman Catholic church and of the Benevolent and Protective Order of Elks

He married September 18 1876 Margaret, daughter of Francis McGrath, of Erie,

A. J. McHugh.

Pennsylvania Children 1 Francis D, now a resident of Uniontown 2 Anna married Dr P A Larkin, of Uniontown 3 Albert J, of whom further 4 Margaret, residing at home 5 William A, Jr, now a physician in Philadelphia Pennsylvania, a graduate of the University of Pennsylvania 6 Edward L, a student at St Vincent's College, near Latrobe, Pennsylvania

(III) Albert James, son of William Armistead and Margaret (McGrath) McHugh, was born at Connellsville Fayette county, Pennsylvania, December 24, 1881 When he was ten years old he removed with his father to Erie, Pennsylvania, but they afterward returned to Fayette county and lived at Uniontown At Erie and at Uniontown he attended the public schools After leaving school and until 1901 he was a clerk in his father's hotel at Uniontown His father having sold the hotel and organized the Fayette Brewing Company he joined his father in the management of the brewery In 1910 he came to Fairchance, Fayette county, Pennsylvania where he conducts one of the best hotels in the county He was from 1896 to 1900 a noted bicyclist, and won many prizes and medals in contests in western Pennsylvania He is a member of the Catholic Mutual Benefit Association and an honorary member of Uniontown Lodge, Benovolent and Protective Order of Elks All the family are members of St John's Roman Catholic Church at Uniontown

He married, April 27 1903 Katharine, daughter of Leopold and Katharine (Becker) Kuth Her paternal grandparents, John and Theresa (Kleinmacht) Kuth, were born in Baden, Germany, and married in Germany, in 1838 Several years later they came to the United States They settled in Cleveland, Ohio, but after a short stay in America returned to Germany, where John Kuth died in 1893 Children, so far as known to us 1 Leopold, was a baker at Greensburg, Pennsylvania, in 1870 but removed to Uniontown where he followed the same trade We suppose him also to have been born in Germany and to be the older of these brothers He married November 4, 1869, Katharine, daughter of John and Katharine (Steinmetz) Becker, who was born in Kittanning, Armstrong county, Pennsyl-

vania, April 18, 1851 John Becker was a stonemason builder, and contractor of Kittanning, both he and his wife were of German birth Children of Leopold and Katharine (Becker) Kuth married Albert James McHugh, William, Alice, Charles, Rose Josephine, Clara, Gertrude, Amelia, Leona 2 John born in Baden, July 1, 1850, came to the United States in 1864, married, July 24, 1883, Elizabeth Becker

Children of Albert James and Katharine (Kuth) McHugh Katharine, born January 19, 1904, Margaret, September 20, 1906, Albert James, born June 25, 1909, died December 10, 1910

CHALFANT The first Chalfant of the line herein recorded to appear in Fayette county was Chads Chalfant, who came from Chester county, Pennsylvania The Chalfants of that county descend from John Chalfant, who obtained a warrant for two hundred and fifty acres of land in Rockland Manor, October 22, 1701, having settled there two years previously He died in August 1725 leaving sons John and Robert Chads Chalfant sprang from this family and probably obtained his name from the marriage of his father with a daughter of the Chads family of Chads' Ford, Chester county The Chads descend from Francis Chads who came from Wiltshire England, in 1684, and after his second marriage in 1695 to Grace Marple settled on the Brandywine at the ford that bears the family name Chads' Ford His son, John Chads built the old stone house at the north end of the village of Chads' Ford and established a ferry across the creek This name is also written Chadds, Chadsey and Chadsi, but the emigrant wrote it Chads The intermarriage between the families cannot be given, but the supposition is strong that in that way the name Chads came into the Chalfant family

(I) Chads Chalfant was born at Chads' Ford, Chester county, Pennsylvania, about 1750 He grew to manhood there and married, then with his bride started westward in search of land and a home, even though it was to be in the wild and unsettled country He located in Brownsville township, where he and a Nathan Chalfant both owned farm land When the village (now borough) of Brownsville was first started they were buyers of several lots In 1788 Chads Chalfant had a farm one mile from the village, but was the owner of several town lots In 1804 he donated to the Methodist Episcopal church the lot on which their church stood, and also owned a lot opposite the Masonic Hall His name appears in a list of "Taxables in Brownsville in 1818" although he always remained on the farm Nathan Chalfant lived in the village and carried on boat building Chads Chalfant was a wheelwright by trade and probably had his shop on the farm, as he is not named among those in business in the village He was a member of the Masonic order, worshipful master of Brownsville Lodge No 60 that commenced work January 23, 1794, under a dispensation of the Grand Lodge of Pennsylvania On June 14, 1811, he sold for fifty dollars the lot on Church street where the Masonic Hall was erected in 1834 He was a devoted Methodist, an exhorter and local preacher He hewed and hauled the logs of which the first church was built, and was buried in the rear of the stone church that followed the rude one of logs The pulpit in the present First Methodist Episcopal Church of Brownsville is directly over his remains His wife, a Miss McManna was an intensely devout, pious woman, and had read the Bible through fifty times She read it through once on bended knees, assuming that attitude of prayer at each reading The Chalfant home was much used for religious meetings, and was a favorite stopping place for itinerant ministers of the gospel They had one daughter, Elizabeth, who married Wesley McCracken Their sons were James, Robert, Mordecai, Abner, Basil and Walter B

(II) Walter Brown, son of Chads Chalfant, was born in Brownsville township, Fayette county, Pennsylvania, May 8, 1794, died October 16, 1865 He was a farmer of Jefferson township, and a man of strong deep, religious temperament He was a devoted Methodist, and like his parents most hospitable and generous in entertaining the ministers who came to his neighborhood He was a strong abolitionist, and fought earnestly against human slavery, otherwise he was very independent in politics and not bound by any party prejudice He married, March 24 1816, Mollie Budd Brown, born at Mount Holly, New Jersey, December 9, 1793, died May 25, 1875 Children Eliza, born February 8, 1817, Chads (2), born October 1, 1818 (q v) Samuel B September 24, 1820, James W of whom further, Fletcher F May 8, 1825. Henry Swatzer, March 23, 1828, Margaret, December 19, 1829, Charles B, October 21, 1832, William B, January 17, 1835, Duncan, October 25, 1836, Anna Swatzer, February 11, 1840

(III) James W, son of Walter B and Mollie B (Brown) Chalfant, was born in Jefferson township Fayette county Pennsylvania, July 5 1822 died 1891 He was educated in the public school and spent his life engaged in agriculture His leaning was toward the Methodist Episcopal church He was a member of the Independent Order of Odd Fellows, and a Republican in politics, and served as town supervisor He married, in 1858, Margaret Lee, born in Jefferson township, Fayette county, in 1840, died 1909, daughter of Francis Lee and Martha Moorehouse Children Martha A, born 1859, married, 1880, William H Bradman, Walter B of whom further, Frances L, born August 25, 1862, Mollie B, 1865, Chads W, 1867. Haddie, 1869, Harry S, 1871, Fred J, 1878

(IV) Professor Walter Brown Chalfant, son of James W and Margaret (Lee) Chalfant, was born in Jefferson township, Fayette county, Pennsylvania, August 25, 1860 His early and praparatory education was obtained in the public schools, followed by a course at Duff's Business College at Pittsburgh whence he was graduated with honors, class of 1883 After graduation he established a school for business instruction at Verona Place, continuing same until 1891, when he returned to Duff' Business College as an instructor and superintendent in charge of the graduate department In three years he prepared and examined over 600 students for graudation He continued there until 1894, then until 1908 was expert accountant, and for one term attended the law department of Michigan University In 1908 he established Chalfant's Business Col-

Joseph Chalfant

lege at Brownsville, a most successful and high grade school for instruction in business branches and methods Not only is Professor Chalfant a capable instructor and head of his institution, but he is one of the most expert accountants in Western Pennsylvania, and one of the most rapid and accurate calculators in the whole country In 1896 he discovered a new and entirely original method of proof that can be applied to all the fundamental rules of arithmetic, and proof of any mathematical calculation obtained in one-fifth the time consumed by any other method He also has formulated a rule for obtaining the exact gain or loss from double entry books, a method far in advance of any found in the latest and best works on bookkeeping He is an active Republican and an attendant of the Methodist Episcopal church He is unmarried

(IV) Fred James, youngest brother of Professor Walter B Chalfant, is a graduate of Chalfant's Business College, class of 1894 He held various positions, and in 1899 was appointed postmaster at Braznell, Fayette county, the appointment being made on his twenty-first birthday, being then the youngest postmaster in the United States He has held in recent years clerical positions in the state senate, and is secretary of South Brownsville Fire Department and Relief Association He is a member of Brownsville Lodge No 60, Free and Accepted Masons, of which Chads Chalfant was the first master and belongs to the Central Presbyterian Church He married, in 1901 Sarah V Pringle, of West Brownsville, born January 7, 1878 Children Helen, born December 12, 1904, James, July 15, 1908

(III) Chads (2) Chalfant, CHALFANT eldest son of Walter B Chalfant (q v) and Mollie B (Brown) Chalfant, was born in Jefferson township, Fayette county, Pennsylvania, October 1 1818 He married Malinda Shearer, born in Fayette county, where she died at the age of seventy-seven years Children 1 Elizabeth, born 1842, married, 1866, Thomas H Cline, and resides in South Brownsville Pennsylvania children 1 Etta, born 1867, married O E Hibbs, a merchant of Uniontown, and has Vera Bell,

born 1888, died 1898 Blanche, born 1891, Thomas, 1894, 11 Kate born 1869, died June 5, 1909, married E M Garwood, and has Esther E born 1888, died 1900, Carl, born 1892 died 1894, Marie E, born 1895, 111 Lavinia, born 1870, graduate State Normal School at California, 1892, married the same year, Rev James Hamilton, pastor of Carmichael Cumberland Presbyterian Church, children John and Robert, died in infancy, James, born 1894, Elizabeth 1897, Mary, 1901, William Chalfant, 1903, Roland, July, 1906, 1v John L, born 1875, graduate of Duff's Business College, June 2, 1912, married Nellie G Hess, child, Clark H, died in infancy, v Malinda died in infancy 2 Joseph Walter, of whom further 3 Rebecca born 1846 died January 1910 4 James Fletcher, born 1850, resides in Charleroi Pennsylvania, married (first) Margaret Fuller, who died in 1875, (second) 1883, Eliza Reeves, children 1 Ira born 1873 died 1899, 11 Malinda B born 1874 married William Albright, has Rebecca and Mildred, 111 Joseph, born July 13 1884 1v Floyd, July 13 1889 5 Frederick S, of whom further 6 William Henry, born 1854, a farmer died 1884 7 Ira born 1857 died 1893

(IV) Joseph Walter, son of Chads and Malinda (Shearer) Chalfant was born on the old Shearer homestead in Fayette county Pennsylvania December 10, 1843, died May 5 1888 He attended the State Normal School, and afterward Meadville College but finished his course at Mount Union College For two years he taught in Peoria, Illinois, and afterward in Jefferson township Fayette county Pennsylvania Owing to delicate health and a love of nature, he bought a farm in Redstone township, Fayette county, and raised cattle, sheep and horses until his death For some years he was town assessor he also held the office of tax collector He was a member of the Redstone Presbyterian Church

He married September 4, 1873 Elizabeth Anna, daughter of James Madison and Nancy Jane (Steele) Bigham She survives him and is now living at Brownsville Fayette county The name Bigham is said to be another form of Bingham and the family is thought, though this is by no means cer-

tain, to be descended from Sir John de Bingham, who came over with William the Conqueror, and received estates near Sheffield,
Yorkshire, England It is said that one of
his descendants .Thomas, went to Ireland
about 1480 and that the Irish branch of the
family, from which the Westmoreland
county Bighams come, is descended from
him   James Madison Bigham was of the
Westmoreland county, Pennsylvania, family   There is a Connecticut Bingham family, of Sheffield, England, descent   The
name was perhaps Saxon, and assumed by
the Norman soldier from his estate Nancy
Jane (Steele) Bigham was the daughter of
William and Sarah (Elliott) Steele   Children of James Madison and Nancy Jane
(Steele) Bigham   Elizabeth Anna, mentioned above, married Joseph Walter Chalfant William Steele, living at Belleflower,
Illinois Norah Gillette, died at Canton,
Ohio, Sarah Marie, married James Barnaby,
lives at Alliance, Ohio, John Newton, lives
at Alliance, Ohio, Charlotte May, married
Rev Charles Russell Carlos, lives at Vallejo
California, James Elliott, died at the age of
ten

Children of Joseph Walter and Elizabeth
Anna (Bigham) Chalfant   1 Carl Dudley,
born November 23, 1874 died October 22,
1896 2 Florian, born February 7, 1877, 3
John, March 27, 1879 4 Myrtle, March 14,
1880 5 Lloyd G, January 30 1883 6 Benjamin S, August 21, 1884, died November
19, 1891

(IV) Frederick Shearer, fifth child of
Chads (2) and Malinda (Shearer) Chalfant,
was born in Jefferson township Fayette
county Pennsylvania, January 25, 1850, twin
of James Fletcher Chalfant He was educated
in the public schools and grew to manhood
on the home farm When a young man he
came to Brownsville and engaged in the
coal business, also conducting a livery He
was very successful, being an active energetic capable man of business He was a
Republican in politics, and in November,
1895 was elected sheriff of Fayette county,
serving until January 1, 1899 He made a
vigorous, efficient sheriff, giving general
satisfaction to all having business with
the sheriff's office   He was a member of the Methodist Episcopal church,
and a useful, consistent Christian man
He married (first), in 1871, Josephine
Breckinbridge of Jefferson township, Fayette county, who died in 1882 (second),
July 18, 1895, Ella Hill, born in Dunbar
township, June 20, 1870, daughter of Colonel
Alexander J Hill, for many years superintendent of the Fort Hill works of the Rainey
Bank Coal and Coke Company at East Liberty, Fayette county The title of colonel
is honorary, and inherited from his father,
Colonel Alexander McClelland Hill, son of
Rev George Hill, of Scotch-Irish descent
(see Hill) Mrs Ella (Hill) Chalfant survives her husband, a resident of Brownsville, Pennsylvania Children of Frederick
S Chalfant and his first wife 1 Chads (3),
born 1872, died 1895 2 Claude born 1874,
died in infancy 3 Carl Wilson, born 1876,
died April 26, 1900, deputy sheriff of Fayette county under his father, married, May
28, 1896, Sadie Hill one child Chads (4),
died in infancy 5 Lillian Frances, born
1880

(The Hill Line)

(I) Rev George Hill was born in York
county, Pennsylvania, in 1764, and moved
with his father and family to Georges Creek
township, Fayette county He studied divinity and became a member of the Presbyterian church, and was for many years
pastor of Ligonier Valley Church in Westmoreland county, Pennsylvania He married Elizabeth, daughter of Alexander Mc-
Clelland

(II) Colonel Alexander McClelland Hill,
son of Rev George Hill, died in 1863, aged
about sixty years He was in early life a
tanner but later a large land owner and
prosperous farmer His Dunbar township
farm of three hundred and fifty acres
was underlaid with the best of coking coal,
as were other farms he owned of smaller
area He was one of the pioneer coke manufacturers of Fayette county, and very
prominent in the development of the county
and in political life He was a strong and
early advocate of the extension of the Baltimore & Ohio railroad through Fayette
county, and aided all early enterprises possible He was a strong Democrat, and
twice represented Fayette and Westmoreland counties in the state legislature He

was faithful to his constituents and made an excellent record as a legislator He served in the house, 1851-1852, and in 1854 and again in 1860 was the successful candidate of his party for state senator He married and had issue

(III) Colonel Alexander J Hill son of Colonel Alexander McClelland Hill, was born at Laurel Hill, Fayette county, Pennsylvania, December 19, 1836, died August 18 1894 He was educated in the public schools, Duff's Business College or Pittsburgh, and Laurel Hill Academy He was a farmer in early life but for many years connected with the Rainey Company as superintendent at the Fort Hill works He was an active Democrat, and once the candidate of his party for the state legislature He was a man of high character, and like his father a man of strong friendship, and like all strong characters aroused the enmity of weaker men He was a member of the Presbyterian church and of the Masonic order He married (first) Caroline Braden Strickler, born in Fayette county, Pennsylvania, December 14, 1836, died March 16, 1879, daughter of Stewart and Mary (Newcomer) Strickler and granddaughter of Jacob Strickler Stewart Strickler was born at New Salem near Uniontown, Pennsylvania, February 17, 1812 His mother died when he was sixteen years of age, leaving himself and eight sisters He worked on a farm by the month and later bought and sold eggs and poultry, taking them down the river in a rude boat of boards He worked and saved until he got a start in life He bought land in small quantities at first and made coke which he shipped by flatboat to Cincinnati, Ohio, and prospered In 1855 he purchased a tract of eighty acres of coal land, and in 1857 put in operation eighty coke ovens, later selling his plant and land for $80,000 About 1867 he moved with a part of his family to Middle Tennessee, where he died Stewart Strickler married in 1835 Mary Newcomer of Tyrone township, who bore him two sons and six daughters, the eldest being Caroline B wife of Colonel Alexander J Hill Their children 1 Harry Braden, born October 29 1864, died July 28, 1891 2 George Johnson, born October 19, 1865, deceased 3 Alexander S,

born October 20, 1867, now a resident of Latrobe, Pennsylvania 4 Mary, born May 27 1869, died in infancy 5 Ella, of whom further 6 Lyman Strickler, born August 12, 1871, died in infancy 7 Sadie, born November 10, 1872, married, May 28, 1896, Carl Wilson, son of Frederick Shearer Chalfant (see Chalfant IV), who died April 26 1900, child Chads Chalfant, died in infancy Colonel Alexander J Hill married (second) Josephine Francis, who died in March, 1894 Child James Francis Hill, now residing in Brownsville, Pennsylvania

(IV) Ella, daughter of Colonel Alexander J and Caroline Braden (Strickler) Hill, was born June 20 1870, married, July 18, 1895, Frederick Shearer Chalfant, whom she survives Children Alexander Hill, born May 2 1896, Josephine, Jan 2, 1898 died Jan 6, 1898

CHALFANT The earliest Chalfants in Fayette county, Pennsylvania, were Chads and Nathan Chalfant, who settled at Brownsville, Pennsylvania The Chalfants of this sketch descend from George who was probably a son of Nathan Chalfant (See Chalfant on preceding pages)

(I) George Chalfant was a farmer of Redstone township, Fayette county, Pennsylvania He was also a stone mason, varying his building with farming operations all his life He was a Democrat in politics and a member of the Presbyterian church He died at the age of seventy-seven years, and his wife at eighty years Children 1 Finley, of whom further 2 Parker married Mathilda Wilson, conducted a general store at New Salem, both deceased 3 Hannah married William Meredith a merchant of Cambridge, both deceased 4 Eliza, deceased, married Andrew Hanna, a farmer of Ohio 5 Harriet, married James Henshaw a farmer of Fayette county both deceased 6 Griffith, deceased a farmer of Ohio, married Anseline Reeves 7 William a farmer in Ohio married Maggie Doff, deceased

(II) Finley, son of George Chalfant, was born in Redstone township, Fayette county, Pennsylvania His education was obtained in the public schools of Fayette county He was always associated with the Democratic party, and rose to a position of political im-

portance in the county, holding the offices of
county auditor, road supervisor and justice
of the peace of Redstone township, Fayette
county He is a member of the Presbyterian church of which he has for some time
been an elder He married Prudence,
daughter of Philip Grable Children 1 Joseph Newton, of whom further 2 Prudence 3 Nimrod, deceased 4 Earhard
5 Esther, deceased married Daniel Mc-
Donald, and lived in Brownsville, Pennsylvania 6 Rebecca married Harvey Chubbuck, deceased 7 Sally 8 Thomas, deceased 9 Hannah, deceased married Jonathan C McCormick, deceased, a farmer of
Redstone township

(III) Joseph Newton, son of Finley and
Prudence (Grable) Chalfant, was born in
Redstone township Fayette county Pennsylvania, September 27, 1844 He has followed farming all his life, which has been
passed in Fayette county He is a member
of the Democratic party, and at one time
held the office of school director in the independent district at New Salem He is a
member of the Patrons of Husbandry and
belongs to the Presbyterian church A good
citizen, a successful tiller of the soil his
reputation throughout the country is without a blemish

He married Jane Violet Swan, born in
Fayette county, July 4, 1849 daughter of
Presly Swan who died in Kansas, married
(first) Maranda Hibbs, (second) Clarissa
Carter Children of Presly Swan by first
wife 1 Sarah Anne born May, 1844, lives
in Uniontown, Pennsylvania married Joseph Campbell (deceased), a farmer of Fayette county 2 Jane Violet (of previous
mention) 3 Richard lives in Colorado
married Catherine Barom (deceased) 4
John married Harriet Chalfant (deceased)
Child of Presly Swan by second wife Maranda, married Fred Herr, a farmer in Kansas Children of Joseph Newton and Jane
Violet (Swan) Chalfant 1 James P, born
April 23 1876 a farmer of Fayette county,
married Nora Craft, children Clark Newton James Edward, and twins George Finley and Samuel Parker 2 Earl Newton,
born November 16, 1881, died November
18, 1903 3 Joseph Morgan born December
22, 1883 lives with parents 4 Louise Vio-

let, born September 22 1887, lives at home.
5 Arthur Greeg, born August 21, 1890 lives
in Montana

DUNN There are several families bearing this name in Fayette county,
mostly of Irish and Scotch descent Grandfather Dunn, the founder of
this branch, was born in county Down, Ireland, about the year 1780, came to the
United States before marriage and settled
in Jefferson township, Fayette county Pennsylvania He owned his farm and after
marriage took his bride to his own home
He was a Democrat in politics, and was a
man of good character and industrious habits His children Robert, James, Thomas
W of whom further, Mary Ann, married
Robert Layton, Eliza married Thomas
Cooke, of Tippecanoe Pennsylvania, all are
deceased

(II) Thomas W Dunn, son of the emigrant was born in Jefferson township, Fayette county, Pennsylvania in 1810, died
March 1896 He passed his life in Fayette
county engaged as a laboring man in various occupations He was a Democrat in
politics and served as tax collector of his
township Both he and his wife belonged
to the Methodist Episcopal church He married (first) Rachel Bradman who bore him
nine children He married (second) Sevilla, daughter of William Pence William
Pence was born in Germany coming to the
United States when a young man He was
a saddler by trade and after settling in
Fayette county worked at his trade until
death He is buried in Fairview cemetery,
Jefferson township, Fayette county Children of Thomas W Dunn by first marriage
1 Gilmore, died in the United States army
2 John, died aged sixteen years 3 Priscilla,
deceased 4 Annie deceased 5 Thomas
now living at Lisbon Ohio 6 Rachel deceased 7 William L, deceased 8 Mary
Jane, deceased 9 ——, died in infancy
Children by second marriage 10 Franklin, died in Fayette county, Pennsylvania
11 George W, a blacksmith, now residing
at Laurel Hill, Fayette county 12 Margaret, deceased 13 Agnes, married John Dennis and lives in Dunbar township, Fayette
county 14 James H, of whom further. 15.

Charles E, a blacksmith, member of the firm of J H Dunn & Brother 16 Joanna, married Isaac Ball, of Dunbar township 17 Lulu, deceased 18 John E, living in Fayette county 19 Ella, married George Woodward and lives at Donora, Pennsylvania

(III) James H fourteenth child of Thomas W Dunn and fifth child of his second wife, Sevilla (Pence) Dunn, was born in Franklin township, Fayette county, Pennsylvania, December 24, 1861 He was educated in the public school, and worked at farming until he was sixteen years of age He was then apprenticed to the blacksmith s trade under Thomas G King of Uniontown After serving his years of apprenticeship he worked as a journeyman for a time, then established a shop of his own at Tippecanoe, Fayette county, where he remained eighteen months He was then in business with Robert Hogsett, of Lemont, Fayette county, until 1897 then sold out and located in business alone at No 163 East Main street, Uniontown, buying out the former owner He remained there six years He then bought his present place of business of William McCormick and in 1905 admitted his brother, Charles E Dunn, as partner, the firm being known as J H Dunn & Brother They conduct a large and prosperous business and are leaders in their line Mr Dunn has real estate investments in Uniontown, and is a keen, reliable man of business He thoroughly undertands his trade and does nothing but honest work He is a member of the Baptist church, the Royal Arcanum, and a Democrat in politics His residence is at No 227 Main street, where he built a good house in 1904

He married, June 22, 1883, Charlotte born in Fayette county, daughter of Jacob and Julia Markley, an old Fayette county family Children 1 Lillian, married Newell R Allton of Uniontown who she survives child, James N 2 Paul a student at Uniontown high school 3 Roy, attending the grade school

(III) Charles E fifteenth child of Thomas W Dunn and sixth child of his second wife, Sevilla (Pence) Dunn, was born in Franklin township, Fayette county, Pennsylvania June 15, 1864 He was educated in the public school, and on arriving at suitable age began learning the blacksmith s trade with W H Wilhelm, of Uniontown He spent one year with him, then two years in the blacksmith's shop of the H C Frick Coke Company He then entered the employ of the Stewart Iron Company, remaining sixteen years In 1905 he entered into a partnership with his brother, James H Dunn, already established in business in Uniontown forming the firm of J H Dunn & Brother general blacksmiths Mr Dunn is an expert worker in iron and steel and allows nothing but first-class work to leave their shop He is a Democrat in politics and with his wife belongs to the Presbyterian church He is a member of the Royal Arcanum He is interested in Uniontown real estate His home is at No 15 Winona street, which he bought in 1902

He married, September 23, 1886, Sarah R born in Fayette county daughter of William H and Sarah Yardley Children Bertha R, born 1896, Ruth E, 1909

DUNN

Probably no state in America has more profited through emigration from Ireland than Pennsylvania, and no section of any state to a greater extent than Western Pennsylvania Hardy sons of Scotch-Irish parentage have made glorious records in the upbuilding of the western counties and the pages of history teem with names that are yet familiar ones, coming among the earliest settlers, these advance agents of civilization suffered and bravely endured all the dangers and privations—even the portion of the pioneer—and thousands gave their lives that fields might supplant the forest, comfortable homes the tepee, and iron rails the tangled trail along which lurked the savage things of the forest

(1) Among those who came at an early day was Samuel Dunn born in the North of Ireland who settled in Washington county, Pennsylvania, where he cleared a farm and lived until his death Among his children was a son Daniel

(II) Daniel son of Samuel Dunn was born in Washington county, Pennsylvania in 1807, died 1862 He secured a limited education in the schools of that period, but in the greater school of actual experience gained a knowledge and acquired a physique that more than compensated for the loss of advantages. He cleared and tilled the soil, and from pioneer conditions gained a competence and an honored name. He became a large land owner, and in his quiet, retired manner exercised a great influence in his community. He sought no public office, but devoted himself to his business and family. He married Sarah Baker, born in Washington county 1812, died 1897, daughter of David Baker, born of English parents, a farmer and cabinet maker. Children: Edmund, of whom further; Margaret Minton, Emmeline Day, and others.

(III) Edmund, son of Daniel Dunn, was born in Washington county, Pennsylvania, in 1840. He was educated in the public schools, after which he entered Waynesburg College, completing the course but not graduating. He was a farmer in his earlier youth, but when he reached manhood the great civil war claimed him, and in August, 1862, he followed the example of thousands and tens of thousands of his race that rallied to the defense of their country's flag. He enlisted in Company K, Sixteenth Regiment Pennsylvania Volunteer Cavalry, and fought until the war closed. His regiment was attached to the Army of the Potomac, and from 1863 until the close of the war was engaged in all historic battles fought by that army. After the war closed he received an honorable discharge and returned home. Soon afterward he settled in Missouri, where he engaged in farming. He did not long remain there, but returned to Pennsylvania, and in 1873 established a mercantile business in Connellsville. This he has successfully conducted until the present time, being one of the oldest established dry goods merchants in the city. He is a thoroughly capable, energetic, reliable man of business, and enjoys the utmost confidence of his community. He is a member of the Methodist Episcopal church and in politics is a Republican. He married, in February, 1866, Rhoda Louisa Yeagley, born in Fayette county. Children: 1. Harry, born January 6, 1868; educated in the public schools and Allegheny College, and now associated in the dry goods business with his father. He is a Republican, and a member

of the Methodist Episcopal church; married 1897, Mae B., daughter of Lloyd Johnston, a retired capitalist. 2. Sarah Phoebe, resides at home. 3. Elizabeth, deceased.

STICKEL The Stickel family of Connellsville, Pennsylvania, descends from an ancestry long seated in Germany. The founder in the United States, August Stickel, was born in that country in 1843, a posthumous child; when he was but an infant his mother also died and he was left to the care of an aunt, and on her death two years later to the civil authorities. He received a good education and became an expert draughtsman. He served the required number of years in the German army, attaining the rank of lieutenant. His proficiency as a draughtsman commended him to the topographical department, and he was placed in charge of maps. In 1874 he came to the United States and the same year was married, at Meyersdale, to Catherine Dahl, who came to the United States a short time before the arrival of Mr. Stickel. The young couple began housekeeping in Allegheny county, Pennsylvania, and during the great flood at Butchers Run lost all their household goods, and other property. After the flood they moved to Mill Run where he established a store. He was successful and was interested in several mercantile enterprises. He again met with misfortune from the elements, but this time fire instead of water, and for a second time lost his property, but undismayed he began business anew, continuing with great success until 1904, when he retired from active business life. He was president and a large stockholder in the McFarland Lumber Company; head of the mercantile business of the A. Stickel Company, operating four stores, which were located at Mill Run, Bear Run, Rogers Mill and Indian Creek. On retiring he disposed of his interests in the company which was then organized as A. Stickel and Company. He also disposed of his interest in the lumber company. He, however, retained his holdings in the Westmoreland Grocery Company and in other less important enterprises. He was an energetic, capable man of business and was held in highest esteem

in business and financial circles He was
a Democrat and always took a deep interest
in public affairs He served as auditor of
Springfield township, Fayette county, for
fifteen years and held other township offices During the thirty-four years that
he resided in Mill Run he became deeply
interested in the welfare of his neighbors
and employees, rendering them useful assistance by advice and often more substantial
evidence of his interest He was a member
of the German Lutheran church, and as long
as health permitted attended services at
Connellsville, there being no congregation
of that denomination at Mill Run Up to
his fifty-sixth year Mr Stickel had never
known a day's illness, but during the last
two years of his life he was in very poor
health During the summer of 1910 he spent
five months at Cambridge Springs for the
benefit of his health, but although under the
care of the best medical practitioners he was
doomed He died suddenly, February 9,
1911, while conversing with his wife at the
residence of his son, August Stickel, No
1008 Chestnut street, Connellsville He married in Meyersdale, Pennsylvania, 1874, Catherine Dahl, whom he had known in Germany and came to the United States to
marry, she having preceded him with her
parents She survives her husband and resides in Connellsville Children 1 F W,
now a member of A Stickel and Company
2 Mollie married C W Gerret, of Pittsburgh 3 Ida, married Dr D Allison Walker, of Heckla, Pennsylvania 4 August C of
whom further 5 Otto 6 Milton 7
Charles, a student at the Carnegie Technical
School in Pittsburgh

(II) August C, son of August Stickel,
was born at Mill Run, on March 7, 1880
He was educated in the public schools of
Mill Run Springfield township Fayette
county, Pennsylvania, and finished his education at the State Normal School at California, Pennsylvania After working for
three months for the Western Pennsylvania
Street Railway Company, he accepted a position as traveling salesman for a Connellsville wholesale grocery house continuing
for five years He became a member of the
A Stickel Company at Mill Run and leaving the road, devoted himself to the interests

of that company, which was composed of his
father and his older brothers He was also
interested in the MacFarland Lumber Company and in the Indian Creek and Ligonier
Valley Railroad Company These interests
he still retains and is also president of the
Stewarton Lumber Company, secretary and
treasurer of the Superba Coal Company,
secretary and treasurer of the Stickel and
Buttermore Lumber Company, and has
other interests of a minor nature He is a
Democrat in politics He married September 25 1907, Sarah Etta, a daughter of E
S Showalter of Uniontown They have
two children Eugene Sturgis, born July 23,
1908, August, born December 20 1911
Mrs Sarah Etta Stickel was born at Mill
Run, Pennsylvania, and educated at Mill
Run Her father was a school teacher many
years, his father, James W was one of the
oldest school teachers in Fayette county
Mrs Stickel was a school teacher several
years before her marriage

This famous Scotch family was
REED planted in America at the same time
with Breckenridge, Parker, Bruce
and many others whose ancestors were as renowned in their native land as their descendants have been in this country
(I) The immigrant ancestor was James
Reed born near Edinburgh, Scotland where
he followed the trade of a carpenter He emigrated to the United States in 1785 the voyage taking three months He was the holder
of an original patent to five hundred acres of
uncleared land in Washington county Pennsylvania, called Mount Hope, and this tract still
remains in the family He introduced several
innovations in the county, owning the first two-
story house ever built there The furniture
also was his own work, the house being furnished throughout in black walnut The windows were of glass arranged on pulleys, very
unusual at that period After his arrival his
house was the only one on which he worked,
as he devoted most of his time to clearing and
cultivating his land but when his sons became
old enough to share in the responsibility of
maintaining the home, he did more work at his
trade He built the first court house in Washington county, and shortly before his death built
a large brick house, which has always been

the family home and is now over one hundred years old He also operated a carding mill on his farm and did work for the neighbors from miles around He was a Democrat, but took no active part in politics beyond casting his vote for honest, upright men for public office In religious faith he was a Presbyterian and a strong follower of John Calvin He died on his farm, aged sixty-six years He married Jessina Parker Children 1 John, died aged ninety-four years married Anna Smiley and lived on a farm in Washington county 2 Samuel, married Mary Ann Vincent and lived on half of the home farm, which he had inherited 3 Parker of whom further 4 Jane married Thomas Trussle, a carpenter, and moved to Missouri 5 Nancy, married Jacob Donaldson, a farmer and lived in Hickory, Pennsylvania, later moving to Allegheny county, Pennsylvania

(II) Parker, son of James and Jessina (Parker) Reed, was born on the old homestead in Hopewell township, Washington county, Pennsylvania, March 16, 1811, died March 17, 1871, in the same house in which he was born He became a successful sheep raiser owning some valuable stock and taking special pride in his Spanish Merinos, whose wool brought him a fancy figure As old age approached he gave over the care of his farm to his sons and obtained the agency for the first mowers and reapers which appeared in the county In politics he was a Democrat, but during the civil war was a sincere and hearty supporter of Abraham Lincoln His interest in religious matters has always been wide and sympathetic For forty years he was ruling elder in the Upper Buffalo Presbyterian Church, and for nearly all of that time was superintendent of the Sunday school He always was the delegate of the church to the synod and twice was a representative in the general church assembly when it was held at New Orleans and New York He married Jane A Bryce born near West Alexander Virginia, now West Alexander, Pennsylvania, June 7, 1811, died April 9, 1892, daughter of Rev John and Jane (Stockton) Bryce Rev John Bryce was born in Harford county, Maryland When he was very young his parents moved to Washington county, Pennsylvania and here he received his early education under the teaching of the Rev Joseph Smith The influence of the teachings of this

good and pious instructor was seen in the next step of the young man's career, the study of theology in preparation for the ministry He received his license from the Presbytery of Redstone in 1788, and a short time later was ordained a minister of the Gospel He was admitted a member of the Ohio Presbytery and established a church at West Alexander and the Forks of Wheeling, where he remained for twenty years also preaching in Greene county and the surrounding county He married Jane Stockton, born near West Alexander, who was a descendant of Frances McKamie, of Welsh descent, one of the founders of the first Presbyterian church established in America at Snow Hill, Maryland Children of Rev John Bryce 1 John, settled in Belmont, Ohio, where he engaged in farming, married Annie Byers and has a grandson, Rev James Byers Bryce who preaches near Pittsburgh 2 Rebecca, married Samuel Frazier, a farmer, and moved to Muskingum county, Ohio 3 Frances (Fannie), married Joseph Blaney, a farmer, and died near West Alexander 4 Alice, married William Craig a farmer 5 Margaret 6 Jane A, of previous mention Children of Parker and Jane A (Bryce) Reed 1 John B, of whom further 2 Parker, born December 4, 1841, moved to Pawnee county, Kansas, and is engaged in the farming implement and hardware business at Larned married Hannah Walker 3 Rebecca, born February 29, 1848, married Samuel P Wilson they live on the old home farm in Washington county, which he purchased from the heirs 4 Henry, born May 17, 1852, married Anna De Mont of Kansas he is an extensive landowner and capitalist of Larned, Kansas 5 Luther born October 2, 1854 owns a large cement manufacturing plant at Osceola, Kansas

(III) Rev John B Reed son of Parker and Jane A (Bryce) Reed, was born on the old "Mount Hope" farm in Hopewell township, Washington county Pennsylvania, April 5, 1839 His early life was spent on the farm, attending the public school situated thereon and the Academy in Upper Buffalo In the fall of 1858 he entered the junior class of Washington College and was graduated in 1860 He then entered the Western Theological Academy, from which he was graduated in May, 1863, having received his license to preach at the end of his second year in the Theological Seminary

At the time of his graduation Rev Adam Terrence pastor of the Presbyterian church at New Alexandria, Westmoreland county, Pennsylvania, had gone to war with a regiment of that county as chaplain and Rev Reed was offered his pulpit which he accepted and filled for one year On December 31, 1863, he received a call to the First Presbyterian Church of Parkersburg West Virginia, remaining there eight years His next two charges were the First Presbyterian Church of Sistersville West Virginia, where he remained eleven years, and the First Presbyterian Church at Fairmont, West Virginia, where he was pastor six years His present church is the Laurel Hill Presbyterian in Franklin township, Fayette county, known as the first Presbyterian church built "west of the mountains," erected in 1772

At the time of the arrival of Rev Reed the church was in anything but a flourishing condition, but under his guidance it has prospered spiritually and financially, becoming a great power for good in the community The membership has been increased by over two hundred A new brick church was erected in 1897, a parsonage built the same year, a house built for the sexton, a new ten-acre cemetery laid out adjoining the old, and independent of all these improvements the church has eight thousand dollars out at interest The Rev Reed's twenty-four years of service in this community have borne abundant fruit and although he is in his seventy-third year his life is still as useful to his parishioners as it was in the first days of his ministry His advice is still as eagerly sought and as willingly given, his aid implored and as lovingly extended as when he shepherded his first flock in the mountains of Virginia

He married, May 12, 1864, Belle Shields born in New Alexandria, Westmoreland county Pennsylvania, February 18, 1841, daughter of James M and Elizabeth Shields, both born in Westmoreland county, of Scotch-Irish descent, he a farmer and elder in the Presbyterian church Children 1 Effie born May 6, 1865, married Dr W A Hopwood, of Uniontown 2 Helen, born November 24, 1869, married Dr H J Bell of Dawson Pennsylvania 3 Cora, born May 23, 1871, married Ellis Phillips, a farmer of Franklin township 4 Georgia, born October 24, 1875 married Rev Dr F M Silsley, pastor of the First Presbyterian Church of Seattle, Washington

5 Edna born November 11, 1879, married Dr J Melvin Smith, of Philadelphia, Pennsylvania

---

HIGBEE Edward or Edwin Higby, emigrant ancestor of Edward C Higbee, of Uniontown, Pennsylvania was born in England and settled in New London, Connecticut, in 1648 The records state that he sold his house there for ' Five bushels of wheat and a dog," September 7, 1649, which would indicate, either an inferior house or a superior dog In 1674 he was an innkeeper at Middletown, Connecticut He had a deed dated October 15, 1664, from Seankeet, an Indian Sachem of Hartford, for land "Adjoining Jonathan Gilberts" in Hartford In 1666 he was "Free of Taxes ' by vote of the court for making and maintaining the way over Pilgrims Harbor About 1675 he moved to Jamaica, Long Island and in 1683, and as late afterward as 1709, he was living at Huntington, Long Island He married Lydia Skidmore and was a brother-in-law of Edward Adams, son of John Adams, grandson of Jeremy Adams, according to a power of attorney given by Adams to Higby in February, 1696 or 1697, and filed at Hartford (see Hartford probate records vol 1, p 288) Lydia his wife joined the church at Middletown September 30 1674 coming thither from the First Church of Hartford, and with her six children was dismissed to the church in Jamaica, October, 1677

(II) John, son of Edward or Edwin Higby, was born 1658 died in 1688 He married, May 1, 1679, Rebecca, daughter of Samuel Treadwell of Fairfield Connecticut The Inventory of his estate was dated December 28, 1688 as taken by John Hall, Francis Whitmore and Nathaniel Stow (vol 2, Hartford probate records p 7) When his wife died she was succeeded in the administration of her husband's estate by her son Edward Children John, Edward, of whom further Thomas

(III) Edward, son of John Higby was born 1684 baptized August 24 1684 He and his wife joined the Middletown church, April 26, 1713, and were dismissed, December 19, 1773, as original members of the new church at Westfield, Connecticut, where he died November 21, 1775, in his ninety-second year He appears to have been one of the owners of the

"Golden Parlour Mining Company," of Wallingford, April 27, 1737, but the record may refer to a son or nephew. He married, November 29, 1706, Rebecca Wheeler, who died October 22, 1772, at Middletown, Connecticut. Children: 1. John, born at Middletown, July 16, 1707, died in 1790; married, March 9, 1730, Sarah Candee. 2. Isaac, of whom further. 3. Rebecca, born 1715. 4. Sarah, 1721. 5. Stephen, 1730. 6. Daniel, moved to Lewis county, New York.

(IV) Isaac, son of Edward Higby, was born in 1709 at Middletown, Connecticut. He married, in 1730, Dinah Elton. Children: Jane. Isaac: Samuel, of whom further; Joseph, Noah, Rebecca, Daniel, Jane.

(V) Samuel, son of Isaac Higby, was born 1732. He married, in 1758, Rebecca Doolittle. Children: Samuel, of whom further; Ruth, Lemuel, Timothy, Isaac, Sylvester.

(VI) Samuel (2), son of Samuel (1) Higby, was born August 14, 1758, died April 23, 1843. He was a soldier of the revolution, serving as private in Captain Hearst's Connecticut Troops, Colonel Erastus Wolcott's regiment, in the siege of Boston, 1776. He was pensioned in his later years and was on the list of New Haven, Connecticut. pensioners in 1832, and again from Milford, New Haven county, in the list of 1840 (see revolutionary roll of Connecticut. pp. 383, 654 and 660). He married, in 1783, Hannah Gilpin. Children: Betsey, born July 20, 1784; Hannah, June 16, 1786; Roxby, September 1, 1788; Samuel Gilpin, March 17, 1791, died 1863, married, in 1814, Lucy Marlett; Isaac Riley; Lucy, April 27, 1794; Abigail Riley, January 13, 1797; Hervey, January 21, 1801, banker and financier, died April 29, 1853, married Charlotte Baldwin; Benjamin, of whom further.

(VII) Benjamin Higbee, youngest child of Samuel (2) Higby, was born in Milford, New Haven county, Connecticut, July 11, 1804. With him the family makes its advent in Fayette county, Pennsylvania, and the name changes its orthography to Higbee. He married (second) Elizabeth Ball, who bore him four children. By his first marriage two sons were born. Children of second wife: Elizabeth, deceased; Sarah, married Elwood Crawford; Israel, of whom further; John.

(VIII) Israel, son of Benjamin Higbee, was born in July, 1835, died October 19, 1910. He was educated in the public schools, and spent his life in Fayette county, Pennsylvania. He was a wagonmaker by trade, but later a farmer. In 1890 he moved from Jefferson to Lower Tyrone township, Fayette county, where he resided until his death. He was a man of high character with all the excellent traits of his Scotch-Irish ancestry. He married Eliza Jane Carter, born November 9, 1833, who survives him, daughter of Zephaniah Carter, a miller and merchant of Brownsville, Pennsylvania, and his wife Mary, daughter of William and Mary Patterson, all of Fayette county, old, prominent and well known families. The Pattersons were early settlers of Western Pennsylvania and Mary Gibbon Patterson is said to have ruled the first sheet of white paper made west of the Allegheny mountains. Children of Zephaniah and his first wife, Mary (Patterson) Carter: Amanda; Eliza Jane, who married Israel Higbee. He married (second) a Widow Tiernan. Children: Harriet, married Captain H. B. Cook, of Brownsville, and Josephine, married ex-Sheriff Isaac Meason, of St. Louis, Missouri. Children of Israel and Eliza Jane Higbee: Edward Carter, of whom further; Oliphant P., born October 22, 1871, now a farmer of Lower Tyrone township, Fayette county; he married Harriet, daughter of Daniel S. and Sophia Strickler.

(IX) Edward Carter, eldest son of Israel and Eliza Jane Higbee, was born in Jefferson township, Fayette county, Pennsylvania, October 28, 1869. He attended the public schools until he had exhausted their capacity to advance him, then for one term attended Merrittstown Academy. After teaching one year he entered Mt. Union College at Alliance, Ohio, being then sixteen years of age. He remained at college three years. After leaving college he was appointed professor in Monongahela College at Jefferson, Pennsylvania, remaining two years. After teaching one term at Waynesburg College he began the study of law, and on March 1, 1896, entered the law office of Judge S. Leslie Mestrezat (now supreme court justice of Pennsylvania), and studied under his able direction until admitted to the Fayette county bar, June 11, 1897. At the same term he was appointed by Judge Ewing to conduct his first case. On September 27, 1897, he opened offices in Connellsville, Pennsylvania, as junior member of the firm of Fulton & Higbee. On February 1, 1900, this partnership was dissolved and the firm of Sterling, Higbee &

Dumbauld organized In 1903 W H Brown became a member of the firm, continuing until his death in 1907 In 1909 Mr Dumbauld retired and R S Matthews was admitted In 1911 Charles L Lewellyn became a partner, but the firm name remains the same, Sterling, Higbee & Matthews The firm maintain offices in both Connellsville and Uniontown, practice in all state and federal courts, being one of the strongest and most successful legal firms in the county

Mr Higbee has always been a Democrat, and though not active in politics has frequently been on the stump In 1898 he was elected solicitor of Connellsville, and served in that capacity for ten years He successfully conducted the litigation establishing the right of the city to the land known as the "public ground" He served for six years on the Connellsville school board being president three years, and since 1903 has been a director of the First National Bank at Connellsville His chief concern, however, is his profession in which he has attained high standing He is learned in the law, skillful in its application and strictly honorable in all his dealings Since 1897 his home has been in Connellsville, where he has been a potent factor in public affairs, his deepest interest, perhaps, being in the cause of public education and the improvement of school facilities He is an Ancient Accepted Scottish Rite Mason

He married, September 22, 1897, Emma Lint born July 15 1871 daughter of William and Jennie (Kennison) Lint, of Lower Tyrone township, Fayette county Children Donald Mestrezat Ruth, Brown, Edward Sterling, Emily Jean

---

EDWARDS This family name is found in early days, not only in New England but in Virginia in old King William and Stafford counties The Stafford county family later settled in Kentucky, where a descendant married Elizabeth, daughter of Robert E Todd and sister of Mrs Abraham Lincoln Another descendant of Hayden Edwards the Stafford county Virginia, settler, was Benjamin Edwards, of Montgomery county, Maryland Another Edwards family was of Louisa county, Virginia John was a common name in these Virginia Edwards families and there is no doubt but what John Edwards, of Preston county Virginia, was a descendant of one of them, but no record can be found by which he can be definitely traced

(I) John Edwards, when a man grown, settled in Preston county, Virginia, where he was a farmer and landowner Later he moved to Fayette county, Pennsylvania where he continued farming operations until his death He is buried with his wife in Connellsville, Pennsylvania Children 1 Squire, of whom further 2 Green Ashbald, served as a private in the Union army during the civil war, dying shortly after his return from the army 3 Thomas Jefferson, married Susan Saylor and died without issue she survives him 4 Salathial, deceased married and left a son 5 Rebecca Jane, married Henry Hileman, both died near Brownsville, Pennsylvania 6 Mary Ann married —— Lint they died near Dawson, Fayette county, their six children are all deceased

(II) Squire, eldest son of John Edwards was born in Virginia, January 9 1831, died in Dunbar township Fayette county, Pennsylvania, December 27, 1907 He came to Fayette county with his parents and became a farmer owning about two hundred acres of land in Dunbar township, which he cultivated until his death He was a Democrat serving as school director, collector of taxes and poor director He belonged to the Presbyterian church, his wife also being a member He married, in 1858, Clarissa Leighty, born in Dunbar township Fayette county Pennsylvania, January 25 1841 who survives him, a resident of Connellsville, Pennsylvania She is the daughter of Henry and Margaret (Barnes) Leighty, and granddaughter of Jacob Leighty of German descent, who came to Fayette county from near Bradford, Pennsylvania Jacob Leighty was a farmer and an early settler of Fayette county, where he died He is buried in the Leighty family cemetery on one of the farms now owned by the J W Rainey Company His son, Henry Leighty, became a wealthy and influential farmer of Fayette county He married (first) Sarah Smith who bore him eight children He married (second) Margaret Barnes Sechrist daughter of Jacob and Mary (Stauffer) Barnes, residents of Canada and Pennsylvania, and widow of John Sechrist Children of Mr and Mrs Sechrist Ann Mary and Lydia all deceased Children by her second husband Henry Leighty Joseph, now living in Kansas Christopher, also living in Kansas, Peter, living in Missouri,

Sarah, deceased, married (first) Andrew Work, (second) James Middleton; Clarissa, of previous mention, widow of Squire Edwards. Henry Leighty died in 1844, aged sixty-two years. His widow married (third) George Boyer and lived near Dunbar, Pennsylvania, on a small farm. She had no issue by this marriage and died in 1882, aged nearly eighty-two years. Children of Squire and Clarissa Edwards: 1. John, an undertaker and furniture dealers of Vanderbilt, Fayette county, Pennsylvania. 2. Margaret, married Joseph G. Strickler, both deceased. 3. Elizabeth, died in infancy. 4. George, deceased. 5. Frank, resides in Vanderbilt and is foreman on the Pittsburgh & Lake Erie railroad. 6. Alvin C., of whom further. 7. Zella, married Alfred W. Hair and resides in Franklin township, Fayette county. 8. Ada, a school teacher, making her home with her mother. 9. Clara, a stenographer, also living at home. 10. Robert, died in infancy.

(III) Alvin C., son of Squire and Clarissa (Leighty) Edwards, was born in Dunbar township, Fayette county, Pennsylvania, July 10, 1868. He grew to manhood on the home farm, and received his education in the public schools. He devoted his entire life to farming, but did not become a landowner until 1908, when he purchased a farm of about one hundred and thirty-two acres, his present home, which he had rented for many years. On his farm is a valued sand deposit, from which he ships many carloads of sand annually. He is a director of the Union National Bank of Connellsville and a capable and successful business man. He is a public-spirited citizen, extremely generous, and of a quiet, contented spirit, enjoying the company of his books, and of an intelligent and genial disposition. He is a Democrat, and a member of the Presbyterian church, his wife of the Methodist Episcopal church. He married, February 21, 1895, Bird C., daughter of Samuel Crossland. Children: Samuel C., born May 14, 1896; Eliza C., August, 1898; Mary Frances, September, 1907.

FINLEY   The Finleys of Fayette county, Pennsylvania, descend from a Scotch ancestor, Michael Finley, born in Scotland, or possibly Ireland, of Scotch parents, in the decade 1680-1690. He lived in county Armagh, Ireland, from whence he emigrated to America, landing at Philadel-phia, Pennsylvania, September 28, 1734, with wife and seven sons (possibly eight). He first settled on Neshaminy creek, in Bucks county, Pennsylvania, afterwards in New Jersey, and later in Sadsbury township, Chester county, Pennsylvania, where he lived from 1737 to 1747. Children, all born in Armagh, Ireland: 1. John, was killed by Indians in Lurgan township, Cumberland county, Pennsylvania, where he settled before 1744; married Martha Berkley and had issue; his descendants are found South and West. 2. Samuel, D.D., LL.D., born 1715, died in Philadelphia, July 17, 1766; he was president of Princeton College, 1761-66, a man of deep learning and a powerful preacher, an ordained minister of the Presbyterian church. He married (first), September 26, 1744, Sarah Hall, born 1728, died July 30, 1760; married (second), Ann, daughter of Matthew Clarkson, of Philadelphia; left issue by both marriages. 3. William, died 1800; a farmer of Chester and Adams counties, Pennsylvania, later of Augusta county, Virginia; married (first) ——; (second) Catherine, daughter of Samuel Culbertson, of London Grove township, Chester county, Pennsylvania. 4. Michael (2), a farmer of Chester county, Pennsylvania; married Ann Lewis; their eldest son, Joseph Lewis Finley, was lieutenant, captain and major in the revolution. 5. Rev. James, of whom further. 6. Clements, born March, 1735, died August 11, 1775, in South Huntington township, Westmoreland county, Pennsylvania; married, January 12, 1761, Elizabeth Carnahan, and left issue. There is some doubt as to whether Clements was a son of Michael, or a grandson, and son of John Finley. The strongest inference is as given. Of the other children of Michael Finley there is no record.

(II) The Finleys of Fayette county descend through Rev. James Finley, fifth son of Michael Finley. He was born in county Armagh, Ireland, February, 1725, died in Rostraver township, Westmoreland county, Pennsylvania, January 6, 1795. He came to America with his father and brothers in 1734. He received a good education and became a regularly ordained minister of the Presbyterian church, and was for many years pastor of the East Nottingham church, Cecil county, Maryland, Eastern Shore, 1752-83, and of Rehoboth and Round Hill churches, Westmoreland county, Pennsylvania, 1783-95. He played an important part in the early settlement of Fayette county, Pennsylvania, particularly in Redstone township, where he was the first of the family to arrive in 1765 He made a wide circuit through the county. preaching here and there, but on the lookout for a good location He is said to have been the first minister of the Gospel (except army chaplains) who ever penetrated Western Pennsylvania He tarried about a month on his first visit, then returned to his church in Maryland, but came again in 1767 and again in 1771, each time on a preaching mission His first favorable opinion of the country was confirmed by each succeeding visit, and in 1771 he made a large purchase of land on Dunlap's creek, within the present limits of the townships of German Redstone and Menallen He returned east and in 1772 came again, bringing his fourteen-year-old son Ebenezer, a farm hand, Samuel Finley (not a relative), and several negro slaves Rev James was at no time an actual settler of Fayette county, but his son Ebenezer always remained and was the real pioneer Finley Rev James Finley was regularly settled pastor of Rehoboth church, in Westmoreland county Pennsylvania, in 1783 continuing until his death in 1795 It is worthy of remark that from his first coming in 1765 until 1783 thirty-four families connected with his church in Cecil county, Maryland, removed to Western Pennsylvania These families scattered and were the nucleus from which later sprang Presbyterian churches at Chartiers Cross Creek, Rehoboth, Laurel Hill and Dunlap s Creek Of the thirty-four families named, twenty-two of the heads of these became ruling elders of the churches named at their organizations

Rev James Finley married, in 1752, Hannah Evans, born 1715, died April 1, 1795, daughter of Robert Evans Children 1 Rev John Evans born July 6, 1753, died in Ohio after 1813, he was pastor of Faggs Manor Church, 1781-93, removed to Bracken, Mason county Kentucky, thence to Red Oak, Ohio, married a daughter of Job Ruston, of Chester county 2 Samuel Robert, born December 19, 1754, died October 25, 1839 3 Margaret, born September 5 1756, died May 10 1836, married Colonel John Power, of Westmoreland county, Pennsylvania 4 Ebenezer, of whom further 5 Hannah born June 20 1764 died before 1820, married John Robinson 6 Joseph, born

December 13, 1766, died June 3, 1860, married (first), a Miss Veech, (second) Frances Moore 7 James born January 14, 1769, died November 17, 1772 8 William, June 10, 1772, died August 20 1857 married (first) Sarah Patterson, (second) Margaret Wilson 9 Michael, born March 24. 1774. died July 29, 1850 married (first) Eleanor Elliot, (second) Mrs Mary Plumer Smith

(III) Ebenezer third son and fourth child of Rev James and Hannah (Evans) Finley, was born in Cecil county Maryland December 30, 1758 died January 18, 1849 He came to Fayette county with his father in 1772 and settled on lands in Redstone township, purchased by his father in 1771 Ebenezer was a daring, hardy lad, and amidst his pioneer surroundings rapidly developed stature and strength Samuel Finley, who came at the same time, but not a relative, was in charge of the farm, aided by his negro slaves brought from Maryland Samuel was drafted for militia duty but Ebenezer was allowed to go as his substitute While at Fort Wallace a rider brought news of the approach of Indians Young Finley was one of the party of twenty men who left the fort, and soon came upon a large body of Indians before whom they retreated, keeping up a running fight Finley's gun would not go off, and in stopping to fix it he fell behind the others An Indian with a leveled gun was about to shoot him, when a settler s shot struck him Finley ran closely pursued, and soon caught up with the hindmost man, who received the tomahawk, intended for Finley, in the back of his head Close pressed, but protected by the fire of a comrade, he safely crossed the bridge and reached the fort A remarkable case of premonition or telepathy or call it as one may, must here be recorded During young Finley s running fight and narrow escapes, just mentioned his father, Rev James Finley, three hundred miles away had a strange and undefinable impression that his son was in great danger, but could form no distinct conception of its nature or cause He fell to his knees and spent a long time in earnest prayer for his son, arising with the comfortable feeling that the danger was past He made a note of the time, and when a few weeks later he received a letter from his son giving an account of his narrow escapes from death, he saw that the time corresponded exactly with his own strange experience Rev Finley was a man of absolute truth

—the reader must settle for himself what was the cause of this wireless intercourse between father and son and separated by three hundred miles of space

Ebenezer Finley grew to be a man of importance in his community His home was in Redstone on Dunlap's creek, where at an early day he erected a grist mill and a saw mill He married four wives, and all rest in Dunlaps' Creek churchyard He died January 1 1849, aged eighty-eight years He was an elder of Dunlap's Creek Presbyterian Church for seventy years, and for half a century ruling elder He married (first) Jane Kinkaid, died June 5 1793, (second) Violet Lowry, died November 11 1804 (third) Margery Cunningham born 1770, died January 27, 1822, (fourth) Mrs Sarah Jones, born September 14, 1769 died January 24 1848 Children of Ebenezer Finley, by first wife, Jane Kinkaid 1 John Evans, born November, 1783, died March, 1793 2 James Elliot born November, 1784, died 1861 a farmer of Menallen township, Fayette county 3 Elizabeth born December 1786, died July 1860 4 Joseph, born March 8, 1788 died December 1848 5 Hannah, born October, 1791, died March, 1793 Children of second wife, Violet Lowry 6 Rebecca, born October, 1795 7 Hannah (2), born October 10, 1796 8 William born August, 1798, moved to Ohio, where he died 1865, married Rhoda Harris 9 Samuel born July, 1800, moved to Ohio, where he died 10 Jane, born 1802, died August, 1890, married John Hibbs, and lived in Redstone township 11 Ebenezer born October 24 1804, and lost his mother the following November 11 he was a farmer of Menallen township, Fayette county, died December 28, 1891, married, February 9 1826 Phoebe Wood Ward Children by third wife, Margery Cunningham 12 Eli H, born April 6, 1807, died January 7 1892 a farmer of Menallen township, married a Miss Baird 13 Robert, of whom further 14 Margaret, born November 29 1810

(IV) Robert, thirteenth child of Ebenezer Finley, and second child by his third wife, Margery Cunningham was born in Redstone township, Fayette county, Pennsylvania, April 4, 1809 died October 7, 1874 He was educated in the public schools and grew to manhood at the home farm He became a farmer on his own account, owning three hundred and twelve acres of good land, well stocked and improved

He was a man of industry and strictly temperate, having little patience with tipplers, laggards or spendthrifts He was a successful business man, but very quiet and peaceful He was a Republican in politics, serving as school director He was a member of the Dunlap's Creek Presbyterian church, as was his wife He served the church in Redstone as trustee and was very active in church work For forty-five years he was a member and for thirty-five years a trustee He was broadminded and charitable a judicious counsellor and a genial companion His hospitality was proverbial, and his friends were legion He married (first), January 23, 1833, Catherine Carothers who died June 19, 1842 (second) May 13 1845 Anna, daughter of Samuel and Margaret Hertford, both born in Fayette country, but lived all their lives in Luzerne township where they owned a good farm, they were members of the Methodist Episcopal church, their children 1 Thomas, moved to Illinois 2 William, lived in Luzerne township, but in old age moved to Brownsville Pennsylvania 3 Lawrence, moved to Ohio 4 Naomi married Thomas Dunaway, and moved to Ottawa Illinois 5 Mary, married a Lawrence, and moved to Iowa 6 Anna (of previous mention)

Children of Robert Finley and his first wife, Catherine Carothers 1 Ruth, born March 13, 1834, died June 9, 1842 2 Mary Margery, born October 25, 1835 died March 26, 1902, married Jeremiah Baird, eleven children 3 Samuel E born March 15 1838 married Sarah Burchinal 4 Ebenezer born September 6, 1841, died November 1 1842 5 Catherine died June 9, 1842 Children by second wife Anna Herford 6 William Herford died young 7 Thomas W, born June 18 1848, married August 28, 1884 Jennie Smiley, he lives on the old Finley homestead 8 John E of whom further 9 Margaret E, born March 29, 1851, married James G Wilson 10 Naomi, born February 11 1852, died August 1, 1852

(V) John E son of Robert Finley and his second wife Anna Herford, was born in Redstone township, Fayette county, Pennsylvania September 23, 1849 He attended the Pleasant Valley subscription school and spent four years in attendance at Merrittstown Academy in Luzerne township riding three miles to school every day He then became his father's

Wm Elliott Finley

farm assistant continuing until the death of the latter in 1874 He then purchased one hundred and fifty-seven acres of the old William Stone farm in Menallen township, on which the Stone tannery was located The farm was underlaid with the Pittsburgh nine-foot coal vein, and Mr Finley disposed of several acres of the coal only receiving therefor $1,000 per acre He has continued the cultivation and improvement of his farm all through life, and still makes it his home and chief business concern He is a Republican in politics but has never sought or held public office Mr Finley is an elder of the Second Presbyterian Church of Uniontown, his wife also being a communicant of the same church He has also been connected for several years with the Patrons of Husbandry, an order that has greatly benefited the agriculturist in many ways

He married, September 23, 1873, Josephine Hazlett, born in Franklin township Washington county Pennsylvania, October 1, 1846, daughter of Samuel (2) and Jemima (Condit) Hazlett, both born in Washington county, her father was son of Samuel (1) Hazlett born in Ireland, emigrated to the United States and settled in Washington county Samuel (2) Hazlett was the owner of a good farm of one hundred and ninety-six acres in Washington county which he cultivated until death He was a Democrat in politics, and a Presbyterian of the most rigid type His wife Jemima was a daughter of Isaac Condit and of Irish descent Children of first wife Eliza, Ann William, Elizabeth, Caroline and Charlotte all deceased Children of his second wife Samuel J, deceased a farmer on the old Washington county homestead Di I C now of California, John M, deceased, a soldier of the civil war, enlisted in Company K, Sixteenth Regiment, Pennsylvania Cavalry, saw hard service, and was in many of the famous battles of the war including Gettysburg, Josephine (of previous mention), James K, now manager of a company farm near Jeannette, Pennsylvania, Ruth E, now residing with her sister Josephine

Children of John E and Josephine (Hazlett) Finley 1 Winona B, born May 16, 1876, married Thomas Holland, a civil engineer of Uniontown, in the employ of the H C Frick Company, children Wilbur F and Rosa L 2 Anna Myrtle, born June 7 1878, resides with her parents at the home farm

FINLEY For complete early history of this fine old Scotch-Irish and early Fayette county family, see sketch of John E Finley in this work The line of descent from Michael Finley, the emigrant ancestor, is through his fifth son, Rev James Finley, whose third son Ebenezer, married (third) Margery Cunningham Ebenezer Finley had by his first three wives fourteen children of whom Eli H was the twelfth, and first of the three borne by his third wife His full brother, Robert Finley, is recorded at length in sketch mentioned

(IV) Eli H eldest son of Ebenezer Finley and his third wife Margery Cunningham, was born in Redstone township, Fayette county, Pennsylvania April 6, 1807 died January 7, 1892 He grew to manhood at the home farm and received the usual education of a farmer boy of that period After arriving at manhood he settled in Menallen township Fayette county, where he purchased and cultivated a farm the remainder of his days He was energetic and capable, conducting his farm operations successfully He was quiet and retiring in disposition and was held in high esteem among his neighbors He and wife were members of the Presbyterian church He married Maria, daughter of Aaron Baird Children 1 Margaret married Jefferson Burnett and moved to Iowa where both died 2 Mary married James Corder and moved to Illinois, where both died 3 Fairmine, married J P Brown, whom she survives, a resident of New Salem, Pennsylvania 4 Anna, married Jacob Brown he lives in New Salem, she is deceased 5 Dr Robert E was a dentist of Coshocton Ohio died December 31, 1903 6 William E, of whom further

(V) William Elliott, youngest son of Eli H and Maria (Baird) Finley was born in Menallen township Fayette county Pennsylvania April 7, 1843 died March 11 1905 He was educated in the public school and remained at the home farm until his departure for the front during the civil war He enlisted in August 1861, in Company I, Eighty-fifth Regiment Pennsylvania Volunteer Infantry, serving three years and four months when he received his honorable discharge He was severely wounded at the battle of Fair Oaks and was confined in the hospital at Philadelphia for three months before he was able to rejoin his regiment After the war he returned to Fayette county and for seventeen years thereafter he cultivated his father's farm.

Immediately after the sale of the farm and the erection of the Buffington Works thereon, he moved to Uniontown, where he engaged in teaming very successfully until his death. He was a man of high standing in his community, faithful and upright in all his business engagements and highly esteemed. He was a Republican in politics and served as assessor and borough auditor. He was a member of the Grand Army of the Republic and of the Presbyterian church.

He married, April 6, 1870, Mrs. Rachel C. (Moore) Sharpnack, born in German township, Fayette county, daughter of Abraham Moore and widow of Jasper N. Sharpnack. She is a great-granddaughter of Captain Cowan, an officer in the revolution. She is also a great-granddaughter of Captain John Moore, and his wife Margaret (Colvin) Moore, who came from Maryland in 1765 and settled in Redstone township, Fayette county, on a tract yet owned in the Moore family. Aaron, son of Captain John Moore, married Mary Haney and had: John, William, Abraham, Margaret and Mary. Abraham, son of Aaron Moore, was born in Fayette county, May 17, 1823, died August 28, 1902. He was a farmer of Fayette county and a man highly esteemed. He married Adeline McClean, born in Westmoreland county, Pennsylvania, April 2, 1823, died December 24, 1894, daughter of John and Rachel (Cowan) McClean, old settlers of Westmoreland county. She was one of a family of eight children: Gibson, Samuel, William, Thomas, Mary, Isabel, Adeline and Rachel. Children of Abraham and Adeline (McClean) Moore: John Seymour, a farmer of German township; Aaron, deceased, and Rachel C. (see forward).

Rachel C., daughter of Abraham Moore, married (first), October 1, 1868, Jasper N. Sharpnack, born in Fayette county, son of John and Sarah Sharpnack. On October 12, just twelve days after his marriage, he was drowned. She married (second) William Elliott Finley, of previous mention. She is a member of the Presbyterian church and since she became a widow has resided at her home No. 64 South Mount Vernon avenue, Uniontown.

RICHEY   This old Fayette county family is of Scotch-Irish descent. The first of whom we have record is James Richey, who is named on a list of early Connellsville occupations as a "forge carpenter." He was a flat boat builder, a thriving industry in the early days. It was commenced by the westward bound emigrants and traders, who coming across the Alleghenies and over the state road, striking the river at Connellsville, found it a cheaper and easier means of transporting their household goods and merchandise. In the succeeding years it was prosecuted as a regular business by enterprising business men of the town, the Richeys, Millers and Whites building flat boats that carried the pig iron stacked along the banks of the Youghiogheny and floating it down to Pittsburgh and other river points. He continued in active business until compelled to desist by old age.

He married a Miss Sherbondy and had sons: John, David, Hunter, Andrew F., colonel of a militia regiment raised to resist invasion during the civil war. He early settled in West Virginia and at the opening of the civil war purchased the *Fairmont Virginian*, a most pronounced southern paper, changed its name to the *Fairmont National* and edited it as the first and only Republican paper in this country. He was a member of the first convention called to divide the state of Virginia, and was so useful and influential that at his death, November 21, 1867, it was said in the *Wheeling Intelligencer*: "No man in West Virginia will be more widely missed or made greater sacrifice for the cause which he espoused." He married Laverna P. Barnus and left issue.

(II) David, second son of James Richey, was born in 1809 in Connellsville, Pennsylvania. He was a mine worker and lived in Allegheny, Westmoreland and Fayette counties. He was a Democrat and a Baptist. He married Sophia Eicher, born in Westmoreland county, Pennsylvania, daughter of John Eicher, a farmer of that county. Children of David Richey: Hiram; John J., of whom further; Mary, married James Latimer, of Fayette county; Margaret Jane, married James Echard, of Connellsville; Joseph, of near Connellsville; Francis Marion, a carpenter of near Pennsville, Fayette county; James and Maria, both died in infancy.

(III) John J., second son of David and Sophia (Eicher) Richey, was born in Connells-

Abraham Moore

ville, Pennsylvania, March 4, 1839 He was educated in the public school, and in early life lived principally on a farm He continued farming as an occupation, working for others until 1887, when he bought a farm of one hundred and twenty-eight acres in Bullskin township, upon which he has since successfully conducted a line of general farming In politics he is a Democrat and active in township affairs, having served as road supervisor for seven years and as school director He enlisted, in 1862, in Company F, 168th Regiment, Pennsylvania Infantry, for nine months, at the expiration of which time he was honorably discharged

He married (first) Melvina Hutchinson, born in Fayette county daughter of William Hutchinson, an old settler of the county He married (second) a widow, Mrs Christina (Rist) Sharp, died in 1900 daughter of Peter and Sarah (Galley) Rist Children of first wife 1 Melvina, resides in Pittsburgh, unmarried 2 David, a farmer of Fayette county married Catherine Cable 3 Joseph, a pipe fitter of Pittsburgh, married Carrie Dethorn 4 Annie, married Robert Harbuck and lives in Pittsburgh 5 Lindley married Iva Sanders and lives in Fayette county 6 Sophia Alice, married Guy Bogardus a Baltimore and Ohio engineer, resides in Pittsburgh 7 Margaret, died in infancy Children of second wife 8 Charles, married Myrtle Jouthers and lives in Connellsville where he is a motorman on the street railway 9 Frank a farmer, married Winifred Bell deceased 10 Ewing Porter, a street car conductor married Lottie Cooper and lives in Connellsville 11 Cora, resides at home

---

CUNNINGHAM The Cunninghams of Fayette county descend from James Cunningham born in Ireland Through intermarriage they are connected with some of the oldest families of the county notably the Craft family, early settlers at Brownsville The Cunninghams were an old and prominent family in Ireland, holding position under both church and state appointment

(I) James Cunningham, great-grandfather of the present generation, lived and died in Ireland He was a landholder, married and reared a large family, including a son William the founder of this branch in Fayette county

(II) William son of James Cunningham, was born in Ireland where he was educated and grew to manhood When a young man he came to the United States, finally settling in Luzerne township, where he operated a distillery and a general store with profit He married Mary Gallagher and had issue 1 James, of whom further 2 Ann married James Work 3 John married Mary Muir, children William Jane, Robert Eliza, died unmarried, Elizabeth all deceased except Jane

(III) James son of William and Mary (Gallagher) Cunningham was born in Luzerne township, Fayette county Pennsylvania July 25, 1812 died April 8, 1888 He was educated in the public school, and on arriving at suitable age was apprenticed to learn the blacksmith's trade He became a skilled worker in iron and steel following his trade until 1850, when he purchased a good farm in the township, spending his after years engaged in its culture While his early school advantages were limited, he so improved himself by later study and reading that he became an unusually well informed man His penmanship was remarkably fine, while in mechanical skill he was unsurpassed by any smith in the county He was a Democrat in politics, active and influential in party councils He was elected and served as county commissioner, also as county auditor, he held several township offices was for many years a member of the school board, serving as president of the board, and for ten years was justice of the peace He was ever afterward known locally as "Squire" Cunningham and was the dread of the evildoers

He married Rosanna M Muir born March 25 1811, died September 8 1885 Children 1 Mary Jane, born November 3, 1836, married, 1859, Isaiah Newton Craft, born at the Craft homestead, April 21, 1837, died December 8, 1910, son of Daniel Craft He attended the old Bunker Hill school, and while still a young man purchased a farm near Lock No 5, which he cultivated until his father's death, when he returned home and managed the home farm for the remainder of his life Besides the general farming and stock raising operations which he conducted on the home place, his only other business venture was in 1874, when he opened a mercantile store in partnership with Alfred Cunningham at Belle Vernon From 1866 he was a member of the Cumberland Presbyterian Church and was active in managing finances during the building of the Hopewell church For over twenty years he was an elder in the church and for the same length of time was superintendent of the Sunday school In politics he was a Democrat and at various times held the offices of school director, tax collector, inspector and judge of elections He was an excellent type of citizen, unfalteringly performing his civil duties and giving the best of his time and efforts to his church and Sunday school work His influence throughout the township was enormous and always enrolled on the side of the weak and defenceless in the cause of right Children of Isaiah Newton and Mary Jane (Cunningham) Craft Ewing Oscar, died 1910, Harry died aged three years 2 John, born September 27, 1838, died 1910 3 Martha A, of whom further 4 Sarah Ann, born August 21 1843, died August 27, 1900 5 Alfred, born August 1, 1845 died February 11 1905 6 Ann Eliza, born March 14 1850 lives on the old Cunningham homestead

(IV) Martha A, third child and second daughter of James and Rosanna M (Mun) Cunningham was born in Luzerne township, Fayette county, Pennsylvania, April 16, 1841 For many years she was teacher in the local schools but for the past fifteen years has been directing the management of her estate, on which she and her widowed sister reside

RALSTON The Ralstons of Connellsville are of Scotch ancestry and parentage The first of this branch to come to the United States was Hugh Ralston born in Edinburgh Scotland in 1822, died 1906 He was educated and grew to manhood in Scotland came to the United States in 1849, and settled in New York City He entered the employ of the New York Central railroad and for almost half a century was section foreman on that road He married Margaret Fitzsimmons, born in County Caven Ireland, 1824, died 1907 daughter of Patrick Fitzsimmons, who came to the United States about 1843, settling in the Province of Quebec, Canada, purchasing a farm on which he lived until his death He married in Ireland and had issue Margaret was about eighteen years of age when her parents went to Canada, but did not accompany them, remaining in New York City with friends and there married Hugh Ralston He was a Presbyterian, she a Catholic

Children Hugh (2), now living at Bristol, Quebec, Canada, Henry died aged two years, Mary Jane married J M McLean and lives in Toronto Canada Rachel, married John Roy, a farmer and merchant of Bristol Canada

(II) John White, third son of Hugh and Margaret (Fitzsimmons) Ralston was born at Hudson, Columbia county, New York, October 6 1854 He was educated in the public schools, and while yet a boy began business life as clerk in a general store in Hudson He remained there in New York state until 1880, when he came to Fayette county and entered the employ of the H C Frick Coke Company as pay roll clerk at Broadford soon after becoming bookkeeper He remained there about five years then was promoted chief clerk at Trotter, Pennsylvania, remaining there about eight years He was then transferred to Mount Pleasant and made chief clerk of the Southwestern Connellsville Coke Company, a subsidiary company, remaining there until 1901 In 1901 he was in the employ of Stuart Coal Mining Company, situated at Landstreet Somerset county Pennsylvania who enlarged and reorganized as the Somerset Coal Company of which Mr Ralston was made chief clerk and confidential bookkeeper with residence at Somerset Pennsylvania In 1904 J F McCormick secretary and treasurer of the Connellsville Machine & Car Company, died and the position was offered Mr Ralston who accepted under the advice of his father-in-law, James McGrath president of the company He took up his residence in Connellsville the same year and continued secretary and treasurer of the car company until 1905 when he was appointed secretary and treasurer of the Fayette Brewing Company of which he was a stockholder He is now the active secretary and treasurer of both companies The brewing company's plant is located at Uniontown the car company s at Connellsville Both are prosperous concerns and afford ample scope for Mr Ralston's abilities as an executive officer which it may truthfully be said are of a high order He is a Republican in politics and with his family is a member of the Church of the Immaculate Conception of Connellsville (Roman Catholic) He also belongs to the Knights of Columbus, the Catholic Mutual Benevolent Association and the Holy Name Society

He married, October 11 1883 Frances Ophelia McGrath, born in Connellsville, daughter of James and Jane (Clark) McGrath James McGrath was born in Ireland in 1836 and in 1849 came to the United States, locating in Buffalo, New York where he learned the trade of machinist in the shops of the Buffalo Steam Engine Company He next entered the employ of the Pennsylvania railroad and in 1859 came to Connellsville to take charge as foreman of the Smith shops of the Pittsburgh & Connellsville railroad In September 1865 he formed a partnership with Bernard Winslow and under the firm name of McGrath & Winslow leased land on Water street erected shops, and began the manufacture of railroad frogs and switches also tools for oil wells This concern has passed through many changes of name and ownership, but Mr McGrath has always retained principal ownership In 1870 the business was incorporated as the Connellsville Machine & Car Company, with Mr Mc Grath president, which position he yet holds He is a member of the Church of the Immaculate Conception and a Democrat in politics He married, January 11, 1859 Jane Clark born in Ireland daughter of Thomas and Margaret Clark Their children 1 Mary Margaret, married A B McHugh, whom she survives a resident of Connellsville 2 Fannie Ophelia, of previous mention 3 Eleanor Ann, married J T Rush superintendent of Hostettler Coke Company at Whitney Pennsylvania 4 Amelia, married Thomas Madigan whom she survives, a resident of Connellsville 5 Kate, married Charles W Patterson, of Connellsville 6 Charles C, superintendent of Connellsville Machine & Car Company, married Anna Quinn 7 John T

Children of John White and Frances Ophelia (McGrath) Ralston Margaret Eleanor, James Hugh John Rudolph born 1890, Charles Clark 1892 Paul Henry 1896, May Frances, September 25, 1902

HOOPER This is a purely English family, the children of Thomas J Hooper, of Connellsville being the first American-born generation of this branch The family trace an English ancestry back many generations, the men of the family holding positions in the mechanical world far above the average

(I) Thomas Hooper, born in England was a man of education and superior mechanical intelligence He was a mine foreman in England until 1881 when he came to the United States, locating in Fayette county, Pennsylvania, where he was a valued employee of the H C Frick Coal & Coke Company He met his death through injury at the Leith mine October 5, 1895 Both Mr Hooper and his wife were members of the Established Church of England (Episcopal) He married, in England, Maria Richards, who died March, 1907 Children 1 William R 2 Thomas J of whom further 3 Sidney | 4 Anna M married Harry White, now of San Antonio, Texas 5 Beatrice E, married John H May, of Youngwood Pennsylvania 6 Edith married Charles Harford, of Uniontown Pennsylvania 7 Leah, deceased married F H Detwiler

(II) Thomas J second son of Thomas and Maria (Richards) Hooper, was born in London, England February 12 1866 He was educated in the Zetland public school of Yorkshire and chose a mercantile life At the age of eighteen years he came to the United States (1884), following his parents who came in 1881 He finally located in Oskaloosa, Iowa, where for two years he was engaged in the shoe business He later came to Uniontown, Pennsylvania where he was engaged in the same business about five years as a salesman He then located in Connellsville, Pennsylvania, entering the employ of Johnston & Norris of that city as a salesman He continued with that firm about ten years, when opportunity offering he purchased the interest of Lloyd Johnston and became junior member of the firm of Norris & Hooper This firm continued in successful business until September, 1910 when it was dissolved, Mr Norris retiring and W R Long purchasing his interest, becoming junior member of Hooper & Long The store does a strictly retail business and is a well known, thoroughly established concern ranking high in public favor Mr Hooper is a Republican in politics and has served his city as councilman and as school director He is a member of the Presbyterian church, and is the present (1912) worshipful master of King Solomon's Lodge No 346 Free and Accepted Masons He is a companion of the Connellsville Chapter, Royal Arch Masons and a Knights Templar of Uniontown Commandery In the Scottish Rite he has attained the thirty-second degree, belonging to Uniontown Lodge of Perfection and Pittsburgh Consistory

He married, January 14, 1889 Rachel E

Cropp, born in Dunbar township, Fayette county, Pennsylvania, daughter of Joseph and Sarah Cropp, of Dunbar township. Children: 1. Albert J., born October 31, 1890; educated in public schools and business college; now engaged with his father in the shoe business. 2. Clarence T., born July 15, 1892; a medical student at the Jefferson Medical School, Philadelphia. 3. Bertha M., born October 19, 1895. 4. Robert, born July 8, 1900. 5. Sarah, born February 10, 1903. 6. Ella Belle, born August 28, 1905, died March 31, 1909.

RHODES This name, spelled by the emigrant both Roads and Roades, is found also as Rhodes and Rhoades. The founder of the Rhoads family of Philadelphia and Pennsylvania was John, who signed his will Roades. He was born in county Darby, England, about 1639. The family in that county is an ancient one and is said by Burke to have descended from Gerard de Rodes, of Horn Castle, county Lincoln, in the time of Henry II. The settlement of Pennsylvania created wide interest among the Friends in Darby, and as a result many emigrated to the land of Penn. Among these was John (2) Roades, son of John (1) Roades. Two years later Adam, another son, came to Pennsylvania. The coming of these boys influenced the father to dispose of his English estate and join them. He came about 1696 and purchased land on High (now Market street), Philadelphia, where he is first found officially in 1698. In 1700 he sold his Philadelphia property and moved to Darby, where he bought a farm, and died in 1701. His will, signed "John Roades," made October 20, 1701, proved October 22 of the following month, mentions sons Jacob, John, Adam, Joseph, and daughters Mary and Elizabeth. Joseph, the youngest son, received his Chester county farm. The name is spelled in the body of the will "Roads." No wife is named, she no doubt having preceded him to the grave. Her name was Elizabeth. Their nine children, all born in England, are in order of birth: Adam, Mary, John (2), Elizabeth, Jacob, Abraham, Sarah, Hannah and Joseph. The four sons all married and founded families whose descendants are found in many counties of Pennsylvania.

(I) The family in Connellsville was founded there by Henry Rhodes, of Germantown, Pennsylvania, a descendant of John Roades, the founder. The coming to Fayette county of Henry Rhodes was in 1800, when his daughter Mary married Joseph Smith, who came to investigate a land purchase made by his father, John Smith, of Germantown. The history of this purchase is interesting: Colonel Hayes, a revolutionary officer, owned, at Barren Run, near Smithtown in Rostraver township, Westmoreland county, Pennsylvania, a tract of about twenty-two hundred acres. There he built a log house, the first in the locality. Later he sold his holdings to one Shields, who in turn sold the tract to one Backhouse. The latter died before payment was made and Shields, being in need of money, advertised it for sale at Greensburg, the county seat; there being no bidders, he obtained authority from the court to offer it for sale in Philadelphia, where it was sold in 1798 to John Smith. In 1800 John Smith sent his son Joseph out to investigate his purchase. The latter, before starting on this long trip, married Mary Rhodes and together they came to Western Pennsylvania and founded the family later so numerous in and around Smithtown. This brings the narrative to the coming of Henry Rhodes, then a resident of Germantown. He accompanied his daughter and son-in-law on their western journey in 1800, no doubt taking his own family along, or bringing them soon after. He lived in the old log house built by Colonel Hayes and later bought a farm, on part of which Smithtown now stands. He had nine children: John, Michael, Peter, Henry, all of whom founded families, and five daughters, who married: Joseph Smith, Peter Sowash, Jacob Fullmer, Solomon Hough and Michael Warner. Henry Rhodes, Jr. bought land along the river known as the "Heltervan tract," part of which he sold to his brother John.

(II) John, son of Henry Rhodes, purchased a part of the "Heltervan tract" from his brother Henry, married, and there reared a family consisting of Betsey, Samuel, Abraham, Henry John and Joseph.

(III) Joseph, son of John Rhodes, a farmer of Westmoreland county, became a wealthy and leading man in his community. He married and left issue, including Joseph.

(IV) Joseph (2), son of Joseph (1) Rhodes, (this name is also spelled in Westmoreland county, Rhoades) was born at Smithtown (now in South Huntington township, Westmoreland county) He was a farmer and distiller, justice of the peace and a member of the Universalist church He served three years in the civil war in Company B, 77th Regiment, Pennsylvania Volunteer Infantry receiving honorable discharge at Nashville, Tennessee, June 22, 1865 He married Susanna Rowe, now deceased They had nine children, one being Henry

(V) Henry (2), son of Joseph (2) Rhodes, was born June 9, 1866 He was educated in the public schools, and began business life as manager of the store operated by the Youghiogheny River Coal Company He later formed a partnership with Irwin Smith, and until 1900 they operated a general store at Blythedale In that year they sold out to the Pittsburgh Coal Company, and Mr Rhodes settled in Connellsville with his family He purchased the general store of I C Smutz and continued in business until 1910 He then engaged in real estate and insurance, until April, 1912, when he embarked in the grocery business He is an active Democrat and was school director of New Haven borough before consolidation He is prominent in the Masonic order, being a past master and holding the thirty-second degree of the Ancient Accepted Scottish Rite in religious faith a Methodist He married Mollie, daughter of John Branthoover, for many years foreman later superintendent of a coal company in Indiana county, Pennsylvania His first wife died young, leaving a daughter Mollie aforementioned, born in Indiana county, December 28, 1867, who is still living and, like her husband, a devoted Methodist Children of Henry and Mollie Rhodes Roy Otis of whom further Freda, Joseph, Gertrude, Marguerite

(VI) Roy Otis, eldest son of Henry (2) Rhodes, was born at Smithtown Pennsylvania, April 20 1887 He was educated in the public school of Blythedale, and began business life as a clerk in his father's store continuing until he was nineteen years of age He then spent two years at Valparaiso University (Indiana), after which he returned to the store He acquired a knowledge of stenography and for six months held a position at Dunbar as stenographer On May 5, 1911, he opened a gentlemen's furnishing store at No 809 West Main street Connellsville, where he is still located in successful business He is a Democrat and in

November, 1911, was the candidate of his party for city auditor, failing of election by but two votes He is a member of the Methodist Episcopal church, and one of the popular rising young business men of Connellsville

THOMPSON The Thompsons of Uniontown Pennsylvania, herein recorded, have an ancestry traced to many lands, paternally of Scotch-Irish blood and maternally of German and Holland Dutch, the Markles coming from Alsace and Amsterdam In this country the Markles settled in Berks county, Pennsylvania, the Thompsons coming in from the South, residing for a time in Westmoreland county, Pennsylvania, then going to the "dark and bloody" battle grounds of Kentucky

The founder of the family in Westmoreland county, Pennsylvania, William Thompson, great-grandfather of Josiah V Thompson, came to Mount Pleasant from the Cumberland Valley of Pennsylvania, from the Big Spring Presbyterian Church congregation near Chambersburg, Pennsylvania He served throughout the revolutionary war from beginning to end, serving in the battles of the Brandywine and Germantown in 1776, and those of Trenton and Princeton in 1777, and also at Yorktown where Cornwallis surrendered He married Mary Jack of Scotch-Irish and Huguenot descent, daughter of John Jack who was prominent in drafting the "Hannastown Declaration" in 1775, which preceded both the Mecklenberg Declaration and the Declaration of Independence given to the world at Philadelphia, Pennsylvania July 4 1776 Mr Thompson removed to Kentucky after the close of the revolutionary war became a comrade in arms of Daniel Boone and died in Mason county of the state he helped to create and settle There are many Thompson families of different branches and nationalities, the name being found in England Ireland and Scotland In Fayette county Pennsylvania, it is well known and none is more honored

(II) Andrew Finley, son of William Thompson was born in Kentucky in 1789, died in Westmoreland county Pennsylvania, in 1825 He served as a soldier in the war of 1812 with three of his brothers He was taken prisoner when Hull surrendered at Detroit, and after his release tramped on foot to Westmoreland county, where relatives were living There he married Leah, the twenty-second and youngest child of Caspard Markle, of Westmoreland county, a native of Berks county, Pennsylvania (see Markle), and with her on horseback over the wilderness trail; she died in that state in 1824. He then returned to Westmoreland county, Pennsylvania, accompanied by his two younger children, and there his death occurred. Children of Mr. and Mrs. Thompson: William L., died aged twenty years in Missouri; Mary, married J. P. Crothers, of Fayette county, Pennsylvania; Jasper Markle, of whom further.

(III) Jasper Markle, son of Andrew Finley Thompson, was born near Washington, Mason county, Kentucky, August 30, 1822, died March 15, 1889, at his residence in Menallen township, Fayette county, Pennsylvania, two and a half miles west of Uniontown. When he was three years of age, his parents being deceased, he was taken to Westmoreland county, Pennsylvania, where he resided with his grandmother, Mary Markle, until her death in 1832, when he went to reside with a cousin, General Cyrus P. Markle. He was educated in the old subscription school and spent his early life in farming, clerking and bookkeeping, on the farm and in the store and paper mills of his cousin. In April, 1850, he located in Redstone township, Fayette county, Pennsylvania, where he purchased a farm, but soon sold it and later in the same year moved to Menallen township, where he purchased a farm two and a half miles from Uniontown. Here he resided, farmed and dealt in live stock until 1862. In that year he was appointed by President Lincoln collector of internal revenue for the twenty-first Pennsylvania district, in which office he served most effectually for four years, then resigned and returned to his home and farm. He collected and paid over to the government during his four years' service over $2,000,000, having in one day collected $100,000 on whiskey alone. He held two commissions under President Lincoln, covering his four years as collector and receiver of commutation money.

In 1863 he became one of the organizers and original directors of the First National Bank, which is now the leading financial institution of Uniontown. He was elected president of the bank, June 11, 1870, and continued at its head until 1889, the year of his death. This bank was established in 1854 by John T. Hogg as

one of his chain of private banks; later it was owned by Isaac Skiles, Jr., until 1864, when it was organized as a national bank, its number on the list of national banks being 270. Under President Thompson the bank prospered and entered upon its most successful career. He was a wise financier and laid deep the foundations upon which a great financial edifice has risen. He was also president of the Uniontown Building & Loan Association, director of the Fayette County Railroad, president of the Fayette County Agricultural Society, trustee of Washington and Jefferson College, and a director of the Western Theological Seminary in Allegheny City, Pennsylvania.

He was a Whig in politics until the formation of the Republican party, then cast his lot in the new party. In 1868 he was a presidential elector and cast his vote for General U. S. Grant for president. In 1873 he was elected to the state legislature from Fayette county, reversing a normal Democratic majority of one thousand votes by a majority of 1,031 for himself. For nearly thirty years he was ruling elder in the Presbyterian church of Uniontown, of which he was an active and honored member for almost forty years. He continued in active work until March, 1889, when he died of pneumonia on his hurried return from a business trip from Florida and Alabama, having caught a severe cold in Kentucky which developed so rapidly that he died the evening following his return home. His was a strong character, and if a reason can be given for his success in life it was due to his strict attention to business and his devotion to duty. He was consistent in his religious obligations, and was most generous and unostentatious in his charities.

He married, in February, 1846, Eliza, youngest daughter of Samuel and Ruth (Elliott) Caruthers, of Sewickley township, Westmoreland county, Pennsylvania, a ruling elder in the Sewickley Presbyterian church. The mother of Samuel Caruthers was a daughter of Lieutenant John Potter, first sheriff of Cumberland county, Pennsylvania, in 1750 to 1756, and her brother, General James Potter, was a trusted officer and friend of General Washington during the revolution. Children of Mr. and Mrs. Thompson: 1. Ruth A., educated at Washington, Pennsylvania, Female Seminary; married, in 1875, Dr. J. T. Shepler, of Dunbar, Pennsylvania. 2. Lenora M., educated at the same institution as her sister; married, in 1873,

Eliza Thompson

John A Niccolls, of Brownsville, Pennsylvania 3 William M whose sketch follows 4 Josiah V , of whom further

(IV) Josiah Vankirk son of Jasper Markle Thompson was born in Menallen township, near Uniontown, Pennsylvania, February 15, 1854 He attended the public schools and lived on the home farm until he entered Washington and Jefferson College, Washington, Pennsylvania, whence he was graduated in June, 1871 On November 11 of that year he entered the employ of the First National Bank of Uniontown as clerk, his father being then president of the bank On April 3 1872 he was promoted teller, and on June 5 1877, following the death of James T Redburn, was made cashier March 15, 1889, his father died, and on April 2, 1889, he succeeded him in the presidency and still remains (1912) the honored head of that most wonderful financial institution, which according to the government reports, has more surplus and profits in proportion to capital than any other national bank in the United States, and the bank examiner says that it pays the largest salaries to the minor employees of any bank in the country The capital stock is $100,000 In 1907 its surplus was $1,100 000 which means that every one hundred dollars of stock has a real book value of eleven hundred dollars The surplus now (August 28 1912) is $1 512,000 In addition the bank pays a semi-annual dividend of eleven per cent or twenty-two per cent annually There is just one reason for this and that is Josiah V Thompson To lead from a country town over six thousand national banks, many of them with greater capital, much larger deposits, and located in the very center of the business of the nation needs a reason and you have it in Mr Thompson himself

First let us explain what Mr Thompson and the First National Bank does not do No loans are made for more than the legal six per cent rate, nor is a bonus ever asked or taken from borrowers If you get the money at all you get it regular and no bonus inducement can tempt a dollar from their vaults , again, no deposits are received except subject to check no interest being paid on deposits no matter how large Employees are never put under bond Mr Thompson hires no one until satisfied that he is thoroughly trustworthy and of the right mettle, then he is placed on his own sense of duty and honor No one has ever gone wrong in the entire history of the First National Bank,

but all are required to abstain from drink and tobacco in every form, this on the ground that such habits are not conducive to success in business or growth in morality

The things that President Thompson and the First National Bank do are many, and from them can be gleaned why the bank leads the Roll of Honor issued by the United States government The high salaries paid insure the best service Old employees are rewarded for faithful service by being made participants in the profits of his large, lucrative individual coal operations This policy has been extended to depositors, particularly women with limited incomes whom he has allowed to share in the same manner until they have become financially strong through their small investments There are at least four hundred depositors to whom he has afforded opportunity for profitable investment This generous policy has enriched many and built up a loyal host of depositors and workers for the advancement of the bank This policy of generous advice to investors has ever been carried to those of another class There are many men in his community to whom unsecured advances of money have been privately made in times of financial distress which have placed them again on a safe footing This, of course, is the personal affair of Mr Thompson, but Mr Thompson and the First National Bank in Uniontown are synonymous terms, but the greatest factor is his wonderful capacity for work and his power of inspiring his subordinates with enthusiasm and zeal

It is not uncommon for Mr Thompson to work continuously in his private office at the bank for a week without as much sleep as would amount in that period to one good night's rest He personally attends to all his own correspondence and writes his own letters Frequently on his return home from an absence of a day or two he will drive to the bank after a lunch at his home, Oak Hill to see what letters demand his attention There may be one hundred and fifty of them but every one will be answered before the light above his desk is turned out, daybreak often finding him at his desk When this happens he usually makes the best of the situation and again goes to work with the bank force for another day's business without having either rest or sleep It is not uncommon, when work is very pressing, to even follow this by another night's work at his desk, then going home for a couple of hours sleep to be back again at 9 A M to begin again The spirit of emulation aroused by the knowledge all the employees have of the stiain and severity of Mr Thompson's work has much to do with the success of the bank, naturally all wishing to keep pace with the president, but none can do it, try as they may He can go sound asleep in a second anywhere, and when he awakens it is with every faculty and instinct alert with life He will fall asleep standing in the public bank room writing a letter, nap, perhaps, for fifteen minutes, and on awakening resume instantly the writing of his letter just where he dropped it, without having to read it over to pick up the thread of his thought

In his enormous coal and land operations he personally attends to all the detail, whether he is in them alone or with others All his associates do is to put in their share of the purchase money When the deal is closed each partner gets a statement of the essential details and a memorandum that such an amount of money has been placed to his credit in the First National This is usually his original investment plus a handsome profit, often many times the sum invested His operations are startling He has bought and sold most of the coking coal deposit of Fayette county and still owns many acres In Greene county his coal acreage is immense He is also a very large owner of Washington and Allegheny counties, Pennsylvania, and of West Virginia coal lands He is undoubtedly the largest individual owner of the valuable thick vein coking coal lands in the United States, and has an enormous fortune, which he is credited with having accumulated by fair means, without having wronged a single person or having enjoyed any exclusive legislation or social or commercial advantages

Another marked feature of his personality is his remarkable memory Of the two thousand notes held by the First National Bank he can name from memory every maker and endorser and give their address On one occasion he entertained at his residence at Oak Hill a party of Cleveland capitalists to whom he had sold a $3 000,000 tract of coal On being asked concerning his trip around the world, beginning in 1903 and continuing fifteen months, he took his questioners to nearly every quarter of the globe, naming not only the places visited, but the date and details associated with each place He stated that he had not kept a diary further than that each day he noted the number of miles traveled His ability to read nature is wonderful, and seldom is he wrong Many loans are made by the First National Bank with no security beyond Mr Thompson's knowledge and belief in the man In 1901 he conceived the idea of an eleven-story building as a suitable home for the First National Bank The population was then seven thousand, four hundred and thirty-three, and only the Carnegie building in Pittsburgh was the superior of this proposed building as recently as 1890 But he reasoned that the First National Bank had made its money in Uniontown and that it was meet and proper that this able and progressive bank should foster home investment and give Uniontown what it greatly needed—a modern office and apartment building The plans were drawn by the World's Fair architects, D H Burnham & Company, and the building when completed was unsurpassed in the United States or in the world for utility and convenience It houses a thousand persons, and from morning until night is a scene of continuous activity In no city in the world of its size can such a commercial building be found A fitting home for the greatest bank and a fitting monument for the man who inspired it The bank building has a frontage of 150 feet on Main street, and runs back 150 feet to Peter street

The public service of Mr Thompson has been weighty and valuable He served on the commission that freed the Monongahela river from the heavy burden of toll, was a member and president of the city council from 1892 to 1900, a period of great improvement in the city, was president of the News Publishing Company, president of the Union Cemetery Company, and has aided and abetted every legitimate enterprise in his city which has been offered to him for support

Mr Thompson married, December 11, 1879, Mary, daughter of John and Sarah (Redburn) Anderson She died August 8, 1896 Children Andrew A, born October 25, 1880, John R, born October 6, 1882

(The Markle Line)

The progenitor of the Markle family in Westmoreland county, Pennsylvania, was Christian Markle, born in Alsace, Germany, 1678 To avoid religious persecution following the Revocation of the Edict of Nantes he fled to Amsterdam, Holland, where he married Jemima Weurtz, a sister of an admiral in the Dutch navy In 1703 he came to America, settling at Moselem Springs, Berks county, Pennsylvania, where he purchased fifteen hundred acres of land He was a coach maker and established on his farm a wagon-making shop, a blacksmith shop and a grist mill

Caspard, youngest son of Christian Markle, was born in Berks county Pennsylvania, 1732, died at Mill Grove, Westmoreland county, Pennsylvania, in 1819 He owned, with Judge Painter, large tracts of land on Sewickley creek, extending for several miles

He erected a grist mill on the creek, which traversed his homestead and made some of the first flour manufactured west of the mountains, this he transported in flatboats to New Orleans In 1819 the citizens erected a monument to him to commemorate his early connection with flour making west of the Alleghenies He married (first) Elizabeth Grim, and moved to Westmoreland county His wife died there, and in 1776 he returned to Berks county, where he married (second) Mary Rothermel and again returned to Westmoreland county He had by both wives twenty-two children, the youngest being Leah, wife of Andrew Finley Thompson (see Thompson)

Several of the Markles were soldiers George Markle was a soldier of the Indian war and fought at the defense of Wheeling Another George Markle was a revolutionary soldier and fought at Brandywine Jacob Markle was in the naval service under Commodore Barney Another member of the family, Abraham Markle, came from Germany and settled in Canada and was a delegate to the provincial parliament In the war of 1812 he came to the United States and became a colonel in the American army The British government confiscated his property in Canada but the United States gave him four sections of land near Fort Harrison, in Indiana

THOMPSON (IV) William M , son of Jasper Markle (q v) and Eliza (Caruthers) Thompson, was born November 13, 1851, in Menallen township, Fayette county, Pennsylvania. Being the eldest son, responsibilities came to him at an early age, but he was eager to be useful, and in addition to his school work became a most useful assistant, even while yet a growing boy He attended the public schools of Menallen township and later Madison Academy in Uniontown After finishing his preparatory course he entered Washington and Jefferson College, from whence he was graduated, class of 1871 After graduation he returned to the home farm and took full charge of its operation His father at that time was deeply engrossed with his affairs of the bank and gladly surrendered the management of his agricultural interests to his son So good a manager was he that the farm of one hundred and sixty acres, when he took it as a young man, had been increased to an estate of seven hundred acres at his father's death This land all lay in fertile portions of Menallen and South Union townships By his father's will William M inherited four hundred and fifty acres, including the homestead, which has ever since been his home He has devoted his entire life to agriculture and its kindred pursuits Besides caring for his own estate he also has the management of several hundred acres belonging to the brother Josiah V Thompson He has taken a deep interest in high grade stock and has a herd of short-horned cattle on his farm that experts pronounce the finest among the many fine herds of short-horns in the state of Pennsylvania He carries this same idea of excellence through all his stock breeding and farming operations, and is a perfect type of the prosperous modern American farmer In most comfortable circumstances financially, he is in position to follow modern progress in all lines pertaining to his business and to prove by actual experiment the value of the different methods in fine stock breeding, rotation of crops, selection of seed etc These experiments he is constantly carrying on his being almost an experimental farm for that section He has raised the standard of the agricultural methods of his township and freely gives of his experiences for the benefit of his neighbors

He is a Republican in politics and although deeply interested in public affairs, never desired or sought public office. He stands for what is pure and honest in local government and wields an influence exerted only for good. He is a member and an elder of the First Presbyterian Church of Uniontown and interested in all god works. While not deeply interested in business other than agriculture, he yet holds a position in the directorate of the First National Bank of Uniontown and the same position in the Richhill Coke Company.

He married, January 12 1887 Catherine Mays Ruple, born in Washington county, Pennsylvania, daughter of General James B and Sarah A (Mays) Ruple. Children, all born in Menallen township, Fayette county, Pennsylvania and living at home 1 Helen Ruple, born November 9, 1887, graduate of Washington Seminary 2 Jasper Markle, born January 5 1889, a student at Washington and Jefferson College 3 Catherine M, born January 26 1895, student at Washington Seminary

(The Ruple Line)

The Ruples, originally from Germany, settled in Philadelphia where Baltus Ruple, the founder of the family, was born in about the year 1740 Shortly after the revolution he moved to Morris county, New Jersey, where he lived until 1794, when he came to western Pennsylvania locating in Washington county near the line of Morris and Finley townships, two miles north of Prosperity Village. He died there the following year. He was twice married his second wife being Anna McCallum, the mother of his five children Colonel James, David, Elizabeth Mary and Margaret By his first wife he had John, Ruth and Samuel. His widow married (second) Major Charles Cracraft, a pioneer and Indian fighter who on several occasions was captured by his red foes but always escaped

(II) Colonel James Ruple, eldest son of Baltus Ruple, was born in Morris county, New Jersey, February 18 1788. He was six years of age when his father came to western Pennsylvania, where he received a fair education and grew to manhood on the homestead farm. Before attaining his majority he went to the town of Washington where he learned the carpenter's trade with Samuel Hughes He became a leading contractor and builder

of Washington county, continuing until a few years prior to his death, when he became a brick manufacturer on a large scale Shortly after the war was declared against Great Britain in 1812 he enlisted as a volunteer and was chosen first lieutenant of Captain Sample's company, and upon the formation of the regiment was promoted adjutant He was in service at Black Rock (Buffalo) on the Niagara frontier and served until the troops were discharged from duty there In 1814, when the city of Washington was reported threatened, he quit his business uniformed his apprentices and started with them to the seat of war They were, however, ordered to return before reaching the state line Shortly afterward a volunteer regiment was formed and Mr Ruple was elected its colonel In 1817 he was elected coroner of Washington county, holding the office three years In 1828 he was appointed clerk of the county courts by Governor Shultz, and in 1830 was reappointed by Governor Wolf, serving six years In January, 1839, he was appointed to the same office by Governor Porter and in October of the same year was elected under the provisions of the amended state constitution, serving three years He died January 8, 1855 He married, in 1809 Diana Goodrich, born in New York state near the Connecticut line a descendant of William Goodrich, who came from England to New England in 1643 with his brother John William Goodrich married Sarah Marvin and became a man of consequence in Connecticut His son John married Rebecca Allen and lived in Weathersfield Connecticut Their son Jacob, born November 27, 1694, married Benedict, daughter of Nathaniel and Mehitable (Porter) Goodwin and lived in Wethersfield and Windsor, Connecticut Their son Elijah, born July 3 1724, married August 20, 1752, Margaret Gillett resided at Windsor, Connecticut and Hancock, Massachusetts Their son Jesse born October 28 1759 died September 21, 1852, married, January 16, 1782 Dinah or Diana Bishop Their daughter Dinah or Diana born January 16 1789 died December 14 1885, aged ninety-six years married Colonel James Ruple She came to Washington county, Pennsylvania, with her parents shortly after the year 1800 Children of Colonel James Ruple 1 Elizabeth, deceased, married John Ruth, of Washington county, Pennsylvania 2 James B, of whom further 3 Minerva, married Henry M Buston, whom she survives, a resident of Ohio 4 Joseph C, died in Washington county, Pennsylvania 5 Dr Samuel H, a practicing physician of Illinois 6 Sarah, deceased, married Wilham Acheson 7 Rebecca, married Rev L P Streator, of Washington, Pennsylvania 8 Anna, married John D Brading, of Washington, Pennsylvania 9 John, resides in Washington, Pennsylvania 10 David, deceased 11 Henry 12 Ruth

(III) General James B Ruple, son of Colonel James Ruple, was born June 3, 1812, in Washington county, Pennsylvania, died March, 1901 At the age of twelve years he became his father's assistant in the manufacture of fanning mills The wire screens used had to be bought for cash in Pittsburgh, and, times being hard, father and son attempted to make wire screens themselves The experiment was a success, and when prosperity again came to the country in 1826 they did a good business among the millers of that section They made all kinds of milling wire screens, sieves riddles, etc, later adding wire rat and mouse traps

When a boy of fourteen he was afflicted with a disease that left him a partial cripple for several years When more advanced in years he became a clerk in the county offices In 1832 he moved to Greenbrier county, Virginia, where he engaged in the manufacture of fanning mills, continuing until 1835 or 1836 At the request of his friend John A North clerk of the court of appeals for the western district of Virginia, he accepted a situation in the latter's office continuing a few years, then returning to Washington Pennsylvania Here he was clerk in the post office then the heaviest distributing office in the country He spent the following summer working out of doors at carpentering and in the winter he went south to Louisiana Here malaria drove him north again, and in the fall of 1837, in company with T B Bryson he engaged in cabinetmaking, but was compelled again by his health to abandon business In January, 1839, he was appointed to a clerkship in the office of the secretary of state at Harrisburg, serving under Governor David R Porter until 1845 Prior to this he had bought a half interest in the Washington Examiner and for four years was connected

with that journal in partnership with T W Grayson In 1852 he was appointed deputy sheriff by John McAllister, sheriff of Washington county, serving three years He was then acting prothonotary of the court of common pleas during the illness of W S Moone In 1857 he was elected to that office and re-elected in 1860, serving in that office eight years in all Like his father, he was a Democrat, but in 1854 he split with his party and ever after acted with the Republican party In February, 1867, he was appointed by President Andrew Johnson as assessor of internal revenue of the twenty-fourth Pennsylvania district, serving four years He later lived a retired life He gained his military title of general by service in the National Guard of Pennsylvania In 1836 he was elected captain, and in 1846 was appointed by Governor Shunk a member of his staff with the rank of lieutenant-colonel In 1855 he was commissioned brigadier-general of Pennsylvania militia

General Ruple married, September 24 1839 Sarah A daughter of Charles Mays, one of the oldest settlers of Washington county, Pennsylvania Children 1 Charles M, now an attorney of Washington, Pennsylvania 2 James Goodrich, district passenger agent of the Pennsylvania railroad, located at Pittsburgh 3 Virginia, married Rev J J Jones, of Washington, Pennsylvania, whom she survives 4 Anna M, of Washington, Pennsylvania 5 Frank W, of Columbus Georgia, connected with the Georgia Central railroad 6 Catherine Mays, of previous mention, wife of William M Thompson 7 Etta, married D A J Culbertson, of Washington, Pennsylvania

HARMAN The Harmans, originally from Germany settled at an early date in Westmoreland county, Pennsylvania, where Andrew Harman was born, lived and died He was a farmer and dealt largely in live stock He raised a great deal of stock on his own farm, which, with his purchases he formed into droves and sent on the hoof to eastern markets Until the railroads came they had to be driven the entire distance He served in the war between the states, and was a man of influence in his town He married Mary M Shaffer Children 1 Henry, of whom further 2 John, a farmer of Donegal township, Westmoreland county 3 Pamina, married John Getemey whom she survives, a resident of Latrobe, Pennsylvania

(II) Henry, a son of Andrew Harman, was born in Donegal township Westmoreland county, Pennsylvania, in 1844 He learned the carpenter's trade, and also owned and conducted a farm when a young man In 1880 he moved to Mount Pleasant, Pennsylvania After the Johnstown flood he engaged in the rebuilding of that town, carrying on a large contracting and building business He is now living practically retired He and wife are members of the Methodist Episcopal church In politics he is a Democrat He married Mary Barkley, born in Donegal township, in 1844, died May, 1898, daughter of John Barkley, a farmer of Donegal township, of an early Westmoreland county family Children of John Barkley and wife 1 Hiram, now a farmer of Donegal 2 Mary, of previous mention Children of Henry and Mary Harman 1 Ezra N married a Miss Hoyman and resides at Mount Pleasant, Pennsylvania, he is a well-to-do real estate dealer, specializing in farm property 2 Fimma, married W S Huffman, a livery man of Mount Pleasant, Pennsylvania 3 Allen, resides in Connellsville Pennsylvania, baggage master with the Baltimore & Ohio railroad, married a Miss Critsner 4 George a Pennsylvania railroad employe living at Youngwood Pennsylvania, married a Miss Seamon 5 Elizabeth, died 1903 married Isaac Bungard 6 Isaac, died 1903, w s a liveryman of Mount Pleasant, Pennsylvania, married Miss Hood 7 Minnie married W E Rumbaugh, and lives at Mount Pleasant, Pennsylvania 8 John Henry, of whom farther

(III) John Henry, youngest son of Henry and Mary (Barkley) Harman, was born in Westmoreland county Pennsylvania August 7, 1874 He was six years of age when his parents left the farm and located in Mount Pleasant where he attended the public school, graduating from the high school in 1893 After leaving school he began learning the carpenter's trade, working under the instructions of his father He became an expert workman and was placed in charge of his father's building operations From 1897 to 1902 he was employed in the planing mill of

J W Ruth, of Scottdale, Pennsylvania In 1902 he came to Uniontown, where he installed the saw and planing mill equipment of the Carroll Lumber Company and was manager of that plant for eighteen months In 1903 he was graduated after a seven years' course in architecture with the International Correspondence School of Scranton, Pennsylvania, and in April 1904 formed a partnership with W B Jamison, opening an architect's office in Uniontown The new firm won successful recognition and continued as partners until 1910, when they dissolved, Mr Harmon continuing the business alone He has risen high in his profession, and maintains offices both in Uniontown, Pennsylvania, and Morgantown, West Virginia He has grown steadily in public favor, and with his practical knowledge of constructive building and his skill as a designer makes a most capable superintendent of buildings committed to his care and oversight He has designed many churches, schools, business blocks and fine private residences in Uniontown and elsewhere always with the greatest satisfaction to the owners He designed the clubhouse for the Uniontown Club, also the landscape gardens surrounding it He operates over a wide territory and everywhere may be found evidences of his taste and skill He is a member of Great Bethel Baptist Church and of the Order of Heptasophs In politics he is a Democrat

He married, August 15, 1896, Clara daughter of Louis and Lydia (Koontz) Simpson, both residents of Uniontown Louis Simpson now retired was for twenty years a foreman at the Mount Pleasant Coke Works for the H C Frick Coke Company Mr Harman built his present residence at No 129 Evans street, Uniontown in 1908 Children Louis, born November 28, 1898, Arthur, August 15, 1900 Ralph September 12, 1909

EGNOT The earliest ancestor of this family of whom record is found is Michael Egnot, a farmer and landowner in central Austria, Hungary He remained in Hungary all his life and married Julia ——— Children 1 Michael (2), of whom further 2 John, emigrated to the United States when twelve years of age, resides in Allegheny City, where he holds a position as clerk in a mercantile house 3

Anna, came to the United States and settled at West Butler, Montana, where she married John Garber, a farmer 4 George, died in infancy

(II) Michael (2), son of Michael (1) and Julia Egnot, was born in the central part of Austria about 1864 He was educated in the common schools of his native province, and about 1882 emigrated to this country with his brother John settling in Tyrone township, Fayette county, Pennsylvania where he found employment at one of the blast furnaces for about eighteen months When he was unable to find any more employment there he moved to Braddock, Pennsylvania, where he held the same position for the following four years He then worked in a pipe mill at McKeesport for three years He showed no disposition to remain for any length of time in one particular situation, but after being employed at the Nellie Mines for three years, he gave up his roving life and remained at Juniata for twenty years Here he was engaged in drawing and leveling coke About 1895 he purchased property at Duquesne, Pennsylvania, and in 1903 bought a house with about an acre and a half of land attached near Juniata He has been steadily adding to this until now he owns thirty acres, all of which he cultivates While the wisdom of living an unsettled life as he did might be doubted by some, it is nevertheless true that his prosperous condition justifies his wandering His only relative in this country is a cousin John, a son of his father's brother He is a Republican in politics and a member of the Roman Catholic church

He married, at McKeesport, about 1887 Mary, daughter of John and Susan Monsky children 1 John emigrated to the United States but returned to Austria after five years where he died 2 Susan, married John Dubinsky lives at Charleroi, Pennsylvania 3 Eli, married Mrs Anna Monchan 4 Peter, married Anna ——— and lives at Juniata 5 Mary (of previous mention) Children of Michael (2) and Mary (Monsky) Egnot 1 Michael (3), married Anna Slukey now deceased, had one daughter who died at birth He is employed at Juniata Coke Works 2 John yard foreman at Juniata Coke Works 3 Mary 4 Andrew 5 Anna 6 George 7 Susan 8 Margaret 9 Paul

The Colonial ancestors of the SACKETT Sackets and Sacketts of America came from England The Sackets, Sacketts and Sackvilles of England trace descent from a common ancestor whose forbears were natives of Normandy The name Sackett originated from one whose pursuit was the sacking of wool for shipment In the records of early days Adam S Sackere (Adam, the Sacker) is met with, as one busied not in the care of shearing sheep, but as one engaged in the purchase and shipment of wool This man, whose father or grandfather came to England with Wilham the Conqueror, is recognized by the Sacketts and Sackvilles of England as their common ancestor Just when or under what circumstances the last syllable was changed from "er" to "ett" and "ville" does not appear

Few families have played a more important part in founding developing and maintaining our republic than the descendants of Simon Sackett, of Cambridge, Massachusetts, and John Sackett, of New Haven Connecticut, brothers, who landed at Plymouth, Massachusetts, from England, with Roger Williams No authentic records have yet been discovered which establish beyond question the name of the father of Simon and John Sackett, the accepted tradition being that they came from the Isle of Ely, Cambridgeshire, England In the early records the name is spelled with the final double "t"

(I) Simon Sackett sailed with his brother John December 1, 1630, on the ship "Lyon," from Bristol, England, arriving at Boston February 5 1631 He settled at Newtown (three years later renamed Cambridge), where, with six other "principal gentlemen" he erected a substantial dwelling In the laying out and founding of the town he was an important factor, but the exposure and privations of his midwinter voyage on the "Lyon" had undermined his health, which continued to decline until October, 1635, when he died On November 3 following his widow, Isabel Sackett, was granted authority by the court to administer on his estate It was at this same session of court that the infamous decree banishing Roger Williams from the colony was entered John, brother of Simon Sackett, followed Roger Williams to Rhode Island, and later was a prominent citizen of New Haven, Connecticut, and a founder of the Sackett family of Connecticut Widow Isabel Sackett's name appears on the Cambridge records February, 1636 In June of that year she joined Rev Hooker's company with her two sons and traversed the wilderness to Hartford, Connecticut, where she became the second wife of William Bloomfield Children of Simon and Isabel Sackett Simon (2), born 1630, died July 9, 1659, married Sarah Bloomfield, John, of whom further

(II) John, son of Simon Sackett, was born at Newtown (Cambridge), Massachusetts, 1632, and so far as is known was the first white child born there He was taken to Hartford, Connecticut, by his mother, who remarried, and in 1653 John Sackett was a resident of Springfield, Massachusetts Here he married, and a short time afterward sold his land and moved to a property he had purchased at Northampton, fifteen miles up the Connecticut river Here he lived until 1665, when he again sold out and moved to a farm purchased near Westfield Massachusetts, on what are now called Sackett's Meadows There he built a house and barn, which were burned by the Indians October 27, 1675 He lost a large amount of other property at the same time and all his cattle, which were driven off He rebuilt his house and barn and also erected a saw mill In 1672 he was chosen selectman of Westfield, holding that office as late as 1693 His wife died in 1690 and he remarried, continuing to reside on his farm until his death His will, dated 1718, was probated in 1719 He married, November 23 1659 (first), Abigail Hannum, born 1640, died October 9, 1690, daughter of William and Honor (Capen) Hannum He married (second) Sarah, daughter of John Stiles and widow of John Stewart Children of first wife 1 John, born November 4, 1660, died December 20, 1745, married Deborah Pelley 2 William, of whom further 3 Abigail, born December 1, 1663, died July 3, 1683, married John Noble 4 Mary died in childhood 5 Hannah, born March 7, 1669, died August 30, 1740 6 Mary, born June 8, 1672, married Benjamin Moseley 7 Samuel, born September 16, 1674, married Elizabeth Bessell 8 Elizabeth, died young 9 Abigail, born 1683, married David King

(III) William, son of John Sackett, was born at Westfield, Massachusetts, April 20, 1662, and met his death by drowning in the Connecticut river at Deerfield, March 28, 1700, while on his return from a wedding with a party of relatives and friends He married (first) December 26, 1687, Sarah Crain, who died soon after, (second), 1689, Hannah, daughter of Isaac and Hannah (Church) Graves, and granddaughter of Thomas Graves, "the emigrant" Children of William and Hannah Sackett Joseph, born May, 1690, died 1756, married Abigail ——, Hannah born June, 1692, Rebecca, born September 18, 1694, died September 15, 1872 married F Dewey, Jonathan, of whom further

(IV) Jonathan, son of William Sackett, was born at Westfield, Massachusetts, March 20, 1696, died September 1, 1773 He grew to manhood in Westfield, but after his marriage moved to a small farm in Hebron, Connecticut, where he lived the remainder of his days He married (second) January 28, 1725, Ann, daughter of Zebulon and Experience (Strong) Filer His first wife, Abigail Ashley, died within a year after her marriage Children of Jonathan and Ann Sackett 1 Ann, died in infancy 2 Jonathan (2), born December 26, 1727, died 1777, married Hannah Phelps 3 Justus, born March 9, 1730, died March 16 1815, married Lydia Newcomb 4 Reuben, of whom further 5 Aaron, born August 5, 1735 6 Anne, August 23, 1738 7 Hannah, August 13, 1740 8 Rebecca, April 14, 1743 The last four are all supposed to have died in childhood

(V) Reuben, son of Jonathan Sackett, was born at Swansea, Massachusetts, June 17, 1732, died June 5 1805 He resided with his father at Hebron, Connecticut, later in East Greenwich, that state He married, December 21, 1752, Mercy Finney, who died aged seventy-one years, daughter of John and Ann (Toogood) Finney, of East Greenwich Connecticut Children 1 Samuel, born April 5, 1754, of whom further 2 Alexander, March 6, 1758 died Nav 7 1829, was a revolutionary soldier, married Patience —— 3 Aaron December 26, 1760 4 Cyrus, January 5, 1764 5 Anne, April 10, 1766 6 Lucinda, January 23, 1769 7 Violet, July 18, 1771

(VI) Dr Samuel Sackett, son of Reuben Sackett, was born April 5, 1754, died February 13, 1833 In his diary, still preserved he says he was born at East Greenwich, Kent, Litchfield county, Connecticut On

August 2, 1774, he was living in Spencertown, Connecticut He studied medicine, and during the revolutionary war served in the Continental army as surgeon On February 10, 1777, he was married, and in 1780, in company with his brother Aaron, he came to Western Pennsylvania In a letter still preserved, dated Shistee Settlement, Youghiogheny county, October 27, 1780, he writes to friends in Connecticut "I do not think I can cross the mountains back home until spring There are no doctors here between Pittsburgh and Wheeling, and all the way is thickly settled It is a healthy looking country I do not think I will get much to do until I get acquainted with the people Tell Jonathan Hamilton I think this is the best place for land jobbing in the thirteen states, and in case of invasion by Indians it is supposed that fifteen hundred men would rid them out" In the family record, under date of September 15, 1781, he writes We set out from New England to come to Redstone township, and arrived at Beesontown, or Uniontown, on October 16, 1781 The following children were born at Beesontown Betsey, April 4, 1782, Lucinda, March 5, 1784, Alexander, January 10, 1786, Mary Anna, September 3. 1788 On November 10, 1788, we moved to Georges creek, Fayette county, Pennsylvania, where the following children were born Annie, November 9, 1790, Lydia, November 22, 1792, Samuel, September 21 1795, Sarah, October 20, 1797, married Dr Louis Marchant, of Huguenot descent" These entries are in the doctor's handwriting His eldest son, Alexander, born in Pennsylvania, studied medicine with his father and served as surgeon in the war of 1812 He was attached to General Harrison's command and died of fever at Fort Meigs, aged twenty-seven years His first born son Reuben (not named previously) learned the printer's trade in Pittsburgh in 1802 at the *Gazette* office In 1803 he went to Alexandria, on the Red river, Louisiana, where he was thrown from his horse and killed being then aged forty-nine years His second son, David (not mentioned previously), learned the saddler's trade in Pittsburgh and later studied medicine with his father He located in Centerville, Indiana, where he died, aged eighty-four years His children Guilema, Elizabeth, James, Alexander, Emily, Mary,

Martha, David, Margaret and Agnes

Dr Sackett was probably the first physician to practice in Fayette county He was skillful, successful in his practice and held in highest esteem He moved in 1788 from Uniontown to the fame yet known as the old Sackett homestead on Georges Creek, one mile south of Smithfield He continued his practice and cultivated his farm until his death in 1833 Dr Sackett's wife was Sarah Manning, to whom he was married in Sharon Connecticut by Rev Smith February 10 1777 Children (not previously mentioned) Reuben born January 16, 1778, died 1823 David Filer January 18, 1780, died 1864 married Martha Milliken They were born at Kent, East Greenwich, Litchfield

The Sacketts have in their possession many souvenirs of the good doctor, dating back into the eighteenth century There are nineteen copies of the *Pittsburgh Gazette* to which paper he was a subscriber, and on which his son was a compositor, dates 1794, 1795 and 1796 There are fourteen letters over one hundred years old written him from friends in Connecticut There are $700 in Continental money the largest note being for $80, the smallest two shillings Probably this money represents his pay as surgeon in the army There is a doctor's account book printed in London in 1603, and an account book of Dr Sackett's in which the oldest date is 1774

(VII) Samuel (2), son of Dr Samuel Sackett, was born in Georges township, Fayette county, Pennsylvania, on the home farm September 21 1795, died April 27 1860 He grew up on the home farm and was educated in the schools available at that early day Being the youngest son, he remained with his parents, and after his father's death became the owner of the homestead While yet a young man he left the farm and for a few years conducted a general store in Smithfield Later he returned to the farm, where his after life was spent He was a man of quiet tastes and habits, a great reader and lover of history He was an ardent Whig, and strongly opposed to human slavery, being classed among the then despised abolitionists He and his wife were members of the Presbyterian church He married Priscilla Caldwell, born July 24 1811 died April 1881, daughter of William and Rachel

(Cross) Caldwell Children 1 Alexander, born November, 1832, died February, 1900, he was a machinist and resided in Pittsburgh, unmarried 2 William, born July, 1834, he was a farmer and stock raiser of Georges township, now living retired in Smithfield, Pennsylvania, married Millie Everhart, who is also living, children Hugh, who owns the farm settled by Samuel Sackett in 1788, Marchant and Carrie 3 Lucinda, born March 14, 1836, died August, 1911, married, October, 1856, Laurence Crawford, who survives her, he was formerly a merchant of Greensboro, Greene county, Pennsylvania Children Ortella and George Harry 4 Elizabeth C, of whom further 5 Louisa, born March 3, 1844, now resides in Smithfield, Pennsylvania

(VIII) Elizabeth Caroline, fourth child of Samuel and Priscilla (Caldwell) Sackett, was born in Smithfield, Fayette county, Pennsylvania, May 9, 1839 Her early life was spent on the old homestead in Georges township, where she was educated at Georges Creek Academy She married, March 3, 1859, William Nixon Brownfield (see Brownfield) After her husband's death Mrs Brownfield moved to Uniontown, Pennsylvania, with her daughters, where she has resided since 1898, at No 12 Nutt avenue She is a member of the Methodist Episcopal church and a most vivacious, courteous, charming lady of "ye olden time "

BROWNFIELD The Brownfields of Fayette county, Pennsylvania, are of English, Scotch-Irish blood They were originally natives of Scotland, where the father of Charles Brownfield, the emigrant, was born They settled in Ireland and were members of the Scotch Presbyterian church The Scotch family trace to George Brownfield, a native of England, who was a soldier under Cromwell, and after the revolution fled to Scotland

(I) Charles Brownfield was born in Ireland, where he grew to manhood Prior to the American revolution he emigrated to America with other members of the family, settling near Winchester, Virginia, finally coming to Fayette county, Pennsylvania, being persuaded to this latter step by Colonel Burd (his sister's husband), the builder of Burd's Fort and Burd's Road in Western

Pennsylvania, the fort being built at the mouth of Redstone creek Charles Brownfield built his cabin on his own land, where stands Brownfield station on the Southwest Pennsylvania railroad, was several times dislodged and driven off by the Indians, but at last fixed his abode in peace and safety The first title in fee simple given for land in Fayette county is that of Charles Brownfield to George Troutman, dated November 21 1783 He married and had sons, Robert, of whom further, and Thomas (q v) Another account of the origin of the family was written by Joseph Brownfield, a son of Basil and great-grandson of Robert (1) Brownfield He says "The origin of the Brownsfields is One Brownsfield, an Irishman, went to Scotland and married a Scotch lady by name of Grier, and had a son, Robert, who came to America with a wife and family He came to Fayette county and camped under a large white oak tree east of Smithfield, about one-half mile east of where grandfather and grandmother Robert and Mary Brownfield are buried He was my great-grandfather, and had a son named Robert, who was my grandfather This same Robert married Mary Bowell, whose mother's maiden name was Jane Lamont "

(II) Robert, son of Charles Brownfield, was the settler in Fayette county alluded to as camping and making his first home under the spreading branches of a white oak tree in Georges township, near Smithfield He married and had a son Robert

(III) Robert (2), son of Robert (1) Brownfield, was born in Fayette county, Pennsylvania, where he spent his life engaged in farming He married Mary, daughter of Thomas and Ann Bowell, whose parents emigrated from Wales to America at an early date Among the children of Robert and Mary Brownfield was a son, Basil

(IV) Basil, son of Robert (2) Brownfield, was born on the homestead farm near Smithfield, Fayette county, Pennsylvania, March 2, 1796, died at his farm in South Union township, August 21, 1881 He received a limited education in the early subscription schools but the absence of book learning was more than compensated for by a quick, active brain and an unusually retentive memory He worked on the home farm until about twenty years of age, then began an unusually active and successful life By industry and rare business tact he won his way to fortune until at the age of thirty-five years he was accounted wealthy in a local sense At about the age of forty he became involved, through much endorsing and bail giving for others, in extensive litigation, which financially embarrassed him and caused him to mortgage much of his real estate Finally, however, he managed to lift his burdens During this period of financial difficulty his business complications became numerous and vexatious, and a career of litigation in his history was inaugurated which won for him a remarkable distinction in the courts, and till the day of his death a career in which he was for the most part the victor by one means or another Litigation became a recreation to him, obviously a necessity to his happiness, strong willed, aggressive and of a strong intellect, he used these weapons to fight the battle of life, making, as all strong characters do, hosts of enemies, but also an army of friends, and many, neither enemies nor friends who admired his pluck and diplomacy, however much they may have questioned the propriety of some of the weapons with which he fought His great experience as a litigant made him familiar with the legal principles and knowledge of common law, and his quick mind was not slow to take the measure of the lawyers who frequented Fayette county court house He held most of them in royal contempt, one of his expressions concerning them was that they were not fit to feed stock " He had at one time owned thousands of acres of land on the mountains, and here and there made clearings, put up cabins and got tenants to occupy them Almost invariably these "savages" of the mountains would quarrel with him and launch suits at law to avoid payment These very people would stop at his fireside turn their horses into his pasture and eat at his table on their trips to and from the court house Some of his bitterest legal fights were with men who thus took advantage of his well-known hospitality and good nature Yet he at times became so wrought up by the vileness of men and methods employed against him that he forgot his great virtues of benevolence, social virtue and rigid sense of justice, and that he stooped to the same questionable methods and used the weapons

his enemies delighted in But he was always better than his surroundings, and at his death the *Genius of Liberty* said four days after his death "His neighbors bear testimony that he was a man of good impulses and was always ready to forgive an injury when approached in the right way * * * He was a pleasant, agreeable gentleman, and his home was always open for the reception of his friends and neighbors"

He was a great reader, especially of the Bible, which he could quote at length, and at eighty-six years was as full of vigor and aggressiveness as many a man of forty He was publicly known as "Black Hawk," a name which associated with his will and brawn bore terror to evil doers He was a member of the Baptist church, and exceedingly liberal to the poor He married March 2 1820, Sarah Collins died October 1 1870, aged sixty-eight years, daughter of Joseph and Margaret (Allen) Collins, of Union township. Joseph was a son of John Collins, who came from Ireland when a boy Margaret Allen was a daughter of Major Isaac and Margaret Allen, of English descent Isaac Allen was a major in command of American troops at the battle of Saratoga an event he survived only a few years Margaret Allen was a girl of twelve at the time of Burgoyne's surrender, and after the death of her father, Major Isaac Allen, she came with her mother and an old aunt, Whitesides (also mother's maiden name) to Uniontown then Beesontown Joseph and Margaret Allen Collins lived at what was then known as Gaddis Fort Children of Basil Brownfield 1 Joseph Collins, born November 29 1821 died May 2 1905, married Martha Chipps, he became a large land owner of Fort Worth, Texas 2 Robert born October 28 1822, married Phoebe daughter of Isaac Brown of Georges township 3 Margaret C, born February 2, 1825 married Jehu, son of Colonel Benjamin Brownfield 4 Mary born April 19 1827 died February 3 1857, married Isaac Hutchinson born at Trenton New Jersey 5 Eliza, born November 4 1829 died unmarried July 20, 1853 6 Sarah N, born March 9 1832, died July 4, 1883, married William F Core, and moved to Texas 7 Ruth, born October 23 1834, died January 10 1884, married Joseph, son of William Barton 8 William N, of whom further. 9. Isaac Allen, born April 27, 1839, died December 29. 1897; a veteran of the civil war; married Sarah J. Burchfield, of Allegheny county, Pennsylvania. 10. Lydia Caroline, born November 15, 1842; married Thomas McClelland. 11. Harriet Helen, born April 30, 1845, died March 22, 1879, unmarried.

(V) William Nixon, son of Basil Brownfield, was born March 26, 1836, died January 11, 1889. He was educated in the public schools and grew to manhood on the home farm. After his marriage he purchased a farm of one hundred and thirty acres (to which he afterward added) one mile south of Uniontown, on the Morgantown road in South Union township. He enlisted, August 28, 1862, in Company F (Captain Springer's) Fourteenth Regiment, Pennsylvania Volunteer Cavalry, and served until the close of the war. He was wounded at the battle of White Sulphur Springs, South Carolina, but being only a flesh wound he soon recovered, although his health was seriously impaired by his army life and he was never again physically strong. After the close of the war and the grand review in Washington, he was honorably discharged and returned to his home. He resumed the cultivation of his farm, but his energy and habits of industry caused him to frequently overwork himself and for many years prior to his death, January 11, 1889, he was an invalid.

He was a Republican in politics, and a member of the Baptist church. He married, March 3, 1859, Elizabeth Caroline Sackett, who survives him. (See Sackett-Brownfield VII.) Children: 1. Sarah, residing at home. 2. Jane, residing at home. 3. Mary E., married Levi Brown, a retired farmer of Uniontown. 4. Dona B., died in 1880, aged fourteen years. 5. Basil B., a sketch of whom follows. 6. Harriet Helen. married Harry Gans, a civil engineer of Uniontown. 7. Lucinda C., married John Jeffries and resides in Uniontown. 8. Joan, married John Grant Pullman, an electrical engineer and contractor of Pittsburgh. 9. Margaret C., residing at home. 10. Edward, died in infancy. 11. Samuel Sackett, a civil engineer and superintendent of the Fort Palmer Coal Company at Ligonier, Pennsylvania; he married Lou Blank, of Greensburg, Westmoreland county, Pennsylvania; one child, William N.

(VI) Basil B., son of William Nixon and Elizabeth Caroline (Sackett) Brownfield, was born in South Union township, Fayette county, Pennsylvania, March 12, 1870. He attended the Hatfield district school in South Union, obtaining a limited education only. He grew up on the home farm, and when but a young boy began learning the carpenter's trade, becoming an expert workman. He was but fourteen years of age when he obtained his first contract, which was the erection of a large double house for William O'Connell, who believed in the boy and in his mechanical ability. The contract was faithfully performed, and this act of Mr. O'Connell's so won the boy's heart that they were always the closest of friends until Mr. O'Connell's death. This contract was the foundation of his fortune, and from that start he has, as a boy of fourteen, gone forward to a most successful career as a contractor and builder. He has been continuously engaged as a contractor, save two years, when he was engaged as building carpenter by the H. C. Frick Coke Company. In 1895 he moved to Uniontown, where he had erected a handsome home at No. 318 South Morgantown street. He has inherited a goodly portion of the shrewdness and business capacity of his grandsire Basil, and has acquired a competency through his own industry and ability. He has dealt largely in unimproved real estate, building suitable houses thereon and selling them to desirable owners. He is a Republican in politics, but never sought or desired office. He served for nine years in the Tenth Regiment, Pennsylvania National Guard, and was called out with his regiment at the great Homestead strike. Both Mr. Brownfield and wife are members of the First Methodist Episcopal church of Uniontown.

Mr. Brownfield has devoted a great deal of time to travel in the United States and has a valuable collection of curios collected by him; also a fine and valuable collection of coins and antiques, and is well considered as an authority on the latter. He is a man of warm, sympathetic nature, and has been a benefactor to many of small means in various instances, aiding them to the acquisition of a home.

He married, April 16, 1895, Ada C. Clark, born in South Union township, Fayette coun-

Isaac. H. Brownfield

ty, daughter of John and Hannah (Farr) Clark John Clark is a farmer of South Union township and a veteran of the civil war Mrs Brownfield was educated in the public schools and Madison Academy, of Uniontown, Pennsylvania, then taught school in South Union township for several years before her marriage Children of Basil B Brownfield Ruth, born January 16, 1896 died April 7, 1900, William, born February 27, 1902, died September 1, 1903

(II) Thomas Brownfield, son of Charles Brownfield (q v), was born near Winchester, Virginia, and after his marriage came in 1805 to Fayette county, Pennsylvania He at first re ited and afterward bought the White Swan Tavern in Uniontown, of which he was proprietor until his death in 1829 The land on which he settled was bought from the sons of William Penn, and part of it is yet owned by his great-grandson Isaac H Brownfield He married Miss McCoy, and had sons Ewing, John, Isaac and others

(III) Isaac youngest son of Thomas Brownfield, was born at the Brownfield homestead in South Union township, Fayette county, Pennsylvania, April 15, 1782, died at the homestead April 25 1859 He was a farmer all his active years By a first marriage he had a daughter He married (second) a widow, Mrs Jane (Reynolds) Gaddis, born December 12 1780, died August 15 1862 Children 1 Isaac (2), of whom further 2 Jane, born July 9, 1821, married Thornton Fisher, both deceased 3 William, born January 2 1825, died unmarried, aged twenty-four years

(IV) Isaac (2), son of Isaac (1) Brownfield, was born at the homestead in South Union township, Fayette county, May 10, 1818, died there September 11, 1890 He was educated not after the manner of the farmer boy of that early period, but in a private school He grew up a farmer and inherited the home farm which was always his home He was a Whig later a Republican, and an attendant of both the Baptist and Presbyterian churches his wife being a member of the latter He married Elizabeth Beatty, born in Virginia, died at the home farm, September 19, 1888, daughter of William and Mary Tarr Beatty William Beatty was a carpenter, living in Virginia, later came to Fayette county, where he died at Hopwood, while yet a young man, his

children Mary Ann, married Jesse Sackett, Elizabeth, of previous mention, Harriet, married Mr Crayton Hannah, married Aaron Hutchinson, Lucinda, married Alfred Gorley, Nancy, married Andrew Lenox Lydia, married James Frazier William, died in childhood Children of Isaac (2) and Elizabeth (Beatty) Brownfield 1 Jane, died unmarried 2 Mary Ann died young 3 Mahnda, resides at New Florence, Westmoreland county, Pennsylvania 4 William, now a farmer of South Union township, married Mary Derrick 5 Elizabeth, resides in South Union township 6 Isaac, died young 7 Isaac H, of whom further 8 Anna, married Newton Crossland, now a coal dealer of New Florence Pennsylvania 9 Harry L died aged three years

(V) Isaac Hopwood son of Isaac (2) Brownfield, was born at the old Brownfield homestead, in South Union township Fayette county Pennsylvania, January 17 1861 He was educated in the public schools later entering Mount Union College, Alliance, Ohio, whence he was graduated class of 1887 After leaving college he taught school one year in Ohio and two years in South Union township then returned to his boyhood occupation, farming He soon however, became actively engaged in coal operations and coal land dealing He was for fifteen years sole owner and manager of the Brownfield Coal & Coke Company part owner of the Lafayette Coke Company which he sold to the Atlas Coke Company, and also owned the River View Coal & Coke Company, sold to the Southern Consolidated He is president of the Cameron Coal & Coke Company, which corporation is not at present active He has retained the management of his farm through all these years of active business life, and resides in a beautiful modern home erected by himself He is a man of wealth and influence, highly esteemed by all He is a Republican in politics served as school director seven years and now serves in the same office after re-election for a six years' term He is a member of the Masonic order and of the Methodist Episcopal church He married May 8, 1886, Mary A McClean, born in Mount Union, Ohio (now sixth ward of the city of Alliance) daughter of Edwin and Maria (Miller) McClean Edwin McClean was a farmer who late in life moved to Alliance, where he died aged seventy years. Maria Miller was born near Benton, Ohio, and died aged seventy years. Their children: Jesse, married Rhoda Hopkins, both deceased; John, a practicing D.D. S. of Washington, D. C.; Samuel, a blacksmith of Alliance, Ohio; Hugh, married Etta Heiserman, and resides in Alliance; Mary A., of previous mention; Frank, a fruit farmer of Cuba; married Clara Oyster.

Children of Isaac H. and Mary A. (Mc-Clean) Brownfield: 1. Frank W. born October 18, 1886; now a farmer; married (first) Maude Fell; child: Donald, died in infancy; married (second) Mary Kramer; child: Gladys, died in infancy. 2. William Watson, born June 11, 1888; graduate of Ohio State University, class of 1912. 3. Samuel M., born November 25, 1889; graduate 1912, New York School of Electricity. 4. John A., born September 26, 1891, died in infancy. 5. Isaac Hopwood (2), born May 21, 1893. 6. Marie, born January 10, 1895. 7. Charles E., born March 30, 1897. 8. Paul, born February 28, 1900, died in infancy. 9. Martha, twin of Paul. 10. Mary Ruth, born April 8, 1902, died in infancy. 11. Arthur McKinley, born July 22, 1905. 12. Mary Frances, born April 5, 1911.

BROWNFIELD (IV) Isaac Allen Brownfield, ninth child of Basil Brownfield (q. v.) and Sarah B. (Collins) Brownfield, was born April 27, 1839, died December 29, 1897. He grew to manhood on the old Brownfield farm, and received his education in the public schools. He was barely of age when the war between the states broke out and called the patriots of the north to the field of battle. He enlisted in Company A, First Regiment, West Virginia Cavalry, fought three years, when he was promoted to the rank of lieutenant. He was then ordered to Tennessee, where he was in charge of wagon transportation. He served until the close of the war, receiving honorable discharge. He fought at Antietam and in many other battles and skirmishes, proving a brave soldier and an efficient officer. After the war he returned to his farm of two hundred and thirty-six acres in South Union township, continuing there until his death. He was a Republican in politics, served twelve years as school director, and was a member of the Baptist church, his wife a Presbyterian. He

married Sarah B., daughter of Levi Berchfield, a blacksmith and farmer of Allegheny county, Pennsylvania, who died aged seventy years. He married Eliza Lusk. Their children: Thomas; Phineas; Sarah B., wife of Isaac Allen Brownfield and the only living member of the family of children; Mary, Kate and Edward. Children of Mr. and Mrs. Brownfield: 1. Levi (better known as Lee), of whom further. 2. Basil Allen, of whom further. 3. Frederick, died aged twelve years. 4. Wade, died in infancy. Mrs. Sarah B. (Berchfield) Brownfield, aged sixty-three years, resides at her old home, the Brownfield homestead in South Union township.

(V) Levi (Lee), eldest son of Isaac Allen and Sarah B. (Berchfield) Brownfield, was born at the home farm in South Union township, Fayette county, Pennsylvania, July 1, 1870, where he has lived all his life. He was educated in the public schools, and has always been an agriculturist. He is a successful farmer, owning one hundred and two acres. He is an upright, highly respected citizen of the community in which he is well known as "Lee" Brownfield. He is a Republican in politics, but is strictly a private citizen, never having sought or held public office. He served four years in the Pennsylvania National Guard. He married Jessie Dolores Forsythe, born at Morris Cross Roads, Springhill township, Fayette county, Pennsylvania, April 7, 1887, daughter of John Ellsworth and Eliza M (White) Forsythe. Eliza M. White was born in Kingwood, West Virginia, June 29, 1863, died August 27, 1910. Children: 1. Jessie D., wife of Levi Brownfield. 2. Luna, born April 10, 1889. 3. Alice, September 15, 1890. 4. Florence, June 6, 1892, died March 19, 1894. 5. May, January 6, 1894. 6. Edna, September 15, 1896. 7. John, April 24, 1902. These children are all residing in Uniontown except Mrs. Brownfield. Child of Levi and Jessie D. Brownfield: Joseph, born August 27, 1910.

(V) Basil Allen, second son of Isaac Allen and Sarah B. (Berchfield) Brownfield, was born in South Union township, Fayette county, Pennsylvania, July 26, 1872. He was educated in the public schools, and after finishing his school years cultivated the home farm for twenty years. He then contracted a severe attack of "gold fever," which was not cured until after a year spent in Alaska in search of the elusive yellow metal He returned home minus about four thousand dollars, but with an experience well worth the cost, and well contented to follow the less romantic, but much more profitable calling of a Fayette county farmer He returned to the home farm has dealt extensively in timber land and conducting a general contracting business He owns a good farm of one hundred acres, which he profitably cultivates in connection with his other activities He is a Republican in politics, but has never sought public office He served in the Pennsylvania National Guard for ten years, mustered out as first sergeant

He married May 31, 1901, Anna Myrtle Endsley, born in Luzerne township, Fayette county, Pennsylvania, August 19, 1880, daughter of John W Endsley, now a farmer and threshing machine operator of Georges township, aged fifty-eight years He married Mary Jane Balsinger, born in Luzerne township, Fayette county, Pennsylvania, died aged fifty-six years, being killed by a horse Their children 1 Laura, married Charles Barbour, now a clerk in Toledo, Ohio 2, James, now a farmer of North Union township, Fayette county, married Minnie Daniels 3 Margery, deceased, married Ewing Walters, now living in Masontown, Pennsylvania 4 Anna M, wife of Basil Allen Brownfield 5 Frank, now in charge of the air shaft at Redstone Mines, married Bessie Ryan, and lives in Uniontown 6 Noah, foreman in a laundry at Uniontown, unmarried ,7 Russell, a carpenter of Georges township 8 Lola, married Thomas Collier, an engineer lives in Georges township Child of Basil A Brownfield Sarah Jane, born March 17, 1902

KELLY The Kellys of Connellsville, Pennsylvania, descend from Irish ancestors who settled in Maryland about sixty years ago and founded a family of enterprising, steadfast men and women

(I) The American ancestor, Michael Kelly, accompanied by his wife Mary, came to the United States in 1850, locating at Mount Savage, Maryland Michael was a farmer and soon became the owner of a good farm on which he lived and died After his death his farm was found to be underlaid with valuable coal veins

(II) John W, son of Michael Kelly, was born at Mount Savage, Maryland, 1861 He attended the public schools and learned the trade of brickmaker, later learning the carpenter's trade He came to Pennsylvania when a young man and was, in addition to his trade of carpenter, a stationary engineer employed by the Bessemer Coke Company He is a member of the Catholic church He married, in Uniontown, Pennsylvania, Alice Ambrose, born in Fayette county, Pennsylvania, 1861, a member of the Episcopal church, daughter of James and Mary Jane (Shaw) Ambrose Mary Jane Shaw's father built the tavern at Sea Wright, which he kept for many years, also was a toll taker on the "old pike" James Ambrose was a stage driver in the early days running between Cumberland Maryland, and Pittsburgh, Pennsylvania, later a farmer He was born in Scotland and came to the United States about 1840 He died at Vanderbilt, Pennsylvania Children of John W and Alice Kelly William Edward, of whom further, Katherine a teacher

(III) William Edward, son of John W Kelly, was born in Fayette county, Pennsylvania, March 11, 1887 He was educated in the New Haven (now Connellsville) high school, and after finishing his studies became general ironworker, employed in various Connellsville shops On September 1, 1910, he was appointed manager of the Connellsville Iron Works, a position he still most capably fills He is a Republican in politics and a member of several secret societies He belongs to the Episcopal church Mr Kelly is unmarried

---

JOHNSON The early history of this family is somewhat obscure Various descendants give varying traditional accounts, and in former printed works dealing with Fayette county families discrepant statements are made The time of the coming of the immigrant ancestor to America is given as early in the eighteenth century, he came from Scotland or Ireland, he was very young when he came, his father, according to one version, died on the route to America, a German family brought him up, he lived somewhere in Eastern Pennsylvania So far there seems to be agreement, but an attempt to fill out this bare outline with the living details soon meets bewildering contradictions. The paucity of written records in a pioneer community, save in exceptional cases, like those of Massachusetts and Connecticut, and the natural direction of the interest and attention of the pioneers of a new civilization toward the present and the future, therefore away from the past, quite explain this phenomenon. Of few of the Western Pennsylvania families can the histories be clearly and positively traced in the eighteenth century; the peculiarity of the present case is only in the number of definite but disagreeing traditions. On one other point there is enough agreement to make a good probability, namely, that the immigrant married into the German family by whom he was brought up.

A probable family line is as follows:

(I) Peter Johnson, perhaps the immigrant ancestor, but more probably his son, was born in Eastern Pennsylvania, and came to Fayette county, Pennsylvania, in 1790. He was a farmer and a Mennonite. Whom he married is not known. Children: Jacob, married Susanna Bixler; David, of whom further.

(II) David, son of Peter Johnson, was a large land owner in Nicholson township, Fayette county, Pennsylvania, to which he had come on foot from Hagerstown, Maryland. To each of his six sons he gave two hundred and fifty acres of land, and only within a few years has this land been alienated from the Johnson family. The name of his wife is not known. Among his sons was Peter, of whom further.

(III) Peter (2), son of David Johnson (and commonly called Peter of David), was born about 1800. and died on his two hundred and fifty acre farm, received from his father, in Nicholson township, in 1885. He was a Democrat, never aspiring to office. He married Rebecca Fast, born about 1806, died in 1882. Children: David; Francis, of whom further; Magdalena; John, deceased; Mary Ann, deceased; Jacob, deceased; Elizabeth; Margaret; Miles; Daniel J.

(IV) Francis, son of Peter (2), and Rebecca (Fast) Johnson, was born in Nicholson township February 2, 1837, died in German township, Fayette county, Pennsylvania, August 31, 1909. He was brought up in Nicholson township, and attended the district school. He cultivated a farm near Mason-

town and died near where German township adjoins Masontown. At different times he held many township offices, though they came to him unsought. His friends were always numerous, and he is said never to have had an enemy He was a member of the Free and Accepted Masons and of the Independent Order of Odd Fellows. In German township he was active in politics as a Republican He married (first) Hannah, born about 1840, died on the home place November 17, 1887, daughter of ———— and Martha Ache. Her father was a farmer in Nicholson township and there died. Children of ———— and Martha Ache: Louisa, lives in German township, near Masontown; Hannah, married Francis Johnson; Jefferson, deceased. Mr. Johnson married (second) in 1890 Sarah (Moser) Galley; she married (first) Joseph Galley. Children of Francis Johnson, all by his first wife and all living: 1. Lowrey, married Mattie Deffenbaugh; he is a contractor and builder and lives on Lake street, Chester, Alabama. 2. Allison D., born July 5, 1866; married, October 28, 1892, Lucinda Kine; he is a furniture dealer at Myersdale, Somerset county, Pennsylvania. 3. Emerson Ache; he married Laura Wright; they live at Uniontown, Fayette county, Pennsylvania, where he is bookkeeper for C. O. LaClair & Company. 4. Miles Lester, of whom further. 5. Cora, married Charles E. Moser, a farmer, and they live in Iowa. 6. Lindsey, married Pearl McCann; he farms on the home place, near Masontown. 7. Clayton S., married a Miss Provins; he is a dentist at Brownsville, Fayette county, Pennsylvania. 8. Myrtle, married Norman Speicher; they live at Myersdale.

(V) Miles Lester, son of Francis and Hannah (Ache) Johnson, was born at Masontown December 23, 1872. His early years were spent on the home place and he received a public school education in German township. In 1892 he graduated from Redstone Academy. For the next two terms he taught school in German township. Going to Philadelphia for the study of dentistry, he graduated from the Philadelphia Dental College in 1898, receiving the decree of Doctor of Dental Surgery. For one year he practiced with Dr. J. W. Jaco at Uniontown. Since that time he has practiced at the same place by himself, having his dental office at No. 23

West Main street He is a Republican The earlier generations of the Johnson family were disposed toward the Mennonite religion, but the present family are members of the Third Presbyterian Church, Uniontown

Dr Johnson married, June 8, 1899, Lida Jane, born at Uniontown September 3, 1872, daughter of Samuel A and Emma (Marcy) Loughman Her father was a blacksmith, who died at Uniontown in February, 1900, aged fifty-four years, her mother was a native of Jefferson township, Greene county, Pennsylvania, living at Uniontown Mrs Johnson was the only child Child of Dr Miles Lester and Lida Jane (Loughman) Johnson Miles Lester, Jr, born January 25, 1901

HOWARD Of this name, historic both in England and in America, the origin is doubtful Danish, Saxon and Norwegian derivation have all been suggested Havard or Haavard is said to have been a common personal name among the Northmen; it is thought to be the source of the English name Howard, having been left by them in Northumberland and East Anglia Authentic records of the Howard family extend no further back than the thirteenth century when the Howards rose into eminence in Norfolk There are several New England families of this name, and probably others in other parts of the country Their connection with the famous English family would be probable, but could probably not in any case be proved Of Americans of this name General Howard was a notable soldier of the civil war

(I) Absalom Howard the first member of this family about whom we have definite information, settled before the revolution in what is now Greene county, Pennsylvania Thus he was one of the first settlers in Western Pennsylvania He cleared a large tract and was a farmer all his life It is not known whom he married but he had a son, Absalom, of whom further

(II) Absalom (2) son of Absalom (I) Howard, farmed on the same lands as his father had occupied The name of his wife is not known, but he had a son, Denune, of whom further

(III) Denune son of Absalom (2) Howard, was born probably in Greene county,

Pennsylvania, in 1802, died in April, 1876 He attended the subscription schools and learned the trade of a cooper About 1825 he left Greene county to settle in Nicholson township, Fayette county, Pennsylvania At Jacob's Creek he established himself in the cooperage business, and he continued in this the remainder of his life For many years he made barrels at the cement mill, where the Howard Carriage Company's factory now is, at Uniontown, on West Peter street Later he removed to Masontown, German township, and there he had a shop until his death Several of his sons learned the cooper trade, and with their help he carried on a large factory at Masontown He was an old line Whig, afterward a Republican but held no office Both he and his wife were Dunkards

He married Sarah Haught, born in 1811, died in 1904 She was a remarkable woman Her industry was exceptional and her ambition corresponded It is estimated that she wove enough carpet to reach from Uniontown to Philadelphia She was also excellent as a manager With her other abundant labors she raised a family of sixteen children To her encouragement her husband and children owe a great part of their achievements With all, consecrating and elevating all, she was a woman of great piety Children 1 Naomi, married Benjamin Schaefer, deceased he was engaged in the glass business, his widow lives near Point Marion, Fayette county, Pennsylvania 2 Mary, married John Steele, he was a farmer, his widow now lives at Uniontown 3 James Madison, born August 17, 1840, married, November 10, 1861, Susannah Miller, he lives at Masontown is an extensive manufacturer of wagons and vehicles and the wealthiest man in his township, a Republican in politics 4 Abigail, deceased married Absalom Longanecker 5 Sarah Jane deceased, married A J Lowe 6 Jacob Denune, married Mary Knight, he lives in Belleview, Pittsburgh, and is engaged in the cooperage business 7 Absalom, of whom further Nine others, deceased

(IV) Absalom (3), son of Denune and Sarah (Haught) Howard, was born at Masontown, December 29 1850 He was brought up at Masontown and learned the trade of cooper from his father For many years he worked for his older brother, James Madison Howard in his wagon factory at Masontown

In 1881 he moved to Smithfield, Fayette county, Pennsylvania, where he carried on for himself the business of coopering and manufacturing wagons Later he bought and for many years operated a general store at Smithfield, and he is now living a retired life at that place He is a Republican and has served as tax collector The Methodist church claims the allegiance both of himself and of his wife He married Rebecca Jane, born in Georges township, Fayette county, Pennsylvania, near High Horse June 3 1852, daughter of Alfred and Mary Core She is now living at Smithfield Alfred Core, her father died in May 1911, in the eighty-fourth year of his life, his widow is still living at Smithfield, having reached the age of eighty-one years Both were of Fayette county birth and of Scotch-Irish descent Mr Core was a prominent farmer in Georges township, from whence he removed to Smithfield where he served for twenty-five years as justice of the peace All his life he was an auctioneer and through his activity in that occupation knew everybody for forty miles about Children of Alfred and Mary Core Emma married James W Abraham, they live at Smithfield, and he is a passenger conductor on the Pennsylvania railroad, Rebecca Jane married Absalom Howard Children of Absalom and Rebecca Jane (Core) Howard 1 Alfred Core, of whom further 2 Orville McCormick, born October 21, 1878 unmarried, about 1898 he came to Uniontown and worked for seven years in the shoe department of Maurice Lynch's store he then attended the dental department of the University of Pittsburgh, graduating in 1908, and he became partner of his older brother in dental work in Uniontown, he now has a large practice He is a member of Fayette Lodge, No 651, Free and Accepted Masons, Lodge of Perfection at Uniontown, and of the Consistory in Pittsburgh He is a member of the Methodist Episcopal church 3 Leroy Downey, born October 19 1882, he is a physician having graduated in 1906 from Jefferson Medical College at Philadelphia with the degree of doctor of medicine, and lives and practices at Fairmont Marion county West Virginia, married Pearl Sturgis child Martha Rebecca 4 Lindsey Graham, born February 8, 1889, he is engaged in the insurance business

at Johnstown, Pennsylvania 5 John Calvin born August 24, 1891, he works at the Union Supply Company's office at Uniontown

(V) Alfred Core, son of Absalom (3) and Rebecca Jane (Core) Howard, was born at Masontown, August 10, 1876 He grew up at Smithfield attending the public school there Coming as a growing boy to Uniontown, he worked for seven years in the shoe department of Maurice Lynch's store, two of his brothers afterward did the same thing that department having been for twenty years managed by one of the Howard family He then entered the dental department of the Western University of Pennsylvania, now renamed the University of Pittsburgh, from which he graduated in 1901 and received the degree of Doctor of Dental Surgery For one year he practiced at Smithfield He then opened his office at Uniontown, where he has had from that time a continuous, growing and successful practice In 1908 he took into partnership his brother Orville McCormick Howard and they work under the name of Howard Brothers Dr Howard is a member of Fayette Lodge, No 651, Free and Accepted Masons of the Chapter, Commandery and Lodge of Perfection at Uniontown and of the Consistory at Pittsburgh, also of the Independent Order of Odd Fellows He is a member of the Laurel Club of Uniontown In politics he is a Republican Dr and Mrs Howard are members of the Methodist Episcopal church

He married, November 29, 1910 Estella Frazee born at Hopwood Fayette county, Pennsylvania daughter of James Ross and Martha (Frazee) Barnes Her father is a leading coal magnate of Uniontown and Hopwood Child James Ross Barnes, born November 25 1911 The Howard home is at No 95 East Main street, Uniontown

BOYD The Boyds came to Fayette county from the Shenandoah valley of Virginia the family seat being near Winchester They were an influential family, and of frequent mention in Virginia records The founder of the Fayette county family was William Boyd, who moved from the Shenandoah valley to Fayette county, Pennsylvania, in 1784, settling in Bullskin township there he founded the Boyd family,

made illustrious by his sons, grandsons and great-grandsons His farm "Springhill,' on Mounts Creek," consisted of two hundred and forty acres, which was patented to him in June, 1786, by the government, is yet owned in the family He bore a commission as justice of the peace, dated 1792 He was a man of education, and held high positions in the township He was a slave owner, and brought with him from Virginia several slaves, and six negro children were registered as having been born to these between 1795 and 1809 He died in 1812 and was buried on the homestead farm He married and had issue Thomas, John Robert, James, William, Jeremiah and a daughter The eldest son Thomas, inherited the homestead, and died in 1855 John died in 1857 Robert, of further mention James died in Tyrone township William moved to Ohio Jeremiah became a physician

(II) Robert, son of William Boyd was born in Bullskin township, Fayette county, Pennsylvania, where he was educated and grew to manhood After his marriage he settled in Menallen township, where he became a prosperous farmer and a leading citizen He was one of the associate judges of Fayette county, appointed in 1841, serving until 1845 He married and had issue, including a son William

(III) William (2), son of Judge Robert Boyd was born in Menallen township, Fayette county, Pennsylvania, and there received his education and followed the calling of a farmer He was well-to-do and a man of influence in his town He was a Democrat and a man of correct Christian life He married Jane C Burgess, and left issue

(IV) Albert Darlington, son of William (2) and Jane C (Burgess) Boyd, was born in Menallen township, Fayette county, Pennsylvania, December 31, 1845 He was educated in the public schools, alternating his winter terms of study with summer work upon the farm He obtained a good English education and when a young man taught several terms in the township schools of Fayette county and one year in Connellsville He supplemented his public school study with two terms at Morgantown Academy (West Virginia), and while still teaching began the study of law under the able preceptorship of Judge Alpheus E Wilson He prosecuted his

legal study with all the energy of his nature, and in 1869 passed the required examinations and was admitted to the Fayette county bar He made rapid progress in his profession after locating at Uniontown, was admitted to all federal and state courts of the district, and commanded the patronage of the best class of clients His natural oratorical gifts brought him into prominence as a public speaker, which in turn so impressed the rank and file of his party that in 1871 he was chosen the Democratic candidate for district attorney He was elected by a handsome majority, serving with distinction until 1874 He then retired to private practice, and did not again appear prominently in public life save as chairman of the Democratic county committee until 1898, when he was elected state senator by an overwhelming majority from the district comprising the counties of Fayette and Greene He ably represented his district in the senate, served on important committees and as a legislator added to the fame already gained as a lawyer He continued in active practice until his death Senator Boyd was learned in the law, and seemingly carried the contents of his valuable law library in his head so ready was he with quotation of precedent in cases of similar import, printed and used as judicial authority He had a large practice, and was so unselfish that his memory is lovingly cherished by men then young at the bar whom he helped with their first cases Among the older strong men of the bar he stood without a superior, either in legal attainment or in political prominence He began practice at the age of twenty-four, and in his second year successfully prosecuted a murderer defended by the ablest Uniontown lawyers For many years he was engaged in nearly every noted criminal case in Fayette county, either for the prosecution or for the defense He gradually withdrew from criminal practice and devoted his talents to civil law, securing even higher position in that branch of his profession than as a criminal lawyer He was essentially the lawyer, his political offices coming to him as a tribute from his fellow citizens and not as the rewards of a self-seeking politician He was very popular and had a host of loyal friends, to whom he also was most devoted He was a good citizen, always interested and helpful in all public improvement and a willing

worker for the public good   His estate,
Locust Hill," in the east end of Uniontown,
was purchased shortly after his marriage, and
there he spent his happiest hours

He married, September 21, 1872, Annie
Elizabeth, daughter of Robert Patterson, of
Uniontown, who survives him, a well-known
lady of Uniontown (See Patterson IV) She
was born in Uniontown, Pennsylvania, educated in Uniontown schools, now a member
of the Presbyterian church and allied societies
Children, all born in Uniontown 1 Edward
Wilson, a well-known lawyer, associated with
his father until the death of the latter 2
Samuel Patterson an attorney, associated
with his father and brother in legal practice
until the latter's death 3 Albert Darlington a
civil engineer, of Uniontown, Pennsylvania
4 Wallace Burgess, a civil engineer, now of
Oklahoma 5 Mary Elizabeth, wife of Charles
S Bowman, one child, Charles S, Jr

(The Patterson Line)

There is a tradition in the Patterson family
that they have been in Ireland since the
planting of Ulster, and ever since that time
inhabitants of Manor Cunningham, that
their crest was a boar's head, very likely
there was more than that, but that is the
only part handed down in their family

It is a matter of history that a Patterson,
Robert or James, was one of a company of
gentlemen that came over from Scotland at
the invitation of Charles the First, in the
year of 1613 Each of these gentlemen was
assigned lands, and Patterson was given land
afterward called Manor Fort Cunningham
This historical fact agrees with the tradition
in the family of Robert Patterson's ancestors
Another Patterson came over in 1614 and
settled on another quarter called Mone-
gragam, but not far from Robert hence it is
to be presumed that they were brothers

(I) The first ancestor whose name we have
was James Patterson, who married Matilda
Bredin, or Breading, or more likely Braddon
(the same as the novelist) Mr Drummond
Grant, an authority, writes that Braddon is
more likely to be the proper spelling of the
name and the others are corruptions The
children of James and Matilda (Braddon)
Patterson that we know of were James, Samuel and William There may have been
others

(II) Of these James, the eldest, inherited
Drumonghil, the home   He married Margaret MacIvaine Of her family nothing positive is known except that she was the daughter of John MacIvaine, for whom their eldest
son was named James Patterson, of Drumonghil, was always called Esquire, or Squire
It was not a title, but was applied by the
people to large wealthy farmers My in-
formant says that it was not only because of
his wealth, but of his superior education re-
finement and manner of dress He had three
sons and one daughter, Matilda, or Matty,
who married a farmer named McMonigal and
later came to the United States, where they
were last heard from in New Orleans

John, the eldest son, inherited Drumonghil
He married a widow named Elizabeth (Betty)
Rankin, who had one child, a daughter He
had no children of his own, and it is said was
not happy, having married a woman consid-
erably older than himself He sold Drumonghil and went to Sydney, Australia, in company with a friend named John Moore, who
later returned to Manor Cunningham after
making considerable money and married
John Patterson's wife was to have gone to
Sydney later on, but for some reason never
went, and his family never knew what became of him eventually

Henry (Harry), the second son, went into
the navy, and by his ability won a lieutenancy
which he later resigned He married a widow
named Sarah Wallace After his marriage he
lived and died at Doorable, having no children His widow inherited all of his property

(III) James, the third son, married Sophia
Stewart, daughter of Alexander and Mary
(Calhoun) Stewart, and had born to them
nine children, five sons and four daughters,
two of the latter, Sarah and Matilda Anne,
dying quite young The eldest daughter,
Margaret, married Jeremiah Ralston, and
Mary, the youngest living, married John
Fritz, both of Philadelphia, neither had any
children Of the sons James, the eldest, with
a cousin, Alexander Stewart, came to Philadelphia the year following his father's death
with Captain Foster, and through Captain
Foster's influence secured a position to build
a section of the Erie canal west of Harrisburg James never married and died in Philadelphia Alexander, the second son, was in
the Mexican war, he never returned to Phil-

adelphia, and the last heard from him was a letter written home after the war, but giving no information as to his intentions for the future Samuel, the third, and William, the fourth, sons, owned and sailed a schooner between Philadelphia and the West Indies with which they brought fruit, etc, etc, to the Philadelphia markets Samuel was married, but had no family, William was married and left two sons, of whom nothing is known Samuel and William both died in Philadelphia Robert, the fifth son, came to the then west, Pittsburgh, Pennsylvania and later on to Uniontown John, the sixth son, married and had three children, two daughters, Margaret and Mary, and one son, Henry John died in Philadelphia of paralysis

James Patterson, after his marriage to Sophia Stewart, rented a farm called Unity and resided there until after the birth of Robert, the fifth son, when he was appointed purveyor, or buyer for the line of vessels plying between Liverpool and Philadelphia owned by the firm of Foster & McCorkell Henry Foster, of this firm, being a cousin of Sophia (Stewart) Patterson The supplies for these vessels included all kinds of live stock, which were driven to Moville and there shipped by tender to the ships

After his change of business he moved back to a farm at Drumonghil, on which was a corn mill and some tenant houses, where he employed a large number of people to care for his stock and to go with him to the weekly fairs, as was the custom,, to buy supplies to provision the vessels and to drive home such stock as he purchased He usually carried a large amount of money on his person, but he was so well known and so universally liked that there was no danger in his so doing It is related that the footpads of which there were many in those days, would just say, "Sure 'tis only Shamus O'Pettherson, God bless him!" Then Patterson would give them some drink money and pass on He did many things that called for presence of mind and bravery, one of which caused the peasantry to make verses about him, calling him the bravest man in the north of Ireland

During his last buying excursion he was seized with a fever and was brought home by coach unconscious He never rallied, and died in less than a week The physician pronounced it spotted fever

His wife, knowing very little about his business, was at a great disadvantage, and it is said was grossly imposed upon After a hard struggle she concluded to come to Philadelphia with her children, bringing with her the children's nurse, Katy McDermott After their arrival in Philadelphia she was assisted a great deal by her cousin, Henry Foster, in the management of her family She died of yellow fever contracted in visiting the schooner of Samuel and William at the wharf in Philadelphia

(IV) Robert Patterson, the fifth son of James and Sophia (Stewart) Patterson, was born on the farm called Enity, March 4, 1808, at Manor Cunningham When two and a half years old his father removed to Drumonghil, where they resided until his father's death, and later the family removed to Philadelphia, Pennsylvania He attended a day school in Manor Cunningham for a while, which was taught by a priest He then went to school in Raphoe for six months and was later tutored by the Rev Alexander Rentoul in company with Jack Rentoul (John, later a Presbyterian minister), the minister's son On coming to Philadelphia work was secured for the older boys in a large white goods manufactory Robert was put to attending a loom, at which he became very expert, and it has been his boast that he has woven many and many a yard of cloth On coming west to Pittsburgh he met Lucinda, daughter of Benjamin Franklin and Ethalinde (Robertson) Winchell, whom he married at her sister's home in Steubenville, in March, 1837 His wife, having lost her parents, made her home with her sister and brother-in-law, Thomas and Maria (Winchell) Frey

After his marriage Mr Patterson rented a farm of Squire Boice at Burgettstown, Washington county, Pennsylvania He was very successful, the business coming to him naturally Their eldest child, Margaret, was born on the farm June 11, 1839 In the autumn of that year there was much talk of the opportunities to make money out in the territory of Iowa He concluded to see for himself, so he sold off his farming implements, disposed of his crops and went to Dubuque, Iowa Arriving there they were much disappointed to find the town consisted of but few houses set on a low mud flat, the country overrun with roving bands of Indians, with the principal business of the country lead mining To make the best he could of the situation he opened up a general merchandising business in one side of his house, and this business he continued until the fall of 1841 In the meantime his wife and child had contracted malaria and were constantly ill with chills and fever, so tiring of this venture they came back to Steubenville, traveling down the Mississippi and up the Ohio river, giving them a long, tiresome trip They remained in Steubenville for a short time considering an offer made to them by an uncle of his wife, William Robertson, of Stafford Court House, Virginia who wanted them to come there and take charge of his large business, which had outgrown his own management William Robertson, in addition to his large plantation and many slaves, was operating seven freestone quarries, the product of these quarries was sent by way of Aquia to the Potomac and thence to Alexandria and Washington, where it was used in some of the finest buildings of the two cities They concluded to go, and found the better way was to go by boat to Parkersburg and across the country by stage and wagon Mr Patterson had gone to secure the tickets for the boat and his wife had left little Margaret in the care of the proprietor s daughter while she attended to some necessary things incident to their journey When she was hastily summoned she found the little child s clothes on fire She was terribly burned and died at 6 o'clock that evening The mother was also badly burned in extinguishing the flames Their journey was delayed until after the burial of the child, who was laid to rest beside her grandmother Winchell in the cemetery at Steubenville Journeying to Stafford county, they found their uncle and aunt, who were delighted to have them, and everything went well for a short time When Mr Patterson suggested some improvement in the work as well as the management of the negroes his uncle did not agree with him, preferring the old rather slipshod way This, of course, led to some hard feeling, and later Mr Patterson concluded that he could not content himself doing work in that way In the meantime another daughter was born to them

Leaving Stafford they went to Baltimore and, not finding anything to suit him in a business way, he went on to Philadelphia to visit relatives After a visit in his old home he concluded that they would try their fortunes in the far west again Traveling over the National Road by way of Cumberland, they reached Uniontown and stopped at the hostelry of "Natty" Brownfield By this time Mrs Patterson was so tired that she insisted that he get into some business in that town and settle down On looking about he found that he could buy out the meat market of Samuel Fisher, the agreement being that Fisher was to continue to take charge of it, and this he did until his death At that time there were few houses that could be rented, so they had to be contented with one on the 'Natty" Brownfield farm outside of the town limits, removing from there after six months to the Benjamin Brownfield house on Morgantown street, opposite the (old) Baptist church, where they resided for about six years On March 1 1849, they moved to the Isaac Wood farm, which they bought, and there lived until the death of Mr Patterson, which occurred June 14, 1904, at the venerable age of ninety-six years and three months his wife having preceded him eight years, passing away August 14, 1896, at the age of eighty-one years

Mr Patterson led a very busy life, and amidst his other pursuits carried on his farming most successfully He was a strong Republican in belief, only once being known to vote the Democratic ticket, and that during the Douglass campaign against the Knownothings He had been most carefully trained in his youth in the Presbyterian doctrines, and although he did not unite with the church until his later years, his life was governed by his early teachings and he brought up his family in the same rigid way and taught them to be strictly truthful and honorable It was said of him that his word was as good as his bond, as many who had business dealings with him could attest He was also very charitable, but always in a quiet, unostentatious way, so that only those that knew him well knew of the many kindnesses he performed He was a great student of the Bible, had a remarkable memory and was also a great reader of current literature, being well posted on all the topics of the day During the last few years of his life he was very deaf, which was a great trial to him, for he dearly loved to discuss the news of the day and was not slow to form opinions, which were shrewd and sound. He was for many years a member of the Scotch-Irish Society.

Robert Patterson and Lucinda, his wife, had six children: 1 Margaret, who was burned to death when about two years of age. 2 Sarah Virginia, who remained at home and ministered to her parents until their death. 3 John William, married Elmyra A Franks, he is a farmer near Martinsburg, West Virginia, has eight children. 4 Annie Elizabeth, married Albert Darlington Boyd, a prominent attorney of Uniontown (see Boyd IV). 5 Robert Ira, married Margaretta Askew, he is a successful business man of Uniontown, has four children. 6 Alexander Hamilton, married Annie J McCray; he is also a farmer near Martinsburg, West Virginia, they have had ten children, one of whom has passed away.

BOYD This is another branch of the Boyd family descending from William Boyd, of Virginia, who came in 1784 a land owner and slave owner of Bullskin township, surveyed to him in June, 1786 as ' Spring Hill."

(II) James, son of William Boyd, was a farmer of Tyrone township, Fayette county, Pennsylvania. He married and had male issue.

(III) George W, son of James Boyd, was born in Tyrone township, Fayette county, Pennsylvania, where he became a prosperous farmer, retiring late in life to Mount Pleasant, Pennsylvania, where he built a large brick house which was his residence until death. He was a member of the Baptist church and a man of influence. He married Martha Smith, February 18, 1846 she was also a Baptist. Children: 1 James Smith, of whom further. 2 Catherine May born 1848, married George Shrader a farmer, and moved to Ohio, both living. 3 Emily, born March 3, 1851, deceased, married John Mock, now a farmer of Ohio. 4 Smith, born April 25 1853 married and now living in West Virginia. 5 Mary, born March 11, 1855, married Peter Lacos of Scottdale whom she survives. 6 Demsey, born August 17, 1857 married Mary McMasters, he is a merchant of Merrittstown, Pennsylvania both living. 7 Martha, born February 7, 1860, married

John Metcalf, a traveling salesman, now residing at Lawrence, Kansas. 8 George M, born December 24, 1861 married and died in Joplin, Missouri.

(IV) James Smith, son of George W and Martha (Smith) Boyd was born near Morgan Station in Upper Tyrone township, Fayette county, Pennsylvania, December 23, 1846. He attended the local public school and grew to manhood on the home farm. After his marriage he lived two years on his father's farm then until February, 1855, lived at Detwiler's Mills as manager of Grandfather Detwiler's farm, and also did the mill hauling. In 1855 he moved with his family to near Cawker City, Kansas, where he purchased one hundred and sixty acres of land. He prospered, and in 1893 purchased an additional two hundred and forty acres on which he moved and lived until 1906. In that year he sold his one hundred and sixty acre farm and bought one hundred acres near Wichita, Kansas. He has devoted himself mainly to raising alfalfa, that wonderful crop that has brought prosperity to the west. He also conducts a line of general farming operations on his two farms. He is a Republican in politics and has served on the school board for many years. He is a member of the United Brethren church, as is his wife.

He married Susan Catherine Detwiler, born at Detwiler's Mills Bullskin township, Fayette county, Pennsylvania, January 13, 1852, daughter of Samuel and grandmother -of Henry and Susan (Stauffer) Detwiler. Henry Detwiler was born in Germany came to the United States about 1800, settling in Bucks county, Pennsylvania. He was a miller, and shortly after coming to Fayette county built a log mill close to the present mill. He also built a log house and cleared part of his land, but confined himself very closely to milling. His children: 1 Samuel, of further mention. 2 Joseph, died a young man. 3 Henry, died a young man. 4 John S, an extensive stock dealer and farmer, owning at his death nearly three thousand acres of good land, he married Catherine Atkinson. 5 Jacob, moved to Wadsworth Ohio where he now resides in 1849 he joined the "goldseekers,' journeyed to California but illness compelled his return, first to Ohio, then to Pittsburgh. 6 Martin, lived and died at Moyer, Fayette county. 7 Betsey, married Henry Fretts and lived in

Fayette county, Pennsylvania, until her death. 8. Sarah, married George Atkinson. Samuel, eldest son of Henry Detwiler, inherited the mill from his father, whose trade of miller he also followed. He built other mills on the site of the old log mill and also carried on extensive farming operations. He is a devoted member of the United Brethren church and a man of considerable influence. He married Elizabeth Fretts, who also survives. Their children: 1. Henry, an attorney of Uniontown, Pennsylvania; married Josephine Van Gundy. 2. Susan Catherine, of previous mention. 3. Elizabeth, died unmarried. 4. John Fretts, a physician of Uniontown, Pennsylvania. 5. Anna, married Frank Burkhart. 6. Joseph M., married Mary Comp. 7. Smith, married (first) Lorena Newcomer, now deceased; he married (second) in June, 1912, Olive Fretts, of Scottdale. 8. Samuel M., married Alice Walters. Children of James Smith Boyd: 1. Albert Mason, of whom further. 2. Harry Ellsworth, born October 3, 1875; now living on his father's two hundred and forty acre farm in Kansas; married Della Cram. 3. Frank Hanby, born January 3, 1878; now assistant superintendent at the Waltersburg Coke Works in Fayette county; married Laura Humphreys. 4. Bessie Marie, born July 7. 1879; married Edward Anderson, an employee in the freight department of the Baltimore & Ohio railroad at Scottdale, Pennsylvania. 5. Samuel Detwiler, born October 31, 1881; now manager of a plumbing establishment at Denver, Colorado; married Mattie Keller. 6. Ruth Van Gundy, born October 14, 1884; residing with her parents. 7. John Clyde, born October 22, 1885; died in infancy. 8. Anna Josephine, born September 12, 1886; married Mark Bohrer, a tinner, now residing at Smith Center, Kansas. 9. Ralph Harper, born October 31, 1890; residing at home; unmarried. 10. Azalia Belle, born April 1, 1893; resides at home. 11. Max Dewey, born May 15, 1896; resides at home.

(V) Albert Mason, eldest son of James Smith and Susan Catherine (Detwiler) Boyd, was born near Morgan Station in Upper Tyrone township, Fayette county, Pennsylvania, August 18, 1874. He was a year old when his parents moved to Detwiler's Mills, where his boyhood days were passed and his early education acquired at the Gault school in Buckskin township. He was ten years of age when the family moved to Kansas, where he completed his studies in excellent public schools. His father then was cultivating about six hundred acres of land, and as the eldest son, Albert M., soon became his valued and trusted assistant. He, however, insisted upon having an education, attended Cawker City high school, where he was graduated in 1894. He then attended Kansas State Normal at Emporia, and taught school for three terms. He returned to Fayette county in 1898 and entered the employ of the Union Supply Company at Leisenring No. 3, remaining eleven months. He then engaged with the W. J. Rainey Company in their store at Elm Grove, Fayette county, as meat cutter. After two years he was appointed payroll clerk, serving as such eleven months, then became yard boss at the coke works, continuing one year. In June, 1903, he was appointed manager of the Elm Grove store, a responsible position, which he now most acceptably fills. His home is in Elm Grove, and he also owns a tract of 320 acres in Kansas. He is a Republican in politics and has served as school director. He is a Mason of high degree, belonging to James Cochran Lodge, No. 614, Free and Accepted Masons, at Dawson; Connellsville Chapter, No. 283, Royal Arch Masons; Uniontown Commandery, Knights Templar; Uniontown Lodge of Perfection, and Pittsburgh Consistory, Ancient Accepted Scottish Rite, in which he holds the thirty-second degree. He is a member of Laurel Hill Presbyterian Church and interested in all the work of his church.

He married, September 19, 1907. Melissa McBurney, born in Franklin township, Fayette county, Pennsylvania, daughter of Robert and Susan (Bute) McBurney. Children: Susan Mildred, born September 15, 1908; Grace Antoinette, November 7, 1911.

BOYD   This branch of the Boyd family is of Irish birth and parentage.

The Boyds were originally from Scotland, but settled in the north of Ireland several generations ago. The first of this line of whom we have record was David Boyd, born in County Down, Ireland, about 1837. He was an only child, received a good education in the public schools, and has always followed farming as an occupation. He yet resides near the scene of birth fairly well pre-

served for a man of his years He is a Liberal in politics, and a communicant of the Presbyterian church He married Anna McBurney, born in County Down, Ireland, died in 1889, aged sixty years Children Archibald, died in Ireland aged twenty-two years, married a Miss Irben Mary William, of whom further Margaret David John Samuel Robert Ellen Jane, died in infancy All of these living children reside in their native land except William, he being the only one who emigrated to the United States.

(II) William, son of David and Anna (McBurney) Boyd, was born in County Down, Ireland, August 2 1866 He attended the public schools of the town and grew up a farmer At the age of twenty, in 1886, he came to the United States, finding his way to western Pennsylvania He entered the employ of the Carnegie Steel Company at Larimer's Station, Westmoreland county, remaining one year, then was transferred to Douglass Station on the Youghiogheny river, remaining twelve years In the early years after coming to Pennsylvania, he attended the night schools, adding greatly to his educational acquirement About the year 1900 he entered the service of the H C Frick Coke Company, continuing until 1911 In November, 1911 he was elected justice of the peace of New Salem, Menallen township, which office now engages his time He was the first of the justices elected under the new law making the term one of six years instead of four He has served as school director and was assessor of district No 3, Menallen township four years, expiring in 1911 He is a Republican in politics and has always been an active party worker He is an elder of the Presbyterian church, his wife and oldest children also being members of that church He is a man of high character and holds the unvarying respect of his community

He married October 6, 1897 Mary Weigel, born in Allegheny City, Pennsylvania (Pittsburgh, North Side), daughter of Conrad Weigel, born in Germany, came to the United States, engaged in mercantile business in Coraopolis, Pennsylvania, where he died at the age of sixty-nine years His wife Mary survives him, and with her youngest daughter, Kate, continues the business established by her husband Louisa the oldest daughter, married Thomas Manning, and resides at Robbin's Station, Westmoreland county, Pennsylvania, Mary was the second of the three daughters of Conrad Weigel Children of Mr and Mrs Boyd 1 Gladys, born July 21, 1897, Winfield Conrad, July 23, 1899, William, November 5, 1901, Joseph David, April 10, 1905, James Samuel, December 10, 1910 The family home is at New Salem.

McFARLAND This family descends from a Scotch-Irish ancestry They first settled in Greene county, Pennsylvania, where John McFarland, grandfather of John J McFarland, of Vanderbilt, Fayette county was born A McFarland figured in the whiskey rebellion in Greene county and was killed in one of the conflicts with the authorities

(II) John McFarland, the first of whom record is found, lived and died in Greene county, Pennsylvania, where he married and left issue

(III) Jacob, son of John McFarland, was born in Greene county, Pennsylvania, in 1823, died 1880 He worked at farming in his younger days, then learned the carpenter's trade, which he followed the remainder of his life, residing at Mapleton, Greene county, and doing an extensive lumber and contracting business He was a Democrat and with his wife a member of the Presbyterian church He married Susan Brown, born in Greene county, Pennsylvania December 17, 1822, died September 4, 1911, daughter of Jonathan Brown of Greene county She was a member of the Methodist Episcopal church Children Rebecca, deceased, Mary Ann, married Job Chisbo John J, of whom further, Jesse, married Jennie Turney James Lindsay, deceased, Caroline, deceased, Sarah Ellen, deceased, Melinda, married E W Waters, Miner, deceased Thomas, deceased, Alice, married W K Shaw, Jacob, married Annie Crowley, William, married Alice Morris

(IV) John J, son of Jacob and Susan (Brown) McFarland, was born in Mapleton, Greene county, Pennsylvania, September 25, 1850 He was educated in the public schools He engaged in the lumber business, operated a planing mill and was a contractor and builder of prominence in Uniontown Pennsylvania In 1892 he engaged in the hotel business, continuing at Uniontown and at Dunbar Pennsylvania until 1900, when he disposed of his interests, came to Vanderbilt,

Fayette county where he has since been the owner and proprietor of the Vanderbilt Hotel He is an active Democrat served six years as mercantile appraiser of Fayette county, was presidential elector in 1896 when William J Bryan made his first campaign for the presidency, delegate to many state and county conventions of his party and is still influential in party politics

He married (first) in 1877, Anna Van Horn, of Westmoreland county, Pennsylvania, who died in 1887 He married (second) Jennie, born May 11, 1865, daughter of Dr B A Feichtner of Somerset county, Pennsylvania Children of first marriage Frank J, now residing in Dunbar, Caroline, married Earl Ober of Uniontown, Anna Winifred, married Harry Cochran, of Dawson, Pennsylvania Children of second marriage Lindsey F born November 18, 1889, John E born December 16, 1896

STRUBLE Frederick Struble, the first member of this family about whom we have definite information, was born in Philadelphia He was licensed in the September sessions of 1806 to keep tavern in Fayette county, and this he did at McClellandtown It is not known whom he married He had a child Asbury, of whom further

(II) Asbury son of Frederick Struble, was born at McClellandtown, January 5, 1809, died December 3, 1889 In German township, Fayette county, he owned five hundred acres of land, and was not only one of the most extensive, but also one of the most successful farmers in the county at that time He was a Democrat He married (first) —— Sprote, (second) Sarah Ann Smith, of Findlay, Ohio Children, seven by first wife and by second wife the following Asbury R born June 21, 1856, George Willey, of whom further. Emma Virginia, married Professor James M Hantz they live at Greensboro

(III) George Willey son of Asbury and Sarah Ann (Smith) Struble was born in German township, April 1, 1858 He was brought up in German township and there he attended public school Afterward he entered the agricultural department of the Pennsylvania State College, where he obtained a scientific agricultural education Returning home he engaged in farming and he has continued steadily in this work, and the combination of sound theory and practical experience has given him great success in agriculture His own home farm, of about three hundred acres, has all been put into an excellent state of cultivation and is one of the finest farms in the county Seventeen acres have been sold from his first holdings, having been bought by the railroad for right-of-way Besides this fine farm, Mr Struble owns one hundred and thirty-seven acres near Merritstown Pennsylvania, five hundred acres in Preston county, West Virginia, and one hundred and sixty acres in South Dakota Naturally he is a well-known man throughout Fayette county He has always carefully studied the business aspect of farming He is a member of the Free and Accepted Masons In politics Mr Struble is a Democrat, and he has served as school director twenty-five years

He married, in September, 1890, Anne, daughter of William McShane, who died November 27, 1911 She was a member of the Presbyterian church Their only child died in infancy

LYNN Judge David Lynn, who was of Scotch-Irish descent, founded this family in America He came from Dublin, Ireland and settled in Frederick county, Maryland, where he became prominent He was a judge under the crown and held office at the time of the Stamp Act agitation

(II) Andrew, son of Judge David Lynn, was born in Ireland and came to Maryland, where he died, leaving issue Andrew (2), of whom further, William and James

(III) Colonel Andrew (2) Lynn, son of Andrew (1) Lynn, grew to manhood in Maryland He came to Fayette county with his brothers, William and James Lynn William was a revolutionary soldier, and settled near Louisville, Kentucky James settled in Indiana, while Andrew remained in Fayette county, where he came in 1761 and entered a large tract of land, as did his brother William, by the method known as "Tomahawking" William's tract was in Washington township, extending to the Monongahela river, including the site of Freeport, now Fayette City When he moved to Kentucky he sold three hundred acres to his brother, Colonel Andrew Lynn His "Tomahawk"

Isaac Lynn

Lewis E Lynn

claim held good until 1769, when he made application to have it surveyed His petition was granted, and on August 2, 1769, it was surveyed, being the first authorized survey ever made by the government in Fayette county under the law of 1769 Besides this the Colonel owned his own 'Tomahawk" claim and several hundred acres in Redstone and Jefferson townships, including a mill site When the revolutionary war broke out Andrew enlisted in the Continental army and rose to the rank of a commissioned officer He served throughout the entire war and was with Washington at Yorktown During his absence from home during the war the authorities compelled his wife to comply with the law requiring every owner of a mill site to either erect a mill or abandon the site to the state She pluckily faced the situation, and by the time her husband returned from the war the mill was completed and grinding flour and feed for the public He resumed his agricultural life and devoted himself to the improvement of his farm He died in 1794, and was buried in the family graveyard on one of his farms, known as Crabtree Bottom, in the "New Purchase," where, about 1814, his excellent wife was laid by his side He married Mary Ashercraft, daughter of Peter and Mary (Ashercraft) Johnson, of Maryland Children 1 Nancy Ann, who became the third wife of the Rev John Corbly, a Baptist minister, at one time her husband was confined in Culpeper jail for preaching the doctrine of complete separation of church and state After his release he came to Greene county, Pennsylvania, where he established the Baptist church at Gerrards Ford, and preached the gospel until his death 2 William 3 Andrew (3) 4 John, who, in the fall of 1791, became a member of the United States service during the Indian uprisings, and was selected as one of eight scouts by his commander at Fort Wheeling, Virginia, to ascertain the movements of the hostile Indians, and while on duty in Ohio was shot through the heart while lying under the same blanket with John Crawford, the latter escaping without injury John Lynn was a warm friend of Crawford's, and upon the birth of a son in Crawford's family he was named John Lynn Crawford, in accordance with a sacred pledge made by Mr Crawford twelve years before 5 Ayers, of whom

further 6 Captain Isaac, who fought with Commodore Perry at the battle of Lake Erie, and won a medal for distinction in that campaign

(IV) Ayers, son of Colonel Andrew (2) Lynn, was born in Redstone township, Fayette county, September 15, 1772, died November 28, 1840 He built a stone house upon his farm in Redstone, which is yet standing and occupied, and there several succeeding generations were also born He was a farmer all his life, owned a large farm and was a prosperous, substantial citizen He was a Whig in politics and always active in public life In religious faith he was a Baptist He married Charlotte McFarran, born in Hancock, Maryland, August 30, 1780, died January 6, 1855, at Canton, Illinois, while on a visit there to her daughter, Nancy C Cochran They left issue as follows John J, Samuel Mc, Nancy C, married a Mr Cochran Louisa J, Mary, Isaac, of whom further, William, Alexander Mc, Andrew, Harriet S, Dr James J and Robert W

(V) Isaac, son of Ayres Lynn, was born in the old stone house on the home farm in Redstone township, Fayette county, Pennsylvania, November 15, 1816, died December 20, 1891 He was a prosperous farmer of Redstone, a Whig in politics, later a Republican, holding many local offices He was a Baptist in religion, and a man of high standing in his community, as the Lynns have always been He married, February 1, 1844, Rebecca, born October 11, 1821, near Greensboro, Greene county, Pennsylvania, died September 27, 1805, daughter of Lewis and Rachel (Jones) Evans In 1898 the family home was established in Uniontown, where the three living daughters reside Children, the first born in the stone house 1 Lewis Evans, of whom further 2 Louisa Johnson, born September 2, 1846 3 Charlotte Jane, born September 12, 1848, died October 10, 1849 4 Rachel Evans, born June 6 1851 5 Eliza Bell, January 28, 1855 6 Robert Wasson, November 14, 1857

(VI) Lewis Evans, eldest son of Isaac Lynn, was born in Redstone township, Fayette county, Pennsylvania, November 22, 1844 He was educated in the public schools and grew to manhood on the home farm, and for many years followed agriculture as an occupation In 1890 he moved to Uniontown, and has since been engaged in coke and coal land operations. He has prospered in business and stands well in his community. He belongs to lodge, chapter, commandery and shrine of the Masonic order, is a member of the Presbyterian church and a Republican in politics.

He married, February 6, 1872, Nancy M., born August 25, 1850, died August 14, 1888, daughter of Jacob and Marjorie (Harper) Henderson, of Dunbar township, Fayette county. Children: 1. Jacob H., born November 20, 1872, in Dunbar township, Fayette county, Pennsylvania, educated in the common schools and entered the University of Virginia at Morgantown. Later he engaged in the coal and coke business, is now located in Bucks county, Pennsylvania, at Langhorne, where he has a fine estate, "Lynnwood." He still holds his interests in the coal and coke business. He married Alberta D. Hogg, daughter of Charles Hogg, of Cadiz, Ohio, no issue. 2. Mary Rebecca, born September 2, 1874, married Dr. Gregg A. Dillinger, of Pittsburgh, Pennsylvania, has one child, Bessie A. 3. Robert I., died in infancy.

This family is believed to be of
DILS   German ancestry, although the name has been greatly changed no doubt since its introduction into this country. The earliest record is of Philip Dils who married Mary Hagar, in what was then Springhill township, Fayette county, and settled in the same township about 1807. He came from near Parkersburg, West Virginia and died in 1857 in Nicholson township, Fayette county where descendants yet reside. He was a successful farmer, and left each of his five children a good farm. Philip Dils and wife both lived to a good old age. Children: Ann, Benjamin, of whom further, Henry, Peter, Mary.

(II) Benjamin, son of Philip and Mary (Hagar) Dils was born in Nicholson township, Fayette county, Pennsylvania, in 1811. He was educated in the public schools of the township, and after leaving school assisted his father on the home farm of one hundred acres. This he inherited upon his father's death and conducted extensive stock raising operations supplying the meat dealers of the nearby towns and also making large shipments to the cities. In politics he was a Democrat and served his township as school director. He married Elizabeth, daughter of George and Hannah (Larch) Gans. Children: Philip, Paul, John, William, George, Benjamin, Mary Ann, married J. A. Gilbert, Hannah married Alexander Moser, Franklin Pierce, Leander, of whom further, Maria, Michael.

(III) Leander, son of Benjamin and Elizabeth (Gans) Dils, was born on the old homestead farm in Nicholson township, Fayette county, Pennsylvania, October 17, 1854. He obtained his education in the public schools, and after reaching man's estate took entire charge of the home farm, later, in 1908, purchasing a farm of one hundred and fifteen acres, which he now conducts very successfully. He is a member of the Patrons of Husbandry and of the Baptist church. His political party is the Democratic. The only office he ever held was that of road supervisor to which he was re-elected several times. He married, in 1881, Elizabeth Poundstone, born October 16, 1858, daughter of William and Mary (De Bolt) Poundstone. Children: 1. Jennie L., married Le Roy Brown. 2. Philip Lawrence died in infancy. 3. Ida, lives at home. 4. Alvin Crow, twin of Ida, lives in Georges township. 5. Leanna Elizabeth, lives at home. 6. Vanie R., lives at home.

On the paternal side
CUNNINGHAM   this family traces to the Emerald Isle, where John (1) Cunningham, grandfather of John A. Cunningham, of Connellsville, was born. John (1) Cunningham came to the United States where he married Anna McClintock, whose father, Alexander McClintock, was born in Ireland, came to the American colonies prior to the revolution, and was a member of General Washington's personal guard, serving seven years, nearly the entire revolutionary period. After the war he came to Pennsylvania, settling in Somerset county on Fort Hill township of Addison, where he made a clearing and cultivated a small area until his death at a log rolling, being caught and crushed under a huge log that caught him unawares.

(II) John (2), son of John (1) and Anna (McClintock) Cunningham, was born in Somerset county, Pennsylvania 1806, died 1875

He was a farmer all his life. He came to Fayette county, where he remained for a time, married and then returned to Somerset county, where he owned a good farm. He was a Republican and always took an active part in public affairs. Both he and his wife were members of the Methodist Episcopal church. He married Elizabeth, born in Connellsville, 1817, died 1898, daughter of George Marietta, of the prominent Fayette county family of that name (see Marietta). Children: Wesley, Fletcher, Brooklyn, Emily, married Frank Roger, Emmitt, John A., of whom further, Coston Melissa, married David Enfield, Mary, Belle, who became the wife of Thomas Grey.

(III) John A., son of John (2) Cunningham, was born in Somerset county, Pennsylvania, April 17, 1851. He was educated in the public schools, worked on his father's farm, and on arriving at man's estate learned the blacksmith's trade at Uniontown and for ten years operated a shop in Somerset county. He then came to Connellsville where he still continued at his chosen occupation, having been continuously in business there except for one year. In 1898 he erected his present commodious shop at No. 402 South Pittsburgh street, and in 1905 built a store building adjoining, now occupied by a grocer. He is a successful man of business. He has always been modern and progressive in his business methods, equipping his shop with all aids in the way of improved machinery and devices. At the time of his coming to Connellsville all smithing was done by hand labor and he was the first to use an engine in the town. In point of years in business he is the oldest smith in Connellsville. He is a member of the Methodist Episcopal church, as is his wife, also of the Independent Order of Odd Fellows and the Knights of the Maccabees.

Mr. Cunningham married (first) in 1873 Margaret Romesburg born in Somerset county. Children: 1 Fletcher, married Gertrude Fleming 2 Thomas married Stella Harland 3 Ethel, married William Young 4 Clarke, married Ella Ansel 5 Homer, married Blake McMillon 6 Bertha resides at home. Mrs. Cunningham died in 1891. Mr. Cunningham married (second) in 1893 Sarah daughter of John Trimpe, of Somerset county, Pennsylvania. Children: Ruth, Paul and Robert.

POUNDSTONE Richard Poundstone, the first member of this family about whom we have definite information, was born in Germany. He came from Germany in 1754, and about 1756 settled in what is now German township Fayette county, Pennsylvania. He married Margaret Baker, who was born in Germany. It is not known how many children they had but among these was George, of whom further, probably also Nicholas Poundstone who married Elizabeth Everly was their child.

(II) George, son of Richard and Margaret (Baker) Poundstone was born in German township, in 1768, died August 2, 1845. Across the mountain, then almost impassable, he drove the first team, and thereafter he did teaming, more or less the remainder of his life. Cumberland, Baltimore and Philadelphia were among the points to which he went by team. He became owner of about six hundred acres of land, and was an influential man in Fayette county. He was one of the founders of the Lutheran church in this county and was its main support. He married Susanna Messmore born in 1771, died in 1834. Children: 1 John of whom further 2 Susan married —— Dundy 3 Jacob born April 10 1795, died December 15, 1868, married, September 27, 1827, Mahala Core 4 Philip married Una Harford 5 Richard married Elizabeth Coftenbaugh 6 George, born September 18 1801, died December 3, 1884, married in 1836 Susan Stumm 7 Katharine married Elias Freeman 8 Margaret, married Augustus Scott.

(III) John, son of George and Susanna (Messmore) Poundstone, was born October 3, 1790, died February 25 1861. He was a farmer, in 1842 he was school director and in 1845 assessor. He was a Democrat and a member of the Cumberland church. He married Nancy Funk born March 22 1794, died February 25 1861. Children: 1 Susanna, born August 9 1813, died December 1, 1840 2 David R., born November 23 1814, died November 11, 1871 3 George, born July 25, 1816, died in August, 1816 4 George, born August 16 1817 died in September 1817 5 John, born May 6, 1819, died in July, 1819 6 Adam M., of whom further 7 Hugh C., born November 7, 1822, died November 22,

1899 8 Nancy J, born December 27, 1824, died November 12 1901 9 Joseph F, born June 17, 1827 living 10 William S, born January 5, 1829 died April 17, 1908 11 Benjamin born December 16, 1830, died in February, 1831 12 John M, born December 3, 1831, died January 15 1832 13 Robert S, born November 30, 1836, died April 13, 1838

(IV) Adam M, son of John and Nancy (Funk) Poundstone, was born September 2, 1820, died April 29, 1892 He was a farmer, and lived on the same farm as his father had lived on, when he died he left it to his two sons, Samuel A and Albert G, who now farm it together He had the education of the district school, was a Democrat and a member of the Cumberland Presbyterian church He married, February 8 1846, Rebecca C, born August 19 1829, died November 1 1852, daughter of Samuel and Elizabeth (Weibel) Allebaugh Children 1 Samuel A, of whom further. 2 ———, died in infancy 3 Albert G, born October 24, 1852, married Mary Elizabeth Deal, of German township They have two children, both unmarried and living at home Anna Rebecca, born December 16 1878, and Estella born August 26 1883

(V) Samuel A son of Adam M and Rebecca C (Allebaugh) Poundstone, was born in German township, February 20, 1847 He is a farmer, and one of the best known men in Fayette county Although he and his brother live on the old place, a portion has been sold from the original one hundred and forty-three acres and the brothers have one hundred and ten acres This farm is near Footdale The coal has been sold to the Eureka Coal & Coke Company Mr Poundstone has worked in the recorder's office at Uniontown for three years, with Henry A Witt, and for another period of three years with Byron Porter also at Uniontown, he was for five years with the Second National Bank at that place He is a member of the Independent Order of Odd Fellows having been initiated in 1868 at Necessity Lodge at Uniontown In politics he is a Democrat and he has served one term as county auditor

JOHNSTON William Johnston is the first member of this family about whom we have definite information It is not known whom he married Children 1 James, deceased, he was a farmer near Pleasant View, Fayette county, Pennsylvania, was unmarried 2 John who went in 1849 to California to dig gold, returned to Redstone township, Fayette county, Pennsylvania, where he became a farmer 3 Philip L, of whom further 4 Lucy, died at advanced age, unmarried 5 Sally, died at advanced age, unmarried 6 Elizabeth died young married George Gehoe 7 Martha, married George Gehoe 8 Robert, who lives on the home farm in Redstone township, where he made a home for his sisters Lucy and Sally, he was unmarried

(II) Philip L, son of William Johnston, was born in Jefferson township, Fayette county, Pennsylvania, April 24, 1824 died March 3, 1910 He grew up in Jefferson township on Little Redstone creek, and when he was a young man learned the trade of cooper, which he followed all his life After his marriage he owned a small place in Washington county, Pennsylvania, above Allenport, soon after this he bought fifty acres near Pleasant View, in Redstone township As long as there was a demand for barrels he worked at his trade and the sons did the work on the farm He retired in 1906 and removed to Brownsville, where he lived for the remainder of his life He was a large, strong and enduring man, weighing one hundred and eighty pounds He was a Democrat Although both he and his wife had been members of the Baptist church, when he removed to Brownsville he presented his letter to the Cumberland Presbyterian church at that place

He married Isabel Maxwell who was born at Allenport April 27, 1829, died December 9, 1911 Her father was born in Ireland, he was a river man and lived at Allenport Her mother was of German birth Their children 1 Thomas, died in middle life, he was a river man on the Monongahela 2 Thornton, captain of a river boat 3 Alexander, served in the civil war and was captain of a river boat 4 Mary married ——— they live at Lacon Illinois 5 Isabel married Philip L Johnston 6 Martha, married Robert Wilson, they live at Fayette City Fayette county, Pennsylvania 7 Jane, deceased married Samuel Mansfield, also deceased they lived at Fayette City 8 Caroline, married (first) Peter Riley, (second) Samuel Fields Mr Fields was a river boat captain, she is now a widow living at Allenport Children of Philip L and Isabel (Maxwell) Johnston 1, Mary married Allison Reppert, lives at Belle Vernon, Pennsylvania 2 Dora B, unmarried, lives at Brownsville 3 Josephine, married Finley Haggerty, he is a farmer in Franklin township Fayette county 4 William E married Bertha Osborne, he is a farmer and lives in Greene county 5 Michael Wolf, died aged thirty-two, unmarried 6 George Maxwell of whom further

(III) George Maxwell, son of Philip L and Isabel (Maxwell) Johnston was born on his father s place in Washington county, on the Monongahela river, one mile above Belle Vernon, November 2, 1866 He attended Spear's school, near his birthplace Also in boyhood he learned telegraphy at West Belle Vernon In 1886 he went to Chicago and was a telegrapher for the Western Union Telegraph Company He followed this occupation until March, 1905, when he returned to Fayette county and bought sixty acres of the old Dunn place in Franklin township Here he still lives He makes specialties of small fruits and garden vegetables He is a Democrat Both Mr and Mrs Johnston are members of the Baptist church at Flatwoods, Fayette county, Pennsylvania He married July 4, 1892, Mary daughter of John and Threna Johnston, who was born near Manitowoc, Wisconsin, April 7, 1866 Despite the name, she is not of the same descent as Mr Johnston Her parents were both born in Norway, although they married after coming to America in Wisconsin Both are deceased the father owned a farm of two hundred acres Children of George Maxwell and Mary (Johnston) Johnston Ruth Marie, born December 14 1894, George Maxwell born July 1896 Edith born April 29, 1898, Esther Matilda, born September 16 1902

This family is native to Fayette SMITH county, Pennsylvania, North Union township, where Robert H Smith was born and has spent his life engaged in farming He married Eliza F Humbert, also born in Fayette county, Pennsylvania Children Peter F, of whom further, Jennie, married Clyde D Kimball, of Dunbar, Pennsylvania William W, in business in Connellsville, Dr Charles H, of Uniontown

(II) Peter F, son of Robert H and Eliza F (Humbert) Smith, was born at the home farm near Dunbar, North Union township, Fayette county, Pennsylvania, April 16, 1857 His early education was obtained in the public school, finishing his classical study at the State Normal School at California, Pennsylvania Having decided upon the profession of medicine, he entered the medical department of the University of Michigan at Ann Arbor, whence he was graduated M D, class of 1887 He began the practice of medicine at Percy, Fayette county, Pennsylvania, continuing there for eight years He then located in Uniontown, Pennsylvania, where he has since been in continuous successful practice He is a member of the medical staff of Uniontown Hospital and a member of the Pennsylvania State and Fayette County Medical societies He served a term as coroner of Fayette county, and is a Republican in politics

He married, June 25 1895 Ruth Eliza Rinehart, of Waynesburg, Pennsylvania Children Charles F and Eleanor Eliza

The McCormicks of McCORMICK Uniontown, Pennsylvania herein recorded, descend from Noble McCormick, of Franklin and North Union townships Fayette county, Pennsylvania There were McCormicks in Franklin township earlier than 1785, the name of James McCormick appearing as a land owner at that date Whether Noble was a son or relative of James is not certain, although the statement is made that Noble McCormick was born in Ireland There are grounds, however, for the belief that he was born in Fayette county, 1790-1800 and that he was a son of James Noble McCormick was a school teacher and a farmer, owning a good farm in North Union township He married (first) a Miss Brown, (second) Sarah Jane McDonald, who bore him a son, Charles, who moved to the state of California Children by first wife 1 Eliza, married Jacob Springer 2 Mary Ellen, married Simon Coborn 3 Rebecca, moved west 4 Anna Maria, married Ellis Springer 5 Thomas, a farmer of Dunbar township 6 Joseph, went west 7 James, went west 8 William Brown of whom further

(II) William Brown son of Noble McCormick, was born in South Union township, Fayette county, Pennsylvania. He grew to manhood at the home farm on the Morgantown road and became a wealthy butcher and cattle dealer. His market in Uniontown occupied the present site of Ritenour's drug store.

After his more active years were over he became an enthusiastic and successful bee farmer and an authority on the honey bee and how to profit by his industry. His apiary was celebrated and attracted interested visitors from all over the state. He was an ardent Democrat and a member of the Methodist Episcopal church.

Mr. McCormick married Susan, daughter of Matthew (1) and Elizabeth (Catlin) Allen, he a farmer of North Union township, Fayette county, where he was born of Irish forbears. Children of Mr. and Mrs. Allen: 1. Matthew (2), served in the Mexican war and never returned. 2. Susan, of previous mention, wife of William Brown McCormick. 3. Mary, married John R. Crawford, a farmer; she is yet living, aged eighty-seven years. Elizabeth (Catlin) Allen died in 1826. By a second wife Matthew Allen had: 4. George, a printer, died aged twenty-five years. 5. Robert J., a school teacher, married Bertha Bunker. 6. Josiah, a farmer. 7. James, died of camp fever during the civil war, in which he served as teamster. Matthew (1) Allen was a son of George and Jane (Paul) Allen. George Allen, born in Eastern Pennsylvania, was one of the earliest settlers in Dunbar township, Fayette county; Jane Paul was born in Fayette county, sister of Colonel James Paul, the noted Indian fighter of the early day. Children of Mr. and Mrs. McCormick:

1. George A., a butcher and three times elected sheriff of Fayette county. He married Alice Barker and lives in Uniontown. 2. Milton Allen, a lumber dealer of Fairchance, Pennsylvania. 3. Mary, married Frank Brooks and lives in Uniontown. 4. Ella, married William Thorndell and lives in Detroit, Michigan. 5. Elizabeth, married Ward Howland and lives in Detroit, Michigan. 6. Sophia, married Frederick Ward, a real estate dealer at East Riverside, New Jersey. 7. William Calvin, of whom further.

(III) William Calvin, son of William Brown and Susan (Allen) McCormick, was born at the old McCormick homestead, just north of Uniontown, Pennsylvania, March 7, 1856, died August 30, 1911. From childhood he was practically crippled by rheumatism and gave little hope of ever being other than a sufferer all his life. He was well educated, and when he was sixteen years of age his father started him in the butcher business at Dunbar, Pennsylvania. Here he remained for several years, his rheumatic troubles disappeared, and he became one of the strongest men in the county. He was stockily built, of medium height and very quick in all his movements. He never liked the butcher business, and when he found himself possessed of perfect health and strength sold out his Dunbar business, settling in Uniontown. There he became a contractor and building supply dealer. He built a store and yards on the lot in the rear of the Brunswick Hotel, which later was partially destroyed by fire. He then rebuilt at the corner of Beeson and East Fayette streets, continuing until 1904, when he erected the extensive buildings along the Baltimore & Ohio railroad track, between Jefferson and Fayette streets, that are still used by his successors in business. He was very successful in this business, becoming one of the leading contractors in his city.

He was in business alone until January 1, 1911, when the press of business and poor health compelled him to admit a partner, John T. Hoover, who took charge of outside activities of the firm. His work as a contractor was exceedingly varied, including street paving, road building, the building of sewers, reservoirs, coke ovens, buildings and all similar construction. In the store and yards department he carried a complete line of builders' supplies. He was a very ardent Democrat, serving for nineteen years as councilman of Uniontown. A feature of his construction work in Uniontown was the erection of private sewers, and his estate is credited with owning more miles of sewer in Uniontown than the city itself owns, and from which a goodly income is derived. He did not confine himself to contracting, but was interested in other Uniontown activities, including flouring mills. He was very public spirited and always ready to lend his support to any legitimate enterprise. He built and operated the first street railway in Union-

Wm C. McCormick

town, a line running the length of the city out to his ball and zoological grounds, 'McCormick Park." Later his railroad was shared by others, known as the firm of Ewing, Hopwood & McCormick About 1880 he became interested with his brother, George H, in undeveloped coal lands They then had little capital, but selected their holdings with great judgment, and held options on thousands of acres of land in West Virginia The panic of 1892 and 1893, however, compelled them to relinquish their holdings, being unable to raise money to meet their payments Those to whom the option finally passed became millionaires, thus justifying the judgment of the McCormick brothers, who would have likewise profited had not the panic overthrown their plans

During the early part of the last decade of the nineteenth century he was appointed by his brother, George A (then sheriff of Fayette county), chief constable of the coal and iron district, to assist in holding in check the strikers of the county, who were boarding railroad trains, riding from place to place and refusing to pay any fares Mr McCormick's assistant was "Indian Tom," a half-breed, who stood six feet ten inches in height, with courage to match his great size Their duty was to ride on the trains and throw off all those refusing to pay fares In 1893, while making an arrest, Mr McCormick had his skull crushed by a beer bottle, which wound resulted in blindness that caused him to spend the last nineteen*years of his life in darkness, although, except for a short time, he continued active in business Just previous to this sad event he had assisted in the capture of the Cooley gang, a notorious band of thieves that had infested the district for some years

To turn to a less serious side of his life, he was known as the "father of baseball" in Uniontown When a young man he was a good amateur catcher, and never ceased to be an ardent lover and supporter of the national pastime He organized the first team to represent Uniontown, "The Uniontown Amateurs," and later organized and managed the first professional team representing Uniontown in one of the minor leagues When a team would languish and drop out he would finance and organize another, start it off successfully, then turn them over to a

manager, always keeping a team in the league The family preserve three large pennants won by his teams in the professional league He built, owned and conducted the first baseball park at Uniontown, having in addition as another interesting feature, a small menagerie and amusements, making it a popular resort The before mentioned street railway was built to connect McCormick Park with the city

He married (first) Margaret Johns, (second) Irene, born in 1864, daughter of William Wyatt, a soldier of the civil war, a teamster and in the early days helped in the construction of the National road The Wyatts are an old Fayette county family Child of first marriage 1 Montgomery Ward, now conducting an employment agency in Uniontown Children of second wife 2 Beatrice, married Frank Filmore Hyde, now a bookkeeper living in New Castle, Pennsylvania 3 Howell Brown, of whom further

(IV) Howell Brown, youngest child of William Calvin and Irene (Wyatt) McCormick, was born in Uniontown, Pennsylvania, February 21, 1885 He was educated in the public schools, Madison Academy graduate, class of 1901, and Virginia Military Academy After three years at the latter school he was obliged to return home, his father's health requiring that he have the constant companionship of his son to guide his steps and assist him in the management of his business affairs He had become familiar with the contracting busines, even as a boy, and was its mainstay during his father's last years He inherited the business interests of his father and is now engaged in making final settlements with his partners He is a clear-headed, energetic young man, and will worthily fill the place made vacant by the death of his father He is a Democrat in politics, a member of the Methodist Episcopal Church and a member of the Fraternal Order of Eagles

He married, March 4, 1907, Gail Lancaster, born in Little California, Pennsylvania, December 1 1890 daughter of Charles and Ida (Trump) Lancaster, born in Washington county the latter still living Children Beatrice, born June 12, 1908, William Howell February 10, 1910 The family home is the old McCormick residence, No 41 Iowa street, Uniontown

The emigrant ancestor of McCORMICK the McCormicks, of Fayette county, Pennsylvania, herein recorded, was Dr John McCormick, who emigrated from Ireland to Virginia between the years 1730 and 1740 In the Orange county, Virginia, records there is a deed, under date of May 21, 1740, from Just Hite to "John McCormick, of Orange county," for three hundred and ninety-five acres of land Later he took up other grants adjoining this property, which was located in that part of Orange county that later became Jefferson county, West Virginia It was on this estate near Summit Point that in 1840 he built ' The White House," which was still standing in 1903 He was a graduate in medicine of the University of Dublin, and brought to this country with him a large and valuable medical library, which at his death was sold to Dr Cramer, then the leading physician of Charlestown He died in 1768, leaving a wife and eight children In his will, made May 8, 1768, and recorded February 8, 1769, he mentions wife Anne and sons James, John, Francis, William, George, Andrew, daughter "Mary Tate, wife to Magnus Tate,' and 'Jean Bryen, wife to James Bryen." His wife and son James were executors of his estate It is indicated that he was married before coming to this country, but the maiden name of his wife cannot be found The descendants of his eight children are scattered throughout many states It is said of the early members of the family that they were singularly unobtrusive people, content in happiness derived from their own family relations, being extremely clannish, both the men and women were strictly honorable, affectionate, domestic and courteous, one of their marked characteristics was a strict regard for the truth One of the heirlooms of the family was an old English prayer book which descended from Dr John McCormick to his son Francis, and was given by him to his son Thomas at his marriage but was unfortunately destroyed during the civil war In it was the family tree on parchment, on another page, Dr John McCormick in a blue broadcloth suit with brass buttons, another, the marriage scene, and yet another, Anne McCormick with a blue bodice and yellow silk or satin skirt, with a branch in her hand and a bud, an-

other, a death scene, coffin, etc, and a notice of dates, births and death beneath The dates were all in the year 1700 Francis, one of the sons of Dr John McCormick, was born April 17, 1734, one of his two wives was a Miss Province, after whom his son Province was named Province McCormick served in the war of 1812 with the rank of colonel The name Province was also perpetuated in the family of William McCormick, but spelled Provance

(II) William, son of Dr John McCormick, was born about 1736, he being the next son to Francis, born 1734 He was probably born in Virginia, as the record of the deed mentioned was 1740 He came to southwestern Pennsylvania about the year 1770, and was the first settler within the limits of the later borough of Connellsville, preceding by a few years Zachariah Connell, in whose honor the town was named William McCormick came to Connellsville from Winchester, Virginia, bringing with him a number or pack-horses, which he employed in the transportation of salt and iron and other commodities from Cumberland Maryland, to the Youghioghney and Monongahela river settlements There were no railroads, and Cumberland was the nearest point on the old National Pike He settled on the Connellsville side or the river, building his first home of logs on the river bank directly opposite the home of Colonel William Crawford, on the west side of the Youghiogheny river, in 1767, at Stewart's Crossing later the borough of New Haven, now a part of the city of Connellsville He died in 1816, aged about eighty years He married Effie, daughter of Colonel William Crawford, the revolutionary officer and famous Indian fighter, whose life and tragic death at the hands of his savage foes has inspired the pen of so many writers Colonel Crawford's coming to Western Pennsylvania antedated William McCormick's by several years, while his coming to Stewart's Crossing was about fourteen years later than William Stewart's, who lived there in 1753 and 1754 Another daughter of Colonel William Crawford married Zachariah Connell who came soon after 1770 and made his home with Colonel Crawford until his marriage to Ann Crawford in 1773, later, between 1773 and 1778, he moved to the east side of the river, locating on a tract of land designated in his warrant of survey as "Mud Island." William and Fffie (Crawford) McCormick had eleven children, including a son Provance

(III) Provance, son of William McCormick, was born July 29, 1799, in Connellsville, where he died in 1887. He was a man of good education and versatile talent. In early life he le rned the carpenter's trade, but after a few years gave it up. He was the first manufacturer of coke in the Connellsville region, and in 1842 built the first beehive oven constructed in the United States. From his small beginning has grown the now enormous output that taxes the carrying capacity of the several railroads entering the coke region of Pennsylvania. For many years he was justice of the peace, and served one term as associate judge of Fayette county. He married Susan Bowers, born near Connellsville, died 1868, of German descent; among their children was a son, Joseph I.

(IV) Joseph Trevor, son of Provance McCormick, was born in Connellsville, Pennsylvania, November 23, 1830, died May 4, 1904. He received a good education in the public schools, and after completing his studies taught school for several years in Connellsville. Later he established in the drug business, continuing for several years, then secured an appointment as draughtsman in the Department of Internal Affairs at Harrisburg, holding it five years. In 1866 he entered into a partnership with James McGrath and established the Connellsville Machine & Car Company, manufacturing all machinery used in the mining of coke and transportation of coal. This was one of the largest enterprises of Connellsville and was always a prosperous one. Mr. McCormick was treasurer, Mr. McGrath superintendent, each owning a half interest, the most important being his connection Mr. McCormick had other and varied interwith the Second National Bank of Connellsville, of which he was president until his death. He was a member of the Masonic order, of which he was one of the charter members in Connellsville. In politics he was always a Democrat. He married, at Connellsville, October 27, 1855, Susan Newmyer, who survives him, daughter of Jonathan and Mary (Stickler) Newmyer, both born in Bullskin township, Fayette county. Jonathan Newmyer

born 1790, was a leading farmer of his township, son of Peter Newmyer, who came from eastern Pennsylvania to Bullskin township during the revolutionary war and purchased a large farm. Children of Joseph Trevor McCormick: 1 Karl C, died 1891. 2 Mary Maud, married Rev John M Scott, children John M, Jean Donald M, Roger M, Karl M, and Malcolm M. 3 Louis Provance, of whom further.

(V) Dr. Louis Provance McCormick, youngest son of Joseph Trevor McCormick, was born in Connellsville, Pennsylvania, August 7, 1866. His early education was obtained in the public schools after which he attended Mt Pleasant Institute in Westmoreland county, Pennsylvania, later attending Bridgeton (New Jersey) Institute, whence he was graduated class of 1886. He chose medicine as his profession and entered Jefferson Medical College, Philadelphia, whence he was graduated M D, class of 1891. He at once began practice, locating at Connellsville, where he is now located and well established as a skillful, popular practitioner. At the outbreak of the Spanish-American war he was assistant surgeon of the Tenth Regiment, Pennsylvania National Guard. He volunteered for service with his regiment, was mustered into the United States service at Mount Gretna, Pennsylvania, May 5, 1898, mustered out August 22, 1899, at San Francisco, California. He served with the Tenth in the Philippines, and was in the battle and taking of Manila by the land forces. He was assigned February 4, 1899, to the United States gunboat 'Laguna de Bay," and during Aguinaldo's insurrection saw active service, particularly between February 4 and the following June, in twenty-six engagements. From August 6 to 14, 1898 he was in charge of the Manila ambulance service. From August 14, 1898, to the following February 5, 1899, he was on duty at the Reserve Hospital at Manila. In August 1899, the regiment returned to the United States and was mustered out at San Francisco. Dr McCormick is still in service in the National Guard as surgeon, with the rank of major. After the war he returned to Connellsville and re-established his practice, having offices in the Second National Bank Building. He is on the surgical staff of the Cottage State Hospital at Connellsville, was president of the board of health for several years, and is a member of the Fayette county and Pennsons, Uniontown Commandery, Knights sylvania State medical societies, and the American medical association He is prominent in the Masonic order, belonging to King Solomons Lodge, Free and Accepted Masons, Connellsville Chapter, Royal Arch Masons, Templar, Uniontown Lodge of Perfection, and Pittsburgh Consistory, Ancient Accepted Scottish Rite, in which he has attained the thirty-second degree, and is a noble of Syria Temple, Nobles of the Mystic Shrine He is commander of the local society of the Army of the Philippines He is a Democrat, but extremely independent in political action

He married, February 1, 1906 Kathryn Felsinger, born in Northumberland county, Pennsylvania, August 8, 1882, daughter of Jacob and Clara Felsinger, both born in Philadelphia Children of Dr Provance McCormick Helen, born January 2, 1907, Martha, March 12, 1909

McCORMICK The McCormicks of Redstone township, Fayette county, spring from James McCormick, who settled at an early date He is credited with the ownership of land in Jefferson township in 1780 and in Franklin township in 1785 In 1787 he was naturalized as a citizen He died in 1847, aged eighty-five years His children, seventeen in number, settled in various parts of Fayette county, several in Redstone township

(II) John C, son of James McCormick, was a house carpenter of Redstone and a farmer noted for the excellence of his agricultural methods In fact, his farm south of Cook's Mills, during his ownership there was regarded as a model He was an ardent Presbyterian, and one of the founders of the Cumberland Presbyterian church of Pleasant View, Menallen township He was assessor of Redstone township in 1847, and also served as school director He died in 1876 leaving issue

(III) Samuel, son of John C McCormick, was born November 2, 1820, died 1881 He grew up a farmer and spent his life engaged in agriculture and kindred pursuits He was energetic and very successful in his business operations He owned the old Sharpless farm,

later bought the old Davis farm (where his children were reared), and finally bought the old Hess homestead near New Salem, where he died in 1881 He was a strong Democrat, and a Presbyterian He married Margaret Hess, born February 4, 1820, died in California Pennsylvania, August 6, 1910 Children 1 Mary, born November 1, 1845, married Henry Johnson, a farmer of Menallen township Fayette county 2 Elliott Evans, of whom further 3 Mary Jane, born June 25, 1857, died April 6, 1897

(III) Elliot Evans only son of Samuel and Margaret (Hess) McCormick, was born in Redstone township, Fayette county, Pennsylvania January 20, 1854 He passed his early life on the home farm and obtained his education in the common schools In after life he became a successful farmer and took an unusual interest in machinery and its application to farming His political party was the Democratic and he and his wife were members of the Methodist church He died April 5, 1890

He married, November 15, 1877, Elizabeth J Scott, born in Butler county, Pennsylvania, daughter of Samuel Scott, who emigrated to Butler county, Pennsylvania, from Scotland Children 1 Elizabeth J, of previous mention 2 Emmett, deceased was a teacher in Butler and Beaver Falls, Pennsylvania 3, Samuel E, a master mechanic near Pittsburgh, Pennsylvania 4 Jennie Porter 5 Annie, married John Wagner, deceased, and lives in Butler county 6 Margaret, deceased Children of Elliot Evans and Elizabeth J (Scott) McCormick 1 Samuel O, of whom further, 2 George E, born August 29, 1880, married July 11, 1903, Ruth Hatfield 3 Emmett Scott, born December 11, 1882 assistant train despatcher on Pittsburgh, Virginia & Charleston railroad at Pittsburgh, Pennsylvania 4 Jessie Brown, born December 3, 1887, associated in seed business with brother at New Salem, married July 17, 1907, Louisa Murphy, daughter of M A Murphy, of Franklin township

(IV) Samuel O, son of Elliot Evans and Elizabeth J (Scott) McCormick, was born in Redstone township, Fayette county, October 3, 1878

He was educated in the public schools of Redstone township and later com-

plcted a course in Duff's business college at Pittsburgh, Pennsylvania. His early life was passed on the home farm helping his father, and upon the death of the latter he took entire charge of the home farm for about two years.

For five years following he was employed by Jesse P. Brown of New Salem, then entering the mercantile business, held a position with the Shamrock Supply Company, leaving there to accept a situation as assistant to the superintendent at the Buffington plant of the H. C. Frick Company. After two years' employment with the Union Supply Company he entered the feed and builders' supplies business at New Salem in partnership with Mr. Stevenson, under the firm name McCormick & Stevenson. They opened their store at Boyd's Mill and at the end of a year Mr. McCormick purchased his partner's interests. He has built up a large and remunerative business, covering all the territory included between Redstone creek on the north, Brownsville on the west, Carmichaels, Greene county, on the south, and Uniontown Pennsylvania, on the east. He is a Republican in politics, and has held several local offices, among them the following: Postmaster at Salem for five years, school director in independent district for four years, and road supervisor of Menallen township, in which capacity he has built the first piece of state road in the county. He is a member of the Christian church in New Salem, is superintendent of the Sunday school, superintendent of the board of finance, and superintendent of the mission school at Shamrock, Pennsylvania. As a power for good in the church his value cannot be overestimated, and his congenial, pleasing manner gives him much liberty and freedom of action in his Sunday school work. He is a fine type of the successful business man, the Christian gentleman and the good citizen.

He married, June 29, 1904, Evelyn B. daughter of Oliver C. a boot and shoe manufacturer of McClellandtown, Pennsylvania and Elizabeth (Huhn) Harn of German township. Children: Evelyn B. (of previous mention), Emmons Blaine, manager of Lamson Store Service Company, Atlanta Georgia. Child of Samuel O. and Evelyn B. (Harn) McCormick: Elizabeth, born October 20, 1907.

FAIRCHILD This family name is of Scotch origin and until the settlement in England was Fairbairn, 'bairn' being the Scotch equivalent of "child." The coat-of-arms is an ancient one, and denotes in heraldry three pilgrimages to the Holy Land and three prisoners taken by knights of the family during the Crusades. Thomas Fairchild, ancestor of the American family, and his first wife, were among the first settlers of Stratford, Connecticut, coming in 1639 from England, where a branch of the Scotch family settled in the fifteenth century. He became a prominent man, and in 1659 the general court honored him with the prefix 'Mr.'

He married (first) in England, about 1639, Sarah, daughter of Robert Seabrook, (second) Katherine Craig, of London, England. He died December 14, 1670, and his widow married (second) Jeremiah Judson. Children of Thomas Fairchild and his first wife: 1, Samuel, born August 31, 1639, said to have been the first white child born in Stratford, Connecticut. 2 Sarah, born February 19, 1641, married Jehiel Preston. 3 John, born May, 1644 died young. 4 Thomas (2), born February 21, 1645, married Susan ——, who survives him and married (second) Samuel Nichols. 5 Dinah, born July 14, 1648 died 1703, married Benjamin Corey. 6 Zachariah of whom further. 7 Emma, born October 1653. Children by second wife: Joseph, born April 18, 1664, John June 8, 1666, Priscilla, April 20, 1669.

(II) Zachariah, son of Thomas Fairchild and his first wife, Sarah Seabrook, was born in Stratford, Connecticut December 14, 1651, died June 3, 1703. He married November 3, 1681, Hannah, daughter of John Beach. She survived him and married (second) May 5, 1708, John Burritt. Children of Zachariah Fairchild: 1 Mehitabel, born March 21, 1682, died September 27, 1684. 2 Hannah, born August 1, 1685. 3 David, March, 1688. 4 Agnes, October 1 1691. 5 Caleb, September 10, 1693, settled at Whippany, New Jersey, and died there May 1, 1777. 6 James, born February 12, 1695. 7 Mary, May 7, 1698. 8 Zachariah (2) of whom further. 9 Abiel, born July 15, 1703.

(III) Zachariah (2), son of Zachariah (1) Fairchild, was born at Stratford, Connecticut, settled at Morris Plains, Morris county, New Jersey, where he died August 6, 1777 He married (first), Deborah ———, born 1707, died April 3, 1757, (second) widow Lydia Hathaway, in August, 1757, she was born 1724, died May 22, 1769 Children of first wife 1 Jane, married Silas Goble, 1744 2 Mary, married Benjamin Hathaway 3 Phineas, of whom further 4 Abigail, married Jonathan Conklin 5 David, born May 6, 1734, married (first) November 9, 1757, Catherine Gregory born March 13, 1735, died February 18, 1800, (second) Nancy Loper 6 Katurah, married Philip Hathaway 7 Rhoda, born November 4, 1737, married Jedediah Gregory 8 Abel, born November 4, 1739, married (first) Esther Gard, (second) Elizabeth ——— With Zachariah (2) and his children the prominence of the Fairchilds as a Morris county, New Jersey, family, began

(IV) Phineas, son of Zachariah (2) and his first wife, Deborah Fairchild, was born 1730, died in Morris county, New Jersey, November 12, 1801 He was a prominent citizen of Morris county, New Jersey He married Sarah ———, born 1729, died November 2, 1811 Children Abigail, born December 24, 1754, married David Hurd, Deborah, born February 22, 1757, married William Hubbard, Sarah, born February 22, 1759, drowned 1769, Mary, born June 12 1761, married Caleb Tuttle, Timothy, born July 22, 1763, married Stephen Mehitabel Tuttle, Stephen, of whom further, Esther, born November 20, 1766, married Jonathan Dean, Charlotte, born October 10, 1768, married Loamm Chesterline, Justus, born July 20, 1771, died November 22, 1772, Sarah, born February 26, 1773, died May 6, 1861, married December 15, 1795, Peter Tompkins

(V) Stephen, son of Phineas and Sarah Fairchild, was born in Morris county, New Jersey, November 30, 1764 He served in the revolution, but not as an enlisted man, being but fifteen at the time, but one of his older brothers in the army was taken sick, and while he was home being nursed back to health Stephen took his place in the army His service was recognized, and in her old age his widow was granted a revolutionary pension, which she drew until her death One of his brothers was with Washington the dreadful winter at Valley Forge Stephen

Fairchild was a shoemaker by trade, and after attaining manhood he moved to Fayette county, Pennsylvania, settling at what is now East Liberty He married, late in life, Elizabeth Jillet Children Twins, Alexander and Andrew, Alexander owned a farm on the mountain above Dunbar, Fayette county, and married (first) Catherine Logan

(VI) Andrew, son of Stephen and Elizabeth (Jillet) Fairchild, was born in Dunbar township, Fayette county, Pennsylvania, June 6, 1823, died June 5, 1892 He grew to manhood in East Liberty, attended the public schools, and in early life worked at cabinet making He then bought a saw mill on Dickerson Run which he operated for ten years He engaged in undertaking, was justice of the peace, and so continued until his death He was a strong Democrat of the Jackson type, and a devoted member of the Cumberland Presbyterian church During the civil war he contracted mail routes in West Virginia, which he sub-contracted to other parties, visiting Buchanan and Beverly for that purpose, and there having exciting adventures with guerrillas He married (first) Eliza Jane Evans, who died at the age of twenty years He married (second) Martha Brewer, born in Perry township, Fayette county, Pennsylvania, 1825, died 1856 He married (third) Sarah Brewer, a sister of Martha his second wife Martha and Sarah were daughters of Aaron and Elizabeth Brewer Their father in early life was a wagoner on the old National Pike but after his marriage settled on a farm in Franklin township, Fayette county In later years he moved to Van Buren county Iowa, where he settled on a farm and died The family were from Eastern Pennsylvania and of German descent Martha Brewer was the second of a family of twelve children Children of Andrew Fairchild and his first wife, Eliza Jane Evans 1 Daughter, died unmarried 2 Susan, after her mother's death was taken and reared by her grandmother Evans, she married Stewart Worthington Children of second wife, Martha Brewer 3 Elizabeth, married Rudolph Wariaka and moved to California, where both died 4 Aaron J, of whom further 5 Joel Evans, now living in California, engaged in orange growing at Redlands, also a carpenter and builder, married Florence Hutchinson Children of third wife, Sarah Brewer 6, Martha died September 9, 1875, aged sixteen years seven months thirteen days 7 Harriet, married Samuel Snedeker, deceased 8 Anna, married Jacob Strawn, and lives in Allegheny county, Pennsylvania 9 Sarah, died in infancy 10 John A, now living at Pocohontas, Illinois, where he owns and operates a flour mill

(VII) Aaron Jillet, son of Andrew Fairchild and his second wife, Martha Brewer, was born at East Liberty, Fayette county, January 11, 1852 He spent his early life at East Liberty and there attended the public schools He learned the trade of carpenter in his father's mill and followed it until he was thirty-five years of age At that time he purchased a small piece of ground near Dickerson Run, to which he steadily added until he owned seventy-five acres Here he engaged in the dairy business for a time with but indifferent success Recently he has been engaged in operating real estate adjoining Dickerson Run, and in this has been very successful He votes the Prohibition ticket and is a member of the Patrons of Husbandry

He married, December 25, 1873, Susan Strickler, born in Franklin township April 12, 1855, daughter of Jacob and Rebecca (Snyder) Strickler Children 1 Leroy Oglevee, born October 30, 1874, married Rachel Johnson, he is a civil engineer in the employ of the Baltimore & Ohio railroad at Chillicothe, Ohio 2 Elbert Strickler, born January 19, 1876, married Anna Simpson, and lives in Wilson Pennsylvania, a contracting carpenter 3 Bessie Pearl, born September 10 1879, married Clyde Brown a farmer of Franklin township 4 Wilford Cleveland, born February 5 1884, civil engineer in the employ of the American Bridge Company at Toledo, Ohio 5 Cora Belle, born October 28, 1887, lives with parents

HAIR The earliest record of this family to be found gives Daniel Hare as the immigrant ancestor from Ireland, settling in Dunbar township He had been a weaver in his native land and soon after settling in Dunbar township was offered a large tract of land for a pony and a web of Irish broadcloth which he had in his possession, but probably from reasons of sentiment refused to accept the offer He was unable to follow his trade in this country and attracted by the fertility of the soil engaged in agriculture, soon owning a great deal of land in the vicinity of Paul Works

(II) Joseph, son of Daniel Hare, was born in Fayette county and married Susan Foster, born in Lancaster county, both are buried in the old Cumberland Presbyterian church cemetery at Vanderbilt Children (This generation spelled the name Hair) 1 Daniel, born and died in Dunbar township 2 David, died young 3 James, moved to Washington county, and there died at a very old age 4 John W, of whom further 5 Susan, born and died in Dunbar and Franklin townships, married John Barricklow 6 Mary, born and died in Dunbar township, married Jacob Leighty died young 8 Elizabeth, deceased, married R M Boyer Joseph Hare was a lifelong Democrat, and served as road supervisor, and once was a candidate for associate judge of Fayette county

(III) John W Hair, son of Joseph and Susan (Foster) Hars, was born in Dunbar township He engaged in farming with his brother James on land given them by their father, who continued to be with them until his death He was a Democrat in politics and held the office of county commissioner for some time and also was school director many years He moved to Franklin township and lived there on the old Rankin farm until the time of his death His only lodge was the Independent Order of Odd Fellows He married Annie Stoner who still remains his widow living in Dunbar township Children 1 Agnes, married George Edwards (deceased) lives at Dickerson Run 2 Emma, married William Work, lives at Cadiz Ohio 3 Alfred W, of whom further 4 Jesse D married —— 5 Christian unmarried and living at home with mother 6 Mary, married David Hughes, a conductor of the Lake Erie railroad lives at Glassport, Pennsylvania 7 Annetta, married Benjamin McManus a telegraph operator lives at Dickerson Run 8 Samuel, engaged in milk business at Dickerson Run 9 John W employed by brother Alfred W 10 Anna Grace, at home Four others died in infancy

(IV) Alfred W, son of John W and Annie (Stoner) Hair, was born in Dunbar township, November 21 1868   He was educated in the public schools of Vanderbilt, and grew to youthful manhood on his father's farm   He was employed for two years as a mercantile clerk by W J Rainey at Vanderbilt, and for the following two years was employed by the Brown & Cochran Coal Company as check-weighman at the Nellie Works   He then moved to Dunbar township, where he rented land and engaged in general farming until 1902, when seeing the possibilities in that section for a reliable dairyman he started a dairy business   In the spring of 1905 he purchased a farm of one hundred fifteen acres near Dawson and has continued in the same business ever since   He keeps a herd of about twenty fine bred Holsteins and Jerseys and does a profitable retail business at Vanderbilt and Dickerson Run   His milk is produced under the very best conditions from high-class stock, and because of the excellency and cleanliness of his dairy facilities, the possibility of contamination is reduced to a minimum

In politics he is a strict Prohibitionist but has never sought public office   He is a member of the local grange Patrons of Husbandry, and both he and wife are members of the Vanderbilt Presbyterian Church   He married November 10, 1892 Zella M Edwards born April 5, 1870, daughter of Squire and Clarissa Edwards (see Edwards)   Children

1   Bessie born February 22, 1895 a student in Dunbar high school   2   Mabel, born February 3 1899, student in public school at East Liberty

The maternal grandfather of Alfred W Hair was Christian Stoner, who was a farmer of Westmoreland county, owning the Freed farm, which is now included in Dunbar township   His children   1   Isaac, living in Dunbar township   2   Cyrus, deceased   3   Abraham died in Missouri   4   Christian, died in the west   5   Levi, died in West Virginia   6   Rebecca (deceased) married J Oglevee   7   Sarah (deceased), married Henry Freed   8   Agnes, twin of Sarah died at very old age, married John D Collins   9   Elizabeth, married Joseph Newcomer, and now lives in the west   10   Annie, of previous mention

From 1798 until 1880 there
McBURNEY   has always been a McBurney in the blacksmithing business in East Liberty, Fayette county, Pennsylvania   The first to settle was Robert McBurney, a Scotchman who came from Maryland in 1798 to visit Robert Boyd, his brother-in-law   He was a blacksmith and on the lookout for a location   He was strongly urged by Boyd and the neighboring farmers to settle in East Liberty who as an inducement offered to fit him up a shop   He accepted their offer, and with his bride soon afterward came permanently to East Liberty   His first shop was in an old building that had been previously occupied as a smithy but for few houses in the village then, but the farm-some time had been abandoned   There were ers were coming in and he had plenty of work   He prospered was justice of the peace, and later engaged in a mercantile business, but also retained his smithy until his death   He married Annie Burford, born in England came to America when a girl with an invalid brother William   locating at Hagerstown Maryland   Her brother died and soon afterward she met and married Robert McBurney   They both lived to an old age, leaving issue William, of whom further, John, Robert (2), Nancy, Esther and Eliza

(II) William son of Robert and Annie (Burford) McBurney was born in East Liberty Dunbar township Fayette county, Pennsylvania, in August, 1807, died there about 1895   He learned the blacksmith's trade with his father, succeeding him in East Liberty and continuing until about 1880, when he retired   He was in active business for over a half century   He was a quiet homeloving man, a staunch Democrat in politics and an industrious capable business man   His home in East Liberty was formerly owned by Samuel Brown a hatter, and is said to have been the first building erected in East Liberty   He married Frances Boyer, born on the farm where Vanderbilt now stands, daughter of George Boyer   Children   1   Robert, now an old man of seventy-eight, living in East Liberty   2   Maria, died in Dunbar township unmarried   3   Mary, married Ayers Hayden, died in East Liberty   4   George, of whom further   5   Died in infancy

(III) George, son of William and Frances

(Boyer) McBurney was born in East Liberty, Fayette county Pennsylvania, January 16, 1843 He was educated in the public school, and early in life became a clerk in his father's store, later becoming a merchant of East Liberty, continuing in successful business until 1902, when he was compelled to relinquish business cares through failing health, and is now living retired in East Liberty He is a Democrat in politics, and has always borne a high reputation in his community He married Nancy Wadsworth, born in Franklin township Fayette county, February 20, 1849, daughter of John, son of Joseph Wadsworth Joseph Wadsworth raised a company in Brownsville to serve in the war of 1812, and went to the front with them He died in 1814 before the war was over, and was buried at Fort Meigs, Ohio His widow, Susan Hartman, married (second) Joseph Evans, of Franklin township John Wadsworth was born in Fayette county, and was a boat builder and riverman He built the flatboats in which he boated coal, etc, down the river to Pittsburgh Later he became a farmer He married (first) Nancy Walker, who died young, (second) Jane Evans, and moved to Illinois, where both died Children of first wife, Nancy Walker 1 Joseph, became a farmer of Kansas, died in Wichita that state 2 Sarah (first) Samuel Harper, (second) Matthew Cunningham 3 Thomas, now a farmer of California 4 William, now living retired in Wichita, Kansas he served four years under two enlistments in the 83rd Regiment Illinois Volunteer Infantry 5 Susan now a widow living in Uniontown, Pennsylvania 6 Jane married William Randolph and resides in East Liberty, Pennsylvania 7 John, a carpenter, now living in Perry, Oklahoma, he is a veteran of the civil war having served in the 112th Regiment Illinois Volunteer Infantry 8 Caroline, married Calvin Harvey, both now living in Illinois 9 Nancy (of previous mention, wife of George McBurney) 10 Emma died aged three years 11 Mary, married Robert Hoke and lives in Westmoreland county, Pennsylvania Children of John Wadsworth and his second wife, Jane Evans 12 Martha, married and lives in Chicago 13 Walker, lives in Chicago Children of George and Nancy McBurney 1 William Wadsworth of whom further 2 John, a clerk in Scottdale, married Catherine

Hixon 3 Ola married William Allen, resides at Clinton 4 Howard, was mercantile appraiser of Fayette county two terms, now an employe of Ogelvie & McClure at East Liberty married Pearl Brasher 5 Anna, married James Dunn, resides in Uniontown 6 Georgia a teacher in East Liberty, resides at home

(IV) William Wadsworth McBurney, eldest son of George and Nancy (Wadsworth) McBurney, was born in East Liberty, Dunbar township, Fayette county, Pennsylvania, April 29 1874 He was educated in the public schools of Vanderbilt, and began his active business life as a farmer working for others In 1906 he purchased one hundred acres of the farm on which he had been employed several years and on which his mother had been kindly reared by Henry Bowman and his sister Eliza He built a modern farmhouse, has his farm well stocked, and in fertile well tilled condition He is a Democrat in politics, and has served the election board He is an attendant of the Baptist church, his wife a member

He married, in 1893, Mary N Cooper, a sister of Ex-Congressman A F Cooper Children 1 Nellie C, born March 16, 1894, now a student in Dunbar township high school 2 Anna Grace, born July 5, 1903 3 Willetta, August 30, 1910

COVER The Covers came to Fayette from Lancaster county, Pennsylvania where John Cover the founder was born He settled first on land in Springhill township that later was set off in Nicholson township He purchased a good farm and was successfully engaged for many years in its cultivation and in the raising of live stock He took great interest in politics, never holding office, but always a strong Democrat He married and had issue Jacob John Betsey married Jacob Snowderly, Michael Samuel of whom further Polly, married Elijah Board Sally, married Peter Walser

(II) Samuel, son of John Cover was born on the old homestead in Nicholson township, Fayette county, Pennsylvania He obtained his education in the public schools and finishing school and engaged in farming following out the plans of his father in regard to the management of the property He held the office of town supervisor and school director, to both of which he was elected as a Democrat. For many years he was a member of the German Baptist Church. He married Mary Newcomer, born in York county, Pennsylvania, 1802, daughter of Jacob Newcomer. Children: 1. John, born 1826, died 1876. 2. Nancy, born 1828, died 1900; married Jacob Fast. 3. Martha, died 1853. 4. Mary, died 1905; married John A. Walters. 5. Betsey, died 1865; married Peter A. Johnson. 6. Jacob, of whom further.

(III) Jacob, son of Samuel and Mary (Newcomer) Cover, was born at the home of his father in Nicholson township, Fayette county, Pennsylvania, June 23, 1842. He was educated in the public schools of the township, and followed farming with his father, later assuming entire control of the home farm. He has several very fine orchards which bear fruit of superior quality. He has served his township as auditor and school director, always acting with the Democratic party. At one time he held the rank of lieutenant in the National Guard, but is no longer a member. He lives a rather retired life, devoting much time to reading and study. The privilege of a college education was denied him, nevertheless he makes books his constant companions and study his unfailing recreation, believing with Cicero, that "one is never alone, having made a friend of literature."

The Leightys of Fayette county, Pennsylvania, are of German ancestry. The first of the family was —— Leighty, who came from east of the mountains during the revolutionary period and bought his land from an earlier settler named Stauffer: hence the land records do not give his name or the date of his coming. He married and had a son Henry, of whom further.

(II) The first record in the county is of Henry Leighty, a wealthy farmer of Dunbar township and the owner of several farms in the vicinity of Vanderbilt. He was a man of influence and of high standing in the township. He married (first) Sarah Smith, born in Dunbar township, the mother of eight children. He married (second) Mrs. Margaret (Varnes) Secrease, a widow. Children of first wife: 1. Henry S., moved to Illinois, went to

California in 1849, returned later to Illinois and is now a wealthy farmer and stockman. 2. Jacob S., now a farmer of Kansas. 3. John, died in St. Joseph, Missouri. 4. William, died in Illinois. 5. Frances, married a Mr. Muriel and lived in Ohio. 6. Elizabeth. 7. Daniel, died in Illinois. 8. Stephen S., of whom further. Children of second wife: Joseph, Christopher, Peter, Sarah, Clarissa.

(III) Stephen S., eighth child of Henry and Sarah (Smith) Leighty, was born in Dunbar township, Fayette county, Pennsylvania, September 13, 1815, died August 10, 1892. He was reared a farmer and followed that occupation all his life. He owned three hundred acres of good farm land underlaid with coal, but sold the coal at the rate of twelve dollars per acre, now worth hundreds. The farm he retained and it is now owned by his son Ulysses Grant. He was a man of industry and thrift, highly regarded for his sterling traits of character. He was a Republican, served as school director, and was a member of the Presbyterian Church of Liberty. He married (first) Eliza Hudson, born in Dunbar township, near the old Barricklow farm, in 1820, died December, 1862, daughter of Jesse and Catherine (Oldshoe) Hudson, both born in Dunbar township: he a farmer. Their children: Eliza, of previous mention; Nathan; Sophia; William and John, twins; Jemima, Jesse, David, Wesley. Children of Stephen S. and Eliza (Hudson) Leighty: 1. William, a retired physician and farmer of Stafford, Kansas. 2. Henry S. residing in Illinois. 3. Zachariah Taylor, of whom further. 4. Stephen S., a retired farmer of Hutchinson, Kansas. 5. Margaret, married Milton Blair and resides in Oklahoma. 6. Rebecca, married Joseph Piersol and resides in Perryopolis, Fayette county. 7. Anna, married Robert Rankin, whom she survives, a resident of Stafford, Kansas. 8. Davis J., married Davis Woodward and lives near Wooster, Ohio. 9. Agnes, married George W. Cox and lives in Woodson county, Kansas. Stephen S. Leighty married (second) Mary Hare, of West Virginia. Children: 10. Emma, married C. A. Guinn of Uniontown, Pennsylvania. 11. Ulysses G., a farmer on the old Leighty homestead in Dunbar township. 12. John, resides in Washington, Pennsylvania.

Jacob Cover

E. T. Leighton

(IV) Zachariah Taylor, third child of Stephen S and Eliza (Hudson) Leighty, was born in Dunbar township Fayette county, Pennsylvania, January 2, 1847 He was educated in the public schools, and early became his father's helper in the farm work starting in the cornfield at eight years of age He has always followed the business of a farmer and has been very successful He owns and resides on the farm which was owned and operated by his father and which has also been his lifelong home He is interested in coal land speculation and in other business affairs He is a member of the Patrons of Husbandry, is a Republican, and with his wife a member of the Presbyterian Church at Leisenring

He married (first) October 19, 1871, Martha Murphy, who died October 24, 1884, daughter of William Robinson Murphy, born near Perryopolis, Fayette county He married (second) December 2, 1886, Anna J Duff, born near Upper Middletown in Menallen township, Fayette county, January 27, 1862, daughter of Hugh Thompson and Diana (Hornbeck) Duff, he born March 21, 1833, in Menallen township she in Washington county, Pennsylvania, died January 29, 1909 Hugh T Duff is a veteran of the civil war and a farmer He is of Irish descent Children of Zachariah Taylor Leighty and his first wife, Martha Murphy 1 Frederick Cooper (q v) 2 Melvina Bella, born August 31 1874, now residing in Illinois Children by second wife, Anna J Duff 3 Mary D born October 13, 1890 4 Sarah, born February 13, 1892, died March 25 1900 5 Esther, born July 25, 1893 6 Howard born June 29, 1897 7 Inez born September 27 1900 8 Z Taylor, born May 29, 1902 9 Lyda, born July 5, 1904

(III) Frederick Cooper LEIGHTY Leighty, eldest son of Zachariah T Leighty (q v) and his first wife, Martha Murphy was born in Dunbar township Fayette county Pennsylvania, near Eagle school house, March 17, 1872 He was educated in the public school (Eagle school) and grew to manhood on the home farm continuing his father's assistant until the spring of 1898, when he married and settled on a farm of one hundred and twenty-eight acres which he had purchased three years previous Since then he has added forty-one acres to his original purchase, erected new buildings, and brought the property to a condition of modern improvements He devotes his acres to general farming and stock raising, having gained a local reputation as a successful agriculturist He is a director of the Dunn Coke Company, and a stockholder of the Union National Bank of Connellsville He is a Republican in politics, but has never sought or held public office He is a member with his wife of the Cumberland Presbyterian church and of the Patrons of Husbandry Grange He married March 31, 1898, Bertha Mae Critchfield, born in Bedford county, Pennsylvania, daughter of Jacob Albert and Ann (Wilson) Critchfield, her father born in Somerset county, Northampton township, September 8, 1852, and for many years interested in the coke business, now a farmer He married (second) a widow, Mrs Mary May Jacob Albert was a son of John J and Julia Ann (May) Critchfield, both old residents of Bedford county John J was for many years an employee of the Pennsylvania railroad Their children 1 William Oliver, settled when a young man in Denver, Colorado, where he now resides 2 Jacob Albert of whom further 3 James Franklin, until recently a resident of Bedford county 4 Winfield Scott, a railway conductor, residing in Altoona Pennsylvania 5 Louis Edward, a resident of Dunbar 6 John Howard a railroad employee of Ellerslie, Maryland 7 Charles died young 8 Ellen 9 Bella 10 Mary 11 Anna 12 Jennie These five daughters all died in one month, victims of the dreaded disease, diphtheria

Jacob Albert Critchfield was born in Somerset county Pennsylvania, September 8, 1852 his wife, Mary Ann Wilson, in Fulton county, Pennsylvania in 1855 They were married in Bedford county and about 1873 moved to Fayette county where they now reside on a farm Mary Ann, his wife, was a daughter of Adam and Rebecca Ann (Peck) Wilson, both born in Fulton county, Pennsylvania, where Adam a farmer and large land owner, died and his widow yet resides, but married again to a Mr Engle, and has John Rachel Anna, William, Reuben and Lucy by her second husband Children of Adam Wilson Mary Ann (of pre-

vious mention); Amanda Ella, married Scott
Rohm; and a son who died in infancy. Children of Jacob Albert and Mary Ann (Wilson)
Critchfield: Charles Wilson; Bertha Mae (of
previous mention), first wife of Frederick
Cooper Leighty; William Grover; Thomas
B., a veteran of the Spanish-American war,
serving in the Philippines, where he was
wounded in battle, but recovered; Edgar
Monroe, enlisted in the United States navy,
served his term and later was accidentally shot
while hunting in Arizona. John J. Critchfield is a son of William Critchfield, born in
Somerset county, a farmer, and for many
years a justice of the peace; he owned a great
deal of land in Somerset county, and there
lived and died; he had three children: 1.
John J. (of previous mention), who was
drafted and served in Company D, 28th Regiment Pennsylvania Infantry. 2. Jesse, also
served in the Union army, was captured in
batle, and later released on parole. 3. Betsey, married John Baidagan, a farmer of Fayette county.

Children of Frederick Cooper Leighty and
his first wife, Bertha Mae Critchfield: 1.
Thomas, born March 13, 1899. 2. Homer
Elroy, August 11, 1900. 3. James Hamilton,
born November 2, 1902. 4. Albert Taylor,
July 21, 1908. 5. Frederick Cooper (2), May
31, 1910.

(IV) Ulysses S. G. Leighty,
LEIGHTY son of Stephen S. Leighty and
grandson of Henry Leighty,
(q. v.), was born in Dunbar township, Fayette county, Pennsylvania, September 14,
1867. He grew to manhood on the home
farm, receiving his education in the public
schools. He continued his father's assistant
until the death of the latter when he purchased
the homestead farm of one hundred and two
acres in Dunbar township, where he still resides. He conducts a general farming and
stock raising business and has always prospered. He also owns ten acres of coal land
in Washington county and has other interests.
He is a Republican in politics, but never
sought public office. He is a member of the
Patrons of Husbandry, and with his wife belongs to the Presbyterian church of Vanderbilt.

He married, December 12, 1889, Frances,
born in Fayette county, daughter of Abra-

ham (2) and Angeline (McBurney) Shallenberger. Children: 1. Byron Scott, born
August 4, 1893, educated in the common
schools and Leisenring high school, but
forced to abandon his studies through eye
trouble. 2. Orland F., born December 29,
1894, a student at Leisenring high school. 3.
Loretta Cora, born April 11, 1900.

Abraham (2) Shallenberger was a renting
farmer of Dunbar township, was a member
of the Disciples of Christ Church, a Democrat
and assessor of the township. He died in
1895. His widow, also a member of the Disciples of Christ Church, survives him, a resident of Vanderbilt, Pennsylvania. Their children: 1. John P., now engaged in the insurance business at Connellsville. 2. Sarah
Melissa, died in infancy. 3. Jennie, married
Samuel J. Moore, who survives her, a resident of Kentucky. 4. Elizabeth, married
Charles Martin and resides at Vanderbilt. 5.
Mary Katherine, married U. S. G. Blair and
resides in Connellsville. 6. Carrie, died in
infancy. 7. Frances, of previous mention,
wife of Ulysses S. G. Leighty. 8. Robert, a
fire boss at Vanderbilt. 9. Abraham, married Huldah Lother and resides at Vanderbilt. 10. Angeline, married Joseph Means,
who survives her. 11. Harry, resides in East
Liberty, Pennsylvania. His wife, Angeline
(McBurney) Shallenberger, was a daughter
of Robert and Melissa (Wilgus) McBurney,
both born in Fayette county, the latter a
daughter of John Wilgus. Robert McBurney was a merchant of East Liberty, Pennsylvania, also a boat builder and carpenter. His
children: 1. Amanda J., married John Parkhill. 2. Ann, married David Randolph. 3.
Angeline, of previous mention, wife of Abraham (2) Shallenberger. 4. John, deceased,
married Susan Wadsworth. 5. Robert, a
farmer of Franklin township, married Susan
Butey.

Abraham (2) Shallenberger was a son of
Abraham (1) and Elizabeth (Wollock) Shallenberger, both born in Connellsville township, Fayette county, Pennsylvania, and a
grandson of Christian Shallenberger, who
came early to Fayette county and acquired a
large tract of land by "tomahawk" right,
which was afterward patented to him. He
came from Lancaster county to Fayette and
at one time kept a tavern at the "Narrows"

neai Connellsville Elizabeth (Wollock)
Shallengerber was of German descent Abraham (1) Shallenberger, son of Christian
Shallenberger, was a blacksmith and farmer
of Fayette county

SMITH 1his branch of the Smiths of
America was early founded in
Fayette county, Pennsylvania,
where the name is publicly perpetuated by the
borough of Smithfield, laid out June 13, 1799,
by one Barnabas Smith The first definite
record in this branch is of Henry Smith, of
German descent He was a farmer of Fayette county, which is said to have been his
native county He married (first) Keziah
Davis, children, all deceased except James
and Mary Elizabeth married —— Speers,
David, Hannah, married Uriah Carter, Eliza
Jane, marr ed Mr Foster, James B Mary,
married Mr Bosley He married (second)
Leah Field Children Milton, deceased,
Estep, deceased, Maria, deceased, married
James Gaddis, Isaac F, died March 14, 1911
Henry P, of whom further He married
(third) Eliza Wilkey Children Elmer, living in Iowa, Alice, married John Cameron,
who lives in Iowa, Lewis, living in North
Dakota

(II) Henry P son of Henry and Leah
(Field) Smith was born on the home farm in
North Union township, Fayette county,
Pennsylvania, October 23, 1835, died at Dunbar, same county, in 1905 ● He attended the
public school nearest his home, and during
his earlier life was a farmer and stock raiser,
owning the old North Union homestead He
then became interested in the butchering business, managing stores at Dunbar and Mount
Braddock for Robert Hogsett In 1879 he
began business for himself, opening a meat
market at Dunbar He was very successful,
and as his sons grew up admitted them to the
business He bought cattle all over Fayette
and adjoining counties also buying live cattle in Chicago, bringing them to Fayette
county in carload lots His relations with the
farmers with whom he did business were of
the most cordial nature, his reputation for
square dealing, being proverbial He was a
man of great energy threw his whole soul
into whatever he had to do, and retained his
interest in his business until the very last, although do ng business in Dunbar, his home

was in Uniontown When really too feeble
to make the journey, he came to Dunbar, was
taken seriously ill, and did not return to his
Uniontown home until carried there by sorrowing friends He was always an active Republican, and in 1893 was a candidate of his
party for county treasurer In 1892 the opposition party had elected their ticket in the
county by handsome majorities yet so great
was Mr Smith's popularity and the confidence reposed in him by the voters that he
was elected by sixteen hundred majority His
vote in Dunbar where he had been so long in
business was practically unanimous Party
lines were forgotten, all seeming anxious to
testify their esteem in this public manner He
was a member of great Bethel Baptist church
of Uniontown, his parents having belonged
to the same church He is buried in Oak
Grove cemetery He married, in 1860, Margery daughter of Lewis Stewart, of Menallen
township, she died in February, 1873 He
married (second) in February, 1882, Jennie,
daughter of Horatio N Griffith, of Georges
township who survives him Lewis Stewart
was born in Fayette county, in early life was
a shoemaker later a prominent farmer He
married Mary Ann, daughter of William
Worthington, a driver on the "Old National
Pike" between Cumberland, Maryland and
Wheeling, Virginia Children of Henry P
Smith and his first wife, Margery Stewart
1 One died in infancy 2 William C, of
whom further 3 Emma married James
Coonms, of Uniontown, now in the employ of
the W J Rainey Coke Company as stable
foreman 4 Harry L, born March 11, 1870,
now a partner with his brother in the meat
business at Dunbar, he married Anna McPherson

(III) William C eldest son of Henry P
Smith was born on the North Union township farm February 2, 1862 being the third
generation born there He grew up on the
homestead farm attending the public school
until eleven years of age when his mother
died He was then taken with his younger
brother and sister into the home of their
grandfather Stewart, where he remained until
1882, attending school and working on the
Menallen township farm of his grandfather
In 1882 he became associated with his father
in the butchering, cattle dealing and meat

market business in Dunbar He continued
this until the death of Henry P Smith in
1905 Since then the brothers have continued the business as partners They are well
established in a modern well equipped market and command a generous patronage
William C Smith was appointed postmaster
of Dunbar in 1906, and is still holding that
office He is a Republican in politics member of the Royal Arcanum, Junior Order of
American Mechanics, and in religious faith
a baptist

He married, October 31, 1886 Luella Taggart, born in Monongahela City, Pennsylvania daughter of A A Taggart, a contractor and builder of Uniontown, who died
in August 1911 Children Iola, married
Ray Guyeton, a druggist of Pittsburgh, Pennsylvania Cecil his father's assistant in the
store Clarence now in the employ of the
Allegheny Supply Company at Pittsburgh
Harold, Eleanor

The first of this name to settle
SPARKS   in Fayette county was Horatio
Sparks, a farmer and tanner
He came to the county early, was first a
Democrat, active in the party, but in later
life a Republican He married Helena Ham-
mond and both died in Fayette county, leav-
ing issue

(II) Samuel Hammond, son of Horatio
Sparks, was born in Fayette county, Pennsylvania, in 1850, died December 7, 1904 He
was reared and educated in Fayette county,
and learned his father's trade tanning Later
he established a tannery of his own in Bullskin township He was also a farmer In
politics he was a Democrat He married Melinda, daughter of Peter Christner now a resident of Indiana Children of Samuel Hammond Sparks William Ketchum, Charles
Boyle, Roy, of whom further, Lida Hammond, Edward, Lena Hammond, Luella B
Maud Kitchen, Francis Davis, Samuel Hammond, Clyde, Harriet

(III) Roy, third son of Samuel Hammond
Sparks, was born at Indian Head, Fayette
county, Pennsylvania, July 28, 1876 He was
educated in the public school and followed
farming industriously until he was twenty-
two years of age

He then came to Connellsville learned the
carpenter's trade, and for five years was with

the Fayette Lumber Company In politics
he is a Democrat

He married, July 28, 1899, Luzetta Viola
Beal, born in Fayette county July 28, 1879,
daughter of William L and Sarah (Miller)
Beal William L Beal was born in Somerset
county in 1839, he served in the civil war
three years and eight months in Company B,
One Hundred and Forty-second Regiment
Pennsylvania Volunteer Infantry, fought at
Gettysburg and was held a prisoner at Belle
Isle for eight months and three days He
married Sarah Miller, born in Fayette county, 1843, daughter of George Miller Their
children Laura Belle, deceased, Nancy
Francina, deceased, Lloyd M Ida N , Luzetta Viola, of previous mention Children of
Leroy and Luzetta Sparks Clarence Brooks,
born February 13, 1900, Audrice May February 6, 1902 Gertrude, May 10, 1904, Dorothy Irene, January 14, 1908, William Hammond November 28, 1910

This branch of the many Brown
BROWN   families of the United States
descend from a Virginia settler
and from that colony came Wendell
Brown and his sturdy sons, Adam, Maunus and Thomas to Fayette county settling
originally on the Provance's Bottom on the
Monongahela Judge Veech says in his
'Monongahela of Old "When Washington's little army was at Fort Necessity or
Great Meadows, the Browns packed provisions beef and corn to him, and when he surrendered to the French and Indians, July 4
1754, they retired with the retreating colonial
troops across the mountain to their old Virginia home ' After General Forbes had re-
established English dominion they returned
but settled not on their old lands, but in what
is now South Union and Georges townships,
where they were the first white settlers
Adam Brown located on three hundred and
twenty-seven acres warranted to him, June
14, 1769 Maunus Brown had three hundred
and six acres warranted to him the same day
Adam Brown "Old Adam '—as he was called
—boasted of having been a king's lieutenant
in his earlier days having probably served
with the Virginia provincials in the French
and Indian wars For his services he claimed
to have received a royal grant of land nine
miles square, extending from near Mount

Braddock along the face of Laurel Hill southward and westward as far as New Salem, and it is said that when this land was being surveyed the surveyor was shot and by whom no one ever seemed to know, thus ended the survey, but it was supposed that the work was done by an Indian The old lieutenant, it is said, induced many Virginia acquaintances of the Browns to settle around him on the grant, the Downards, Greens, McDonalds, McCartys, Brownsfields, Kindells, Scotts, Jennings and Higginsons Out of abundant caution Adam and Maunus Brown did not trust to their tomahawk claim, but entered applications for their land in the Pennsylvania law office, June 14, 1769, and had them surveyed soon after They took no part in the boundary dispute between Virginia and Pennsylvania but it is said that Adam and some of his associates had employed an agent to go to London to perfect the royal grant, but when the revolution ended the King's power in the colonies, they gave up the effort and in due time perfected their titles under Pennsylvania

From this circumstance and from others of little weight arose the allegation that "Old Adam" and sundry of his neighbors were unfriendly to the cause of independence, but there is no evidence that they ever committed any act of toryism The Maunus Browns were never suspected of any lukewarmness for the cause and always retained the fullest confidence of their neighbors The Indians who held the country when the Browns came had one or more lead mines in the mountains, the localities of which they guarded with inviolable secrecy The discovery of these mines by the Browns would have been a valuable acquisition—many efforts did they make to find them and many sly attempts to follow the Indians on their trips to the mines, but without avail Thomas Brown it seems was most persistent and only escaped death at the stake through the intercession of a friendly chief Later he was again caught when there was no intercession near and had all his teeth knocked out with a piece of iron and a tomahawk An instance of savage honesty is told of Brown In a season of scarcity they came to them for food, the old man sold them eight rows of corn—after they had gone he found they had taken just eight rows, no more The Browns held to

their lands, and much of it is yet in the family name This line descends through Maunus Brown

(II) Maunus, son of Wendell Brown with his father and two brothers, was the first white settler in South Union township, Fayette county, Pennsylvania, where he had three hundred and six acres patented him, June 14, 1769 His lands lay in what became Georges township, where he lived until a good old age, possessed much influence and means He married and left issue

(III) Abraham, son of Maunus Brown, was born in Georges township, Fayette county, Pennsylvania, where his entire life was spent engaged in agriculture He owned a farm of three hundred acres, and was highly respected in his neighborhood He was a Democrat and served the township as tax collector and poor director He married Mary Bend Children 1 Benjamin, a farmer, of Georges township, married Elizabeth Franks 2 Isaac, a farmer, owning the land on which the Pence Coke Works are built, he married first a Miss Hutchinson, second the widow of Thomas Grier 3 Maunus, a farmer, of South Union township, married Sallie Franks 4 Abraham 5 Sarah, married Isaac Bailey, a farmer 6 Polly, married Isaac Vance 7 Rachel, married James Higinbotham 8 Clarissa, married Nathan DeFord, and moved to Kansas 9 Susan

(IV) Abraham (2), fourth son of Abraham (1) and Mary (Bend) Brown, was born on the old Brown homestead farm, December 26 (or June 28) 1817, died May 29, 1897 He attended the common schools and became one of the most wealthy farmers of the county He owned at his death seven farms, aggregating eight hundred acres (part of it the old Maunus Brown tract) besides a cash estate of one hundred and fifty thousand dollars He held most of the township offices, and was equally active and influential in the Lutheran church He was a shrewd practical farmer, a good judge of values and a very successful speculator He was very liberal in his donations to all churches and generous to the poor He was a Democrat in politics and very influential in the party He married, November 18, 1841, Hannah Colley, born in Fayette county, Pennsylvania, April 24, 1816, died July 1, 1887 Her birthplace was the old Colley farm along the National Pike just west of Uniontown, where her father, Abel Colley, kept a stopping place for stage coaches, a driver's yard and a house of entertainment for travelers on the Pike He married Nancy Nolen Children of Abel Colley Peter, a farmer of the old homestead, deceased, Levi, a farmer, deceased, Hannah, wife of Abraham (2) Brown, Searight, a farmer of Redstone township, married Catherine Smouse, Jane, married Robert Leedham, a farmer of Fayette county, died in West Virginia Children of Abraham Brown 1 Peter, born February 23, 1843, a farmer of Georges township, married Mary Huldah Lawrence 2 Abraham, born, June 28, 1844, now a farmer of South Union township, married Harriet Core, deceased 3 Searight born October 27, 1846, now a retired farmer, married Laura Dawson 4 Nancy born December 8, 1847, deceased, married Jefferson Walters, a farmer of Georges township 5 George, born June 25, 1849, now a retired farmer married Emma Morgan and resides in Uniontown 6 Isaac, born September 5, 1851, deceased, married Sarah Brownfield, who survived him and married (second) Stephen Wadsworth 7 Levi 8 Mary born March 26, 1855, married (first) William Huston, (second) Bert McMullen and lives in Uniontown 9 Sarah born August 3 1856 married Ephraim Walters, a retired farmer 10 Alfred, born November 9, 1858, now residing upon the old Maunus Brown homestead, married Jennie Brownfield

(V) Levi, sixth son of Abraham (2) and Hannah (Colley) Brown, was born in Georges township Fayette county, Pennsylvania, October 16, 1854 He attended the Walnut Hill district school and grew to manhood on the home farm, always remaining with his parents At his father's death he willed the farm to Levi and his youngest brother, Alfred They divided it, Alfred taking the part on which the old homestead stood and Levi the part where his father had lived Both brothers reside on and cultivate their respective portions Levi Brown is a Democrat in politics, and a successful, energetic and highly-regarded citizen He married, September 12, 1891, Mary Brownfield, born in Fayette county, daughter of William Nixon and Elizabeth Caroline (Sackett)

Brownfield Children William, born August 28, 1892, Playford, February 7, 1894, Elizabeth, April 28, 1896

BROWN This branch of the Brown family of Fayette county, Pennsylvania, came from Maryland, where Banning Brown was born and probably married, he then came to Fayette county, settling in South Union township He was of that famous body of hardy men who drove on the National road in the long ago hauling goods from Baltimore and other eastern points to Wheeling, Pittsburgh, and even as far west as Indiana He continued on "the Pike" for several years, then moved to Licking county, Ohio, where he died He was of English descent, and possessed the characteristics of that race His sons and daughters settled near Newark, Ohio where descendants are yet found

(II) Hugh C, son of Banning Brown, was born in South Union township, Fayette county, Pennsylvania, in 1826, died in 1882 He learned the shoemaker's trade with a cousin S K Brown, and worked at it in his native town for several years He secured a contract from the superintendent, Rev A H Waters, to furnish boots and shoes used at the Orphans' Home at Jumonville, Pennsylvania, and in the execution of that contract moved to Jumonville, where he died He was a veteran of the civil war, serving in Company F, Fourteenth Pennsylvania Volunteer Cavalry, from September, 1862, until the close of the war The Fourteenth was a "fighting regiment," and Company F was engaged in sixty battles and engagements, not including mere skirmishes He was a member of the Methodist Protestant church, and a Republican of the most pronounced type, having been a Whig and antislavery man prior to the formation of the Republican party

He married Phoebe Nesmith, born at Hopwood Fayette county, Pennsylvania, in 1837, died September 29, 1888 daughter of Thomas Nesmith, born near Baltimore, Maryland He was a regularly ordained minister of the Methodist Protestant church and one of the founders of that church He settled at Hopwood, when a young man, where he erected a factory and engaged in the manufacture of horn combs He was also a justice of the peace, thus being legally equipped to mete out to offenders both the law and the Gospel ' He was a soldier of the war of 1812 and drew a pension from the government He was noted for his wonderful memory and his fund of interesting information He was always the center of any group of men who were eager to listen to his tales of travel and adventure, many of them personal experiences and others remembered from his reading He lived in Hopwood until he was seventy-five years of age, then moved to Illinois, settling at Hennepin, where he died at the age of ninety-two years His wife was a Johnson Their children 1 William, was a soldier of the civil war, served in the Eighth Pennsylvania Reserve Infantry, died during the war and was buried at Alexandria, Virginia, married Ellen Hacydore, of Hopwood 2 John, a first lieutenant of the Fourteenth Regiment, Pennsylvania Volunteer Cavalry, during the civil war, married a Miss Hopwood and settled in Cedar Rapids, Iowa 3 James, first sergeant of the Fourteenth Regiment, Pennsylvania Cavalry, serving with his brother in the civil war, married Jane Wyatt, of Uniontown, Pennsylvania, and moved to Oxford, Iowa 4 Drusilla, married Calvin Springer and moved to California, where she died 5 Dorcas, married Rev James Brown, a Baptist minister, and now is living in Confluence, Pennsylvania 6 Ann, married Abraham Hayden and lived at Hopwood, Pennsylvania, where both died 7 Mary, married William Bosley and moved to Hennepin, Illinois 8 Phoebe, of previous mention, wife of Hugh C Brown Their children 1 Thomas Nesmith 2 John, died 1912, married Mary Hayden and lived in Fairmont, West Virginia, where he pursued his calling of mechanical engineer 3 Mary, married C S Gause, a civil engineer of Uniontown 4 William, now a farmer of Shaner Station, Fayette county, married Ruth Smith 5 Hugh C, Jr, deceased, was a machinist, married a Miss Sisley 6 Walker, died in infancy 7 Walter, died in infancy

(III) Thomas Nesmith, eldest son of Hugh C and Phoebe (Nesmith) Brown, was born in Uniontown, Pennsylvania, December 24 1851 He was deprived of early educational advantages, only having limited training at Hopwood public schools, but is a natural student and has acquired a liberal education by self study and reading in certain lines, being exceptionally well informed He learned the shoemaker's trade under the direction of his father, working at that trade until twenty-three years of age He did not like the confinement nor the work itself and decided to use his energy in another direction He began his flower gardening in a small way, building his first greenhouse in 1880 at Hopwood, supplying the dealers in cut flowers and plants at Uniontown with the product of his skill In 1883 he moved his business to Uniontown, built greenhouses and has been continuously engaged there as florist, excepting the year 1904, when he was employed as landscape gardener in Lower California by the Chase Floral Company He does not grow flowers for the trade, nor handle cut flowers, confining his business entirely to plants of every description for bedding and ornamental decorative purposes He is a lover of plants and well informed on all that pertains to their successful culture His business is well established in popular favor and a constantly increasing one While living in Hopwood he was appointed the first postmaster of that village, serving eighteen months He is a Republican in politics and was twice elected justice of the peace, but refused to serve on account of business demands upon his time He is a member, with his family, of the Methodist Protestant church

Mr Brown is a deep student of geology and entomology and is a recognized authority, many well written and learned articles from his pen having appeared in the scientific journals He possesses unusual artistic ability and has on exhibition at the Carnegie Institute in Pittsburgh his paintings illustrating the life history of the butterfly, the only exhibit in the entomological department from Fayette county He also furnishes illustrations in oil for the colored plates used in the entomological journals He also has done some most creditable landscapes in oil In pursuing his favorite scientific studies he was obliged to acquire a knowledge of Latin, which he did thoroughly His collection of butterflies, moths, beetles and insects is one of the rarest and most complete and valuable to be found outside the great museums It fills forty-six full size regular museum cases and a great number of smaller ones, containing fifteen thousand specimens, beautiful and rare, gathered in Europe, Asia, Africa, Central and South America and from the Isles of the Sea, also a fine North American collection, including those of his own Fayette county

Mr Brown is preparing a catalogue of the coleoptera (beetles), found in Fayette county, fully classified, the only work of its kind ever published in the county His geological collection is also an important one, containing mineral specimens from all over the world His library is richly stored with valuable scientific works on the subjects in which he is interested This love of nature is not an acquired one, but is a part of his very nature and is followed solely for the purpose of acquiring a more intimate knowledge of the works of the Creator and of giving that knowledge to the world He is a purely unselfish, self-sacrificing scientist, striving to better understand the wonderful life that surrounds him

Mr Brown married, September 13, 1877, Sarah Louisa Malone, born in South Union township, Fayette county, Pennsylvania, daughter of John William Malone, also a native of Fayette county He was a soldier of the civil war, was captured by the Confederates and sent to the Salisbury prison pen, where he died His widow did not long survive him Their children 1 John William, a farmer of Lower Tyrone township 2 Mary married Jefferson Condon and lives near Tulsa, Oklahoma 3 Sarah Louisa, wife of Thomas Nesmith Brown Their children 1 Florence Fredonia, married D D Weaver, whom she survives, without issue 2 Phoebe Ann, married A B Glick a glass worker, now residing at Tulsa, Oklahoma Children Florence and Thomas

The Nesmith family spring from one of three sources Thomas Nesmith, a rigid Presbyterian, lived near Philadelphia in 1730, whose descendants settled in Maryland and West Virginia It is believed that he is a brother of Deacon James Nesmith, founder of the New Hampshire family of John Nesmith, who was contemporary with the other two mentioned It is not unlikely that Thomas, John and James were brothers, and that Thomas and John emigrated to Pennsylvania with the McKeens in 1728 The family is of Scotch descent, settling in the North of Ireland, from whence they came to America A tradition of the Fayette county branch is that their progenitor (probably the Thomas, previously referred to) was a florist or landscape gardener in Scotland and of him it is recorded in works on horticulture that he seeded an inaccessible crag or cliff by discharging seed from a large bore gun The great painter, Mr Nesmith, was also a Scotchman from this same family The family in Fayette county and West Virginia are known to descend from James Nesmith, of Maryland, who was undoubtedly a son of Thomas Nesmith, of Philadelphia, 1730

CLARK

This branch of the Clark family is of English origin, the one of whom we have record being Richard Clark, who settled in Elizabethtown, New Jersey, in 1678 The Clark estate and mansion was about a half mile northwest of the old Wheat Sheaf tavern He married and had issue

(II) Thomas, son of Richard Clark, resided on the 'Upper road' about midway between Elizabethtown and the village of Rahway, New Jersey He was a farmer married and had at least three sons and one daughter 1 Thomas (of whom further) 2 Abraham, born 1703, a commander of the troops, lived directly west of the homestead and outlived his brother Thomas but fifteen days 3 James, or 'Connecticut Farms,' lived to a great age 4 A daughter, married —— Day

(III) Thomas (2), son of Thomas (1) Clark, was born in Elizabethtown, New Jersey, 1701 He inherited and lived on the homestead farm He was one of the charter aldermen of the borough of Elizabeth His grandson, Dr Abraham Clark, says "He was judge and I believe keeper of the King's Arms, as many muskets and cartouche boxes with the letters G R on their cover remained in the house until used by the patriots " He died September 11, 1765, and was buried very plainly in accordance with an agreement entered into by several of the leading citizens to limit display and pomp at funerals He married and had an only child, Abraham

(IV) Abraham, only child of Thomas (2) Clark was born in Elizabethtown, New Jersey February 15, 1726 He was well educated under competent instructors making a specialty of mathematics and civil law He was of a naturally weak and slender form, and although a farmer pursued in his earlier manhood surveying, conveyancing and the giving of legal advice, the latter service given gratuitously not being a lawyer by profession, yet competent through a course of legal study From the willingness with which he gave his free legal counsel he gained the title of "Poor man's counsellor " He early became prominent in public life, first in Essex county, later in the nation He was elected high sheriff of the county of Essex, New Jersey, was clerk of the colonial assembly at Amboy under the Royal Dominion, but when the coming tempest of war began to agitate the land and the revolution dawned, he, acting under a well settled and solemn conviction of the justice of the colonial cause, appeared in the front rank of the revolutionary phalanx and devoted his remaining years to the service of his country He was an active member of the committee of public safety, a constant attendant at popular meetings and a persevering promoter of patriotic feelings On June 21, 1776, he was appointed by the provincial congress of New Jersey, in connection with Richard Stockton, John Hart, Francis Hopkinson and Dr John Witherspoon, a delegate to the continental congress He was one of the strong men of that body, and with great pride and resolution affixed his signature to that immortal document, The Declaration of Independence " On November 30, 1776, he was again elected by the provincial congress of New Jersey a delegate to the continental congress and continued with the exception of 1779 to be annually re-elected a delegate from New Jersey until November, 1783 In 1788 he again was elected and took his seat in the national legislature He was a true patriot and instrumental in passing many laws that all worked for the public good Two of his sons were officers in the continental army and both were made prisoners and confined in the prison ship, Jersey," where they were most mercilessly treated In June, 1794, at the adjournment of congress, he retired from public life, dying from sunstroke in the autumn of that year He is buried in the churchyard at Rahway, he bestowed numerous benefactions upon this church

In 1749 he married Sarah Hatfield, of Elizabethtown, of the prominent family of that name She was born in 1728, died June 2, 1804, daughter of Isaac Hatfield They had ten children, among them a son, William

(V) William, son of Abraham Clark, The signer," was born in New Jersey and settled in Indiana county, Pennsylvania There was another William Clark in that county at an early date who came from Ireland and founded a numerous family Our William Clark was a soldier of the war of 1812 He lived in Indiana county until his death He married and left issue

(VI) Samuel, son of William Clark, was born in Indiana county, Pennsylvania He settled in Westmoreland county, where he kept one of the old time taverns along the ' Pike " He was a great horseman and dearly loved a horse trade, usually having one or more pending He was very popular in the township and captain of a militia company of which he was very proud, frequently purchasing new uniforms for his men in order to have them present a neat and soldierly appearance on "general training days " He married Mary Lippincott, born in Westmoreland county, daughter of Jesse and Jane Lippincott, both born in Pennsylvania and residents of Westmoreland county She was a member of the Methodist Episcopal church Children of Samuel and Mary Clark 1 Griffith T (of whom further mention) 2 Harriet, married Cyrus Galley of Mount Pleasant, Pennsylvania, a carriagemaker 3 Elizabeth, married John Shehey, of Youngstown, Ohio, both deceased 4 Margaret, married Jacob Hodit 5 Mary Jane, deceased, married Thomas Potter 6 Rachel, now living in Youngstown, Ohio, unmarried 7 William P, a veteran of the civil war, now a justice of the peace of Connellsville and the last male survivor of the family he enlisted in 1862 in Company B, One Hundred and Eighty-sixth Regiment, Pennsylvania Volunteer Infantry, as drummer after a year's service he was made chief musician, a position he held until the close of the war, he took part with his regiment in twenty-four battles, escaping unhurt, he came to Connellsville after the war and has ever since resided there, he worked for many years at his trade of carpenter and cabinetmaker, in 1905 he was elected justice of the peace, he married Elizabeth Nichol and has Della G, married George M Hosack, an attorney of Pittsburgh, Charles deceased, Ellen and Harriet 8 Lucretia, married John Elmer Seton, of Connellsville, both deceased 9 Henry, died in infancy 10 An infant, died at birth

(VII) Griffith T, eldest son of Samuel and Mary (Lippincott) Clark, was born in Mount Pleasant township, Westmoreland county, Pennsylvania, died June, 1896 He was educated in the public schools, and lived at home until the outbreak of the civil war, when he enlisted in Company B, One Hundred and Forty-second Regiment, Pennsylvania Volunteer Infantry, and fought from 1862 until the close of the war, attaining the rank of sergeant He engaged with his regiment in twenty-four important battles, including Gettysburg, and at the close of the war marched with the tattered and torn but victorious armies of the nation down Pennsylvania avenue in Washington in grand review before their great chieftain, Abraham Lincoln, soon to fill the grave of a martyr After the war he came to Connellsville, where for twenty years, until his death, he worked as a carpenter in the shops of the Baltimore & Ohio Railroad Company He was a member of the Methodist Episcopal church, as was his wife, he was also a Republican Sergeant Clark was a good soldier, an upright citizen and a faithful employee He was held in high regard by his fellows and won the confidence of his employers

He married Sophia, daughter of Samuel C Sheffler born in Germany, served in the German army in the cavalry came to the United States, settled in Hempfield township, Westmoreland county, Pennsylvania, where he owned and cultivated a good farm He married a woman who was of German birth, both living to a good age Among his treasures was the sabre that he carried in the German army, which he carefully preserved Children of Samuel C Sheffler Daniel, deceased, Samuel, now superintendent of a bank building at Connellsville, Robert, Israel T, now a farmer near Greensburg, Pennsylvania, Jerome, deceased, Elizabeth, married Henry Pope and lived in Greensburg, Lois, married James Davis, of Greensburg, Sophia, aforementioned, wife of Griffith T Clark, Children of Griffith T Clark Samuel S of whom further, Laura Rebecca, married and lives in Cleveland, Ohio

(VIII) Samuel S, son of Griffith T and Sophia (Sheffler) Clark, was born in Connellsville, Pennsylvania, January 30, 1866 He was educated in the public schools, and after completing his years of study served an apprenticeship of five years with A J Case and learned the trade of harnessmaker He then spent five years with the Connellsville Electric Company, becoming an electrical engineer For three years he worked at steam fitting with the Connellsville Brewing Company, which brings him to the time of the Spanish-American war He enlisted in Company D Tenth Regiment, Pennsylvania National Guard, as sergeant, and with his regiment was mustered into the service of the United States in 1898 The Tenth was sent to the Philippines, but Sergeant Clark was detached and sent back to the United States as a recruiting officer He formed a company which he took to the Sandwich Islands, being for ten weeks acting captain of the company He then continued with them to Manila and served with the Tenth during the Aguinaldo insurrection, being in two engagements with the 'Little brown men' He returned to the United States with the Tenth and was mustered out at San Francisco, August 20, 1899

After his return to Connellsville he entered the employ of the Connellsville Brewing Company as foreman of construction work, continuing eighteen months On January 1, 1901, he was appointed superintendent of the First National Bank Building in Connellsville and so continues He is a Republican in politics, and in religious faith inclines to the Methodist belief of his fathers He is a member of Connellsville Lodge, Benevolent and Protective Order of Elks He is the last surviving male member of this Clark branch, except his aged uncle Squire William P Clark of Connellsville He is an energetic, resolute, upright citizen and held in high esteem He is unmarried

The earliest ancestor of this
BRADY branch of the Brady family, of whom any record can be found, is John Brady, who was born in Ireland and who served in the British army, in which service he was killed He married and had issue

(II) Colonel James Brady, son of John

Brady, was born in Ireland died at Atlantic City, New Jersey, May 29 1911 He came to the United States when but fourteen years of age, he engaged in the printing business in New York and Philadelphia for a time, and also was manager of a hotel in Atlantic City, New Jersey He was owner of the *Sunday Northern* newspaper, and later was an importer of china, with his business located in Philadelphia He has a long and honorable military record, which began when in 1848 he was appointed captain of cavalry in New York City by the governor On July 8, 1861, he was commissioned captain of the First Pennsylvania Artillery, Battery H, and attached to the Forty-third Regiment, Pennsylvania Volunteer Infantry While holding this command he was in the siege of Yorktown, battles of Mechanicsburg and Fair Oaks At the latter battle he was in command of the battery on the right wing of the Fourth Artillery, and held this position after the repulse of the corps until refused aid by the corps commander He was in the right wing of the Army of the Potomac at the Bottoms and Railroad Bridge after the battle of Mechanicsville Through his efforts the cavalry on the right and rear of the army was held in check at the battle of Savage Station On July 2 and 3, 1862, he covered the retreat of troops at Malvern Hill For valiant service in this engagement he was promoted to the rank of major, July 19, 1862 He was assigned to the command of a brigade of artillery, First Division Artillery Corps, ordered to Urbana on the Rappahannock, December 13, 1862, under H T Nagle, chief of artillery Doubleday Division, and in January, 1863 he was in command of the forced march He was chief of artillery in Couch s department in the Valley of the Cumberland during the Gettysburg campaign, and was in charge of the erection works on the south side of the Susquehanna river, which checked the advance of Lee's Cavalry on Harrisburg, September 23 1863 He was promoted lieutenant colonel and placed in command of a brigade of Artillery Reserves of the Army of the Potomac at Mine Run During part of the winter of 1863-1864 he was in command at Brandy Station, while in the spring of 1864 he was in Washington, D C, in command of Camp Marshall, preparing for the Wilderness campaign He

was then assigned to organize and command the Thirteenth United States Colored Artillery at Bowling Green Another recognition of his services was granted when on March 16, 1865, he was made brevet colonel in recognition of his services at Fair Oaks, Malvern Hill and Mine Run He was presented with a sword by the government for bravery and gallant service at the battle of Fair Oaks He had charge of dismantling the rebel works in and around Richmond, after Lee's surrender, with orders to destroy or ship to Washington all guns and munitions of war

Aside from his own service, at one time his wife recruited troops and took them to the front Such a record in the service of the United States has seldom been equalled, and it is a noticeable fact that he was always among the commanders and not the commanded, and, furthermore that not only did he fill the various positions which fell to his lot in a manner satisfactory to his superior offices, but showed such exceptional ability that he was presented with testimonials from the government such as are only conferred on rare occasions At the time of his discharge from the service after the war, he was offered the rank of brigadier general, which he refused, asking only the rank that he held while in the service of his adopted country On all political questions he sided with the Democratic party, and in religion was a Roman Catholic

He married in New York City, October 12, 1849, Winifred Mimnaugh Children Frank, died in United States artillery service, 1874, James, Harry, of whom further, Sarah, Winifred Rachel, Mary

(III) Harry, son of Colonel James and Winifred (Mimnaugh) Brady, was born at Philadelphia, June 13 1863 He attended the public schools in Philadelphia and later with his father moved to Atlantic City He was appointed by the governor of New Jersey as second lieutenant of Sea Coast Artillery and was honorably retired upon commencing the study of medicine In 1897 he was graduated from the Medico-Chirurgical college with the degree of M D and has since practiced in Chester, New Castle and Gallatin, Fayette county, Pennsylvania He has served as deputy coroner in Fayette county, and at present is justice of the peace (1912) In religion he is a Roman Catholic During the Spanish-American war, in 1897, served with the hospital trains service between Philadelphia and Camp Mead, and Florida He is a Republican in politics and a member of the Benevolent Protective Order of Elks

He married, May 3, 1905 Mae, daughter of John S and Mary (Holliday) Gillespie John S Gillespie and the mother of James G Blaine, who was Maria Gillespie, were cousins Children of Mr and Mrs Gillespie Maud, Mae (of previous mention), Madge, Wade Zoe Children of Harry and Mae (Gillespie) Brady   1 Jane, born June 3, 1906   2 Harry Gillespie, born March 16, 1908   3 Mary born November 2, 1909   4 Rose Maxwell, born December 17, 1910

COLLIER The Colliers came to Fayette from Somerset county Pennsylvania, after a previous residence in Kentucky, where the family were among the pioneer families as they were of Missouri Record cannot be obtained farther back than John, grandfather of Merchant Collier, of Georges township

(I) John Collier was born in Kentucky, and died in Addison township, Somerset county, Pennsylvania He followed farming all his life in Addison township, where he came with his family from Kentucky in middle life He was deeply interested in politics, being a strong and enthusiastic Democrat He married and left issue John Joseph Daniel, of whom further Maria, married Samuel Frazer Thomas, died young, Perry

(II) Daniel, son of John Collier, was born in Addison township Somerset county, Pennsylvania, May 9, 1799, died in Georges township, Fayette county, Pennsylvania, January 24 1877 He was educated in the common schools of Addison township and later in life was a stock dealer and farmer For a time he and his sister were joint proprietors of The Burnt House a tavern at Mount Augusta, Henry Clay township later moving to Georges township He married Susan Seaton, born at the Seaton House, Uniontown, Pennsylvania, December 10, 1805, died June 11, 1879, daughter of James C Seaton, born October 26 1780, a hotel proprietor of Uniontown, where he died He married Elizabeth Swann, born December 26, 1779, died February 30, 1860 Children Hiram, Frances born May 6, 1803 died September

25, 1826, Susan, Sarah, married William Crawford, Mary, married William Ingram, Rebecca, married George Martin, Merchant Julia, married Robert Berry, James, John, married Mary Ellen Rose Children of Daniel and Susan (Seaton) Collier 1 Frances, married Allen Johnson 2 Elvira, married (first) Samuel Griffin, (second) Amos Bowlby 3 John J 4 Merchant, of whom further 5 William, married Mary Longnecker 6 Elizabeth, died in infancy 7 Thomas, married Harriet Coffman, and lives retired in Uniontown 8 Daniel, married Louisa Stum 9 James Seaton, married Neal Brown, and lives in Uniontown, retired

(III) Merchant, son of Daniel and Susan (Seaton) Collier, was born in Henry Clay township, Fayette county Pennsylvania, September 3, 1835 He was educated and passed his early years in Georges township, working on his father's farm until he attained man's estate, when he was taken in full partnership in the care and cultivation of the farm Upon his father's death he inherited one hundred acres, to which he added one hundred and fifty acres as well as one hundred and eighty-five acres in Virginia Farming has been his lifelong occupation, and fruitful and successful cultivation of the soil his great delight Although never seeking office, he has ever been an earnest upholder and supporter of Republican principles In religious faith he is a Baptist He married, February 5 1857, Hannah Hustead born in Dunbar township, January 1, 1834, daughter of Robert Hustead, a farmer, born in Georges township, died in North Union township, he married Rebecca Humbert, born in Georges township, died 1910, children Eliza, Jane, Hannah (of previous mention), John William, married Mary Brown, Abraham married Sarah Junk, Moses, married Martha Dunn, James F married (first) Jennie Dearth, and lives in Uniontown, Pennsylvania, (second) (name not known), Robert, died in infancy Alcesta, married Fuller Hogsett (see Hogsett), Mary, married James Curry Of these children, Jane Hannah, James F and Alcesta are living

Children of Merchant and Hannah Collier 1 Frances, married M Taylor Nixon (q v) 2 Daniel, born August 7, 1860, died July, 1908, he married Mary Sesler, who sur-

Merchant Collier

vives him, a resident of Georges township Children Daisy, died aged nine years, Merchant married Belle Newcomer, and farms the homestead, Margaret, died aged four years, Thomas, married Lola Ensley, Grace, Ethel, Mary, Daniel Edgar 3 Alcesta Jane born December 16, 1862, married James V Robinson, a farmer of Georges township, Hannah, resides at home, Rixey Marie, Ruth and Merchant, all living at home 4 Loretta, born October 6, 1865, married Robert Brownfield, a farmer and dairyman of Georges township Children Phoebe, died aged twenty years, Isaac, married Margaret Brown, and is a farmer of Georges township, Hannah, resides at home, Rixey, married George Brown, and has a son, Alfred Benjamin, Ethel, resides at home, Merchant, Robert (2) Rebecca and Benjamin 5 Robert, born June 19, 1867, died January 1, 1869 6 Mary, born January 8, 1869 married (first) Norval N Madera, (second) Robert Kennedy 7 James F born October 20 1871, now engaged in the plumbing and heating business at Hamilton, Ontario married Etta Steel, child Raymond, born 1909

COLLIER (III) John J Collier, son of Daniel Collier, (q v), was born in Fayette county, died in Uniontown Pennsylvania, May 23, 1890 He was a farmer of Georges township, Fayette county, for many years, owning a good farm of one hundred acres In 1870 he established a livery business in Uniontown that he conducted until just before his death twenty years later He was a Republican, and a member of the Methodist Episcopal church He married Annie Laidley, who died July 18, 1879, daughter of Dr Thomas Laidley, a practicing physician of Carmichaels, Greene county Pennsylvania, five of her brothers are yet living (1912) Thomas, John, Charles, James and Wilbur Children of Mr and Mrs Collier William D, a farmer of Somerset county, Pennsylvania, Thomas L of whom further, Frank M deceased, Ella, married J B Adams Susan (Sue), Margaret, married Frank Eddy, of Salem, Ohio

(IV) Thomas Laidley, son of John J and Annie (Laidley) Collier, was born in Uniontown, Pennsylvania December 25, 1860 He was educated in the public schools, his years

of study ending with his fifteenth birthday He began business life as a dry goods clerk in the store of Joseph Horne & Company at Pittsburgh, remaining seven years He then returned to Uniontown where for twenty-five years he was manager of the dry goods department of Hustead, Seamans & Company, later with the Wright, Metzler Company in the same position In 1909 he purchased a jewelry store in the First National Bank Building but did not assume personal charge until November 1, 1911 He has a large store stocked with valuable goods peculiar to the jewelry trade is well established and prosperous He is a Republican in politics and served as school director from 1904 to 1908 He is a member of the Methodist Episcopal church, as was his wife, he also belongs to the Heptasophs and the Royal Arcanum

He married, June 28, 1888 Ella, daughter of Robert and Ella Blackstock, of Pittsburgh, Pennsylvania Children Maude, now a student at Washington and Jefferson college, Helen a graduate of Uniontown high school, Annie, a student in high school, Frank, aged seventeen years, a student in high school, Edward, aged fifteen years, a student in high school

---

COLLIER Barnabas Collier, one of the earliest engineers in the employ of the Baltimore & Ohio Railroad Company lived in Cambria county Pennsylvania During the civil war period he moved to Uniontown, Pennsylvania, corner of Church and Iowa streets About 1870 he moved west with his family, locating in Illinois, where he died His first wife, Mary, the mother of his children, died in Uniontown, his second, Susan died in Illinois He was a member of the Cumberland Presbyterian Church Children Albert, of whom further Edward John all deceased, Sarah married Davis Jones of Denver, Colorado

(II) Albert, son of Barnabas Collier, was born in Cambria county, Pennsylvania, in 1842 He was educated in the public schools, and when a young man went west to Indianapolis Indiana, where he obtained a position as a clerk in a mercantile house When the war between the states broke out he enlisted in Company K, Seventieth Regiment, Indiana Volunteer Infantry, and served three years, attaining the rank of corporal While in the service he visited Uniontown on a furlough to visit his parents and there became acquainted with his future wife After the war he came to Uniontown, where he was a clerk for Charles Rush He was married in January, 1870, and died June 29, 1871, of tuberculosis, resulting from an attack of pneumonia during the war During a part of his military life he was clerk in the United States postoffice at Nashville, Tennessee He was a Republican in politics, a member of the Methodist Episcopal church, and a sterling young man, whose early death cut short a promising career

He married Annie King, born in Uniontown, daughter of Charles and Phoebe A (White) King, and granddaughter of Thomas and Sarah (Hedley) King, who were married in New Jersey, March 25, 1793 Her mother Phoebe A (White) King was a daughter of George and Nancy White, who came from Ireland to this country George White was a student of divinity, preparing for the ministry of the Church of England He participated with all the patriotic ardor of his race in the Irish Rebellion, and was so conspicuous that a reward was offered for him "dead or alive " He took refuge beneath a corn shock at the home of his parents where his little sister, on pretense of gathering flowers, carried food to him After several days he was smuggled in a hogshead aboard a ship bound for America, the captain having been paid a sum of money equal to the reward placed upon his head by the King On arriving in this country he first settled in New York City, subsisting on money sent him from home One gift sent him was contained in a walnut chest in which was a till which was filled with gold guineas and the balance with fine linens made by his devoted mother The chest was preserved in the family until a recent fire in Uniontown destroyed it with many other valuables

He first established a wholesale shoe business in New York with this money, later came farther west and engaged in the milling business When the second war with Great Britain broke out he struck a blow at his old enemy, the King, by enlisting in the American army He there contracted disease, dying while in the service Nancy (Craw-

ford) White, his wife was one of the two daughters of a wealthy Irish land owner Her sister fell in love with and married a worker on her father's estate, which so enraged the father that he drove her from the house The young couple engaged passage for America, and Mary, who had gone to the ship to bid her sister "good bye,' was at the last moment persuaded to join them with a promise that she should be allowed to return right away After arriving at New York she met and married George White, the exiled patriot Their five children are all deceased Phoebe A, married Charles King, of whom further mention, Margaret, Jane, George, Mary

Charles King, born in New Jersey, was a blacksmith and wagon builder He came to Connellsville at an early day, and during the years when the National Pike was the great highway between the east and west conducted a very large and profitable business He was an ardent Whig, one of the only two in Connellsville at that time He was a very genial, popular man, and notwithstanding his unpopular politics was elected collector of taxes

Mr King was known for his charitable traits, he helped many a family with coal and provisions and even money In fact many received assistance that they never knew from what source it came He was a strong advocate of temperance and belonged to the Local Lodge of Good Templars In religious faith he was a Presbyterian, as was his wife Children of Charles and Phoebe A (White) King I Thomas G, deceased 2 Eliza, deceased married Cromwell Hall 3 Sarah, deceased, married John Moore 4 Charles F resides in Uniontown 5 Annie, widow of Albert Collier, of previous mention

Since the death of her husband Mrs Collier has continued her residence in Uniontown where for eighteen years she conducted a successful millinery business She now lives retired at No 31 Jefferson street She is a member of the Methodist Episcopal church, and is held in high regard for her womanly virtue She has a son, Albert B, born December 25, 1871, who resides in Uniontown He married Grace, daughter of the late Robert Knight and his wife, Frances V (Bunting) Knight They have one daughter, Frances, attending high school

Charles King

SNYDER Tracing back less than a century and the ancestors of the Snyder family of Connellsville, are found seated in Saxony, now a part of the great German Empire There the grandparents of Henry P Snyder lived and died They were people in moderate circumstances, but gave their children the advantages of a good education and taught them trades or useful occupations, so that in whatever part of the world they settled they were capable of meeting and overcoming the difficulties that beset the emigrant Through intermarriage this branch connects with the best blood of Western Pennsylvania, tracing to Judge McCormick and through him to that hero-martyr, Colonel William Crawford the renowned Indian fighter and friend of Washington, who at last met an awful death at the hands of his lifetime foes

(I) Christian Snyder, father of Henry P Snyder, was born in Saxony, Germany He received his education in the public schools of that country and learned the trade of stonecutter He served the required term in the militia, and his military papers indicate that he was a model soldier as well physically as mentally His environment ill-suited his ambitions, and in 1845 he emigrated to America The Pennsylvania railroad was then under construction and he found employment at his trade on a section of the line at Lancaster, Pennsylvania He followed the railroad work westward, and in 1850 we find him at Greensburg Pa, in the capacity of a successful contractor, having in five years mastered the language of the country and the business of building its railroads A few years subsequently he came to Connellsville, where he secured extensive contracts for building the Pittsburgh & Connellsville railroad, subsequently absorbed by the Baltimore & Ohio system Here he married and settled down though his business for some years took him to distant states, where he constructed many miles of railroad Later there was plenty to engage his attention at home The coking business developed and he built many coke plants and bridges throughout the county One of his prominent but profitless bridge-building achievements was the Steubenville bridge of the Panhandle railroad, which at the time was one of the wonders of bridge construction because of its height and length The company failed and the contractor got little money and not much honor He continued in active business until the age of seventy-six, when, in a hale and vigorous old age, and under some protest he retired He was naturalized in Dauphin county, Pennsylvania, in 1853 He was a Democrat in politics, but not a strong partisan, and never sought public office, though he was twice chosen a member of the city council He was a member of the Lutheran faith, and died in Connellsville January 20, 1904, aged eighty-six years, highly respected and sincerely mourned for his rugged integrity and sterling worth He married Jane McCormick born in Connellsville, daughter of Judge Provance McCormick and Susan (Bowers) McCormick

Judge McCormick was also a man of energetic and enterprising character, though mild in manner, and held in high esteem for the purity of his character Notwithstanding some claims have been made for pioneer coke manufacturers of the Connellsville region who are said to have made coke on the ground and used it to a very limited extent in local furnaces and foundries, it is a well-established fact that Provance McCormick, John Taylor and William Campbell built the first coke ovens and manufactured the first merchant coke in the Connellsville region Their plant consisted of three ovens just east of Dawson, on the Youghiogheny river They built their own ovens, mined their own coal and made their own coke during one season in the meantime loading it in two barges constructed by themselves These barges they took down the river on the spring rise of 1842 to Cincinnati, where they peddled part of the cargo out for foundry use and traded the balance for a patent iron grist mill that wouldn't work after they had packed it back to Connellsville They gave up the business in disgust Their plant was taken over by the Cochrans, who found ready sale for their product at a good price the following year at Cincinnati, and who came back home, as one of them expressed it, with more silver dollars than he had ever seen before The Cochrans continued in business and made fortunes Their descendants are still represented among the prominent operators of the Connellsville region

Judge McCormick was a son of William McCormick, and a grandson of Colonel William

Crawford, the personal friend and frequent personal representative of General George Washington Colonel Crawford was one of the prominent Western Pennsylvania pioneers He was born in 1732, the same year that gave birth to Washington, and in the same state, Virginia, then Frederick county, now Berkeley county, West Virginia He was the son of a pioneer farmer, and a pioneer he remained to the last His military service began in 1755, when he was commissioned ensign by the governor of Virginia and fought under Washington in the ill-fated Braddock campaign against the French and Indians at Fort Duquesne (Pittsburgh) in 1755 He came out of the battle with honor and was recommended by Washington for promotion He was commissioned captain and accompanied the Forbes Expedition against Fort Duquesne the following year After hostilities ceased he returned to the more peaceful pursuits of agriculture and surveying The Pontiac war again called him to arms, and he rendered efficient service in protecting the frontier from the murderous forays of the Indians Early in 1767 he made a permanent location on the banks of the Youghiogheny, within the present city of Connellsville, then known as Stewart's Crossings, from the fact that William Stewart had lived there in 1753 He supposed he was settling in Virginia, but Pennsylvania established her claim to the territory which was first Cumberland, then Bedford, then Westmoreland, and finally, as now, since 1783, Fayette county Crawford's services as a civilian and soldier were conspicuous and continuous during the years of his residence in the Valley of Youghiogheny In 1770 he was commissioned justice of the peace for Cumberland county When Bedford county was founded, March 1, 1771, he was appointed by Governor Penn one of the justices of the peace for the new county, and in 1773, when Westmoreland was created one of the justices of the court of quarter sessions of the peace and of the court of common pleas As he was first named on the list of justices he became by courtesy and usage the president judge of Westmoreland, the first to hold that office in the county The same year he was appointed surveyor of the Ohio Company by the College of William and Mary In 1774 occurred the Dunmore

and Cresap war, when the celebrated speech was made by Logan, the famed Indian chief and orator Crawford became a conspicuous figure in this war He commanded a company scouting on the Ohio, defended the frontier, destroyed two Mingo villages near where Columbus, Ohio, now stands, and performed many other signal services After the decisive battle of Point Pleasant, fought October 10, 1774, which brought comparative peace to the frontier, he retired again to his home, "Spring Garden," as he had named it Washington was a frequent visitor here, chiefly on business connected with taking up lands Correspondence between Washington and Crawford and the books of Washington show continuous business relations marked by uninterrupted friendship and trust from 1750 to 1774, when the opening of the war of the revolution changed business to war and the sword again took the place of the compass As Washington's agent Crawford was constantly up and down the valleys of the Youghiogheny, Monongahela, Ohio and Kanawha, selecting, locating and surveying lands Correspondence tells of frequent trips to Williamsburg and Mount Vernon and visits to the home of Washington where his business was transacted Crawford also took a prominent part in the boundary dispute between Virginia and Pennsylvania, but upon the opening of the Revolution he dropped county disputes and threw all his energy and patriotism into the cause of Independence He entered the service as lieutenant-colonel of the Fifth Virginia Regiment, but was soon called to the command of the Seventh Soon after he was assigned the duty of recruiting a new regiment He resigned his colonelcy of the Seventh and recruited the Thirteenth Virginia or West Augusta Regiment This was in 1777, under date of February 17 Congress resolved "That 20 000 dollars be paid Colonel William Crawford for raising and equipping his regiment, which is a part of the Virginia war levies ' In August, 1777, with 200 of his new recruits, Colonel Crawford joined the army under Washington, near Philadelphia He rendered efficient service in the movements that resulted in the battle of Brandywine He participated in the battle of Germantown the Long Island campaign and the retreat across New Jersey He was engaged in the defense of Philadelphia and commanded the scouts in Delaware He was in great favor with Washington, who appreciated his courage, sagacity and patriotism Late in the year, an experienced commander being needed on the western frontier, Colonel Crawford was sent to Fort Pitt to take command under Brigadier-General Edward Hand This removal cost him his place in the Continental line which even Washington, much to his regret, could not get restored He was in command of the Virginia militia in the Indian country until the close of the Revolution In 1781 he retired from the service and returned to his home determined to pass the remainder of his days in peace But this was not to be Indian troubles made it necessary to send an expedition to Ohio, and at the earnest request of General Irvine, in command at Fort Pitt, Colonel Crawford took command of the expedition He started with 480 mounted men, the flower of the border, including many of the most experienced Indian fighters of that section The march began May 25, 1782, the objective point being the Indian towns on the Upper Sandusky and its object their destruction While every precaution was taken, the Indians, reinforced by the British Rangers, succeeded in attacking in both front and flank The Americans finally retreated after the loss of about 180 men, including their beloved commander, his son John, his son-in-law Major Harrison, his nephew and Dr John Knight The 'Great Captain,'' to the unspeakable joy of the Indians, was in their hands, and they were determined to put him to death with all the fiendish tortures that devilish malignity could invent Their intentions were carried out to the letter On June 11, at Upper Sandusky, he was burned at the stake After four hours of the most excruciating torture his dauntless spirit took its flight from its cruelly mutilated earthly tenement Dr Knight, who was compelled to witness the torture of Crawford subsequently escaped and gave to history a vivid and circumstantial account of Crawford s frightful end

Colonel Crawford s wife was Hannah Vance Her brother was the father of the Vance family of Tyrone township, and for a century prominent in its affairs She bore him three children John, who accompanied his father on his last fatal campaign, but escaped and subsequently settled on lands

along the Ohio, Sarah, married to Major William Harrison, who also perished in the Sandusky affair, and Effie, who married William McCormick The latter were the parents of Judge Provance McCormick, father of Jane McCormick, wife of Christian Snyder Children Mary, Lillian Elizabeth, married Charles L Gray, George B, died August 7, 1909, and Henry Provance, of further mention

(II) Henry Provance, son of Christian Snyder, was born in Connellsville Pennsylvania, August 2, 1856 He was educated in the public schools and at Mount Pleasant Academy At the age of fifteen he became his father's principal assistant in the management of his numerous interests He acted as bookkeeper and paymaster and did most of the clerical work Just prior to this time he graduated from the commercial school of Thomas P Forsythe, a famous teacher of his time Upon completing the course Mr Snyder was presented with a certificate stating that he was competent not only to keep books but to open and close them and "to settle deranged partnership accounts" This knowledge served him in good stead subsequently, when his activities brought him in contact with numerous diversified industries and actual connection with not a few

In 1878 he began the study of law in the office of P S Newmyer, of Connellsville In 1879 the Connellsville Tribune became financially involved and was sold by the sheriff to satisfy the claims of creditors The machinery and materials were purchased by a small group of progressive and public spirited Connellsville business men who felt that a dead newspaper did not indicate a live town The paper was renamed The Courier and Mr Snyder, who had joined in its purchase, was requested to become its editor He consented to so act temporarily little doubting, in the large confidence of youth, his ability to become a successful lawyer and editor at one and the same time It soon dawned upon him that he could not serve both mistresses He abandoned the law and devoted his energies to making The Courier what some of the highest critics subsequently declared to be 'a model weekly paper" He became sole owner of the paper in 1891 In 1902 a daily edition was established, which soon acquired a phenomenal circulation A

Sunday edition was added in 1906, but the panic of 1907 so limited its advertising revenues that it was discontinued The Courier is a prosperous and influential newspaper The weekly edition is a recognized authority on the statistics of Connellsville coke production and output, its figures having for years been accepted as authoritative by the coke and iron interests, and by the industrial bureaus of the State and the United States and due credit given therefor in their official publications

In addition to the management of his newspapers Mr Snyder has always been connected more or less actively with numerous other business interests He has been engaged in the lumber business in Pennsylvania and the rice business in Louisiana, he has mingled in the management of various industries from a tin plate plant to a ferry company, he has been a bank director and manager of building and loan associations, he was secretary of the first chamber of commerce established in Connellsville, and was for a time president of the present reorganized chamber, he is secretary and a life trustee of the Carnegie Free Library, and a trustee of the Cottage State Hospital He has been active in newspaper association work He has been prominent in the affairs of the National Editorial Association, served as president of the Pennsylvania State Editorial Association early in its career, and is now president of the Western Pennsylvania Associated Dailies, which includes all the leading daily newspapers of Western Pennsylvania outside of Pittsburgh His energies were never confined to a single purpose, yet in all he has succeeded very well, owing chiefly to his keen foresight and restless mental activity

Mr Snyder is naturally very much interested in local history, and has made some valuable contributions thereto in the columns of The Courier A concise but comprehensive historical address on the life and services of Colonel William Crawford, delivered before the Washington County Historical Society, February 22, 1909, excited widespread favorable comment, and applications for printed copies were received by the author from historical societies and universities all over the country

In politics Mr Snyder has been a man of strong convictions and earnest purposes He was reared a Democrat and continued in that faith until 1896, when he refused to support the Free Silver platform of the Democratic party and identified himself with the Gold Democracy Four years later he supported the Republican ticket, and he has been of that political faith since In his political changes The Courier has faithfully reflected his views He never lacked the courage of his views on questions, political or otherwise, and the clientele of The Courier has always respected them, no matter how much it has differed from them, because it has felt that they were the courageous expression of conviction

Mr Snyder has never identified himself with any church or secret society His religion has been as broad as his charity and his home life too happy to make lodge affiliations attractive He is a member of a number of purely social clubs and has been prominent in Connellsville's social life

He married (first) August 24 1886, Jane, daughter of David and Josephine (Emery) Roberts of Connellsville David Roberts was born in Wales, came to the United States, where he married Josephine Emery Mrs Jane Snyder died, 1902 He married (second) January 25, 1905 Katharine McIntyre, daughter of Mrs Alice (Kuhn) McIntyre of McKeesport, a prominent family of Western Pennsylvania, related to the Speer family of Pittsburgh Child of first wife Jean born 1887, educated at National Park Seminary, Washington, and Miss Capron s School for Girls at Northampton, Massachusetts Children of second wife Henry Provance (2), born 1906, Alice Kuhn 1908, Josephine, 1909

SNYDER The Snyders of Dawson, Pennsylvania descend from a German ancestry, the father of Joseph C Snyder being the first of his branch to settle in the United States His grandparents lived and died in Germany Their children John B Louise and Louis, the two latter lived and died in Germany

(1) John B Snyder was born in Essen, Germany, July 1 1831, died in Pittsburgh, Pennsylvania in 1899 He was well educated in the German schools and learned the machinist's trade, working in the great Krupp works at Essen the most famous iron works

in Europe, known perhaps best throughout the world as the plant at which the great Krupp guns are manufactured He married and remained at the Krupp works until 1869, when he came to the United States with his wife and her widowed mother He settled in Pittsburgh, Pennsylvania where he was employed as a machinist until his death at the J & L Iron and Steel works He was a devout member, with his wife of the German Lutheran church He married Amelia Woerman, born at Essen, Germany, May 15, 1839, died in Pittsburgh, May 13, 1887, daughter of John and Louise Woerman both born in Germany, where John Woerman, a farmer, died His wife Louise accompanied her daughter and son-in-law John B Snyder, to the United States Their children Amelia (of previous mention), Matilda, married John Johnson and resides in Baldwin township, Allegheny county, Pennsylvania Tillie married Dietrich Schmidt, and resides in Essen, Germany Augusta married Augustus Prosser, and resides in Pittsburgh, Pennsylvania Children of John B Snyder 1 Hugo died in infancy 2 Albert, died in infancy 3 Joseph (of whom further) 4 Elizabeth, married Charles Ashbaugh head roller in the tin plate mills at New Kensington, Pennsylvania, where the family resides 5 Henry, a bridge builder, resides in New York City

(II) Joseph son of John B Snyder was born at Pittsburgh, Pennsylvania, May 28, 1874 He attended the public schools of that city until he was fifteen years of age then became a wage earner at the Cunningham Bottle Works, remaining one year, then at the McKee Glass Works on Tenth street, Pittsburgh one year then two years at the J & L Iron and Steel works He then decided to learn the machinist s trade, and entering the repair shops of the Pittsburgh & Lake Erie railroad served a four years apprenticeship From 1892 until 1897 he was employed in the McKees Rocks shops on locomotive repairs In 1890 he became foreman of the machine shops of the Pressed Steel Car Company, continuing three years, then returning to the machine shops of the Pittsburgh & Lake Erie Two months after his return he was made foreman at the McKees Rocks roundhouse, holding that position seven years In 1909 he was appointed general fore

man of the Pittsburgh & Lake Erie machine shops at Dickerson Run, Fayette county, Pennsylvania, and so continues He is a most skillful machinist and a capable manager of men His entire record with his company is one of efficiency and honorable service He is a member of Trinity Lutheran Church, Connellsville, Pennsylvania, also of the Knights of Malta, and the Independent Order of Odd Fellows Politically he is a Democrat, and now holds the office of school director at Dawson, Pennsylvania his home

He married January 14, 1897, Anna K L Shulte, born in Pittsburgh Pennsylvania, January 10, 1878, daughter of Henry and Lisetta Shulte both born in Germany, where they were married, came to the United States about 1875, and settled in Pittsburgh, where Henry Shulte died his widow is still living in that city Children of Joseph and Anna K L (Shulte) Snyder Wilbert, born May 15, 1898, Alberta, October 20, 1899, Helen K March 18, 1902 Joseph C (2) May 4, 1904

ARTIS This name dates in Pennsylvania to pre-revolutionary times A William Artis served in the war for independence from Chester county, but the Connellsville family descends from John Artis who came to Fayette county from Virginia at an early date He met his death from a falling tree near the town of Dunbar He married and left issue

(II) Elijah son of John Artis, was born about 1786 He spent his life and died in Fayette county He was a teamster and a worker around the charcoal furnaces, and is said to have been a soldier of the war of 1812 He married Sarah Dillinger, and left issue including Jacob of whom further William, enlisted in Company H One Hundred and Forty-second Regiment, Pennsylvania Volunteer Infantry, and was killed at the battle of Fredericksburg

(III) Jacob son of Elijah Artis, was born in Fayette county in 1816 He was a tinner by trade, and also a stationary engineer He enlisted during the civil war in Company H, One Hundred and Forty-second Regiment Pennsylvania Volunteer Infantry He married Amanda Curry, whose mother Hannah (Bland) Curry, was of the old Virginia family of that name ——— Curry, father of Amanda, was a soldier of the war of 1812, and was one of the defenders of Fort Henry, in Baltimore harbor, when it was attacked by the British. He died shortly after that war, and his daughter Amanda was reared by an uncle, John Bland. Hannah Curry, her mother, then came to western Pennsylvania, and died at Connellsville aged eighty years. Children of Jacob and Amanda (Curry) Artis: 1 William Alexander, of whom further. 2 Oscar, a molder by trade, died in Sacramento California, leaving a daughter. 3 Jacob Emery, now of Connellsville. 4 George, died in infancy. 5 Melissa, married James Cady, of Connellsville. 6 Carrie, married George Critchfield, of Mount Washington, Pennsylvania.

(IV) William Alexander, son of Jacob Artis, was born near Liberty (now Vanderbilt), Pennsylvania October 10, 1846. He was educated in the public schools, but when the civil war broke out enlisted although very young, in the same company as his father and Uncle William—Company H, One Hundred and Forty-second Regiment, Pennsylvania Volunteer Infantry. He was taken prisoner at the battle of Fredericksburg and for two months was confined in Libby prison. After the exchange of prisoners began his name was soon reached, the exchange being in alphabetical order. He then rejoined his regiment and fought at Gettysburg where he received four wounds. Later he was honorably discharged and mustered out. After the war he learned the tanner's trade and also engaged in teaming. In 1882 he entered the employ of the Baltimore & Ohio railroad as wreck master a position he still holds. His work is highly commended by his superior officers who fully appreciate his valuable services in times of disaster to the road. In politics he is a Republican. In fraternal relation he is a member of the Independent Order of Odd Fellows, an order he joined in 1862, and the Union Veteran Legion.

He married, in 1867, Theresa, born in Uniontown daughter of Simon and Mary Ann (Gorley) Samsell. Simon Samsell was born in western Virginia came to Fayette county before the civil war, and served in the Union army. He was a coach builder and merchant before the war, but afterward lived

retired on account of ill health. He died about 1880 his wife Mary A. Samsell died aged seventy-two. They had fifteen children, ten of whom grew to maturity. Children of William Alexander Artis: 1 Walter born July 8, 1870, married Jessie Calhoun children Ada Bertha, Annabel William Robert. 2 Ada Mary June 28, 1873 married Robert Hamman, of Connellsville children Robert, Ada May. 3 Annabel, December 24, 1875, died in youthful womanhood June 30, 1899. 4 Daisy Ellen, born November 15, 1879, died June 13 1910 married John Collins, children Helen William, John James Edward.

RIST

While the spelling of this name would indicate German origin, it was brought to the United States from Scotland, where Conrad and Helen Rist were born, lived and married. On coming to this country they first located in Philadelphia, Pennsylvania where they remained two years, and where Conrad worked at his trade of boat builder or ship carpenter. They then came to Fayette county, where both died. Children: Conrad (2) became a farmer of Kansas where he died. John H., of whom further. Katherine died at Bradford Pennsylvania, married John Orbin. Eliza, died at Bradford, married Henry Orbin.

(II) John H. son of Conrad (1) Rist, was born in Fayette county Pennsylvania died October 26, 1876. He received a good education and for many years engaged in teaching, later became a farmer. He was a Democrat, and a member of the Methodist Episcopal church. Toward the close of the civil war he was drafted and served his term. He married Katherine C. Bally born in Fayette county May 2 1843. She married (second) James E. Sidebottom of Connellsville. Children of John H. Rist: 1 George F. of whom further. 2 Charles H., now living in Conneaut Ohio. 3 John S., now of Cincinnati, Ohio. 4 Molly, married William Cole of Pittsburgh. 5 Anna Kate, died in infancy.

(III) George F. son of John H. Rist, was born in Connellsville March 17, 1864. He was educated in the public schools. His first employment was as a brakeman on the Baltimore & Ohio railroad, later being advanced to conductor. After twelve years' service he left that company and for three years was conductor on the Pennsylvania railroad He then for the next ten years was in the employ of the Pittsburgh & Lake Erie, making his home in West Newton Pennsylvania In 1899 he returned to the employ of the Baltimore & Ohio railroad and until 1910 held the position of conductor In 1910 he left the company, and has since been night watchman at Broad Ford for Overholt & Company In 1909 he was appointed deputy sheriff of Fayette county and is now holding both the last named positions He is a Republican in politics and a member of the Methodist Episcopal church He also belongs to the Independent Order of Odd Fellows and the Order of Railway Conductors

He married, January 9 1898 Anna Mary Nicholson daughter of Peter and Elizabeth (Myers) Nicholson, of Somerset county, Pennsylvania Peter Nicholson is a farmer and large land owner Children of George T Rist Anna Marie, born December 11, 1896 Dewey L November 30 1898 Leo M April 18, 1901, James H, August 23, 1904, John T, December 23, 1907

In the Province of Alsace-
HIRLEMAN Lorraine George Hirleman was born in 1782 of French parentage He grew to manhood there and when Napoleon Bonaparte had so impressed his genius upon France that in 1804 he was crowned emperor George Hirleman became a soldier and devoted follower of that greatest soldier of Europe For four years he followed the fortune of his emperor, years of Napoleon's greatest military glory, including the victories of Austerlitz December 2, 1805, when he defeated the Austrians and Russians, and dictated terms in the Austrian capital, Vienna, Jena where he again defeated them with an added ally, Prussia, captured Berlin, and dictated his terms from that capital These and other battles were participated in by George Hirleman who, during part of his military service, was a part of the emperor's personal guard He left the army before allied Europe had overthrown Napoleon or even occasioned temporary reverse to dim the glory of that great chieftain He saw the abdication, the return from Elba, the one hundred days of restored power the final overthrow at Waterloo, June 18, 1815, and the restoration of Louis XVIII to the throne of France After his marriage George Hirleman came to the United States about 1823 first settling at Germantown Pennsylvania Later he bought a farm near Pottsville which is still owned in the family Here he lived until his death in 1882 lacking one day of being one hundred years and two months of age His wife Martha, preceded him to the grave aged ninety-five years Both retained their power of mind and a goodly amount of bodily vigor until their very last days The old French soldier never tired of extolling the greatness of his beloved emperor, and to gain his friendship it was only necessary to express admiration for Napoleon Children George, died on his farm near Bloomsburg Pennsylvania Henry, Philip, of whom further, Adeline married Frederick Beck, Sarah married George Beck Barbara, now aged eighty years, married Henry Shappell and is the last survivor of the family

(II) Philip son of George Hirleman, was born in Alsace-Lorraine now part of the German empire He came to the United States in the same party as his father and future wife He worked at various occupations, teamster etc finally becoming a boatman on the Schuylkill canal being so engaged until his death in 1861, the result of accidental injury He married in Pennsylvania, Eva Wagner, died in 1902 daughter of German parents, who died in Germany They were both members of the Lutheran church Children Louisa Matilda Edward, now of Reading Pennsylvania, Daniel Thomas of whom further, Sophia, married Abraham Vannatta and died in Connellsville, Pennsylvania, Ella married and lives in Deep Water Connecticut B Frank Philip Jacob, John, died aged four years

(III) Daniel Thomas, son of Philip and Eva (Wagner) Hirleman, was born in Schuylkill Haven, Pennsylvania, December 16 1852 He attended school until he was eight years of age then went on the canal with his father With the exception of two winters he had no further schooling but continued on the canal until 1877 Then he became fireman on the Catawissa railroad, continuing two years From this branch road he was promoted to a run on the main line of the Philadelphia & Reading as conductor, continuing until 1890, except ng three years spent as despatcher at Allentown, Pennsylvania In 1890 he ran for a few months on the Pittsburgh, Fort Wayne & Chicago, then in 1891 located in Connellsville Pennsylvania where for a time ne was in the meat business In 1897 he entered the employ of the Baltimore & Ohio railroad first as brakeman, but was soon promoted conductor In 1901 he resigned and has since been engaged as a public works contractor, being senior member of Hirleman & Guard This is a successful firm and one that has faithfully executed many important contracts with the city of Connellsville for sewer construction etc Mr Hirleman is an Independent in politics For twenty-six years he has been a member of the Order of Railway Conductors and is deputy grand commander of the Knights of Malta

He married, June 1, 1890 Geneva Yates, born in Connellsville daughter of James H and Mary Josephine (Garver) Yates Her grandfather William (2) Yates born in Manchester, England, came to the United States at the age of twenty-one years, joining his parents, William (1) and Margaret (Tinsley) Yates, who had preceded him William (2) Yates was a weaver as was his father and together they operated a factory, manufacturing laces, suspenders, etc He spent two years in Connellsville, but died in Philadelphia, Pennsylvania aged ninety-seven years He married Margaret Graham born near Philadelphia His son James H Yates, was born January 12, 1840 in Somerset county, Pennsylvania He was a railroad man and a soldier of the civil war, serving three years in the Eleventh Regiment Pennsylvania Reserves and one year in the Twenty-second Regiment, Pennsylvania Cavalry He was engaged in thirteen battles including the second battle of Bull Run, Antietam Fredericksburg, the Peninsular campaign Chancellorsville, Gettysburg, South Mountain After the war he conducted a meat market, but later became a weaver, and is now living retired He married, in 1861 in Fayette county Mary Josephine Garver, posthumous child of —— and Mary (Kriseh) Garver Her mother married (second) John Funk, and went west, where she died Children of Daniel Thomas Hirleman I Alta Josephine, born September 10, 1891, married Frank McDiffett and

nas a child, Evelyn M 2 Hilda Margaret born July 11, 1895 3 James Ellis August 23, 1896 4 William Nelson, February 9, 1897 5 Helen Louise, April 22, 1899 6 Gladys July 1, 1901 7 Mildred, August 8, 1903 8 Ruth, November 16, 1904 9 Edythe, September 25, 1906 The first four children have passed through or are now attending the Connellsville High School

HENSHAW The Henshaws of Virginia descend from Joshua Henshaw, of Dorchester Massachusetts, Philadelphia, Pennsylvania, and Frederick county, Virginia He descended from an illustrious English ancestry that is traced to Henry III of England through Catherine, the only daughter of Evan Houghton, of Wavertree Hall and Ellen (Parker) Houghton, of Bridge Hall county of Lancashire England, about the year 1640 Catherine Houghton married William Henshaw, of Poxteth Park, near Liverpool England Mr Henshaw was killed June 20, 1644, at the storming of Liverpool by Prince Rupert, fighting against King Charles I In 1651 his widow died leaving two sons, Joshua aged seven years, and Daniel, five years In 1653 the executor of the estate pretended to send these boys to school in London and afterward reported them as having died of the plague In reality he sent them to New England and placed them in the family of Rev Richard Mather, of Dorchester, near Boston an eminent divine, who educated them with the money forwarded for that purpose Their inheritance was largely appropriated by the executor to his own use, or rather the part which came from the Houghton family—the part which came from the Stanleys reverted to the Stanley family

The youngest of the brothers Daniel died without issue the eldest Joshua married Elizabeth Sumner, of Dorchester Massachusetts, a relative of Governor Sumner, of Massachusetts Children William, born 1670, Joshua 1672 John, of whom further, Elizabeth, Katherine The arms of the Henshaw family are thus described 'Argent a chevron between three Moor hens proper quartering Houghton, Sable three bars argent Crest A falcon proper, billed or beaked and numbered sable, preying upon a bird argent '

(III) John son of Joshua Henshaw, and grandson of William Henshaw, of near Liverpool, England, was born in Dorchester, Massachusetts, in 1860 He moved from there to Philadelphia Pennsylvania where he lived a number of years, and not prospering as he wished, determined to emigrate to the valley lying between the Blue Ridge and Great North Mount in which was called by General Washington in a letter to General St Clair in 1796 "The Garden of America" He bought land from Lord Fairfax, the proprietor, and also bought out some of the settlers and located on Mill Creek Frederick county, Virginia about thirteen miles west of Winchester His eldest son Nicholas also settled there with him, also buying land They erected two houses, also a log grist mill and a saw mill The log mill was replaced in 1828 by a stone mill now in ruins Some of the stones from this old mill were later used in the erection of the new Presbyterian church at Gerardstown, Virginia, being donated by the owner, a descendant This old log mill was a large and prosperous one the flour made there being hauled to Baltimore about one hundred miles away, crossing the Potomac river at Harpers Ferry He married early in life and left male issue

(IV) Nicholas eldest son of John Henshaw, was born about 1705, and was married when he settled on Mill Creek Frederick county, Virginia with his father and brought a family there with him He built a house and was interested in the operation of the old log mill with his father He owned land and was well-to-do His will was probated in Berkeley county, Virginia, August 19, 1777, that county having been set off from Frederick county in 1772 He married Rebecca —— Children John, William, of whom further Eleanor

(V) Captain William Henshaw, son of Nicholas and Rebecca Henshaw was born in 1736 He was one of the most active agents in having the new county of Berkeley erected in 1772, and became one of the most prominent actors in its early civil and judicial history He was a man of wealth as is evidenced by his being bondsman for General Adam Stephens the first sheriff of Berkeley county, the bond being for "One thousand pounds" He was at the battle of Point Pleasant October 10, 1774 and present at the signing of the treaty of peace with the Indians at Camp Charlotte near Chillicothe, Ohio He was lieutenant of the company raised in Berkeley county to serve one year in the continental army On the 4th of October 1776, this company arrived at Bergen Point New Jersey, opposite New York and on the 12th, 13th and 14th were engaged as skirmishers at Kings Ridge There is a tradition in the family that Lieutenant William Henshaw never collected any pay for his revolutionary services He continued in the service and rose to the rank of captain He died in 1799 and is buried in the old graveyard of Christs Church at Bunker Hill, near his home This is a copy of a quaint receipt

June, 1799 Received of Levi Henshaw for a sermon delivered at the burial services read at the funeral of William Henshaw deceased, ten dollars Given under my hand the 14th day of April, 1800

Winchester, $10 00
Frederick county   Alexander Balmain '

He married Agnes (familiarly known as 'Ann' and Nancy '), daughter of William and Mary Anderson Children 1 Nicholas, of whom further 2 Levi, born July 22 1769, died September 9 1843 he was sheriff of Berkeley county Virginia and member of the house of delegates, he married (first) Nancy Davidson, (second) Ann McConnell 3 Hiram married Mary McConnell 4 Adam Stephens 5 Jonathan Seman, married Elizabeth Stafford and settled in Coshocton county, Ohio 6 Washington, settled in Greene county, Tennessee His third wife was a Widow Robinson 7 William Sloughter was a captain of the Fifth Infantry, United States Regular Army, 1808-15, he married Harriet Hyle 8 Urich, married September 29 1807 Elizabeth McDonald 9 Rachel married Joseph Lemmon 10 Rebekah married Lewis Moore 11 Ruhamah, married —— Duncan and settled in Kentucky

(VI) Nicholas (2) son of Captain William Henshaw, was born in 1763 died February 23, 1821 He grew to manhood near Winchester, Virginia, and was twenty-six years of age when he came from the Shenandoah valley in 1789 and patented two hundred and fifty-five acres of land in North Union township Fayette county Pennsylvania, then Readstone township Here he cleared a farm and lived the remainder of his days   He married Margaret McConnell, born 1753 died February 14 1810 and left issue

(VII) William (2), son of Nicholas (2) Henshaw was born in North Union township, Fayette county, Pennsylvania, in 1786, died March 14, 1845   He inherited lands from his father and became one of the prosperous farmers of his township and a man of influence   He was ruling elder of the Laurel Hill Presbyterian Church for many years and an active worker in that church   He married Ann Parker, who died September 27 1845, aged fifty-eight years   Children, all deceased 1 Rebecca married James Campbell 2 James Smith, of whom further 3 Nicholas died unmarried 4 William Harrison, married Elizabeth Foster 5 Clarissa Torence, married Henry Foster 6 Caroline married James Carter

(VIII) James Smith, eldest son and second child of William (2) and Ann (Parker) Henshaw, was born in North Union township, Fayette county, Pennsylvania, November 20, 1809 died there October 22, 1878   He was educated in the public schools of Franklin township   He followed farming all his life, owning a part of his grandfather's farm which the latter divided between James W and his brother William H Henshaw   He was a Democrat in politics serving as school director many years through successive re-elections   He was a member of the local military company but was not in actual war service   He was a member of the Presbyterian church, and a man of very high standing in his community   He married (first) Anna Maria Gray born October 31, 1818, in South Union township, died at the old Henshaw farm in North Union township, October 31 1850 daughter of Nathan and Hannah (Reimer) Gray   He married (second) May 4 1852, Harriet Chalfant, deceased   He married (third) January 16 1868 Maria Jane McDougal   Children by first wife 1 Jonathan Gray died June 2 1867 2 William (3) of whom further   Children of second wife 3 Abigail born January 20 1853 died October 20 1865 4 James Parker, born April 16 1854 died August 16 1854 5 Clarissa, born April 28 1855 died March 30 1904, married Samuel W Dunn 6 Elizabeth born June 24 1857 married Hiram Rankin 7 Samuel Wilson, born November 26, 1859 married Elizabeth

Hankins   Child of third wife 8 Mary Margaret, born June 6 1871, married Elias B Jeffries

(IX) William (3), son of James Smith and Anna Maria (Gray) Henshaw, was born on the farm first owned by his Great-grandfather Henshaw, in North Union township Fayette county, Pennsylvania June 10 1850   He was educated in the public schools of North Union, and remained his father's assistant at the home farm until the latter's death   Under the terms of the will William and Samuel Henshaw received the home farm   William sold his share to Samuel and purchased his present home, a valuable farm in South Union township, near Uniontown, where he has since resided   He is a capable, energetic man of business and has made his life a successful one   He is a Democrat in politics, and a member of Uniontown Grange, No 1103, Patrons of Husbandry   While living in North Union township he was elected supervisor, serving a full term

He married, September 24, 1879, Dorcas Rosetta Hazen born near Smock, Franklin township, Fayette county, Pennsylvania, September 13 1855 daughter of Moses and Caroline (Smith) Hazen   Moses Hazen, born May 3, 1825, died May 3, 1857, a stone cutter and farmer   Moses Hazen joined Brownsville Lodge, No 60   He married Caroline Smith born November 10, 1834 in Franklin township, died June 3, 1901   Children of Mr and Mrs Hazen 1 Dorcas Rosetta, of previous mention 2 James Wilson deceased, married Hannah Alice Crossland   Children of Mr and Mrs Henshaw all living at home except Thomas H, who lives in Philadelphia, and Ruth R, who died December 23 1898 Lulu Belle, Caroline Jane, James Samuel, graduate of Pennsylvania State College, civil engineer, Thomas Hazen, graduate of Bowman Technical School of Lancaster, Pennsylvania Robert Walker Jessie May William Veech, Ruth Rosetta, George Russell, Elmer Wayne

---

HAZEN   The origin of this family beyond the sea has not been traced   Recent information locates a family bearing the name in Newcastle-on-Tyne, England, in the eighteenth century, and possibly the fact may afford a clue to the Eng-

James S Henshaw

lish home of the Puritan Edward Hazen, the emigrant ancestor The first mention of the name which has been found occurs in the records of Rowley, Massachusetts "Elizabeth, wife of Edward Hazen, was buried 1649, September 18 " He was a man of substance and influence in the town was overseer of selectmen in 1650-51-54-61-65-68, and judge of delinquents in 1666 In the records of surveys, February 4, 1661, he appears entitled to "seven gates ' These relate to cattle rights on the town commons, the average number being three, no one had more than seven The inventory of his estate amounted to £404 7s 8d Of his first wife Elizabeth nothing is known further than her recorded death before mentioned He married (second) in March, 1650, Hannah, daughter of Thomas and Hannah Grant He was buried in Rowley, July 22, 1683 His wife survived him and married (second) March 17, 1684, George Browne, of Haverhill, who, September 9, 1693, adopted her youngest son Richard as the sole heir to his large estate She died February, 1716 Children 1 Elizabeth, born March 8, 1650, married Nathaniel Harris 2 Hannah, born September, 1653, married William Gibson 3 John, September 22 1655 4 Thomas, of whom further 5 Edward, born September 10, 1660, died 1748 6 Isabell, born July 22, 1662 married John Wood 7 Priscilla born November 25, 1664 8 Edney, born June 20, 1667, married William Perkins 9 Richland, born August 6, 1669, died September 25, 1733 10 Hepzibah, born December 22, 1671, died November 29, 1689 11 Sarah born August 22, 1673, married Daniel Wicom

(II) Thomas, son of Edward and Hannah (Grant) Hazen was born February 29, 1658, died in Norwich, Connecticut, April 12, 1735 He owned a farm at Rowley at the time of his father's death He moved to Boxford, Massachusetts, prior to March 22, 1690, where he was made a freeman He was dismissed from the church at Topsfield to become one of the charter members of the church in Boxford in 1702, and in 1711 he moved to Norwich, Connecticut, where he died He lived in that part of Norwich called "West Farms " and with three sons was a petitioner for its incorporation as a parish in 1716 The village is now called Franklin He married, January 1, 1683, Mary Howlett who

died October 22 1727 daughter of Thomas (3) Howlett, and granddaughter of Sergeant Thomas Howlett one of the first ten settlers of Agawam (Ipswich), 1632-33, deputy from Ipswich 1635 and Topsfield 1665, and often employed in running lines, locating farms and towns Children 1 John of whom further 2 Hannah, born October 10, 1684, married —— 3 Alice, born June 16, 1686 4 Ednah, married October 21, 1724, Joshua Smith 5 Thomas (2), baptized May 4, 1690, died in Norwich, 1776 or 1777 6 Jacob, baptized April 24, 1692, died December 22, 1755 7 Mary baptized September 9 1694 8 Lydia, twin of Mary, married Benjamin Abel 9 Hepzibah, baptized May 16 1697, married David Ladd 10 Ruth, died in Norwich, February 18, 1740 11 Jeremiah baptized May 3, 1702 These baptisms are all recorded in Topsfield, Massachusetts

(III) John, eldest son of Thomas and Mary (Howlett) Hazen, was born March 23, 1683, on the farm at Rowley, Massachusetts He moved to Norwich and Lyme, Connecticut, where he died He married (first) Mercy, daughter of John and Sarah (Perkins) Bradstreet, and granddaughter of Governor Simon Bradstreet and of Rev William Perkins She died November 22, 1725, in Norwich, where John Hazen married (second) May 31, 1726, Elizabeth Dart Children of first wife 1 John, born February 21, 1711, married March 10, 1734, Deborah Peck (second), Elizabeth Dart 2 Samuel, born May 1, 1713 3 Simon, June 4, 1715 4 Margaret, July 16, 1716 5 Caleb, April 4 1720 married Sarah Hamlin and moved to Carmel, New York 6 Sarah, born 1722 7 Thomas, of whom further 8 Daniel, 1824

(IV) Thomas (2), son of John Hazen and his first wife Mercy Bradstreet, was born at Lyme, Connecticut, February 12, 1722 or 1723 He moved to New Jersey, where he married and had sons born Thomas (2), Aaron, Ezekiel Joshua, Moses, Abraham and David, the latter the pioneer Fayette county ancestor of this branch

(V) David, son of Thomas (2) Hazen, was born February 6, 1770, died in Franklin township Fayette county Pennsylvania, November 11, 1848 In 1808, with his wife and six children, he made the journey from his home in Sussex county, New Jersey, by wagon across the mountains to Fayette county, Pennsylvania, where he purchased a farm in Franklin township, on which he resided until his death. He married in New Jersey, December 6, 1795, Elcy Wintermute, born in New Jersey, June 17 1776, died in Franklin township May 3, 1850. Children 1 George W, born September 2 1796, married Nancy Bowman, of Franklin township, and moved to Belmont county Ohio, where he died leaving issue. The eldest son David, a lawyer by profession lives in Iowa. 2 Abraham of whom further. 3 Thomas, born October 20 1800, married Phebe Cope sister of ex-Sheriff Eli Cope. 4 Elizabeth November 20, 1802 married Jacob Reicheneker, of Brownsville. 5 Mary Ann, February 14, 1805, married Joseph Huston of Tyrone township. Children Clarissa married James Cochran of Dawson, Pennsylvania, Mrs Phebe Martin and John Huston, of Dawson, Pennsylvania 6 Clarissa, October 15, 1807 7 Elcy, 1876-1879, 1810 8 David, March 5, 1814 9 Sarah, February 25, 1818, married (first) John McCormick, (second) Henry Cook

(VI) Abraham, second son of David and Elcy (Wintermute) Hazen, was born in Sussex county, New Jersey, August 22, 1798, died October 7, 1870. He was about ten years of age when his parents came to Fayette county, where his after life was spent. He learned the blacksmith's trade under the instruction of his father but preferred farming and always followed that occupation. He first tilled his father's farm, but in April, 1846, purchased the farm near by on Crabapple run, which he cultivated until his death. He married March 24, 1824, Dorcas Downs, of Redstone township, born November 4 1802 died April 15 1876. Children 1 Moses of whom further. 2 William, born April 11 1827, a farmer, was county auditor of Fayette county, 1857, moved to Washington county, Pennsylvania, where he served a term, 1876-1879, as county commissioner, died July 1 1903 married November 5, 1860 Eliza A Hill, of Washington county. Child Alpha married Dr Eric. 3 George born March 3 1829 a successful farmer and stock raiser of Franklin township, married (first) Mary J, daughter of David Deyarmon, she died January 2, 1875. He married (second) April 17, 1880 Caroline C Carson, of Washington county. George Hazen died July 5 1890 Children of first wife Dorcas Abra-

ham, David, Belle and Elizabeth all of whom married 4 Elizabeth, died May 23, 1833 5 Maria, born December 4, 1833 died April 28, 1912, married November 17, 1855, Jonathan (2) Sharpless, grandson of Jonathan Sharpless, Senior, who came from Philadelphia and was among the early settlers of Fayette county. They have a family and live in Williams county, Ohio Children Elizabeth, Dorcas, Oliver, Minnie, Benjamin, twin of Minnie, and George 6 Thomas, born January 17, 1836, died May 21, 1896, lived on the home farm until 1883, when he sold to his brothers, George and Benjamin and moved his residence to Uniontown, Pennsylvania He was county commissioner in 1878, was connected with the *Genius of Liberty* for more than four years, retiring March 1, 1889 7 Benjamin W, born July 22 1838, a thrifty farmer and stock raiser, owning the old farm on Crabapple run, married, 1862, Edith S, daughter of James and granddaughter of William Piersol, who came from Chester to Fayette county in 1784 Benjamin Hazen died February 25, 1904 Children James P, Annette Ella Wilford (Will) and Leoia 8 David, born August 9 1840, died May 17, 1854 9 Harriet born November 13, 1842, married James, only son of Watson Murphy of Franklin township Children Delmer, Phebe, George, Elizabeth, Dorcas, Annie, Walter, Watson 10 Phoebe, born March 10, 1845, married, April 26, 1881, John Arnold, and lives near Vanderbilt, Pennsylvania

(VII) Moses, eldest son of Abraham and Dorcas (Downs) Hazen, was born in Franklin township, Fayette county, Pennsylvania, May 3 1825, died May 2, 1857 He was a stone cutter by trade, but for several years a farmer and stock dealer He was elected in 1856 auditor of Fayette county, but only lived to serve a year. He married, August 24, 1854, Caroline, daughter of Robert and Rosetta (Shotwell) Smith, of Franklin township Children 1 Dorcas, wife of William Henshaw (see Henshaw) 2 James W, born February 18, 1857, died December 14, 1908, married Hannah Alice Crossland

GORLEY The emigrant ancestor of Thomas Skiles Gorley, of Uniontown Pennsylvania, was his great-grandfather, John Gorley, who came to Pennsylvania with the Scotch-Irish emigration before the revolutionary period and settled in the Cumberland valley, Cumberland county He was a farmer by occupation, and a soldier of the revolution, serving enlistments in Captain John Carothers' company, Cumberland county (Pennsylvania) militia, also a member of Captain Huling's company, with which for a time he was stationed with the troops at Fort Ticonderoga on Lake Champlain After the war he removed to Frederick county, Virginia, settling at New Town, about eight miles southwest of Winchester, where he died He and his wife are buried in the Lutheran burying ground there His children are as follows in order of birth 1 John married a Miss Ferguson, he followed in the footsteps of his father and became a farmer, finally settling near Beaver, Pennsylvania, where he lived and died, to this union were born six sons 2 Jane, who married William Wickersham they emigrated to Chillicothe Ross county, Ohio 3 James, married a lady whose maiden name was Stone, and in 1824 emigrated to Cambridge, Ohio, to this union were born two sons and two daughters 4 Annie, married John Crider, a hatter by trade, they remained and spent their lives in their native town, raising a family of six children, the descendants of this couple at the present day number seventeen great-grandchildren that still reside at New Town (or as it is at present known under the name of Stephen City) 5 Captain Hugh Gorley, from whom the Gorleys of Fayette county, Pennsylvania, descend

(II) Captain Hugh Gorley, youngest son of John Gorley, was born in Frederick county, Virginia, in 1790 and remained there until he had attained the age of twenty-one years His sister Jane (of previous mention) was then living in Chillicothe Ohio, and this no doubt caused him to emigrate to Ohio also Shortly after his arrival there the second war with Great Britain began and he enlisted The story of his enlistment is unusual and well authenticated An artillery company had been raised and was on its way to garrison Fort Meigs, at the mouth of the Maumee river, among the members of the company was a young man who had been drafted into the service very much against his will He was giving so much trouble that the officer in command was compelled to strap him to the

gun carriage When Hugh Gorley saw the young man in such distress and anguish he pitied him and offered to take his place in the company if the officer would release his unwilling member He was accepted, and went to Fort Meigs with the company, while the one befriended went to his home Hugh Gorley remained in the army until Proctor's surrender to General Harrison in the fall of 1813 He then joined a party of men returning to their eastern homes He continued with the party until they reached Uniontown, Pennsylvania where he decided to remain A short time after his arrival he married, and resided there until his death September 10, 1861 He established a boot and shoe manufacturing business and was very successful, employing a large force of men and finding a ready market for his output of goods He was active energetic and enterprising, aiding in every way to develop and advance the interests of his adopted town He owned a good farm of over four hundred acres near Uniontown, and considerable real estate in the town He took active part in public affairs, served in 1828-29 as tax collector of the borough, and was connected with the military, thereby obtaining his title of captain He was an ardent Whig in politics, and a member of the Methodist Episcopal church

He married December 25 1813 at Uniontown, Matilda (Thomas) Hook, widow of Peter Hook (2) who was killed on a Mississippi river boat near New Orleans in the fall of 1810 They had one child, Peter Uriah Hook She was born April 25, 1790 died June 19 1874 She was a daughter of Sheriff William and Ann (Alexander) Thomas, who before coming to Fayette county lived near the Laurel Iron Works near Hagerstown, Washington county Maryland Peter Uriah Hook was a merchant of Uniontown, elected burgess in 1842 and a member of the Pennsylvania house of assembly in 1851 from Fayette county He has many descendants in Fayette county Illinois, and Colorado Children of Captain Hugh Gorley, who died young Eliza Jane died October 16 1815, aged nine months John died March 25, 1818, aged twenty months Jane Eliza died April 14 1839 aged seventeen years seven months twenty-seven days, Louisa, died April 25, 1854, aged twenty-three years five months twenty-five days Those reaching mature years were

1 Ann Mary, born February 14, 1819, died October 29, 1891, married Simon Sampsel, a native of Maryland, he was a carpenter, and for many years worked on the building and repairing of coaches running on the old National Pike, he died May 14, 1878, aged seventy-three years four months nine days Thirteen children were born to this union, nine arrived at maturity George W, born June 23, 1835, Helen Jane, born November 3, 1840, married Crawford Stillwagon, Ann Elizabeth, born November 7, 1841, married George L Rhodes, of Chicago, Illinois, Alice, born January 23, 1844, married Alexander Montgomery Teresa, born March 1, 1846, married William Artis, William, born April 1, 1847, married Amy Brooks, Louisa, born June 7, 1848, married Henry Stillwagon, and at the time of her death, April 8, 1888, was the mother of sixteen children, fourteen of whom were living, Henry Aukerman, born June 11, 1849, married a Miss Shaw John, born December, 1851, married a Miss Robinson

2 James Thomas, born March 29, 1824, died November 9, 1905, he began business life as clerk on a steamboat operating between Pittsburgh and New Orleans, later becoming an owner and running the rivers until the outbreak of the civil war, when he sold his interests and returned to Uniontown where he became a prosperous merchant He was interested in all public affairs, was for ten years a member of the borough council, and for many years director of the National Bank of Fayette county He married, in 1866 Mrs Elizabeth (Miller) Gadd, who died July 25, 1912, in her eighty-third year, widow of Elijah Gadd, to whom she bore a daughter, Fannie March 7, 1854 Children of James Thomas Gorley 1 Richard, born March 28, 1868 11 Charles Holmes, born August 13, 1872, a tailor by trade later hotel proprietor, coke manufacturer and coal land speculator, a very successful operator, married (first) November 15, 1897, Blanche Gregg, who died August 1, 1903, married (second) July 19, 1905, 1 Ethel Westfall, from whom he is divorced, no issue by either marriage 111 Belle, born August 23, 1874, married October 17, 1907, Dr William B Hamaker, of Philadelphia, Pennsylvania child, Helen

3 John Randolph, born February 19, 1826, he learned the shoemaker's trade with his father, which he followed for many years, after his marriage he moved to Muscatine, Iowa, where he was engaged in the grocery business, later removed to Louisville, Kentucky, where he died December 6 1897, he married January 30, 1849, Eliza Murphy, who survives him, a resident of Louisville, daughter of William and Eliza (Miller-Shriver) Murphy Children 1 Lucien B, born February 2, 1850, died December 24, 1886, married Josephine De Lany and had Lily and Joseph 11 James Thomas, born January 2, 1852, a lawyer, of Louisville, Kentucky, unmarried, living with his aged mother

4 Alfred Meason, of further mention

5 Hugh Alexander, born November 25, 1833 he was educated at the old Madison Academy, and learned the trade of printer in the office of the old *Pennsylvania Democrat,* then owned and edited by Jacob Beeson Miller, he then worked for a time in Baltimore, Maryland, later going to Illinois, where he engaged in the dry goods business, after his marriage he caught the gold fever and went to California, going around Cape Horn, he engaged in the dry goods business in San Francisco he was much in public life, was a member of the state legislature of California, representing the district of San Francisco, captain of Company D, First California Infantry fought in the civil war, was a writer of stories and poetry, achieving considerable fame in the literary world, he died in San Rafael, California, September 14, 1907 he was a member of the Loyal Legion and of the Grand Army of the Republic, he married Bell Hamilton, of Michigan, who survives him without issue

(III) Alfred Meason fourth child of Captain Hugh Gorley who arrived at mature years, was born April 25, 1828, at Uniontown, Pennsylvania, died July 13, 1912 He was educated in his native town, and learned the trade of a boot and shoemaker under the direction of his father He followed his trade for many years When the Mexican war was in progress he enlisted in a company forming in Uniontown, as did his brother, John Randolph Gorley, but the company was never called out When the civil war broke out he enlisted in the Eleventh Regiment, Pennsylvania Reserves, June 20 1861, serving until discharged by surgeon's order January 2, 1862 January 29, twenty-seven days later, he re-enlisted in Company K, One Hundred and Twelfth Regiment, Pennsylvania Heavy Artillery, and served until the close of the war He was a Republican in politics and a member of the Lutheran church

He married, December 3, 1848, Lucinda Beatty, born October 5 1830, died April 11, 1903, aged seventy-two years six months, daughter of William and Mary (Farr) Beatty, and granddaughter of William Beatty, a native of old Virginia Mary Farr was a daughter of John (2) Farr, of Lancaster county, Pennsylvania, a son of John (1) Farr, who, although a member of the Society of Friends, joined the continental army and fought for the cause of independence John Farr (2) married Lucinda Hopwood, daughter of John (1) Hopwood, a native of Virginia and a revolutionary soldier He was a son of Moses Hopwood, who came to this country from England early in the eighteenth century Children of Alfred Meason Gorley the first three mentioned dying in childhood George W, died December 24, 1856, Louisa B, January 10 1857, Hattie Elizabeth September 9, 1868 Those who grew to adult age were 1 Thomas Skiles of whom further 2 Alfred Ewing, born February 6 1856, educated in the public schools, learned tailoring, a business in which he has been engaged for many years 3 Mary Matilda, born February 25, 1861 married June 24, 1879, George B Hutchinson, at one time a prominent attorney at the Fayette county bar, children 1 Howard, died aged twenty-one years 11 Hearshel', an engineer on the Pennsylvania railroad in Peail, married J Walter Breakiron also an engineer on the Pennsylvania railroad 1v Helen, married Edward Breakiron assistant cashier of the First National Bank at Smithfield, Pennsylvania v Mary, married James Helmick a plumber of Uniontown vi Virginia unmarried 4 Rose Ella, born December 19 1864 died July 3, 1896, married March 19 1885, Harry L Burnham, for many years connected with the Dunbar Furnace Company children 1 Anna Marceline born March 20, 1886, died July 31, 1886 11 Ewing Edward, born March 10, 1889, married Frances Ayer Hill, born February 5,

1891, one child Ewing in Frank, born August 1, 1891 iv James Hustead, born October 14, 1892 v Charles Henry McCreary, born August 3, 1894 vi Haddie Lilhan, died July 3 1896 aged five months 5 Hugh Alexander, born July 14 1872, he was educated in the public schools and learned the trade of printer in the office of the *Evening Standard* He has always been active in politics has held several local offices and is now member of the city council, elected February 16, 1909 time expires December, 1913 since January 1, 1912 has been president of council in 1912 he was also appointed deputy warden of the Fayette county prison he married in 1892 Anneta May, daughter of Jacob and Katherine (Pence) Dutton children Thomas Skiles, preparing for the profession of civil engineer Ella Katherine Netta May, Annabel, and Helen Pauline

(IV) Thomas Skiles, eldest child of Alfred Meason Gorley was born in Uniontown, Pennsylvania, September 14, 1849 He was educated in the public and private schools, and at the age of eighteen years began learning the trade of printer in the office of the *Genius of Liberty*, under A M Gibson, the owner He afterward went to Altoona Pennsylvania where for about nine months he worked in the office of *The Indicator* then owned and edited by James F Campbell He then returned to Uniontown and finished his trade in the offices of the *American Standard* and the *Genius of Liberty* He then went to Pittsburgh, where on his twenty-first birthday he was out of work and with little money He however secured a position and for several years was employed as compositor on the Pittsburgh dailies He then returned to Uniontown and became foreman of the *American Standard* composing room On March 1, 1889 he purchased from Thomas Hazen a one-third interest in the *Genius of Liberty* forming a partnership under the firm name of Cook, Marshall & Gorley an association that continued four years In October, 1893, the *Evening News* and the *Evening Standard* were consolidated and Mr Gorley was elected secretary treasurer and business manager Under his guidance this has been a very prosperous enterprise, of which he continues the business head He is a Republican in politics, and a member of the Methodist Episco-

pal church   He was made an Odd Fellow
March 4 1871 and is a past noble grand and
representative to the Grand Lodge of Pennsylvania, Independent Order of Odd Fellows,
he was made a Knight of Pythias March 9
1888, and is a past chancellor commander, and
he was also made a Mason February 10 1890

He was married November 6 1878, at
Uniontown, by Rev Robert T Miller, to Annabel Turney, who was born near Uniontown November 30, 1853, daughter of Joseph
Turney, born in Somerset county January 7,
1806, one of nine brothers, sons of John
Turney   He learned the trade of cabinetmaker, but after coming to Fayette county
engaged chiefly in farming   In 1856 he removed with his family to Clark county, Iowa
He was a Whig later a Republican, and very
influential in his community   His home
farm consisting of several hundred acres, was
near Osceola, and there he died in 1883   He
married Sarah Gibson daughter of Joseph
and Rachel (Philips) Gibson   Children Mary
E , Rachel C   Sarah R   Priscilla Daniel P ,
Annabel, of previous mention, Joseph M
and George W   Children of Thomas Skiles
and Annabel (Turney) Gorley   1 Daniel P
Gibson, born September 29, 1879 died July 26,
1883, 2 John Harry born October 24, 1884,
educated in public and private schools and
began business life in 1902 is a clerk in the
drug store of Moser & Springer after remaining two years he entered the employ of
the News Publishing Company as assistant
to his father he married June 5, 1906 Sarah
Cecilia, born November 25 1885 daughter
of Albert Gibson and Elizabeth (Steel) Miller

BRANT   The paternal grandparents of
Samuel E Brant, of Connellsville Pennsylvania, were both
born in England although they met and married in the United States

(I) William Brant born in England came
to the United States when a young man, settling at Buffalo Mills, Bedford county, Pennsylvania, where he became a prosperous
farmer, owning between four and five hundred acres of land   He served in the civil
war with three of his sons, whose term of
service covered the four years of the civil
war, two were wounded but none were killed
The father was active as well as influential in
public affairs   holding several local offices

He lived to a good old age   honored and respected   He married Katherine Miller, born
in England, children Joseph, Henry, a soldier of the civil war, Shannon, also a union
soldier, John, of whom further, Amanda,
Mary Margaret and three others, who died
in infancy

(II) John, son of William and Katherine
(Miller) Brant, was born in Bedford county,
Pennsylvania, August 3, 1849   He has lived
the life of a prosperous farmer, owns two
hundred and twelve acres of fertile land with
modern commodious buildings and is yet engaged in general farming   He is a Republican and has held several township and borough offices, is a member of the Methodist
Episcopal church and of the Independent Order of Odd Fellows   He married Ellen Garber, born in Bedford county, died January 3,
1912, daughter of Joseph Garber, born in
England where he was a miller   On coming
to the United States he settled first at Rox-
ville, then at Accident, Maryland   After following his trade for sixty-eight years he now
resides with his daughter in Bedford county,
aged eighty-seven years   He married and
has issue   Children of John Brant Aaron of
Newark, Ohio, Emma, married W U Sellers, Mina, married W H Fairlamb of St
Louis, Missouri, Samuel Elmer, of whom
further, Dr Morris U, of Buffalo Mills,
Pennsylvania   Grace, married C A Ross of
Washington D C , Mae, resides with her parents, Ray.

(III) Samuel Elmer, son of John and Ellen
(Garber) Brant, was born at Buffalo Mills,
Bedford county, Pennsylvania, August 18,
1876   He was educated in the public school
He learned the carpenter's trade, working
almost exclusively on railroad bridge construction   He was thus employed for eleven
years by the Baltimore & Ohio, and two
years by the Pennsylvania railroad   He took
up his residence in Connellsville in 1892
About 1907 he started in the plumbing business as a member of the firm of Stahl &
Brant, dissolved later and continued the
same business with J A Workman, as Brant
& Workman   In 1910 he started the business
on Church street, that he recently sold to W
E Sellers   He is a Republican and is now
serving his second term as councilman   He
belongs to the Masonic order, the Odd Fellows Maccabees and Eagles

He married, September 17, 1908, Ada Shumaker, born in Hyndman, Bedford county, daughter of John and Sarah Shumaker, old settlers of that county She is a member of the German Reformed church • John Shumaker is living; his wife Sarah died April 10, 1901 Their children Norman R, now of Meyersdale, Pennsylvania, Charles I, deceased, Daisy D, married W Zufall, Ada, married Samuel Elmer Brant, of previous mention, Blanche O, married Henry Purbaugh, Grove C, Virginia L, married John Cook, Justus C Children of Samuel Elmer and Ada (Shumaker) Brant Robert Eugene, born September 10, 1909, Sarah Ellen, March 27, 1911

CRITCHFIELD This family was founded in America by Amos Critchfield, who went from England to Wales, and shortly afterward, between the years 1735 and 1745, came to this country, settling first in New Jersey, later going to the state of Virginia He married and had six sons among them two who settled in Somerset county, Pennsylvania William served in the revolutionary army, settled in Milford township, and founded the family still found there, and Benjamin, of whom further

(II) Benjamin, son of Amos Critchfield, resided in Virginia until the revolutionary period, when he came to Pennsylvania, settling in what is now Northampton township, Somerset county, at or near the village of Glencoe and just east of the Alleghany mountains This part of the county was rough and mountainous the soil not of the most fertile character, but heavily timbered, this fact probably influencing the few settlers who came in at first Chambersburg, Maryland, was then the nearest point to obtain the necessities of life flour and salt The early settlers made lumbering their principal business, gradually clearing farms and becoming fairly prosperous Many, however, became discouraged and abandoned their improvements but Benjamin Critchfield stayed until his death He married and left issue, including a son Absalom of whom further

(III) Absalom, son of Benjamin Critchfield, was born in Northampton township, Somerset county, Pennsylvania, where he grew to manhood and married Later he came to Fayette county, settling in Henry Clay township, where he engaged in agriculture until his death He married —— Roberts and left issue

(IV) James, son of Absalom Critchfield, was born in Somerset county, Pennsylvania, died in Fayette county, Pennsylvania He grew to manhood in that county, learned the carpenter's trade and later became a photographer Later he settled in Henry Clay township Fayette county He served in the civil war in a company of the Pennsylvania troops, and died shortly after the close of the war He and his wife were members of the Methodist Episcopal church He married in Somerset county, Tabitha Younkin, born in that county, daughter of Jacob and Tabitha Hartzell Younkin, both born in Upper Turkey Foot township, Somerset county Her father was a farmer several of her brothers served in the civil war The Younkins are of German ancestry and were early settlers of Somerset county Children of James Critchfield 1 Cyrus Foster of whom further 2 George W, now a resident of Pittsburgh 3 Caroline married Harry G Shepherd, whom she survives 4 James (2) deceased, a resident of Confluence Pennsylvania

(V) Cyrus Foster, eldest son of James and Tabitha (Younkin) Critchfield, was born in Henry Clay township, Fayette county, Pennsylvania July 9 1863 He never attended any school, but has acquired his education by self-teaching and experience He early learned the potter's trade, but followed it for only a short time He then began learning the trade of brass molder, but ill health compelled him to abandon that trade In 1879 he entered the employ of the Baltimore & Ohio Railroad Company at Connellsville as a wiper He was efficient and soon was promoted to engine inspector passing next to the position of traveling car inspector, then brakeman, freight conductor, finally passenger conductor, holding that position until 1903 when he retired from railroad life For the next four years he was proprietor of a hotel at Dawson Pennsylvania, then engaged in the real estate business, and is now associated with the Ohio Fuel Supply Company He is a Republican and a member of the Order of Railway Conductors, the Independent Order of Odd Fellows, the Knights of Pythias

He married, June 1, 1886, Lucinda, daughter of George and Lucinda (Teal) McCormick, and granddaughter of Moses McCormick Both the McCormicks and Teals are prominent Fayette and Westmoreland county families, the latter being the founders of the hospital at Mount Pleasant Moses McCormick, a well-known chair-maker of the early day, married Elizabeth Buttermore, of another prominent family of the county Of their ten children William is the last survivor, now living on a farm at Anderson, Indiana George McCormick was in the butcher business in Connellsville until his death in 1874 Children of Cyrus F and Lucinda Critchfield Edward, born August 18, 1886, died September 17, 1892, Lucinda, born December 17, 1887, died December 19, 1887, Rockwell, born January 5 1889, Hartzell, born September 18, 1891 died February 18, 1892, Foster born April 7, 1895, Clara, November 16 1897 Damon, December 10, 1901

DUGGAN Although of English birth, John Duggan is of Irish parentage and ancestry His father Bartholomew Duggan, was born 1827 in Ireland, moved quite early in life to Minlaton, England, where his son was born In 1864 he came to the United States and in 1867 made arrangements by which he was joined by his family which he had left in England They resided in Noblestown, Pennsylvania, and in 1869 removed to Connellsville Bartholomew Duggan was a miner and always provided well for his family He and his family were members of the Roman Catholic church He died May 3, 1908 He married Mary Cummings, born in Ireland in 1824, and yet living

(II) John son of Bartholomew and Mary (Cummings) Duggan was born in Minlaton, England, June 5, 1857 He was educated in the English parochial schools, and after coming to the United States attended public schools He worked at various occupations during his early life and prior to 1900 was proprietor of the Columbia Hotel in Connellsville In the last named year he began contracting continuing successfully in this line for ten years and has but recently (1912) returned to the hotel business In politics he is an Independent Democrat He has served as councilman and as member of the

Merchants' Association, and was active and helpful in having the bridge between New Haven and Connellsville made free, it having heretofore been a toll bridge The Merchants' Association led in the fight to make it free, and as chairman of the committee of that association Mr Duggan figured prominently in the movement He and his wife are members of the Church of the Immaculate Conception (Roman Catholic) of Connellsville He married, September 26, 1883, Madeline Jeannette Walton, born at Mount Savage, Maryland, daughter of Joseph and Elizabeth Walton Children 1 John, of whom further 2 Madeline, died in infancy 3 Edward, born December 18 1886 4 one, died in infancy, unnamed 5 died in infancy, unnamed 6 Herbert, born August 17, 1894 7 Vincent, June 14, 1897 8 Paul, June 2 1898 9 Gertrude, April 25, 1903 10 Eugene, November 21 1904

(III) John (2), son of John (1) and Madeline Jeannette (Walton) Duggan, was born August 12, 1884, at New Haven, now West Side, Connellsville, Pennsylvania His early education was acquired at the New Haven public schools, graduating with a good standing in the high school class of 1901 He then left home to enter Georgetown University Washington, D C His first course was in the classical department, in which, after having taken his degree as Bachelor of Arts, he took post-graduate work along with similar lines After this solid foundation in liberal studies he entered upon the law course of the university, graduating therefrom in 1906 and was admitted to the bar of the supreme court of the District of Columbia He then returned to Fayette county, Pennsylvania, and continued his legal studies in the office of Cooper & Van Swearengen, and after passing all the examinations with credit was admitted to the bar of Fayette county at Uniontown, in June, 1909 Mr Duggan thereupon opened an office in Uniontown and embarked upon his profession His success has been marked from the first, and he has given many indications of decided ability and an unquestionable promise of future growth He is already a conspicuous figure among his contemporaries at the bar of Fayette county He is attorney for the poor directors of Fayette county and is a member of the board of examiners for the bar of Fayette county He is a Republican in politics, and is a leading spirit in the councils of the party, though he has preferred to dictate policies and shape the activities of the organization to holding office He has in fact, acted as the power behind the throne in the nomination of more than one Republican candidate and exercised a controlling influence in all political matters into which he enters He is a member of the Church of the Immaculate Conception (Roman Catholic), Connellsville, Pennsylvania

Mr Duggan married January 4 1910, Edna Byrne born November 6, 1889, daughter of John R and Joanna (Lynch) Byrne, of Everson, Pennsylvania Mr Byrne is a prominent coal dealer of that region, and is a member of the Pennsylvania state legislature Children of Mr and Mrs Duggan John, born December 2, 1911 Virginia Mary, born June 16, 1912 They reside in Connellsville, though Mr Duggan has his law offices in Uniontown

---

PAULOVITS While Hungary, that land of romance and brave deeds, claims as her own many men of world wide fame, and while the glory of her warriors is as lasting as her own rugged mountains and the songs of her musicians as captivating as the songs of her own native birds, yet it is not a land of great opportunity for those not of the nobility, and many of her sons have left, with regret, their native land and turned their steps westward to that land of greater promise—America

Among those to come to the United States in later years is the Rev R J Paulovits, son of Vincent and Barbara Paulovits, both natives of Hungary, ever their home Vincent Paulovits was a government superintendent of country roads a position of importance He died March 26, 1889 Barbara, his wife died September 23 1879 Children Louis, born March, 1850, Ernest, January, 1855 Vincent, December, 1858, Robert J of whom further Four daughters died in infancy

(II) Rev Robert J Paulovits, youngest son of Vincent and Barbara Paulovits, was born in Hungary June 5, 1863 He was educated in the Archbishop's Lyceum at Esztergom and at once entered the priesthood of the Catholic church for which he had been especially educated He was consecrated and was engaged in priestly offices for the ensuing two

years In 1897 he sailed for the United States, going to Cleveland Ohio where for a year he was assistant pastor of the Hungarian church, St Elizabeth of Hungary He then organized a Hungarian congregation at Toledo, Ohio, erected a church and parish house, school house with meeting hall and house for the school sisters, and left that parish in a healthy spiritual and material condition He next organized a congregation and built a church at Columbus, Ohio, and in 1909 came to Connellsville, Pennsylvania, as a pastor in charge of the Hungarian congregation already established with a church edifice erected Father Paulovits has the spiritual care of two hundred families scattered over four counties, and monthly holds services in Brownsville and Star Junction He is a devoted priest and deems no sacrifice too great where duty calls The church at Connellsville was organized in 1903 and is in a prosperous condition

When Father Paulovits first came to the United States he was the second Hungarian priest to come here from abroad, and was selected for the work because of his great ability as a linguist In the United States he gave the sacraments to his people from Connecticut to Utah He heard confessions in fifteen languages and delivered his sermons in eight different languages, including Latin and Arabic and more modern languages This ability to hold converse with his people in their own tongue not only endears him to them personally, but greatly enhances his value as a spiritual adviser and gains him a wonderful influence for their betterment

---

PORTER It is doubtful if many families can show so many early New England settlers as the Porters Eight men of that name emigrated to America prior to 1653 and all but one of them prior to 1640 Richard Porter settled in Weymouth Massachusetts, in 1653 John Porter was at Hingham, Massachusetts, three miles distant, and is supposed to have been a brother of Richard John Porter settled at Windsor Connecticut, in 1638, previous to this is said to have been of Worcester, Massachusetts Robert and Thomas Porter, brothers, were among the eighty-four proprietors of Farmington, Connecticut, in 1640 This branch of the family is especially noted Robert was the ancestor of President Noah Porter, of Yale College, and his gifted sister, Miss Sarah Porter, who for many years had the most noted private school in the country at her home in Farmington John Porter was admitted to the church in Boston January 23, 1641 John Porter was made a freeman in Roxbury, Massachusetts, November 5 1633 He was a follower of Rev John Wainwright and Ann Hutchinson, suffering banishment to Rhode Island for his religious opinions The David Porter family of whom five generations served in the United States navy reached the climax of its distinction in Admiral David Dixon Porter, whose history is so well known

The origin of the family name is interesting The ancestry of John Porter, of Windsor, is traced through sixteen generations of Englishmen to William de la Grande, a Norman knight who fought with William the Conqueror at Hastings (1066) and was rewarded with estates near Kenilworth, in Warwickshire England His son Ralph or Roger became "Grand Porteur to Henry I, serving from 1120 to 1140 With the adoption of surname the office he held was made the family name Porter The ancient coat-of-arms of this family was Argent on a fesse sable between two or three church bells of the first crest, a portculis argent chained, motto, *Vigilantia et virtuti* The Porters of this sketch descend from John Porter of Windsor Connecticut

(I) John Porter came to New England in 1630, settled first at Dorchester Massachusetts, and is first recorded in Windsor in 1639 He was for that period a man of considerable wealth, as shown by his will His residence was on Little river, near its junction with the Connecticut He died April 22, 1648 his wife Rose died in July, 1647 Children born in England John, born 1620, married Mary Stanley Sarah born 1622 married Joseph Judson Anna, born 1624, married William Gaylor Samuel, of whom further Rebecca 1628 died unmarried Mary, 1630 married Samuel Grant Rose 1632 died 1648, Joseph, 1634 James, 1638 married Sarah Tudor Nathaniel 1640 married Sarah Groves, Hannah 1642 married John Coleman

(II) Samuel, son of John and Rose Porter was born in England in 1626 He was a mer-

chant, and died September 6, 1689 He married Hannah Stanley, sister of his brother John's wife daughter of Thomas Stanley, who came from England in the ship Planter to Lynn, Massachusetts in 1693 She died December 18, 1702 Children Samuel (2), born April 6 1660 married Joanna Cooke 2 Thomas born April 17, 1663, died May 27, 1668 3 Hezekiah born January 7, 1665, married Hannah Coles 4 John, born December 12 1666, married Mary Butler 5 Hannah, born 1668, married John Brown 6 Mehitable, born September 15 1673, married Nathaniel Goodwin 7 Experience, born August 5 1676 married Abigail Williams Ichabod, born June 17, 16—, married Dorcas Marsh 9 Nathaniel born November 15, 1680, married Mehitable Buell 10 Stanley, of whom further

(III) Stanley son of Samuel Porter was born April 1, 1683 He married November 13, 1707, Thankful Babcock (also written early Bodcock) They settled at Coventry, Connecticut, where he was the first town clerk She was a daughter of Jonathan and granddaughter of Robert Babcock who came from England in 1648 He was a captain in the Indian wars Children of Stanley Porter 1, Mercy, born October 10 1708 married Jeremiah Fitch 2 Mary, November 16, 1710 married John Sergeant 3 Jonathan, of whom further 4 Noah, August 24 1715, married Irene Thompson 5, Thomas, September 16, 1723, married Annie Woodward 6, Samuel, August 3, 1725, married Sarah Caulkins 7, Sarah March 25, 1727, married Jonathan Root 8, William, October 13, 1728, married Esther Carpenter 9, Maria, June 18 1731 married Aaron Dewey 10 Bethia July 29 1734 11 Nathaniel, February 15, 1736 12 Elijah, October 12, 1737

(IV) Jonathan, son of Stanley Porter, was born March 20 1713 died March 21, 1790 He married, January 20 1734, Sarah born 1714 died January 21 1806, daughter of Daniel and Sarah (Knowlton) Ladd granddaughter of Nathaniel Ladd, killed by Indians at Maquoit, Maine, August 11 1691 married Elizabeth Gilman, great-granddaughter of Daniel (I) Ladd who came from England in the ship 'Mary and John' in 1634 Children of Jonathan Porter 1 Thomas born March 16 1735, married Zilpah Lyman

Geo. Porter

2 Jonathan (2), September 17, 1737, married Lois Richards 3 Josiah, of whom further 4 Noah, October 6, 1742, married Submit Cooke 5 Sarah, December 6 1744, married Ichabod Jewett 6 Mary, January 29 1748, married Seth Dunham 7 Phoebe, March 11, 1750, married Jonah Carpenter 8 Irena, December 8, 1756, died unmarried, 1790 9 Rebecca 1760, married Solomon Chapin

(V) Josiah, son of Jonathan Porter, was born August 21, 1740 He married (first) in 1784, Lois Carpenter, died April 14, 1786, daughter of Eliphalet Carpenter and a descendant of William Carpenter who came from England in 1638 He married (second) January 10 1787, —— Chubbuck Children by second wife Asahel born March 3, 1786, Abner, June 10 1788 George or whom further

(VI) George, son of Josiah Porter by his second wife, was born October 10 1790, died August 26, 1845 He joined relatives in Oneida and Erie counties New York, later living in Chillicothe, Ohio, where he died

(VII) Edward Tiffin son of George Porter was born in Chillicothe, Ohio, in 1814 died in Indianapolis Indiana in 1842 a merchant of the latter city at the time of his death He married Elizabeth Jane Wilson who survived him and married (second) Eleazar Robinson of Uniontown Pennsylvania, she was a daughter of James Wilson born in Lancaster county in 1764, and came to Fayette county Pennsylvania, 1778 James Wilson became a large land owner and served as justice of the peace of German township from 1807 to 1840 He married (first) Mary H Robb (second) Elizabeth Lowrie By her second husband Elizabeth J Porter had William L Robinson of Pittsburgh, Pennsylvania, and Mary E, wife of Dr A P Bowie of Uniontown Children of Edward Tiffin Porter 1 James Wilson, who in early days was a farmer now a merchant and real estate dealer of Indianapolis Indiana, he served in the civil war, he married Mary Wilson 2 Edward Tiffin was a real estate dealer of Indianapolis Indiana, connected with the Yande family he moved to Junction City, Kansas, and died in California 3 George, of whom further

(VIII) George (2), son of Edward Tiffin and Elizabeth Jane (Wilson) Porter, was born in Indianapolis Indiana October 24, 1835, died August 8 1903 He was brought to German township Fayette county, Pennsylvania, by his mother after the death of her husband, and made his home with his uncle John Wilson He was educated in Dunlap Creek Academy He grew up a farmer, and for twenty years followed that occupation in German township In 1879 he purchased property in McClelland township and there established a general store which he successfully conducted until 1894 superintending his farming operations during the same period He disposed of his mercantile business and in 1895 located in Uniontown where he opened a general real estate and insurance business, building up a large and profitable business, continuing until his death also owning the Star farm and coal lands in Fayette county During his earlier years he taught school in German township He was a member of the Presbyterian church and at McClellandtown served the church as elder After moving to Uniontown he joined the First Presbyterian church of that city and from 1896 until his death was also an elder He was always prominent in the church, and in 1887 was a delegate from Redstone Presbytery to the General Assembly of the Presbyterian church which met at Minneapolis Minnesota that year In politics he was a Republican

He married, May 9 1861 Elizabeth Parshall, born in McClellandtown, German township, Fayette county, March 9, 1836, who survives him, a resident of Uniontown, she is a daughter of Elias Parshall, a wealthy farmer, stockholder and grower of German township (see Parshall XVIII) Children 1 Elizabeth born May 23, 1862 married George Alexander Hogg, and resides in Pittsburgh Pennsylvania, he is a large land owner and heavily interested in steel manufacturing children George Ewing Porter, born March 9 1880 Mildred Elizabeth March 9 1891 Sara Constance February 23 1893, Mary Caroline March 26 1897 Alice Trevor April 9, 1899 and William Cecil, born January 23, 1904 2 Edward Tiffin, born April 3, 1866 formerly a farmer, now assistant general manager of the Union Supply Company he married Julia, daughter of William McShane of German township, children George, born February 2, 1896,

Edward Tiffin, January 7, 1900. 3. George, of whom further mention.

(IX) George (3), son of George (2) and Elizabeth (Parshall) Porter, was born in German township, Fayette county, Pennsylvania, November 21, 1875. He studied in the township schools and later attended the high school in the city of Pittsburgh for two years, then returned to his home and attended Redstone Academy one year. He then entered Cornell University, whence he was graduated four years later with the degree of Mechanical Engineer, class of 1897. He was a member of the Students' Self-Government Council and of the Theta Nu Epsilon fraternity. After leaving the university he entered the employ of the Westinghouse Machine Company, testing gas machines and engaged in experimental work at the Westinghouse plant in East Pittsburgh. He left the employ of that company to become constructing engineer for the then Continental Coke Company. After absorption of that company by the H. C. Frick Coke Company, he continued in the same position for three years. He was with the United States Coal and Coke Company for a time and again with the Frick Company one and a half years. He later located in Uniontown as civil and mining mechanical engineer. He is thoroughly qualified and is considered an expert in his especial lines. He is associated in many undertakings with J. B. Hogg, and in others alone. He is a Republican in politics, and a member of the First Presbyterian church.

He married, March 28, 1900, Mary Moore, born near New Salem, German township, Fayette county, Pennsylvania, September 19, 1877, daughter of Aaron and Naomi (Grove) Moore (see Moore). Child: Virginia Adeline, born April 13, 1909. The family home is at No. 108 Morgantown street, Uniontown.

(The Moore Line.)

Aaron Moore, father of Mrs. Mary (Moore) Porter, was born in German township, Fayette county, Pennsylvania, died there in 1869. He was a farmer and stock raiser. He married Naomi Grove, also born in German township. Children: 1. Mary, of previous mention. 2. Harry Grove, born April 29, 1879; a farmer on part of the Moore homestead; married Margaret Bailey and has

Mary Elizabeth, born December 14, 1910, and John Bailey, born October 15, 1911. 3. Charles A., born September 8, 1881; married Mary Seaton and has Charles Wendell and Mary Seaton, deceased. Aaron Moore was a son of Abraham Moore, a grandson of Aaron Moore, who received a grant of land from William Penn, a part of which is yet the Moore homestead farm in German township, Fayette county.

(I) Through maternal lines Mary (Moore) Porter descends from Thomas Shepherd, who came to America from Shropshire, Wales, with two brothers, John and William, landing near Annapolis, Maryland. Thomas settled at Shepherdstown, Virginia, where he owned about one thousand acres near "Packhorse Ford" on the Potomac river in western Spottsylvania county, Virginia. A settlement of Germans on his farm was called Mechlenberg. He was probably born in 1705, died in 1776. He married Elizabeth, daughter of Robert Van Meter, a wealthy planter of Maryland, who traced his ancestry to the royalty of Holland. She brought her husband a tract of one hundred and sixty-two acres called "Pell Mell," opposite, but a mile below "Packhorse Ford." Thomas Shepherd built a high bluff on the Potomac shore, a stone fort known as "Shepherd's Fort" which stood until 1812. Here the German settlers of Mecklenberg gathered when an Indian alarm was given. After the death of Thomas Shepherd, the name of the settlement was changed to Shepherdstown. Children of Thomas and Elizabeth Shepherd: David, born 1734; Sarah, about 1736; Elizabeth, of further mention; William, about 1741; Thomas, about 1745; John, 1750; Mary, 1752; Martha, twin of Mary; Abraham, 1754; Susanna, 1758. David, the eldest son, moved to Ohio county, Virginia, then including all of now West Virginia and a part of Western Pennsylvania, and settled near Wheeling. He was a large land owner, and during the revolution was colonel of Ohio county troops.

(II) Elizabeth, daughter of Thomas Shepherd, was born at Mecklenberg, Virginia, October 2, 1738, died 1788. She married, May 3, 1762, William Brown, born September 13, 1724, died July 24, 1801. Children: 1. John, born February 16, 1763. 2. Elizabeth, December 27, 1764. 3. Thomas Abraham,

February 25 1767, died November, 1768 4 Mary, of whom further mention 5 Sarah, married William Esty 6 William, born March 24, 1774, died in infancy 7 Shepherd born April 14, 1775, a merchant of New Orleans, killed by a fall in 1817 8 George W (called Harry Washington), born October 22, 1778 living in 1801 9 Hannah Matilda, born November 22, 1781, married Di Adams

(III) Mary, daughter of William and Elizabeth (Shepherd) Brown, was born September 15, 1768, died 1812 She married, February 6 1785 John Grove, a descendant of Hans Groff, sometimes Baron Von Welden of Switzerland, who fled to America in 1696 and some years later settled in Pequa Valley in Lancaster county Pennsylvania It was his son, Jacob, who was the progenitor of the numerous Grove families of Washington county, Pennsylvania Children of John and Mary (Brown) Grove, all born in German township, Fayette county, Pennsylvania 1 Sarah, married Lemuel Hall 2 Jacob, born August 29, 1787 3 Elizabeth, married John Spark 4 Catherine married ——— Auld 5 Shepherd, born March 14, 1793 6 John February 1, 1795, married Anna McQuilliams 7 Samy, married Mary Sprinkle 8 Levi born December 6 1798 9 Hannah M, married Elias Parshall 10 William B, married Nancy Allentar 11 Stephen, married Ann Coldren 12 Harvey, of whom further mention 13 Mary, married John Ground

(IV) Harvey, son of John and Mary (Brown) Grove, was born February 19, 1806 He served as school director and two terms as assessor of the township He married Elizabeth daughter of Thomas Lackey, of German township Fayette county, Pennsylvania Children 1 Mary Louise, married George Hess 2 Naomi, of whom further, 3 Reuben, married Hettie Higginbotham 4 Rhoda 5 Elizabeth, married (first) William Jeffries and moved to Dwight, Illinois, married (second) Henry Coonley 6 Mary

(V) Naomi daughter of Harvey and Elizabeth (Lackway) Grove, married Aaron Moore

(VI) Mary, daughter of Aaron and Naomi (Grove) Moore, married George Porter (see Porter IX)

The Pershall or Parshall PARSHALL family came to England with William the Conqueror and the name Pershale is found on the roll of Battle Abbey, erected on the battlefield of Hastings, 1066 The family is traced to Sir Richard de Pershall, but no records exist covering the period 1066 to the reign of King Edward III, when they are found seated in Staffordshire They had probably been seated there for many generations, as Sir Richard was a knight of great power, being high sheriff under appointment from the King and owned large estates He married Margaret, daughter of Hugh Lord, of Knighton, and added that manor to his possessions

(II) Sir Adam de Pershall, son of Sir Richard de Pershall, succeeded him as high sheriff, and his two wives, both heiresses, added greatly to his already large possessions

(III) Sir Adam (2) de Pershall

(IV) Sir Richard Pershall

(V) Sir Thomas Pershall, Knight

(VI) Nicholas Pershall

(VII) Hugh Pershall, Esquire, the first of the family to reside at Hornsley in Staffordshire He was sheriff under Henry VII, 1489

(VIII) Humphrey Pershall, Esquire, married Helen, daughter of Humphrey Swinnerton, Esquire

(IX) John Pershall, of Checkley married Helena, daughter of John Harcourt, Esquire

(X) Richard Pershall married Isabella, daughter of Thomas Rollerton Esquire

(XI) Richard Pershall Esquire, of Horseley, married Joanna daughter of Sir Edmund Fettiplace, of Berkshire

(XII) John Pershall, Esquire, among the first baronets created by King James I November 25 1612 and four years later was sheriff of the county, married Anne daughter of Ralph Sheldon Esquire

(XIII) Thomas Pershall, born 1596, married Bridget, daughter of Sir William Stafford

(XIV) John Pershall, created a baronet and became Sir John died January 13, 1646

(XV) Sir John (2) Pershall married, in 1660, Frances, daughter of Colonel Thomas Leigh, of Addington in Cheshire He died in 1701

(XVI) Sir Thomas Pershall, died 1712 He married a Miss Metcalf and since then the baronetcy has lain dormant The arms of the Pershall baronets were 'Argent a cross patee fleury one cantor Gules a wolf's head erased of the first" Crest "A wolf's head, sable holding in his mouth a marigold proper The Parshalls of Fayette county descend from Richard Pershall, of the tenth generation preceding He had seven sons and two daughters

(XI) Edmond one of the younger sons of Richard Pershall, went into trade in London, changing the name to Parshall He was a member of the Grocers Guild and flourished during the years of the reign of Queen Elizabeth and under James I He had a son, John

(XII) John son of Edmond Parshall, married and had a son James

(XIII) James, son of John Parshall, was undoubtedly the first of the name in this country, but the date or his arrival the locality or his birth are not even matters upon which traditions throw light The first record of him is a deed dated December 12, 1679 showing he was at that time a resident of Gardiners Island, first called the Isle of Wight After his marriage he moved to Southold, Long Island, where in 1686 his family consisted according to the census of that year, of six white males, two white females three male and two female slaves He made his will in 1692, and died in Southold September 15, 1701 He married Elizabeth, youngest daughter of David Gardiner, proprietor of Gardiners Island who was the first white child born in Connecticut April 29 1636, died July 10, 1689 David was son of Lion Gardiner, first settler on the island in 1639 'And thus was commenced the first permanent English settlement within the present limits of the State of New York" Lion Gardiner came with his wife, Mary (Williamson) Gardiner, from Worden, a town in Holland where his wife was born, to London, England thence to New England dwelling at Saybrook, Connecticut at the mouth of the Connecticut river, where his son David was born He was a native born Scotchman, was associated with the party of Hampden and Cromwell and served in the English army and under the Prince of Orange in

Holland James Parshall named in his will sons Israel and David, also a 'beloved daughter Mary'

(XIV) David son of James Parshall was born in 1682, died January 25, 1725 or 1726 He married, about 1705 Mary, daughter of David and Martha Youngs She was born 1685 died April 21 1725 She was a great-granddaughter of Lion Gardiner, and a daughter of Colonel John son of Rev John Youngs David Parshall's will probated March 16, 1725 or 1726, mentioned sons, David Jonathan and "his daughters" without naming them

(XV) David (2), eldest son of David (1) Parshall, made his will March 11, 1759, it was probated February 28, 1760, and named David (3), Desire, Elias, Sebil, James Mehitable, John, David's wife was Sebil White, to whom he was married December 6, 1736

(XVI) Elias, son of David (2) Parshall was probably born at Southold Long Island, resided there until 1779, then temporarily moved to Connecticut to avoid the British A document extant dated September 21, 1779, recites That he is a friend of the United States that he had lately built a small vessel of twenty tons for trade, that by means of the threats and usage from the enemy, he dared not remain longer on said island and has, therefore, brought over part of his family and effects on board said vessel to this state for liberty of landing and safe protection The council of safety granted his petition, but there are no records to show when he returned to Long Island He married, and had sons Elias (2) Lewis and Daniel, the last two drowned in 1813 with nine others

(XVII) Elias (2) son of Elias (1) Parshall was born on Long Island about 1776, died at McClellandtown, Fayette county, Pennsylvania, 1854 He removed in 1797 to Fayette county, Pennsylvania Until the removal to Fayette county the family had been seafaring men, now they became farmers, builders and merchants They settled in German township where he followed farming and merchandizing He married and left issue, including a son Elias (3)

(XVIII) Elias (3) son of Elias (2) Parshall, was born in Morris county, N J, 1797 died at McClellandtown, Pennsylvania, July 4, 1882 He grew up a farmer and in the

flourishing days of the National Pike operated a number of teams on that historic road He was a large land owner, farmer and stock dealer He became influential and wealthy He was a Whig later a Republican He was one of the pillars of the Baptist church and liberal in his donations He married in 1817, Hannah Matilda Grove, born in Masontown, Pennsylvania, September 1, 1800, died April 28, 1881, daughter of John and Mary (Brown) Grove Children 1 Vincent, born December 12, 1817, he moved to the Shenandoah Valley of Virginia in 1878 purchased an estate of six hundred and eighteen acres and ended his days there, married Eliza Ann Crow and left issue 2 Harvey, born July 19, 1819 died June 5 1822 3 William Grove, of whom further 4 Reuben, born November 9 1823 died unmarried April 26 1884 5 Emily born September 25, 1825, died in Toledo, Ohio, June 12, 1902, married John F Worthington 6 Mary, born August 30 1827, died September 29, 1883 married Thomas W Lyons, and lived in Uniontown, Pennsylvania 7 James M born August 22, 1829, died February 11, 1903 married Mary Higginbotham 8 Maria, born May 7, 1831, died September 16, 1873, married William Porter, and lived at Merrittstown Pennsylvania no issue 9 Hamilton, born January 10 1833, died October 2, 1833 10 Nelson, born February 22, 1834, died July 2, 1834 11 Elizabeth, born March 9, 1836, married George (2) Porter (see Porter VII), and lived in Uniontown 12 Caroline born January 27, 1838 died August 10, 1900, married Thomas N Wettner, and lived in German township, Fayette county Pennsylvania 13 Hannah Matilda, born February 2, 1840, died October 28, 1844 14 Stephen Calvin, born February 13, 1842, died November 9, 1844 15 Sarah Helen born April 11, 1844 married Melancthon J Crow, and moved to Grand Ridge, Illinois, he died April 8, 1884 no issue 16 Luretta, born August 17, 1845, married Dr George Washington Neff, of Masontown, Pennsylvania

(VIX) William Grove, son of Elias (3) Parshall was born in German township Fayette county Pennsylvania, September 14, 1821, died July 4, 1883 He was educated at Jefferson College, read law under General Joshua F Howell, was admitted to the Fayette bar in 1847 and continued in active successful practice all his life He was an active Republican, and influential He served on the county committee was often chairman and a frequent delegate to party, county and state conventions He was an able lawyer and a man of high character He married Martha A Hawks, born February 14, 1836, who survives him, daughter of Jonathan Hawks, a native of Massachusetts Children Three died in childhood Emily, born November 8 1874, died October 8, 1908, married Frank Raymond Crow, children Martha Louisa, born January 10, 1903 and Frank Raymond born May 29 1905 William W, or further mention

(XX) William W, son of William Grove Parshall was born in Nicholson township, Fayette county Pennsylvania, June 18, 1866 He received his early and preparatory education in the public schools of Uniontown, where his boyhood and youth was passed He then entered Cornell University, whence he was graduated B S, class of 1888 He then began the study of law under the direction of W G Guiler, of Uniontown, continuing until his admission to the Fayette county bar in 1890 He at once began the practice of his profession in Uniontown, and continued without interruption up to the present time He is qualified to practice in all state and federal courts and commands a large influential clientele He has large business interests independent of his profession is director of the Second National Bank of Uniontown, president of the First National Bank of Smithfield, director of the McKeefry Coke Company, director of the United Connellsville Coke Company, has a large interest in the Puritan Coke Company, a large operating company, and in various other coal and coke companies of his section He stands high among his professional brethren of the bar, and is an energetic capable man of affairs He is a Republican in politics, has served as a frequent delegate to party conventions and as a member of the Fayette County Central Committee He is a member of the Episcopal church, as is also his wife, both being active and efficient workers His club is the Uniontown Country Both he and his wife are members of the Laurel Club Their house is situated one mile south of Uniontown on the National road, and is a most beautiful and attractive suburban home The property first owned by Elias Parshall, great-grandfather of William W Parshall, in German township, is now owned by W W Parshall

Mr Parshall married, June 11, 1902, Amelia, daughter of Henry and Maria (Dawson) Baldwin, of Springfield, Ohio Children William B (2), born April 30, 1903, Louise B , born December 10, 1904, Lawrence, born May 19, 1907, Henry Baldwin, June 15, 1909 Edward Rodney, October 30, 1910

PORTER
This branch of the Porter family, of which John R Porter is a representative, descends from John Porter, born in England, 1690, came to America and settled at Baltimore, Maryland in 1715

(II) John (2), son of John (1) Porter, was born about 1720 at Baltimore, and settled in Allegheny county, Maryland, in 1782 He married Nancy a daughter of Moses McKenzie, and left eight children

(III) Caleb, son of John (2) Porter, was born in Maryland about 1760 He lived at Ellicotts Mills near Baltimore, Maryland, and about the year 1800 came to Pennsylvania, where he purchased twelve hundred acres of land in Westmoreland county, on which he built a stone house This house with part of the original purchase is yet held in the Porter name He married and had a large family Two of his sons James and Joseph Porter, served in the Union army during the civil war

(IV) Peter, son of Caleb Porter was born about 1795 at Ellicotts Mills near Baltimore, Maryland, died at Jacob s Creek Pennsylvania, July 3 1889 He was brought to Westmoreland county Pennsylvania by his parents in 1800 He followed farming all his life although two of his brothers Ezra and Nathan were pioneer boat builders with yards on the Ohio river, near Pittsburgh In 1847 or 1848 Peter Porter moved to a farm at Jacob's Creek, where he lived until his death in 1889 He was a well known and highly respected man and was successful in his business affairs He married Isabella McCreery born about 1804 at Cherry Tree, Indiana county Pennsylvania, died January 3

1889 They had four sons and four daughters Sons Elliott, Hudson, Elias, deceased he enlisted from Clearfield, Pennsylvania, in the Eleventh Regiment, Pennsylvania Cavalry, and served in the civil war, John Ritchie, of whom further Daughters Harriet, married James I King and resides at Mount Pleasant, Pennsylvania, Emma resides in Pittsburgh, Missouri Margaret, married William Reed of Lafayette county, Pennsylvania

(V) John Ritchie, son of Peter Porter, was born in Westmoreland county, Pennsylvania, August 9, 1844 He was educated in the public schools at Jacob's Creek and remained on the paternal farm until attaining legal age, then entered the employ of the Baltimore & Ohio Railroad Company as fireman on a locomotive He soon left the Baltimore & Ohio for a better position with the Pennsylvania railroad, remaining three years He then returned to the employ of the Baltimore & Ohio and has been continuously with that road until the present date (1912) He has passed through successive grades of promotion in the transportation department, attaining the position of passenger conductor having held the latter position many years, and enjoys the distinction of being the oldest conductor in the company's employ He is well known in his home city and to the traveling public and is held in universal esteem He has had many thrilling experiences in his long career on the rail " not having gained his title of ` veteran ' without experiencing every sensation that falls to the lot of the modern railroad man He is a Democrat and a Mason

He married April 15, 1874, Caroline McBeth, born in Normalville Pennsylvania daughter of John A and Anna (Nickle) McBeth and granddaughter of George Nickle Children 1 Anna Mae born May 25 1875 died February 16 1902 married F T Evans, of Connellsville 2 J Donald, born March 20, 1877, now engaged in the real estate and insurance business in Connellsville, married Myrtle May Pfeifer 3 Roy M died in infancy, April 3, 1878 4 Ralph Ewing born April 28 1879 married Olive Boyd April 15 1907 5 Elmer Reed born September 9, 1885 6 Imogene A , born July 10 1899 7 Kathryn M , born September 18, 1891 .

Porter Homestead

PORTER There are bany different branches of the Potter family in Fayette county tracing to English and Irish progenitors. One branch entered the county from the south another from New York state and still another from Indiana. The larger branch is the southern family, of which Phineas Porter is recorded as being overseer of the poor of Dunbar township in 1803.

(I) Phineas Porter was born in Maryland. He was a tanner. He came to Fayette county about the year 1800 and established a tannery in Dunbar township. All the salt used in the tanning process had to be carried over the mountains on horseback, the tanned leather being sent to market in the same way until the opening of the National Pike about 1822. He married Susan McNutt, who was of Irish descent, the Porters being Scotch-Irish. Children: 1 Phineas, married Hannah Bunker and moved to Appamoose county, Iowa, where he engaged in farming. 2 John, married Lowry and joined his brother in Iowa. 3 Sarah, married Joseph McFarland and moved in the old-fashioned prairie schooner to join her brothers in Iowa. 4 Moses, of whom further.

(II) Moses, son of Phineas and Susan (McNutt) Porter, was born in Dunbar township Fayette county, Pennsylvania, October 16, 1807 died in October 1875. He grew to manhood on the home farm, learned tanning from his father and later the shoemaker's trade, but did not follow it after his marriage. His health failed him and he was obliged to seek out-of-door employment. He was first manager of the "Woolen Mill Farm," on which New Haven was later built. He then cultivated for five years the farm on which the village of Wheeler is built. He prospered and saved enough money to purchase a farm in Dunbar township. He moved to his own farm in 1849, continuing there until his death. He was energetic and thrifty holding the respect of his community. He was a Democrat in politics, serving in the offices of assessor and school director.

He married Elizabeth Murphy, born on the farm on the National Pike now known as the county farm, December 14, 1814, died February 4 1906, daughter of Jacob and Elizabeth (Mason) Murphy. Three Murphy brothers came to Fayette county from Maryland about the time of the American revolution, Jacob, William and Asa. They settled near where Mount Braddock now is and were getting along finely until suddenly attacked by the Indians. Jacob escaped, Asa was killed outright and William hid in a brush pile and was not found. William was so frightened at his perilous adventure that he returned to Maryland and never again returned to Pennsylvania. Jacob Murphy was a well-to-do farmer and owned ten slaves, whom he employed in his farming operations. Elizabeth, his wife, was born in Fayette county in the stone house her father, Isaac Mason, an early iron master had erected in 1802 on the present site of Mount Braddock. Isaac Mason built the first iron furnace erected in Dunbar and operated it many years. Elizabeth (Mason) Murphy was a devoted, prominent Methodist, and on one occasion entertained at her home the entire Methodist conference then in session nearby. Children of Jacob Murphy: 1 Rev Jacob, a minister of the Cumberland Presbyterian church. 2 Ross, married Anna McCormick and moved to Connellsville, Pennsylvania, where he was constable for many years. 3 Thomas, a farmer, married Matilda Patterson, of Perryopolis. 4 Isabel, married John Taylor and died one year later. 5 Sarah, died young. 6 Allen, died young. 7 Elizabeth, of previous mention, wife of Moses Porter. Children of Mr and Mrs Porter: 1 Emily, married J Phinley Patton a farmer, both deceased. 2 Ann H, married William Gaddis, a farmer of North Union township. 3 Susan, married J N Miller a veteran of the civil war and later editor of the Sac Sun, Sac City Iowa, where they now reside. Children: Blaine married Miller Stadt, of Wichita, Kansas. Cuyler, a printer of Wichita. 4 Irwin R, married Joanna Ryner and they now reside on their own farm in Montgomery county, Missouri. 5 Ewing B of whom further mention. 6 Louisa B, resides in Uniontown with her brother, Ewing B. 7 Aaron T, married Lydia Hackney and resides on his farm near Emporia, Kansas. 8 Sarah Ellen, died unmarried.

(III) Ewing B, fifth child of Moses and Elizabeth (Murphy) Porter, was born in Dunbar township, Fayette county, Pennsylvania, February 26, 1850. He was educated in the public school, grew to manhood on the home farm, continuing his residence there until 1881 He then became manager of mine farms for the H C Frick Coke Company, and during the next ten years had charge of forty farms owned by the company In 1895 he became manager of the "Tower Hill' farm of seven hundred and twenty-five acres, continuing there eleven years until 1906, when the farm, rich in coal deposits, was sold, the price paid was twelve hundred dollars per acre Since 1907 Mr Porter has resided in Uniontown in charge of real estate He is a confirmed third party Prohibitionist and for thirty years has voted according to his principles, being one of the oldest voters of that party in the county He was for many years a member of the East Liberty congregation of the Cumberland Presbyterian church, and a faithful, devoted Christian He married, June 11, 1878, Susan Phillips born in North Union township in 1855, daughter of William S and Eliza (Swan) Phillips, both born in that township Child Kennedy F , born March 3, 1879, a farmer of North Union township, he married Ella Dawson and has children William and Robert Ewing The family home of the Porters is at No 78 Mine street, Uniontown

THOMAS The Welsh family of Thomas date far into antiquity While the descendants of Sir Rhys Thomas, E G , who lived during the reigns of Henry VII and VIII of England, claim for him an extant pedigree going back to Adam, the historical line probably begins with Urien Rheged, a British prince, living, according to the best authorities, in the sixth century after Christ While the links connecting him with Sir Rhys may not all be of equal certainty, it is the uniform judgment of all writers upon Welsh history and geneology that Sir Rhys descended from Urien, son of Cynvarch, a prince of the North Britons in Cambria, on the borders of Strath Clyde, who driven out by the invasion of the Saxons in the Sixth century, took refuge in Wales Urien, his eldest son, is called by the Welsh bards brave as a lion, gentle as a maid ' The Welsh name him one of "the three bulls of conflict " and ' the three pillars of battle " His greatest feat was the expul-

sion of the Irish-Scots from the territory between the Tawe and Savery rivers From these early warriors there is an unbroken line of descent to Sir Rhys ap (son of) Thomas, born 1449 He is the acknowledged head of the Thomas family of Wales, from whom the numerous family of Thomas descend He was brave, wise and politic, uniting the branches of his own family and acquiring unbounded popularity He maintained an establishment in keeping with his great wealth, having nineteen hundred tenants bound by their leases to attend him at the shortest call, and, that brief warning having been given, he could bring into the field five thousand disciplined men mounted and armed He took sides with the Earl of Richmond and fought by his side at the battle of Bosworth Field, August 22, 1485 In fact he broke the attack of King Richard on the Earl's person, and is said to have slain King Richard at the moment of his reaching the Earl Be as it may, the new king was very grateful to Sir Rhys, and loaded him with gifts and honors He rose to high power and continued a glorious career as a soldier He was appointed to the highest honors in Wales and there reigned in royal style He is buried in the Church of Grey Friars at Caermarthen, where a most remarkable monument indicates the spot H s will was probated July 5, 1525 He left six sons and three daughters From these sons of Sir Rhys Thomas came the families of Wales bearing the name, and from these latterday families of Wales the many families in the United States These families are found all over the country, Pennsylvania having a family of ironmasters of the name known as the Thomas family of Catasauqua Maryland and Virginia have many families of the name tracing to Wales and some of them to Glamorganshire The family is strong in England and a branch settled in Italy, where they are known as Tomasi The family is also prominent in Wales and exceedingly numerous

The family herein traced from the first to come to the United States, were natives of North Wales the father of John Thomas being a mining superintendent in charge of lead mines until his early death at the age of forty years He lived and died in Wales a man of strong character and a devout member of the established Church of England He had two sons, William Henry and John William Henry emigrated to the United States but after his arrival at Philadelphia all trace of him was lost and nothing can be told of him His younger brother John, who came in 1847, made a diligent search for his brother, but without success It is probable that he went west and founded one of the Thomas families of that section The Thomas brothers of Fayette county, Pennsylvania are of pure Welsh blood father and mother both being born one in North, the other in South Wales The Beynon family also has an ancient Welsh history but theirs is a history of life on the seas Both branches of the family furnished a soldier to the great conflict between the states, while from the same Welsh ancestry came General ('Pap') Thomas the hero of Chickamauga and of many other hard-fought battles The record of this branch of the family in the United States, although covering but two generations, is most creditable and proves that the traits of courage and ambition did not die with the ancient hero, Sir Rhys ap Thomas The American history begins with John, father of John L, William H and Robert O Thomas, of Fayette county, of whose lives a detailed account follows

(I) John Thomas was born in North Wales, January 21, 1821 died in Allegheny county, Pennsylvania January 6, 1906 He attended school in his boyhood but his father died when he was young and the lad early became a wage earner He worked first in the lead mines, but later went to South Wales, where he worked at coal mining becoming a skilled miner He there met his future wife, but they were not married until after coming to the United States In 1841 he emigrated to this country, settling in Pittsburgh, South Side, where he worked at his trade in the old Keeling mines near by He married in 1851 and moved to Coulter Allegheny county, then an inviting coal field convenient to the river He continued a miner all his life becoming mine overseer and having interests in coal mines in that district He prospered and was a highly respected, honorable citizen During the war between the states he enlisted in the Fifth Regiment, Pennsylvania Heavy Artillery, Company F and served over a year, seeing hard service in the Virginia campaign and on detached service in pursuit of Mosby

and his guerillas He was a member of the Methodist Episcopal church, and an active devoted Christian worker For twenty-five years he was superintendent of the Sunday school filling that office continuously during that period

He married, in Pittsburgh, South Side, in 1851 Elizabeth Beynon, born in South Wales in 1826, died in Allegheny county, Pennsylvania, September 7, 1875, daughter of William and Mary Jane Beynon both natives of South Wales Her father was of a Welsh seafaring family, some of them being in command of ships Children of William Beynon 1, William (2), emigrated to the United States and is now in the coal business in Allegheny county, Pennsylvania 2, Ann, married Robert Knox, in their native land but in 1870 came to the United States, settling in Pittsburgh They were then quite aged but being financially independent, came to visit with their children, who had preceded them many years Their children Jane, married and lived in Easton Pennsylvania, where her husband was killed accidentally, she married (second) George Davis, a master roller in the steel mills at Pittsburgh, Thomas a steel roller of Pittsburgh, deceased, Agnes, married Rhinman Buck, a steel worker of Pittsburgh, William, Alice and May remained in Wales 3 Jane married John Morgan, in Wales, came to the United States, settling in Pittsburgh, where he engaged in the retail coal business, owning his own mine 4 Alice, married William Thomas, an iron worker of South Wales where both died, two of their children came to the United States John, an iron worker at Homestead and Alice who later returned to Wales 5, Elizabeth, who married John Thomas, of previous mention After her sister Jane and her husband, John Morgan, came to the United States in 1843, they sent back to Wales glowing accounts to their relatives In 1847 Elizabeth and her mother and uncle William Beynon sailed for the United States, coming on the same boat with John Thomas, who had known them in Wales The Beynons settled in Pittsburgh, where others of their family were living William Beynon, brother of Elizabeth enlisted in Company F Fifth Regiment, Pennsylvania Heavy Artillery, with his brother-in-law, John Thomas, and served during the entire war

Children of John and Elizabeth Thomas
1, Mary Jane born in Pittsburgh, South Side
died aged three years 2, John L, of whom
further 3, William Henry, of whom further
4, Robert O, of whom further 5, James B,
born June 10, 1862, lives at Coulter, Pennsylvania now located at McKeesport, Pennsylvania, cashier for Pittsburgh & Lake Erie
railroad, married Victoria Black, of Coulter,
6, Eliza Jane died aged three years

(II) John L, eldest son of John and Elizabeth (Beynon) Thomas, was born in Birmingham, now South Pittsburgh, Pennsylvania,
June 28, 1854 His parents moved to Coulter,
Pennsylvania, where the lad attended school
five months each winter until thirteen years
of age, then began working in the coal mines
with his father Later he took his brother
Robert O in with him and they worked together in the mines until John L became of
age He then saw that there were better opportunities for an ambitious man as mining
had become so systematized that all that was
wanted was a man to dig, no knowledge of
minerals or expert mining methods being required except in the few positions of fire and
mine boss He had always been fond of commercial arithmetic and well informed in that
branch so decided to enter commercial life
He continued in the mines until he found his
wished for opening with the Baltimore &
Ohio railroad under John L Vaughn station agent at Alpsville, Pennsylvania, who
taught him telegraphy After three months
he was promoted his younger brother, William H taking his former position at the
key John L continued with the Baltimore
& Ohio until June 1 1882, then resigned to
become assistant manager of the Youghiogheny & Ashtabula Coal Company at Guffy
Station, Pennsylvania, remaining there two
years He then resigned having been offered by Division Superintendent Yohe the
appointment of station agent for the Pittsburgh & Lake Erie railroad at Connellsville
West Side (New Haven) After one year
there he was transferred to the station at May-
ville Pennsylvania now called Adelaide, as
chief clerk in the scale office On November
1, 1889, he was appointed general agent for
the Connellsville coke region for the Pittsburgh & Lake Erie and located at Dickerson
Run, also acting as local weigh master for
coal, coke and freight He has held this posi-

tion continuously for nearly a quarter of a
century, and is one of the company's old,
faithful and most trusted employees He has
never regretted the ambition that drove him
from the mine to seek his fortune in the great
business world outside He has risen through
his own well directed energy, and by doing
well each duty that presented itself

He is a Republican in politics, but never
sought public office He became a member
of the Methodist Episcopal church of Connellsville in 1884, and has been a member of
the official board of that church and of the
church at Dawson ever since that date Has
been for several years financial secretary of
the Dawson church, his home being in Dawson, just across the Youghiogheny from his
office in Dickerson Run His method of
keeping the congregation informed as to the
condition of the church finances, and of their
own accounts, is accomplished by mailing
quarterly to each one a printed statement,
showing how every cent received has been
spent and of the condition of their individual
account This plan is worthy of adoption by
other churches as it has proved a valuable
one for the Dawson congregation He is a
member of the Iroquois (a fraternal order)

He married, March 20, 1879 Rebecca H
Shields, born at Greenock, Pennsylvania, September 10, 1859, daughter of Thomas and
Margaret (Walker) Shields, both born in
Paisley, Scotland coming to Pennsylvania
about the year 1856 Thomas Shields was a
coal miner, but became a mine owner and
operated his own plant His children 1,
John born in Scotland about 1850 now a retired coal operator residing in Pittsburgh,
East End, where he conducts a small store
for the sake of keeping his mind employed
He is unmarried 2, Janet, married in her
native land a Mr Welsh and died in 1879 3,
Margaret, married E F Cloman a grocer
of Greenock, Pennsylvania 4, James H, a
retired coal merchant of Pittsburgh East
End and Florida, where he maintains summer
and winter homes he married Abigail Ray
5, Rebecca H, married John L Thomas, of
previous mention 6, Isabella married Henry
Jones, whom she survives, a resident of Mc-
Keesport, Pennsylvania 7 Mary, married
Harry Walthour a railroad employe of Ver-
sailles, Pennsylvania 8 Walter, deceased,
leaving a widow and two sons, now of Mc-

Keesport 9, died in infancy 10, died in infancy The two brothers, James H and John Thomas, have both been conspicuous figures in the coal business in Pittsburgh, being wealthy, influential operators and dealers Children of John I and Rebecca H (Shields) Thomas 1, Mary Belle born October 11, 1880, married William M Shannon a locomotive engineer in the employ of the Pittsburgh & Lake Erie railroad, now residing at Beaver Falls, Pennsylvania child, Helen Rebecca 2 Sibyl M, born May 19, 1882 married Albert E Knight, a bill clerk at the Pittsburgh & Lake Erie scales office in Dawson, children Howard Ellsworth, Raymond Thomas, Fred Ruhl

(II) William Henry, second son of John and Elizabeth (Beynon) Thomas, was born at Birmingham, now Pittsburgh, South Side, August 8, 1856 His parents soon after moved to Coulter. Allegheny county when he attended the public school and at quite an early age began working in the coal mines, continuing for some years in various capacities, from mine boy to skilled miner He followed the example of his elder brother and prepared himself for a business career, learning telegraphy while yet employed in the mines In 1876, when his brother John L was promoted, leaving a vacancy in the Baltimore & Ohio telegraph office at Alpsville, William H was appointed to the vacant key much to the surprise of his brother who did not even know he was an operator, his preparatory study having been carried on quietly without display One year later he was sent to Broadford, Pennsylvania as clerk to the freight agent at that point, continuing in that position two years In 1879 he became station agent at Broadford to succeed F B Hamby, remaining until July 1883 In September of the latter year he entered the employ of the Pittsburgh & Lake Erie railroad receiving the appointment of yard master at Dickerson Run He was on the payroll of the company two weeks before the road was completed to Dickerson Run and ready to operate, therefore he was the first Pittsburgh & Lake Erie employee in the coke region of which Dickerson Run is the centre After six years as yard master he was made special agent for the company, continuing as such four years Then for six months connected with the superintendent's office at Pittsburgh He then

was appointed station agent for the company at New Haven (Connellsville, West Side), a position he now occupies most satisfactorily to his company and the traveling public He is an ardent Republican and active in party work He has served as councilman of New Haven and of Connellsville, was clerk of council, and one year was collector of taxes He is a member of the Methodist Episcopal church, as is also his wife He was made a Mason in 1881 in King Solomon's Lodge, Free and Accepted Masons, is a companion of Connellsville Chapter, Royal Arch Masons, and a Sir Knight of Uniontown Commandery, Knights Templar

He married, at Broad Ford, Pennsylvania, October, 1884 Ella Duke Brandhoover born at West Liberty Pennsylvania daughter of Henry and Mary (Storey) Brandhoover, now deceased Her father was a well-known hotel proprietor, having at different times conducted hotels in Pittsburgh, North Side Elizabeth and Broad Ford, Pennsylvania Both her parents were born in Westmoreland county, Pennsylvania, of German and English descent The family home, on West Main street, Connellsville, was purchased by the Western Maryland railroad in 1911, and a depot building now occupies the site Mr Thomas has secured lots in Greenwood Addition, West Side, and will there erect a modern house He has no children

(II) Robert O, third son of John and Elizabeth (Beynon) Thomas, was born at Coulter Allegheny county, Pennsylvania, June 10, 1860 He attended the public schools at Coulter and when little more than a boy began working in the coal mine with his elder brother, John L Thomas, first as driver, then as digger After his brother left the mine and learned telegraphy Robert O very quietly found means to also acquire the art He secured a position with the Baltimore & Ohio railroad as telegrapher, became an expert despatcher and continued at the key eight years In September, 1888, he resigned and became bookkeeper for the H C Frick Coke Company at their Adelaide plant In the spring of 1889 he was appointed superintendent of that plant continuing seven years, then was transferred to the Mount Pleasant branch having charge of Summit, Eagle and White Plants remaining two years He next was placed in management of the Calumet plant, which he completely rebuilt and managed for five years. In 1901 he resigned and located in the city of Connellsville, where he engaged in the coal and coke business, and so continues a successful man of business and substance. He is a Republican in politics, has served as school director in Connellsville; also was a candidate for nomination for assembly in 1910 on the Republican ticket. In religious faith he is a member of the Methodist Episcopal church, as is his wife. He is a member of the Masonic order, belonging to Connellsville Lodge, Free and Accepted Masons, and the Chapter, Royal Arch Masons.

He married, September 20, 1887, Jennie Coughanour, born in Connellsville December 7, 1863, daughter of Gilbert Lafayette and Rebecca (Norris) Coughanour, of Connellsville. Children of Robert O. Thomas: 1. John Joseph, born April 28. 1890, now engaged with the West Pennsylvania Engineering Corps. 2. Mary Margaret, born October 16, 1894. 3. William Fred, born September 8, 1896; all graduates of Connellsville high school. 4, Robert O., Jr., born February 23, 1903. 5, James Gilbert, December 8, 1906. The family home is at No. 401 East Green street, Connellsville, erected in 1908.

STILLWAGON   A pioneer of this family, who deserves more than a passing notice here in view of the fact that more than one thousand of his descendants are now residents of Connellsville and vicinity, was Peter Stillwagon, Sr., who was born in Germany and came to America about the year 1765. In 1775 he was married to Elizabeth Poole in the German Lutheran church of Philadelphia, Pennsylvania, and in July of the following year he enlisted in the patriot army as sergeant of a company commanded by Captain Holmes. He was also a member of the Fifth Pennsylvania Regiment. He took part in the battles of Colts Neck, Brandywine, Germantown, Trenton, Monmouth and Eatontown; he was captured by the British and confined in an old sugar house in New York for nearly two years. During his absence his home was plundered by British troops and his wife so mistreated that she applied to General Firman for relief, who gave her a home with the wife of Captain Huddy. Just before the

battle of Trenton a company of Tories, commanded by Captain David Smith, again visited the Stillwagon home, plundering it of its remaining valuables and burning it to the ground. Mrs. Stillwagon, hearing of their coming, took her two little children to an adjoining field and watched in anguish while the work of destruction was carried on. She then once more sought refuge in the camp with her husband. The commanding officer treated her kindly and allowed her to stay. She made herself useful by washing and baking for the soldiers and caring for the sick and wounded. At the battle of Monmouth she distinguished herself by her courage and carried ammunition for the artillery. By some she is believed to be the "Molly Pitcher" of historic fame. At the close of the war Peter Stillwagon received an honorable discharge and settled with his family at Deckertown, New Jersey.

Mr. Stillwagon was the father of thirteen children: 1, Daniel. 2, Hannah. 3, William, of whom further. 4, Sarah Ann; married Henry Nash, a Methodist minister, and moved to Tennessee. 5, Mary. 6, Catherine; married a Mr. Conklin, and died at the early age of twenty-two, leaving two children, Daniel and William. 7, Andrew. 8, Peter, Jr. 9, Susannah. 10, Josiah Decker, of whom further. 11, Andrew Poole, married Catherine Buttermore, and removed to the West. 12, Henry. 13, John, died without issue at Broad Ford, Pennsylvania. One of these daughters married Mr. Haven, an Englishman, and lived and died in Connellsville. Among her grandchildren were Mrs. Annie Robbins, deceased; Mrs. Eliza Newcomer, deceased; Mrs. Mary Enos and Mrs. Kate Kurtz. Another daughter married a Mr. Polk and removed to Tennessee.

In 1802 Mr. Stillwagon came to Connellsville, Pennsylvania, and established a home in the neighborhood of Peach and Water streets. The children at this time numbered but nine, four of them having died. By mere chance of fortune Captain David Smith, their old Tory enemy, also came to Connellsville after the war, living with his son, Asher Smith, on the corner of Cottage avenue and East Main street, and it is said upon good authority that some of the plunder of the Stillwagon home was afterward discovered there in an old chest. Peter Stillwagon, Sr., died in Connellsville in December, 1831 His wife Elizabeth, with a marvelous vitality, lived to be one hundred and fifteen years of age Even at that advanced age she was remarkably active and able to attend to many of her household duties One Monday afternoon she was left at home alone and her grandson on his return found the interior of the house on fire Securing help, he put out the flames as quickly as possible, but his grandmother was already dead It is believed that she was smoking a pipe and that sparks from this set her clothing on fire

(II) William, son of Peter and Elizabeth (Poole) Stillwagon, married Margaret Wilson, of Deckertown, and had eleven children Peter, of whom further, Joshua, Sophia, Eliza, married Stephen Robbins, Josiah Decker, married Elizabeth Ficher, Sarah, married Josiah Marietta, mother of a large Marietta family of Connellsville, Henry Nash, married Mary M Curry, he was a soldier in the Mexican war, and received an injury while building a bridge for the artillery before Vera Cruz from which he never fully recovered, Joseph, Mary, John, married Elizabeth Stouffer, William Wilson, married Maria M Rockwell William Stillwagon inherited much of the patriotic fire of his parents and was a veteran of the war of 1812

(III) Peter (2), eldest son of William and Margaret (Wilson) Stillwagon, married Margaret White and had issue

(IV) William P, son of Peter (2) and Margaret (White) Stillwagon, was born in Connellsville, Pennsylvania, in 1844 died October 4, 1893 He was educated in the public school, and in his early life was a contractor and coal operator, conducting the W P Stillwagon Coal Company, later Mr Marietta was admitted as a partner and the name was changed to the Marietta & Stillwagon Coal Company He also had interests in West Virginia coal lands He was a Democrat in politics and a man of influence He married Mary Gregg, born in Connellsville died there in the year 1908 daughter of George and Susan Gregg George Gregg, of Irish descent, was credited by his friends with being the real inventor of the armor-clad vessel which Ericsson later developed into the famous "Monitor' of civil war fame Children of William and Mary Stillwagon 1 Clair, died 1910, married Rose Hanlon 2, Blanche,

married (first) John Woodward (second), William Rice, of Connellsville 3 Anna, married Thomas Crush, of Pittsburgh 4, Larmer, of whom further 5, Edna, married Harry Griffin, of Glassport 6, Rose, married Thomas Maloney, of Pittsburgh 7, William P, now living in West Newton 8, Rockwell, now living in Connellsville 9, Ruth, now living in Connellsville

(V) Larmer, son of William P and Mary (Gregg) Stillwagon, was born in Connellsville, Pennsylvania, February 17, 1878 He was educated in the public school and on arriving at suitable age learned the trade of coremaker and molder, continuing four years with the Boyts Porter Company of Connellsville The succeeding four years he spent in the machine shops of the Baltimore & Ohio Railroad Company at Connellsville, then entered business life He is interested in West Virginia coal lands and is vice-president of the Connellsville Distillery Company In 1911 he began the manufacture of soft drinks, having bought the plant known as Deans Bottling Works, in Connellsville He there carries on every department of soft drink manufacture, including essences and syrups He is a Democrat in politics and a member of Connellsville city council His fraternal order is the Benevolent and Protective Order of Elks He married, in September, 1905, Lily Edwards, born in Connellsville, daughter of Rolla and Margaret Edwards Child Larmer, born January 15, 1908

(II) Josiah Decker Stillwagon, son of Peter Stillwagon (q v) came to Connellsville with his parents and nine of their children, four having died before their emigration from New Jersey The date of their coming is given as both 1815 and 1802, the former being in all probability the correct date He was a teamster on the "old pike," but later confined his teaming to Connellsville and vicinity He was a Democrat in politics and held several township and borough offices He married (first) in Connellsville Elizabeth Rowtruck, of German descent, who bore him 1, Elizabeth, married Samuel Catlin, of Ohio 2, Mary, married William Crossland Josiah D Stillwagon married (second) Elizabeth Coughenour, also of German parentage, children 3, Josiah Decker, whose sketch follows 4, Noah, died a young man 5, Theresa, died in 1861 or 1862, married a Mr Hutchinson 6, John Wesley, of whom further

(III) John Wesley, youngest son of Josiah Decker (1) and Elizabeth (Coughenour) Stillwagon, was born in Connellsville, Pennsylvania, April 2, 1833 He was educated in the public schools and on arriving at suitable age was apprenticed to the blacksmith's trade He became an expert ironworker and continued in Connellsville until he moved to Broad Ford, Fayette county, and established a smithy of his own in that village He continued there for forty years doing the greater part of the horseshoeing and ironwork for that section He also did all the smithwork for the Overholt Distilling Company, when they started in that neighborhood He purchased a small tract of ten acres when he retired from active work, and now resides there with his aged wife He joined the Independent Order of Odd Fellows July 4, 1863, and will soon celebrate his half century of membership in that order He also for many years belonged to the Knights Templar He is a Democrat in politics, and has served as school director He married, September 5, 1855, Elizabeth daughter of Henry (2) Strickler and granddaughter of Henry (1) Strickler, of Pennsylvania Dutch descent and an early settler in Fayette county Henry (2) Strickler was a farmer owning a good farm of two hundred and forty acres He married Susanna Sloanecker and reared a family of five daughters and two sons Children of John Wesley and Elizabeth Stillwagon 1, John Wesley (2) 2, Josiah Decker, now residing in Fayette county, married Margaret Oxley 3, Henry S, now living in Colorado 4, Frank, now living in Dawson, Pennsylvania, married Margaret Spaneyfelt 5 William died December 11, 1911, for twenty years a machinist with the Overholt Distilling Company, married Lily May Nicholson 6, Charles Newton, deceased 7, Walter S, of whom further 8, Mary Eva now living in Dawson Pennsylvania, married John Williams 9, Ernest, now living in Chicago, married Ollie Oxley

(IV) Walter S seventh son of John Wesley and Elizabeth (Strickler) Stillwagon was born at Broad Ford, Fayette county, Pennsylvania, July 1, 1869 He was educated in the public schools and worked with his father at the forge when young He then learned the machinist's trade, working under instruction at both Broad Ford and Connellsville, and later studied plumbing and gasfitting, following that trade five years in Connellsville Later he became a stationary engineer, and in 1889 entered the employ of the Overholt Distilling Company as machinist After being with that company some years he returned to Connellsville for a time, then again entered the employ of the Overholt Company as chief engineer, a position he now most capably fills He is a Democrat in politics and has served in several township offices His orders are the Knights of Malta and the Junior Order of American Mechanics Both Mr Stillwagon and his wife are members of the Presbyterian church

He married, in 1893, Minnie E Newman, born in Fayette county, daughter of George and Lydia Newman Children Wesley G, born December 23, 1892, Oliver, June 28, 1895, Bessie, August 28, 1897, Florence December 17, 1899, Lida, July 25, 1902, Ralph, April 4, 1907, Thomas, March 7, 1910

(III) Josiah Decker (2) Stillwagon, son of Josiah Decker (1) Stillwagon (q v), was born in Connellsville, Pennsylvania, April 8, 1828, died June 8, 1893 He was educated in the public schools, and was one of the prominent men of his day He became a hardware merchant of Connellsville, where he was in continuous business for thirty-three years He was a staunch Democrat and a leader of his party in Fayette county Among offices held were those of postmaster of Connellsville and clerk of the city council He was a Methodist, and for thirty-seven years superintendent of the Sunday school He married Elizabeth Freeman born in Connellsville 1828, died April 7 1874 Among their children was a son, James Emmet, of whom further

(IV) James Emmet, son of Josiah Decker (2) Stillwagon, was born in Connellsville, September 30, 1848, died August 9, 1901 He was educated in the public schools and early in life learned the painter's trade, but never followed it as an occupation He was a strong Democrat, and during President Cleveland's first administration was appointed assistant collector of internal revenue for the Pittsburgh district In 1890 he was appointed superintendent of the Connellsville Water Company a position he held until his death He was elected chief burgess of Connellsville, serving at different times five terms in that office

His untimely death occurred August 9, 1901, being a passenger on the ill-fated Baltimore & Ohio train of Atlantic City excursionists that was wrecked with great loss of life at Confluence, Pennsylvania, on that date Like all the Stillwagons, he was a Methodist He married Mary Elizabeth Walker, born in Connellsville November 26, 1845, who survives him, a resident of Connellsville She is the daughter of David L Walker, born July 23, 1819 died February 2, 1881, probably a descendant of the Walkers of Virginia He was a planing mill operator and general contractor He was a Democrat, and in 1887 was elected sheriff of Fayette county He married Sarah Zarley, born September 8, 1821

Children of James Emmet Stillwagon Olive May, married Herbert Horn, of Pittsburgh, Josiah David, of whom further, John Clark, now of Connellsville, Ernest Lee a machinist, George Freeman, Minnie Hazel, married Joseph C Herwick

(V) Josiah David, son of James Emmet Stillwagon, was born in Connellsville, Pennsylvania, October 7, 1871 He was educated in the public school and began business life as a clerk in his grandfather Stillwagon's hardware store, remaining three years He was then for two years in the employ of the Union Supply Company, then two years with Jamison & Fogg He then secured an appointment as "gauger" in the United States Internal Revenue service, Twenty-third Pennsylvania district, continuing eight years He then succeeded his father as superintendent of the Connellsville Water Works, holding that position until his resignation in 1910

He is now in the employ of the Fayette County Gas Company He is a Democrat in politics, and a member of the Methodist Episcopal church, and of King Solomon's Lodge, Free and Accepted Masons

He married, in February 1893, Mattie (Stillwagon) Stillwagon, a distant relative, daughter of George W and Jane Elizabeth Stillwagon George W Stillwagon was born November 15, 1826, died April 13, 1890 His wife, Jane E, was born June 21, 1829 Children of Josiah D Stillwagon Hazel, born November 11, 1893, Josiah David (2), September 30 1909

HENRY

The Henrys of Fayette county, Pennsylvania, descend from the Henrys of Westmoreland county Pennsylvania who spring from a Scotch-Irish progenitor, Edward Henry He was born in County Down, Ireland, came to the American colonies and settled in eastern Pennsylvania prior to the revolution Several Henrys served in the Colonial army and one Edward Henry who was no doubt the ancestor After the close of the war and late in his own remarkable life, he moved to Westmoreland county, Pennsylvania, where he died many years later, at the great age of one hundred and five years He left issue, including a son Edward

(II) Edward (2) son of Edward (1) Henry, was born in Westmoreland county, Pennsylvania He founded a homestead farm near Madison, where he was engaged in agriculture all his life He married Mary McCauley, and left issue, including sons Adam and Edward The latter born on the homestead farm in 1809 married Susan Coughenour, from the Shenandoah valley, Virginia His son Dr Hugh Henry was a noted physician

(III) Adam son of Edward (2) Henry, was born on the nomestead farm near Madison, Westmoreland county, Pennsylvania, about 1810 He grew up a farmer, and after leaving the paternal roof continued the same business in the township of Penn Later in life he sold his farm in Westmoreland county and came to Fayette, purchasing property in Lower Tyrone Here he lived until death He was a strong Democrat active in public affairs, and a devoted member of the Methodist Episcopal church He married Elsie, daughter of William Campbell a shoemaker, who in his early life was possessed of considerable wealth of which he was robbed Children 1 James Campbell, of whom further 2 Nancy, married John Bryan and lived in Westmoreland county 3 Emery married Elizabeth McLaughlin, is now a retired farmer of Scottdale, he married (second) Mis D Fretz 4, Margaret married George Hagerman of Fayette county 5 Rev Joseph, married California Stone, he is a minister of the Methodist Episcopal church and yet survives 6, Mary, married Samuel Cottom, a farmer of Westmoreland county 7, Jennie, resides in Scottdale, unmarried

(IV) James Campbell, eldest child of Adam Henry, was born in 1830, died May 5, 1893 He attended the district schools in the winter months, and remained on the farm with his father until he was sixteen years of age He then went to Columbus, Ohio, and entered a medical school, there taking a full course and graduating He then returned to Westmoreland county, and for two years studied and practiced under Dr John Stephenson He then settled at Tyrone Mills, Pennsylvania, practicing his profession there four years In 1868 he located at Dawson, Fayette county, where he continued in active practice until his death a quarter of a century later He was a skillful practitioner, and had the confidence of his community He had a very large practice and worked very hard to meet the demands made upon him He was a member of the Presbyterian church, and a very strong Democrat He married, December 29 1863 Mary L Cunningham born in Westmoreland county, daughter of Barnett and Mary (Chain) Cunningham, the latter born in Columbiana county, Ohio, the former in Westmoreland county After their marriage in Ohio they came to Westmoreland county, where Mr Cunningham bought a farm of one hundred and thirty acres which he kept well stocked with choice live stock, both horses and cattle They were both members of the Presbyterian church he was an elder for twenty-one years He was a son of Joseph and Keziah (Norris) born in Fayette county, Lower Tyrone township The Cunninghams were of Scotch-Irish descent Mary Chain was a daughter of Hugh and Margery (Cunningham) Chain, both born in Columbiana county, Ohio, where they both died The Chains were early settlers in Ohio Children of Barnett and Mary (Chain) Cunningham   1, Joseph Chain, married Mary McCrary   he was a farmer and saw mill owner   2, Keziah Jane, married Daniel Fritz (both deceased)   they owned a fine farm in Westmoreland county, near Scottdale   3 Margery Eliza, married William Hearst a farmer in Westmoreland county East Huntington township both deceased   4 Hugh, died aged four years   5 Cyrus died aged two years   6, Mary (of previous mention) wife of James Campbell Henry   7, Amos, married Mary Nelson, whom he survives, a retired farmer of Washington county   8, Anna married John Hardy, who survived him and

married (second) Martin Wurtz, of Greensburg, who survives her since February 11, 1912   9, Barnett, married Julia Hardy, who survives her, a farmer   10 Thomas Jefferson, was a farmer of Iowa   he married ——— Mason   11, William Wilson married Maria Shellenberger, who survives him on their Westmoreland farm   Children of Dr James Campbell and Mary (Cunningham) Henry. 1, Winnie Ione, born February 5, 1865 died May 5, 1868   2, Mary Estelle, born March 11, 1868   married H Clymer Painter, of Greensburg, a hardware merchant   3 Lettie F   born October 11, 1870, died October, 1890   4, Robb Dejarmon, of whom further 5, Carl Cunningham, born April 15 1875, married Letta Kater (or Cator) and resides at Belle Vernon, Pennsylvania, a locomotive engineer   6, Zola, born April 5, 1880   7, James Roy, born November 28, 1883, Zola and James R reside with their mother in Dawson

(V) Robb Dejarmon, fourth child and eldest son of Dr James Campbell Henry, was born in Dawson Fayette county, Pennsylvania, December 19, 1873 He attended the public schools, and while yet a boy worked in the local printing office At the age of fifteen years he began working for the Baltimore & Ohio Railroad Company as assistant station agent, learned telegraphy, and remained at the Dawson station five years Since leaving railroad employ he has been engaged with the Cochran interests, first as bookkeeper The First National Bank of Dawson was organized in 1891, and in 1896 Mr Henry came to the bank as bookkeeper, in 1905 he was made assistant cashier, and in 1910 was promoted to cashier He is a Democrat in politics and has served on the school board for twelve years He is a director of the Tri-State Candy Company of Connellsville, Pennsylvania, a member of James Cochran Lodge No 614 Free and Accepted Masons, Connellsville Chapter, No 283, Royal Arch Masons, Uniontown Commandery, Knights Templar Uniontown Lodge of Perfection, and Pittsburgh Consistory, Ancient Accepted Scottish Rite in which he has attained the thirty-second degree He also belongs to the Royal Arcanum and the Grand Fraternity In religious faith he is a Presbyterian, belonging to the Dawson congregation

He married June 30, 1908, Grace E Shroyer, born in Dawson, November, 1883, daughter of Charles O and Katherine (Walker) Shroyer Charles O Shroyer is the present recorder of wills of Fayette county Children Katherine Louise, born July 4, 1909, Mary Margaret, March 18, 1911

HENRY The Henrys of this sketch descend from George Henry, a Scotch-Irishman, who came from Philadelphia to the town of Bedford, Bedford county, Pennsylvania, and became a prominent land owner He married Elizabeth Havener, of German descent Sons Dr James Alexander, George, daughters Elizabeth Rebecca, May, Jane and Sarah

(III) William, grandson of George Henry, was born in Bedford county, Pennsylvania, where he grew to manhood Later, in company with his brother John he moved to Somerset county, where they became prosperous farmers each owning one thousand acres in Middle Creek township where they were the first settlers He was a Democrat, and both he and wife Mary were Lutherans Children 1, Joshua, now a farmer of Sabetha, Kansas 2, Harmon, died at Sabetha, Kansas 3 Rose Ann married Solomon Garrett, of Somerset county 4, A daughter, deceased 5 Marion of whom further

(IV) Marion, son of William Henry, was born in Middle Creek township, Somerset county, Pennsylvania, January 30 1840 He attended the public schools, and has always been devoted to agriculture and kindred pursuits He inherited a portion of the original homestead and added to it by purchase until he owned three hundred acres of the original tract He cultivated this successfully, but in latter years disposed of all but one hundred and thirty-four acres, on which he now resides He is a Democrat and a member of the Lutheran church He married Mary Fosbrink, born in the town of Holland Germany, December 25 1836 daughter of Garrett and Mary (Riggrear) Fosbrink, both born in Germany emigrated to the United States in 1836, when their daughter Mary was three months of age Garrett Fosbrink was a farmer and owned his own farm in Somerset county Pennsylvania His wife Mary was a daughter of Henry Riggrear born in Germany In 1836, with his wife Elizabeth, and Garrett

Fosbrink, with his family (a party of ten) he left Hanover, Germany, and after a voyage of fifty-four days landed at Baltimore, Maryland Here they purchased wagons and teams, coming in that way to Somerset county over the National Road, then being built He joined his four sons, Henry, Fred, Barney and Dietrich, who had preceded him to Somerset county, prospered, and sent home the money that brought their parents over The whole colony of Fosbrinks and Riggrears settled nearby in Somerset county, where Henry Riggrear died aged ninety-four years, his wife, Elizabeth, at the age of eighty-one years Garrett Fosbrink, born 1799, died 1856, Mary Riggrear, his wife, born 1816, died 1886 After they had been in Somerset county about ten years, Garrett bought a farm of one hundred and twenty-seven acres in Upper Turkeyfoot township, where he died, as did his wife Previous to coming to the United States he had served six years in the German army They were members of the Lutheran church Their children 1, Henry, born in Germany, a farmer of Donegal, Westmoreland county Pennsylvania, where he died 2 Mary (of previous mention), wife of Marion Henry 3 Garrett (2), a veteran of the civil war, serving in Company G, One Hundred and Sixteenth Regiment, Pennsylvania Volunteer Infantry died and is buried at Myersdale Pennsylvania 4 Harmon, a veteran of the civil war, serving in the Sixteenth Regiment Pennsylvania Volunteer Cavalry died in Fayette county, a gardener 5, John Three other children died in infancy Children of Henry and Elizabeth Riggrear, 1, Elizabeth married Henry Coleman, of Somerset county, where both died 2 Frederick, married Anna Struckoff, both died in Somerset county 3 Henry married Elizabeth Seifringhouse 4, Barney, married Katherine Leary 5 Mary (of previous mention) wife of Garrett Fosbrink 6 Elizabeth married John Lucas 7 Katherine married Diedrich Uphouse 8 John, married Mary Shope 9 Dietrich, died in Kansas the only one of the family to leave Somerset county, he married Sarah Shawley 10 Anna married Henry Hofelt Garrett Fosbrink had three sisters 1 Katherine married Henry Nearman a blacksmith of Baltimore, Maryland 2, Mary married Joseph Newmeyer, a silversmith of Baltimore 3 Elizabeth, married Henry Fogarding, a gardener of Baltimore

Children of Marion and Mary Henry 1, John, a blacksmith and farmer, near the home farm in Upper Turkeyfoot, Somerset county 2, Joshua, a carpenter of Scottdale, Pennsylvania 3, Hiram, a farmer of Upper Turkeyfoot, Somerset county 4, James, a stonemason, living at the old home in Somerset county 5, Jacob C, of whom further 6, Mary, married Harrison Mognet, a farmer of Upper Turkeyfoot, Somerset county 7, Kate, married Charles Henningkemp a stationary engineer, living at Centreville, Pennsylvania

(V) Jacob C, fifth and youngest son of Marion and Mary (Fosbrink) Henry, was born in Middle Creek township, Somerset county, Pennsylvania November 23, 1870 He was educated in the public school nearby, and after a boyhood spent on the farm began learning the carpenter's trade under the instruction of his brother-in-law, Harrison Mognet His hours of labor were from sunrise to sunset, his wages fourteen dollars monthly He was a natural mechanical genius, and so soon mastered the details of building construction that after one year with Mr Mognet he began contracting and employed his former boss to work for him He continued contracting in the neighborhood of his home for five years, then in 1900 moved to Connellsville, Pennsylvania, where for six months he worked as journeyman for John Curry & Son He then began contracting and building on his own account, continuing successfully until 1907 In that year he was appointed superintendent and general manager of the South Connellsville Lumber Company, conducting a general building and retail lumber business The present officers of the company are Michael Hurley, president, Jacob C Henry secretary and superintendent, \ H Soisson, treasurer The company's offices and yards are in South Connellsville Mr Henry is a member of the Methodist Episcopal church, as are his wife and children In politics he is an independent

He married September 26, 1900, Mary Susan Younkin, born in Somerset county, Pennsylvania daughter of Michael Younkin, born September 25, 1875 at Kingwood, Somerset county and Maria McClintock Clawson Younkin, born in Upper Turkeyfoot, Somer-

set county, in 1835 Michael was a son of Frederick and Sarah Younkin, both born in Somerset county, he is a farmer Michael Younkin when fourteen years of age was taken to Terre Haute, Indiana, by his father, but when the latter returned Michael did not accompany him He lived in Kankakee, Chicago, Iowa, Indian Territory and in Arkansas He was a stage driver for many years in Iowa and Indian Territory, and passed an adventuresome life in the west and southwest for thirty-five years A yearning for family and home then overtook him, and he returned to Somerset county He found his father alive, and was persuaded by the latter to again settle down in his native county and become a farmer He died in Somerset county in 1873 He married a widow Mrs Anna Maria (McClintock) Clawson, and had Fred, now an attorney of Connellsville, and Mary Susan, wife of Jacob C Henry Their children Leona Fern, born February 21, 1902, Ray, February 27, 1904, Glen, March 8, 1908 The family home is at No 359 East Main street, which Mr Henry purchased in 1901

SHERRARD This family (often spelled Sherred and Shearer), is said to have been of Huguenot ancestry, fleeing from the north of France to Scotland, settling in the Lowlands Later a colony composed largely of Sherrards settled in County Derry, Ireland, in and around the village of Newton Limavady There William Sherrard was born in 1720, owned a farm by freehold right and carried on linen weaving or manufacturing, employing many hands At the age of thirty years he married Margaret Johnson, a lady of fortune and good family He died in 1771, a wealthy man, leaving the freehold of one hundred and thirty-three acres to his sons John and James, and to each of his daughters two hundred guineas William Sherrard had a brother Hugh their father being the emigrant from Scotland in 1710 Hugh Sherrard settled after his marriage near Coleraine across the Bann Water His son, also Hugh Sherrard emigrated to America in 1770 settling on Miller's Run in Washington county, Pennsylvania This Hugh had several sons, one of whom, William was killed by the Indians on Raccoon creek, near Florence It was at the house of this Hugh Sherrard that John Sherrard (of further mention) stopped on his return from the disastrous Crawford expedition Children of William Sherraid, all born at Newton Limavady, County Derry, Ireland 1 John, of whom further 2 Elizabeth, born 1752, married a McConkey, emigrated to America, all trace lost 3 Margaret, born 1755, married and came to the United States 4 James, born 1757, by his father's will he remained in possession of the freehold lease In 1785 he visited the United States with his mother, but both returned to Ireland and nothing more is known of either of them Tradition says James came again to the United States after the Irish rebellion of 1798 5, Mary, born 1760, married and came to the United States

(II) John, eldest son of William and Margaret (Johnson) Sherrard, founder of this branch of the family in the United States, was born in County Derry, Ireland, in 1750 died April 22, 1809, buried at Smithfield Ohio He grew to manhood at Newton Limavady (located about ten miles from Londonderry), and at the age of twenty-two years lost his father Even before this he had been anxious to come to America, and in 1772 he sold his share in the freehold estate (left him by his father) to his mother for two hundred guineas With this and some other money he sailed for America in August, 1772, in the ship 'Wolf," arriving at Philadelphia late in the following October He remained there all winter, and in the spring of 1773 started to seek his fortunes west of the mountains He settled in Fayette county, near Laurel Hill, making his home with George Paull He purchased in 1773 a tract of 3,000 acres, but was superseded in its ownership by Thomas Gist, who held a king's patent In March, 1774, he joined a party going to Kentucky, remaining until June, when the Indians drove them out Returning to Fayette county, he selected a new farm of fourteen hundred acres, going to Virginia to take out his claim He then settled for a time in Lancaster county, Pennsylvania, continuing until the spring of 1775, when he enlisted in a volunteer company of militia called the "Flying Camp of Pennsylvania" After serving actively for a year or more he returned to Lancaster county, where he was made a naturalized citizen, June 13 1777, and remained until 1778, then again re-

turned to Fayette county, taking up his residence again with the family of George Paull, who was buried the day of his return from Lancaster county He remained there about four years, and in the fall of 1782 joined many of his neighbors in the ill-fated "Crawford expedition,' but escaped uninjured, returning safely to Fayette county stopping for a day with his relative, Hugh Sherrard, in Washington county In 1784 he married Mary Cathcart and settled on a cleared farm of sixty acres three miles southwest of Uniontown, on the Connellsville road He continued in Fayette county until 1794 when he sold everything he owned in Pennsylvania, intending to move to Kentucky, but his land there had been taken by others, and for the next three years he was employed at Mason's Furnace, then worked on farms in Fayette county, later moving to Ohio, where he died He was a hard working man but a poor business manager and had a hard time earning sufficient to support his family He died in Smithfield, Ohio, and is buried in the old Quaker graveyard there His wife Mary Cathcart, whom he married May 5, 1784 died October 27, 1833 and is buried at Laurel Hill, Fayette county, she was born near Enniskellen, County Fermanagh Ireland, September 28, 1751, daughter of Alexander and Ann (Gamble) Cathcart, who were married March 17, 1743

Children of John and Mary Sherrard 1 William Johnson, born May, 1785, died November 7, 1820, unmarried 2 David Alexander C, born September 2, 1786, married (first) March 14, 1816, Elizabeth Irvine born 1786, died June 9, 1855 (second) February '15, 1858, Martha Watt, died June 2, 1880 3 John James, born October 28, 1787, married Sarah Harrah 4 Robert Andrew, born May 4, 1789 married (first) May Kithcart, (second) Jane Hindman 5 Ann, born December 6, 1790, died in infancy 6 Thomas Guthridge, of whom further

(III) Thomas Guthridge, youngest child of John and Mary (Cathcart) Sherrard, was born March 18 1793 in Fayette county, Pennsylvania near Mason's Furnace He grew up on a farm, and when a young man made several trips south, freighting flour down the Ohio and Mississippi with very indifferent success On one of these trips, in company with his oldest brother William, the latter was drowned Later Thomas G moved to Green Creek, Sandusky county, Ohio, where he entered three tracts of eighty acres each including a good mill site He moved there May 3, 1823, and on March 23, 1824, his body was found in the Sandusky There were circumstances that looked like foul play, but the verdict of the coroner's jury was "accidental drowning ' He was an industrious, energetic business man, living in friendly intercourse with all his neighbors, being affable, courteous and kind to all He married, September 20, 1820, his second cousin, Rebecca, daughter of Alexander and Mary (Gamble) Conn, who survived him and married (second) in 1834, Samuel Junk of Fayette county, Pennsylvania, she died October 13, 1873 Children 1 William Johnson, born October 22, 1822, died without issue, April 22, 1872 2 Thomas Guthridge (2) of whom further

(IV) Thomas Guthridge (2), posthumous son of Thomas Guthridge and Rebecca (Conn) Sherrard, was born October 17, 1824, in Dunbar township, Fayette county, Pennsylvania, died March 22, 1874 After her husband's tragic death his mother returned from Ohio to Fayette county where about ten years later she married Samuel Junk The boy continued at home, his stepfather's assistant, until he was of legal age, then began working as a farm hand for his uncle, David A C Sherrard He then married, and after another year with Mr Sherrard moved to a fifty-acre farm located where the village of Juniata now stands This property belonged to his wife, having been received from her father To this Mr Sherrard added seventy-two acres, and also purchased one hundred and fifty acres of David A C Sherrard He became very prosperous and prominent in public affairs He was a man of large athletic proportions and of genial, companionable nature, having many friends

He was a strong Democrat and served as county director of the poor and school director He was a member of the Presbyterian church having been brought up in that faith by his mother who was a devoted Christian They both belonged to the Laurel Hill congregation

He married, March 9, 1850, Mary Ann Henderson, born in Dunbar township, Fayette county March 8, 1830, died December 23, 1910, daughter of Stuart and Anna (Hunt)

Henderson Stuart Henderson emigrated to the United States when a young man, settling first at Erie, Pennsylvania, and then coming to Dunbar township, Fayette county, where he became a most successful farmer and land owner, holding title to between three and four hundred acres of land on ' the Summit," He and his family were members of the Presbyterian church at Laurel Hill Children 1 Nancy, born November 1, 1807, married John Work, a farmer of Dunbar township 2 Thomas, born November 30, 1809, a farmer of Knox county, Illinois, where he died 3 Stuart, born March 11, 1812, died in Knox county, Illinois, where he was a farmer 4 Isaac, born June 23, 1814, a farmer of Menallen township 5 Alexander, born November 22, 1816, a farmer of Redstone township, married Phoebe Cratt 6 Harvey, born March 11, 1818, a farmer of Franklin township 7 David, born January 26, 1822, a farmer of Knox county 8 Jacob, born March 23, 1824, a farmer of Dunbar township 9, Dr Joseph, born October 19, 1826, practiced medicine in Illinois, moved to Fayette county, where he died 10 Mary Ann (of previous mention)

Children of Thomas Guthridge (2) and Mary Ann (Henderson) Sherrard 1 David Cathcart born March 12, 1851, died at Los Angeles, California November 25, 1881, married Mary Jane Hankins, who died April 12, 1885 Children Rachel, Thomas G and Mary Ann, all deceased 2 Alexander Conn, or whom further 3 Rebecca Ann, born January 15, 1855, died December 11, 1870 4 Nancy, born January 23 1857, married October 10, 1878, Peter Preston Humbert, a farmer near Little Washington Pennsylvania, children Thomas S Martha Jane, Joseph A and Elsie May 5 William Johnson born January 7, 1860, a farmer of Franklin township 6 Martha Jane born June 26 1862 died December 28, 1883 married, May 4, 1882 Guthrie W Curry a farmer and banker of Aurora, Nebraska 7 Jacob Henderson, born January 17 1863 died July 17 1883

(V) Alexander Conn son of Thomas Guthridge and Mary Ann (Henderson) Sherrard, was born in Dunbar township, Fayette county, Pennsylvania, December 28, 1852, in a log cabin now the site of the Juniata mine shaft His early life was passed on his father's farm, and his education was received at the Sandy

A. C. Sherrard

Hollow schoolhouse in Dunbar township Upon the death of his father the care of the home fell upon his shoulders, and for two years he cultivated the farm, moving in 1877 to Dunbar township and purchasing one hundred and thirty-seven acres of rich fertile land On this in 1892 he built a beautiful country home and lives there at the present time In politics he is a Democrat, and is one of the leading business men of the county Besides owning valuable coal lands in Greene and Washington counties, he holds directorships on the boards of the following institutions Washington Coal and Coke Company, Washington Run Railroad Company, First National Bank of Dawson, Union National Bank of West Side, Connellsville, Cochran Coal Company of Morgantown, West Virginia, and is also director and president of the Little Kanawha Coal Company of West Virginia

He married August 26, 1875, Elizabeth (Cooper) Pollock, born February 15, 1853, died January 26, 1906, daughter of Rev David H and Elizabeth (McMullan) Pollock Her father was pastor of the United Presbyterian church of Laurel Hill for many years Children of Alexander Conn Sherrard 1 Margaret Jane, born January 28, 1877 graduated from Washington Seminary, June, 1899, lives at home 2 Thomas Guthrie born May 23, 1879 died March 10, 1882 3 David Pollock, born December 23, 1880, died April 22, 1881 4 Mary Ann, born January 27, 1882, graduated from Washington Female Seminary, June 1903, lives at home 5 John Core, bookkeeper in First National Bank Dawson, Pa, born April 24, 1883, married Helen Quay, and lives in Connellsville 6 William Johnson, born January 10, 1885, graduated from Carnegie Technical Institute, June 1912 7 James Espey (q v) 8 Jacob Henderson, born July 21, 1889, graduated from Washington and Jefferson College, June 1912 9 Elizabeth Pollock, born April 8, 1891, attends Washington Female Seminary lives at home 10 Nancy Eleanor born April 6 1895, also a student at Washington Female Seminary, lives at home

(VI) James Espey, son of Alexander Conn and Elizabeth (Pollock) Sherrard, was born in Dunbar township, Fayette county, Pennsylvania, February 21, 1887 His early years were spent in Dunbar township attending public school in that township and making a

hand on his father's farm in vacation seasons He also attended the graded school at Vanderbilt, Pennsylvania, and graduated in 1906 from the Dunbar township high school For one year he attended Washington and Jefferson Academy, then took a course of four years at Washington and Jefferson College, graduating in 1911 with the degree of Bachelor of Arts Since graduation Mr Sherrard has been reading law at Uniontown, in the office of Reppert Sturgis & Morrow, and expects to be admitted to the bar—perhaps in the fall of the present year (1912) He is a Democrat He and his wife attend the First Presbyterian Church at Uniontown

He married June 21, 1911, Pauline Levaughn, daughter of Ralph and Margaret Jane (Stevens) Watson, who was born at Washington, Pennsylvania, October 1, 1891 Her parents are living at Washington, where her father is superintendent of an oil company, he was born at Olean New York, in 1868, and his wife is about one year his junior Children of Ralph and Margaret Jane (Stevens) Watson Pauline Levaughn, married James Epsey Sherrard, Mildred Stevens, Dorothy Deane Child of James Espey and Pauline Levaughn (Watson) Sherrard Jane Elizabeth, born June 18, 1912

McCLINTOCK This family is of that sturdy North of Ireland stock, a blending of Scotch and Irish blood that, transplanted to America in the eighteenth century, produced a race of hardy pioneers that, particularly in Western Pennsylvania, has brought fame and much material good to the commonwealth The ancestor of this family was John McClintock, who settled in Cumberland county, Pennsylvania, prior to the revolution, and was a soldier of that war His name is found on the payroll of Captain John Nelson's company, April 9 to June, 1781, Cumberland county militia The gun he carried is yet preserved in the family He may be the John who married Mary daughter of John Williamson, born in Dublin, Ireland came to Pennsylvania in 1730, settling at Chester, where he married Mary Davidson, who came from Derry, Ireland She died, aged ninety years John McClintock married Mary Williamson before 1771 and died in Somerset county, Pennsylvania

(II) John (2), son of John (1) McClintock, the Cumberland county farmer and soldier and Somerset county hunter and trapper, was born about 1800 in Cumberland county, settled in Somerset county, Pennsylvania, where he was engaged in farming He married —— Silbaugh, of German parents, who came to Pennsylvania before the revolution, settling later in Somerset county, where the wife of John (2) was born, they had William, Robert S, of whom further, Jane, Harriet, Esther and Cassie Of these Cassie and Jane are yet living (1912)

(III) Robert S, son of John (2) McClintock, was born in Somerset county, Pennsylvania, 1840 He grew up familiar with horses and farm labor, and after his marriage went to the state of Iowa, where he remained several years In Iowa he was a stage coach driver, making long drives between the Mississippi and Missouri rivers with mail and passengers When railroads were built through Iowa the reign of the stage coach was ended, and the hardy, picturesque drivers were compelled to seek other employment Mr McClintock returned to Pennsylvania and purchased a farm in Westmoreland county, where he died June 5, 1907 He carried on a teaming business in connection with his farm for many years prior to his death He was a strong Democrat, and held many local and county offices—constable, county supervisor, etc He enlisted in the Union army, but disability caused his early retirement from military life Both Robert and his wife were members of the Methodist Episcopal church He was of a genial, generous nature, and had many warm friends He married Charlotte Burgess, born in Somerset county, 1836, died 1888, daughter of William Burgess, a blacksmith near Listenburg (now Dumas), born in England and came to Pennsylvania when a boy He married and had six children William, Thomas, Nancy, Charlotte, Hylie and Owen, all deceased Children of Robert S McClintock William, Cynthia, Charles S, Mary, Elizabeth Milton H and Robert E, of whom further, Florence, Duella

(IV) Milton Howard, sixth child of Robert S McClintock, was born in Westmoreland county, Pennsylvania, September 26, 1868 He was educated in the public schools and after completing his studies began working in a printing office, where he learned type-setting, and worked for five years as a compositor on different papers in Pittsburgh and until 1888 In that year, September 22, he entered the employ of the Baltimore & Ohio railroad as brakeman and flagman, and in 1891 was promoted to be freight conductor, a position he now holds He owns a good farm in Lafayette county, six miles from Connellsville Since September, 1888, he has made that town his residence He is a Socialist in political faith and a supporter of the Methodist Episcopal church He married, May 21, 1890, Mary Ada McCoy, born July 27, 1869, in Connellsville, daughter of James and Margaret McCoy, and granddaughter of Matthew and Martha McCoy Matthew was born in Scotland, a cooper by trade, came early to the United States, where he married Martha Harr James McCoy was born in Fayette county, in March, 1838 He was a cooper by trade and served in the civil war as a private in a Pennsylvania regiment of heavy artillery, he died January, 1906 Martha, his wife, was born 1838 and survives him

Children of Milton Howard McClintock: 1 Lillian Gertrude, born May 10, 1892 2 Ruth Charlotte, September 18, 1895 3 Howard Ray, May 28, 1898 4 Edgar Melvin, December 15, 1901 5 Sarah Leona, August 16, 1903 6 Margaret Kathryn, November 29, 1904 7 Ernest Merle, April 9, 1905 8 Mary Elizabeth December 19, 1911

(IV) Robert E, seventh child of Robert S McClintock, was born in Fayette county, Pennsylvania, January 10, 1879 He was educated in the public schools of Belle Vernon and at West Newton, Pennsylvania, and although reared a farmer entered the employ of the Baltimore & Ohio railroad in 1899, beginning as a brakeman and working his way upward until in 1902 he was promoted a conductor, a position he now holds He is a Democrat and a member of the Methodist Episcopal church His wife is a Baptist He holds membership in the Order of Railway Conductors and has served the order officially

He married, August 18 1904, Sadie A Malone born in West Newton, Pennsylvania, daughter of John W and Mary A Malone; her father was born in Westmoreland county, her mother in Greene county, Pennsylvania

Children of Robert E McClintock 1 William Emmett, born May 23, 1906 2 Walter Clyde, February 21, 1908 3 Raymond Franklin, August 7, 1910 4 Calvin Haremcame, June 16, 1912

THEAKSTON

The Theakstons of this sketch descend from John Theakston, born in England He had sons, Robert of whom further, Philip, John, William H, of whom further They came to Washington county, Pennsylvania at an early date, becoming prosperous farmers of that county

(II) Robert, son of John Theakston, was a farmer of Washington county, Pennsylvania, and a member of the Wesleyan Methodist Episcopal church He died in July, 1865 He married Emily Ramage, who died in April, 1865 Children Selby, William Lyle, of whom further, Samuel Lewis, deceased, Andrew, deceased, Emma, Lucius, deceased, Minerva M L, Robert, deceased

(III) William Lyle, son of Robert and Emily (Ramage) Theakston, was born in Washington county, Pennsylvania, July 8, 1851 He was educated in the public schools and had spent his life engaged in farming and in the livery business He now resides in West Brownsville, Pennsylvania, a Republican and a member of the Methodist Episcopal church He married Lenora Herrington, born in 1849, daughter of George Herrington, of Greene county, Pennsylvania, and his wife, Christina (Williams) Herrington, both of whom died in Brownsville, Pennsylvania Children of William L Theakston Frederick, born 1873, living at Speers, Washington county, Carl, born 1876, died 1906, Harry A, of whom further, Minnie, born 1882, married Homer Wolford, child George

(IV) Harry Adelbert, youngest son of William Lyle and Lenora (Herrington) Theakston, was born in West Brownsville Washington county, Pennsylvania, June 20, 1879 He was educated in the public schools and grew to manhood in his native town He worked at various employments during his earlier years, including seven years in the Hotel Aubrey and two years in Westmoreland county, Pennsylvania In 1907 he became proprietor of the Atwood Hotel in West Brownsville, which he still conducts He is a Republican in politics and a member

of Brownsville Lodge, No 1356 Fraternal Order of Eagles

He married, December 27, 1900, Emma Voss, born in Germany in 1876, daughter of Frederick Voss, who came from Germany to Washington county in 1884, and now resides in Uniontown, Pennsylvania Children William Carl, born December 21, 1902, David Voss, December 19, 1908

(II) William H Theakston, grandfather of the present generation, and son of John Theakston (q v), came to the United States with his brothers, Robert, Philip and John, all settling in Washington county, Pennsylvania, where they ever afterward lived William H Theakston was a prosperous farmer, a Republican and a member of the Methodist Episcopal church His wife, Eliza (Bowen) Theakston, was a native of West Virginia

(III) Oliver J, son of William H and Eliza (Bowen) Theakston, was born in Washington county, Pennsylvania, died in East Bethlehem township, that county, in 1879 He was educated in the public schools, finishing his education at the Pennsylvania State Normal School at California He was engaged for a number of years as a teacher in the public schools, later engaging in mercantile life, establishing in Fredericktown, where he was a well-known prosperous merchant until his retirement in 1876 to his father's farm, where he resided until his death He married Nellie, daughter of William Boyd, she died in 1876

(IV) Frank B, only child of Oliver J and Nellie (Boyd) Theakston, was born in Fredericktown, Washington county, Pennsylvania, March 8, 1876 He was an infant when his mother died and but three years old when his remaining parent died and left him to the care of relatives, Townsend H Theakston and an aunt, Mary F Theakston, who cared for him during his early years He was educated in the public school at Westland, Pennsylvania and for one year attended Washington and Jefferson College, but resigned a college in favor of a business career He entered the employ of Erasmus Kaiser, the leading jeweler of Brownsville, Pennsylvania, and under his capable direction learned the jeweler's trade in all its detail He remained with Mr Kaiser twelve years, until 1904 On the 15th of October that year he began business for himself in the same line in the Iron

Bridge Building in Brownsville, where he is now well established and prosperous He is a Republican in politics and a member of the Presbyterian church He is prominent in the Masonic Order, belonging to Brownsville Lodge, No 60, Free and Accepted Masons, Brownsville Chapter, No 164, Royal Arch Masons, St Omer Commandery, No 7, Knights Templar, Syria Temple, Nobles of the Mystic Shrine, of Pittsburgh In Scottish Rite Masonry he has attained the fourteenth degree in Uniontown Lodge of Perfection

He married, September 23, 1908, Jean B, daughter of John and Elizabeth Crasser, of Lonaconing, Maryland

This family, of Scotch-Irish an-
BLACK cestry and marked with the
strong qualities of that sturdy race, is one of the very oldest in Pennsylvania, dating as far back as 1730 Their its members have from the beginning been prominent in legal, political and business life and leaders in every department they entered

(I) The first of the family in Somerset county was James Black, of Scotch-Irish ancestry, who is mentioned as an early settler in Stony Creek township in 1770, he having emigrated from Adams county, Pennsylvania His farm was seven miles east of the present village of Somerset, close to the old Bedford Pike He was a tanner, and had a tanyard in Stony Creek, mentioned as early as 1798 His house was the first voting place in the entire county He married Jane McDonough from near his old home along Marsh Creek, Adams county, and left issue

(II) Henry, son of James Black, was born February 25, 1783, in Stony Creek township, Somerset county Pennsylvania, and died in 1842 He owned a large farm which he personally conducted, although he was at the same time busied with large affairs He was a man of liberal education, served for twenty years as an associate judge of the county, and was a member of congress at the time of his death He married, and among his children were sons James (of whom further), and Jeremiah S Black The latter named became one of the most distinguished men of his day He was born January 10, 1810, he rose to a first place at the Pennsylvania bar, was a president judge at the age of thirty-two, he argued many important constitutional cases

before the supreme court of the nation He was attorney-general in the cabinet of President Buchanan, and was nominated to the supreme court bench, but this was on the eve of the outbreak of the civil war, and he was not confirmed on account of the absence of the southern senators who had withdrawn to ' go with their states " He died August 19, 1882, leaving a widow, Mrs Mary (Forward) Black and four children, a son, Chauncey Forward Black, was a leading Democratic statesman, and lieutenant-governor of Pennsylvania

(III) James, son of Judge Henry Black, and brother of Judge Jeremiah S Black, was born in Stony Creek township, Somerset county, Pennsylvania, between 1812 and 1815 and died at Somerfield, Pennsylvania, at an advanced age His boyhood home was a fine farm on the Bedford Pike, near or a part of the original Black family homestead, settled by his grandfather He later moved to Somerfield, Addison township, Somerset county, where he owned and operated a pottery and tannery He married Catherine Johnson, and they both died in Somerfield They were members of the Methodist Episcopal church, and they reared their family in their own faith Children

1 George J, born June 6, 1842, died November 20, 1902 He succeeded to his father's business, and for several years conducted the pottery and large general store at Somerfield Later he moved to Myersdale and established a pottery for the manufacture of stoneware, and also kept a general store He was prominent in public life, in 1887 he was elected county treasurer and served three years, in 1896 he was elected associate judge and served five years, and at the time of his death he was collector of taxes for Myersdale borough He was a Republican in politics and a member of the Methodist Episcopal church He married, in 1851, Sarah Margaret Bradfield, of Loudon county, Virginia Children Alverda G, married George Hopwood, of Uniontown, Mary, married Robert H Koontz, Annie, Susan L, married William T Hoblitzel, of Myersdale, James Hamilton, a successful business man of Myersdale, Frank B, one of the great coal operators of his section, J Milton, a coal operator of Somerset

2 Albert Gallatin, the only living member

of the family, now a retired merchant of Confluence, Pennsylvania, founder of the business now conducted by his sons under the firm name of A G Black s Sons Company He married Esther Brownfield, who belonged to one of the most prominent families of Fayette county, and in fact, of the state Albert Gallatin Black is the father of thirteen children, eight of whom are still living Named in the order of their birth they are as follows Virgil Maro Black, who married Mollie Pullin, and is a member of the firm of A G Black s Sons Co , Fannie Black, who married T J Schaffer, of Pittsburgh, but now resides at the home of her father, Martha Jane Black, died unmarried, Catherine Black, died in infancy, Thomas William Black, married Lillian Dorothea Flannigan, and is a member of the firm of A G Black s Sons Co , Maud Eliza Black, died in infancy, John Franklin Black, married Mary Reynolds, and is in business in Dickerson Run, Pennsylvania, Maggie Long Black, died in infancy, James Harry Black, married May Friend, and is a business man of Friendsville, Maryland, Charles Egbert Black, a member of the firm of A G Black s Sons Co , and whose wife was —— James, of Connellsville, Pennsylvania, Susan Etta Black, married A B Kurtz jeweler, of Connellsville, Pennsylvania, Edgar Brownfield Black married Hattie Farmer, Uniontown, Pennsylvania, is also a member of the firm at Confluence, Pennsylvania, Mary Clyde Black, died quite young

3 Newton H , of whom further

4 James S , one of the earliest bankers of Myersdale, member for many years of the banking firm of Philson, Black & Co , now the Citizens' National Bank of Myersdale, married a daughter of Samuel Philson

5 Sarah Ellen, married James S Hook, of Cumberland, Maryland, they later located at Somerfield, Pennsylvania

6 Charlotte, married (first) James Hamilton, (second) Charles H Rush, a merchant of Uniontown

7-8 Daughters died in their teens

(IV) Newton H , third son of James and Catherine (Johnson) Black, was born in Somerfield, Somerset county, Pennsylvania, and died November 5, 1895 He was educated in the public schools and was for a time employed in his father's store Later he went to Uniontown as a clerk for his brother-in-law, C H Rush He later established himself in business, having first a store in Hopwood and later in Uniontown, also conducting coal operations, having a mine near the former place He was a successful business man and was held in high esteem He was a Republican in politics and a member of the Methodist Episcopal Church He married Alcinda F Hopwood, born in Hopwood, Fayette county, daughter of Gaddis and Nancy (Costolo) Hopwood, the father a native of Fayette county, the mother of Laurel Iron Works, Monongalia county, West Virginia , her father was a local preacher of the M E church and a deeply religious man, died in the prime of life in 1849 his widow long surviving him and dying in 1904, aged eighty-three years Children Alcinda F , married Newton H Black, Caroline, burned to death at the age of five years, William Costolo, died of fever contracted in the army in the civil war, Nannie G , married Dr T F Farmer, who survives her a resident of Confluence, Pennsylvania

Children of Newton H Black 1 Herbert G , born October 26, 1871, died August 23, 1895, unmarried 2 George A , an orange grower of the Salt River Valley, residing in Phoenix, Arizona, married Ada Beam, of McKeesport, Pennsylvania 3 William Costolo, of whom further 4 Paul, born July 31, 1877, died October 10, 1895 5 Nannie H , born August 25, 1880, died September 6, 1895 6 Alfred H , died December 5, 1883, aged one year

(V) William Costolo, third son of Newton H and Alcinda (Hopwood) Black, was born in Hopwood, Fayette county, Pennsylvania, April 1, 1875 He was five years old when his father removed his mercantile business to Uniontown where the lad was educated in the public schools, later taking a business course at Redstone Academy In 1891, at the age of sixteen, he entered the employ of the Baltimore & Ohio railway as clerk in the Uniontown ticket and freight office, holding that position five years On July 31, 1896, at the age of twenty-one, he was promoted to the important position of ticket and freight agent in the same office, and in which he remained for three years resigning in 1899 to enter the employ of Armour & Company as assistant cashier at their Uniontown branch and later was appointed cashier in their office at Grafton, West Virginia   During the years 1901-02 he was payroll clerk at Plant No 2, Continental Coke Company, during its construction and early operation   On February 11, 1902, he was appointed teller of the Citizens' Title and Trust Company at Uniontown, and the following year was elected assistant secretary and treasurer, a position he has acceptably filled to the present time   He is also president of the Huntington Bank Book Company of Huntington, Pennsylvania, and treasurer of the Waltersburg Coke Company, operating a one hundred and fifty oven plant at Waltersburg   He is a Republican in politics, and has served this city as school director for two terms, is a member of Fayette Lodge, No 228, F and A M, Union Chapter, No 165, R A M, Uniontown Commandery, No 49, Knights Templar, Caldwell Consistory, Bloomsburg, Pennsylvania, Ancient Accepted Scottish Rite, thirty-second degree, and of Syria Temple, A A O N M S, Pittsburgh

Mr Black married, December 1, 1903, Anna G Burnham, born at Connellsville, Pennsylvania, daughter of John H and Laura S Burnham, her father is a machinist, formerly of Pittsburgh, later of Connellsville, now residing in Uniontown, Pennsylvania   Children John Newton, born October, 1905, died same year, William Costolo, born December 2, 1906, Herbert Hopgood, July 7, 1911   The family home is at No 240 East Fayette street, Uniontown

SMITH   There are many families bearing the name Smith to be found in Fayette county and Georges township   Every nation has contributed to the group for does not the name come from "The Smith that forgeth by the fire?"   And as every nation had a smith, so with the adoption of surnames, every nation had a Smith

The town of Smithfield is named in honor of Barnabas Smith, who laid it out June 13, 1799, on land obtained from the father-in-law, Jonathan Reese   Although the Brownfields owned all the land around the village, it has been named Smithfield from the first   Barnabas Smith married Elizabeth Reese and became the head of a large family of descendants

(I) Squire Solomon Smith was a well-to-do farmer of Georges township, and an active and ardent Democrat   He held the office of justice of the peace several years, and was known locally as Squire Smith   He also served as a school director and was a man of strong, upright character   He married (second) Mary Hayden, born in Georges township, daughter of John, son of William Hayden, who came from the east to Georges township in 1781   The village of Haydentown was laid out by John Hayden in 1790 on his own land, patented in 1787   Children of "Squire" Solomon Smith two by a first wife   Jonathan, married Hannah Riffle and lived in West Virginia, Margaret married Jacob Johnson, a farmer of German township, Fayette county, Elizabeth married Jacob Hayden, Albert H, of whom further, Keziah, married Lucien Leech, of Smithfield, Mary Louise, married Albert Johnson, a farmer, near Bethelboro, Fayette county, Pennsylvania

(II) Albert H, only son of 'Squire" Solomon Smith by his second wife, Mary (Hayden) Smith, was born in Georges township, Fayette county, Pennsylvania, August 12, 1843, died September 12, 1909   He was well educated in the public schools, and grew to youthful manhood on the home farm   At the age of seventeen years he began teaching in the public schools, continuing for thirty terms   During this long period he taught in many schools, establishing a reputation for marked ability as an instructor   In 1890 he retired from pedagogy and entered the employ of the H C Frick Coke Company as bookkeeper   He was employed by different plants owned by the company, finally being located at the Davidson's works near Connellsville, where he continued until his death   He was highly regarded in his community, being a man of more than ordinary attainment intellectually and of high moral character   He was a Democrat in politics and was the candidate of his party for county superintendent of schools in one campaign, failing, however of an election, the whole party ticket being defeated at that election

He married February 29, 1865, Mary Ellen, daughter of Moses and Louisa (Bailey) Nixon   Moses Nixon was a farmer of Fayette county, owning a farm in Georges township that later was sold to the Oliphant

Furnace Company, their plant being erected thereon He died in 1859 Louisa Bailey was a daughter of Eli and Perry (Gregg) Bailey, a Quaker family, formerly of Greene county, Pennsylvania, later of Georges township, Fayette county, where they owned a large farm Children of Moses and Louisa Nixon 1 William, married Mary Means and lives in the state of Montana 2 Frances, married Azell Freeman and resides at Mount Pleasant, Henry county, Iowa 3 Perry Louise, deceased, married William Dawson and lived in German township, Fayette county 4, Amanda, married Charles Freeman and resides in Denver, Colorado 5, Presley, deceased, married Carrie Presley and removed to Mount Pleasant, Iowa 6 Emily, married Jacob Painshaw and resides in Mount Pleasant, Iowa 7 Moses Taylor, a farmer of Georges township, married Fanny Collins 8 Mary Ellen, married Albert H Smith, of previous mention She survives her husband and resides with her son, Daniel Ray Smith, in Connellsville 9 Samuel Gregg, a farmer of South Union township, Fayette county, married Anna Williams 10 Anna Virginia, married Thomas Ringman, a farmer near Mount Pleasant 11 Victorine, married William Lawhead, of Uniontown, Pennsylvania 12 Died in infancy 13 Died in infancy 14 Died in infancy 15 Died in infancy Children of Albert H and Mary Ellen Smith 1 Walter Scott, born November 29, 1868, now of Owego New York 2 C Sheldon, born June 29, 1870, now residing in McKeesport, Pennsylvania 3 Samuel W, born January 30 1874 now of Uniontown, Pennsylvania 4 Bessie May, born August 20, 1879, resides in Mount Sterling, Pennsylvania 5 Ida Victorine, born January 23 1881, died May, 1881 6 Daniel Ray, of whom further mention 7 Albert Presley, born November 22, 1893

(III) Daniel Ray, sixth child of Albert H and Mary Ellen (Nixon) Smith, was born at Highhouse, near Uniontown, Pennsylvania, July 10, 1885 He was educated in the public schools of the different towns in which his parents resided during his boyhood, completing his studies in the Connellsville schools After arriving at a suitable age he began learning the plumber's trade, serving his apprenticeship under F T Evans, with whom he remained seven years Having now the expert knowledge and experience necessary, he located in Dawson, Pennsylvania, and began business for himself He shortly afterward returned to Connellsville, where on May 15, 1910, he established in business at No 313 West Main street, conducting a general plumbing business and dealing in gas fitting and plumbing supplies, becoming well known and building up a good business He is a Democrat, but independent in local politics He belongs to the Christian church He is unmarried The family home is at No 406 Highland avenue, where he resides with his widowed mother

STONE This family name is one found in every part of the United States, and is one particularly honored Congressmen, senators and governors are frequent in the list of noted men of the name, while literature, journalism and the professions have gained added lustre from their achievements

This record deals with a West Virginia-Pennsylvania branch although the principal character was born in the state of Missouri Western Pennsylvania has furnished the world with startling instances of the rapid development of men from depths of comparative obscurity to heights of dazzling altitude, but conditions of exceptional opportunity and special privilege added largely to their undoubted ability In the career herein traced conditions exceptionally unfavorable had to be overcome and success literally forced from unwilling fortune How well a crippled boy has fought the battle of life gained the victory and reached an honorable position at little over forty years of age is a story worth the telling

(I) Henry Stone, the first of the line here under consideration was a native of Germany, from whence he emigrated to this country in young manhood, locating in Loudon county, Virginia, where he engaged in agriculture After remaining there a few years he removed to Monongalia county, West Virginia, and there he also engaged in farming, added to which he did considerable teaming in the early days of the National Pike His death occurred on his farm of forty acres, located near Maidsville which he owned and tilled He married Margaret Murphy Children Joseph served in the war of 1812, John,

served in the war of 1812, Jacob, served in
the war of 1812 George, Henry, James, of
whom further, Sarah Polly

(II) James, son of Henry and Margaret
(Murphy) Stone, was born near Maidsville
on the old Stone farm in 1806 died in 1872
He was educated in the common schools of
the neighborhood, and later learned the trade
of carpenter, which he followed in connection
with farming continuing thus throughout the
active years of his life He was a Democrat
in politics He married Jane Childs a native
of Fayette county, Pennsylvania, daughter of
Abram Childs who lived near the White
Rocks Children of Mr and Mrs Stone
Sarah married Joseph Parker Joseph married Margaret Parker, John, unmarried, who
was last heard of in Iowa in 1872 Emanuel,
married Jane Humphrey Solon, of whom further Theodore married Julia Wade

(III) Solon, son of James and Jane (Childs)
Stone, was born at Maidsville West Virginia,
September 13, 1841 He grew to manhood
in his native state and followed farming
When the war between the states called for
every man to show his colors, he enlisted in
the Union army, June 7, 1861 as a private of
Company A Sixth Regiment West Virginia
Cavalry at Morgantown, West Virginia He
served his three years' term of enlistment and
was honorably discharged at Wheeling August 13, 1864 He re-enlisted at New Bright-
ton, Pennsylvania, September 28, 1864, in
Company K, Fiftieth Regiment, Pennsylvania
Volunteer Infantry, to serve "during the war"
He was honorably discharged and mustered
out at Harrisburg, Pennsylvania June 9 1865,
the war being over He was engaged during
his first engagement in many battles and
skirmishes, including the battles of McDowell,
Franklin, Cross Keys Cedar Mountain Bull
Run (first and second) Hedgeville Rocky
Gap, Mill Point, Droop Mountain, and rode
in the noted "Salem Raid" During his second enlistment he fought at Hatchers Run
Petersburg Virginia, Fort Steadman and at
the battles just preceding Lee's surrender
His service was long and arduous, serving in
both branches cavalry and infantry

He resided at various times in the states
of West Virginia Pennsylvania and Missouri,
and after the war he removed to Iowa where
he engaged in farming Later he moved to
Missouri where he engaged in railroad con-

struction He returned to West Virginia in
1873 and was engaged in farming there until
1879, when he removed to the Connellsville
coke region and was employed as manager
and in different capacities in the coke and coal
fields since that time He is a member of
the Church of Christ (Scientist), and in political faith is a Republican

Mr Stone married, at Bald Hill Greene
county, Pennsylvania, January 31, 1866, Zana
Magdelena Dean, born at Maidsville, West
Virginia, June 17, 1847, eldest daughter of
Samuel Dean, born at Maidsville, a farmer
all his life, a Democrat, and a member of the
Methodist church, he married, at Smithfield,
Pennsylvania, in 1843, Elizabeth Dusenbe ry
Children of Mr and Mrs Dean Sam M,
Katherine, Mary L and Zana M Isaac Dean,
father of Samuel Dean, married Zana Lazelle daughter of William and ——— (Car-
hart) Lazelle Isaac Dean was a son of John
Wilson Dean Elizabeth (Dusenberry) Dean
was a daughter of Samuel and Dorothy
(Breakiron) Dusenberry, the latter a daughter
of Frederick and ——— (Carr) Breakiron.
Samuel Dusenberry was a son of John Dusen-
berry, who married Sarah Carhart This ancestry carries to the earliest colonial days and
includes English and French progenitors
Children of Mr and Mrs Stone Frantz Sie-
gel born December 7 1866, Oliver Perry,
July 14 1868 William Arthur of whom further James Francis September 13, 1872,
Elizabeth Jane, March 12, 1875 Zana Mary,
September 13, 1877, Clyde Victor, May 10,
1880, Ella May, May 31, 1882, Sarah Love,
December 4 1884 Euphemia, January 15,
1886 Samuel Mack May 22 1889, Minnie
Ann, July 28 1891

(IV) William Arthur son of Solon and
Zana M (Dean) Stone, was born in Carroll
county, Missouri July 17, 1870 He attended
the public schools of Hopwood, Fayette
county, Pennsylvania but being one of the
eldest of a family of twelve, he was compelled to seek employment at an early
age He was but ten years of age when he
began work in the coke yard at McClure
Station Westmoreland county Pennsylvania
He followed coke burning and mining until
he attained the age of seventeen years, then
began working in a saw mill where he had
the great misfortune to lose his left leg This
was a most serious handicap for the young

man, as his education at that time was exceedingly limited. But the loss of his leg, or the lack of education did not mean that there was no future for one so ambitious, and stouthearted. As soon as he had recovered from his accident he began attending school in Hopwood, under the instruction of Nixon Canan, who took a deep interest in the boy, and whose kindly interest Mr Stone has never forgotten. Later he took a special course of three months under the direction of Miss Hannah Jeffries, whose aid was of greatest value. Lack of means now compelled him to quit school and again become a wage earner. In his crippled condition few occupations were available, and as the one offering the best inducements he chose subscription book selling. The book he gave his principal effort to sell was the "Golden Censor," whose contents he committed to memory. He sold a great many copies of this and other works of a general nature. When delivering he seized the opportunity to become familiar with their contents, and many nights were passed in this way, not for the sake of reading, but to add to his store of knowledge. This course of reading was most beneficial and strengthened his mental equipment as nothing else within his means could. He became known as a successful salesman, and his services were secured by the Union Publishing Company of Chicago to appoint and manage agents. He accumulated a few hundred dollars, which he invested in a grocery business and lost. He then became an itinerant vendor of specialties, spending five years in street selling in the different cities of the United States. He again accumulated some capital and located at Hopwood, Pennsylvania and again engaged in storekeeping. To this he added timber speculation. He prospered, and became financially interested in the People's Bank of Fayette County at Uniontown afterward merged with the Citizens' Title & Trust Company of that city, of which he is vice-president. Mr Stone has other business interests of importance, being heavily interested in the mining and manufacturing of coke. Starting most humbly and meeting with the most unfriendly fortune at the outset of his career, he has attained a position of trust and honor solely through his own indomitable will, his untiring industry and the courage to take up arms against adverse fortune. His career is an object lesson

in "grit" that will nerve others to greater effort. He is a member of the Methodist Protestant church, and a Republican in politics.

Mr Stone married, at Buffalo New York, August 16, 1893, Bertha May Ingles, born in Hopwood, Fayette county, Pennsylvania, November 12, 1876, daughter of Andrew Stewart and Charlotte Jane Ingles. Andrew S Ingles was a merchant, now a real estate dealer of Uniontown, Pennsylvania. Mrs Stone is an only child, a sister having died in infancy. Children of Mr and Mrs Stone. Wendell Allen, born April 22, 1894, Bertha Yolande, January 31, 1897. Nina Ethelyn, December 28, 1898, Arthur Elwood, April 7, 1901, Albert Thomas May 13 1903.

FUEHRER This family springs from one of the numerous Fuehrer families of Germany, descendants of Johan Michael Fuehrer, a royal landscape architect who died December 12, 1720 at Minden in Westphalia, Prussia, Germany. His descendants are found among the highest classes in Germany and include officials, army officers and many professional men. They are so numerous throughout the Empire that they have held annual reunions for several years, and have a regular organization. The secretary of the association is a minister of the gospel Rev A Fuehrer, residing at Klein Schmalkalden, Germany, who has a genealogical family tree of all those with whom he is in correspondence. Any of the family who will write him (in German) and can give him the place their father or grandfather was born can obtain a great deal of information. A small fee, less or about a dollar annually, will obtain permanent membership in the association.

(I) The Fayette county family descend from John Fuehrer born near Berlin, Germany, thirty miles distant in a small village, December 14, 1818 son of a German farmer who lived and died in his native land. John Fuehrer grew to manhood in Germany, where he received a good education and learned the tailor's trade. In 1836, being then aged eighteen years, he left home and fatherland coming to the United States, settling finally in Schuylkill county, Pennsylvania, at the town of Maqua where he opened a custom tailor shop. He combined with his business the teaching of instrumental music, principally the violin, and was an accomplished performer on many brass and stringed instruments He enlisted as a musician during the war between the states, being attached to the band of the Eleventh Pennsylvania Regiment, Colonel Coulter, of Greensburg, Pennsylvania, commanding He became leader of the band and served his whole term of enlistment with the Eleventh Regiment After becoming a naturalized citizen he became affiliated with the Democratic party, but cast his vote for Abraham Lincoln in 1860, and ever afterward acted with that party After he married he moved to Burkeville, Virginia, settling on a farm which he cultivated until his death He married, in Schuylkill county, Pennsylvania, Margaret Rhinemuller, born in Germany, in an adjoining province to her husband's birthplace, September 27, 1827, died in Virginia, daughter of Nicholas Rhinemuller, a small farmer of Germany, where he lived and died Children of John Fuehrer 1 George, of whom further 2 John W, a resident of Adelarde, Pennsylvania 3 Augusta, married Thomas Cann, of Richmond, Virginia, 4 Peter a farmer near McKeesport, Pennsylvania 5 Richard Coulter, a resident of Richmond, Virginia 6, Lewis, a resident of West Leisenring, Pennsylvania 7, Harry, a resident of McKeesport, Pennsylvania

(II) George, eldest son of John and Margaret Fuehrer, was born in Schuylkill county, Pennsylvania, July 17, 1848 He was educated in the public schools of Schuylkill and Carbon counties, attending until the age of thirteen years then became a breaker boy at the anthracite coal mines, attending school at night He next became mule boy, driving both in and outside the mines, then ran a mine pump for a time, which ended his mining career He obtained a position driving a delivery wagon then as clerk in a Luzerne county store He then formed a partnership with another young man, and pooling their savings had sufficient capital to start a small country store They prospered in business and added a saw mill to their operations In 1881 he came to Fayette county, Pennsylvania, and soon secured a good position as manager of a store at Leisenring, No 1, for the Connellsville Coke and Iron Company He continued in this position eight years then became yard boss at Morgan Sta-

tion for the H C Frick Coke Company He then resigned and came to Connellsville, where he began business as an insurance solicitor In a short time he established his own office and insurance agency, to which he added real estate dealings in 1896 He prospered, and still continues both lines, insurance and real estate, having built up a strong agency representing the best foreign and home companies His real estate operations as owner and dealer have been many and varied in character, but skillfully managed and profitable He has been located in the Title and Trust Company Building since 1900, having been the first tenant to occupy offices in that edifice He is a member of the German Lutheran church, and in politics a Republican He belongs to lodge and chapter of the Masonic order, the Knights of Pythias, Heptasophs and Royal Arcanum

He married, October 17, 1870, Margaret Johnson, born in Schuylkill county, Pennsylvania, daughter of Thomas and Mary Johnson, her father was born in England, her mother in Germany Children 1 Dora, born July 28, 1871, died March 31, 1873 2 Caroline (Caine), born May 10, 1873, married Charles Michael 3 Charles W, born March 19, now living in Youngwood, Pennsylvania 4 Anna Margaret, born May 30, 1877, married Clarence Marietta 5 George H, born November 6, 1879, married Mattie Pane, Child George (3), born July 28, 1905 6 Bessie May, born November 11, 1881, married Harry Kencaid, of Youngwood, Pennsylvania Children Paul, Helen, Donald 7 Mary Gertrude, born July 26, 1884, died December 31, 1886 8 Bertha Blaine, born June 13, 1892 9 Ralph Howard, born December 3, 1894

BARBER There are several distinct families of this name in the United States—the Barbour family of Virginia, which claims descent from John Barbour, one of the earliest Scotch poets and historians,—the New Jersey family, the Rhode Island family, and the Pennsylvania family A fifth family came to America from Scotland in which were three brothers,—James Barber, who settled in New York, David and John, who settled in Centre county, Pennsylvania Judge John Barber held the first court in Bellefonte, Pennsylvania, in

1800 The spelling of the name in the early records of Virginia was Barber Some time previous to the year 1688 Robert "Barbar," a cordwainer, came it is supposed from Yorkshire, England, and settled in the vicinity of Chester, Pennsylvania He was a member of the Society of Friends and soon became prominent in the Chester meeting The earliest record found of him is in the minutes of a Quarterly Meeting, held in Walter Faucit's house in Chester, on the sixth of the twelfth month, 1687 He was one of the committee appointed to supervise the building of the first meetinghouse in Chester and was taxable in 1693 He built a substantial brick house on the northeast corner of Edgmont avenue and Second street, adjoining the latter day Edgmont House in the city of Chester He married Hannah Ogden in 1690 and died without issue in the year 1709

(II) Robert (2), second son of John "Barbar,' of Yorkshire, England, came to Pennsylvania about 1699, to join his uncle Robert "Barbar," mentioned above, as an apprentice to the shoemaker's trade At the death of his uncle, Robert, he inherited a considerable portion of his estate and soon took his uncle's place in public and religious affairs He seems to have entered actively into politics at an early age He was a candidate for sheriff in 1719, was elected coroner of Chester county, October, 1721, elected member of the board of assessors of Chester county, 1721 It was while acting in this capacity that he discovered the land on the Susquehanna that he afterward purchased In 1726 he took up five hundred acres, where the city of Columbia now stands John Wright and Samuel Blunston left Chester and Darby for Conestoga in order to begin a settlement at Shawanah, upon the twelfth day of September, 1728 The tradition is that Robert Barber preceded them and selected the site They were all members of the Society of Friends He moved just below where Columbia now stands in 1728, taking a certificate from the Chester Meeting, but never delivered it to any meeting in Lancaster county He continued in politics, and at a council held in Philadelphia, May 8, 1829 was appointed the first sheriff of Lancaster He was for many years one of the foremost men of Lancaster county in all public enterprises, but gradually withdrew from public notice, devoting the latter

years of his life to the care and support of his large family He died at Columbia, Pennsylvania, September, 1749 aged fifty-seven years He was buried in the old "Brick Graveyard,' but being a Friend his grave was unmarked He married, May 17, 1718 Hannah, daughter of William Tidmarsh Children Eleanor, born 1718, John, 1720, Robert, of whom further, Thomas, born 1724, Nathaniel, 1727 Elizabeth, 1729, Mary, 1732, Sarah, James, Samuel

(III) Robert (3), son of Robert (2) and Hannah (Tidmarsh) Barber was born in Chester, Pennsylvania, October 10, 1722 He was the first lieutenant of the first company formed at Timicum Island, Pennsylvania, 1775, of which his brother, James, was captain, his brother, Samuel, second lieutenant, and his son, John, a private He took the oath of allegiance to the State of Pennsylvania, July 1, 1777 He received sixty-two acres of ground from his mother, October 14, 1761, and built the brick house still standing in Columbia He died there, October 4, 1782 He married, September 26, 1746, Sarah, born December 2, 1729, died October, 6, 1793, daughter of Samuel and Elizabeth (Wright) Taylor Children 1 Hannah, born September 17, 1747, died in infancy 2 Eleanor, born 1749 3 Hannah (2) died in infancy 4 Robert (4) of whom further 5 John, private in the Hemphill township company in 1775 fought at the battle of Long Island, 1776, died November 20, 1796, unmarried 6 Samuel, born 1756 died unmarried, 1801 7 Hannah (3), born 1758 died 1803 8 Thomas born 1760, died 1827 9 Elizabeth born 1762, died 1838 10 James, died in infancy 11 Sarah, born 1766, died unmarried, 1841 12 Susan, born 1769 died married, 1824 13 Rhoda, born, 1775, died unmarried, 1849

(IV) Robert (4), eldest son of Robert (3) and Sarah (Taylor) Barber, was born in Columbia Pennsylvania, August 28 1751 He took the oath of allegiance to Pennsylvania in Hemphill township, July 1, 1777 In company with his brother, Thomas, he moved to Northumberland county (now Union), Pennsylvania in 1785, in which year he was taxed on four horses, two cows and five hundred and eighty acres of land In 1791 he built a sawmill on his farm on White Spring Run In 1797 he built a grist mill on the same stream. In 1805 and 1806, in partnership with Solomon Heise of Columbia, he built on Penn's creek the largest flouring mill in his county, also a sawmill. He served as a magistrate several years, being commissioned justice of the peace for Buffalo township, November 29, 1792. He occupied the same farm fifty-six years. He was known far and near as "Squire" Barber, a man of strong character and great influence among the early settlers. He died in Union county, Pennsylvania, November 27, 1841. He married, September 23, 1775, Sarah, born in Columbia, Pennsylvania, May 19, 1754, died May 25, 1818, daughter of Dr. Samuel and Mary Bethel Boude. Children: 1. John, died in infancy. 2. Samuel, born 1777, died 1782. 3. Sarah Boude, born January 10, 1779, died November 2, 1860, married Benjamin Chambers. 4. Mary Boude, born November 13, 1780, died May 1, 1852, married Joseph Chambers. 5. Eleanor, died in infancy. 6. John. 7. Thomas A., born February 20, 1785, died April 5, 1872, married Elizabeth Clingan. 8. Samuel, born June 21, 1787, died March 24, 1846, married Mary Van Valzah. 9. Elizabeth, born February 28, 1789, died unmarried July 5, 1867. 10. Hannah, born March 9, 1791, died unmarried July 26, 1826. 11. Eleanor, born April 21, 1793, died unmarried August 25, 1872. 12. James Wright, born in Buffalo Valley, August 5, 1795, moved to Stephenson county, Illinois, in 1843, died May 30, 1877; married a relative, Susan Barber.

(V) This generation settled in Greene county, Pennsylvania. The records are incomplete and the name cannot be supplied, although it is believed to have been John. The settlement was in Cumberland township, prior to or about 1800. The Greene county settler married and left issue.

(VI) Henry Barber, son of the foregoing, was born in Cumberland township, Greene county, Pennsylvania, in 1810. He was reared a farmer and for several years was so engaged. He then learned the trade of coppersmith, which he followed in connection with farming. He married and had issue: John; Joseph; Robert; Andrew, of Dearthstown, Pennsylvania; Fannie, married Jarrett Cumley, lives in Masontown, Pennsylvania; Lavina; James M., of whom further.

(VII) James M., son of Henry Barber, was born in Greene county, Pennsylvania, October 3, 1841. He moved in 1863 to German township and from there to Luzerne township, Fayette county, where he now resides. He is master of two trades, that of stone mason and carpenter. He has a long and honorable record in the civil war, enlisting at its outbreak and serving through its entire four years. In politics he is a Democrat, and in religious faith Presbyterian. He married, 1862, Rebecca, born in Maryland, died April 26, 1837, daughter of Caleb Lancaster, a farmer of Maryland, who after his daughter's marriage moved to Fayette county. Children: 1. John W., of whom further. 2. Mary, born 1864, married Calvin Norman and lives in German township. 3. Henry, a farmer of Luzerne township. 4. Maria, married Andrew Griffith, and lives in Luzerne township. 5. Elizabeth, married Luther Hunter. 6. Ettie, married Louis Gadd, a merchant of Luzerne township.

(VIII) John William, son of James M. and Rebecca (Lancaster) Barber, was born in German township, Fayette county, Pennsylvania, March 19, 1863. When he was five years of age his parents moved to Luzerne township, and there in the public schools he obtained his education. For a time he conducted a store, but in 1903 sold out and purchased a farm of one hundred and ten acres, on which he now conducts general farming operations, specializing, however, in fruit-growing. He takes great pride and delight in his orchards, which are the best and most productive in that section of the county. He is a Democrat in politics, and in religion a member of the Church of the Brethren. He married Margaret Burwell, born in Greene county, daughter of Abner, a farmer and Lucinda (Kepler) Burwell. Children: John, lives in Brownsville; Henry, Jacob, James, Lucy, Mary, Ruth; all living at home excepting John.

SELLERS

Philip Henry Sellers was born in 1704 at Weinheim, Germany. This date is obtained from the records of Indian Creek church, Franconia township, Montgomery county, Pennsylvania, where it is stated he died in 1769, aged sixty-five years. Philip H. spelled his name Soller, but the English form is invariably Sellers. His arrival in

Pennsylvania is recorded in "Colonial Records of Pennsylvania," vol ii, p 332 September 11, 1728, a number of Palatines with their families, about ninety, immigrated in the ship, 'James Goodwill," David Crocket, master, from Rotterdam, last from Deal, whence she sailed June 15 The name of Philip Heinrich Sellers appears in the list He was married before coming to Pennsylvania, the Christian name of his wife being Catharina Several of their children were born in Germany After spending a short time in Philadelphia he purchased a tract in Bucks county on the north branch of the Perkiomen He died in 1769 and is buried in the graveyard of Indian Creek church, Franconia, Bucks county, Pennsylvania He was survived by his wife, Catharina who died in 1773 Both their wills are on file in Philadelphia Children Philip, Leonard Philip Henry, John, Paul, Peter, Jacob, Elizabeth, Magdalena and Margaret It is from one of these sons that William U Sellers descends, probably through Jacob, who settled first in Juniata, now Mifflin county, descendants settling later in Bedford county Little is known of the grandfather further than he was a wheelwright, married, and died in Bedford county, leaving issue

(II) Augustus Sellers was born in Bedford county, Pennsylvania He worked on the home farm later learning the cooper's trade which he followed until enlisting as a soldier in the civil war He was a private of One Hundred and Forty-second Regiment, Pennsylvania Volunteer Infantry, and served three years and six months He saw hard service with the Army of the Potomac and fought at Bull Run, Antietam, Gettysburg and many other battles and skirmishes After the war he returned to Pennsylvania and engaged in the manufacture of lumber He now lives on a small farm at Ursina, Pennsylvania, and does a general teaming business He is a Democrat, and a member of the Methodist Episcopal church He married Sarah daughter of William Lenhart a crippled shoemaker who gave two of his sons to his country Others of his sons enlisted, but two were killed in battle, the others returning in safety She is a member of the Methodist Episcopal church Children of Augustus Sellers William U of whom further, Jennie E, resides at home, Lee, a hotel

keeper at Confluence Their first born, a daughter, died in infancy

(III) William U eldest son of Augustus Sellers, was born in Somerset county, Pennsylvania, November 8 1869 He was educated in the public schools of Ursina, and he entered the employ of the Baltimore & Ohio railroad as a boy In 1884 he entered the train service and has passed through several grades of service, now being a freight conductor Since entering the train service he has made his home in Connellsville He is a member of the Order of Railway Conductors, the Fraternal Order of Eagles and the Knights of the Maccabees He is a Democrat and an attendant of the Methodist Episcopal church, of which his wife is a member

He married, June 10, 1896, Emma Brant, born at Bedford Mills Bedford county, Pennsylvania daughter of John and Ella Brant Children Ruth Mae born July 24, 1898, Frank H October 11, 1902 Charles Samuel, November 14 1904, Martha Virginia, August 18, 1910

JOHNS The American progenitor of the Johns family in Uniontown was Napoleon Johns, born in France, emigrated to the United States, settling first in New Jersey, later in Fayette county Pennsylvania He married and had issue

(II) Major Peter A Johns, son of Napoleon Johns, was born in New Jersey and came to Fayette county, Pennsylvania, with his parents, when a boy He was well educated and secured an appointment to the United States Military Academy at West Point, where he passed four years and was graduated After some time spent in the army he resigned and was otherwise engaged until the outbreak of the Mexican war when he enlisted as a private and served with distinction, being mustered out as first lieutenant He returned to Fayette county after the war, and a few years later began the study of law in the office of Joshua Howell, a leading attorney of Uniontown He continued his legal study until December 7, 1857, when after examination he was admitted to the Fayette county bar He began and continued practice in Uniontown until his death, although much of his time was spent in the public service of his county and State He served one term as register and recorder of

Fayette county, eight years as postmaster of Uniontown under President Grant's administrations, and was several times elected to the state legislature from Fayette county. When the war between the states broke out, he at once offered his services, entered as lieutenant of the Eleventh Pennsylvania Reserves, served until the close of the war, when he was mustered out as major. He died September 20, 1876, leaving a record of unsullied manhood and faithful official and military service.

He married Susan Marietta, born in Fayette county, Pennsylvania, died January 4, 1897. Children: Napoleon, died in childhood; William, died in childhood; Mary, died in childhood; Emmett, deceased, married Mary Ashcraft and had a child, William, all are deceased; Frank, deceased; Marietta, deceased, succeeded her father as postmaster; George, deceased; Charles, deceased; Margaret, living in Derry, Pennsylvania; Phillip Sheridan, deceased, married and left two daughters, Geraldine and Georgie; Peter A., of whom further.

(III) Peter A. (2) (Doll), youngest child of Major Peter A. (1) and Susan (Marietta) Johns, was born in Uniontown, Pennsylvania, October 13, 1861. He was educated in the public schools, finishing his studies at Madison academy, Uniontown. He learned the printer's art, but did not continue at his trade very long. He invested in a draying outfit and for two years was engaged in that business. Since 1886 his life has mainly been given to the public service of Fayette county. In that year he was appointed chief deputy, under Sheriff Miller, resigned March 4, 1887, to become court crier (Mr. Johns was the first Republican to serve in that office in Fayette county). He continued court crier until November, 1889, when he resigned to become deputy collector of internal revenue for the western district of Pennsylvania. He served in this position until 1892, then resigned and engaged in the hotel business in Somerset county, Pennsylvania. He remained at the hotel until 1896, when he sold out his interests, returned to Uniontown, where in January of that year he was appointed chief deputy under Sheriff Fred S. Chalfant, serving during Mr. Chalfant's term of office. In 1898 he was a candidate at the primaries for the nomination for sheriff, but lost by a narrow margin. In 1899 he was nominated by the

Fayette Republican county convention for the office of register and recorder, winning against two competitors, on the first ballot by a vote of 126 out of 156 delegates. On motion of the defeated candidates his nomination was made unanimous. The campaign following was hard fought, but in the final summing up Mr. Johns led his Democratic opponent by 857 votes. He filled the office most efficiently for three years, and after retiring again engaged in the hotel business.

He opened and maintained a house of entertainment in Uniontown until 1907, when he sold out for the third time. He contested for the office of sheriff of Fayette county. He was the successful candidate for the nomination and at the ensuing election led all other Republican candidates on the ticket, and won by a majority of 1,520. He entered upon the duties of his office, January 1, 1908. He was the last sheriff of Fayette county to serve under the old "Fee bill" system and the first under the law making the sheriff's term of office four years. He has established several precedents that are worthy of mention. He is the first sheriff who did not live in the jail, but kept there a warden and matron. He appointed the first woman deputy sheriff in the county (his daughter, Lucy Beach Johns), and the first woman clerk ever to serve in the sheriff's office (Miss Martha Grier, of Dunbar township).

He has given the county efficient service in every position he has ever filled and retired from office with the entire respect of the courts he served and the people whose interests were committed to his care. He has always been a strong party man and has done valiant service in upholding Republican principles in his county and state. He can always be found in the thickest of the fight and has been the leader in many a hard fought political battle. In 1909 and 1910 he was chairman of the county committee and a delegate to the Republican national convention at Chicago in 1912. Victory has not always followed in his path, but he is a good loser and is ready for the next battle of the ballots. He is now (1912) closing up the unfinished business of the sheriff's office recently quitted. He is a member of the Benevolent and Protective Order of Elks, and trustee of Uniontown lodge.

He married, September 20, 1882, Mary Knight Cunningham, of Uniontown Children Marietta, died March 4, 1894, Lucy Beach, the first woman deputy sheriff in Fayette county, Druanna

---

ELY This ancient English family traces authority to Nicholas De Ely, who was Bishop of Worcester, 1268, and of Winchester until his death, 1280 There is a great deal written also to show the descent from a Norman youth, Tasillo, who appeared at Buda, the capital of Hungary, in 550 A D, and took service under the Hungarian monarch, Theodoric, who gave him the hand of his daughter, Brunehilda, in marriage The name is found in all periods of English history after the eleventh century and was borne by many eminent men

The American ancestor is Richard Ely, of Plymouth, Devonshire, England, who emigrated to America between 1660 and 1663, his son, Richard, accompanied him He was for a time in Boston, later settling at Lyme, Connecticut He was a widower when he came to New England, his wife Joanna (maiden name supposed to have been Phipps) having died in Plymouth, England, January 7 1660 He had an estate of three thousand acres of land, including what was later called Ely's Ferry He took part in public affairs, was a devout Christian and lived a Godly life He married (second) in Boston in 1664, Mrs Elizabeth Cullick, widow of Captain John Cullick, who for some time was secretary of the Colony of Connecticut and one of the most noted men in the Colony She died November 12, 1683, he died November 24, 1684 Children, all by first wife 1 Richard, of whom further 2 William, baptized October, 1647, died 1717, married Elizabeth Smith 3 Judith, baptized September 6, 1652, died June 21, 1655 4 Daniel, died in infancy

(II) Richard (2), son of Richard (1) Ely, was born in 1636, baptized in Plymouth, England, June 19, 1637 He accompanied his father from England and resided with him at Lyme He married Mary Marvin, born 1666 eldest daughter of Lieutenant Reinold Ely, a large land owner and prominent in town affairs, and his wife, Sarah (Clark) Ely, of Lyme Children 1 Samuel, born October 21, 1686, married Jane Lord 2 Mary, born

November 29, 1689, married ———— Niles 3 Sarah, born June 13, 1695, married General Jonathan Gillett 4 Richard, of whom further

(III) Deacon Richard (3) Ely, youngest son of Richard (2) Ely, was born at Lyme Connecticut, October 27, 1697, died February 24, 1777 He was a man of deep piety and great Christian activity He was generally known as Deacon" perhaps to distinguish him from his cousin, Captain Richard Ely He married (first) Elizabeth (Phoebe) Peck, who died October 8, 1730 He married (second) October 26, 1732, Phoebe Hubbard, of Middletown, Connecticut, fourth in descent from George Hubbard, one of the original settlers of Hartford, Connecticut She died August 28, 1779, aged sixty-eight years (tombstone) Children of first wife 1 Elizabeth, born October 11, 1724, married Colonel Samuel Selden, captured at the battle of Long Island and died a prisoner in New York 2 Esther, died aged ten years 3 Ezra, born January 22, 1728, married (first) Sarah Starting, (second) Anna Starting 4 Mary, died in infancy Children of second wife 5 Richard, born September 30, 1733, married Jerusha Selden 6 Seth, of whom further 7 Elihu, died in infancy 8 Elihu, born November 15, 1737, married Anna Ely 9 Josiah, born July 20, 1739, married (first) Phoebe Dennison, (second) Elizabeth Ely, widow of Reuben Lord 10 Robert, born June 26, 1741, married Jerusha Lay 11 Phoebe, born May 16, 1743, married James D Colt 12 Hepzibah, born June 6, 1745, married John Pratt 13 Rev David, born June 7, 1749, married Hepzibah Mills All the children of Deacon Richard and Phoebe Hubbard lived to an advanced age, all met in 1813 at the home of the eldest brother, Rev Richard Ely and the youngest brother, Rev David Ely, of Huntington, Connecticut, preached a sermon on the occasion, he being then near seventy years of age

(IV) Seth, second son of Deacon Richard (3) and Phoebe (Hubbard) Ely, was born in Lyme, Connecticut, December 11, 1734, died January 3, 1821 After his marriage he settled in North Lyme where both are buried He was appointed captain in the Third Company of the town of Lyme in the Third Connecticut Regiment He married Lydia Reynolds born at Norwich, Connecticut, Decembei 16, 1736, sixth daughter of John and Lydia (Lord) Reynolds, died March 23, 1815 Children 1 John, born 1763, graduate of Yale, 1786, and a minister of the Congregational church, married Mary Lord 2 Seth of whom further 3 Richard, died aged four years 4 Richard (2), died in infancy 5 Ebenezer, died unmarried 6 Lydia, born September 12, 1766, married Judge Matthew Griswold, second son of Governor Matthew Griswold 7 Abigail born 1768, married George Beckwith 8 Phoebe, died aged seven years 9 Deborah, born December 19 1781, married Enoch Sill

(V) Seth (2), second son of Seth (1) and Lydia (Reynolds) Ely, was born at North Lyme, Connecticut, 1764, died 1847 He settled in Lyme after marriage, later migrating to Ripley New York He is called Colonel Seth by some writers He married, in 1799, Phoebe Marvin, born 1772, died 1852, daughter of Elisha and Elizabeth (Selden) Marvin, a granddaughter of Colonel Samuel Selden, of the revolution Children 1 Selden, born March 7, 1800, married Stalira Esther Griffin and lived in Ripley, New York 2 Elizabeth Colt, born 1802, died 1855, married, 1832, Rufus Hills 3 Phoebe Hubbard, born 1804, married Matthew Griswold 4 Lydia, died in infancy 5 Seth Elisha of whom further 6 Ebenezer born 1811, died 1822 7 Abigail Deborah, born 1813, died 1879, married (first) 1848, Henry M Gregory, married (second) 1865, Abner Lord Ely

(VI) Seth Elisha, son of Seth (2) and Phoebe (Marvin) Ely, was born in 1808 in New York state He came later to Fayette county, Pennsylvania, where he was living in 1829 He married and had issue including a son, Washington, of whom further

(VII) Washington, son of Seth Elisha Ely, was born in Fayette county, Pennsylvania, May 10, 1829 He was educated in the public schools, and learned the carpenter's trade He was a soldier of the civil war, serving a full term of enlistment In 1853 he was living in Wood county, West Virginia, later returning to Fayette county, Pennsylvania He was a Republican in politics He married Sarah McClain, born in Fayette county, Pennsylvania, in 1835 Among their children was Joseph Seth, of whom further

(VIII) Joseph Seth, son of Washington

and Sarah (McClain) Ely, was born in Wood county West Virginia, September 17, 1853 In 1855 his parents moved to Meigs county, Ohio, and in 1865 returned to Fayette county, Pennsylvania He was educated in the public schools of Ohio and Pennsylvania, and has spent his mature years engaged principally in agriculture and contracting operations, also extensively interested in lumber and stone He is a Prohibitionist in politics, and a member of the Methodist Episcopal church He has served as tax collector of the borough of Point Marion since 1901 He married

Children Carrie May, born May 29, 1877, John W, December 28, 1878, Nina V, May 6, 1882, Sarah G, November 2, 1884, died December 24, 1885, Russell, April 28, 1888, died January 28, 1892

LINDSAY The Lindsays of Connellsville, Pennsylvania, herein recorded are of direct Irish ancestry, for many generations natives of the Emerald Isle but beyond that tracing to the Lindsays of Scotland, a family of prominent mention in Scotch history The first of his branch to come to the United States was John, the father of John (2) Lindsay, of Connellsville, Pennsylvania James Lindsay, his paternal grandfather, was born, lived and died in Ireland, leaving issue

(II) John, son of James Lindsay, was born in Ireland and remained in his native land until about 1840, when he emigrated to the United States in a sailing vessel that consumed eight weeks on the passage After landing he made his way to Western Pennsylvania, where he was employed as a teamster for several years, then entered the employ of the Pittsburgh, Fort Wayne and Chicago Railroad Company at Allegheny City (now Pittsburgh, north side), continuing until stricken with a partial paralysis that left him incapable of physical effort He lived in this helpless condition fourteen years, dying in 1889, the direct cause being a broken leg, the result of a fall He was a member of the Reformed Presbyterian church, as was his wife He married, in Pennsylvania Margaret Smith, also born in Ireland, who died in 1887 Her father died in Ireland, and she came to the United States with her mother Children, all born in Pennsylvania 1 James, a resident of Wilkinsburg, Pennsylvania 2 John (2), of whom further 3 Elizabeth, married John McCune 4 Jane, married ———— Keeelty and resides in Norfolk, Virginia has children

(III) John (2), son of John (1) Lindsay, was born in Allegheny City (Pittsburgh, north side), Pennsylvania, in 1850 He was educated in the public schools, and when quite a young man learned the carpenter's trade with Smith Crisswell & Company, prominent contractors of that section In 1876 he came to Connellsville, entered the employ of the Baltimore & Ohio Railroad Company as a carpenter, and so continues at present (1912), having in 1886 been promoted foreman His term of service with the company covers a continuous period of thirty-five years, which entitles him to the well-earned title of "veteran " He is a Republican in politics, and a member of the Methodist Episcopal church He married, September 18, 1879, Mary B Cooley, born in Connellsville, daughter of William and Letty Cooley, oldtime residents of Fayette county Children 1 Bessie D, died aged five months, July 10, 1881 2 John Howard, born April 18, 1882, now chief clerk of division engineer, Baltimore & Ohio, at Connellsville 3 Mary M, born October 12, 1884, died September 22, 1889 4 Helen E, born March 21, 1891 5 Gertrude, January 29, 1894

HOOP The Hoop family of Connellsville descend from German ancestors, John Hoop being of the second generation in the United States

(I) Conrad Hoop his father, was born in Germany, and in 1844 came to the United States, settling in the state of Maryland He worked at various occupations such as brewing, coal mining, etc, until 1863 He then came to Connellsville, where for twenty years after he was successfully engaged in the grocery business He was a member of the Presbyterian church, and an energetic upright man of business He married Mary Landis, born in Germany, came to the United States where she had relatives living in Cumberland, Maryland, and died in 1895 Children John, of whom further, Conrad, Henry Mary, Elizabeth, Katherine and Margaret, both deceased, a son, died in infancy

(II) John, eldest son of Conrad and Mary (Landis) Hoop, was born in Allegheny county, Maryland, January 20, 1848 He was educated at the Poplar Lane school house On arriving at suitable age he learned the blacksmith's trade at Uniontown, Pennsylvania, beginning in 1867, and serving an apprenticeship of three years In 1870 he came to Connellsville, where he established a shop and smithing business, continuing successfully until the present time In 1911 he erected his present commodious shop on South Fourth street, having previously been located on Main street He is now one of the oldest smiths in the city and commands an extensive patronage He is a friendly rival of John Cunningham for the title of "the oldest smith,' both having served their terms of apprenticeship in Uniontown, and both locating in and passing their business lives in Connellsville He is a member of the Presbyterian church and a Republican He has held public office almost continuously, serving in about every borough office except mayor or chief burgess He was a member of the first common council, elected after the consolidation of the Ashman addition to the borough of New Haven with Connellsville, and has served several terms in that body He is a man of thoroughly businesslike habits and is highly regarded

He married, October 17, 1870, Sarah Ann Caruthers, born in Uniontown, Pennsylvania, daughter of John Caruthers, who came there from New Jersey Children 1 John II, married Lillian Zoller, and now resides in Beaver county, Pennsylvania Child John G 2 James C, deceased 3 William C, married Margaret Soles, and now resides in McKeesport, Pennsylvania, child, Harriet 4 Charles Centennial, born in 1876, married Anna Davis, and now resides in California, Pennsylvania, children, Sarah V and Charles 5 Clarence E, resides in Beaver county, unmarried 6 Della Mae residing with her parents

BRITTON The emigrant ancestor of the Brittons of South Brownsville, Pennsylvania, was George Britton, born in Fermanagh county, Ireland, in 1794, died in West Brownsville, Pennsylvania, in 1859 He married there in 1824 Catherine Laud, born in County Cavan in 1806, died in 1872 He was a miller and lived in Ireland until May, 1848, then he came to the United States, settling in Washington county, Pennsylvania In September of the same year his wife and six children came, leaving two, William and George, in the old country   The following year, 1849, they joined the others in Washington county

Children   1 Jane, married James Brown and lived in New Castle, Pennsylvania, children   Charles, John, a member of the Pennsylvania legislature, twice elected mayor of New Castle and two terms postmaster of the same city, Lizzie, Kate, James, Ella   2 William, of whom further   3 George, now living in West Brownsville, married (first) Elizabeth Watkins, children Cornelius, James and Richard, married (second) Harriet Claybaugh, children Nellie, Catherine, Georgianna   4 Margery, married John Watkins and had fourteen children   Susan, Catherine, George, Eliza Jane, Henrietta, William, Elizabeth, Matilda, John, Mary, Annie, Daisy, Charles, Mary   5 John, married Anna Britton, children, Charles, George, Lillian, William   6 Ann, married James Cauthers, child, James B, now a lawyer of New York city, graduate of Amherst college and Columbia university   7 Catherine, married William Noble, no issue   8 Ellen, married, February 15, 1866, James Williams, of West Brownsville, who died February 6, 1912, enlisted in August, 1862, in Company B, Twenty-second Pennsylvania Cavalry, serving until the close of the war, he was in railroad employ for twenty-three years, later a grocer

(II) William, son of George and Catherine (Laird) Britton, was born in County Fermanagh, Ireland, in 1832   He came to the United States in 1849 and later settled in Greene county, Pennsylvania, where he worked in a distillery   He remained in Greene county until after his marriage, then moved to South Brownsville, Fayette county, thence to Washington county, returning later to South Brownsville, where he died in 1909   He was engaged in the distilling business all his life   He was a Democrat in politics, and a member of the Episcopal church   He married Melinda South, born in Greene county, Pennsylvania, died in South Brownsville in 1910   Children   1 Anna, married John G Crawford   2 John G married Ella Springer of South Brownsville   he was superin-

tendent of the Pittsburgh & Morgantown Packet Company many years, and for several years was pilot from Pittsburgh to Louisville, and one of the best known river men of the day   3 Ruth, married Robert Crawford   4 Catherine   5 Elizabeth   6 William D, of whom further

(III) William Duncan, son of William and Melinda (South) Britton, was born in Washington county, Pennsylvania, near the old National road, June 20, 1868   He was educated in the Brownsville public schools, and until he was seventeen years of age lived on a farm   He then became engineer on river boats owned by the Pittsburgh, Brownsville & Geneva Packet Company, and for fifteen years was chief engineer on river boats running south from Pittsburgh   For the past two years he has been engineer for the Brownsville Brewing Company, having charge of the engine room of the refrigerating department, the largest ice plant in the county used in connection with the brewing business   He owns the old homestead in South Brownsville, which is still the family home   He is a Democrat in politics, and a member of the Episcopal church, Brownsville lodge, No 60, Free and Accepted Masons, Brownsville Chapter, No 164, Royal Arch Masons, and the National Association of Stationary Engineers

He married, in 1904, Daisy daughter of Allen J and ——— (Day) Mowl, of early Washington county families   Allen J Mowl survives his wife, a resident of Washington county   Child of Mr and Mrs Britton Elizabeth, born December 25, 1908

ROWE   The Rowe family of Uniontown are of English parentage   Isaac Rowe, of London, England, came to the United States in 1873 and settled in Cleveland, Ohio, where he had banking connections   In 1874 his wife and family joined him in Cleveland where he died two years later   He married Sarah Thoroughgood, who yet survives him, a resident of Cleveland   Children   Isaac O, deceased, Frank W, of New York, Ernest H, of whom further, Gilbert W deceased

(II) Ernest H, son of Isaac and Sarah Rowe, was born in London, England, April 20, 1872   His boyhood was spent in Cleveland, Ohio, where he was educated in the public schools, graduating from the high school with the class of 1889 For ten years he was connected with the brokerage and insurance business in Cleveland and during that period attended the night law school of Baldwin University, being graduated and receiving his law degree in 1902 He has never practiced law, but all his business life has been as indicated For ten years he was an active, working member of the Cleveland Chamber of Commerce, serving on important committees and becoming thoroughly familiar with the workings of a modern chamber of commerce in a progressive American city In 1909 he received a call from the city of Lorain, Ohio, to become secretary of the Chamber of Commerce of that city He remained there one year, then came to Uniontown in 1910 to accept a similar position He has placed the business organization of the chamber in a healthful working condition and the interests of Uniontown have been greatly advanced The matter of civic progress and expansion is one that Mr Rowe has carefully studied and he has developed an ability that has produced satisfactory results His powers of organization have brought him prominently forward and other associations of business men have placed confidence in his ability He is secretary of the Coke Producers' Association of the Connellsville region, secretary of the Automobile Club of Fayette county and secretary of the Fayette County Road Supervision Association He has allied himself with national and civic associations and derives from them the advantages such bodies confer He belongs to the American Association of Commercial Executives the American Academy of Political Science and the American Civic Association He is active and energetic along lines of commercial development as well as in civic or political improvement Another association for the public good in which he is actively interested is the Uniontown Library Association He is independent in political action, throwing the weight of his influence and position in favor of conservative businesslike conduct of public affairs He is an active member and lay reader of St Peter's Episcopal church of Uniontown, of which his wife is also a communicant

He married, June 26, 1901, Osyth, daughter of William and Florence (Secord) Callory, of Niagara Falls, Ontario, Canada Children Victoria, born May 24, 1904, Osyth, born December 16, 1905, died October 10, 1910, Patricia, born December 11, 1910

NIXON This family is said to be of Scotch ancestry There was a John Nixon, of Ridley, Delaware county, Pennsylvania, a member of the Society of Friends in 1683, of whom little is known There is a theory that he was the father of Richard Nixon, father of Colonel John Nixon, born in Chester county, a noted merchant of Philadelphia, and one of the founders, in 1770, of the Friendly Sons of St Patrick He was chairman of the Committee of Public Safety during the revolution, and lieutenant-colonel of the Third Pennsylvania Battalion, in the defense of the Delaware river in 1776 and 1777 He it was who on July 18, 1776, read to the people of Philadelphia, for the first time, the Declaration of Independence, using a platform built for another purpose in state house yard The Nixons of Uniontown descend from the Philadelphia and Delaware county family They are Scotch-Irish, their progenitors settling in Ireland before coming to America There is a William Nixon found in Georges township, Fayette county, Pennsylvania, in 1787, a property owner

(I) The earliest record of this branch is of Samuel Nixon a farmer of Georges township, justice of the peace, and from 1828 to 1841 associate justice of the Fayette county court of common pleas and quarter sessions He was a prominent man, married, and left issue

(II) James, son of Samuel Nixon, was born in Georges township, Fayette county, Pennsylvania, December, 1828, died November, 1894 He was educated and passed his minority in his native county After his marriage he moved to Westmoreland county, remaining, however, but a few years He then returned to the Nixon homestead in Georges township, Fayette county, where he engaged in agriculture until his death He was a Democrat, active and influential in public affairs In 1886 he was elected commissioner of Fayette county, serving three years He and all the members of his family were members of the Cumberland Presbyterian church He married Sarah Jane Zerley, who survives him, a resident of Fairchance Pennsylvania She was born January 1, 1836 Children 1 Dorcas Ann married Harmon Custer, and resides in Galesburg, Illinois 2 Hannah P, married Ambrose Bradley, of Altoona, Pennsylvania 3 Jennie, married Robert Goldsboro of Fairchance, Pennsylvania 4 William S, of whom further 5 James, now of Allegheny county, Pennsylvania 6 Sarah, married Richard Goldsboro, of Fairchance Pennsylvania 7 Charles B, residing in Fairchance 8 Alice, deceased, married Samuel Aitis

(III) William S, son of James and Sarah Jane (Zerlev) Nixon, was born in Westmoreland county, Pennsylvania, May 19, 1862 He was educated in the public schools and passed his earlier years at the home farm in Georges township, his parents returning there while he was a child He began business in 1886 at Fairchance, Pennsylvania, establishing a meat market In 1890 he went to Denver, Colorado, where he was engaged in the grocery business two years In 1892 he returned to Fairchance and opened a meat market, continuing until 1896, when he sold his business He engaged in the undertaking and livery business in Fairchance, building up a prosperous business, and in 1908 sold out and came to Uniontown He there opened an undertaking establishment, with a livery stable in connection He is a graduate of the Barnes School of Embalming, and has been very successful in the two branches of his business, both being conducted on thoroughly modern lines The serious duties of his profession have been attended to with great zeal and carefulness, and his handling of the delicate and difficult problems connected with funerals has been done with the greatest consideration and respect for all concerned He has every facility of the up-to-date undertaker, and with his first-class appointments has secured a fine trade in the undertaking line in Uniontown He is a member of the First Presbyterian church in which he is an active worker, and is a member of the Royal Arcanum

He married (first) April 4, 1883, Rhoda, daughter of Jacob and Melinda (Kendall) Dawson, of Georges township, Fayette county, of the well-known and prominent Dawson family, she died March 19, 1896 He married (second) April 23, 1900, Mary A, daughter of Captain James and Jennie (O'Donovan) Abraham, of Georges township Children of first marriage 1 Ray Dawson, now living in Fairchance, Pennsylvania 2 Elenora, living at home Children of second marriage 3 Janet II 4 William S 5 James A 6 Donald R

NIXON In a list of settlers in Georges township Fayette county, Pennsylvania, in 1787, is found the name of William Nixon, where he came from is not known He owned land in Georges township and was a farmer there until his death He was a Whig and a deacon of the Presbyterian church It is said by one authority that he died on the ocean while returning to his native land He married and left issue Hannah, married Dr J Cory, Moses, of whom further Jane, married Howard Griffith, Isaac, Samuel

(II) Moses, son of William Nixon, was born in 1812, died in Georges township July 22, 1857 on the home farm which now bears the name "Oliphant farm" He received his education in the public schools of his native township, and in his later life followed the occupation of a farmer He was at one time a member of the state militia, and in religion he and his wife were Cumberland Presbyterians He married Louisa Bailey, born in Greene county, Pennsylvania, but who moved to Fayette county when very young, daughter of Eli, a farmer in South Union township, and Perrie (Gregg) Bailey Children of Mr and Mrs Bailey 1 Presley, married and lives in the west 2 Jesse 3 Ellen, married Harriott Gaddis 4 William, married Jenny Patterson 5 Louisa, of previous mention 6 Eliza, married William Barnes 7 Ruth Ann, married Ellis Linn 8 Emily, married William C Dixon They are all deceased Children of Mr and Mrs Nixon 1 William, married (first) Mary Means, (second), Mattie Richardson, and lives in Montana 2 Francis, married Azel Freeman, deceased 3 Perrie, deceased married William Dawson 4 Amanda, lives in Denver, Colorado, married Charles Day Armond, deceased 5 Emily, married Jacob Renshaw, and lives in Winfield, Iowa 6 Moses Taylor, of whom further 7 Ellen, married Albert Smith, of Connellsville, Pennsylvania 8 Samuel G (q v) 9 Presley, deceased, mar-

W. S. Nixon

*Mr. and Mrs. M. T. Nixon
and Grandchildren*

ried Carrie Robinson 10 Anna, married Thomas Ringland, a farmer of Winfield, Iowa 11 Victoria, married William Lawhead, deceased, lived at Uniontown, Pennsylvania

(III) Moses Taylor, son of Moses and Louisa (Bailey) Nixon, was born in Georges township, Fayette county, Pennsylvania, March 22, 1849 His entire life, with the exception of three summers, when he was in Iowa, has been passed in Georges township, where he received his education He has owned a farm since 1889 and is to-day one of the county s most energetic, enterprising and successful farmers, having all modern equipment and improvements upon his farm and a group of buildings so unlike many tumbledown farm houses that they would do credit to any village or town Cleanliness is the slogan in everything attempted and everywhere is seen the glittering of freshly applied paint His interest in politics, local, state and national, is great, and he has held several offices as a Republican, among them being school director, to which he has several times been re-elected, a member of the election board, tax collector, on the county poor board for three years and at present is roadmaster With his wife he is a member of the Presbyterian church

He married, September 19, 1878, Frances Collier born in Georges township, July 23 1858, daughter of Merchant a farmer in Georges township, and Hannah (Hustead) Collier Children of Mr and Mrs Collier 1 Frances, of previous mention 2 Daniel, born August 7, 1860, died July 7, 1908, married Mollie Sesler 3 Alsesta born December 16, 1862, married James Robinson a farmer of Georges township 4 Loretta, born October 6 1865, married Robert Brownfield, a farmer of Georges township 5 Robert, born June 19, 1867 died January 11, 1869 6 Mary, born January 8, 1869, married (first) Norval Medara, (second) Robert Kennedy 7 James F born October 20, 1871, married (first) Ella Steel, (second) ———— Children of Mr and Mrs Nixon 1 Louisa, born October 30, 1879, married Albert Thomas, children May Thomas, born October 29, 1899 and Bessie Thomas, born July 22, 1901 These children live with their grandparents, who take great

delight and pride in them 2 Hannah May, born July 4, 1881 married D F Swaney, road supervisor of Georges township Children Daniel and Earl

(III) Samuel Gregg, son of Moses and Louisa (Bailey) Nixon, was born in Georges township, Fayette county, Pennsylvania, December 11, 1852 He was educated in the public schools and remained at the home farm with his parents until manhood After his marriage he began farming operations for himself in South Union township, where he owns a good farm and is successfully engaged in farming and live stock He married, October 30, 1880, Anna Williams, born in Uniontown December 1 1854, daughter of Isaac and Martha (Lancaster) Williams Isaac Williams was a brick manufacturer for forty years, and founded the business now conducted by his sons He retired from business fifteen years preceding his death in Uniontown November 21, 1893 Children of Mr and Mrs Williams 1 Thomas B deceased, married Emma Sheets, who survives him, a resident of Morgantown, West Virginia 2 Lewis, married Rebecca Clark, both deceased 3 Josiah V, married Ellen Derrick, deceased, he resides in Uniontown, is a brick manufacturer 4 Elliott, married Ada Bailey, he is a brick manufacturer of Clarksburg, West Virginia 5 Marjorie died in in fancy 6 Jenny, married Perry Markle, a real estate dealer of Uniontown, Pennsylvania 7 Anna, of previous mention wife of Samuel G Nixon 8 Emma, married George Brooke, a merchant of Uniontown 9 Julia, married Marshall Brooke, a farmer of Somerset county, Pennsylvania 10 Rev Charles, a minister of the Protestant Episcopal church, living near Philadelphia, Pennsylvania 11 Harry bookkeeper for the Elkins Coal and Coke Company married Grace Kiddie Children of Mr and Mrs Nixon 1 Pearl born September 23, 1881, married Charles Clark, a lawyer of Uniontown children Martha, born 1005, Helen, 1907, Mary, 1908 2 Jessie, born September 7, 1883, residing at home 3 Ray, born August 1, 1884, married May Browning, child Ray (2), died in infancy 4 Martha Jane, born July 25, 1885, resides at home 5 William Moses born October 10, 1887, died in infancy 6 Paul, born December 28, 1890 7 Julia born April 26, 1893

8 Perrie D , born August 22, 1895 9 Ruth, born November 28, 1899

This branch of the Don- DONNELLY nelly family descends from Michael Donnelly, born in Ireland, who with his wife, formerly a Miss Hastings, came to the United States in 1823 They settled in Susquehanna county, Pennsylvania where he was one of the pioneer farmers

They were both devout members of the Roman Catholic church, and Michael Donnelly was a Democrat He died at his farm and is buried at Fredsville, Pennsylvania, she died in 1871 aged eighty-one years Children who grew to maturity John, Michael, Patrick, Dennis, Martin, of whom further, Edward, James, Margaret, Eliza, Bridget

(II) Martin, son of Michael Donnelly, was born in Ireland and came to the United States with his parents in 1823, then but a child He was educated in the public schools of Susquehanna county, and in his earlier years was a farmer and lumberman In 1849 he moved to Binghamton New York, remaining until 1855 when he returned to Susquehanna county In 1856 he went west, settling in Oconto county, Wisconsin, remaining until 1859, when he again returned to his boyhood home in Pennsylvania Later, in 1871, he located in Scranton, where he died February 7 1908

Martin Donnelly married Margaret died July 31, 1906, daughter of Thomas and Honora (McDonald) Sheahan, both born in Ireland came to the United States, settling at Silver Lake, Susquehanna county, Pennsylvania Thomas Sheahan died in Grand Rapids, Michigan, aged ninety-three years His wife died in Meadville, also at an advanced age Children Philip, James, a contractor in Iowa, Patrick, Thomas, Margaret, of previous mention, Mary, Eliza living at Grand Rapids, Michigan, Honora, living in Port Colborne, Canada Children of Martin and Margaret Donnelly 1. Mary J , born February 3 1848, in Susquehanna county 2 James E , January 27, 1850, at Binghamton, New York 3 John J , of whom further 4 Anna Eliza, January, 1855, in Susquehanna county 5 Thomas P , 1857, in Wisconsin, killed on the Baltimore & Ohio railroad in Pennsylvania, February 6, 1893 6 Nellie,

born May 30, 1861, in Susquehanna county 7 Joseph E , April 30, 1863, in Susquehanna county 8 Lucy, born 1865, died young

(III) John J son of Martin Donnelly, was born at Binghamton, New York, February 10, 1853

He attended the public schools and worked on the farm until he was sixteen years of age He then entered the train service of the Delaware, Lackawanna & Western railroad as brakeman. He later came to Connellsville, and on May 1, 1873, entered the employ of the Baltimore & Ohio Railroad Company In 1874 he was promoted to conductor, continuing with the company ten years and one month He then resigned, and for sixteen years was engaged in the bottling business in Fayette county He spent nine years in the lumber business, two years in contracting and is now living retired He is a Democrat and has served the city of Connellsville as auditor for two terms of three years each He is a member of the Roman Catholic church

John J Donnelly married, January 6, 1876, Lena Bower, born in Germany February 6, 1856, daughter of John and Katherine Bower John Bower was born in Germany in 1808, came to the United States and settled in Alleghany county, Maryland, in 1863, where he worked at his trade of miller, later moved to Bedford county, where he engaged in farming until his death in 1881 His wife Katherine was born in Germany in 1823, died in Bedford county in 1884 Children Charles, Louis, John, Laurence, deceased Frederick, deceased, and Lena, of previous mention Children of John J and Lena Donnelly 1 William H born October 15, 1876, married Mary Jones, children Margaret J , born December 25, 1902 Marie November 18, 1904, John J , September 11, 1907, Eleanor, March 14, 1910 2 Joseph E , born January 17, 1878 3 Dodie Frances, February 10, 1880, married September 5, 1906, D J Lambert, and has a son, John, born February 10, 1910 4 Nellie Mary, born February 10 1882, married, November 4, 1910, M M Patterson, and has a daughter, Louisa, born April 7, 1911 6 Charles F , born August 28, 1889 7 Albert V , May 31, 1891 8 Margaret G December 1, 1893 9 Eugene H , October 26, 1895, died March 30 1897

O'CONNOR This is a famous name in Ireland, and was borne in the United States by one of the greatest lawyers of the New York bar, Charles O'Connor, a descendant of the Irish family The father of Bernard O'Connor, of Connellsville, Pennsylvania, Peter O Connor, died in 1871 in Ireland, where his life had been spent His widow, Mary (Murtha) O'Connor, came to the United States, where she lived with her children until her death in 1887 Peter O'Connor was a farmer and small landowner He married (first) ———— McCluskey, children John, who came to the United States and was never heard from, Bridget and Peter, died in infancy Children by his second wife, Mary (Murtha) O Connor 1 James, lives in Ireland and farms the old home acres 2 Michael, died in Ireland, leaving six sons and two daughters 3 Alice, married John Riley and lives in Ireland eight children 4 Mary, married James Rock and died leaving two children in the old country 5 Margaret, died in infancy 6 Francis, came to the United States and settled in Connellsville, Pennsylvania, married ———— and has five sons and three daughters 7 Patrick, came to the United States and resides in Pittsburgh, Pennsylvania, with a family of six sons and two daughters 8 Rose married (first) in Pennsylvania, James O'Freil, he died at Mount Pleasant, Pennsylvania she married (second) Lawrence Megan 9 Bernard, of whom further 10 Katherine, came to the United States, married John Lynch, of Pittsburgh Pennsylvania, has four living children parents and children were all members of the Roman Catholic church

(II) Bernard, youngest son of Peter and Mary (Murtha) O'Connor, was born in County Cavan, Ireland, November. 1855 He received his education in the village school in his native land and under a private tutor, at his own expense In 1881 he came to the United States and located in Connellsville, Pennsylvania, where he was employed for one year and seven days as a coke drawer by the Cambria Iron Company He then entered the service of the Baltimore & Ohio railroad as foreman of a construction gang and laid the first section of the double track between Connellsville and Pittsburgh Later for a year was timekeeper for the W J Rainey Coal Company, then for six months was patrolman on the Connellsville police force In 1885 he bought seventy-five acres of the old Rogers homestead, 'Cross Keys," and for four years was engaged in dairy farming In 1889 he discontinued dairying, but remained owner of the farm until 1908 About 1888 he began contracting in a small way, but his business so increased that in 1900 he gave up the farm, built a brick residence at No 201 North First street, Connellsville, West Side, which has since been his home He continued in business very successfully, and in 1909 formed a partnership with J W Madigan, under the firm name of O'Connor & Madigan For four years, 1904 until 1908, he was proprietor of the Victoria Hotel in Connellsville, then returned to contracting He is a member of the Roman Catholic church, the Holy Name Society and the Benevolent and Protective Order of Elks In politics he is an independent

He married, May 12, 1882, at St Patrick's Cathedral, New York city, Rose, born in County Monaghan, Ireland, daughter of James and Rose Cassidy, who both died in Ireland Children 1 Florence, married J W Madigan 2 Mary, died aged fourteen years 3 Alice, died in infancy 4 Anna, resides with her parents 5 Charles, in business with his father 6 Laura, graduate of State Normal School at California, now a teacher in the Connellsville schools 7 Katherine, a graduate of the State Normal School at California 8 Bernard P student in the Connellsville high school 9 William, student in the Connellsville high school

DUNAWAY The earliest available record of this family is of Matthew Dunaway, who in early life lived near Pittsburg, Pennsylvania, but in 1812 moved to Fayette county After a year spent in Luzerne township, at Gray's Landing, he moved to Greene county, Pennsylvania, where he spent several years In 1835 he again came to Fayette county, purchasing a farm of two hundred acres near Merrittstown, on which he erected a fine brick residence, later owned by Jefferson Hibbs He was a successful business man, industrious, quiet and unassuming, highly respected by all who knew him He died at a good old age, as did his wife Annie He was a Democrat, and a Presbyterian Children 1 John, of

whom further 2 Thomas, died in La Salle
county, Illinois 3 Jacob, died in Cass county,
Illinois 4 Jesse Evans, died in Iowa 5
James, lived in Cass county, Illinois 6 William, born in Nicholson township, Fayette
county, Pennsylvania, March 23, 1812

(II) John, eldest son of Matthew and Annie
Dunaway, was born in Fayette county Pennsylvania, November 4, 1801 He was educated in Fayette county, but after his marriage removed to Greensboro, Greene county,
where he was a stage driver and farmer He
married Margaret Robinson born October 3
1801, died October 4 1888 Children 1
Thomas born January 2 1828, died April 7
1889 2 Catherine, born January 24 1830
3 Nancy, September 4, 1832 4 James, October 16, 1837 5 Allen, August 24 1840,
died June 15, 1904 6 John W, born September 13 1847 7 Alexander, of whom further

(III) Alexander son of John and Margaret (Robinson) Dunaway was born in Luzerne township Fayette county, Pennsylvania,
April 3 1849 died in Fairchance, Pennsylvania, January 5 1905, of paralysis He was
educated in the public schools of Greensboro,
Greene county, where his parents moved
when he was quite young He began business in Greensboro when a young man, engaging in the drug business, continuing there
very successfully until 1896 In that year he
moved to Fairchance, Fayette county, where,
with a cousin C W Weltner, of Uniontown,
he owned and operated a distillery until four
months previous to his death, when the partnership was dissolved He was a very successful business man, and death came very
unexpectedly his plans having been laid for
spending the winter in the south He was
a member of Fairchance borough council, and
deeply interested in the welfare of this
borough

He was a member of the Royal Arcanum
and of other societies He married Hannah E Ewing, born March 23, 1854
daughter of E A and Mary Ann (Hibbs)
Ewing of Greensboro, and granddaughter of
James Ewing born in Ireland died in Fayette
county Pennsylvania Children of E A
Ewing

Harriet E John Andrew, Horace Greeley,
Laura Edward, William, Annabella, and
two died young Children of Alexander

Dunaway 1 Minor Gray, born August 16,
1879, died November 15, 1911, a druggist 2
Catherine, born September 2, 1881 3 Warren Gordley, of further mention

(IV) Warren Gordley, youngest son of
Alexander and Harriet E (Ewing) Dunaway,
was born in Greensboro, Greene county,
Pennsylvania, December 19, 1885 He was
educated in the public schools, attended the
Uniontown high school He has been since
1911 manager of the Dunaway Drug Store in
Fairchance He is a Democrat in politics,
and served the borough as tax collector for
a term of three years He is a member of
the Knights of Pythias, the Patriotic Order
of America, and an attendant of the Presbyterian church He is unmarried

---

DILWORTH

The Dilworths are found
in Bucks county, Pennsyl-
vania, at an early day
James Dilworth married about 1681, Ann
Wain, and came from Thornbury, in Yorkshire, England to Bucks county, where he
died in 1699, leaving William, Richard, Jane,
Hannah, Jennet, Rebecca and James William married Sarah Webb, settled in Birmingham James Dilworth believed to be a son
of William, married, in 1745, Lydia Martin,
and is said to have built the first log cabin
where Dilworthstown, Chester county, now
stands and the tavern building in 1758, although there was no license there until after
his death Charles, eldest son of James Dilworth, was justice of the peace, and took an
active part in the revolution, for which he was
disowned by the Society of Friends It is
from this Chester county Dilworth family that
the Dilworths of Connellsville descend Their
parental grandfather settled in Ohio with his
wife Rebecca, who lived to be nearly one hundred years of age

(II) George M Dilworth was born at
Mount Pleasant, Ohio where he succeeded
his father in the mercantile business He was
a prosperous merchant, and held a high position in his town He was a director of the
First National Bank, and for twenty-five years
was a member of the school board, also serving in many positions of trust He was a
member of the Presbyterian church, and helpful in church and town affairs, being a man of
great public spirit He married Evelyn Hogg,
born in Mount Pleasant, Ohio, where they

both grew to adult years, married and died, he in 1888, she in 1880. Her father, John T Hogg, was an early settler at Mount Pleasant, a leading merchant, and a well-known influential man in that section. Children of George M Dilworth 1 William R. of Alliance, Ohio 2 Cassie, married Arthur Murdock, of Denver, Colorado 3 Anna, resides in Denver 4 Winfield S. resides in Denver 5 Ellen, married B F Montgomery and resides in Los Angeles, California 6 Desso K., of whom further 7 Ada, married Charles Van Peltz

(III) Desso Kirk, youngest son of George M and Evelyn (Hogg) Dilworth was born in Mount Pleasant, Ohio, August 14 1858. He was educated in the public schools, finishing his studies at the high school. He learned telegraphy, and for some time was in the employ of the C & P Railroad Company as operator, but resigned to become bookkeeper for the stove works at Martins Ferry Ohio. In 1884 he came to Pennsylvania and was engaged with the Rainey Coal Company of Moyer, and for four years with the Connellsville Glass Company, later returning to the Rainey Company as manager of their office business at Mount Braddock, Pennsylvania, a position he yet holds, being one of the oldest employees of the company, as well as one of the most capable and efficient. He is a member of the Presbyterian church, as is his wife, and of King Solomon's Lodge, Free and Accepted Masons. In politics he is a Republican.

He married September 18, 1890, Maud L, daughter of John and Eliza (Barnes) Montgomery, of near Belle Vernon, Pennsylvania. John Montgomery was a millwright and contractor, building many of the grist mills of western Pennsylvania. He was a member of the Presbyterian church as was his wife Eliza. He died July 2, 1881, she January 20, 1902. Their children James Clarinda. Franklin Hannah Nancy, Theodore John David, Richard Maud L (of previous mention), Isadore and Belle.

Children of Desso K and Maud L Dilworth 1 John Montgomery, born August 8, 1891, graduate of Connellsville high school class of 1911 2 Desso Kirk (2) born December 6, 1897. Mr Dilworth lives at No 201 Washington avenue, Connellsville, where he erected his present residence in 1902

DE TEMPLE This family descends from Jacob De Temple, member of a wealthy, influential and aristocratic family of Belgium. He located in the north of France, where he established and operated extensive iron works. These works were highly profitable until the French revolution, when, with other French families of wealth, he fled to Switzerland, where he found asylum for only a few months. Being compelled to leave Switzerland, he went to a Rhine province in Germany, where he remained until the downfall of the revolutionists and restored peaceful conditions made it again safe to return and reopen his iron works. He continued in business until his death. He married, and among his children was a son Joseph.

(II) Joseph, son of Jacob De Temple, worked with his father in the management of the iron works in northern France, and on the death of the latter continued their operation. He married Eva Monbier, and had six sons, all of whom served in the French army under Louis and under Napoleon III. Children John of whom further 2 Alexandre, served in the Marine Corps (artillery) and was in the regiment that escorted the body of the great Napoleon from St Helena to the magnificent monument in Paris, the Hotel des Invalides, where the body was laid at rest, December 15, 1840 3 Louis, also served in the Marine Corps 4 Nicholas, served in the Fifty-ninth Regiment of Infantry 5 Joseph (2), served in the Thirty-third Regiment Infantry 6 Michael, served in the Thirty-third Infantry

(III) John, son of Joseph De Temple, was born in 1808, in northern France, in the department from which came Lafayette. He was a worker in the family iron and steel plant with his father and brothers. He was a soldier under the Citizen King Louis Phillipe, the "King of the French," that being the title under which he was allowed to reign after the July revolution of 1830 which dethroned Charles X. John De Temple served eight years with the French army in Africa, in the Fifty-eighth Regiment (infantry). He married Catherine Bon born in France in 1812, daughter of Nicholas Bon a soldier under Napoleon I. His brother, Peter Bon was with Napoleon on his disastrous invasion of Russia, was captured by Cossacks at Moscow, escaped, and after the burning of that city struggled homeward to France with the badly broken French army, suffering as he was from a bad wound in the face Nicholas Bon, after leaving the army, engaged in the grocery business, he married Eva Schmelk of German (or Dutch) descent Children of John De Temple and Catherine Bon 1 Joseph, died in infancy 2 John, of whom further 3 Catherine, married Michael Gradeau, a soldier of France killed in the Franco-Prussian war 4 Alexander, came to the United States in 1870, now living in Connellsville, unmarried

(IV) John (2), son of John (1) De Temple, was born in northern France, February 24, 1844 He received a good education, and after completing his studies and until 1868 worked in the iron and steel mills, held for three generations in his immediate family In 1868 he came to the United States settling at that Mecca of the steel worker, Pittsburgh, remaining there one year when he came to Connellsville entering the employ of the American Steel Company as hammerman When the Connellsville branch was discontinued, Mr De Temple began building coke ovens and continued for many years, making that his specialty He became known all over the United States where coke is made, and has erected ovens in all sections of the coke field In 1905 he made a tour of Europe, going alone and although over sixty years old, visited all the countries of Europe except Russia, Spain and Turkey He is a Republican, and with his wife belongs to the Roman Catholic church

He married, March 2, 1867 in the city of Nancy France Catherine Luffer who died in 1902 he married (second) Anna Mary Smith Children all by first wife John (3) a railroad man married Emma Rhodes Theresa deceased Mary married Patrick Handlin Louis, a boilermaker, now living in New Orleans

---

WORK The Work family came to Fayette county from "over the mountains," having been residents of Lancaster county, Pennsylvania, prior to their removal west The first settlement was made by Joseph Work the great-grandfather of Judge James Clark Work, of Uniontown

(I) Joseph Work, of English parentage, was a resident of Lancaster county, Pennsylvania, as early as 1755 He had brothers, Samuel and Robert, and in 1766 they came with their few belongings to Fayette county, having made the journey over the mountains on horseback Samuel took up land in Dunbar township, where in 1799 he was assessed as having "one slave, four horses, four cattle and three hundred and eighty-two acres of land " Robert settled in North Union township, about two miles north of Uniontown In the tax list of 1793 he is assessed as a single man Joseph settled near what is now Vanderbilt, in Dunbar township, Fayette county, where he is on the first assessment roll of the township, bearing date 1799, as owning four horses, six cattle and three hundred acres of land He had children James, of whom further, John, located in Washington county, Pennsylvania, Adam and Alexander, farmers of Dunbar township, Andrew, of Franklin township, Mary, married Thomas Miller, of Harrison county, Ohio, Esther, married William Dugan, of Dunbar township

(II) James, son of Joseph Work, was born in Dunbar township, Fayette county, Pennsylvania He married Mary Ellen Dugan, also born in Fayette county After marriage they moved to Harrison county, Ohio, where they remained several years, then returned to Dunbar township, where he owned the farm now the property of his grandson, Judge Work, of Uniontown James Work was a man of weak frame and delicate health, which threw the greater burden of farm work upon his sons Children Catherine, died unmarried, John, of whom further, Ellen, married William Griffith, a farmer of Dunbar township, Nancy, married Samuel J Cox, a tailor of Brownsville Pennsylvania, Joseph W, a prosperous farmer of Fayette county, married a Miss Murphy, Mary, died unmarried

(III) John, eldest son of James and Mary Ellen (Dugan) Work, was born at Cadiz, Harrison county, Ohio, December 30, 1818, died January 3, 1900 He was nine years of age when the family returned to Fayette county where he attended the subscription schools for a limited time Owing to his father's health the burden early fell upon his shoulders, being the eldest son, but he was made of manly material and bore his burdens bravely When not engaged at work on the

home farm he worked for nearby farmers at wages of thirty-five and fifty cents a day At nights he studied by the light of the wood fire and so educated himself that he taught two terms in the district school ' When but a young man he bought a little farm three miles northwest of Dunbar, on which he was able to make a first payment He was known from boyhood as a good judge of stock, and at the age of twenty-five years he was chosen by Greenberry Crossland to take charge of his droves of cattle while being driven over the National Pike to eastern markets—Baltimore, Philadelphia and New York So capable was he that he was taken into partnership with Mr Crossland, an alliance that existed fifteen years He then retired and formed a partnership with his father-in-law, Charles McLaughlin, continuing the same business In both these associations Mr Work superintended the driving of the stock and its sale in eastern markets In those days drafts were unknown, and the money received was brought back by Mr Work in gold and bills, carried on his person or in his saddle bag Though he carried hundreds or thousands of dollars in this way over "the pike," where he was well known, he was never molested nor did he ever carry a revolver The droves often exceeded two hundred head and the returns were very large Mr McLaughlin retired about 1870, Mr Work continuing until 1882 During the war the business was very profitable, and they continued their drives to market even after the railroads came He was a very active, energetic man, weighing over two hundred pounds but his large frame carried no extra flesh He stood six feet high and was built in perfect proportion He was strong and robust, continuing active until his last illness He was a Whig, later a Republican, and with his wife belonged to the Presbyterian church

He married Sarah McLaughlin, born in Dunbar township, Fayette county, Pennsylvania, in 1826, died April 16, 1894, daughter of Charles and Mary (Swearingen) McLaughlin Charles McLaughlin was a son of the emigrant from Ireland, who settled first in Lancaster county, Pennsylvania, but after about seven years there crossed the mountains to Fayette county, making the journey on horseback He settled near Laurel Hill in Dunbar township, where he died Charles

McLaughlin was born in Lancaster county, but his childhood and after life were spent in Fayette county He grew up on the farm, but early in life began hauling produce to eastern markets, returning loaded with goods for the merchants of his section After the National Road was opened he was a wagoner on that historic thoroughfare for several years He also engaged with his son-in-law, John Work, in cattle dealing He owned a good farm, on which he lived and made the base of his operations The family were members of the Presbyterian church His wife, Mary (Swearingen) McLaughlin, was of German descent, hers being a well known county family Children of Mr and Mrs McLaughlin 1 William, married Emma Gaddis, they lived and died on their farm in Dunbar township, she died in 1912 2 Sarah, of previous mention wife of John Work 3 Samuel, a farmer of Dunbar township, married Eliza Clark, both deceased 4 Elizabeth, married William Whitehill, a farmer of Dunbar township, later of near Marengo, Iowa, where both died Children of Mr and Mrs Work 1 Mary Elizabeth, died aged nineteen years 2 Ellen, married George W Barricklow, now a retired farmer of Kansas City, Missouri 3 William, died in 1888, was a farmer of Menallen township, Fayette county, he married Harriet Hankins, who also died in 1888 4 Anna M married John M Henshaw, a farmer at Scenery Hill, Washington county, Pennsylvania 5 Charles, died in infancy 6 James Clark of whom further 7 Sarah Belle, married James A Chalfant, a merchant of South Brownsville Pennsylvania 8 John, of whom further 9 Clara, married Adam Nicholson, a farmer of Franklin township, Fayette county 10 Samuel, died in infancy

(IV) Judge James Clark Work, sixth child of John and Sarah (McLaughlin) Work, was born on the farm he now owns, settled by his grandfather in Dunbar township, Fayette county, Pennsylvania, February 8, 1859 He attended the Sandy Hollow district school, and after a preparatory course entered Waynesburg College, where he pursued a classical course and was graduated, class of 1884 He was a member of the Union Literary Society while in college and took an active part in society work In the fall of 1884 he entered the law school of the Uni-

458 PENNSYLVANIA

versity of Michigan at Ann Arbor, continuing one year. He then, in the fall of 1885, entered the law school at Yale University, passing the examination for entrance to the senior class. He was graduated LL. B., class of 1886. Before leaving New Haven he passed the required examination and was admitted to practice in the supreme court of Connecticut. He then returned to Fayette county, locating in Uniontown, entering the office of Alfred Howell, then a leader of the Fayette county bar. He familiarized himself with Pennsylvania law and procedure, and on December 6, 1886, was admitted to the Fayette county bar. In January, 1887, he opened a law office in Uniontown, where he practiced his profession alone until 1889. In that year he formed a law partnership with William A. Hogg, continuing for three years as Work & Hogg. The partnership was dissolved and he resumed practice alone, never again having a partner. He was an honorable, successful lawyer and always stood high at the bar. In 1907 the Pennsylvania legislature passed an act creating a separate orphans' court for Fayette county, and in May, 1907, the governor appointed James Clark Work judge of that court, to serve until a successor was duly elected and qualified. He was sworn in June 5, 1907. The party primaries having been held, the Republican county committee met and nominated Judge Work to succeed himself. The Democratic county committee endorsed the nomination, although the candidate was an uncompromising Republican, and had done more than any other man to wrest party control of Fayette county from them. The Prohibition party and the Citizens' party also endorsed his candidacy, so he was the unanimous choice of the county. This evidence of popularity and appreciation one seldom sees equaled in public life. At the following election sixteen thousand five hundred votes were cast, and of these greatly over fifteen thousand bore the name of Judge Work. He thus became judge of the orphans' court by an almost unanimous county vote for a term of ten years. Prior to the appointment of a temporary judge by the governor and after the passing of the act creating the Fayette county orphans' court, the Bar Association of Fayette county met and recommended the appointment of James Clark Work for the position.

This evidence of the high appreciation of his brethren of the bar was a graceful compliment and very gratifying to the recipient.

Judge Work is a staunch Republican. He cast his first presidential vote for James A. Garfield, and in 1893 was chosen chairman of the Fayette county Republican committee, serving until 1895. In 1893, under his leadership, the first Republican county ticket passed the ordeal of the ballot box successfully. In 1894 the victory was duplicated and Fayette became a debatable instead of a sure Democratic county. In view of this fact the endorsement of Mr. Work for the judgeship was indeed high appreciation.

He is an attendant of the First Presbyterian church of Uniontown, and belongs to Fayette Lodge, No. 228, Free and Accepted Masons, Uniontown Chapter, Royal Arch Masons, Uniontown Commandery, Knights Templar, Uniontown Lodge of Perfection and Pittsburgh Consistory, Ancient Accepted Scottish Rite, in which he holds the thirty-second degree. He is a member of the American, State and Fayette County Bar associations, Uniontown Country and Laurel clubs. He is a trustee of Uniontown Hospital and a director of the Second National Bank. Judge Work inherits the stature of his sire, stands six feet tall and carries with it a personality that marks him a man of influence and worth. His career on the bench has been a dispensation of justice, and for him the "recall" hath no terrors.

Judge Work married, April 16, 1903, Mrs. Edwina (Null) Fuller, born in Westmoreland county, Pennsylvania, daughter of Harrison Null of Greensburg, Pennsylvania.

(IV) John, son of John and Sarah (McLaughlin) Work, was born in Dunbar township, Fayette county, Pennsylvania, September 8, 1864. He received his education at the Sandy Hollow" and "White Schools." He engaged in farming on his father's land and remained with his parents until the death of his mother, April 6, 1894. Upon the death of his father he inherited the estate of two hundred and twenty-four acres, on which he erected several new buildings, which have all the latest improvements. Aside from his farms he is interested in the coal lands of his native state. He is a supporter of Republican principles and has served as school director. He is a member of the Local Grange,

Patrons of Husbandry, and with his wife a communicant of the Laurel Hill Presbyterian church

He married, October 23, 1901, Annie E, daughter of Thomas L and Sarah (Parkhill) Phillips Children Sarah, born October 27, 1902, died November 20, 1903, Mabel Ruth, born February 3, 1906, James Clark, born September 12, 1908

The paternal grandfather of Annie E Phillips was Ellis Phillips, a native of Washington county, Pennsylvania, later of Fayette county, where he became a farmer and a large and influential landowner He married Phoebe Lilly, and with her was a member of the Society of Friends His children 1 Ruth, born at Brownsville, where she died, married Charles Swan 2 Solomon, a bachelor, died aged eighty-one 3 William, a farmer, living near Uniontown, he married a Miss Swan 4 Elizabeth, died unmarried, lived with her brother Solomon 5 Thomas, of whom further 6 James, married Sarah Duggan, lives near Washington, Pennsylvania 7 Martha, married Charles Hilles, resides near Bourbon Indiana 8 Ellis, a physician, married Ada McIlvane and lives at Columbus, Ohio

(II) Thomas, son of Ellis and Phoebe (Lilly) Phillips, was born in Fayette county, Pennsylvania He followed the trade of carpenter for a short time and then took up farming on the old homestead in Franklin township He operated the first coal bank in Fayette county, supplying the county for miles around with the ever necessary "bottled sunshine" He was one of the county's most prominent and influential men He married Sarah Parkhill Children 1 Elizabeth, married John S Junk, deceased of Uniontown, Pennsylvania 2 Annie E, of previous mention 3 Ellis, married Cora Reed, lives on a farm in Franklin township

MILLARD The Millards of Connellsville, Pennsylvania descend from a long line of English ancestors The father of the American family was a gallant officer of the English army who upheld his country's honor on many battlefields The family for many generations were residents of Portsmouth, England They were always an adventurous family and followed the flag of their country on sea and land wherever duty called James B Millard is the first of his family to come to the United States, none of his seven brothers and sisters settling in this country

His father, William Millard, was born in Portsmouth, England, about 1816, died in 1866 He was a commissioned officer in the English army, and fought under the banner of St George all through the Crimean war to its finish at Sebastopol When the great mutiny occurred in India he was with the army that marched to the relief of Lucknow, and witnessed the terrible punishment meted out to the leading mutineers After passing through all the perils of war he returned to England and died a peaceful death He married Emma Brookman, who survived him many years but remained a widow until her death Children William, Edward, deceased, Joseph, George, deceased, John, James B, of whom further, Alfred, Emma None of these children came to the United States except James B

(II) James B, sixth son of William Millard the English soldier, was born at Portsmouth, England, April 22, 1855 He was educated in the schools of Liverpool, England, to which city his parents removed when he was a young child After completing his school years he entered the employ of a butcher in Liverpool, and for thirteen years was engaged in that business In 1881 he came to the United States, locating finally at Connellsville, Pennsylvania, entering the employ of the Baltimore & Ohio Railroad Company at the paint shops, remaining with that company five years For the next eight years he was employed in the machinery department of the Leisering Company He then engaged in catering for five years, having a restaurant in Connellsville In 1899 he purchased the bottling business of J J Donnelly, and is yet engaged in the manufacture and bottling of mineral waters of different kinds, with home and factory on Trevor street He has prospered in his various activities, and has varied investments in other of Connellsville enterprises He is a Republican in politics, and has taken an active part in the city government In 1906 he was elected councilman an office he has held continuously until the present date (1912), and since March, 1910, has been president of the council He is a firm advocate of good government, and has always stood for the best methods in administering the affairs of his city In religious faith he is an Episcopalian He is past exalted ruler of Connellsville Lodge, Benevolent Protective Order of Elks, having twice held that office, is also a Knight of the Maccabees and Order of Moose

He married, March 26, 1880, in England, Annie Kyle, born in England, daughter of Christopher and Martha Kyle Children John, born January 18, 1881, died October, 1891, James, born July 12, 1883, Anna Belle, born May 29, 1888, Helen, born March 29, 1892, Zoe, born May 9, 1894, Harry, born August 21, 1898

PORT This family came to Connellsville from Blair county, Pennsylvania, where Levi Walter Port was born in 1830, where he was educated and learned the trade of merchant tailor He came to Connellsville in 1891 and was in business there, later at Dawson, Fayette county, where he died April 30, 1909 He was a veteran of the civil war, a Republican and a member of the United Presbyterian church He married Martha Smith, born February 15, 1843, a member of the Methodist Episcopal Church Children Clarence Albert, of whom further, William James, deceased, Mae, Sarah, Levi Walter (2), Frank, Lloyd, Nancy, Lena; and three died in infancy

(II) Clarence Albert, eldest child of Levi Walter and Martha (Smith) Port was born in Tyrone, Blair county, Pennsylvania, February 13 1865, died November 3, 1909 He was educated in the public schools, and learned his father's trade and business—merchant tailoring He continued in business with his father until 1890, when he located in Connellsville, where he engaged in business until his death He was a Republican and a member of the Methodist Episcopal church He married, November 26, 1891, in Connellsville Clara Belle Foster born in Franklin township, Fayette county, Pennsylvania, March 20, 1866, daughter of George and Martha (Norris) Foster and granddaughter of Henry Foster, born in Franklin township December 25, 1797, and great-granddaughter of David Foster, of Lancaster county, Pennsylvania, and one of the early settlers of Fayette county Pennsylvania, where he died November 5 1817 Henry Foster died February

5, 1881, married Magdalena Barricklow, born in Franklin township, Fayette county, about 1798, died November 13, 1840 The children David, George, Henry, William, James, Margaret, Benjamin, Susan, Catherine He married a second wife, Martha McKnight Their children Thomas, Robert, Sarah, Magdalena, Mary Ellen, Matilda George Foster was a farmer, a Democrat, and a member of the United Presbyterian Church He died in Connellsville, September 25, 1909 He married Martha Norris, who died July 9, 1876 Their children John Henry, Sarah Jane, Mary Catherine, George, Ewing Paull, Harriet and Clara Belle, who married Clarence Albert Port Their children Clarence Albert (2), born June 7, 1892, Harold Foster, July 31, 1894; Irene, June 9, 1897, Milton Arnold, November 3, 1899, died March 6, 1901, Frederick Roehm, born April 20, 1902 Mrs Clara B Foster Port survives her husband and resides in Connellsville

BRICKMAN The Brickmans of Connellsville, Pennsylvania descend maternally from Adam Rubel a farmer of Bavaria, Germany, and a soldier in the Crimean war He married and had a family of nine children, one, Adeline coming to the United States She married Jacob Zimmer and lived in Wheeling, West Virginia They descend paternally from George Brickman, born in Bavaria Germany, where he lived and died He was a stonemason· a man of good education and industrious, thrifty habits, belonging to the Presbyterian church He married Margaret, daughter of Adam Rubel, of previous mention George Brickman died 1868 his wife surviving until 1873 They were the parents of thirteen children, one only coming to the United States, Jacob of whom further

(II) Jacob son of George and Margaret Brickman, was born in Bavaria Germany, where he received an excellent education, served in the German army and followed the occupation of farmer In 1871 he came to the United States and located at Wheeling, West Virginia being then a young man He entered the employ of the Baltimore & Ohio railroad, entering the woodworking shops, where he learned the carpenter's trade After one year in Wheeling he was transferred to the Connellsville shops, continuing in the same

employ until 1910, when on account of age
and poor health he was retired on a pension
His entire life in the United States has been
spent in the carpenter shops of the Baltimore
& Ohio, and his pension is the reward that
the company gives for long and faithful service He is a Democrat, and has served the
city of Connellsville as councilman and on
the school board He is a member of the
German Lutheran church, the Knights of
Pythias, Knights of Malta, and the German
Mutual Aid Society He married July 2
1876, Sophia Snyder, born in Cumberland,
Maryland, daughter of John B and Elizabeth
Snyder, both born in Germany, coming to
the United States about 1850 Children 1
George W of whom further 2 Mary, now
a teacher in the public schools of Connellsville 3 Margaret, residing with her parents
4 Nellie, now a bookkeeper in Connellsville
5 Carl now a bookkeeper in New York City
6 William, traveling salesman for the Westmoreland Grocery Company 7 Albert, graduate of Connellsville high school, class 1912
Two other children died in infancy

(III) George W, son of Jacob Brickman,
was born in Connellsville Pennsylvania,
April 29, 1877 He was educated in the public schools of that city, and began business life
as a clerk in a grocery store In 1905 he established for himself at the corner of North
Pittsburgh and Peach streets, where he has
since conducted a successful grocery business
In politics he is a Democrat, and is a member of the Knights of the Maccabees He is
unmarried

MILLS This branch of the Mills family
was founded in the United States
by Joseph Mills, born in England, about the year 1830 He obtained an
expert knowledge of coal mining in his native land later coming to the United States
and settling in the anthracite coal region of
Pennsylvania Lackawanna county He obtained employment in the mines, where his
knowledge of mine gases and proper methods
of tunneling enabled him to secure the highest wages He died in 1878 He married
Jane McDugall born in the North of Ireland
in 1831, died 1883 of Scotch ancestry She
grew to womanhood in Ireland, emigrating to
the United States with a colony of Scotch-
Irish Presbyterians, locating in Scranton,

Pennsylvania, where she was married Their
only child who survived infancy was Thomas,
of whom further

(II) Thomas, son of Joseph and Jane (Mc-
Dugall) Mills, was born in Scranton Pennsylvania, February 25, 1871 He was several
years of age when his father died, and twelve
years of age when his mother died, leaving
him without a relative in the United States
Thrown thus early upon his own resources, he
was obliged to take such work as offered
He worked among the farmers of the country
in different places until he was nineteen years
of age, receiving at first very small wages and
often nothing but his board In 1890 he secured a position with the Scranton Electric
Light and Water Company, one of the first
electric companies formed in the United
States He began trimming street lamps, and
gradually gained a knowledge of all branches
of the electrical business, as at that time there
were no specialists the company requiring
each employee to be capable of handling any
part of their work Under such conditions
he gained a thorough knowledge of the electrical business Two years later he went to
Cleveland, Ohio, remaining two years in the
employ of the Cleveland Electric Light Company, now known as the Cleveland Illuminat-
ing Company He next obtained a position
in the electrical department of the Electrical
Street Railway Company, and later was appointed chief electrician with the American
Steel Wire Company In 1904 he located
in New York City where he was in charge
of wiring for the electrical department of the
subway In 1908 he came to Connellsville,
where he was appointed superintendent of the
armature winding department of the West
Penn Railroad Company In 1909 he established a plant for the repairing of all electrical
mining machinery In 1910 this business was
incorporated as the Wells-Mills Electric Company, with G W Wells as president, and Mr
Mills, vice-president This company deals in
all forms of electrical supplies, wires and in-
stalls electrical machinery, and do all forms
of electrical repair work Their services are
in demand for repair work within a radius of
one hundred miles They have also added a
garage which has proved a very successful
department Naturally of a mechanical turn
of mind, Mr Mills excels along electrical
lines, having learned the business from its

practical side   He is a Republican, but extremely independent in political action, voting for the best men, regardless of party   He is an attendant of the Lutheran church, of which his wife is a member

He married, October 7, 1895, Lily M Rupert born at Stroudsburg, Pennsylvania daughter of Byron and Elizabeth M Rupert, of Pennsylvania German stock from the Allentown, Pennsylvania, district, her father is a farmer   Children of Thomas and Lily M Mills   Herbert born August 9, 1904, Helen, March 10, 1906

CAMPBELL-SWAN   The Campbells, of Uniontown, Pennsylvania, herein recorded, descend from Rev Isaac Campbell, born in Scotland, died in Maryland 1784   He was ordained and licensed by the Lord Bishop of London to officiate in Virginia July 6, 1747   He was rector of Trinity Parish, Newport, Charles county, Maryland, 1748, was a member of Charles county committee of safety, November 24, 1774, and was loyal to the Colonies all through the struggle for independence   After 1776 he had a school at his residence   He published a work on "Civil Government" in four volumes   In 1779 he was elected rector of the parish by the board of trustees, having previously had the living from Governor Ogle   He served the parish thirty-six years   At his death he left a large estate in Virginia, about three thousand three hundred acres, which he divided equally among his sons also a large plantation in Maryland, on which he lived and which he divided between his daughters   His widow survived him but a short time   His estate was appraised March 7, 1785   He married 1755 Jean Brown born at Rich Hill, Charles county Maryland June 1 1728 died 1784, daughter of Dr Gustavus Brown, of Charles county Maryland born in Scotland   Rev Isaac Campbell left sons William, Gustavus Brown Isaac, James, Richard Henry, and John M

Abel Campbell the founder of this family in Fayette county, was a grandson of Rev Isaac Campbell through one of these sons supposed to be Isaac Campbell

(III) Abel grandson of Rev Isaac and Jean (Brown) Campbell, was born about 1770 in Charles county Maryland and in early life settled in Fayette county, Pennsylvania   He was a member of the Society of Friends, and became a wealthy farmer of Fayette county   He died aged eighty-nine years   He married Martha Dixon   Children   1 Lewis, of whom further   2 Elizabeth, married (first) Samuel Mitchel, (second) Etaka Hyatt   3 Mary, married William Price

(IV) Lewis son of Abel and Martha (Dixon) Campbell, was born in Fayette county, Pennsylvania, July 1, 1795, died aged eighty-nine years   He was an extensive farmer and large landowner cultivating his fertile acres until his health gave way, then turned the farm over to his sons James and Joseph M   After the death of the latter the heirs in 1898 sold the homestead to the Fayette Coal & Coke Company   He was a Whig in politics, later a Republican

He married Deborah Antrim, daughter of the early Antrim family of Fayette county   Children   1 Martha, married Jesse Coldren   2 Susan A, married Nathaniel Gray   3 James, died at the age of seventy years, a bachelor   4 Mary Ann, married Elliott Hibbs, of Uniontown, and is the only survivor of these children   5 Joseph Morgan, of whom further   6 Elizabeth, died in infancy   7 Milton, died in infancy

(V) Joseph Morgan, son of Lewis and Deborah (Antrim) Campbell was born in New Salem, German township, Pennsylvania, April 11, 1841 died January 5 1894   He was educated in the public schools and grew to manhood on the home farm, later becoming its manager in association with his brother James   Afterward he was sole manager, continuing until his death   He was a successful farmer and a lover of fine live stock, keeping nothing but the best breeds in his fields or stables   He was interested in the First National Bank of Uniontown and was a member of the board of directors for nearly a quarter of a century   He was always active in politics and served one term of three years as auditor of Fayette county   He was kind-hearted and generous always willing to aid a neighbor in any way possible   He was a Republican in politics and was a Quaker in church faith but attended meetings at the Presbyterian church   He married, June 5, 1873 Sallie Ann Swan, who survives him   She is the daughter of Presley G and Miranda (Hibbs) Swan   (See Swan VI)

Joseph M. Campbell

The family of Swan is of English origin, but the ancestor of the Swans of Pennsylvania herein recorded was one of the one hundred English families whom King James of England placed in possession of an equal number of confiscated Irish estates At what time Richard Swan came to America there is no record, but he settled in Hanover township, Lancaster county, Pennsylvania, prior to 1738 His sons were 1 James, born 1711, in Ireland, died December, 1741 2 Moses, of whom further 3 Joseph, born 1715, resided in Franklin county, Pennsylvania 4 William, born 1719, in Ireland married Jeannett Shields, and died in Franklin county, Pennsylvania, January, 1773, leaving issue 5 Richard, born 1725, in Ireland, was a merchant of Philadelphia Pennsylvania, and was one of the signers to the non-importation resolutions of 1765 6 Alexander, born in Ireland, in 1727, settled in Hanover township, Dauphin county, Pennsylvania, married Martha Gilchrist, and died March, 1778, leaving issue

(II) Moses son of Richard Swan, born in Ireland, in 1713, settled in Paxtang township, Lancaster county, Pennsylvania, about 1730 He married, in 1737, Jean Barnett Children Hugh, born 1738, John of whom further, Isaac, born 1742 died unmarried, Catherine born 1743, married Thomas Porter, William, born 1745, married Martha Renick Joseph born 1747, Moses, 1749, Jean, 1751 Margaret 1753 Richard 1757, married Catherine Boggs

(III) John, son of Moses and Jean (Barnett) Swan was born in Paxtang, Pennsylvania, 1740 He settled in Maryland, going from thence to western Pennsylvania, where he was the first permanent white settler in Greene county This honor is disputed, but there seems to be no evidence of earlier permanent settlement although there were others who passed over and camped for a time on the same territory John Swan, the first settler in Cumberland township and one of the first who settled in the county, was there as early as 1767, and looked with an eye of satisfaction on the stately forests of the valley of Pumpkin Run, and to give notice to all comers that he had chosen that location for himself placed his mark upon it by blazing the trees around a goodly circuit This method of marking a tract was called a "tomahawk improvement," and though it carried no legal title from state or Indians, yet it gave a title which it was not so safe for a rival settler to disturb and was universally respected

In 1768 John Swan returned with Thomas Hughes, later Jacob and Henry Van Meter came, having made the trip from Maryland, with their families, settling along the banks of Muddy Creek near (now) Carmichaels John Swan brought a number of slaves with him, who cleared the forests and cultivated the ground There was no trouble at first with the Indians, but in 1774 Logan made his raid and began a reign of terror A fort was built on John Swan's farm for a place of refuge that was known as Swan's and Van Meter's Fort John Swan had sons John, Thomas, Charles, and others

(IV) Colonel Charles Swan, son of John Swan, was born in Maryland and early came with his father and the Van Meters to Greene county He made the journey with the Van Meters, and one of them, Sarah, his future wife, then a girl of ten years, rode the entire distance on horseback with the party An oath of allegiance to the state, by Henry Van Meter (father of Sarah), a warrant for one thousand acres of land to Charles Swan, on the payment of four hundred pounds, a receipt for one dollar subscription to the Pittsburgh *Gazette*, dated July 15, 1795, to Charles Swan notification to Colonel Charles Swan, dated 1810, of the passage of an act granting two thousand dollars for Greensburg Academy at Carmichaels, provided that the Episcopal church, of which Colonel Swan was an active member would allow the use of its church edifice are all preserved in Greene county records Colonel Charles Swan was a leading character in the county, and a man of wealth He married Sarah Van Meter, with whom he made the journey to Greene county in childhood

(V) Robert son of Colonel Charles and Sarah (Van Meter) Swan, died December 29 1873 He married in 1818 Susanna Gregg, who died in 1866, aged seventy-one years Children Presley G, Sarah Ann, Charles H, Alford G, Ruth William, Emily

(VI) Presley G son of Robert and Susanna (Gregg) Swan, was born in March 1821, died in 1891, he married Miranda Hibbs, of Red-

stone township, Fayette county, Pennsylvania
Children Richard, married Catherine Boram,
Jane Violet, married Joseph N Chalfant,
John Hibbs, married Harriet Chalfant, Sarah
(Sallie) Ann, married Joseph M Campbell
(see Campbell V)

CAMPBELL This is a Scotch name of
high distinction, the
Campbells being a High-
land clan, noted in their home, and whose descendants have been eminent in other parts
of the world According to their tradition,
the clan Campbell is of Irish origin, being descended from the great King Heremon, who
reigned in Ireland from 1699 to 1683 B C
Heremon's descendants form by far the most
illustrious line in Ireland, and his ancestry
is traced by the Irish chroniclers to Adam
without a single break As Pennsylvania has
received from early days a large Scotch in-
fusion, it is not strange, but rather what
should have been expected, that Campbell is
a common name in the state, and Fayette
county has its due proportion of Campbells
As, however, the present family came into
Pennsylvania from Ohio and was settled in
that state at an early date, it is probable that
its first American seat was Connecticut, and
that state has a Campbell family from at
least as early as 1719 of Irish origin from
county Ulster, the immigrant ancestor being
Robert Campbell, who arrived at New London, Connecticut, about 1719

(I) William Campbell, the first member of
this family about whom we have definite information, was born July 11, 1761 He lived
in Ohio and was a farmer He married Ruth
Crawford, who was born March 26, 1764
Children Mary, born October 22, 1791,
James C , February 17, 1793, Ephraim, June
10, 1795, William (2), of whom further, Margaret, born June 22, 1798, Elizabeth, February 16, 1800, Ruth, July 19, 1801; Regal,
June 15, 1803, Rachel, May 5, 1805, Abel,
October 26, 1807, Benjamin, August 14,
1809

(II) William (2), son of William (I) and
Ruth (Crawford) Campbell, was born August 13, 1796, and died December 19, 1875
He was brought up and educated in Ohio, in
which state he was a farmer of moderate
means Having farmed in Ohio for some
years, in 1822 he removed to Perryopolis,

Fayette county, Pennsylvania About a mile
from Perryopolis he settled on a farm of
about one hundred and sixty acres, which
had once been part of the estate of George
Washington, and here he became an experienced and successful farmer An old Whig,
he was in his later days a Republican In
religion he was a Quaker He married Mary,
daughter of Caleb and Martha Antram, who
was born August 31, 1797, and died April 22,
1872 This family we suppose to be an offshoot of the Antrims, Antrams and Antrums
of New Jersey, these are all sprung from two
brothers, John and James, who were among
the earliest of the Quaker settlers of West
Jersey, their descendants have been among
the sturdiest and strongest supporters of that
belief in the colony and state, and from them
have come several citizens of prominence
Caleb Antrim was a Quaker, he was born
February 9, 1756, and died February 2, 1842,
his first wife, Sarah, died October 22, 1792,
and his second wife, Martha, born in 1763,
died July 21, 1834 By these two wives he
had nine children Children of William (2)
and Mary (Antram) Campbell 1 Morgan
born January 18, 1825, married Priscilla
Sharpless, three children 2 Robert, born
June 24, 1826, married Elizabeth Price, three
children 3 Ruth, born October 28, 1828,
married John Henderson, no children 4
Caleb born February 14, 1830, married Mary
Gaddis 5 Reuben B , born October 14,
1831, married Jane Haggerty, they are living
in Illinois, and have had six children 6 Benjamin, born September 2, 1833, died in 1834
7 Joseph, born April 15, 1836, married Sarah
Blaney, one child 8 Eliza Ann, born August
4, 1838 married William A Blaney 9 Samuel, of whom further 10 Clark B , born
April 16, 1842, married, October 31, 1878,
Susan C Smith, two children

(III) Samuel, son of William (2) and Mary
(Antram) Campbell was born near Perryopolis August 4, 1840 He was brought up in
Perry township, living on his father's farm
until he was twenty-five years old, and attended school in this township At the age of
twenty-five he bought a farm for himself
For the last seventeen years (1912) he has
lived on the old Poundstone farm, near Mc-
Clellandtown, its extent was formerly eighty-
five acres but part has been sold away, the
fifty-seven acres which remain are all under

cultivation, and there is a gas well on the farm Part of the house is more than one hundred and fifty years old Mr Campbell is a Republican, and has served one year as school director He is a Presbyterian He married (first) January 1, 1867, Hannah G, daughter of John and Mary (Gallagher) McCombs, who died January 14, 1892, (second) September 10, 1895, Hannah, daughter of George and Susan (Stumm) Poundstone, who was born November 21, 1848 Her father, grandson of the first George Poundstone, was born September 13, 1801, and died December 3, 1884 He married, in 1836, Susan Stumm, who was born August 2, 1806, and died February 28, 1884 Children of George and Susan (Stumm) Poundstone Mary, born February 26, 1838, died January 1, 1899, married David R Coffman, eight children, Elizabeth, born November 29, 1839, died January 16, 1911, married David R Coffman, Margaret, born October 16, 1841, married John H Long, two children, John H, born June 17, 1841, died July 30, 1845, Catharine, born January 6, 1847, died December 9, 1865, Hannah, married Samuel Campbell (see Poundstone) Samuel Campbell has no children by either marriage

---

GILMORE This branch of the Gilmore family descends from James Gilmore, born in Ireland, came to America during the revolutionary war, settling in Somerset county, later in Washington county, Pennsylvania, where he died

(II) John, son of James Gilmore, was born in Somerset county, Pennsylvania, in 1780, died in Butler county, Pennsylvania, 1845 He passed his boyhood and days of youthful manhood in Washington county, obtaining an education and preparing for the profession of law He was admitted to the bar at the age of twenty-one years, and soon afterward began the practice of law in Pittsburgh, Pennsylvania In 1803 he married in the town of Washington, Pennsylvania, and the same year settled in Butler, Pennsylvania, having received the appointment as deputy attorney-general He served several terms in the legislature from Butler county, was speaker of the house in 1821 and most prominent in the legal and political history of Butler county during the first twenty-five years of its ex-

istence as a separate political diversion He was the first congressman elected from Butler county, he was a Democrat and an Episcopalian He married Eleanor Spence Anderson, a native of Maryland Children 1 Samuel A, of whom further 2 John, died young 3 Frank, died young 4 Alfred, born in Butler, Pennsylvania, studied law with his brother, Samuel A, and was admitted to practice March 15, 1836, he became a successful lawyer and a politician, serving in congress, 1849-51, later he became a resident of Philadelphia, Pennsylvania, then of Lenox, Massachusetts, where he died about 1890, he married Louisa Grant, whom he met in Washington while serving in congress 4 Anna Lena, married Eugene Ferrero, a lawyer of Butler county

(III) Judge Samuel Anderson Gilmore, son of John Gilmore, was born in Butler, Pennsylvania, January 21, 1808, died in Uniontown, Pennsylvania, May 16, 1873 He was educated at Jefferson College, studied law under the direction of his father, and was admitted to the bar January 8, 1828 He practiced in Butler, becoming very well known and popular He was elected to the legislature 1836 and 1837, and was secretary to the constitutional convention of 1838 In 1848 he was appointed judge of the territory forming the fourteenth and twenty-seventh judicial districts by Governor Shunk, when that office became an elective one In 1851 he was easily elected president judge, an office he held until death After his appointment as judge he lived in Washington, Pennsylvania, one year, then located in Uniontown He was the ideal judge, learned in the law, impartial and a hater of wrong or injustice He endeavored to see that justice and equity prevailed in every case that came before him, and had the unvarying respect of the lawyers whose cases he sat in judgment upon He was a Democrat in politics and a member of the Episcopal church

He married Elvira A Plumer, born in Venango county, Pennsylvania, November 26, 1827, who survived her husband until October 25, 1892 (see Plumer) Children of Judge Samuel Anderson and Elvira A (Plumer) Gilmore 1 Eleanor A, married A J Mead, deceased a grain dealer of Kansas City, she now resides in Uniontown 2 Arnold P, deceased a physician of Chicago.

Illinois, specializing in diseases of the eyes and ear, he married (first) Fanny Gilbreath, of Erie, Pennsylvania, (second) Lena Marsh 3 John, of whom further 4 Lida G, widow of Arthur Weir Bliss (see Bliss IX), she survives her husband, a resident of Uniontown 5 Henry Plumer, of Fairmount, West Virginia 6 Patti Adams, married George B Kaine, deceased, three children 7 Gweenthleen, married Raymond W Green, one child, Samuel 8 David Watson 9 Eleanor

(IV) John (2), son of Judge Samuel Anderson and Elvira A (Plumer) Gilmore, was born in Uniontown, Pennsylvania, at the "Gilmore Mansion," February 22, 1855, died September 2, 1907 His early education was obtained in the public school, his preparatory at the Hills School, Pottstown, Pennsylvania, after which he entered Lafayette College, from whence he was graduated After completing his college course he began business life as a hardware merchant at New Castle, Pennsylvania, in partnership with Fred Plumer, a relative of his mother Later he sold his interest to his partner and began farming He was very successful in his farming operations, and continued for several years He later returned to the hardware business, forming a partnership and trading under the firm name of Gilmore & Frey They purchased the hardware stock and good will of Z B Springer in Uniontown, and there Mr Gilmore was very successfully engaged in business until his death He had other important business interests outside his hardware store He was interested in farms and fine stock raising, organized the Gilmore Coal & Coke Company and also had coal interests in both Fayette and Greene counties He was a prosperous, influential citizen and held leading positions in his city He was a Democrat in politics, but was never an aspirant for public office In religious faith he and his wife are Episcopalians

He married, April 16 1874, Mary, born in Uniontown, daughter of Louis D and Isabella B (Frey) Beall (see Beall) Children of Mr and Mrs Gilmore 1 Guy B, born September 14, 1876, married Nella Epperson, and resides in Sumpter, South Carolina, children John A and Wiliam E 2 Samuel Anderson, born May 30, 1879, an attorney of Pittsburgh, Pennsylvania, married Mary G Taylor

(The Plumer Line)

Mrs Elvira A (Plumer) Gilmore was a descendant of Francis Plumer, one of the founders of the town of Newbury, Massachusetts, 1635

(I) Nathaniel Plumer, the first of the name in Pennsylvania, was born in Newbury Massachusetts, was a commissary in Braddock's army and quartermaster of Forbes army

(II) Nathaniel (2), son of Nathaniel (1) Plumer, settled in western Pennsylvania and purchased four hundred acres of land, embracing part of the site of Mount Washington, now one of the wards of the city of Pittsburgh, and settled thereon in 1789

(III) Samuel son of Nathaniel (2) Plumer, married Patty Adams and settled in Jackson township in 1800

(IV) Arnold, son of Samuel Plumer, was born June 6, 1801 He was educated in the public school and by his mother and grew to manhood on the farm He early took a deep interest in politics and became a recognized leader of the Democratic party He was but twenty-two years of age when he was elected sheriff of Venango county On January 25, 1830, Governor Wolf appointed him prothonotary and clerk of the several courts, recorder of deeds and register of wills, which office he held six years In 1836 he was elected a member of the Twenty-fifth Congress On March 20 1839 he was appointed by President Van Buren United States marshall for western district of Pennsylvania, which office he held until May 6, 1841 In October, 1840, he was elected a member of the Twenty-seventh Congress December 14, 1847, he was again appointed United States marshall, serving until April 31, 1848, when he resigned to accept the office of state treasurer of Pennsylvania, to which he had been elected by the legislature of that year After the close of his term in the state treasurer's office he returned to private life and business He retained a lively interest in politics and was a warm personal friend of President Buchanan, whose candidacy he was largely instrumental in promoting He was slated by the president for a cabinet appointment, but positively refused to allow the president to appoint him He was a strong man and of strong character Had he possessed the advantages of an education, there were no heights to which he could not have risen

He married, January 6, 1827, Margaret, daughter of George McClelland, of Franklin, Pennsylvania. His was the first death to break the family circle, April 28, 1869. The courts of the county adjourned out of respect to his memory, and deepest regret was heard everywhere. Children of Arnold and Margaret (McClelland) Plummer: 1 Elvira A., of previous mention, wife of Judge Samuel A. Gilmore. 2 Samuel, was a lawyer of Franklin county, Pennsylvania, married ————, their only son Lewis M. Plumer, is a leading attorney of Pittsburgh, Pennsylvania. 3 Margaret, married Henry Lamberton, a lawyer of Carlisle, Pennsylvania, later lived in Winona, Minnesota. 4 Eliza, married Rev. Richard Austin, of Uniontown, a minister of the Baptist church. 5 Arnold, married Rachel Smith, he was a merchant of Franklin, Pennsylvania. 6 Henry married Lily Davenport, of Erie, Pennsylvania, he was a lawyer of Franklin, Pennsylvania, moved to Germantown, Pennsylvania, where his wife and children yet live.

(The Beall Line.)

The arms of the Beall family are Three white bells on a blue shield. The above arms are the same as those accredited to Robert Bell, of Scotland in the year 1427. These Bells are on the list of the annuity clans in West Marches in 1587, the Bells lower is mentioned in the acts of parliament in 1481. The American ancestor, Colonel Ninian Beall, came from Scotland in Calvert county, Maryland, in 1655. On first coming to Maryland he signed his name Bell and it would seem to have been carelessness of clerks in the record offices that caused the change to Beall as he afterward wrote it. In Maryland he soon became a leader in the military affairs of the province, which fact indicates previous experience in such matters. In 1676 he was commissioned lieutenant of Lord Baltimore's yacht or vessel of war, called the "Loyal Charles of Maryland." He took an active part in the revolution of 1689 led by Goode, who it is said called Major Ninian Bell his "Argyll", after the great Scotch covenanter. He was appointed major in 1689, and in 1690 was one of twenty-five commissioners for regulating affairs in Maryland until the next meeting of the assembly in 1692 when he was appointed high sheriff of Calvert county. The year following he was designated colonel, and

in 1697 was one of the board of commissioners to treat with the Indians. An act passed in 1699 reads "An act of gratitude to Colonel Ninian Beall." After reciting his valuable services the act awards "75 pounds sterling to be applied to the purchase of three serviceable negroes."

In this same year he was appointed commander-in-chief of the Rangers. In 1696 he had taken the oath as member of the house of burgesses for Calvert county, and was also the first representative elected for Prince George county. Although he was an elder of the Presbyterian church he signed a petition in 1696 to the king for the establishment of the Church of England in Maryland. Five years later he donated half an acre of land in Prince George county for "Ye erecting and building of a house for ye service of Almighty God." He always remained a loyal Presbyterian and kept the Presbyterians on the Patuxent together until the arrival of Nathaniel Taylor who came over with a congregation of Scots from Fifeshire in 1690. He was a man of wealth and devised to his children many thousands of Maryland's most fertile acres.

His son, Colonel George Beall, inherited part of the tract granted to his father called "The Rock of Dumbarton" on which the city of Georgetown is built, a town founded by Colonel Ninian Beall. 'Scharf's History of Maryland' states that Colonel Ninian Beall about the year 1678 induced Presbyterians to settle around and upon the locality where the cities of Washington and Georgetown, D. C., now stand.

Colonel Beall died at the age of ninety-two years. He was buried on the home plantation, and when in recent years his remains were removed, owing to the growth of Georgetown, where his home was situated, it was found that he was six feet seven inches in stature and that his Scotch red hair had retained all its fiery hue. There is one gift of Colonel Ninian Beall to the church he loved that deserves especial mention. This was a handsome silver service made by a celebrated London silversmith in 1707 and presented to the Patuxent Presbyterian church. The service was sent to the church at Bladensburg originally part of Patuxent parish, after the church at Upper Marlboro was abandoned. Part of the service has been lost, but in 1888 two chalices and a handsome tankard were in use by the church, which is now located at Hyattsville So far as known this is the oldest silver service in the United States He has a distinguished posterity—most of the alliance of children and grandchildren were with Scotch families who had settled in Prince George county, in the part called New Scotland Two of his daughters married Magruders, another a Belt, another an Edmondson Eliza Ridgely Beall, his great granddaughter, married Colonel George Corbin Washington, son of Colonel William Augustine and Jane (Washington) Washington, fourth child of Augustine Washington, the elder half brother of President George Washington Although born in Virginia, Colonel George Corbin Washington, who married Eliza Ridgely Beall, adopted Maryland as his home and represented the Montgomery county district three successive terms in congress He died in Georgetown in 1854

Seven members of the Beall family were officers in the continental army, three of them becoming members of the "Society of the Cincinnati " A grandson of Colonel Niman Beall was the founder of the city of Cumberland, Maryland

Louis D Beall, father of Mrs Mary (Beall) Gilmore, and a direct descendant of Colonel Niman Beall, was born in Allegheny county, Maryland, coming to Fayette county, Pennsylvania, about 1840-45, and locating in Uniontown, where he died in 1871 He was a merchant for many years, later engaging in stock dealing He was a man of high character and strict integrity, a citizen of value to his town His wife, Isabella B (Frey) Beall, born in Allegheny, Maryland, died in 1874

Children of Mr and Mrs Beall 1 Clarence H , now living retired in Uniontown, Pennsylvania, married Elizabeth Smith 2 Louis Erwin, after several years of service in the postal and naval departments of the United States at Washington, D C , returned to Uniontown, Pennsylvania, where in company with Judge Nathaniel Ewing he founded the Hygeia Crystal Ice & Cold Storage Company, a prosperous company of which he is now the head, he married, in December, 1884 Harriet Morgan Clark, children Louis Erwin, Jr , Priscilla McKeag and Edward

Clark 3 Lilli, married (first) Lieutenant Lyons, (second) Colonel Wilson Vance 4 Mary, of previous mention, married John Gilmore, whom she survives, a resident of Uniontown She is a member of the Episcopal church, and a lady highly esteemed for her many womanly virtues

BLISS The name Bliss is not of frequent occurrence in English history It is supposed the family was of Norman origin and that the name was originally Blois gradually modified to Bloys, Blyze, Blysse, Blisse and in this country to Bliss Sir John Burke's "Dictionary of Peerages" (page 74) states that the ancient house of Blois was founded in England at the coming of the Conqueror and that the founder was called Blois after the city or that name in France Several English works on heraldry describe the coat-of-arms of one branch of the family thus. "Blisse or Blyse —Argent one a bend cottised, azure, three garbs or Crest A garb or guillims "A Display of Heraldry" (1724) p 127, says ' He beareth, Sable a bend Vaire, between two fleur de lis or, by name of Bloys This coat was granted or confirmed to ———— Bloys of Ipswich in the county of Suffolk by Sir William Segar " This is identical (except in color) with that now claimed and used by the American family

The American history of the family begins with Thomas Bliss, of Belstone parish, in the county of Devon, England Very little is known of him except that he was a wealthy land owner, that he belonged to the class called Puritans on account of the purity and simplicity of their forms of worship, that he was persecuted by the civil and religious authorities under the direction of Archbishop Laud and that he was maltreated impoverished, imprisoned and finally ruined in health and purse He is believed to have been born in the decade, 1550-60, and that he died about the time his sons Jonathan and Thomas emigrated to America 1635-40

(II) Thomas (2), son of Thomas (1) Bliss, was born in Belstone parish, Devonshire, England, about 1580-85 He married in England, 1612-15, Margaret ———— to whom were born six children before coming to America He endured the persecutions meted to his father and brother George and finally was compelled to leave England He sailed from Plymouth in 1635 with his younger brother George and their families and in due season arrived in Boston He settled at Braintree, Massachusetts, later at Hartford, Connecticut, where he died in 1640 His widow Margaret (thought to have been Margaret Lawrence) was a woman of great force of character and after his death managed the affairs of the family with great prudence and judgment She sold the Hartford property in 1643 and moved to Springfield, Massachusetts, thirty miles or more up the Connecticut river, a journey of seventy-five days through the forest She purchased a large tract of land there, part of which is now Main street, Springfield, Massachusetts She lived to see all her children grown up, married and settled in homes of their own except Hannah, who died aged twenty-three years She died in Springfield, August 28, 1684, after a residence in America of nearly fifty years, forty of which she was a widow Children Ann, Mary, Thomas, Nathaniel, Samuel, of whom further, Sarah Elizabeth, Hannah and John

(III) Samuel son of Thomas (2) Bliss was born in England in 1624, died March 23, 1720, aged ninety-six years He married, November 10, 1664-65, Mary Leonard, born September 14 1647, died 1724, daughter of John and Sarah (Heath) Leonard Children Hannah, born December 20, 1666, Thomas, of whom further, Mary, born August 4, 1670, Jonathan, January 5, 1672, Martha, June 1, 1674, Sarah, September 10, 1677, Experience, April 1, 1679, Mercy, July 18, 1680, Ebenezer, July 29, 1683, Margaret, September 11, 1684, Esther, April 2, 1688

(IV) Thomas (3), son of Samuel and Mary (Leonard) Bliss, was born in 1668, died November 10, 1733 He was born, lived and died in Springfield, Massachusetts He married Helen Caldwell Children Hannah, born August 12, 1699, Samuel, March 5, 1701, Martha, January, 1703, Thomas, April 20 1704, Icabod, December 19, 1705, Rachel, September 8, 1707, Abel, February 18, 1708-09, May, October 21, 1710; Timothy, March 2, 1713, Daniel, of whom further, Aaron, 1717, Edward June 24, 1719, Elizabeth, November, 1722

(V) Rev Daniel Bliss, son of Thomas (3) and Hannah (Caldwell) Bliss was born in Springfield, Massachusetts, June 21, 1715, died in Concord, Massachusetts, May 11, 1764 He was graduated at Yale College in 1732, ordained to the ministry, March 7, 1739, and was pastor of the Congregational church of Concord from 1738 to 1764 He was a personal friend of the great Whitefield and like him was bold, zealous, impassioned and enthusiastic in his preaching He was one of the most distinguished of the clergy, who in his day were denominated "New lights" by their opponents, and was several times before a council on account of difficulties in doctrinal points His last and most powerful sermon was delivered, March 11, 1764, in the presence of Rev Whitefield, and so impressed him that he remarked ' If I had studied my whole life I could not have produced such a sermon " A few days later Rev Bliss sickened and died

He married, July 22, 1738, Phoebe Walker, of Stratford, Connecticut, born 1713 died in Concord, July 2, 1797 Children 1 Daniel, born March 18 1740 2 Phoebe, October 21, 1741, married Rev William Emerson, pastor of the church of Christ, successor of her father as pastor of the Concord church 3 John, July 11, 1743 4 Thomas Theodore, of whom further 5 Hannah, March 22, 1747 6 John, died in infancy 7 Samuel, born November 19, 1750 8 Martha, November 5, 1752 9 Joseph, July 23, 1757

Shattuck's ' History of Concord' says "Mr Ebenezer Hartshorn made Mr Bliss coffin—five hundred broad headed coffin nails and five hundred small white tacks were put on the cover and gloves and jewelry were given (to the bearers) at the funeral "

(VI) Captain Thomas Theodore Bliss, son of Rev Daniel and Phoebe (Walker) Bliss, was born at Concord, Massachusetts, May 21, 1745 He learned the trade of shipwrights which he followed in his earlier years He held two commissions as captain in the American army during the revolutionary war One from the congress of Massachusetts bay, the other from the continental congress The latter was signed by John Hancock and gave him command of a company of artillery He was a brave but unfortunate officer On the first campaign into Canada he was taken prisoner by the English at Three Rivers, with all his company, and was held a prisoner during the war He married a Miss Bartlett in Concord and died in Cambridge, Massachusetts, September 1, 1802 The Boston records show the marriage there, June 25, 1789, of a Thomas Theodore Bliss to Huldah Delano This is believed to have been a second marriage of Captain Thomas Theodore Bliss Children 1 Theodore, of whom further 2 Thomas, born February 3, 1767, died 1839, he moved to Charlestown, New Hampshire, Auburn, New York, and in 1836 to Allegan, Michigan, being shipwrecked on his way at Thunder Bay, Lake Huron, married Priscilla Howe, of Boston 3 Eliza, married a Mr Goff, of Maine 4 Phoebe, married, January 1, 1797, Captain William Cunningham, of Boston 5 Ann (or Hannah), married a Mr McIntosh from Maine

(VII) Captain Theodore Bliss, son of Captain Thomas Theodore Bliss, was born March 17, 1766, died March 17, 1831 He served three years as a private with Massachusetts troops during the revolution and was present at the surrender of Burgoyne at Saratoga He was for many years captain of a vessel engaged in the merchant service, sailing from the port of Philadelphia, Pennsylvania He married, July 18, 1793, Sarah Jones, of Bristol, who died in New York in the autumn of 1834 Children 1 Theodore Edward, born at Bristol, April 26, 1794, died in New York city, January 16, 1851, married, May 19 1823, Elizabeth Whitney, of Derby, Connecticut, no issue 2 Sarah, died young 3 Sarah Ann, born January 7, 1802, died September 10, 1872, married, April 26, 1827, Thomas Dean, of Boston, three daughters in 1881 were living at No 35 West Thirty-ninth street, New York city 4 Robert Lewis, of whom further 5 Rosa Elizabeth born 1806, died September 3, 1832, married in New York, December 30, 1825, Samuel Butcher, of Sheffield, England 6 Samuel Potter, born 1808, last heard from at Evansville, Indiana, in 1836

(VIII) Dr Robert Lewis Bliss, son of Captain Theodore and Sarah (Jones) Bliss, was born in Bristol, England, October 5, 1803, died in Florence, Alabama, April 4 1872 He prepared for the profession of medicine and practiced at Florence, Alabama He married in Florence March 19, 1835, Susan Collins, born October 8 1807, daughter of Dr John P and Eliza Collins, of Cookstown, Ireland

Children 1 Theodore, born December 29, 1835 2 Rev John Collins, born May 20, 1837, graduate of Western Theological Seminary at Allegheny, Pennsylvania, in 1862, pastor of the Independent Presbyterian church at Carlisle, Pennsylvania, in 1867 accepted a call to the pastorate of the Independent Presbyterian church of Plainfield, New Jersey, in 1857 he instituted the Jaynes Hall Union prayer meetings in Philadelphia, Pennsylvania, that were the means of great good, he married, May 5, 1864, Mary N. Pechin, of Philadelphia, children Collins Pechin and Edmund 3 Sarah, born January 1, 1839, died July 27, 1873, unmarried 4 Arabella Pillar, born August 13, 1840, died February 7, 1843 5 Robert Lewis, born June 4, 1843, married, at Farmersville, Tennessee, Dora M Watkins, children Theodore Dean, May Watkins, Susan Collins, Fanny Watkins 6 Thomas Pillar, born August 13, 1845, died April 4, 1863, unmarried 7 Arthur Weir, of whom further

(IX) Arthur Weir, son of Dr Robert Lewis and Susan (Collins) Bliss, was born at Florence, Alabama, June 1, 1847, died in Atlantic City, New Jersey, August 25, 1903 He was a very bright, intelligent boy and prepared for college at home At age of sixteen years he entered Princeton University beginning with last half year of the sophomore class He was graduated with the class two and a half years later, having completed the prescribed classical course After graduation he returned south, taught at Bolivar, Tennessee, one year, then came to Uniontown, Pennsylvania, where he engaged with the Dunbar Furnace Company as bookkeeper at their Dunbar plant While occupying this position he became of legal age and cast his first vote He remained with the Dunbar Furnace Company several years, gradually rising to more responsible positions Later he resigned and formed a partnership with George C Marshall and the two young men began the manufacture of fire brick with plant at Dunbar They prospered wonderfully, again and again enlarging their plant, the development of the coke industry creating a great demand for their product After many successful years in business as fire brick manufacturers, they began the manufacture of coke, they found this business profitable and became one of the most extensive coke producing firms in Fayette county They owned large plants at Percy Oliphant and at many other points in the county, all producing merchantable coke Mr Bliss continued actively in business until his death in 1903 He resided in Uniontown at the old Judge Gilmore mansion, the childhood home of his wife, and one of the fine resident locations of Uniontown He was a most capable and energetic man of business, farseeing and wise in management of his large interests He was a Democrat in politics, and a member of the Episcopal church

He married, January 6, 1881, Lida G Gilmore, born in Uniontown, Pennsylvania (see Gilmore) Children Adele and Florence

---

McLAUGHLIN Robert McLaughlin was born in the state of New Jersey, resided in Fayette county, Pennsylvania, and there founded a family After settling in Franklin township, Fayette county, he engaged in farming, but spent his last days in Ohio He was a Democrat, and a member of the Presbyterian church He married Ann Barricklow, born in New Jersey in 1800, and had issue, including a son, Robert (2), of whom further

(II) Robert (2), son of Robert (1) McLaughlin, was born in Fayette county, Pennsylvania, in 1824, died in 1900 He attended the public schools, and afterwards learned the stone mason's trade, an occupation he followed many years He was a Democrat in politics, and a member of the Methodist church, his wife was of the Presbyterian faith He married Susan Gilleland, born in Fayette county about 1828, died in 1882, aged fifty-four years, daughter of William and Mary Gilleland both of whom died in Fayette county Children 1 Mary Ann, born 1848, died 1876 2 Isabell, born 1849 3 Rebecca 1852 4 Mariah, born 1854, died 1857 5 John, born 1856 6 Elizabeth, 1859 7 Lindley B, 1861, now of West Virginia 8 Robert E of whom further 9 Charles, born 1865, died 1867 10 James, born 1868, died 1889 11 William, born 1869 12 Emma, born 1871, died 1889

(III) Robert E, eighth child and third son of Robert (2) and Susan (Gilleland) McLaughlin, was born in Franklin township, Fayette county, Pennsylvania, March 30, 1863 He was reared on the home farm, attended the public schools and completed his education at Mt Union (Ohio) College After leaving college he entered the employ of James Cochran & Sons Company, continuing with them fourteen years as yard foreman He is a Democrat in politics, and was elected justice of the peace of Dunbar township in 1901 and still holds that position In 1905 he was elected chief burgess of the newly created borough of Vanderbilt and wisely guided its affairs during his term of office He is a member of the following fraternal orders Independent Order of Odd Fellows, Junior Order of American Mechanics, Knights of the Mystic Chain, Modern Woodmen of America, Loyal Order of Moose, Knights of Pythias

He married, in 1883, Frances Boyer, born in Vanderbilt, Pennsylvania, September 26, 1869, daughter of Robert and Elizabeth (Sinclair) Boyer, both born in Fayette county, and both deceased She is a granddaughter of George Boyer, a former farmer and tax collector of Dunbar township Children of Robert E McLaughlin Orville Pearl, born 1884, Grover Cleveland, 1885, Bessie Emma, 1887, formerly a teacher in the Vanderbilt schools now teaching in Franklin township, Elizabeth Idessa, born 1890, Eva Louisa, 1892, Mary Nevada, 1895, Helen Rhea, 1900, Henry Etta, 1902, Frances Roberta, 1908

DUNN This branch of the Dunn family in Connellsville descends from Thomas Dunn, born about 1745, in County Down, Ireland, and his wife, Mary Caldwell, born in Scotland He came to western Pennsylvania in 1772 and took a patent from the government for four hundred and sixty-four acres of land in Fayette county, now in Franklin township He was a soldier of the revolution and one of the great army of Fayette county hardy pioneers After settling on his land he did not wait to erect a dwelling, but made the family home in a stable for a year after their arrival in order to get in a crop The following year he put up his log cabin, and also a wagon shop as he was a wheelwright by trade, continuing in business until his death in 1800 Four years before his death he erected the stone house which his grandson Thomas (2) occupied He died aged fifty-five years His wife, Mary (Caldwell) Dunn, born January

20, 1746, survived him until 1824 Seven of his twelve children were sons, and all but two of them moved to the state of Ohio early in life. These two, John and Samuel, worked the old farm together for several years, then Samuel took the western fever and, selling his interest to John, also went to Ohio

(II) John, son of Thomas (1) Dunn, was born in Franklin township, Fayette county, Pennsylvania, on the old homestead farm, where he died October 21, 1861 He was a farmer and a soldier of the war of 1812 He continued on the old farm after all his brothers had moved to Ohio, and ended his days in his native township He married (first) in 1815 Mary Smith, who died June 5, 1835, she left children Sarah, Elizabeth, Mary Jane, Nancy, Thomas (2), of whom further, Rebecca, Robert, moved to Kansas, Harriet He married (second) Mary Oldham, who died in 1843 and he married (third) Catharine Scott, who survives him

(III) Thomas (2), son of John Dunn, was born in the old homestead in Franklin township, Fayette county, Pennsylvania, April 7, 1824, died 1882 He was a farmer of Fayette county all his life He was a member of the United Presbyterian church, in early life a Whig, later a Republican and a Prohibitionist He married, February 4, 1844, Eleanor Scott, born near Masontown, Fayette county, in 1822, died 1894, daughter of Thomas and Catharine (Foster) Scott, who both lived and died in Fayette county Children Marion Crawford, killed at the battle of Murfreesboro during the civil war, Eleanor, Elspay, Mary, Major, and Robert The last survivor now resides at Atlantic City Children of Thomas (2) Dunn John Alexander, born 1845, now deceased, Agnes R, born 1846, died 1911 Thomas Scott, of whom further, Mary Catherine, born 1849 Samuel Watson born 1855, deceased, William Caldwell born 1857, Ann Elizabeth, Harriet Isabel, killed in a runaway 1879, Robert C, born 1861, Major Elsworth, 1862, William C Harry Grant, 1866

(IV) Thomas Scott, son of Thomas (2) and Eleanor (Scott) Dunn, was born on the old homestead farm in Franklin township, Fayette county, June 7, 1848 being the third generation born there after the settlement by his great grandfather Thomas (1) Dunn He was educated in the public schools, and

chose farming as his occupation in early life, but soon became employed in saw milling and lumbering, a business he has carried on for over forty years He also has large coal and real estate interests In 1909 he moved from Franklin township, taking up his residence at 314 South Eighth street, Connellsville, Pennsylvania He was a Republican in earlier life, but since 1877 has been a third party Prohibitionist and a leader in the party He has been the candidate of the Prohibition party for every important office in the county This is purely a matter of principle with him, as an election is not even among the possibilities He is an elder of the United Presbyterian church, of which his father and grandfather also were elders He has always been interested in Sunday school work, having served as superintendent for many years

He married, in 1869 Jane A Murphy, of Fayette county, born September 27 1848, daughter of Robinson and Margaret (Frazer) Murphy, early settlers of the county Children of Thomas Scott Dunn 1 Clarence Edgar, born 1869, died in infancy 2 Olive Bell, born 1871, married in 1897, Dr J O Arnold, of Philadelphia, Pennsylvania 3 Thomas Bryson born 1875 now cultivating a farm in Franklin, married 1898, Ethel Arrison 4 William Robinson, born 1877, resides on homestead farm 5 James H, born 1881, married Annie E McBurney, December, 1906 6 Harriet, born 1884, married William B Downs, of Connellsville, May, 1906

STONER   The Stoner family is one of the old families of Bedford county, Pennsylvania, the earliest ancestor, name unknown, coming from Switzerland

(II) Christian Stoner, son of the emigrant, was a farmer of Bedford county until 1799, when he moved to Westmoreland county, settling in East Huntington township, where he secured title to three hundred acres of good land, and followed farming until his death in 1814 Prior to his demise he divided his farm among four of his sons, John, Abraham, Jacob and Daniel His wife, Barbara Shank, came from Bedford county with him and died in Westmoreland Children John, a farmer of Westmoreland county, and a Mennonite, married Magdalena Fox, Abraham, Christian (2), of whom further, Jacob, Daniel; Henry, David, Barbara, married John Wertz, Elizabeth, married Christian Sherrick, Anna, married John Rudabuck

(III) Christian (2), son of Christian (1) and Barbara (Shank) Stoner, was born in Bedford county, October 10, 1793 When six years old his parents moved to Westmoreland county, settling in East Huntington township near Scottdale, at what is known as "Stoner's Settlement " Here he grew to manhood and resided until his marriage, when he moved to Dunbar township, settling in 1817 on the old Stauffer farm, which he obtained through his wife, Annie, daughter of Christian and Agnes (Overhault) Stauffer Annie Stauffer was born February 5, 1798, died October 9, 1865 They were both Presbyterians Children of Christian (2) Stoner· 1 Abraham, married Margaret Mackey, settled in Illinois, going thence to Missouri, served four years in the confederate army, died at Eureka Springs, Arkansas 2 Christian S, married Mary Shellenbarger, and moved to Illinois, where he died, two of his sons, Caleb R and Martin S, served in the union army 3 Mary, married Abraham Galley, and resided in Franklin township, Fayette county 4 Sarah, married Henry N Friede, and lived in Bullskin township, Fayette county, where her husband died 5 Agnes, twin of Sarah, married John Dudley Collins, and lived in Dunbar township 6 John W, married Margaret Ogleive, and moved to Kansas about 1875, he served in the civil war in the Sixth Regiment, Pennsylvania Heavy Artillery, both deceased leaving a large family of grown children 7 Rebecca, married Joseph Ogleive of Dunbar township, a merchant of Vanderbilt 8 Elizabeth, married Joseph Newcomer, and moved to Kansas, where he was killed by a train 9 Levi, of whom further 10 Isaac F, married (first) August 11, 1859, Rachel Ball, who died January 25, 1882, he married (second) March 9 1884, Mrs Leah (Sipe) Ficher, widow of Andrew Eicher, a union soldier killed in front of Petersburg, and daughter of Peter and Rebecca Sipe 11 Annie, born October 4, 1839, married John W Hair, and lived in Franklin township, Fayette county 12 Cyrus born October 6, 1842, died unmarried in Dunbar township, aged thirty-three years

(IV) Levi, ninth child of Christian (2) and Annie (Stauffer) Stoner, was born in East Dunbar township, Fayette county, Pennsylvania, about 1836, died in Sistersville, West Virginia, in 1904 He followed farming in early life, then became a teamster He served two terms as constable, and spent the last fourteen years of his life in Sistersville He served three years of the civil war in the One Hundred and Forty-second Regiment, Pennsylvania Volunteer Infantry, and was wounded at the battle of Gettysburg He was a Republican in politics, and a member of the Methodist Episcopal church He married Catherine Shaw, born in Fayette county, Pennsylvania, November 5, 1840, who survives him, a resident of Sistersville, a member of the Baptist church She is a daughter of Nathan Shaw, an early resident of Connellsville and a riverman for many years Children William, Cyrus M, of whom further, Charles Bell, deceased, Catherine, Nathan, Lulu, an infant, twin of Lulu, Frederick, Joseph, deceased

(V) Cyrus Millard, second son of Levi and Catherine (Shaw) Stoner, was born in Fayette county, Pennsylvania, March 25, 1861 He attended the public school of Connellsville until he was a lad of twelve years of age. For a time he was connected with the National Locomotive Works, but left there and went to the oil fields in Butler county, returning he entered the employ of the Hazelwood Oil Company as an apprentice to the machinist's trade He has been with Boyts, Porter & Company since 1882, now thirty years He has been promoted several times, and is now (1912) superintendent of the Connellsville plant, a position he most capably fills He is a Republican in politics, and attends the Lutheran church

He married, August 23, 1883, Emma Dawson, born in Connellsville, July 25, 1864, daughter of Robert and Nancy Dawson They were early Fayette county settlers of Scotch-Irish descent, the American ancestor being John Dawson, who came to the American colonies from Whitehaven, England, early in the eighteenth century Nicholas Dawson served with Washington in 1764 and during the revolution, he was in Crawford's defeat, and narrowly escaped capture while helping a bewildered soldier Children of Cyrus Millard and Emma (Dawson) Stoner 1 Edna May died in infancy 2 Alberta, born July 27, 1884   3 Sadie, born June 15, 1887, married Carl W Foore, of Bedford county, Pennsylvania, and has   Emma Jane, born May 4, 1911

This branch of the Brown fam-
BROWN   ily descends from Joshua
Brown, born in England, in 1764   He came to the United States, settling in Fayette county, Pennsylvania, where he became wealthy and prominent   He owned at one time one thousand acres of land, several slaves, and two hotels   Much of his land was under cultivation, and in addition to managing his farming operations he also conducted both hotels   He was interested in the early establishment of banks, and seems to have been a man of great energy and quick discernment   His slaves were freed by law, but he kept them in his employ as long as they wished to stay   He died in 1819   He married (second) Catherine Achards, born in Germany, who lived to be one hundred and one years of age   By a first marriage he had nine children, by his second, three

(II) Rev Benjamin F Brown, son of Joshua and Catherine (Achards) Brown, was born in Georges township, Fayette county, Pennsylvania, August 20, 1816 died February 23, 1906   He was educated in the township schools and reared upon the farm   He was ambitious to become a minister, and in furtherance of his ambition studied and read until his mind was richly stored   He accomplished a course of theological study and received from the Baptist church a license to preach   Later he was ordained and admitted to membership in the Monongahela Baptist Association   He filled appointments in Maryland, West Virginia and Fayette county, Pennsylvania, besides work in missionary fields   He was a faithful minister and sound exponent of Baptist doctrine, as well as an eloquent pulpit orator   He retired to his farm in Georges township in 1895 and spent his remaining years in practical farming, the occupation of his early manhood   He inherited one hundred and sixty acres from his father, to which he added one hundred and twenty-five acres more   also considerable town property   He served the township as tax collector and supervisor   He married, April 5, 1838, Maria, daughter of John and

Catherine Lyons   She was born in Springhill township in 1819, died 1892   Children, Thomas J, deceased, John L, George W, of whom further, Sarah A, Mary C, Rebecca J, deceased, Orpah, deceased, Benjamin O, Ada M

(III) George W, son of Rev Benjamin F Brown, was born in Georges township, Fayette county, Pennsylvania   He was educated in the common schools, and has spent his life in the pursuit of agriculture   He now owns and cultivates the old Brown farm in Georges township, first patented to his grandfather, Joshua Brown owned next by his father Rev Benjamin F Brown and now by himself   He is a Democrat in politics, and a member of the Presbyterian church   He married Mary C, born in Westmoreland county, Pennsylvania, daughter of Benjamin Rotharmel   Children   Minnie, married Charles E Morton of Georges township, Anna M, married Ashbel F Conn of Springhill township, Fannie, married James E Hanly, of Uniontown; Edward D of whom further, Roy J, of Georges township, Ora S, of Smithfield borough

(IV) Edward D, son of George W Brown, was born on the homestead farm in Georges township, Fayette county, Pennsylvania, June 19, 1877   He was educated in the township schools, taught for four years, then entered the State Normal School at California, Pennsylvania, whence he was graduated, class of 1900   Later leaving Normal School, he taught for two years, having in 1901 begun the study of law under the guidance of D M Hertzog, of Uniontown   On November 2, 1903, he was admitted to the Fayette county bar, and at once began the practice of his profession, locating in Uniontown   He has been admitted to practice in all the state and federal courts, and is well established in his chosen profession   He has business interests of importance outside of his law practice, together with coal land interests in West Virginia   He is a Republican, served on the executive committee of the Republican county committee, and is a member of Uniontown city council   He belongs to the Fayette County Bar Association, the Independent Order of Odd Fellows, and is an active member of the Presbyterian church, as is his wife

He married, July 20, 1898, Alice, daughter of Daniel P and Ella (Lyons) Morgan, of

E. D. Brown

Springhill township, Fayette county, Pennsylvania Daniel P Morgan was a farmer and cashier of the First National Bank of Smithfield He was a son of William and Sarah Ann (Stentz) Morgan, who were married in 1846 His grandfather was Colonel John Morgan, a soldier of the war of 1812 and the Mexican war He was a son of David Morgan, who came to Fayette county in 1788 and took up land on Grassy Run The Morgans are of Welsh extraction Children of Edward D Brown Morgan H, born October 14, 1902, Lauretta, born September 14, 1906

The Hetzels of Connellsville, HETZEL Pennsylvania, descend from a long line of German ancestors native to the town of Mulheim, province of Wittenburg, and for three generations at least engaged in the slaughter and sale of meats The American ancestor, Jacob Hetzel, was born in Mulheim, Germany, where he grew to manhood and followed the business of his fathers He came to the United States in 1846, having been preceded by his son John the previous year He settled in West Newton, Westmoreland county, Pennsylvania, where he lived a retired life until his death in 1859 His wife survived him until the following year They left issue, four daughters and two sons, all came to the United States except Jacob

(II) Jacob (2), son of Jacob (1) Hetzel, was born in the town of Mulheim province of Wittenburg, Germany, in 1819, died there in 1863 He was a butcher and operated a retail meat market in Mulheim He married Mary Slotterbeck, born in Wittenburg, died in Mulheim, Germany, aged sixty-three years Children Jacob, deceased, John T, of whom further, Catherine, deceased, Jacobine, deceased, Barbara, unmarried, living in Germany, Louisa, married Mark Slagle and lives in New York city, Mary, married John Stroebel and lives in Germany, Wilhelm, of whom further

(III) John T son of Jacob (2) Hetzel, was born in Mulheim Wittenburg, Germany, October 12, 1846 He was educated in Germany and worked with his father in the meat market in Mulheim until he was fourteen years of age, when the father died and the business was continued by his eldest son, Jacob John

T Hetzel remained with his widowed mother until he was twenty-one years of age, then was compelled to enlist and perform his years of service in the German army After serving one year he became so filled with the idea of coming to the United States and joining his uncle, John Hetzel, in Connellsville, with whom he was in correspondence, that his mother secured his release from the army by purchasing a substitute In 1868 he sailed for the United States His regiment, the First Wittenburg Infantry was badly cut up at the battle of Metz in the Franco-Prussian war, only eighty men of the regiment coming out of that battle unharmed After a voyage of fifty days he landed in Baltimore, Maryland, and at once came to Connellsville, Pennsylvania, where for a year he worked for his uncle, John Hetzel, in his meat market He then worked for two years in Pittsburgh at the same business, then returned to his uncle's employ, continuing until his marriage in 1872 During this period he attended night school in Connellsville and improved his knowledge of English In 1872 he opened a meat market in the borough of New Haven (Connellsville, West Side) continuing until 1885, when he built a brick residence and store at the corner of Main and Third streets, where he is now in prosperous business and is highly esteemed He is a Republican and has served four terms in the city council and on the school board He and all his family are members of the Trinity Lutheran church

He married, February 4, 1872, Sarah Ann Blough, born in Fayette county, Pennsylvania, daughter of Benjamin and Mary Ann (Coughanour) Blough Children 1 Louis, died aged two years, nine months and twenty days 2 Charles, now living in Pittsburgh 3 John 4 Mamie, married E H Dillenbach, of Allegheney City 5 Harley, now associated in business with his father married Belle Rout born in Fayette county children Thelma, Grace and John 6 Saylor

(III) Wilhelm son of Jacob (2) and Mary Hetzel, was born in Germany, July 8, 1861, died in Connellsville, Pennsylvania, September 23 1892 He was educated in the excellent schools of his town, and continued his residence there until shortly after his marriage, when with his bride he came to the United States, settling in New Haven, now

Connellsville, West Side, where he worked for two years for his brother, John T, there engaged in the butcher business He then started a meat market on his own account on Pittsburgh street, Connellsville, continuing until his death from typhoid fever after an illness of seven weeks He had built up a prosperous business, and was one of the leading dealers in his line He was a Republican, but gave his time entirely to his family and business, taking little part in public affairs He was a member of the German Lutheran church, as was his wife, but since her husband's death Mrs Hetzel has been connected with the English Lutheran church He married, in Germany, Margaret, daughter of Philip and Margaret (Snyder) Kraft, both natives of Germany, where the mother died Philip Kraft, a shoemaker, survives her, now aged seventy-five years He married (second) Philipena Hay, and has Sophia, Katherine and Beana Children of Wilhelm Hetzel 1. Philip Wilhelm, of whom further 2 Louis, now a resident of Mount Vernon, New York 3 Lena Louise 4 Fred, now a student at Gettysburg College

(IV) Philip Wilhelm, son of Wilhelm and Margaret (Kraft) Hetzel, was born at Connellsville, West Side, September 6, 1884 He attended the Connellsville schools, was a student for two years in high school, then entered Pittsburgh College of Pharmacy, whence he was graduated April 12, 1905 Immediately after graduation he entered the employ of Graham & Company, druggists of Connellsville, a position he now holds He is a duly registered pharmacist and thoroughly familiar with all the requirements of his profession He served in Company D, Tenth Regiment, National Guard of Pennsylvania, two years, eight months, advancing from private to first lieutenant, resigning on account of the demands of his business He is a member of the English Lutheran church and in politics a Republican He is a member of the Masonic Order and of the Heptasophs His college fraternity is Beta Phi Sigma

(II) John, son of Jacob (1) Hetzel, was born in the town of Mulheim, province of Wittenburg, Germany, March 9, 1822, died in Connellsville, Pennsylvania, in 1900 He was educated in Germany and learned the butcher business with his father, also serving the required years in the German army In

1845 he emigrated to the United States, settling in the German community at West Newton, Pennsylvania He established a meat market there and was in business until 1867, when he moved to Connellsville, where he opened a market on Main street, which he successfully operated until his death He was one of the founders and pillars of the German Lutheran church of Connellsville and a Democrat He married (first) in Germany Barbara Hengstettler, born in the same province as her husband, about nine miles from the town of Mulheim, in 1827, died in Connellsville in 1861 He married (second) Sarah Fulmer, born in Westmoreland county, Pennsylvania, died 1873, daughter of Henry Fulmer, born in Germany He married (third) Maria Iferd, born in Rockport, Somerset county, Pennsylvania, died 1880, daughter of John Iferd, a farmer, born in Germany, died in Fayette county, aged ninety years Children of John Hetzel and his first wife 1 Catherine, deceased, married John Trainer, and lived in Georgia 2 Mary, married Morris English, of Connellsville, whom she survives 3 Caroline, married Quitman Marietta, of Connellsville, whom she survives 4 George, of whom further 5 Jacob, died in infancy 6 John S, a butcher of Connellsville, died in 1908 7 Frank, now a butcher in New York city 8 Anna, now of Pittsburgh 9 Rose, married Robert Andrews and lives in Alabama 10 Barbara, married John Lesby, of Pittsburgh, whom she survives Children of second wife 11 Henry, now living in Connellsville 12. Jacob, now a butcher of Waynesburg, Pennsylvania 13 William, now a butcher of Wheeling, West Virginia 14 Lizzie, died aged eleven months 15 A son, died unnamed Children of third wife 16, Edward Uriah, of whom further 17 Charles, deceased 18 A daughter, died unnamed

(III) George, son of John Hetzel by his first wife, Barbara (Hengstettler) Hetzel, was born in West Newton, Westmoreland county, Pennsylvania December 2, 1854 He was educated in the public schools of West Newton and Connellsville and at an early age became his father's helper in the meat market He thoroughly learned all branches of the business, and on arriving at man's estate opened a meat market for himself on North Pittsburgh street, remaining in that location three years He later handled wholesale meats, and later had another retail shop In 1899 he was appointed city night watchman, and in 1909 was appointed chief of police, a position he now most ably fills He is a Republican, and a member of Trinity Lutheran church, of the Knights of the Maccabees, and Woodmen of the World

He married, May 1, 1881, Catherine Hall, born in Connellsville, daughter of John and Elizabeth (Dawson) Hall, both born in Fayette county Children 1 Cora Edna May born May 21, 1883, married (first) Clarence Mosholder, accidentally killed she married (second) Harry Mosholder, children Clarence (by first husband), Samuel and Lulu 2 George Quitman, born August 8, 1890 3 Lena Pearl, born October 25, 1896

(III) Edward Uriah, son of John Hetzel and his third wife Maria (Ifred) Hetzel, was born in Connellsville, Pennsylvania, September 16, 1874 He was but six years of age when his mother died, and after attending the public schools he became his father's assistant in the meat market until 1896 He then spent three years working in other markets until 1899, when he opened a retail meat market on Pittsburgh near Main street On March 24, 1911, his shop was destroyed by fire He is a Republican and a member of the Connellsville city council He is a member, with his family, of Trinity Lutheran church His fraternal orders are the Benevolent and Protective Order of Elks and Knights of the Maccabees

He married, November 18, 1900, Amelia Hyatt, born at Draketown, Somerset county, Pennsylvania, daughter of J Lewis and Alcinda Hyatt J Lewis Hyatt is a merchant of Draketown Child Margaret Marie, born January 14, 1902

CAMPBELL This good old Scotch family name was introduced into Uniontown, Pennsylvania, by Benjamin Campbell, born in Scotland He came to the United States and to western Pennsylvania by way of Hagerstown, Maryland, traveling by packhorse with his few belongings over the old National Pike He settled in Uniontown among the very earliest comers and lived there the remainder of his life He was a silversmith and watchmaker, and among the articles carried in his pack was a set of tools pertaining to this trade There was not, however, any visible opening for a jeweler at that early day, therefore he took up land and in other ways provided for his large family, consisting of wife and eleven children He was active and prominent in the early life of Uniontown and left an honored name that is still an influential one in the community A clock made by the old pioneer is one of the treasured ornaments of his grandson's law office

(II) Dr Hugh Campbell, son of Benjamin Campbell, was born in Uniontown, Pennsylvania, May 1, 1798, died 1895 He was educated in his native town and at Jefferson College, Cannonsburg, Pennsylvania, graduated in medicine, 1818, at the University of Pennsylvania, and became a leading physician of Uniontown, where he practiced until 1860 He was a warden of the Western Penitentiary, 1865 Like his father, he was a devout and rigid Presbyterian, and an elder in the church He was a fine scholar and linguist With others he led in the early temperance movement in Fayette county He was greatly beloved in the community, being most sympathetic and tender in his ministrations He married (first) Susan Baird, of Washington county, Pennsylvania, who with her infant child died a year after marriage He married (second) Rachel, born in Baltimore, daughter of Samuel Lyon, born in Carlisle, Pennsylvania, of Irish parents She survived him a few years Several children of the second marriage died in infancy Those who reached maturity were Samuel now deceased, Susan Baird, married James Allison, both now deceased, William Ward a Presbyterian minister, now residing in Wilmington, Delaware, Benjamin, now living in Uniontown, Edward, of whom further, Hugh, now deceased Sarah Louise unmarried residing in Washington, District of Columbia

(III) Judge Edward Campbell son of Dr Hugh and Rachel (Lyon) Campbell, was born in Uniontown, Pennsylvania July 24, 1838 He was educated in private schools, and for six years attended Madison College then newly founded in Uniontown He then began the study of law under the preceptorship of Nathaniel Ewing for many years a leading attorney of Uniontown now deceased After due course of preparatory study, Mr Campbell was admitted to the Pennsylvania bar, and began the practice of his profession in Uniontown, his lifelong home At the outbreak of the civil war he answered the call for three months' men made by President Lincoln in April, 1861 As there still seemed need for soldiers he re-enlisted for three years in Company E Eighty-fifth Regiment, Pennsylvania Volunteer Infantry, and served until November 22, 1864, the date of his honorable discharge He entered as a private and was mustered out as lieutenant-colonel of his regiment, receiving his last promotion October 16, 1863 He saw hard service with the Army of the Potomac and earned his successive promotions by 'gallant and meritorious conduct" After the war closed he returned to his interrupted law practice Having been admitted to practice in all state and federal courts he soon established a large business In 1866 the death of Judge Samuel A Gilmore left a vacancy on the county bench and he was appointed, by the Governor of Pennsylvania, presiding judge to fill the unexpected term He was, while on the bench, the youngest presiding judge in the state, being only twenty-eight years of age He has continued in practice all his life and has secured an enviable reputation as a learned and skilful lawyer The law has been to him a jealous mistress and has had his entire devotion Keenly interested in all that pertains to the welfare of the city, state or nation, he has never sought public preferment, preferring the quieter walks of life He is a Republican and a member of the Presbyterian church

---

                    The Hathaways of Union-
HATHAWAY   town, Pennsylvania, came
                    to Fayette from Greene
county, Pennsylvania, the settler in the latter county, being it is supposed, of a branch of the Hathaways of western New York If this be correct, they are descendants of John Hathaway the first of the name in this country He was born in 1617, came from London, England in the ship "Blessing" in 1635, married Hannah Mallett, and settled at Barnstable, Massachusetts He left a son John, born August 16 1658, who married and lived at Freetown Massachusetts His son Jacob, born 1680, married Philippi Chase Their son Isaac (2) born 1705 married Mae Sarah Makepeace, their son Isaac (2), born 1729, married Phoebe Bailey, their son Isaac (3),

born 1755, married Jemima, daughter of Nathan Comstock, who moved in 1796 from Adams, Massachusetts, to western New York, with a large family Their son, Isaac (4) Hathaway, born January 2, 1787, at Cambridge, Vermont, died at Farmington, New York April 10, 1858 He married, January 18, 1807, Nancy Richmond Isaac (4) Hathaway was of the seventh generation in America and if the theory is correct, he was the father of John Hathaway, who settled in Greene county, the grandfather of Charles Hathaway, of Uniontown, Pennsylvania

(VIII) John, son of Isaac (4) Hathaway, was born in Farmington, New York, about 1820 He was an early merchant and large land owner of Carmichaels, Greene county, Pennsylvania, where he married and left issue Samuel, deceased, of further mention, Jacob, William and Lawrence, all living at Carmichaels, Greene county, Pennsylvania, another living in Missouri

(IX) Samuel, son of John Hathaway, died at Carmichaels, Greene county, Pennsylvania, in 1909 He was a man of education and good business ability, owning and operating a jewelry store and watch repairing establishment at Carmichaels until his death He was a Republican in politics He married Ella Jolliff, born in 1853, daughter of James and Mardelia (Wylie) Jolliff, he coming to Carmichaels from West Virginia, she the daughter of an old settler of Greene county, and a justice of the peace James Jolliff was a blacksmith In 1888 he came to Uniontown with his daughter, Mrs Hathaway, and her son Charles, and followed his trade there until his death in 1889 His wife Mardelia survives, aged seventy-seven years Children of Samuel and Ella Hathaway 1 Harold, born February 28, 1878 2 Charles of whom further

(X) Charles youngest son of Samuel and Ella (Jolliff) Hathaway, was born at Carmichaels Greene county, Pennsylvania, April 16, 1880 He was educated in the public schools of his native town and Uniontown, graduating with the class of 1897 from the high school He then entered the employ of Conwell & Strickler, shoe dealers of Uniontown He remained with that firm until 1901, when Mr Conwell retired on account of ill health and he was admitted to a partnership with Mr Strickler This association existed from January, 1901, to May of the same year The erection of the First National Bank building having thrown John M Campbell out of a business location, he purchased Mr Strickler's interest 'in the shoe business of Strickler & Hathaway, the new firm, Campbell & Hathaway, continuing a successful business until January 1, 1910, when Mr Campbell sold to his partner and Mr R G Weltner, who have since continued under the same name, although incorporated

Their business is large and prosperous, the store being modern and finely stocked In politics Mr Hathaway is a Democrat, but strictly independent in local politics He is a member of Fayette Lodge, No 228, Free and Accepted Masons, and Uniontown Lodge of Perfection, Ancient Accepted Scottish Rite In religious faith he is a Methodist

RIDGWAY The American ancestor of the Ridgways of Connellsville, David Ridgway, was a native of Ireland, and after coming to the United States settled first in Philadelphia, later coming to Greene county, and, it is said, made the journey westward on foot He was a shoemaker by trade, and followed that occupation until his death His wife, Lydia, born in Ireland, made the journey across the mountains with him, and died in Greene county, at the great age of ninety-six years They were the parents of nine children, all deceased excepting Miles M Ridgway, of Des Moines, Iowa, and Mrs Maria Grimes, of Waynesburg, Pennsylvania, since died, June, 1912

(II) Job son of David and Lydia Ridgway, was born in Greene county, Pennsylvania, April 30, 1814 There most of his life was spent engaged in farming He was a Democrat in politics, and a member of the Methodist Protestant church He married Sarah Hook, born in Greene county, February 18, 1818, daughter of William and Katherine (Kent) Hook, both born in Pennsylvania Children of Job and Sarah (Hook) Ridgway 1 Katherine, died in infancy 2 Lydia, died 1911 3 Eliza Horn, living in Kansas 4 Samuel, died of typhoid fever in the Union army during the civil war 5 Charles 6 Craven, a veteran of the civil war 7 James, died in infancy 8 John H of whom further 9 Vienna, now living in Greene county, Pennsylvania 10 Thomas, now living near Pitts-

burgh, Pennsylvania 11 Lucy, now living in Connellsville

(III) John Hook, son of Job and Sarah (Hook) Ridgway, was born in Greene county, Pennsylvania, March 27, 1852 He was educated in the public school, and at the age of sixteen began work on a farm Later he was employed at Mount Pleasant with the Limestone Quarry Company, and two years with the Charlotte Furnace Company In 1880 he entered the employ of the H C Frick Coke Company, with which corporation he is still connected after a service of thirty years He resides at No 10 Eighth street, Connellsville, is a Democrat in politics, and while living at Mount Pleasant served as inspector of elections His wife is a Dunkard He married, in 1879, Katherine Sailor, born in Fayette county, June 7, 1861, daughter of Levi and Louise Sailor, an early county family Levi Sailor deceased, his wife Louise still survives him Their children Elmer, George, Mary, Melinda Charles, Robert, Katherine and Cleveland

Children of John Hook Ridgway 1 Eliza, born January 22, 1881, married John Gosset 2 Minnie, born August 27 1883, married Harmin Michaels, children Rose, Irene, Marshall Gilbert David 3 Charles F born July 3, 1885, now living in Connellsville 4 William, born May 6, 1887, died young 5 Jesse, of whom further 6 George, born January, 1890, died young 7 Mary, born January 7, 1892, married John Meader, April 16, 1911 8 Theresa, born September 3 1894, died September 23, 1904 9 James, born August 27 1896 10 John, born May 28, 1898 11 Katherine, born September 23, 1900 12 Lucy, born August 6, 1902

(IV) Jesse, son of John H and Katherine (Sailor) Ridgway, was born in Mount Pleasant, Pennsylvania, December 28, 1888 He was educated in the public schools of Fayette county, and began business life as a laborer On September 23, 1907, he entered the employ of the Baltimore & Ohio Railroad Company as locomotive fireman and so continues In politics he is a Democrat On April 12, 1912, he was elected financial secretary of the Brotherhood of Firemen and Enginemen He married, January 25, 1911, Rose Marie Meader born in Ligonier, Pennsylvania, daughter of John G and Susannah A Meader John

G Meader was born in Germany, came to the United States, and was engaged as a jeweler His wife, Susannah, was born in Pennsylvania She survived her husband and married (second) Christian Meader, brother of her first husband Children of John Meader Albert, John Monroe and Rose Marie, of whom above Children by second husband Mary Frances, deceased, and Carl Child of Jesse and Rose Marie (Meader) Ridgway Rose Alice, born December 31, 1911

AUGUSTINE The American ancestors of the Augustines of Uniontown came to America from Holland during the latter part of the eighteenth century They were accompanied by their son Peter and his wife, Anna Augustine, who located in Somerset county, Pennsylvania Peter Augustine became a large land owner, prosperous farmer, justice of the peace, and prominent in local affairs He was a Whig in politics, and with his wife actively upheld and followed the teachings of the Lutheran church Their children Abraham, died in Somerset county, John, died in Garrett county, Maryland, Daniel, of whom further, Jacob, died in Turkeyfoot township, Somerset county, Peter, died in Agency City, Iowa Daughters Diana, Mary, Elizabeth and Anne, four others probably died young

(II) Daniel, son of Peter and Anna Augustine, was born in Somerset county, Pennsylvania, in 1818, where his life was passed and death occurred October 18, 1899 He became a wealthy farmer and live stock dealer, and like his father, influential in his community He was a Whig in politics until that party was supplanted by the Republican party, then became a leader of the new organization He was a member of the Methodist Episcopal church as was his wife, both being active workers He married Mary Miller, born in Somerset county, Pennsylvania, in 1824, died December 11, 1890 She was one of a family of ten, and of German descent, her forbears being early settlers of the county Children Alcinda, deceased, married Milford Watson, Perie, unmarried, Minnie, resides in Somerset county, unmarried Laura, married Justice T H Anderson, of Washington, D C, Ross, resides at Addison, Pennsylvania, unmarried, Jasper, of whom further

(III) Jasper, youngest son of Daniel and Mary (Miller) Augustine, was born in Addison, Somerset county, Pennsylvania, April 10, 1856 He was educated in the public schools and at Beaver College, Pennsylvania He began business life as his father's assistant in his extensive farming and cattle dealing operations The Augustine estate was one of the largest in the county, comprising twenty-seven farms, aggregating fifty-four hundred acres The care of his estate, which was not compact, devolved in great measure upon the younger man, and the renting, buying, selling and general upkeep were his particular charge This early training under the wise guidance of his capable father developed an energetic, efficient business man and prepared him for the business he has always followed—real estate dealing and its management His home is in Uniontown, Pennsylvania but from early spring until late in the fall he occupies his beautiful home on the National Road, twenty-four miles east of Uniontown This house is one of the famous brick taverns of the halcyon days of "The Pike," was built about 1818, remodeled by Mr Augustine, and now surrounded by an estate of sixteen hundred acres and is an ideal summer home He is a member of the Methodist Episcopal church, as is his wife, and has always supported Republican party principles

He married, January 1, 1885, Mary Maude Cunningham, born in Armagh, Indiana county, Pennsylvania, October 24, 1865, daughter of John Hutchinson and Martha (Elliott) Cunningham, granddaughter of William and Esther (Hutchinson) Cunningham, of Indiana county, Pennsylvania, and great-granddaughter of Hon Hezekiah Cunningham, of Huntington county Pennsylvania, one of the first members of the legislature Esther was a daughter of Robert Hutchinson and granddaughter of Cornelius Hutchinson, a soldier of the revolution The Hutchinsons are of English descent, and are first found in Western Pennsylvania in Westmoreland county Martha Elliott was a daughter of Alexander and Margaret Morrow (Bell) Elliott, of Indiana and Westmoreland counties, Pennsylvania John Hutchinson Cummings was born in 1837, his wife in 1844 Both were born and raised in Indiana county After marriage they lived in Indiana county until 1869, when they went to Johnstown, where they have since resided He is a lumber dealer and prominent in the business world For many years a member of the firm of Nutter, Cunningham & Co, and now connected with the Johnstown Pressed Brick Company Both are members of the Presbyterian church Their children Mary Maude, wife of Jasper Augustine, Clara Francena, wife of Clarence Harmony, of Johnstown, Pennsylvania

Children of Jasper and Mary M Augustine 1. John Daniel, born November 19, 1885, educated at Pennsylvania Military College and University of Pennsylvania, married Julia E Ross, of Addison, and resides on his farm in Somerset county, Pennsylvania 2 Thomas H, born April 23, 1890, graduate Chester (Pennsylvania) Military Academy, now residing in Uniontown, Pennsylvania 3 Ross Quay, born July 16, 1892, graduate of Keskeminita Springs School, now a student at Lafayette College 4 Jasper Clarence, born April 10, 1896, student in Uniontown high school 5 Edgar Elliott, born March 30, 1898, student in Uniontown school

---

SEARIGHT Worthy deeds of noble men are the beacon lights of time They create the atmosphere in which our race progresses as the years revolve Every good action, whether it was performed last year or centuries ago, helps to make the present better than the past, and all finer minds are deeply stirred by the record of such actions nobly done It has been truly said that any people who take no pride in the great achievements of remote ancestors will never accomplish anything worthy of remembrance by remote descendants This is equally true of families and of individuals The best and purest part of our human nature rises up in admiration and stands in honest pride before the record of good deeds done by those through whom we inherit life and being Every soul worthy of his inheritance is ready and anxious to do what he may to perpetuate the memory of those who have "gone before," as well as to emulate their virtues and kindly benefactions In doing this he gathers strength for his own lifework and transmits inspiration to unborn generations In it he finds pleasure and duty so strangely mingled as to form a composite whole, a complete and perfect unit This natural feeling of reverence for worthy ancestors has led to many and varied attempts to give it adequate expression Among these are compilations of family history and genealogy, which are met with quite frequently in recent years The best example of this kind of work is an issued volume entitled ' A Record of the Searight family in America "

Its contents comprise an ideal history of a family connection which now extends into half the states of the American Union, and has furnished some of the best, most useful and most distinguished citizens of the great Republic Every branch is carefully traced, and all known facts regarding each member are succinctly given The work also embraces a historical retrospect of this well known Scotch-Irish family as far back as the siege of Derry (1688), when a number of the Searights were engaged in the defense of that ancient stronghold, having espoused the cause of William, Prince of Orange, against James II

The name was formerly spelled Seawright, and in its original form was Sievewright and Seabright The Searight family is of Dalraidain Scotch-Irish origin, and has for its crest a thunderbolt and for its motto *Deum timete* (fear God) They are of that wonderful Scotch-Irish race which in its career among the nations of the earth has been fitly compared to the Gulf Stream in its course through the regions of the ocean To trace the making of the Scotch-Irishman, one must follow a restless Celtic race from Gallatia into the British Isles, where they founded their great college of Icolmkill, and three centuries later planted the seed bed of the Scotch-Irish race in Strathclyde and in Northumbria Here followed a Brito-Scot and Anglo-Norman fusion which in 1605 was transplanted into Ulster of the North of Ireland, and modified by the choicest elements of the Puritan, the Huguenot and Hollander, to form the Ulsterman, who then driven by persecution settled our western border and became the Scotch-Irishman of history, so

named from the dominating strain of his
blood and the land from which he came
He protected the borders from the Indians,
fought in the Revolution (never produced a
Tory), won the west, developed his great
racial characteristics of independence, education and scriptural faith, and has fought
in every war of the Republic The descendants of Sir Edward Seabright (Seawright,
Searight) went to Strathclyde, thence to
Ulster, and some members of the family
that settled in West Ulster served in the
defense of Londonderry

(I) One of the descendants above mentioned was William Seawright, born about
1720, came from county Donegal, North of
Ireland, about the year 1740, and settled in
Lampiter township, Lancaster county,
Pennsylvania He was at the time of his
death (1771) a prominent citizen and landholder of that county He sought religious
liberty in the new world, where he was destined to found a family whose name should
be written high on the rolls of fame in the
new Republic whose birth he did not live
to see Shortly after his settlement in Pennsylvania, he married Anne Hamilton, a descendant of the powerful dukes of Hamilton
of Scotland She came from Belfast Ireland, at the same time as her husband, and
settled in about the same locality, near Lancaster City She was accompanied to America by her brothers, William and Hugh,
and a sister Mary Her brother William
was the grandfather of the distinguished
governor of South Carolina in Calhoun's
day, who was known as the Nullifier Governor, in consequence of his having advocated the nullification of certain laws passed
by Congress which he considered adverse
to the interests of the people of the south
The ancestors of the Hamilton family came
from Scotland to Belfast, Ireland, when it
became the refuge for persecuted Covenant-
ers They were a part of the historical
Scotch family of Hamiltons, one of whom
was chosen as the husband of Queen Mary,
and another as the husband of Queen Elizabeth Family tradition and family history
also teach that Alexander Hamilton, of Revolutionary fame, was connected with this
same Lancaster county family of Hamiltons
Children of William and Anne Seawright

1 Mary, married John Glenn, the Glenns
are extinct, and are mostly buried in Pe-
quea churchyard, Lancaster county, Pennsylvania 2 Esther, married Gilbert Seawright, who was the founder of the large
family of Seawrights in and around Carlisle, Cumberland county, Pennsylvania 3
Anne, married William Woods, and removed from Lancaster county, Pennsylvania, to Albemarle county, Virginia, where
they died, two children Alexander and
Seawright, born in Lancaster county, Pennsylvania, they later settled in Fayette county, Kentucky, and subsequently removed to
Illinois, where the former died in Jo Da-
vies county and the latter in Greene county 4 William, of whom further 5 Alexander, married a Miss Logan, and removed
to Augusta county, Virginia, children William, Alexander and Margaret, who removed with their families to Henry county,
Tennessee, about the year 1826, where some
of their descendants are living at the present time

(II) William (2), son of William (1) Seawright, the American ancestor, was born in
1753, died in 1824 He learned the trade of
fuller He moved from Lancaster county,
Pennsylvania, to Augusta county, Virginia,
returning to Pennsylvania later and settling
in the Ligonier Valley, Westmoreland county, where he built and operated a fulling
(cloth) mill until his death He was a Presbyterian, like his father, and was for many
years an elder of that church He married,
in 1784, Jean, daughter of Samuel and Catherine (Seawright) Ramsey Children 1
Samuel married Mary A Wilson, and after
1810 settled in Tippecanoe county, Indiana
2 Alexander, married Catherine Jones, first
settled in Brooke county, Virginia, and
afterwards removed to Morgan county,
Ohio 3 William, of whom further 4
Mary 5 John 6 Hamilton 7 Archibald
The four latter named remained in the Ligonier Valley and died without issue They
are buried by the side of their parents in
Pleasant Grove graveyard, about five miles
from the town of Ligonier

Samuel Ramsey, father of Jean (Ramsey)
Seawright was a man of wealth and gave
largely of his means to aid the cause of independence He was a prominent citizen of

Wm Searight

Cumberland county, Pennsylvania, and was the owner of the famous "Letort Springs" tract near Carlisle, where he lived and died He married Catherine Seawright, daughter of William Seawright, who came from Donegal, Ireland, about 1740 and settled in Leacock township, near Lancaster City, Pennsylvania, where he lived and died He was for many years a landholder and prominent citizen of Lancaster county In the revolution of 1688 the ancestors of William Seawright threw themselves into the cause of William of Orange Some of them were driven within the walls of Londonderry when its gates were closed against James the Second, some afterwards died in the besieged city, while others of them survived the siege William Seawright married Catherine Jackson, also a resident of the North of Ireland, and they were the parents of one child, Catherine, who married Samuel Ramsey and they were the parents of children, namely Jean, aforementioned as the wife of William Searight, Catherine, died unmarried, Margaret, died unmarried Esther, died unmarried, Elizabeth, died unmarried, Samuel married a Gettysburg lady, no children, Archibald, married Margaret Dean and their grandchildren are now residents of New Bloomfield, Perry county, Pennsylvania, Seawright, married a member of the Pittsburgh family of Dennys After the death of his wife Catherine, Samuel Ramsey married (second) the Widow Macfeely, grandmother of General Robert Macfeely, commissary general of the United States army, Washington, D C

(III) William (3) Searight, son of William (2) (q v) and Jean (Ramsey) Seawright, was born near Carlisle, Cumberland county Pennsylvania, December 5, 1791 died August 12, 1852 He received a plain English education, but he was endowed with the precepts of stern integrity, industry and honor, the elements of his future success in business and of his elevated character He learned the trade of fuller and dyer of cloth At the age of twenty-one years he came to Fayette county Pennsylvania, his entire stock in trade being an expert knowledge of his trade, a keen sense

of honor, and a stout heart He arranged a lease of the Hammond fulling mill, later was a partner in the operation of the old Cook's mill, on Redstone creek, operated another fulling mill at the mouth of Dunlap Creek, and subsequently rented another mill on the George Washington farm near Periyopolis This was accomplished in a few years, the young man becoming the largest fulling mill owner and operator in Western Pennsylvania He continued in business until, with rare foresight, seeing that the fulling mill must fall before the modern factory system of the east, sold his milling interests and became one of the principal commissioners of the National road and the Erie extension of the Pennsylvania & Ohio canal He also purchased a farm and hotel on the National road and founded the village of Searights, named in his honor, and there made his permanent settlement He was gifted with rare sagacity, universal business ability, undaunted courage, became a leading business man of his county, and was intimately connected with the foremost of her institutions He was a man of sympathetic nature and his private charities were many He stood high in church and community life, all realizing in him a friend and counselor in whose fidelity they could with safety confide

Mr Searight was a prominent and zealous old-time Democratic politician, and wielded a wide influence On one occasion he rode on horseback from Searights to Harrisburgh, a distance of over two hundred miles, to assist in the preparation to nominate General Jackson for the presidency He was an intimate friend of the late Simon Cameron, ex-United States senator from Pennsylvania, and had close political relations with the leading politicians of his day In the early history of Fayette county, political conventions of both parties were accustomed to meet at Searights and plan campaigns A memorable meeting, of which Mr Searight was the chief instigator, was held there in 1828, known as the "Gray Meeting" from the name of the keeper of the hotel at that time, John Gray At this meeting the Jackson and Adams men met to test their strength They turned out in the meadow below the hotel, formed in rank and counted off, the Jackson men outnumbering their opponents decisively, and it was regarded as a great Jackson victory In the political campaign of 1836 a large Democratic meeting was held at Uniontown, and the delegation from Searights bore a banner with the inscription, "Menallen the battle ground of the Gray Meeting"

The many similar political meetings with which Mr Searight was identified prove the esteem in which he was held by the citizens of the county by all parties But Fayette county although the first, was but little in advance of other communities to learn and admire his worth He early became known and appreciated throughout the entire state He was appointed commissioner of the Cumberland road (National road) by Governor Porter, a position he held for many years In 1854 he was superseded by Colonel William Hopkins, of Washington, Pennsylvania Subsequently an act of the legislature placed the road in the hands of trustees appointed by the courts, and these trustees restored William Searight to the commissionership, the duties of which office he continued to discharge with great fidelity and industry He was thoroughly familiar with all the hills and valleys of that grand old thoroughfare, once so stirring and active, but now still and grass-grown Previous to his appointment as commissioner of the National road he was a contractor on the same He was one of the contractors who built the iron bridge over the mouth of Dunlap creek, between Bridgeport and Brownsville, and was also a contractor on the Erie extension of the Pennsylvania and Ohio canal At the time of his death he was the candidate of the Democratic party for one of the most important offices in the state, that of canal commissioner To this office he would have undoubtedly been elected, after his death Colonel William Hopkins, of Washington county, was nominated by the Democratic party for the same office, and was elected by a large majority

Mr Searight was a man of the most generous and humane character ever ready to lend his counsel his sympathies and his purse to the aid of others Though a strong political party man, yet he always treated his opponents with courtesy In religion

he was like most of the race to which he belonged, imbued with Calvinism The brightest traits of his character were exemplified in his last hours So far as human judgment can decide he died a Christian His aged widow often quoted an expression he made as he was approaching the sad realities of death, which gave her great comfort It was this "Our prayers have been answered, I feel that if I should die to-night, the Lord will receive me into His Holy Kingdom" Although death plucked him from the very threshold of earthly honors, yet it caused him no regrets The Kingdom into which he was about to enter presented higher honors and purer enjoyments To him they offered

"No midnight shade, no clouded sun,
But sacred, high, eternal noon"

Mr Searight married, March 25, 1826, Rachel Brownfield, born at Gainsboro, Frederick county, Virginia, February 7, 1805, daughter of Thomas and Elizabeth Brownfield, of Uniontown, Pennsylvania Children 1 Thomas B , of whom further 2 Ewing B , of whom further 3 Jean of whom further 4 William, of whom further 5 James Allison, of whom further 6 Elizabeth S , of whom further

Mr Searight died at his residence in Menallen township, August 12, 1852 A more emphatic eulogy than is in the power of language to express was bestowed upon him on the day of his funeral by the assembling around his coffin to perform the last sad duty of friendship of as great, if not a greater number of citizens than ever attended the funeral ceremonies of anyone who had died within the limits of Fayette county Among that vast assemblage were both the patriarchs of the county and the rising youth who came to give their testimony to the lofty worth in life of the distinguished dead A few days after his death a large meeting of the citizens of Fayette county, irrespective of party, convened at the court house for the purpose of bearing suitable testimony to his memory and character The following gentlemen were chosen officers Hon Nathaniel Ewing, president Hon Daniel Sturgeon (ex-United States senator), and Z Ludington, vice-presidents John B Krepps and R P

Flenniken, secretaries On motion of Hon
James Veech (later author of "Monongahela of Old) a committee of resolutions,
composed of leading citizens, was appointed,
which committee presented the following
preamble and resolutions, which were unan-
imously adopted

'When a valuable citizen died, it is meet that
the community of which he was a member mourn
his loss A public expression of their sorrow at
such an event is due as some solace to the grief of
the bereaved family and friends, and as an in-
centive to others to earn for their death the same
distinction
In the recent death of William Searight, this
community has lost such a citizen Such an event
has called this public meeting, into which enter no
schemes of political promotion no partisan purposes
of empty eulogy Against all this, death has shut
the door While yet the tear hangs upon the cheek
of his stricken family, and the tiding of death are
unread by many of his friends we his fellow-citi
zens neighbors friends of all parties, have as-
sembled to speak to those who knew and loved him
best, and to those who knew him not, the words of
sorrow and truth, in sincerity and soberness Therefore as the sense of this meeting
"Resolved That in the death of William Searight, Fayette county and the commonwealth of
Pennsylvania have lost one of their best and most
useful citizens The people at large may not realize
their loss, but the community in which he lived,
over whose comforts and interests were diffused
the influences of his liberality and enterprise feel
it, while his friends, of all classes parties and
professions to whom he clung, and who clung to
him mourn it
"Resolved That while we would withhold our
steps from the sanctuary of domestic grief we may
be allowed to express to the afflicted widow and
children of the deceased our unfeigned sorrow and
sympathy in their great bereavement and to tender
them our assurance that while in their hearts the
memory of the husband and father will ever be
cherished, in our hearts will be kept the liveliest
recollections of his virtues as a citizen and friend
'Resolved, That among the elements which must
enter into every truthful estimate of the character
of William Searight are a warm amenity of manner, combined with great dignity of deportment
which were not the less attractive by their plain-
ness and want of ostentation, elevated feelings
were pure than passionless high purposes with in-
tiring energy in their accomplishment an ennobling
sense of honor, and individual independence which
kept him always true to himself and his engagements, unfaltering fidelity to his friends a liberality which heeded no restraint but means and
merit, great promptness and fearlessness in the discharge of what he believed to be a duty private or
public guided by a rigid integrity which stood all
tests and withstood all temptations honesty and
truthfulness in word and deed which no seductions
could weaken or assaults overthrow in all respects

the architect of his own fortune and fame These,
with the minor virtues in full proportion are some
of the outlines of character which stamped the man
whose death we mourn, as one much above the
ordinary level of his race
'Resolved, That while we have here nothing to
do or say as to the loss sustained by the political
party to which he belonged, and whose candidate
he was for an office of great honor and responsibility we may be allowed to say that had he lived
and been successful with a heart so rigidly set as
was his with feelings so high and integrity so firm,
and withal an amount of practical intelligence so
ample as he possessed his election could have been
regretted by no citizen who knew him, and who
placed the public interests beyond selfish ends and
party success As a politician we knew him to hold
to his principles and party predilections with a tenacious grasp, yet he was ever courteous and liberal
in his deportment and views toward his political
opponents
'Resolved That in the life and character of
William Searight we see a most instructive and
encouraging example Starting the struggle of life
with an humble business poor and unbefriended
with an honest mind and a true heart with high
purposes and untiring industry, he by degrees
gained friends and means which never forsook him
He thus won for himself and family ample wealth,
and attained a position among his fellowmen which
those who have not had the best advantages our
country affords, might well envy That wealth and
that position he used with a just liberality and influence for the benefit of all around and dependent
upon him Though dead, he yet speaketh to every
man in humble business 'Go thou and do likewise
and such shall be thy reward in life and in death '
"Resolved, That the proceedings of this meeting
be furnished for publication in all the papers of
the county and a copy thereof, signed by the officers,
be presented to the family of the deceased "

STIDGER—One of the later and most
powerful of the races of the human family
is the English and the making of the Englishman can be traced from the cradle and
nursery of the human race in Central Asia
away into five great climate zones around
whose settlement centers grew race masses
Three were in Asia one along the Nile, the
other on the shores of the Mediterranean,
where civilization had its birth and the two
great groups of modern nations, the Latin
and the Greek had their rise

Of the fierce Northland German races
that swept from the Mediterranean to the
Baltic, one was Teutonic, whose unconquer-
able tribes settled largely along the north-
ward waterways from the heart of the great
German forest Three of these tribes, the
Angles, Jutes and Saxons, stretched west-

ward along the North Sea coast from the mouth of Elbe river to that of the Weser The Angles gave their name to the country, the Saxons theirs to the language, while the Jutes were so few in numbers as to stamp their name in no prominent way, and were even denied mention in the name of the new race, which at the time of their conquest by the Normans was called Anglo-Saxon The Anglo-Saxon had driven the Briton from the land, but when in turn they were conquered by the Dane and Norman, they remained, and in one hundred and fifty years had so largely absorbed their last conquerors that there were an Anglo-Saxon and Norman Dane people that became known as English when they aided the Barons, on June 16, 1215 to compel King John to sign the Magna Charta, which secured many liberties for all the people of England, which country had formerly been called Angleland From the granting of the Great Charter the Englishman rapidly developed those magnificent and powerful traits of character for which he is noted all over the world

From this wonderful English race was descended Mrs Rachel (Brownfield) Searight-Stidger born in the village of Gainsboro Frederick county Virginia, February 7 1805, died at her home at the west end of Main street, Uniontown, Pennsylvania, January 3 1893 Her lineage is traced back to the origin of the Society of Friends in the early part of 1600 From thence through equally reliable sources, in parish and other records, her lineage can be traced into the same family of Fishers of which John Fisher, Bishop of Rochester who was beheaded by Henry VIII in the early part of the year 1535, was a member Through her grandmother Mary Butler, her lineage is also traceable through the same reliable sources into the family of which Bishop Butler, of "Butler's Analogy" fame, was a member

Her great-grandfather, Thomas Butler, was born at Hanley on the Thames England His first settlement in America was in Middletown, Bucks county, Pennsylvania, after which he removed to Chester, Delaware county, same state He married, seventeenth day, fourth month, 1731, Rebecca Gilbert in the Middletown meeting house

Children Joseph and Mary Mary married Barak Fisher, and they removed from Bucks county, Pennsylvania, to Frederick county, Virginia, in 1763, where they raised a large family, one of whom, Elizabeth, married Thomas Brownfield, a native of Frederick county Virginia, and they were the parents of Rachel, aforementioned Barak and Mary (Butler) Fisher settled on Back creek, near the village of Gainsboro, Virginia The ruins of the old house in which they lived when they first removed from Pennsylvania to Virginia can yet be seen, and the old farm upon which they originally settled is still in possession of some of their descendants Barak Fisher died in 1784, and his wife in 1800 Barak Fisher was the eighth child of John and Elizabeth (Scarborough) Fisher

Thomas and Elizabeth (Fisher) Brownfield with their children, Catherine Rebecca, Sarah, Mary, Ewing, Rachel, removed from Virginia to Uniontown, Fayette county, Pennsylvania They traveled over what was known as the old mail route road, the old Braddock road and the old Nemacolin road At this time Rachel was about six weeks old She received the education the schools of that day afforded In her girlhood days she sang in the Methodist church choir and she was one of the young girls selected to strew flowers in the pathway of General Lafayette when he visited Uniontown in 1825 On March 25 1826, she married (first) William Searight of Menallen township, to which place she removed immediately after her marriage She married (second) in 1858, Harmon Stidger, M D, of Canton, Ohio, and removed with him to that city She resided in Canton during the civil war and watched its progress with great interest She resided in Canton until 1869, at which time she purchased what is known as the "Roberts property" situated at the west end of Main street Uniontown, Pennsylvania, and returned to the old town in which she had passed her earlier years, to live the remainder of her life amongst her old friends and early acquaintances, and from that year until her death lived within one hundred feet of the spot on which she landed in 1805, an infant in her mother's arms

Rachel Searight Slidger

Yours truly

T. B. Searight

Soon after her first marriage and removal to Menallen township to live she became a member of Grace Episcopal Church, in Menallen township, and continued, a faithful member of the Episcopal church during her entire after life She was confirmed by Bishop Onderdonk whilst the Rev Mr Freeman was rector of Christ Church Before the building of the present Grace Church at Menallen, services were frequently held at her home Mrs Searight-Stidger was quiet, gentle and patient, never neglecting a duty, nor failing in an act of kindness, or lacking on any occasion in any courtesy of life Her life spanned one of the most wonderful periods in human history At her birth there was not an iron ploughshare in the entire world, nor was there a steamboat steamship locomotive nor railway train, telegraphing and telephoning were unknown most of the inventions in machinery and nearly all the appliances for comfort and convenience were also unknown The improvements in agriculture mining manufacturing etc were all made during the span of her life What a privilege and yet what a responsibility to be permitted to live so long and witness so much Her remains were interred in Grace Church burying ground January 7, 1893 and the funeral services were conducted by the rector of St Peter s Episcopal Church Uniontown and the rector of Christ s Church, Brownsville •

(IV) Colonel Thomas SEARIGHT Brownfield Searight eldest son of William (3) (q v) and Rachel (Brownfield) Searight, was born at Searights, Menallen township, Fayette county Pennsylvania February 20, 1827, died in Uniontown, Pennsylvania, April 3, 1899

He was reared on his father's farm, and successfully prosecuted his academic studies at Dr Wilson s Academy and Madison College at Uniontown He entered Washington and Jefferson College, May 1 1844, and was graduated in the class of 1848 Among his classmates was Judge Slagel of Pittsburgh, Hon John Murray Clark, and James G Blaine, later the famous statesman, who was one of his most intimate friends, and who graduated one year earlier He read law with Judge James Veech a learned historian and able jurist, author of Monongahela of Old," and was admitted to the Fayette county bar in 1850 In the following year, his father being the proprietor of the *Genius of Liberty*, the organ of the Fayette county Democracy, Thomas B Searight assumed charge of the paper as editor and conducted it until the beginning of the war against the south, a period of ten years In 1857 he was elected prothonotary re-elected in 1860, in 1881 and in 1884, at that time being the only man in the county who had ever served four terms in that office In 1863 he represented Fayette county in the house of representatives of the state legislature, and was re-elected in 1864 Two years later he was chosen state senator from the district composed of Greene, Fayette and Westmoreland counties He was a leading member, as well as one of the acknowledged leaders of his party on the floor of the house and senate, serving on many of the important committees, took a prominent part in all important legislation, and was generally successful in securing the passage of measures that he favored and advocated Active in behalf of the interests of the people of his district, he received many manifestations of regard from Governors Curtin and Geary, and, on the proposition to ratify the fourteenth and fifteenth amendments to the constitution of the United States, his speeches in all the debates arising thereon were able and conspicuous against their ratification by the legislature of Pennsylvania He was a delegate to the Pennsylvania Democratic state conventions of 1857-60-63-69-92, and also to the National Democratic conventions at Chicago that nominated General George B McClellan and Grover Cleveland for the presidency in 1864 and 1884 In all the political campaigns since 1848 he took a leading part in Fayette county, and in various parts throughout the state Without solicitation on his part, he was appointed in 1873 by President Grant surveyor-general of Colorado, and served as such for three years In 1883 he received the Democratic nomination for the judgeship of the Fourteenth Judicial district, but opposing influences in an adjoining county and dissensions in his own party in Fayette count prevented his election

Colonel Searight was a humanitarian in the broadest sense, his benefactions often being in excess of his ability to give He was a member of St Peter's Episcopal Church

In politics he believed in the principles of Jefferson as enunciated by Jackson, and after a careful study of all political parties his early principles became his mature convictions As a Democrat, he advocated state sovereignty, but did not believe in secession, and was as liberal in the financial support of his party as he was fearlessly outspoken in his political views As a political organizer he had no superiors in Fayette county, which he controlled largely according to his will during the thirty years of his active life, most of which was spent in holding important offices whose every duty he discharged efficiently and satisfactorily

He was a magnanimous political opponent when the smoke of battle cleared away, and while other men of Fayette county held higher offices, none made a greater impress as a potent factor in the political life of the county Colonel Searight's aggressiveness was doubtless hereditary as well as his qualities of leadership inherited from his ancestors of the warlike clan of Hamilton of Scotland Colonel Searight's tastes were more political and literary than legal yet he practiced successfully before the different county, district and supreme courts of Pennsylvania He was a member of Fayette Lodge No 228, Free and Accepted Masons and also of Fort Necessity Lodge, No 254 Independent Order of Odd Fellows

A grand page in the history of the new world is Colonel Searight's story of the 'Old Pike or National Road," which great thoroughfare was so important to the early development of his country and so powerful in strengthening the bonds of the Union, and around which cling a wealth of romance and many facts stranger than fiction There are but two great highways noticed in history, one of the Appian Way, the "Queen of Roads " of which no account has been preserved, and the other the 'National Road " whose history is only told by Colonel Searight, who was born and reared on its line and who spent his entire life amid scenes connected with it, some of which were very familiar to his fellow college student James G Blaine whose letter concerning a trip over the 'Old Pike' is given

Stanwood, Bar Harbor Maine,
September 8th, 1892

Hon T B Searight,
Uniontown Pa

My Dear Friend I have received the sketches of the 'Old Pike" regularly, and have as regularly read them, some of them more than once, especially where you came near the Monongahela on either side of it, and thus strike the land of my birth and boyhood I could trace you all the way to Washington, at Malden, at Centerville at Billy Greenfield's in Beallsville, at Hillsboro (Billy Robison was a familiar name), at Dutch Charley Miller's at Wards at Pancake, and so on—familiar names forever endeared to my memory I cherish the desire of riding over the 'Old Pike" with you, but I am afraid we shall contemplate it as a scheme never to be realized

Very sincerely your friend
JAMES G BLAINE

The "Old Pike" has been favorably received and highly commended by the book reviewers and the reading public, and it deals with every character and phase of life of fifty years ago, while its historic pages are rich with incident, accident and anecdote and sometimes relate tragic events as well as humorous incidents While remembered in the future as a strong political leader and recollected as an able lawyer, yet the memory of Thomas B Searight will ever be kept bright through the future as the author of the "Old Pike," which will be his monument—enduring and indestructible —for all time to come

Colonel Searight married, October 29, 1857, Rose, only daughter of Hon Robert P Flenniken who was born in Greene county, Pennsylvania, 1804 died in San Francisco, California 1879 Mr Flenniken was minister to Denmark under President Polk Children Emily, William, Robert, Anne

Colonel Searight's remains after beautiful and impressive funeral services at St Peter's Church, were entombed in a tasteful spot selected by himself in Oak Grove cemetery, and near the "Old Pike" whose history he wrote so well and about which he loved to converse so much

Ewing B. Searight

Jean R. Shuman

Capt William Searight

(IV) Ewing Brownfield
SEARIGHT Searight second son of
William (3) (q v) and
Rachel (Brownfield) Searight was born at
Searights, Menallen township, Fayette
county, Pennsylvania, September 5, 1828
died February 26, 1902 He was educated
in the common schools and grew to manhood on the home farm He engaged in
agricultural pursuits, which he followed
successfully throughout the active years of
his life

He was also connected with the "Old
Pike' as superintendent, his tenure of office
being noted for efficiency served Menallen township as auditor for ten years
school director from 1869 to 1875, and was
for three years a director of the Fayette
County Home He was the owner of farm
and coal lands, and was a man of high
standing in the community He was a
staunch Democrat, and with his wife an
ardent member of Grace Episcopal Church,
near the front door of which he is buried
near his father and mother

Mr Searight married, February 3 1859,
Elizabeth, only daughter of Zadoc and Lydia Jackson Children 1 Rachel, born August 26, 1860, died August 11, 1882, she
married Charles J McCormick and left a
son, Searight Ray, born August 1 1882 2
William, born August 11, 1863, married,
February 20 1890, Miss Jennie Louise Patterson, a beautiful and accomplished
daughter of Sidney Patterson, ex-president
of a Dunbar bank William still lives on
the "Old Homestead," and is a very highly
respected citizen

(IV) Jean, daughter of Will-
SHUMAN iam (3) (q v) and Rachel
(Brownfield) Searight, was
born in Menallen township Fayette county,
Pennsylvania, September 15, 1830 She received her education at Washington Female
Seminary, then under the charge of Mrs
Sarah R (Foster) Hanna, who was a well
known teacher and a prominent member of
the Seceder church, of Western Pennsylvania

She married April 25, 1849 Captain
Thomas Shuman of Brownsville who
died February 11, 1878 Soon after her hus-

band's death, Mrs Shuman removed to
Uniontown where she has resided ever
since To the union of Thomas Shuman and
Jean R Searight were born eight children
William Searight Florine Emma Virginia
George Bowman, Thomas, Elizabeth Sea-
right, Rachel Searight and Samuel Ramsey,
all living excepting William Searight

(IV) Captain William Sea-
SEARIGHT right, third son of William
(3) (q v) and Rachel
(Brownfield) Searight, was born at Searights, Menallen township, Fayette county,
Pennsylvania, June 28, 1834, died July 31,
1881

He was educated at Dunlap's Creek Academy, and Washington and Madison Colleges
(Pennsylvania), and in 1853 was appointed
cadet at the United States Military Academy, West Point from which he resigned
one year later He then took a thorough
commercial course, after which he entered
the employ of Governor Black, of Nebraska
as clerk, and also served in that capacity for
his brother in the prothonotary's office at
Uniontown, Pennsylvania In 1861, at the
beginning of the civil war, he enlisted in
Company G, Eighth Pennsylvania Reserves,
Captain Oliphant He was made first sergeant, and became a popular drill officer, his
West Point schooling now bringing results
Upon his captain's promotion, leaving a
vacancy, he was advanced over the senior
officers and elected to the rank of captain
Sickness compelled him to resign but upon
regaining his health he again enlisted as a
private in the Eighty-eighth Pennsylvania
Regiment, serving until 1865 Under President Johnson's administration he served efficiently as a departmental clerk at Washington, D C In 1869 he became local editor of the Genius of Liberty, and made
that paper one of the best known ablest,
and most popular papers in Western Pennsylvania From that time until his death,
Captain Searight (familiarly known as "B")
was prominently connected with the Uniontown and Pittsburgh papers He was a
member of the Grand Army of the Republic,
and of other local organizations He was
kindly-hearted and generous, having a wide
circle of friends who cherish his memory

(IV) James Allison Sea-
SEARIGHT right, fourth son of William (3) (q v) and Rachel
(Brownfield) Searight, was born on the Searight homestead, Searights, Menallen township, Fayette county, Pennsylvania, September 13 1836

His early education was obtained in the
township public school, and in 1850 he began an academic course at Dunlap's Creek
Presbyterian Academy After leaving the
academy he entered the employ of John
T Hogg at Brownsville, then engaged in
the banking business He then became a
student at the Iron City Business College
of Pittsburgh, and in 1859 entered the preparatory department of Kenyon College
class of 1863, where he was a classmate of
E L Stanton son of the great war secretary, Edwin M Stanton During his college course, Lorin Andrews, president of
that college resigned his position and raised
a regiment with which he marched to the
front, but he was soon brought home and
entombed near Rosse Chapel, Gambier,
Ohio

Two years after his graduation he entered the Philadelphia Divinity School,
but ill health compelled him to leave in a
short time and he was forced to abandon
all thought of following the sacred calling
of the ministry After some time spent in
Washington D C, in the general land office. he returned home, and in 1871 established a real estate and insurance agency
in Uniontown, where he has represented
some of the leading insurance companies
of Europe and the United States, and in
which city he has since been identified with
many of the leading industries In 1873 he
joined with others in organizing and securing a charter for the People's Bank of
Fayette County, of which he was soon after
elected cashier Upon the death of the president, Colonel Ewing Brownfield, in 1880,
he was elected to succeed him in the president's office He remained at the head of
this bank until it was merged into the Citizens' Title & Trust Company, and gained
enviable distinction as a careful and conservative financier

Mr Searight has pronounced literary talent and has contributed many well written
articles to the press He spent several years
in collecting data for the history of the
"Family of Searight in America," which he
wrote in 1893 His book has received commendation from scholars and the press, and
is to be found in many of the leading libra-
ries of the world It has also been widely
distributed among the various branches of
the Searight family in America, and it will
stand as an enduring monument to the Searight name as long as the English language
is either read or spoken A number of
paragraphs which appear in this sketch of
the Searight family have been copied from
a review of the above-mentioned book by
W Scott Garner, of West Virginia

Mr Searight has been active in important
diocesan conventions of the Episcopal
church in Pennsylvania, he was a member
of the council when the first division of the
Diocese of Pennsylvania was made, again
when Dr Kerfoot was elected bishop of
Pittsburgh, again when Dr Whitehead was
chosen bishop of the same city, and served
on the committee that notified the bishop of
his election

Mr Searight is a member of St Peter's
Protestant Episcopal Church, has been active and useful in the local work of the same
and has served in prominent church office
He was the first member of the Scotch-
Irish Congress, elected from South Western
Pennsylvania He is a life member of the
Sons of the American Revolution, a life
member of the Historical Society of Pennsylvania, and has contributed liberally to its
collection of valuable works, and a member
of the Fayette County Historical and Genealogical Society He is a Knight Templar
Mason and a Jeffersonian Democrat He
takes a keen interest in the history of his
nation and state, also in the Scotch-Irish Society of America He is modest and retiring
in nature, but a man of sterling worth and
an honor to the race that claims him He is
well known in his city, where his worth is
fully appreciated

(IV) Elizabeth, youngest
COLVIN child of William (3) (q v)
and Rachel (Brownfield) Sea-
right, was born at Searights, Menallen township, Fayette county, Pennsylvania, Febru-

James A. Seavight

Elizabeth S. Colvin

aıy 17, 1839

She received her education at Washington Female Seminary, then under charge of Mrs Sarah R (Foster) Hanna; a Scotch-Irish teacher of ability and reputation She married, January 7. 1869. Joseph T Colvin, president of the Pittsburgh Bank of Commerce, later president of the Tradesmans' National Bank of Pittsburgh Mr and Mrs Colvin resided since their marriage in Pittsburgh, Pennsylvania She died November 18, 1908, and is buried in ' Homewood Cemetery,' Pittsburgh, Pennsylvania She like her sister, Mrs Shuman, was held in high esteem by all who knew her

---

The American ancestor of BRINKER the Brinkers of Uniontown, Pennsylvania, herein recorded, was Henry Brinker, born in Germany, who came to America with his parents at an early day, and settled in Butler county Their names or place of settlement are not known, but Henry Brinker is first found in Westmoreland county He married Elizabeth Henry, and left issue, one son being Stephen John, mentioned below Four of his sons served during the entire civil war period in the Union army They were Carson B , Joseph H , deceased, Simon, deceased , and Columbus, deceased The daughters were Louisa, deceased, Margaret, deceased, Rebecca, deceased

(II) Stephen John, son of Henry and Elizabeth (Henry) Brinker, was born in Westmoreland county, Pennsylvania He served during the entire period of the civil war

He married Alice daughter of Peter and Jane (Richey) Leezer, both born in McKeesport, Pennsylvania Jane Richey was a daughter of Abraham Richey Children of Stephen John Brinker 1 Harry L , now chemist for the Ohio Steel Works at Youngstown, Ohio 2 Laura Jane, married John K Griffith, of Uniontown. Pennsylvania 3 William H now of Uniontown 4 Henrietta, deceased 5 Samuel P , of whom further 6 Lottie, unmarried

(III) Dr Samuel P Brinker, youngest son of Stephen John Brinker, was born at Tarr Station, Westmoreland county, Pennsylvania, July 13, 1876 He was educated in the public schools and at Greensburg Seminary, whence he was graduated, class of 1899

He then entered the College of Physicians and Surgeons, Baltimore, Maryland, whence he was graduated Doctor of Medicine, class of 1905 For one year after graduation he was connected with Bay View Hospital, Baltimore He was then in Wheeling, West Virginia, for a time at the Emergency Hospital He was duly certified to practice by the State Medical Board of West Virginia, and the same year took the examination prescribed by the State Medical Board of Pennsylvania, who in 1906 duly certified his fitness to practice in the state of Pennsylvania In the spring of 1907 he began practice in Normalville, Pennsylvania, continuing until November 1911 when he came to Uniontown where he is well established as a skillful, capable physician

He is a member of the American Medical Society, the Pennsylvania State and Fayette County Medical Societies, the Independent Order of Odd Fellows, Royal Arcanum, and Royal Order of Lyons, of which he is medical examiner In politics he is a Republican, but takes little part in political affairs beyond exercising his right of franchise as an intelligent and patriotic citizen

He married, November 28, 1907, Amy Zoe, daughter of William Henry (2) and Mary Agnes (Alfred) Waggy, of Weston, West Virginia, and granddaughter of William Henry (1) and Agnes (Alfred) Waggy, who came from Germany and settled in Weston, West Virginia Her grandfather was a large slave owner and a prominent citizen William Henry (2) Waggy was born near Weston, where he still resides Children of Mr and Mrs Waggy Lilhan May, married M W Smith, now of Baltimore, Maryland, Effie A , married D B Givens, of Weston, William T , deceased, Amy Zoe, of previous mention, Stella Agnes, married K E Anderson, of Oklahoma, James Henry, of Pittsburgh, Pennsylvania, Delphi Denella, married Clarence B Butcher, of Weston Dr Samuel P Brinker and his wife are members of the Methodist Episcopal church of Uniontown

LUTTERMAN The family is of German ancestry, long seated in the Fatherland

The earliest of whom we have record is August Lutterman, a collector of taxes under the government, who lived and died in Germany leaving issue He held office under King George V until the fall of the Hanoverian monarchy

(II) Arnold, son of August Lutterman was born in Hanover Germany, in 1833 He was educated in his native land, and when a young man came to the United States settling in Cincinnati Ohio He learned the trade of molder and now resides at Dawson, Fayette county, Pennsylvania He is a member of the German Lutheran church

He married in Cincinnati Ohio, Amelia daughter of Fred and Mary Nolte Fred Nolte was a well-to-do farmer of Northwestern Indiana, and a veteran of the civil war, enlisting at Tell City, Indiana, and received severe wounds at the battles of Bull Run and Gettysburg Children of Arnold Lutterman August, deceased, Arnold, married Mabel ——, Oscar, deceased, Oliver, deceased, Walter, deceased, Harry T, of whom further, May, now living in Toledo Ohio, married Charles Palmer, three children, Nannie, deceased, Carrie, deceased

(III) Harry T, son of Arnold and Amelia (Nolte) Lutterman, was born at Cincinnati, Ohio July 18, 1873 He was educated in the public schools of that city, and in private schools, and in Merrill Business College of Stamford, Connecticut He began business life as an accountant, continuing several years

In 1909 he came to Connellsville and established the Model Dye Works at No 406 South Pittsburgh street, of which he is proprietor and manager He is a member of the Methodist church and of the Masonic Order, in politics a Democrat He has traveled extensively in almost every state in the Union and is a well educated and thoroughly informed man He married May 29, 1912 Anabel, eldest daughter of James B Millard, of Connellsville, Pennsylvania

STRICKLER Another branch of the Strickler family descends from Conrad Strickler born in Germany, through his son Conrad (2) Strickler There are said to have been seven brothers named Strickler who settled in Lancaster county, Pennsylvania, later coming to Fayette county They were all large men except the youngest, who was called "Little Dave"

(II) Conrad (2) Strickler kept a drover's stand and house of entertainment on the "Pike" between Connellsville and Uniontown, was also a farmer and built flat boats, freighting on the Youghiogheny and Ohio rivers He married Elizabeth Varns and had issue Jacob, of whom further, Mary married William Snyder Conrad, now living in California, a fruit farmer, Henry, died young, John, died aged twenty years, Elizabeth, married Parkhill Blair, David married Lyda Strickler, Samuel, now living near Vanderbilt, Pennsylvania, Sarah, married John Guiler, whom she survives

(III) Jacob, son of Conrad (2) Strickler, was born in Dunbar township, Fayette county, Pennsylvania, August 20, 1822, died May 17, 1908 He worked for his father until his marriage, then moved on the Henry Galley farm, remaining one year He then bought one hundred and twenty-eight acres in the eastern part of Franklin township, and a few years later purchased the Oglivee farm lying in both Dunbar and Franklin townships In 1892 he built a frame house on the farm, letting his son William have the red brick mansion—here he lived until his death He was Presbyterian in religion, his wife a German Baptist or "Dunkard" He was a Democrat in politics and served as school director While he was a very well-to-do farmer he made most of his money in cattle raising and dealing, having engaged in that line very largely

He married, October 10, 1850, Rebecca Snyder, born February 14, 1831, who survives him residing in Fayette county, daughter of David and Susan (Hepler) Snyder and granddaughter of Lewis Snyder, born in Germany, who came to America and settled in Lancaster with his parents, who died and left him without resources He was bound out to a cooper who taught him his trade He later came to Fayette county where he owned a good farm in Tyrone township, operated a cooper's shop and made a specialty of bee culture He was a German Baptist as were the members of his family David Snyder, his son, was a farmer of Tyrone township, owning his own farm He married Susan Hepler, who died aged sixty years leaving an only child Rebecca, who married Jacob Strickler David Snyder married (second) Sarah Cumberland and died near Mount Pleasant at the foot of the mountains Their only child Sidney married James Wiedman and now lives in Mount Pleasant Children of Jacob and Rebecca Strickler 1 David, born July 24, 1851, married (first) Lena McGinnis, (second) Mary Downs, and now lives on his truck farm near San Francisco, California 2 Conrad, born April 6, 1853 married Sarah Foster and now lives at Smithfield, Ohio 3 Susan, born April 12, 1855, married Aaron J Fairchild and lives on their farm in Dunbar township 4 John, born May 3, 1857, resides at the home farm in Franklin township with his aged mother he is unmarried 5 Elizabeth, born September 12, 1858, married William Foster and lives at Smithfield, Ohio 6 Sarah, born May 5, 1861 married George Bute now the owner of four hundred and eighty acres of land near Omaha, Nebraska, on which he resides 7 Joseph G, of whom further 8 Benjamin Franklin, born •January 9 1865, married Nan Hornbeck and lives in Franklin township 9 Flora, born October 11, 1867, married J H Edwards, an undertaker of Vanderbilt, Pennsylvania 10 Jesse O, born March 14, 1869, married (first) Nora Core, (second) Margaret Lewis he is a farmer near Curfew, Franklin township 11 William, born May 26 1871, married Anna Cowan and lives in Dunbar township, a farmer 12 Anna, born February 25, 1875, married Dr Jesse Cogan and resides in Dawson, Pennsylvania

(IV) Joseph G, son of Jacob and Rebecca (Snyder) Strickler was born at the Strickler homestead in Franklin township, Fayette county, Pennsylvania, May 29 1863, died October 14, 1911 He attended the public school, and grew to manhood at the old farm first purchased by his father When

Jacob Strickler purchased the Oglivee farm, Joseph G became manager of the homestead, continuing seventeen years In October, 1901, he bought a tract of eighty-four acres in Franklin township, part of the old Henry Snyder farm In 1902 he moved to this farm on which he resided until his death He also owned eight hundred acres of Texas land and one hundred and fifty acres of West Virginia coal land He was a Democrat in politics, serving three terms as school director He belonged with his wife to the Presbyterian church He was a hard working, energetic man, very strong and hearty, but died very suddenly

He married Margaret Edwards, born in Dunbar township, Fayette county, Pennsylvania, August, 1861, died August 15, 1909, daughter of Robert and Claussa Edwards— he born in Virginia, came to Fayette county when young, became a prosperous land owner and farmer also justice of the peace, being well known as "Squire" Edwards His children J H, funeral director of Vanderbilt, Pennsylvania, Margaret, of previous mention, George, deceased, Zella, married Alpheus W Hair, Alvin, now living at Crossland Junction, Fayette county, Ada, a school teacher of Connellsville, Pennsylvania, Albert, unmarried

(V) George W only child of Joseph G and Margaret (Edwards) Strickler, was born on the old Strickler homestead in Franklin township, Fayette county, Pennsylvania, May 17, 1882 He was educated in the Jefferson school in his native township and at Ada, Ohio After finishing his studies he returned to the home farm and became his father's assistant In 1905 he visited California, remaining a year or more, working on fruit farms and cattle ranches, increasing his store of practical knowledge as well as touring the state and visiting relatives In 1907 he returned home and assisted in the farm labor until his father's death in 1911, when he became sole owner by inheritance He continued at the old farm, a prosperous, modern agriculturist He is a Democrat in politics, and a member of the Presbyterian church His fraternal society is the Loyal Order of Moose

He married Lucy Clelland born in Preston county, West Virginia, daughter of

Frank Clelland, a veteran of the civil war, now living in Dunbar township Children of George W Strickler Virginia, born January 5, 1910, Olive, February 8 1911

STRICKLER   The Stricklers of Fayette county descend from Conrad Strickler, born in Germany, who emigrated to Pennsylvania where he died Early settlers in Fayette county were Abraham, Jacob and Henry Strickler, who were large landowners in Upper Tyrone township

(I) This branch descends from Henry Strickler, a prosperous farmer of Upper Tyrone, where much of his property is yet held in the Strickler name He married and had issue, including a son, Henry R

(II) Henry R, son of Henry Strickler, was born in Upper Tyrone township, Fayette county, Pennsylvania, where he lived and died in 1894 He inherited the Strickler homestead and was a man of influence and means

He was a member of the Methodist Episcopal church and in 1821 auditor of the township He married Susanna Slonaker, also born in Upper Tyrone Children 1 Fanny, married Henry Orbin, now a farmer of Nebraska 2 Elizabeth, married Wesley Stillwagon, and lives in Upper Tyrone township 3 Mary, deceased married Thomas Orbin, who died in a southern military prison during the civil war 4 Susanna, died aged sixteen years 5 George W, of whom further 6 Rist D died unmarried 7 Nancy Jane, married Benjamin Rist, a farmer of Upper Tyrone, both deceased 8 Catherine, married James Kaine, now owning and operating a horse ranch in Kansas 9 Rebecca, married Michael Darrh, a locomotive engineer living in Hazlewood, Pennsylvania 10 Sarah Ann, married J C Moore and lives in Vanderbilt, Pennsylvania

(III) George W, eldest son of Henry R and Susanna (Slonaker) Strickler, was born at the old Strickler homestead, in Upper Tyrone township, Fayette county, Pennsylvania, May 2, 1841, died April 10, 1912 He was educated in the "Ridge" school, under the tuition of John Rist Being the eldest son he remained upon the home farm, after his marriage he continued to reside there, but in another dwelling In 1879 he moved to Georges township, Fayette county, where he rented the Jacob Franks farm, continuing there for ten years In 1889 he returned to the home farm and managed it for his aged father, until the latter's death, when it was willed to George W Strickler, with the provision that he pay the other heirs stated sums He was a Democrat in politics, and with his wife had been a member of the Christian church for forty years He was also a member of the Royal Arcanum

Mr Strickler married, May 22, 1863, Margaret S Cochran, born in Lower Tyrone township, Fayette county, March 15, 1845, daughter of Mordecai Cochran (see Cochran III)

Children of George W and Margaret S (Cochran) Strickler 1 James C, born March 22, 1864, died October 26, 1866 2 Lenora, born November 19, 1865, died December 20, 1868 3 Alice, born September 17, 1867, married George Newman and resides at Continental Works No 1, Fayette county 4 An infant son, died at birth, April 8, 1869 5 Lutellas C, born February 25, 1870, now residing in California, unmarried 6 Edward, born November 20, 1872, now a railroad contractor, living in Tacoma, Washington, married Florence Rider 7 George, born November 19, 1873, residing at home, unmarried 8 Hugh, born July 24, 1875, now a coal miner of Lower Tyrone township, married Rose Gault 9 Iva, born July 28, 1877, married Harry Laughrey, cashier of the Title & Trust Company, of Scottdale, Pennsylvania 10 Walter, born June 3, 1879, now residing on a homestead claim in Montana, unmarried 11 Roy, born May 29, 1885, now a farmer of South Union township, married Bertha Sease 12 Lloyd, born June 29, 1887, a stationary engineer in a lumber camp in Washington, unmarried, resides in Tacoma

Mrs Margaret S Cochran Strickler, survives her husband and continues her residence on the farm in Upper Tyrone township She is a lady of rare charm of manner and a true exponent of the virtues of the Cochran race who have ever been men and women of distinction

G. W. Strickler

Mrs. M. S. C. Strickler

(The Cochran Line)

(I) John Cochran came to the American colonies about 1745, settling in Chester county, Pennsylvania

(II) Samuel, son of John Cochran, born July 24, 1750, was a soldier of the revolution, serving with a company enlisted in Cumberland county, Pennsylvania He fought at Paoli, Brandywine and Germantown, and spent the winter with the hardy, tried patriots under Washington at Valley Forge He married (first) a Quakeress, Esther, daughter of Daniel John Her father was brought to Pennsylvania by William Penn to preach to the Indians and Quakers One of his grandsons, Gideon John, was sheriff of Fayette county about 1850 Samuel Cochran came to Fayette county after the revolution and settled in Tyrone township, where he purchased a three hundred acre tract from Joseph Huston, where he lived until his death He willed the homestead part of his landed possessions to his youngest son, Mordecai, and the remainder to his oldest son James The latter died a bachelor in 1875, aged ninety-two years, having always lived with his brother Mordecai, to whose oldest son, James W, he willed his estate Mrs Esther (John) Cochran died October 8 1802, leaving six children James, Samuel, Isaac, Thomas, John, Mordecai, of whom further Samuel Cochran married (second) Agnes —— who bore him one child Esther, who married John Strickler, of Tyrone township

(III) Mordecai, youngest son of Samuel and Esther (John) Cochran managed the Cochran farm, which was located at the western outcrop of the Connellsville coking coal deposit In addition to his farming operations he embarked about 1845 in the manufacture of coke, an industry that has brought millions upon millions of dollars to the Connellsville region He purchased a tract on the Youghiogheny river, and erected four coke ovens that being the beginning of the plant which, in its later development, was known as the Sterling Mines, situated below Broad Ford, in Tyrone township These ovens were operated continuously until 1868, when he sold them to his sons James W, Alexander C and Lutellas Cochran He sent the coke down the Youghiogheny to the Monongahela and Lower Ohio, until the 1860 decade, when shipments began by rail Mordecai Cochran after settling his coking interests in 1868, continued his farming operations until his death, December 29, 1880 His three sons added a large amount of coal land to the plant, in association with W H Brown, of Pittsburgh, as Brown & Cochran, enlarged and expanded the business, and until 1873 did the largest coking business in Pennsylvania The firm was dissolved by the death of W H Brown and Alexander C Cochran The business, however, remained in the family, and through James, a nephew of Mordecai Cochran, and his descendants, has brought fame and fortune to this justly celebrated Fayette county family Mordecai Cochran married Susannah Welch, who died August 12, 1873 Children Three died in infancy, Esther, married R Q Fleming, and died in 1872, Alexander C, died May 30, 1873, James W, died April 20, 1888, Lutellas, died September 25, 1892, Mary Ann, Margaret S, of previous mention, now widow of George W Strickler, Melinda, married Hugh S Darsie, Catherine D, married Jacob Harris, Alice C, married Isaac N Beighley and Mark M, a leading lawyer of the Fayette county bar and a prominent business man, married (first) Emma J Whitsett, (second) Mary Schell

STRICKLER Jacob Strickler was born in Bucks county, Pennsylvania, son of German parentage He grew to manhood in his native county and was reared in the Menonite faith, to which he always adhered He was the owner of Bucks county property which he sold, and about the year 1789 moved from Bucks county to Fayette county, Pennsylvania On December 22, 1791, he purchased a tract of three hundred and ninety-four acres near Scottdale On this there was a great deal of timber and a water power which he utilized to furnish power for a saw mill and a grist mill both located on Jacobs Creek He converted his timber into lumber as rapidly as possible and ran the grist mill in grinding for the general public He did not come empty handed to Fayette county and added largely to his estate before his death He was a Whig in politics and held a good position in the county He married Elizabeth Stewart, a daughter of Jacob Stewart, of Scotch parentage Jacob (2), her brother, was a landowner a surveyor, and in 1797 established the first newspaper in Fayette county, *The Fayette Gazette* and *Union Advertiser*, published at Uniontown A sister of Elizabeth Stewart married John, a brother of Jacob Strickler Children of Jacob and Elizabeth Strickler Elizabeth, married Moses Vance, Mary, married Alexander Long, Jacob B, David, a cabinetmaker

(II) Jacob B, son of Jacob and Elizabeth (Stewart) Strickler, was born in Upper Tyrone township, Fayette county, Pennsylvania, October 30, 1791, died August 31, 1874 He worked for his father on the farm and in the mill, inheriting at his death one hundred and sixty-five acres of the paternal estate which seems to have been equally divided by Jacob among his five children Jacob B was a Whig in politics, later a Republican, and a local preacher of the Methodist church He drove whiskey from his harvest fields by raising the wages of his men He married Mary Fiscus born October 18, 1790, died September 12, 1868, daughter of Charles and Serviah Fiscus, of Westmoreland county Children I Joshua, of whom further 2 Alexander a merchant of Mount Pleasant, Pennsylvania, his lifetime home 3 Henry, deceased 4 Maria married Dr Covert and lived in Pittsburgh, where both died 5 Susan, married John Sherrick, moved to Illinois, where both died 6 Anna, married a Mr Gorby Three children died young

(III) Joshua son of Jacob B and Mary (Fiscus) Strickler, was born in Fayette county, Pennsylvania, January 21, 1821 died August 24, 1910 He was a wagoner on the national pike until 1850, when he married and moved to a small farm in Luzerne township, where he lived happy prosperous and contented for half a century He made a specialty of raising fine merino sheep, with which he was very successful In the year 1900, just fifty years from his taking the farm, he moved to a good home he had purchased at No 28 Ben Lomond street, Uniontown, where he lived until his death,

ten years later, in his ninetieth year He was a Republican and an official member of the Methodist Episcopal church, always active in church work, as was his wife He was hospitable, generous and a man of high character, attaining a competence through his own energy He married, January 31, 1850, Elizabeth, daughter of Benjamin and Abigail (Randolph) Covert, who lived for many years in Fayette county, near the Monongahela river, owning and operating their own farm Their children 1 Elizabeth, now widow of Joshua Strickler, whose devoted wife she was for sixty years 2 Richard, lived and died in Fayette county 3 Mary, married David Wakefield Children of Joshua and Elizabeth Strickler 1 An infant died unnamed 2 Mary Abigail, born December 4, 1852, married Albert D Conwell, whom she survives 3 Benjamin C, born October 3, 1855, resides in Uniontown, married Velma Nealon 4 Jacob Arthur, born November 10, 1858, lives in Uniontown, married (first) Mary Bowlby, by whom one child was born Bryan, he married (second) Mary Stevens 5 Edward Everett, of whom further 6 Randolph J, born April 20, 1869, a farmer of Greene county, Pennsylvania, married Jessie Goodwin, one son 7 Frank, born November 3, 1872, died in January, 1875

(IV) Edward Everett, fifth child of Joshua and Elizabeth (Covert) Strickler, was born on the home farm in Fayette county, Pennsylvania, along the shores of the Monongahela river, December 4, 1860 He was educated in the public school, attended the State Normal at California two terms, the University of West Virginia, one term and Duff's Business College, from whence he was graduated in 1882 After completing his studies he entered the employ of Conwell & Strickler, shoe dealers of Uniontown, continuing with them as clerk for about eight years He then became bookkeeper in the National Bank of Fayette County and in 1903 was promoted teller, which position he now holds (1912) He is also director and secretary of the Mount Hope Coal Company, and interested in Uniontown real estate He is a member of the First Presbyterian Church, and belongs to the Royal Arcanum

He married, September 3, 1886, Mary Dawson, born in Fayette county, daughter of Louis M and Mary J Dawson, an old Fayette county family Children Eugenia Marguerite, born June 3, 1887, married Albert F Miller, of Riverside, California, child, Dorothy Marguerite, born January 1, 1912, Edgar E, October 4, 1902 The family home is a beautiful brick residence on South Mount Vernon avenue

---

McCORMICK This branch of the McCormick family descends from Moses McCormick, a chair maker and prominent citizen in the early day He married —— Buttermore, and left issue Jacob, George of whom further, Andrew, John, William, Eliza married Henry Shaw, Katherine, married Jacob Dull, Mary, married John Freeman, Sarah, married Reuben Shaw, (second) John Stillwagon The only living child is William, now residing near Anderson, Indiana

(II) George, son of Moses McCormick, was born in Fayette county, Pennsylvania, died in Connellsville, July 1, 1878 He was for many years engaged in the butcher business in Connellsville, was also a chair maker and a skillful glazier He was a Democrat, and both he and his wife members of the Methodist Episcopal church He was a quiet retiring man, of excellent reputation He married Lucinda Teel, died June 30, 1886, whose father was a soldier of the war of 1812 After that war he retired to Westmoreland county, where he died He was born in Ireland as was his wife Lucinda, but they met and married in Pennsylvania Children of George McCormick, Mary, deceased, Moses, deceased, John T Hurst, Emma married Rockwell Marietta, Elizabeth, deceased, Noble, of whom further, Matilda, deceased, Frank, deceased, Lucinda, George

(III) Noble, son of George and Lucinda (Teel) McCormick, was born in Connellsville, Pennsylvania, February 2, 1853 He was educated in the public schools, and began business life on the railroad He served on the Connellsville police force and for several years has been engaged in the retailing of liquor He is a Democrat in politics He married September 15, 1873, Priscilla Spriggs, born in Wales, daughter of Charles Spriggs, born in England, of English parents, but moved to Wales, where he married and raised a family Children of Noble McCormick Edward, a boss boiler maker at the Baltimore & Ohio shops, Henry, George Walter and Maude, all deceased, Norah, widow of Guy Percy, has a son, Cooper

---

LECKEMBY The Leckembys of Connellsville, Pennsylvania, descend from an English mill worker who married, lived and died in England Children Thomas, died in England, the others, John, William (of further mention), and Hannah, all came to the United States John Leckemby now lives at Dunbar, Pennsylvania, Hannah married Robert Shelley, and lived in Westmoreland county, Pennsylvania, until her death

(II) William Leckemby, born in England, November 18, 1842, was educated and married in his native land In 1868 he came to the United States, locating in Philadelphia, where he was employed in one of the stocking mills of that city He soon afterward left the city and was next at Ursina, Pennsylvania, where he helped to build the Brooks tunnel He then settled in Meyersdale, Somerset county, Pennsylvania, where for sixteen years he was employed in the coal mines, then for eight years was at Blairsville, Pennsylvania, in the hotel business, then for eight years at New Brighton, in the same line, now living there retired He is a Republican, and always active in local affairs serving as school director, supervisor and tax collector He married Jane Thomas, born in England, one of a large family, she being the only one to come to the United States Children James Edward, of whom further, Joseph Herbert, deceased, Anna, married Austin Miller, of Meyersdale, William Henry, now living in Cumberland, Maryland, Carrie, died in infancy, Molly, deceased, Lucretia, married Walter Stitt, deceased, she lives in Blairsville Pennsylvania, John F, now living in Youngstown, Ohio, Alice K, married Edward Weller, Katherine (now deceased), married Dr Norman Lewis, of

Hooversville, Pennsylvania Both William
Leckemby and wife are members of the
Episcopal church

(III) James Edward, son of William
Leckemby, was born in Philadelphia, Pennsylvania, March 27, 1869 He was educated in the public schools of Ursina and
Meyersdale, Pennsylvania, but at twelve
years of age left school and began working
in the coal mines, continuing until 1896
He then entered the employ of the Baltimore & Ohio railroad as brakeman In
1900 he was promoted conductor, a position
he now holds Since 1902 his home has been
in Connellsville, now at No 909 Sycamore
street He is a Republican, and a member,
with his wife, of the Reformed church, he
also belongs to the Brotherhood of Railway
Trainmen He married, June 11, 1891,
Martha Witt born Meyersdale, Pennsylvania, daughter of William (2) and Martha
(Ankney) Witt, and granddaughter of William and Martha Witt, old settlers of Somerset county, Pennsylvania Their children
John, William (2), and Susan Martha Ankney was a daughter of John and Elizabeth
Ankney, also an old Somerset county family William (2) Witt, born in Somerset
county, was a coal prospector, died 1883
His wife Martha was born and married in
Somerset county, and still survives Children 1 Minerva, married Benton Younkin
2 George R was a sergeant in the regular
United States army, serving in Montana,
now living at Meyersdale 3 William G,
now living at Jenner, Pennsylvania 4 Edward, living in Waterloo, Iowa 5 Silas,
now living in Meyersdale 6 Samuel, died in
infancy 7 Martha (of previous mention)
Children of James Edward and Martha
Leckemby Robert Ross, born January 16,
1892, Merle Ray, April 5, 1894, Eva Mae,
March 27, 1896, Mary Alice, June 11, 1898,
James William, April 17, 1900, Harry Edward, November 6, 1902, Leroy, July 26,
1906

The Langleys of Fayette
LANGLEY   county descend from German forbears, who settled
in Eastern Pennsylvania Their first settlement was made in Redstone township, when
John Langley came at quite an early day

He was a stonemason by trade He owned
a fertile farm of one hundred acres, and later
purchased a farm of one hundred and sixty
acres in German township He followed
his trade and also cultivated his farm all
through life He prospered and held honorable positions in his community He was a
Whig in politics, but took little part in
public affairs He married Phoebe ———
and had issue 1 John, a wealthy farmer
of Illinois 2 Aaron, of whom further 3
Hiram, born February 13, 1821, married
(first) Rachel Moore and had four children,
(second) a widow, Elizabeth Johnson 4
Betty, married Aaron McKnight and had
three children 5 Hannah, married Robert
Blakeley

(II) Aaron, son of John and Phoebe Langley, was born in German township Fayette
county, Pennsylvania, October 7, 1818, died
July 25, 1906 He attended the public
schools in German township, and in that
township lived on and cultivated a farm all
his life In politics he was a Republican
and at one time was supervisor of roads, he
was a member of the Presbyterian church
He married Margaret Moulten born December 15, 1818, died July 23, 1888, daughter
of John Moulton Children of Mr Moulton
1 Rachel, married Robert Moss, of Redstone township, and had four children 2
Elizabeth, married Henry Martin and lives
in Illinois 3 Annie, married Louis Haney
and lives in the west 4 Margaret, of previous mention 5 Avarilla 6 John M, married a Miss Campbell and had seven children 7 Joseph Children of Aaron and
Margaret (Moulten) Langley 1 Mary,
born January, 1848, married (first) Manasa
Sedgwick and had two children, married
(second) David Davidson and had one child
2 Sallie Annie, married Christopher Woodward and had one son 3 Avarilla, married
Abraham Moore and had two children 4
Alice, married Elijah Tracy and had eight
children 5 Eliza, married John Frost and
had eleven children 6 Charles, married
Anna Frost and had one child 7 Alexander, of whom further

(III) Alexander, son of Aaron and Margaret (Moulten) Langley, was born in German township, Fayette county, Pennsylvania, July 4, 1861 He was educated in

the public schools of his native township, and after leaving school became a farmer, cultivating the one hundred and fifty-three acres inherited from his father with such success that he is considered one of the best and most uniformly successful farmers in the county. His farm is richly underlaid with coal, which is operated by the H C Frick Company he having disposed of the rights in 1898. He is a Republican in politics. He married October 24, 1890, Ida Frost, born in Menallen township, August 28, 1866, died June 19, 1909, daughter of William B Frost, a merchant of Uniontown. Children 1 George Washington, born February 22, 1892 2 Aaron born March 15, 1893, 3 John born March 6, 1895 4 Margaret, born January 15, 1897 5 Emily Ruth, born December 11, 1899, died February 3, 1912.

STOUFFER The Stouffer family is of German origin, and on coming to the United States settled in Lancaster county, where the grandparent of James W, and George F Stouffer, lived prior to settlement in Fayette county in 1806

(II) John D, son of John Stouffer was born in Lancaster county, Pennsylvania, in 1803, and when three years of age was brought to Fayette county by his parents He grew up a farmer, and also was a miller, but devoted most of his time to agriculture He was a Whig, later a Republican and a member of the Presbyterian church He died in 1879 He married (second) Betsey daughter of Joseph H Cunningham, a farmer and devout Presbyterian of Tyrone township, Fayette county she died in 1856, aged fifty-three years He married (third) Eleanor Fleming, and left issue

(III) James W, eldest son of John D and Betsey (Cunningham) Stouffer, was born in Dunbar township, Fayette county, Pennsylvania, March 25, 1845 He was reared on the home farm, educated in the public schools, and followed the vocation of a farmer until 1871, when he came to Connellsville, Pennsylvania, and for one year was a clerk in the employ of John Coulson, then with Spears & Company at Dunbar one year In 1875 he moved again to Connells-

ville, where he established a livery business which he conducted most successfully until 1904 He kept a first-class livery and was rewarded with a generous patronage In 1904 he was elected street commissioner of Connellsville, a position he now holds He is a Republican in politics, and previous to his election as street commissioner, served two terms in the city council He is a member of King Solomon's Lodge, No 346, Free and Accepted Masons, Connellsville Chapter, Royal Arch Masons Uniontown Commandery, No 49, Knights Templar, Connellsville Lodge, No 386, Independent Order of Odd Fellows, and of the Methodist Episcopal church He married, March 25, 1875, Elizabeth Pritchard, born in Connellsville, in 1850, daughter of Benjamin and Harriet (Freeman) Pritchard, early settlers of Connellsville where both died Of their six children George F and Clara are living, both residents of Connellsville, children both born in Connellsville 1 Charles H, born December 4 1875, educated in the public schools, now a letter carrier in the United States post office at Connellsville, married Emma Keck, of Connellsville, and has James Keck, born December 7, 1906 2 Harriet Freeman, born May 13, 1877 married A H Murrie, of Martins Ferry, Ohio, now chief clerk at the Laughlin Works of the American Sheet & Tin Plate Company The family home is at No 412 South Pittsburgh street, Connellsville, where he built a residence in 1889

(III) George Fleming Stouffer, son of John D and Eleanor (Fleming) Stouffer was born in Dunbar township, Pennsylvania, July 9, 1862 He was educated in the public schools of Dunbar township and New Haven (Connellsville, West Side), continuing his studies and helping on the farm until he was fifteen years of age He then began learning the carpenter's trade, which he followed eighteen years He also was a painter, a trade he followed three years For ten years he was engaged in pattern making, and for two years he was with the Boyts-Porter Company He is now with the Boyts-Porter Company as pattern maker and has been with that house in all about four years He has resided in Connellsville since boyhood, and since 1886 at No

225 East Fairview street He is a Republican in politics and both he and wife are members of the United Presbyterian church

He married August 5, 1884, Maria B Harris, born in Butler county, Pennsylvania, September 14, 1859, daughter of Perry Oliver and Eliza Jane (Miller) Harris, he born in Butler, his wife in Clarion county, Pennsylvania He was a soldier of the civil war, was taken prisoner, and died in Andersonville prison His wife died in 1903 Their children Mary E, Ella Jane, Anna B, and Maria B Children of George Fleming and Maria B (Harris) Stouffer 1 Arthur Harris, born June 27, 1885, educated in Connellsville, now a civil engineer, married Margaret Lewis, of Pittsburgh, Pennsylvania, where they now reside 2 Homer, born November 15, 1888, died August 8, 1893

This family early appears in the SMITH records of Georges township, Fayette county The town of Smithfield was laid out by Barnabas Smith June 13, 1799, on a tract of land called "Beautiful Meadows" that he had received with his wife, Elizabeth Reese They are believed to have been the parents of Henry Smith a property holder in Georges township, Fayette county, Pennsylvania He was later a farmer of North Union township, where he died He married (first) Keziah Davis, (second) Leah Fields, who was the mother of his children, (third) Eliza Melkey He was a deacon of the Baptist church, which he also served as trustee Children Henry P, Isaac F, Elias Melton, of whom further, Maria Estep, and Melvina, the latter the last surviving child She is now living at North Union township

(III) Elias Melton, son of Henry Smith and his second wife Leah Fields, was born in North Union township, Fayette county, Pennsylvania, in April, 1839, died May 19, 1879 He was educated in the public school and went directly from the schoolroom to the army during the civil war He enlisted in the First Virginia Cavalry During an action his company was ordered to dismount and fight as foot soldiers In obeying the command his horse reared and fell on him

inflicting injuries from which he never fully recovered He, however, served out his period of enlistment, three years, then returned and thereafter was a farmer of North Union township He was a Republican in politics and a member of the Baptist church He married Antridge, born in North Union township, daughter of Peter Pegg, a farmer and stock raiser of that township, who died at the age of seventy years, married Agnes Bosley, and had children William, Edward, deceased, Antridge (of previous mention), Jane, deceased, Mary Ann, George, Peter (2), Jacob, deceased, Franklin, James, Louisa, Fuller, Samuel, and one who died in infancy Children of Elias Melton and Antridge Smith 1 Clara, married Arthur Carstead, a farmer, lives at Atwater, Ohio 2 Child who died in infancy 3 Hannah, married William H Graham, a gauger in the United States internal revenue service, resides in Uniontown 4 James B, of whom further 5 Louisa, married Charles Keys, a market gardener of Connellsville, Pennsylvania 6 Elias Melton (2), a house painter, married Myrtle Robbins, lives at Point Marion, Fayette county, Pennsylvania 7 Fanny Leah, married Andrew O Bryson, a farmer of North Union township 8 Charles Henry, a market gardener of North Union township, married Lulu Bryson 9 William A, a farmer on the old Smith homestead in North Union township, with his mother who is aged seventy years (1912) She is a Presbyterian

(IV) James Benton, son of Elias Melton and Antridge (Pegg) Smith, was born in North Union township, Fayette county, Pennsylvania September 26, 1867 He was educated in the public school, and grew to manhood on the home farm He began his business life as a market gardener and a dairyman, and now owns a farm of eighty-three acres, which he conducts as a dairy farm, marketing his entire product among the hotels of Uniontown He is a successful, progressive farmer and conducts his business on approved modern lines of feeding and sanitation His farm is underlaid with coal, partly by the Pittsburgh vein, but largely by the Freeport vein He is a Republican in politics and a member of the Presbyterian church

1912

Dreaming of the days when he was a Soldier Boy.

1862.

Enlisted for three years or during the war.

J. Robinson Balsley, Company H, 142nd Regt. Pa. Vols.

Mr Smith married, October 10, 1895, Sarah, born in Menallen township, Fayette county, April 18, 1869 daughter of William H Gaddis, a farmer of Menallen township, now aged seventy-four years He married Grace Louisa Preisol, a great-granddaughter of Jonathan and Edith (Nichols) Sharpless, and their children were 1 Howard, now living in Colorado a carpenter, gold miner and real estate dealer 2 Ida May, died in infancy 3 Anna Florence, died aged seven years 4 Sarah (of previous mention) 5 Grace Lulla, married Amzi Vail, a farmer of Menallen township 6 Jonathan now a farmer near Carthage, Missouri 7 Mabel Ray, married Melvin H Bryson, a farmer of Menallen township Children of James Benton and Sarah (Gaddis) Smith, all born in North Union township 1 Harold A, born August 5, 1896 2 Hazel Grace, twin of Harold A 3 Mabel Louise, born July 18, 1898 4 James Benton (2), born April 1, 1901 5 Edith Sharpless, born October 6, 1902

BALSLEY Nothing can be told of the paternal ancestry of this family except that tradition says the emigrant ancestor came from Bavaria, in Europe The name has been anglicized and so changed that the identity of the original bearer cannot be discovered This record begins with Samuel Balsley, who came to Fayette county and had four sons who are believed to have been born in this country There is no record of his wife Sons George H, of whom further 2 John (q v) 3 William, an auctioneer of the county 4 Hiram, who lived in New Philadelphia

(II) George H Balsley, eldest son of Samuel Balsley, was born February 14, 1800, in Fayette county, Pennsylvania, died October 10, 1871 He was a carpenter and contractor of Connellsville where most of his life was spent He built a residence at the forks of the Mount Pleasant road about 1830, where all but three of his fifteen children were born This old homestead of the Balsleys is still standing He married Sarah Shallenberger, born in Fayette county, February 12 1804, died August 8, 1880 Children 1 John, born May 29, 1822, died in Dayton, Ohio, in 1882 2 David, born November 22, 1824, died in infancy 3 Elizabeth, born January 14, 1826, died 1900, married George Buttermore, of Mt Pleasant, Pennsylvania 4 William Yantz, born May 24 1828, died in infancy 5 Daniel, born January 20, 1830 6 Kell, April 20, 1832 7 Sarah, June 29, 1833, died in April, 1877, married Brookly Buckingham, of Connellsville 8 Captain Joseph, born November 9, 1835, died May 2, 1912, an architect and builder of Chicago, Illinois, married Adelia Hadley, of Ohio 9 Christain, born August 21, 1837, a carpenter and builder of Connellsville 10 George H (2), born March 31, 1839, died aged two years 11 Catherine, born May 8, 1841, died June 23, 1881, married Rev Wesley C Harvey, a minister of the Baptist church 12 J Robinson, of whom further 13 Weimer born May 24, 1845 14 Samuel, December 21, 1846, died young 15 Benjamin, born January 22, 1848, died on the same day as his brother Samuel

(III) J Robinson twelfth child of George H and Sarah (Shallenberger) Balsley was born in Connellsville, Pennsylvania, December 13, 1843 He was educated in the public schools, attending the old Pireical Quaker Grave Yard Rock Ridge schools the few years allotted him for study and school work

He worked with his father until the outbreak of the civil war, when, not yet nineteen years of age, he enlisted in Company H, One Hundred Forty-second Regiment, Pennsylvania Volunteer Infantry, as a private He was mustered out, with an honorable discharge, January 25, 1865, with the rank of first sergeant He saw hard service with the army of the Potomac, sharing the fortunes of that army until the battle of Gettysburg, where in the first day's battle, July 1, 1863, he was desperately wounded in both thighs and fell about two hundred yards from where General Reynolds was killed It will be remembered that the first day of fighting was in favor of the Confederates, and as they drove the Federals back, three of their lines of battle passed over the prostrate body of J Robinson Balsley After the enemy had been driven back he was found still alive by the Union searchers and taken to the hospital improvised at the Catholic Church in Gettysburg, where he lay until the 17th of July, hovering between life and death, when he was taken to the Cotton Factory Hospital at Harrisburg Pennsylvania but youth and a hardy constitution triumphed, and in the latter part of December, 1863 he was sent to the Cliftburn barracks at Washington, D C although utterly unfit for the hardships of camp At first he had no blankets furnished him, but later this was remedied He was attached to Company A, Seventh Regiment Veteran Reserves, and was called to the front when Stuart's Cavalry made its daring raid in the vicinity of Washington He continued in the service until January 25, 1865 His brother, Captain Joseph Balsley served in the Twenty-seventh Regiment Indiana Volunteers

Sergeant Balsley returned to Connellsville, after being mustered out of the service, and for a time was in the employ of the Baltimore & Ohio Railroad Company Later he entered the employ of James Calhoun & Company, becoming superintendent of their planing mill He continued with them until 1882 when he purchased the old plant of David Walker & Company, in Grape Valley, and began business for himself as principal owner and manager of the Youghiogheny Lumber Yard, using the old buildings for planing mill and shops and the old Fuller Tannery grounds as his lumber yard On the northwest corner of his property he erected a new building, using the first floor for offices and the second for a finishing shop for fine work Later he erected a two-story building on Pittsburgh street, on part of the plot now covered by the McClenathan Block, which he used as office and supply house

About the same time he admitted Dr S S Stahl to a partnership continuing as J R Balsley & Company until 1892, when the business was sold to J C Munson and others and Mr Balsley retired from business for a few years In 1898 he again established in business under his old firm name, "The Youghiogheny Lumber Yard," locating in Connellsville, West Side, where he is yet in successful operation, specializing in every form of builders' supplies and "no order too

small or too large' for his careful consideration

He was a good soldier and as a good citizen has given much time and attention to the welfare of his city He has served as councilman and school director, giving to each office the same careful attention as to his own private business He has not allowed his successes of the past to lure him into inaction, but each day finds him at his place of business and bearing his full share of present day responsibilities While memories of the past are dear to him, he plans as hopefully for the future as though his allotted 'three score and ten" had not nearly expired

He lacks little more than a year of having completed a half century of membership in the Independent Order of Odd Fellows, and for years has been a member of the Christian Church (Disciples of Christ) Politically he has always been a Republican

He married November 24 1867, Catherine A Francis, born in Connellsville, April 29, 1847, died November 25, 1908 daughter of Robert W and Elizabeth (Radcliffe) Francis Robert W Francis was born May 5, 1797, Elizabeth Radcliffe, August 10, 1806 Their children

1 Walker F who was born December 23, 1828 2 William, born March 29, 1832 3 Mary Jane, July 25, 1836 4 Isaac, December 10, 1838, died in the hospital at City Point during the civil war, was first lieutenant Company H, One Hundred Forty-second Regiment, Pennsylvania Volunteer Infantry 5 Victoria born August 16, 1844 6 Catherine A (of previous mention) Children of J Robinson and Catherine A (Francis) Balsley 1 Isaac F, born September 12, 1868, now a resident of Wilkinsburg, Pennsylvania, married Ammaretta Wymer, of Connellsville, and has J Robinson (2), a student at Cornell University, and Anna Maude 2 Charles H, born June 30, 1870, now associated with his father in the lumber business, married Viola Keenan, of Connellsville, and has Catherine A and Raymond 3 Beatrice V, born March 4, 1876, married Charles H May, of Connellsville, who died July 26, 1911 4 Benjamin, born June 17, 1872, died in infancy

(II) John Balsley, son of
BALSLEY Samuel Balsley (q v) was
born in Somerset, Somerset
county, Pennsylvania, came to Fayette county, and settled in Connellsville, where he
died He was a carpenter, and later established a wheelwright shop, there building
and repairing wagons He married Eliza
Bolley, and left issue

(III) Thomas, son of John Balsley, was
born in Connellsville, Pennsylvania, December 6, 1833, where he died June 16, 1894 He
attended the public school, and learned the
carpenter and wagon making trades with
his father an occupation he followed all
his active life He was a natural mechanical genius, and besides his building and contracting was a good gunsmith and cabinet
maker He was a Democrat, and a man of
high character He married Louisa Cramer, born in Dunbar township, Fayette
county, April 26, 1839, who survives him,
a resident of Connellsville (see Cramer)
Children of Thomas and Louisa (Cramer)
Balsley 1 Amanda, born January 19, 1860,
deceased, married J D Wilson 2 Jennie,
born June 22, 1862, died in infancy 3
Eliza, born November 1 1861, married David Percy, of Connellsville 4 Louise, born
November 11, 1867, married Edward Frock,
of Uniontown 5 Samuel L, of whom further 6 Worth K, of whom further 7
Charles M, of further mention 8 John,
born April 31, 1881, deceased, a teacher, and
at the time of his death, principal of the
Third Ward public school of Connellsville

(IV) Samuel Long, eldest son of Thomas
and Louisa (Cramer) Balsley, was born in
Connellsville, Pennsylvania, October 14,
1870 He was educated in the public school,
finishing his studies at Connellsville high
school He learned the carpenter's trade
with his father, continuing until 1888 when
he entered the employ of the Connellsville
Planing Mill Company, and nearly completed a quarter of a century's service with
that company He was promoted shop foreman in 1904 In June, 1912, he and his
brother W K Balsley, entered into partnership under the name of Balsley Bros,
general contractors and builders He is a
member (as is his wife) of the English Lutheran church, he belongs to the Knights of

Pythias, and is a Democrat in politics He
married, November 5, 1898 Anna Wiant,
born in Connellsville, died August 11, 1911,
daughter of Paul and Ella Wiart Children
Thomas, born March 11, 1900, Louisa, February 14, 1909

(IV) Worth K, sixth child and second
son of Thomas and Louisa (Cramer) Balsley, was born in Connellsville Pennsylvania, April 24, 1875 He was educated in the
public schools of Connellsville, and at the
age of eighteen years began learning the
carpenter's trade under the instruction of
his father, continuing one year He then
entered the employ of Calhoun & Company
in their planing mill, and for thirteen years
worked in about every capacity that mechanical ability was required During the
last three years with the company he was
outside foreman In 1904 he started in business for himself as a builder and contractor, and still continues in successful business operation He has become well known
as a reliable, capable contractor and keeps
a force of men continually employed He is
interested in undeveloped coal lands in
Greene county, Pennsylvania, and is a stockholder in the Dunlap Coal Company In
1906 he erected his present, but has in
course of construction another residence on
Snyder street, which he will soon occupy
He is a Democrat, but extremely independent in political action, voting in local and
county affairs for those whom he considers
best qualified to fill the offices He married,
Thanksgiving Day 1906, Mary Ray, born
in White Haven, England, February 13,
1879, daughter of John and Sarah (Crosier)
Ray, both born in England John Ray was
a coal miner in England, holding the positions of pit boss and fire boss In 1881 he
came to the United States and settled in
Fayette county, where he has worked in the
Dunbar Wheeler and Morrell mines He
is now living in Greenwood, a suburb of
Connellsville His wife Sarah is deceased
Children, all living in Greenwood with their
father, except William John an engineer
in the employ of the Baltimore & Ohio railroad, William, now of Pittsburgh, Pennsylvania, James, deceased, Clarence, deceased
Sarah, Jane, Stella and Mary Children of
Worth K and Mary (Ray) Balsley Mar-

garet Louise, born October, 1907, died April, 1908, Ray Herbert, born February 4, 1909, Helen Elizabeth, April 11, 1910

(IV) Charles M, seventh child of Thomas Balsley, was born in Connellsville, Pennsylvania, October 3, 1877. He received his education in the public schools and on arriving at suitable age began learning the blacksmith's trade under the instruction of J W Buttermore, of Connellsville. After completing his years of apprenticeship he worked as a journeyman smith until March, 1903, when he established his own shop and business on Apple street, in Connellsville. He remained in that location in prosperous trade until the autumn of 1911, when he moved to a larger and better equipped shop that he had built on his own land at Snydertown, in the suburbs of Connellsville. He is well established in public favor and has a steady, reliable patronage. He is independent in politics, voting for the man best fitted to faithfully perform the duties of the office aspired to. In religious faith he is a Lutheran. He married, September 17, 1902, Ada S Kinney, born in Salt Lick township, Fayette county, daughter of John and Rachel Kinney. Her father died when she was six months of age. Mr Balsley has no children, but has an adopted son, Robert, born August 3, 1906, who bears his name

(Kramer-Cramer Line)

Louisa Cramer Balsley descends from a paternal German ancestor and maternally from Ireland, her grandfather Brown being born there and the emigrant to Pennsylvania. The German ancestor was Joseph Kramer born in Germany, came to the United States and settled in Lancaster county, Pennsylvania. His wife Sophia was also born in Germany. They both died in Lancaster county

(II) Henry Cramer, son of Joseph Kramer, was born in Lancaster county February 24, 1786, died in Fayette county, September 7, 1845. His parents died when he was quite young, and he was reared by an uncle who deprived the lad of the estate left him by his father. He was apprenticed to a tailor and worked at that trade until the war of 1812 when he enlisted and served until the unusual hardships of army life in Canada caused him to take quiet leave and return to the United States. He settled in Fayette county, where he married in 1821, and later established a fulling mill in Dunbar township, where he died in 1845. He married, November 21, 1821, Jane Brown, born in Fayette county, December, 1802, died September 5, 1880, daughter of William and Jane Brown, who came from Ireland about the year 1800, settling in Fayette county. Mr Brown was a weaver of linen and woolen goods. He died May 11 1829, his wife March 16, 1837. Children of Henry and Jane (Brown) Cramer 1 Mary Ann, born March 16 1823, married Harvey White, of Connellsville 2 William, born April 1, 1825, now deceased, lived at Vanderbilt, Pennsylvania 3 Joseph, born December 28, 1829, was a teacher in the Connellsville public school 4 Eliza Jane, born March 10, 1832, died February 15, 1842 5 Henry, born April 2, 1834, died February 3, 1842 6 Clarissa, born September 18, 1836, died 1842 7 Louisa (of previous and further mention) 8 Sarah, born September 15, 1841, married Joseph M Graw

(III) Louisa, daughter of Henry and Jane Cramer, was born in Dunbar township Fayette county, Pennsylvania, April 26, 1839. She was six years of age when her father died, and until eleven years of age the family continued in the Dunbar township home. In 1850 her mother moved with children to Connellsville, where Louisa Cramer was married to Thomas Balsley, March 6, 1858. They resided at No 440 East Fairview avenue for thirty years, until the husband's death, and Mrs Louisa Balsley continues her residence there. She and all her children are members of the Lutheran church. Thomas Balsley was baptized in the Presbyterian church but never formally joined the denomination

HAINES This family is of English ancestry and traces in England to an early date. It is spelled both Haynes and Haines in early records, seemingly as the person writing it was inclined, as the same family names are written both ways

(II) The progenitor of this branch is Richard D Haines, born in Lincolnshire,

England, son of Peter Haines He emigrated when a young man to the United States, settling in Virginia, owning a plantation in Spottsylvania county He learned the millwright's trade in England and after coming to Virginia built several mills in his county He prospered in business, and died on his own plantation at a good old age His wife Lucy was born in Spottsylvania county, daughter of Peter Wren, a Virginian of English descent Children 1 John Franklin, living in Madison county, Virginia 2 Sarah Martha, married Christian S Brown, of Pennsylvania 3 James Walter, of whom further 4 Angeline, deceased 5 Lucy Mary, deceased 6 Joseph Van Buren a farmer of Spottsylvania county Virginia

(III) James Walter, third child and second son of Richard D Haines, the emigrant, was born in Spottsylvania county, Virginia, August 26, 1836 He grew to manhood on the paternal plantation, and after finishing his school years learned his father's trade, millwright He became an expert workman and in 1855 spent two years in Texas erecting mills and milling machinery In 1857 he joined a party going from Texas to the Pino Alto range of mountains in Arizona in search of gold That country then was in an exceedingly wild and unsettled condition, the Indians often hostile and the danger great Notwithstanding all this he remained in that country several years with some success, returning to Texas at the outbreak of the civil war He reached Houston, Texas, where he found the entire city given over to a celebration of the great victory won by the Confederates at Bull Run He at once enlisted in Company A, Fifth Regiment Texas Infantry, then being recruited in Houston and composed of the best class of young men in the city He followed the fortunes of the Confederacy through four years of hard service, served under General Robert E Lee in his invasion of Pennsylvania in Longstreet's division and under the gallant Pickett was one of that doomed but immortal division that as a last resort, on the third day of battle, was sent on that wonderful charge against the Union centre strongly intrenched and supported by batteries Of Mr Haines' regiment only one-third came back after a display of courage that still electrifies the world He came through the war without serious injury, and after Appomattox returned to his Virginia home, but the devastation of war had not spared that section and later he located in Cumberland, Maryland, where he worked at his trade and in the mills, sawing lumber for use in building construction In 1871 he moved to New Haven, then a separate borough, now a part of the city of Connellsville, where he entered the employ of the Baltimore & Ohio Railroad Company as shop machinist, remaining sixteen years He then went with the Calhoun Planing Mill Company as machinery man, continuing with them thirteen years In 1904 he retired and now is making his home with his son, James L Haines, in Connellsville His life has been full of adventures and changes, but now at seventy-five years of age he is well preserved and vigorous

He married, after the war, Annie Laura McCarty, born in New Winchester, Virginia, June 5, 1838, died in Connellsville, August 9, 1892, daughter of Timothy and Ann (White) McCarty, born in Bantry, county Cork, Ireland, where they married They came to the United States about 1830, Timothy, aged twenty-one years, his wife, a little younger They were on the ocean two hundred and forty days, experiencing frightful storms, one of eight days' duration that swept them far off their course They finally landed and the young couple, after a stay in Newfoundland, Canada, made their way to Virginia where Timothy McCarty engaged in farming and working at his trade of stone mason During the civil war their farm, lying in the midst of the war zone, was often the scene of actual warfare and on one occasion their barn was used as a field hospital Timothy McCarty died August 21, 1883, in his seventy-fourth year, Ann, his wife, July 18, 1887, in her seventy-seventh year Three of four sons served in the Confederate army Children of Mr and Mrs McCarty 1 Cornelius H, born in Newfoundland, Canada December 21, 1832, died in Orlando, Florida, December 3, 1910 2 Joanna, born August 18, 1834, at Boston, Massachusetts, died at Stephens City, November 15, 1895 3 William, born October 26, 1835, died in Pennsylvania 4 Annie Laura, of previous mention 5 Timothy, born January 20, 1840, died in Mexico, Missouri, August 2 1881, he was a soldier of the Confederate army fought under General Stonewall Jackson, was wounded seven times during the war and finally lost an arm at Gettysburg, which ended his military career 6 Joseph, born January 12, 1842, died January 16, 1842 7 Joseph, born February 1, 1843, died in Mexico, Missouri, June, 1893, was a soldier of the Confederacy, serving under General Stonewall Jackson 8 John, born April 14, 1845 9 James, November 5, 1847 10 Ellen, September 7, 1849, died near Monongahela City, Pennsylvania, September 13, 1874 11 Thomas, born September 12, 1851, died near Mexico, Missouri, September 6, 1885 12 Mary Catherine (Craig) born at Bartonville Springdale, Frederick county, Virginia, May 25, 1854, died in June, 1912 Children of James Walter and Annie Laura (McCarty) Haines 1 James L, of whom further 2 Albert M, of whom further 3 Walter W, of whom further 4 Margaret, married Richard Cunningham, a locomotive engineer or Connellsville 5 Charlotte Gertrude, married Charles N Vance, a locomotive engineer of Pittsburgh, Pennsylvania

(IV) James L, eldest son of James Walter and Annie Laura (McCarty) Haines, was born in Spottsylvania county, Virginia, October 23 1866 The family made several moves and when he was five years of age they settled in Connellsville, West Side (then New Haven) He attended the public schools until reaching the age of sixteen years, then began working in Squire & Nables brickyard during the summer season Later he entered the Baltimore & Ohio machine shops, where he served a four years' apprenticeship at the machinist's trade, and spent the next thirteen years in the company's brass foundry until it was removed from Connellsville to a more favorable location He then spent eighteen months in Pittsburgh, in the foundry of Tutman & Hogg, following this with fifteen months with the Baltimore & Ohio as fireman The ensuing three years he was moulder for the Connellsville Machine & Car Company In 1898 he entered the employ of Boyts Porter & Company, at the Yough Pump Works, and is still with them as moulder at their foundry He is an expert at his business, and has few superiors He is a Republican in politics and a member of Trinity Lutheran Church, Modern Woodmen of America, and the Heptasophs

He married, December 4, 1890, Minnie Hay, born in Donegal township, Westmoreland county, Pennsylvania, daughter of Harmon and Missouri Wringler Hay (see Hay) Children 1 Helen May, born March 13, 1892 2 Sadie Frances, in Allegheny county, Pennsylvania, February 15, 1894 3 Mary Bell, October 28, 1898 4 Harmon Franklin, August 9, 1899 5 Charles Edward, December 31, 1901 6 Ralph William, twin of Charles Edward 7 Emma Lou, born April 29, 1904 8 Clifford, March 31, 1906 The family are members of Trinity Lutheran Church

(IV) Albert M second son of James Walter and Annie Laura (McCarty) Haines was born at Summit Point, Virginia, February 18, 1872 He was but a babe in arms when his parents came to Connellsville, settling on the West Side, then New Haven He attended the public schools and when yet a boy began to learn carpentering When thirteen years of age he began working in the planing mill of Calhoun & Company, remaining in their employ thirteen years, becoming a skilled mechanic in all forms of mill and constructive carpentry He also during this period completed a special course with the Scranton School of Correspondence which fitted him for a higher position In 1903 he was one of the organizers of the Connellsville Construction Company, of which he is treasurer and general manager This has been a wonderfully successful company, their offices on the fourth floor of the First National Bank Building being always the scene of great activity They keep from fifty to seventy mechanics constantly employed, the number sometimes running to two hundred and fifty Started at a period of unusual building activity in Connellsville they secured an immediate foothold and have constantly advanced until it is the leading construction company in the city

The officers are President, F F Evans, vice-president, C N Hyatt, secretary, D E Treher, treasurer and general manager, Albert M Haines To the success of this company the mechanical and executive ability of the general manager has materially contributed He is a member of the Presbyterian church, the Independent Order of Odd Fellows the Heptasophs, and a Republican in politics

He married, October 30, 1895, Etta Jean Hawkins, born August 1, 1871, at Mill Run, Fayette county, Pennsylvania, daughter of Thomas and Rebecca (Rowan) Hawkins Thomas Hawkins was born in Ireland and is now engaged as a mine broker Rebecca (Rowan) Hawkins was born in Springfield township, Fayette county, Pennsylvania Mrs Etta Jean Haines is a member of the Presbyterian church They have no children

(IV) Walter Wheeler, third son of James Walter and Annie Laura (McCarty) Haines, was born in Connellsville, West Side (New Haven), June 8, 1876, in a little log house just across from the Baltimore & Ohio shops He attended the public schools until he was thirteen years of age, then became messenger boy at the general offices of the Baltimore & Ohio Railroad Company Later he worked in the repair shops, then returned to his position as messenger boy During this period he had acquired a knowledge of telegraphy, and in 1894 was appointed operator for the Baltimore & Ohio at Layton Pennsylvania In 1895 he returned to Connellsville where he remained as operator until 1902 In that year he was wire chief of the Baltimore & Ohio, in 1904 appointed despatcher at Connellsville, and in 1911 sub chief despatcher at Connellsville, and in 1912 chief despatcher He is clear-headed and efficient, handling the business of his division with skill and promptness He is prominent in the Masonic Order, belonging to King Solomon's Lodge, No 346, Free and Accepted Masons Uniontown Lodge of Perfection, Pittsburgh Consistory, Ancient Accepted Scottish Rite in which he has attained the thirty-second degree He is a Republican

He married, April 25, 1908, Estelle Laverne Barnette, born in Connellsville

daughter of William and Elizabeth D (Van Swearingen) Barnette, both born in North Union township, Fayette county Pennsylvania William Barnette was engaged in the grocery business in Connellsville for twenty years, partner of J D Frisbee, then was in the grocery business alone, and in 1908 established a bakery at Uniontown He died December 28, 1911 His wife Elizabeth D, survives him She is a daughter of William S and Dorcas (Bryson) Van Swearingen, of an early county family, descending from Garret Van Swearingen, said to have been a younger son of a noble family of Holland, was well educated and came to America, settling in New York Of his descendants Captain Van Swearingen was the first to settle in Western Pennsylvania a noted revolutionary officer and captain in the equally celebrated Eighth Regiment Pennsylvania Line and particularly distinguished himself under the command of General Gates at the battle of Saratoga A latter day descendant and brother of Mrs Elizabeth D Barnette is John Quincy Van Swearingen, the ablest lawyer of Uniontown and an honored and respected member of the Pennsylvania bar

SOISSON This family, so prominent in the business history of Fayette county, Pennsylvania, springs from an ancient French family of Alsace, although their ancestral province has reverted to its original owners after a long period under the French flag Part of the indemnity exacted by Germany from France after their conquest of that county in 1870-1871 was the cession of Alsace-Lorraine, ancient German possessions

The earliest record we have is of Joseph Soisson, a well-to-do merchant of Alsace On his mother's side he was a relative of the great Philadelphia banker, capitalist and philanthropist, Stephen Girard, his mother bearing that name previous to her marriage The Girard family of Bordeaux, France, were wealthy, and when the hot-headed Stephen, at the age of fourteen years, demanded a portion, his father purchased three thousand dollars' worth of goods and sent him away with them on a ship bound for one of the French colonies in the West

Indies A daughter of the same family was the mother of Joseph Soisson He married Margaret Kinstof Christophe, born in the same province They lived to a good old age, rearing a family of six children 1 John, born in Alsace, France where he grew to manhood and received his education He emigrated to the United States in 1847, settling in Cambria county, Pennsylvania, near Nicktown, where he engaged in farming He married in his native land, Magdalena Lambour, who accompanied him to the United States Children 1 Nicholas Louis, born November 19, 1852, now resides at St Louis Missouri, married and has nine children, 11 John E, born March 3, 1855, married and has four children, 111 Anthony, born August 12, 1856, a farmer, married and has twelve children, iv M J, born February 1, 1858, now engaged in the express and storage business in Pittsburgh, Pennsylvania, v Mary Magdalene, born February 27, 1859, married October 24, 1876, M J Kersch, and has fourteen children 2 Joseph, of whom further 3 Peter, whose sketch follows 4 Lizzie, born in Alsace, France, April 18, 1833, married, in Germany, February 17, 1858, Joseph Schlosser She came to the United States later in life with her two younger children and now resides with her brother, Joseph, in Connellsville Children Laura, Margaret, Joseph, Leo and Katherine 5 Leon Joseph, born at Wahlscheid, Germany, April 22, 1838 He grew to manhood in his native land and came to the United States, settling in Fayette county Pennsylvania, with his brother Joseph, in whose employ he continued until his death November 21 1911 He married, in 1868 Barbara Snyder, of Nicktown, Cambria county, Pennsylvania Children 1 Louisa born May 13, 1869 married Thomas Collins—seven children, 11 George Peter, born July 4, 1870 married Clara May Carven, six children, 111 Franklin F, born January 25, 1872, married Gertrude Rhodes, no children, iv William J, born November 22 1873, married, in 1898, Myrtle Younkin seven children, v Sylvester, born August, 1875, married Nellie Denver, no children vi Edward, died 1882, vii Emma, died 1882, viii Elizabeth, born December 27, 1878, married Victor

Sims, no children, ix Bertha born March 15, 1882, married Charles McCarthy, two children, x Louis, born July 17, 1884, married Kate Collins, xi Agnes, born August 31, 1886, married Lorance Coyles, two children, xii Ambrose, born August 3, 1886, married Pearl Weis, xiii Andrew, born June 11, 1891, xiv Ella, born May 31, 1895 6 Margaret, born in Alsace, married Charles Walter and yet resides in their native province in the village of Wahlscheid, one child

(II) Joseph (2), second son of Joseph (1) and Margaret K (Christophe) Soisson was born in Wahlscheid, Alsace, France, January 9, 1829 He was educated in his native province and learned both the German and French languages At the age of twenty he came to the United States, landing at New York City after a voyage of forty-two days made in a sailing vessel He could speak no English, but soon acquired a sufficient vocabulary for his needs He soon left New York, where he worked at tinning, going to New Jersey, where for eighteen months he was engaged in the manufacture of building brick He had now learned the language and determined to still further prospect for a favorable location, for he had determined to become a manufacturer He came as far west as Hollidaysburg, Blair county, Pennsylvania, finding employment at brickmaking with Charles Hughes Here he became thorough master of all details of the business He then went south looking for a location but after going as far as New Orleans and not finding a suitable opening, he returned to Mr Hughes, who had formed a partnership with Dr Roderick and was extending his business in all directions Mr Soisson became an agent for the firm, selling brick and taking contracts After two years as agent he purchased Dr Roderick's interest, the firm becoming Hughes & Soisson They operated the plant at Plane No 8 near Hollidaysburg Pennsylvania, until 1860, then established another plant at Miltenberg Hughes & Soisson conducted a very successful business until 1869, when they dissolved by mutual consent For six years, until 1875, Mr Soisson continued the business alone He then formed a partnership with Messrs Spiggs and Wilhelm, and

Joseph Sisson

erected a large plant at White Rock near Connellsville This continued until 1879, when Mr Soisson and his son, John F, absorbed the entire business and launched the firm of Soisson & Son In 1872 a partnership had been formed with John Kilpatrick and John Wilhelm, trading as Soisson, Kilpatrick & Wilhelm This firm had erected an extensive plant at Moyer, Fayette county This plant, after a successful career, was merged with Soisson & Son and the entire business incorporated under the title of The Joseph Soisson Fire Brick Company, with Joseph Soisson, president This is the largest brick manufacturing company in the county and conducts an enormous business They manufacture at their different plants all kinds of bricks and for all purposes, building brick, fire brick, coke oven brick, pavement brick and tile, all of a quality that has built up their market and holds it Their six plants have a combined daily capacity of one hundred thousand brick

In 1873, Mr Soisson first made Connellsville his home, and has continuously resided there until the present date (1912) He and his seven sons, all capable active men of affairs, have been potent factors in the development of Connellsville The father, as years accumulated, withdrew from the more active field, leaving to the sons the burden of the business He took a great interest in borough affairs, contributing liberally of time and money to those enterprises that promised a benefit to his city When the Humbert Tin Plate Company was organized and when the Slaymaker-Barry Lock Company came to Connellsville, seeking a location and local aid, he was the first of the moneyed men of the city to extend a helping hand His contribution to the fund to purchase a site was a large one, and the influence of his name still more helpful, and these industries were able to establish large, well equipped plants, employing a large force of men He was a director and stockholder of the Humbert Tin Plate Company until its absorption in 1899 by the tin trust, The American Tin Plate Company He was a director and first vice-president of the Slaymaker-Barry Company for many years These are only solitary instances and could

be further multiplied, any enterprise that appealed to his business judgment has had his support He went outside his realm of business and became one of the founders of the Yough National Bank of Connellsville He was a director when it was the State Bank, and since becoming a National Bank its honored president This bank stands among the leading financial institutions, which proves his breadth of mind and the versatility of his genius He is a most generous giver to charity and is liberal in all things His career is an inspiration and a great object lesson to the ambitious Industry and clean living are the lessons his life teaches to the young man who would emulate him When such a goal can be won by a young man, a stranger in a strange land, without even a knowledge of the language of those around him, exceptional merit in that particular young man must be the explanation of his success, not luck or fortuitous circumstances He won success, deserves it and all wish him many years more to enjoy it In 1907 he gave downtown Connellsville a modern place of amusement by building the Soisson Theatre He is a Democrat, casting his first presidential vote for James A Buchanan, of Pennsylvania He is a member with his entire family, of the Church of the Immaculate Conception (Roman Catholic)

He married, March 21, 1853, at Hollidaysburg, Pennsylvania, Caroline Filcer, born in Centre county, Pennsylvania, daughter of Thomas and Margaret Filcer   Children

1 Elizabeth, born 1854, married Hugh King, a blacksmith of Connellsville

2 John F, born at Plane No 8 on the old Portage Road near Hollidaysburg in 1856, died in Connellsville in November, 1899 He was identified with the brick manufacturing business with his father, and for thirty years was a leading citizen and prominent business man of Fayette county He was treasurer and general manager of the Joseph Soisson Fire Brick Company, president of the South Connellsville Lumber Company, president of the South Connellsville Building and Loan Association director of the Second National Bank, director of the Youghiogheny Light, Heat and Power Company, director of the South Connellsville

Suburban Street Railway Company, director of the Connellsville News Publishing Company, of which he was a founder He joined with his father and brothers in the development of South Connellsville and aided in the planting of the industries there He was a member of the Church of the Immaculate Conception, the Knights of Columbus and the Catholic Mutual Benefit Association He married Emma C Whitney, children John Whitney, Hilda A, Emma, Irene and Adrian

3 Anna M, married John F Gilligan, a foundry and machine shop proprietor of Latrobe, Pennsylvania, eight children

4 Margaret M, married Joseph Madigan superintendent in the Pittsburgh Brewing Company at Connellsville

5 William Filcer, born at Incline No 8, Blair county, Pennsylvania, August 2, 1862, now residing at No 122 Peach street, Connellsville He was educated in the public school and for two years attended St Vincent's College near Latrobe, Pennsylvania He worked for the Soisson Fire Brick Company in 1881, then became bookkeeper for the firm of John D Frisbee in Connellsville, continuing until August 31, 1885 He then formed a partnership with J C Lytle and as Lytle & Soisson conducted a retail boot and shoe store in Connellsville, continuing until 1890, when he withdrew and became bookkeeper for Joseph Soisson & Sons, with a one-third interest in the firm upon the incorporation of the Joseph Soisson Fire Brick Company, he was elected secretary, continuing until 1899 when he was elected general manager and treasurer He was interested in the development of Connellsville and South Connellsville, and with his father and brothers secured the industries of that borough He is a director and vice-president of the Yough National Bank director and president of the Inter-Railway Coal Company director of the Connellsville Suburban Electric Railway, the Sunshine Coal & Coke Company, the O'Brien Coal Company, the Yough Heat Light and Power Company, the Connellsville Merchandise and Supply Company The Connellsville Building and Loan Company, president of the Soisson Summer Home Company sole owner of the Lang Coal and Sand Company, and is a stockholder in the Midland Coal & Coke Company the Stewart Creek Coal Company, the Connellsville, Machinery & Car Company, the Citizens National Bank, the Connellsville White Sand Company, director of the Yough Plumbing Company president of the Rocks Coal Company He is a member of the Church of the Immaculate Conception, a Knight of Columbus, a Catholic Mutual Benefit Association and a Democrat in politics

He married (first) in 1887, Jennie, daughter of Robert Lang Children Cyrilla Margaret, born November 27, 1888, Robert Regis, July 22, 1890, Basil Joseph, April 25, 1892, Ignatius Lang, August 9, 1894, Marie Genevieve, April 9, 1896, Anena Caroline, August 5, 1898, Anna Marian, September 27, 1901, Elnor Regina, February 27, 1904, William Edison, February 21, 1906, Fred Filcer December 29, 1907 Jennie, his wife, died January 26, 1908 He married (second) Jennie M Wyeth, a widow, daughter of James and Adelia Madden, of Harvard, Illinois, June 6, 1910, by Rev Father Cusack

6 Joseph N, born at Oakdale, Fayette county, Pennsylvania, August 16, 1864 He was educated in the public school of White Rock, later attended public school of Connellsville and the parochial schools In 1881-82 he was a student at St Vincent's College near Latrobe After leaving college he was taken into the brick manufacturing business with his father and elder brothers He was stationed at the fire brick manufacturing plant at Volcano, Fayette county, where after five months' experience, at age of nineteen years he was placed in charge of the plant He was next put in full charge of the new plant being erected at Davidson's Station, north of Connellsville After the completion of that plant, one of the six operated by the Joseph Soisson Fire Brick Company, he went west spending three years at Kansas City, Missouri, engaged in contracting brick construction, stores blocks and dwellings He then returned home and was made superintendent of another Soisson plant, the Fire Brick Works at Rankin Fayette county He remained in charge of that plant until its destruction by fire These works

were not rebuilt and after the sale of the ground, etc, he returned to Connellsville In 1896 he was again made superintendent ot the Volcano plant of the Joseph Soisson Fire Brick Company, and in 1909 he was elected assistant general manager of that company The plant at Volcano is the largest ot the five plants now operated by the company, is equipped with all modern brick making machinery and has a capacity of 25 000 daily The company manufacture here only coke oven brick Mr Soisson has other business interests, notably the O Brien Coal Company of which he is president The company is a prosperous one, owning and operating large properties in Somerset county, Pennsylvania He is a Democrat in politics, casting his first presidential vote for Grover Cleveland He served on the borough council of Rankin, Pennsylvania, and is active in county politics He is a member of the Church of the Immaculate Conception and of the Knights ot Columbus He married, April 16, 1897, Mary T, daughter of Bernard and Mary Callahan Her father is a mine inspector Children Paul B born February 4 1898, Joseph Cail June 2, 1900, Albert James May 29 1903, Electra Margaret, May 20, 1911 The family residence is at No 208 East Washington street, Connellsville

7 Leo Joseph, born at Miltenberg, Fayette county, Pennsylvania, (then the family home) July 17, 1866 *He was but three years of age when his parents moved to their Connellsville home, where he grew to manhood He was educated in the public and parochial schools of Connellsville, and at St Vincent s College where he spent fifteen months as a student After completing his studies he began business life as a tinner He learned his trade under the direction of Robert Greenland, continuing with him two years He then founded a partnership with Lynn Fitzmeier and established a tin and metal business under the firm name of Soisson & Fitzmeier He continued in business thus for two years, then sold his interest to Louis Balsley He was then engaged at his trade two years He next joined his father and brothers in brick manufacturing a business he was thoroughly familiar with, having worked with his father

in boyhood and learned all parts of the business In 1894, when Mr Kilpatrick's death left a vacancy in the Joseph Soisson Fire Brick Company's office of superintendent of the Davidson plant, he was elected to fill the vacancy He has filled the position most capably and at the present date (1912) is still in office He is energetic and full of vigor, understanding the manufacture of fire brick thoroughly, his plant being largely devoted to the manufacture of fire brick used in coke oven construction He is a Democrat in politics and a member of the Church of the Immaculate Conception He married, April 22, 1889, Annie Edith Whipke, born at Ohiopyle, Fayette county, daughter of John and Eliza Whipke Her father is a veteran of the civil war and a contractor, now residing at Hazelwood, Pennsylvania Children Harold Gray, born February 21, 1891, Mary Edith, June 8, 1892, Minnie Venetta, December 15, 1893, Bessie Arvilla April 21, 1896, Frances Eliza, October 7, 1898, David Thuraphine, February 20, 1901, Josephine Filcer, March 21, 1903, an infant, deceased, born June 13, 1905, John Leo, August 19 1906, Ralph Edward January 11, 1909 The family home is at No 1140 South Pittsburgh street

8 Charles E, born at Gibson Station, Fayette county, Pennsylvania (the family home just prior to the removal to Connellsville), June 16, 1868 He was educated in the public schools of Connellsville and during the years 1866-67 was a student of St Vincent s College After completing his studies he at once joined with his father and brothers in their extensive brickmaking operations He was first employed at the Volcano plant, continuing until 1889, when he was appointed clay manager in charge of the fire clay mines at Bear Run, Fayette county Here the clay is taken from the banks and shipped to the six plants of the Joseph Soisson Fire Brick Company He has about seventy men under him, which force keeps the plants supplied with the kind of clay used, principally fire clay Mr Soisson is a capable manager and fills his positon most effectively He is a director and treasurer of the Soisson Summer Home Company, a corporation owning a tract of land three-quarters of a mile east of Con-

nellsville, that they are developing as a summer resort and home A club house has been erected, fishing grounds stocked and many improvements begun He is also a director of the Connellsville Building and Loan Association He is an Independent in politics, selecting his candidate for personal fitness, regardless of his party He is a member of the Church of the Immaculate Conception, as are the members of his family He married, June 26, 1888, Mary Elizabeth Shoup, born in Connellsville, daughter of Daniel F and Sarah Jane (Saylor) Shoup Her father is a coal miner, residing in Connellsville Her mother, Sarah J Shoup, was born in Fayette county, descending from the Saylors of Somerset county, of German-French ancestry Children Henry William, born March 11, 1889, married Nellie Lane, of Scottdale and has Joseph and Henry W (2), Archibald Edward, born September 8, 1891, Leroy Dallas, August 9, 1894, Raymond Daniel Joseph, October 31, 1896, Otto Charles, January 27, 1899, Anthony Saylor, October 14, 1901, George Clarence, April 12, 1904 Emma Louise Caroline, October 25, 1906 The family home since February 2, 1900 has been at No 211 Prospect street, Connellsville

9 Caroline, born in Connellsville, Pennsylvania, November 10, 1870 She married Joseph L Stader, undertaker and livery man of Connellsville

10 Robert W, born in Connellsville, Pennsylvania, November 28, 1872 He was educated in public schools and St Vincent's College He began business life in the Yough National Bank of Connellsville, of which he is now teller He is a member of the Church of the Immaculate Conception

11 Vincent H, born in Connellsville, Pennsylvania, at that part of South Connellsville known as White Rock, February 18, 1875 He attended the public school at Gibson Station and spent six years in the Connellsville parochial school, then was a student at St Vincent's College for three and a half years After leaving college he joined the civil engineering corps of S M Foust, and later that of William Henderson After two years in engineering works, he became secretary of the South Connellsville Lumber Company, continuing until

1899 in charge of the office work of that company In November, 1899, his brother, John F Soisson, died and Vincent H was elected to succeed W F as secretary of the Joseph Soisson Fire Brick Company, which position he now most capably fills He is also treasurer of the South Connellsville Lumber Company, stockholder in Sunshine Coal & Coke Company, and interested in other enterprises of importance He is a Democrat in politics and has served Connellsville as city auditor He is a member of the Church of the Immaculate Conception, the Catholic Mutual Benefit Association, the Knights of Columbus and the Benevolent and Protective Order of Elks He married, June 19, 1909, Mary E Reynolds, born in West Virginia, January 15, 1878, daughter of John F Reynolds, a retired foreman of the Baltimore & Ohio railroad shops at Connellsville Children Mary Caroline, born April 19, 1901, Vincent Joseph, October 2, 1903, Margaret, August 20, 1906, Elizabeth, December 4, 1908, John R, May 27, 1911 The family home since 1908 has been at No 214 East Fairview avenue, Connellsville

SOISSON (II) Peter Soisson, son of Joseph Soisson (q v), was born in Alsace-Lorraine, France, (now Germany) in the town of Walscheid, August 20, 1830, died May 30, 1896, at Connellsville, Pennsylvania He grew to manhood in his native province, where he was educated and became proficient in both the French and German languages In 1851 he came to the United States, settling near Hollidaysburg, Blair county Pennsylvania, where his brother Joseph had preceded him and was engaged in brick manufacturing He entered the employ of Hughes & Roderick, later Hughes & Soisson He continued with the latter firm until 1862, then moved to Gibson, Fayette county, Pennsylvania (now South Connellsville), where he began business for himself as a brick manufacturer, his brother Joseph having located at Miltenberg nearby, in the same business In a few years Peter Soisson gave up brick manufacturing and engaged in the butcher business for John Hetzel, of Connellsville Soon afterward he secured a controlling interest in the old Snyder Brewery, then located where the Connellsville Distillery now stands. He operated the brewery until it was destroyed by fire, then leased and for five years operated the old Calhoun Flouring Mills at New Haven (Connellsville, West Side). He then formed a partnership with William Cope, of Uniontown, and for several years they successfully conducted a general live stock, wholesale and retail meat business. Mr Soisson devoted his energies to the buying of stock and the wholesale department. Mr Cope to the retailing. After a few years the firm dissolved, Mr Soisson forming a partnership with Rockwell Marietta and J D Madigan and operated the Connellsville Brewery (now owned by the Pittsburgh Brewing Company), continuing until his final retirement. He was a member of the Church of the Immaculate Conception (Roman Catholic), a public-spirited citizen active and helpful in advancing the business interests of Connellsville. He was a Democrat in politics, but never accepted public office.

He married Louisa Houck, born at Gallitzin, Cambria county, Pennsylvania, October 23, 1840, daughter of Joseph Houck, born in Lebanon, Lebanon county, Pennsylvania in 1813 a shoemaker by trade. He married, in 1840, Katherine Buser or Basier, born in 1822, in the Kingdom of Bavaria, Germany, daughter of Peter and Barbara Buser or Basier who came to the United States in 1832, settling at Johnstown, Pennsylvania. Peter Buser or Basier, born on the banks of the Rhine, was for twenty years a soldier of France, serving under the great Napoleon and was with him at Moscow, suffering all the horrors of the famous "retreat," reaching France in safety. Later he served in Spain, was made prisoner, but escaped, and on foot traversed the long distance to his home, swimming the rivers, arriving footsore and tattered. Joseph and Catherine Houck after their marriage, moved from Johnstown to an unsettled portion of Cambria and lived on a farm near Nicktown. Later they moved to Gallitzin, Pennsylvania, then returned to the farm at Nicktown, and in 1888 located in Connellsville.

Pennsylvania, where Joseph Houck died in 1899, aged eighty-six years. The Houcks were all German Lutherans, in the early family, but Joseph after his marriage became a Roman Catholic, which is the family religion in his branch. His wife died in Connellsville, June 28, 1901. His only brother, David Houck, went west, and never was again heard from. He had no sisters. He was a son of George Houck, born in Lebanon, Pennsylvania, also a shoemaker. He married Elizabeth Patterson, born in England, June 8, 1784, coming to the United States when a child. He died January 30, 1856, aged seventy-two years, two months and six days. His wife Elizabeth died August 28, 1863. They were very strict members of the German Lutheran church. George Houck was a son of David Houck, who emigrated to this country from Germany in early days and was one of the early settlers of Lebanon county, Pennsylvania.

Joseph and Katherine (Buser or Basier) Houck had issue Louisa, of previous mention, wife of Peter Soisson, Barbara, died aged twenty years, Helena, married James McConnell, of Tiffin, Ohio, Isadore, died in infancy, John, a farmer of Moyer, Pennsylvania, married (first) Mary Crook, (second) Mrs Julia Hogg, George, married Rachel Wills and resides on his farm near Nicktown, Cambria county, Pennsylvania, Margaret, married Sylvester Burse, a farmer of Nicktown, Mary, married Osborne McKeen, of Grundy Centre, Iowa, Jane, married Henry Arble, of Du Bois, Pennsylvania, Peter, a carpenter of Braddock, Pennsylvania, married Mary Marshall, Joseph, married Catherine Giesler, of Hastings, Pennsylvania. Children of Peter and Louisa (Houck) Soisson 1 Catherine Sylvester, born April 26, 1860, married Michael Weidinger, of Connellsville, Pennsylvania 2 Mary Martin, born May 24, 1864, married George Werner, of Derry Pennsylvania 3 William Henry, of whom further 4 Ida, born August 25, 1870, married Daniel Milhelm and resides at Fairbanks, Pennsylvania 5 Augustin D, of whom further 6 Gertrude, born May 10 1874, resides at home in Connellsville 7 Theresa, born May 9, 1877, married James Gibson and resides in Los Angeles, California

(III) Augustin D , son of Peter Soisson, was born in Connellsville, Pennsylvania, December 15 1872   He was graduated from the Connellsville high school, class of 1890, and at once began his business career as his father s assistant at the brewery, continuing until the death of the latter in 1896 He then became superintendent of the branch brewery at Uniontown, Pennsylvania, remaining there two years, then returning to Connellsville   In 1909 he became proprietor of the Royal Hotel at Connellsville and so continues in successful operation   His hotel is well patronized and bears a high reputation for excellence   He is a director of the Title and Trust Company of Connellsville, director of the Connellsville Manufacturing Mine and Supply Company and a stockholder of the Colonial National Bank   He is a Democrat in politics, served as a member of the city council and was chief burgess 1905-06-07, being the first Democrat to be elected to that office in the eighteen years preceding 1905, also the first burgess of the consolidated boroughs of Connellsville and New Haven, and signed the act of consolidation making Connellsville a city of the third class   He is a member of the Benevolent and Protective Order of Elks, the Heptasophs, Eagles ad Royal Arcanum

He married, February 10, 1902, Mary G , born in Connellsville, daughter of Rockwell Marietta   Children   Marietta Demetrius, born April 23, 1904, Emma Louise, August 27, 1906

SOISSON   (III) William Henry Soisson, son of Peter (q v) and Louisa (Houck) Soisson, was born in Blair county, Pennsylvania, at Plane No 6, March 23 1866   When he was two years of age his parents moved to Fayette county, settling at White Rocks, now South Connellsville   He first attended the public school at Gibson Station, then for a few years the parochial schools, completing his studies at Connellsville high school, whence he was graduated class of 1883 That same year he began business life in the John D Frisbee department store as bookkeeper and cashier   He remained in that responsible position for fifteen years,

until 1898   He then acquired an interest in the brewing business established by his father, and became secretary and treasurer of the Uniontown branch of the business. In 1899 the entire brewing plants of the Soissons in both Uniontown and Connellsville were sold to the Pittsburgh Brewing Company, William H Soisson remaining with that company for two years in charge of their offices at Connellsville   In 1901 he joined in the organization and incorporation of the Connellsville Manufacturing & Mine Supply Company   He was elected a director of that company, and at the first board meeting was chosen secretary and treasurer, a position he most efficiently filled

The company manufacture all kinds of mine machinery, hoisting and pumping devices   Their plant and offices are situated between South First and Fourth streets, Connellsville, West Side, and have doubled in size since organization   Their products are sold throughout the United States, Mexico and Canada   This is one of Connellsville's most prosperous and successful business enterprises and shows wonderful progress in the first decade of existence   Mr Soisson is a stockholder and director of the Title & Trust Company of Fayette County, and financially interested in many other enterprises   He is a man of strong executive ability, well fitted by disposition and training for the important positions he occupies He is a steadfast Democrat, and actively interested in party success   He is a member of the Church of the Immaculate Conception   His fraternal orders are Knights of Columbus, Benevolent and Protective Order of Elks and the Catholic Mutual Benefit Association

Mr Soisson married, August 15, 1910, Geula Flynn, of Philadelphia, Pennsylvania, born in Clearfield county, Pennsylvania, daughter of the late Anthony and Mary (Sturtevant) Flynn   Child   William Henry, Jr , born in Connellsville, Pennsylvania, May 18, 1911

(The Flynn Line)

(I) Geula (Flynn) Soisson is a granddaughter of John Flynn, born in Rosscommon county, Ireland, who came from a well known and influential county family   He came to America settling at New Brunswick, Nova Scotia, where he owned considerable land   He married Avesia Kingston, daughter of an English army officer, her mother having been a relative of Lord Stanley, of the Isle of Wight

(II) Anthony, son of John and Avesia (Kingston) Flynn, was born in New Brunswick, Nova Scotia, later becoming a prominent business man of Clearfield county, Pennsylvania   He married Mary Sturtevant, born at Crown Point, New York, daughter of Allen Stewart Sturtevant, a descendant of an old colonial family   Allen S Sturtevant married Hannah Jackson, who was a descendant of the old colonial Lewis family   The Sturtevants, under the varied spellings of their name, were prominent in the revolution, one being an aide to General Allen Stewart, a name that has ever since been perpetuated in the Sturtevant family

In a list of taxpayers of
NICOLAY   Lower Turkey Foot township,   Somerset   county,
Pennsylvania, in 1796, are the names of John Nicola and Henry Nicola   They were probably in that county at an earlier date, as there were white settlers in Turkey Foot as early as 1768   The Nicolas, now Nicolays, came originally from France, driven by religious persecution under Louis XIV to Holland, and coming thence to this country   The first records found of the family are those of John and Henry Nicola abovementioned   They are supposed to have come to Somerset from Juniata county, Pennsylvania   They were known as "Dutch," and were hard-working prosperous farmers   John Nicola married and had male issue, including a son   John (2), of whom further

(II) John (2) Nicolay, son of John (1) Nicola was born in Juniata, Pennsylvania, about 1794   He was but a babe when his parents came to Somerset county, where his after life was spent   He became a farmer and a land owner   He married Mary Ansel, who died aged eighty-seven years, he died aged sixty-five years   Children   1 David married Sarah Johnson, and settled in Upper

Tyrone township, Fayette county   2 Henry, of whom further   3 John, married Mary Tresler, and lived on the home farm in Somerset county, where he was killed by a falling tree   4 Simon enlisted in the One Hundred and Forty-second Regiment Pennsylvania Volunteer Intantry, during the civil war, was captured and confined in Libby prison, where he died after seven months' imprisonment   5 Margaret, married John May, and lived in Springhill township, Fayette county   6 Tillie, married John Mease, a farmer of Milford township, Somerset county   7 Sarah, married Moses Romesburg, a farmer of Lower Turkey Foot township, Somerset county   8 Catherine, married John Himebaugh, a farmer of Somerset county, she is the only living one of these eight children (1912)

(III) Henry, son of John (2) Nicolay was born in Lower Turkey Foot township, Somerset county, December 9, 1824, died in Springfield township, Fayette county, Pennsylvania, October 8, 1904   He attended the district school, and remained on the home farm until he was twenty-two years of age   He then came to Fayette county and located in Springfield township working as a farmhand for two of the old families there, the Linels and the Longs   He saved his money, purchased land in the township, married and became a prosperous farmer, owning at the time of his death three hundred and twenty-five acres of improved land   He was a quiet industrious man, very domestic in his tastes and loved his home   He was a Democrat, although the others in his family were Republicans   He was a member of the Methodist Episcopal church, and a man held in high esteem for his many manly traits   He married Catherine May, born in Springfield township, July 23, 1825, died March 20, 1911, surviving her husband seven years   She was a daughter of Michael and Christina (Parker) May, and granddaughter of Jacob May, born in Juniata county Pennsylvania, settling in Lower Turkey Foot township, Somerset county, when Michael was a boy   At that time the country was a forest, abounding in every form of wild game, and Michael became famous as a hunter   After he grew to manhood he married and moved to Springfield township, Fayette county, where he became the owner of a farm of four hundred acres He died aged eighty-seven years His wife Christina Parker, was born in Belfast, Ireland Their children were 1 John, married Margaret Nicolay, and lived in Springfield township 2 Jacob, died a young man, unmarried 3 Leonard, married Elizabeth Imel, and lived in Springfield township, served through the entire period of the civil war in the One Hundred and Forty-second Regiment Pennsylvania Volunteer Infantry 4 Margaret, married (first) Henry Davis, (second) William Johnson, moved to Illinois, where she died 5 Elizabeth, married Henry Imel and lived in Illinois and Nebraska 6 Catherine, of previous mention, married Henry Nicolay 7 Helen, married Nathan Long, and moved to Illinois Children of Henry and Catherine Nicolay 1 Margaret, born July 12, 1851, deceased, married John Welsh, a farmer of Springfield township, Fayette county 2 Oliver Franklin M, of whom further 3 An infant died unnamed 4 Anna born July 14, 1860, married John Saylor, and now resides on their large farm near Mill Run, Springfield township, Fayette county

(IV) Oliver Franklin M only son of Henry and Catherine (May) Nicolay was born in Springfield township, Fayette county, Pennsylvania He attended the Younkin public school, then held in an old log cabin which burned and was replaced by a more modern building He still further pursued his studies at the local normal schools and Waynesburg College, and began teaching at nineteen years of age He taught three years in Springfield township ten years in Stewart township, three years in the borough of Ohiopyle and three years in Lower Tyrone township During these years he worked at farming during the summer months After his marriage he moved to Stewart township Fayette county, where he purchased a farm of three hundred acres, but continued his teaching during the winters In 1885 he succeeded in having a post office established at Nicolay, named in his honor In 1893 he sold his farm and moved to Ohiopyle Pennsylvania, remaining two years In 1895 he moved to the village of Stickel, in Lower Tyrone township, where he established a small gro-

cery store, but still continued teaching After enlarging his store, adding full general lines and agricultural implements, he devoted himself to mercantile pursuits Mr Nicolay's farm, adjoining the village of Stickel, is underlaid with coal, and he operates a coal bank for local supply From 1895 to 1901 he was postmaster at Stickel, He is a Democrat in politics, and served as school director in both Stewart and Lower Tyrone townships In 1897 he was elected justice of the peace, and has since served continuously through several re-elections He and family are members of the Methodist Episcopal church He is a member of the Independent Order of Odd Fellows, Lodge No 499, of which he is a charter member, and of the local grange, Patrons of Husbandry

Mr Nicolay married, January 2, 1876, Martha Williams, born at Kingwood Somerset county, Pennsylvania, January 28, 1857, daughter of Daniel and Elizabeth Williams, both deceased Her father was a farmer of Somerset, later of Stewart township Fayette county Children of O F M Nicolay 1 Minnie born August 10 1877, married William D Hixon a farmer of Lower Tyrone township 2 Homer, born February 17, 1879 died June 7, 1882 3 Roxana, born September 30 1880, married Charles Moon, a farmer of Lower Tyrone township 4 Roy Vincent, born June 14, 1883, married Lizzie Hixon, and lives in Uniontown, Pennsylvania is a commercial traveler 5 Awilda, born May 3, 1889, is now preparing for the profession of graduate nurse at Battle Creek, Michigan

GANS
This family was founded in Fayette county, Pennsylvania, by George and Joseph Gans born in Germany, from which country they fled to escape persecution They settled at or near Antietam, Maryland, where they remained about ten years In 1784 they came to Fayette county, settling in Springhill township, where each took up about four hundred acres of land that was surveyed to them by the government Both married and founded families

(I) The founder of the branch herein recorded was George Gans, who died in

1807 He was a member of the German Baptist church (Dunkard), although most of his children and their descendants became members of the Christian church (Disciples of Christ) He married and left issue Jacob Joseph, Daniel, George, Margaret, married A Getzendaner Anna, married A Greenley and lived in Greene county, Pennsylvania Elizabeth, and William These sons later in life all settled in the west except William

(II) William, youngest child of George Gans, was born in Springhill township, Fayette county Pennsylvania, 1789, died there in 1867 He grew up on the farm near Morris Cross Roads, which is still owned in the family He later became its owner and spent his entire active life engaged in its care and cultivation He married Magdalene, daughter of George Custer, born in Philadelphia, Pennsylvania December 3, 1744, died on his farm in Georges township, Fayette county, Pennsylvania December 5, 1829 He was a large healthy man and the father of fifteen children He was the fourth son of Paul Custer, who married Sarah Ball, daughter of Colonel William Ball, of Lancaster county, Virginia, and a sister of Mary Ball, the second wife of Augustine Washington, and the mother of George Washington the "Father of his Country" Mary Ball married Augustine Washington March 6, 1731, and died August 25, 1789 Her son, George Washington, was born February 22, 1732 He was a first cousin of George Custer, father of Magdalene, wife of William Gans Children of William Gans 1 Dr George, many years a practicing physician of Moundsville, West Virginia 2 Dr Daniel settled near Canton Ohio, where he practiced medicine married Margaret Hanna children Henry C, of Youngstown Ohio Emmet and Mrs Olive Muckley both of Cleveland Ohio, Elizabeth married Judge Krichbaum of Canton, Ohio 3 Jonathan a farmer moved to Missouri, but later returned to Fayette county, where he died married Sarah Eberhardt, her father was a farmer of Nicholson township Fayette county and a veteran of the civil war 4 Altha owned the farm in south Fayette county, where Gans Station is now stand-

ing and named in his honor 5 Lebbeus Biglow, of whom further 6 Mary Ann, married William P Griffin, who lived on his own farm in Nicholson township for over sixty years 7 Lydia, married James C Ramsey, a farmer of Springhill township

(III) Lebbeus Biglow, fifth son of William and Magdalene (Custer) Gans, was born in Springhill township, Fayette county, Pennsylvania, March 31, 1825 He was educated in the common school, grew to manhood on the home farm, and later purchased the homestead property He was a prosperous farmer and added an adjoining one hundred and thirty-four acres, which gave him three hundred acres of the best farm land in southern Fayette county He later in life devoted his attention more to the raising of fine live stock than to agriculture, but he was all his life a farmer A feature of his farm was a sugar maple grove containing two thousand trees which yielded a good profit annually He was a member of the Presbyterian church, and held in high esteem by his neighbors He married (first) January 6, 1848, Elizabeth J, daughter of James C Ramsey, children 1 Dorcas Ann, married T F Protzman, many years a merchant at Morris Cross Roads 2 Elizabeth J married W Morgan Smith, of Mount Pleasant, Pennsylvania 3 A son, died in infancy He married (second), October 10, 1868, Emily S, daughter of Henry B Goe, of Allegheny City, Pennsylvania, born in Fayette county, on the farm now owned by H B Goe, December 28, 1803 died November 1, 1889 He was a farmer in Jefferson township in early life, but about 1865 moved to Pittsburgh Pennsylvania, where he died He left the farm to engage in oil production, having oil interests in McKean county He married Catherine Shotwell, born at the Shotwell farm in Franklin township, December 28, 1806, died August 11, 1889 They were married in 1824, and spent sixty-five years of married life together They were both members of the Christian church

The Goe family came originally from Scotland the emigrant settling in Jefferson township on land yet held in the family name Children of Henry B Goe 1 Henry

B (2), moved from Pittsburgh to Bradford, Pennsylvania, about 1880, engaged in oil production, and soon afterward died, married Lydia White, of Connellsville, children Henry B (3), Gertrude, Elizabeth, Catherine 2 John S, lived and died in Jefferson township, a fancy stock and cattle dealer, married and left children Dorcas, wife of John H Gans, Emma V, widow of John Moore of Georges township, Eva Catherine and Irene of Uniontown, also John S Jr, who died in the west 3 Robert S, a farmer on the old home farm in Jefferson township, married Heater Higginbotham, children James H, Henry B, of Jefferson township, Ada, wife of Attorney Robert M Curry, of Pittsburgh, Cora, wife of Dr Lloyd Trowbridge, of Piqua, Ohio 4 Joel S, died in Pittsburgh 5 Susan, married John Newcomer, she survives him and has lived for over fifty years on Main street, Connellsville, Pennsylvania, children Mrs L F Ruth and Mrs W Foley 6 Sarah, married Robert Elliot a farmer of Jefferson township, both deceased, children Henry and James living in Iowa, Lawrence and George, of Jefferson township, Fayette county Charles S, of Clarksburg, West Virginia, Frank Mary, Catherine and Martha, the last four live in Greenwood, Delaware 7 Emily S (of previous mention), wife of Lebbeus B Gans 8 Rose, married John D Bailey (deceased), he was a broker belonging to the Pittsburgh Stock Exchange, and for many years was known as the oldest member of the Exchange 9 Laura, resides in Pittsburgh, unmarried Children of Lebbeus B Gans and his second wife Emily S Goe 1 Henry B, a civil engineer, living in Uniontown, Pennsylvania, married Harriet Brownfield 2 William L of whom further 3 Catherine (deceased), married William H Morgan, of Morgantown, West Virginia, who survives her with one child, Emily Josephine 4 Dr Robert A a physician of New Salem, Fayette county Pennsylvania, married Laura Buckley, of Omaha, Nebraska

(IV) William L, son of Lebbeus B and Emily (Goe) Gans was born on the farm settled on by his great-grandfather, in Springhill township, Fayette county, Pennsylvania January 12 1873 He was educated in the public schools in Springhill township and Bethany College, West Virginia whence he was graduated, class of 1895, after a course in the liberal arts He was a member of the college Neotrophian Literary Society and an active worker After finishing his college course he began a course of legal study under the direction of Howell & Reppert, in the latter's law offices at Uniontown, Pennsylvania In 1897 he was admitted to the Fayette county bar, and at once began practice in Uniontown, where he has been constantly engaged in his profession ever since In 1906 he formed a law partnership with Thomas P Jones under the firm name Gans & Jones, which continued until the death of the latter October 24, 1911 Mr Gans has since been practicing alone He is well established in a good business, and is a leader among the younger professional men of his city He is secretary and a director of the Fairchance & Smithfield Traction Company, and has other business interests He is a Republican in politics, and has served as councilman in Uniontown He is a member of the Central Christian Church and the lodge, chapter and commandery of the Masonic order, York Rite also a thirty-second degree Mason of the Ancient Accepted Scottish Rite, Pittsburgh Consistory

He married January 10, 1900, Lucy Brooke, born in Uniontown, Pennsylvania, January 5, 1876 daughter of Frank L and Mary (McCormick) Brooke of Uniontown She is a member of the Methodist Episcopal church Child William Paul, born April 19, 1903 The family home is in South Union township

---

COLBORN This name with many variations of spelling may be traced to Edward Colborn, who came from London, England, in the ship "Defence" in 1635, settling at Ipswich, Massachusetts

(II) Robert, son of Edward Colborn, of Ipswich, settled at Concord, Massachusetts, married Mary Bishop

(III) Edward (2), son of Robert Colborn, was born in Massachusetts, married Mercy Buttrick

(IV) Samuel, son of Edward (2) Colborn, was born in Concord Massachusetts, died at Hampton, Connecticut He married November 17, 1727 Elizabeth Halt

(V) Michael, son of Samuel Colborn, was born in Connecticut, lived and died in Woodbridge, New Jersey, married Sarah Mitchell

(VI) Robert, son of Michael Colborn, was born in New Jersey, January 16, 1753 At the age of eighteen he was apprenticed to a foundry man who taught him the trade of forgeman He married in New Jersey, and with wife and three children settled in Turkey Foot township, Bedford, (now Somerset) county, Pennsylvania, where he engaged in farming and working at his trade of blacksmith He was one of the founders of the first church in Somerset county, built in 1775, and known as the Baptist church in the "Jersey settlement" During the revolution he returned to New Jersey with others originally from that colony, and enlisted as a private in Captain Joseph Luse's company, Morris county, New Jersey, and served every alternate month for four years After the war he returned to Somerset county His farm near Draketown, worked by his sons while he wrought at the forge, is yet known as the "Colborn farm" He died May 16, 1836 He married Effie Wortman, born in Morris county, New Jersey, 1753, died in Somerset county, November 25, 1826

(VII) Abraham, son of Robert Colborn, was born in Somerset county, Pennsylvania, December 23, 1789, died on his farm in Turkey Foot township, in same county, October 11, 1843 He was a farmer, and deacon and elder of the Baptist church He married Eleanor Wood Mansey, who died July 11, 1858, nine children

(VIII) Sylvester, son of Abraham Colborn, was born in 1808, on the parental farm in Turkey Foot township, Somerset county Pennsylvania, where he continued his residence until moving to a good farm of his own He lived and farmed in Somerset county all his life He married Olive Rush, and left issue

(IX) David L, son of Sylvester Colborn, was born April 3, 1827, died 1868 He was educated in the public school and grew to youthful manhood on the parental farm He purchased a farm in Somerset county which he cultivated until his death He married when young (his wife being but seventeen years of age), Julia A Dull (or Doll) of German descent born in Somerset county, in 1833, died 1894, daughter of George and Catherine (Walters) Dull Catherine was a daughter of George and Catherine Walters, of Somerset county George Dull was a skilled blacksmith, a large landowner at Mill Run, Springfield township, Fayette county, Pennsylvania, justice of the peace and holder of several township offices, he died November 18, 1880 He married a second wife, Mrs Margaret Bell Lyman Children of George Dull by first wife, Catherine Walters Daniel W, Uriah, Romanus, served in the civil war, was captured by the Confederates and died in a military prison, Jacob, William H (All the foregoing were veterans of the civil war and are all deceased), John, a farmer, yet surviving, Julia A (of previous mention), Rebecca, deceased, Mary C deceased, Lucinda, married Alexander Brooks, and lives in Scottdale Pennsylvania Children of David L and Julia A (Dull) Colborn 1 Lavinia, died in infancy 2 Rev Lafayette S, now a minister of the Baptist church, located in Alexandria, Ohio 3 Willis D of whom further 4 George W, for twenty years an employee of the Rainey Coal Company, Bullskin township, Fayette county 5 Walter S, a merchant at Mill Run, Pennsylvania 6 Andrew Jackson, of whom further 7 Anna, died in 1868, two weeks after her father's death 8 Sylvester, died in infancy

(X) Willis D, second son of David L and Julia Ann (Dull) Colborn, was born in Somerset county, Pennsylvania October 17 1855 He was educated in the public schools of Somerset county He took especial interest in bookkeeping, in which he perfected himself, and in 1881 entered the employ of the Rainey Coal and Coke Company, at Moyer, Fayette county, as bookkeeper, continuing until 1902 In 1903 he became associated with the Fayette County Gas Company, beginning as cashier, and is now superintendent of the Connellsville division He is a member of the Christian church, and the Knights of the Maccabees, in politics a Democrat

He married, August 3, 1882, Emma B Echard born in Fayette county, Pennsylvania, October 3, 1861 daughter of Jacob and Nancy (Rhinehart) Echard, of Fayette county (see Echard) Children of Willis D Colborn Robert Pattison born October 8, 1883, now living in Pittsburgh, Pennsylvania, John G born February 6, 1885 James E, born January 9, 1889, now living in Greensburg, Pennsylvania, Harry G, born July 25 1890 Eleanor, June 1892, Ann Mary, August 5, 1898

(X) Dr Andrew Jackson Colburn sixth child of David L Colborn, was born in Somerset county, Pennsylvania, April 11, 1863 He was five years of age when his father died, and shortly afterward his widowed mother brought her family to Mill Run, Fayette county, where her father, George Dull, resided Here Andrew J was educated in the public schools, and began business life as a clerk in the general store of A Stickle, remaining five years, he then spent two years in Connellsville as clerk for J A Zimmerman He then returned to Mill Run, established a general store, and during President Cleveland's first administration (1885-1889) was postmaster He later sold out his business and until 1896 was clerk for W J Rainey, was manager of the Ohio Coal & Coke Company's store, then again clerk for Mr Rainey During these years he had been a student of medicine and in 1896 he entered the medical department of the University of Baltimore, whence he was graduated M D in 1898 He at once began practice, locating at Ohiopyle Pennsylvania, where he remained until 1901 He then took a post-graduate course at Maryland Medical College, and returned to Ohiopyle, continuing until January 1 1905 when he sold his practice and located in Connellsville, where he has been in successful practice He is a member of the Fayette county and Pennsylvania State medical societies, the Independent Order of Odd Fellows, Knights of Malta, Fraternal Order of Eagles Fraternal Order of Owls, the Royal Arcanum, Knights of the Maccabees, Children of Ben Hur, and Knights of the Mystic Senate In politics he is a Democrat and in religious faith a Baptist

He married, August 5, 1883, Mary A Tannebill, born in Somerset county, Pennsylvania, September 4 1860, daughter of Eli and Jane Tannebill Eli Tannebill enlisted from Fayette county and was killed in the civil war Children of Dr Andrew Jackson Colborn 1 Bessie, born July 31, 1884, married Frank W Daley, of Ohiopyle, Pennsylvania 2 Harry Earl, born November, 1885, died 1892 3 Roy T, born 1887, died 1890 4 George Dull, born June 19, 1889, graduate of Mt Pleasant Institute 5 Mary Edith, born June, 1895 6 Leah, born 1900

ENOS

This family is of English descent, their progenitors, early settlers of Somerset county, Pennsylvania The first of whom we have record is Jonathan Enos son of the English emigrant He was a blacksmith of Somerset county, coming when a young man in 1840 to Connellsville, where he established a smithy on the north side of East Main street, in the block numbering in the two hundreds He died in Connellsville, September 18 1876 He married, in Connellsville, Mary Keepers, also of Somerset county, daughter of Thomas Keepers, who came from Somerset to Connellsville and kept a tavern in the early eighteen hundreds The Keepers were of German descent After the death of her husband Mrs Mary Enos moved to Northumberland county, Pennsylvania Children of Jonathan Enos, living in 1900 1 George, of whom further 2 Emma E, married Henry Kurtz of Connellsville 3 Dr Joseph B, of Charleroi, Pennsylvania 4 Mary E, married J K Taggart, whom she survived 5 Edgar Jonathan born August 1, 1865, a blacksmith of Connellsville, married, August 24 1887 Sarah Luella, daughter of Abraham H and Mary (Dillinger) Sherrick of Pennsville Pennsylvania children George, Mary Lucile and Ora Caroline

(III) George, eldest son of Jonathan and Mary (Keepers) Enos was born in Connellsville April 11, 1849 died there October 12 1905 He attended the public school and learned the blacksmith's trade with his father, with whom he worked for several years, finally establishing a shop of his own

A. J. Colborn M. D.

Later in life he associated with Henry Wilhelm and contracted the erection of coke ovens They built a great many all over the coke regions of Pennsylvania, also in Pocahontas and Bramwell, West Virginia He continued in active business nearly to the end of his life He was a Democrat, and served on the city council He married Elizabeth Wilhelm, born in East Liberty (Pittsburgh East End), Pennsylvania, 1850, died 1884 daughter of John and Mary Wilhelm John Wilhelm was born in Germany and settled in West Newton, Pennsylvania with his parents He married there, and prior to the civil war came to Connellsville, where he built the "Yough House," and was the proprietor for several years Later he sold out and built a brick house on East Main street, where Lytle's drug store now is, which was considered the best house in the town at that time He was a pioneer in the manufacture of fire-brick in this vicinity in association with Joseph Soisson and Kilpatrick He held several styles of patents on the beehive style of coke oven, and was the pioneer in that form of oven construction He was also one of the pioneer railroad constructors and built the Baltimore & Ohio railroad between Connellsville and Indian Creek After the completion of his section he rode on the first locomotive to attempt the bridge crossing Indian Creek The structure was not strong enough to carry the weight of the engine, which crashed through, fell to the creek bottom, killing all on board except Mr Wilhelm, who received injuries that eventually caused his death He was a member of the German Lutheran church, as was his wife Mary she was born in Germany, but met and married John Wilhelm at West Newton, Pennsylvania Children of George Enos, John Jonathan, and George W of whom further

(IV) John Jonathan, eldest son of George and Elizabeth (Wilhelm) Enos, was born in Connellsville Pennsylvania March 22, 1874 He was ten years of age when his mother died and was taken by his grandmother Wilhelm then living in Allegheny Pennsylvania He remained there until he was seventeen years of age receiving a good education in the schools of Allegheny

and Oakland At the age of eighteen he returned to Connellsville where he learned the blacksmith's trade under the instruction of his father, whom he succeeded after the latter gave up the shop and became a coke oven builder He continued one year only in business in Connellsville then for eighteen months was in the employ of the Electric Metal Works at Erie, Pennsylvania He again returned to Connellsville, where he established a livery and boarding stable, to which he has added general teaming, street paving cellar excavating, etc His home is in Snydertown, a suburb of Connellsville, where he erected his present home in 1905 He is a Republican, and a member of the Lutheran church He married, March 27, 1895, Olive C Wilt, born April 23, 1875 in Pittsburgh, Pennsylvania, daughter of Albert and Mary (Dunn) Wilt James Wilt was an engineer on the Baltimore & Ohio, and met his death in a railroad accident when his daughter Olive C was a young child Children of John J Enos Mary Elizabeth born December 7, 1895 John Clyde, May 8, 1904

(IV) George W Enos, youngest son of George and Elizabeth (Wilhelm) Enos, was born in Connellsville, Pennsylvania January 5, 1879 He was five years of age when his mother died and left him to his father's care He attended the public schools, and at an early age was taught the blacksmith's trade by his father He was an adept pupil, and while yet a growing boy was considered an expert smith He married when eighteen years of age, and continued the Enos shop established by his father on South street, where he is now in successful business He is a Republican, and a member of the Lutheran church He married, February 11, 1897, Blanche Shaw, born September 15 1879, in Connellsville, daughter of George W and Emma Shaw

George W Shaw is a descendant of Nathan Shaw, born in Scotland, came to the United States with his brother James and settled in Massachusetts The Shaws were of English ancestors who for two generations prior to Nathan Shaw had been seated in Scotland Nathan (2), son of Nathan (1) Shaw was born in Massachusetts was a mill sawyer He came to Fayette county,

Pennsylvania, when a young man, and owned a saw mill at Tale's Hollow in the mountains seven miles east of Connellsville His wife Catherine was born in Fayette county Four of his sons, Solomon, James, Lester and David served in the Mexican war, the latter killed in battle George W, son of Nathan (2) Shaw was born near Connellsville, Pennsylvania, 1822 He was a stone mason and bricklayer working at his trade in Connellsville until his death, excepting the time spent in the army He enlisted in Company C, Eighty-fifth Regiment Pennsylvania Volunteer Infantry, under Captain Treadwell He enlisted in Somerset county, taking with him several men from Connellsville He was wounded in the arm at the battle of Cold Harbor, but after recovery rejoined his regiment and served until the close of the war, attaining the rank of sergeant He was a Republican, and served as town constable In religious faith he was a Methodist He married Ellen Cunningham, born in Dunbar township, Fayette county, and their children were

George W (2), of whom further, Dorcas, married J W Bishop of Connellsville, Belle, married Hugh Stillwagon, Nathan, served eight years in the United States regular army, and died aged thirty years, Clara, married David Randolph, of Connellsville Jennie, married Frank Holland, of Connellsville, Mary, married Dr F N Sherrick, of Connellsville George W (2) son of George (1) Shaw, was born in Connellsville July 4, 1849 He attended the public schools and learned the blacksmith's trade at the National Locomotive Works at Connellsville working there four years In 1875 he entered the employ of the Baltimore & Ohio Railroad Company as blacksmith at their general repair shops at Connellsville In 1884 he was promoted foreman of the blacksmithing department, holding that position until 1896 He was then for eight years with the Connellsville Machine and Car Works as blacksmith, four years with the American Tin Plate Company, and now is with the Sligo Steel and Iron Company He is a Republican in politics

He married, May 15, 1872, Emma Ross,

born May 15, 1859, in Connellsville, daughter of Captain Henry and Nancy (Secrist) Ross, both born in Pittsburgh Henry Ross was an Ohio river steamboat captain Children of George W (2) Shaw Gertrude, born November 12, 1874, married Thomas Cordner (or Gardner), of Connellsville, Edward, born September 12, 1875, resides in Connellsville, George W (3), born April 4, 1877, died in infancy, Blanche, born September 15, 1879, of previous mention, Charles N, born April 1, 1882 married Emma Lamley, Fred, born September 12, 1884, Bessie, February 17, 1888

Children of George W and Blanche (Shaw) Enos Helen Gertrude born November 17 1898, Jean, August 17, 1901 George, September 13, 1903, Charles, July 15, 1908

This is a good old
DEFFENBAUGH G e r m a n family planted in Fayette county by Conrad Deffenbaugh, a native of Germany After his emigration he settled in Eastern Pennsylvania, later coming to Fayette county, where he married Margaret Riffle They settled on new land and endured all the dangers and privations of the pioneer They had a family of seven children

(II) Jacob, son of Conrad and Margaret (Riffle) Deffenbaugh, was born in Fayette county in 1776 He learned the blacksmith's trade and was one of the most expert iron workers in the county He made axles, chains, and other needed articles, shipping to river points He prospered and owned three farms of one hundred acres each He was a Whig in politics, and a Presbyterian in religion He died 1854 He married Eva Everly, who bore him eleven children

(III) Jacob (2), son Jacob and Eva (Everly) Deffenbaugh, was born in German township, Fayette county, Pennsylvania, October 26, 1806, died October 25, 1886 He followed farming all his life, moving to Nicholas township in 1833 and purchasing a farm of two hundred acres, conducting general farming and stock raising In politics he was a Republican, and a Presbyterian in religion, holding the office of elder in that church throughout his entire mature life

He married September 5, 1833 Sarah Hertzog born in Springhill township, August 22, 1809, died March 19 1859 Children 1 Mary L, born January 26, 1835, died November 17, 1896 2 Sarah Jane, born March 12, 1837, died November 21, 1849 3 Louisa, born April 10, 1839, died August 18 1840 4 John born May 30, 1841 died March 11, 1844 5 William H, of whom further 6 Margaret, born July 22, 1846, died November 11, 1849 7 Rev George, born October 26, 1850, has been a missionary among the Indians in Idaho and Oregon, but has abandoned that because of ill health, and now has a charge near Portland, Oregon

(IV) William Henry fifth child of Jacob (2) and Sarah (Hertzog) Deffenbaugh was born August 19, 1843, in Nicholson township, on the old homestead He was educated in the public schools of Nicholson township, later attending Dunlaps Creek Academy, at which institution his brother prepared for the ministry Leaving school he worked on his father's farm for a time, finally superintending the entire farm In 1885 he sold his farm and Greeley-like "went west," returning two years later and establishing in the mercantile business at New Geneva

In 1894 Mr Deffenbaugh built a handsome residence in the town but in 1901 heard the call of country life and purchased a farm of one hundred acres in Westmoreland county remaining there until 1909 He then moved to Geneva, where he lives a quiet life, retired from active business affairs When a lad he belonged to Captain W S Crait's volunteer company and attempted to enlist in the regular army, but was rejected because of his youth He is an elder in the New Geneva Presbyterian Church an office he holds for life In politics, the Republican party claims his allegiance He was town assessor for one term, and now holds the secretaryship of the board of education He holds an enviable position in New Geneva and is respected and admired as a public spirited Christian gentleman

He married, December 16 1886 Katherine Ann Irwin, born March 23, 1857, daughter of William Irwin, of Stewartsville, Westmoreland county, Pennsylvania Children 1 Edward Robbins, born December 31, 1887, a prospector in Alaska 2 Louis M, born December 23, 1892, attends Kiskiminitas school

DEFFENBAUGH (III) Nicolas Deffenbaugh, son of Jacob (q v) and Eva (Everly) Deffenbaugh, was born in German township, Fayette county, Pennsylvania, in May. 1816, died March 26, 1888 He obtained his education in the public schools and then occupied himself on the home farm leaving that to conduct his own He raised much fine cattle, growing their feed on the farm He was a member of the Cumberland Presbyterian Church and a Republican in politics, holding the offices of school director and clerk of the board He married April 25, 1844, Henrietta, daughter of Thomas and Sarah Shroyer Children 1 Henderson S of whom further 2 John M, born 1850, lives at Seattle, Washington 3 Thomas J lives in Indiana 4 Marietta, married Morgan Wilson and lives in German township Her mother makes her home here

(IV) Henderson Stewart, son of Nicolas and Henrietta (Shroyer) Deffenbaugh, was born in German township, Fayette county Pennsylvania, March 25 1845 He received his education in the public schools and became a farmer in Menallen township moving to German township only to return to Menallen township, where he conducted the Thaw farm for four years In 1902 he purchased the old Griffin farm of one hundred and seventy-five acres in Nicholson township and since 1903 has made that place his home

He engages in general farming and is a very successful stock raiser He is a member of the Presbyterian church and a Republican in politics having served in the capacity of school director, farm supervisor and other township offices He married January 7, 1869, Margaret Moore born in German township June 17, 1846 daughter of John A, a farmer and Jane Moore They have had a family of eight children, seven of whom are living

DEFFENGAUGH

(II) Anthony Deffenbaugh son of Conrad Deffenbaugh (q v), was born about 1790, in German township, Fayette county, Pennsylvania, where he died He always followed the farmer's occupation, living a simple, peaceful and contented life He married Susan Bowman Children John, Henry, of whom further, George¹ Christopher, Solomon Maria, married John Johnson

(III)Henry, second son and child of Anthony and Susan (Bowman) Deffenbaugh, was born in German township, Fayette county, Pennsylvania, 1824 died May 14, 1901 He obtained a public school education in his native township With the love of the soil strong in his blood and with the example of past generations to follow, it is not remarkable that he should decide to follow farming, beginning as his father's assistant He later moved to Waynesburg, remaining there until 1854 when he purchased a farm in Nicholson township, and at his death was considered one of the most successful farmers in the township He was a member of the Lutheran church and a Republican in politics Universal and sincere respect was his in all circles in which he moved He was revered as a conscientious and earnest church worker, an upright and honorable man in business dealings, and loved as a fond, dutiful husband and father He married Margaret Durr born in Springhill township daughter of Samuel Durr Children Maria, lives on the old homestead, Salena born December 8, 1853, died September 1, 1882 Sylvanus C, of whom further

(IV) Sylvanus C, son of Henry and Margaret (Durr) Deffenbaugh, and twin of Salena was born in Nicholson township Fayette county, Pennsylvania, December 8 1853 He attended the public schools of his native township, and until the death of his father assisted in the work of the farm Since then he has conducted general farming and stock raising operations on the same land His efforts in both directions have been unusually productive of good results He married in 1880, Emma Baker, born in Springhill township, Fayette county,

Pennsylvania, July 15, 1854, daughter of George and Margaret (Sargent) Baker Children 1 Earl, born August 10 1884, lives at home 2 Lola, born December 19 1892 3 Nellie, born November 16, 1897, attends public school

---

BOWMAN

This branch of the Bowman family descends from Christopher Baumann, born about 1733, in Germany, near Ems His father was a man of importance and the owner of a silver mine named Mehlbach situated in the mountains near Ems Tradition says he had three sons, of whom Christopher was the eldest, that these sons were required to work the mine in person Having been bothered for sometime with water in the mine, the boys became discouraged, and Christopher, with his younger brother, resolved to come to America, which they did in 1754

(II) Christopher Baumann, aforementioned settled in Bucks county, Pennsylvania, where he was successful, and in a few years returned to Germany, sold out his interest in the silver mine, and returned to America, bringing his remaining brother It may here be said that one brother settled in Massachusetts, the other "went west," while Christopher remained in Bucks county In 1759 he married Susan Banks, of Scotch descent Later he settled at Mount Bethel in Northampton county, where he bought a farm and lived for thirty years In 1800 he joined his son, Rev Thomas Bowman in Briar Creek township Columbia county He died at Queenshocking Valley, seven miles north of Williamsport, Pennsylvania, in 1806, while on a visit to friends His wife Susan died at Briar Creek in 1816, and is buried at the Old Stone Church graveyard They both were aged seventy-three years at death Christopher being ten years her senior Children 1 Rev Thomas Bowman, born December 6 1760 died April 9, 1823 father of Bishop Bowman, who at his death was the venerated senior bishop of the Methodist Episcopal church 2 Rev Christian Bowman, born 1761, died January 26 1831 3 Mary, born 1762, married James Stackhouse 4 Susan, buried in Queenshocking Valley, Pennsylvania

5 Lydia, died at Briar Creek, 1813, married (first) Jacob Mack, (second) John Hoffman 6 Jesse, born June 10, 1769, died May 16, 1828 7 Susan, died at Nescopek, Pennsylvania 8 John, of whom further 9 Orne, lived near Muncy, Pennsylvania

(III) John, son of Christopher Baumann, was born in Northampton county, Pennsylvania about 1772, and lived near Town Hall, Pennsylvania This generation always spelled their name Bowman, all the other children of Christopher following the change from Baumann John Bowman married and had issue, including a son John (2)

(IV) John (2), son of John (1) Bowman, was born in Eastern Pennsylvania about the year 1800 When a young man he settled at Brown s Run, Fayette county, where he purchased land and followed farming until his death He married Catherine Wall, and left issue, including a son, James A

(V) James A, son of John (2) Bowman, was born on the homestead farm at Brown s Run, German township, Fayette county, died 1880 He attended the public school, and on arriving at a suitable age learned the stonemason s trade He married, and began housekeeping on the 'Old Ephraim Waller s" farm near Fairview Church, where he lived until after the birth of Aaron W, his fourth child He then moved to Masontown He was drafted near the close of the war, served till its close then returned to Masontown, where he lived the remainder of his life He was a Democrat, and with his wife belonged to the Cumberland Presbyterian Church He married Huldah Walters born near Masontown Fayette county, daughter of Jacob and Prudence Walters, both born in Western Pennsylvania Jacob Walters was a tailor, and had a shop in Masontown Children of James A Bowman 1 M H, now living in Uniontown, Pennsylvania 2 Josiah now in the grocery business at Morgantown, West Virginia 3 John F, now a bricklayer living in Charleroi, Pennsylvania 4 Aaron Walters, of whom further

(VI) Aaron Walters youngest child of James A and Huldah (Walters) Bowman,

was born near Masontown Fayette county, Pennsylvania, April 27, 1856 He attended the public schools of Masontown, and early in life began working with his father at the stonemason's trade He was too frail in body, however, for so arduous an occupation, and later secured a clerkship with the Dunbar Furnace Company at Dunbar, Pennsylvania, remaining two and a half years He next was clerk in the dry goods store of Hopwood & Miller at Uniontown, Pennsylvania remaining in that employ three years He next spent six months with the Dunbar Furnace Company in their store at Fairchance, then returned to Uniontown where he formed a partnership with C D Kramer and established a dry goods business, which partnership continued two years, Mr Bowman then selling out to his partner He next was manager for Robert Hogsett, a merchant of Mount Braddock, one and a half years In 1889 he entered the employ of the Union Supply Company, as first clerk of store No 3 at Monarch, Pennsylvania, and later became manager of the company stores at Adelaide, remaining there five years then returned to Monarch and assumed the management at that place for five and one-half years After leaving Monarch he assumed the management of Continental No 1, at Uniontown, Pennsylvania, staying there about two years In 1904 he was appointed manager of the store at Davidson, a suburb of Connellsville, and so continues His long service with the Union Supply Company has brought him substantial reward, and he is rated a most efficient business manager He resides in Connellsville, where he erected a residence in 1905 at No 503 East Cedar street He is an Independent in politics voting for the best candidates, but is a Prohibitionist in sentiment He is a member of the Christian church (Disciples of Christ) at Connellsville

He married, September 28, 1887, Laura Ethel Lloyd, born in Monongahela City, Pennsylvania Children 1 Catherine Adele, born July 22, 1888 died November 27, 1909 2 James Allen, born January 6, 1890 now a student at Pennsylvania State College 3 Huldah Louise, born June 24, 1892 died March 3, 1895 4 Hugus Jenkins, born June 6, 1895   5 Arthur Willis, July 16 1897   6 Mary Ethel, January 26, 1902, died February 18, 1906

The American ancestor of GIBSON this early and prominent Fayette county, Pennsylvania, family was James Gibson, born in Ireland, came to Pennsylvania in 1770, and settled in Chester county, where he owned land   In 1776 he enlisted in the continental army and served until the final surrender at Yorktown   Two of his brothers were compelled to serve in the British army, having been taken by a "Press gang" in the old country These two settled in Virginia after the war, where most of their descendants now live In 1790 James Gibson left Chester county and settled in Luzerne township, Fayette county   In 1792 he married Mary Lackey, and founded the Fayette county family   He was a hard working honorable farmer and left a posterity endowed with sterling elements of character

(II) Alexander, son of James Gibson, was born in Luzerne township Fayette county, Pennsylvania, 1797, died July 12, 1875   He spent his early life on the farm, and obtained an education in the subscription district school   He remained on the farm until he was twenty years of age, then engaged in freighting by wagon between Baltimore and Wheeling, Virginia   In 1819 he began freighting south from Baltimore, going as far as Nashville, Tennessee, where for two years he was engaged in trade with the Cherokee Indians in partnership with Levi Crawford   In 1823 he returned to Fayette county, where he purchased a farm in Luzerne township and spent the remainder of his life engaged in farming and stock raising   He was an energetic capable man of business and prospered to that extent that he was able to give each of his children a good start in life, when they were ready to leave the paternal roof   He never took prominent part in public life and was so fair in his own dealings and so emphatically opposed to contention of any kind that he never had a law suit   In his religious life he was consistent and actively connected with the Cumberland Presbyterian Church He is buried in Hopewell cemetery

He married June 24, 1824, Mary Hibbs, of Redstone township, Fayette county, Pennsylvania, who survived him until January 25, 1876   Children   James G, of whom further, Margaret J, married William H Miller, Mary A, married Oliver Miller, children   Albert G and Emma S, Albert M, married Alice Frey, child, Nelue

(III) James G, eldest son of Alexander Gibson, was born in Luzerne township, Fayette county, Pennsylvania, September 16, 1826, died February 26, 1908, buried in Hopewell cemetery   He was the owner of a fine property and a large number of cattle, and amassed a considerable fortune in coal speculation   He served as president of the Millsboro National Bank and director of the Second National Bank of Brownsville   Mr Gibson was well known, not only in the community where he resided for many years, but in the surrounding communities   He married (first) Mary Rodgers, who died in 1860, leaving two children   John A, of whom further, and Mary R   He married (second) Rebecca J Haney, now deceased

(IV) John A, son or James G Gibson, was born in Luzerne township, Fayette county, Pennsylvania, April 12, 1858   He was educated in the public schools, and grew to manhood on the home farm   After his marriage he continued in the same occupation, now owning six hundred acres of land In 1909 he retired from active farming and erected a modern residence in Brownsville, which is now his home   He is a capable business man and has lived a successful, useful life, honored and respected   He is a director of the Second National Bank or Brownsville, also director of First National Bank of Millsboro, and held in high esteem by his business associates   In political faith he is a Democrat, but never sought public office   He is a member of the Methodist Episcopal church, to which he has belonged for many years

He married, November 9, 1892, Stella M Vernon, born in Luzerne township Fayette county, Pennsylvania, July 11, 1868, daughter of Andrew and Margaret (Mobley) Vernon, both deceased   Children   Margaret, born January 23, 1894 a student in Brownsville high school, Mary, born March 11, 1898, died April 12, 1899

James G Gibson

SHERRICK Sometime during the eighteenth century, three brothers, Joseph, Ulrich and ———— Sherg, came from Switzerland to America, settling in Lancaster county, Pennsylvania The elder of the brothers, Joseph, a widower, brought with him five sons Joseph, Henry, Jacob, John and Christian, (perhaps also daughters)

(II) The eldest of these sons, Joseph Sherg, was a Mennonite preacher, and many of his descendants yet cling to that faith. He moved from Lancaster to Fayette county, and on his journey was accompanied by his wife, Anna Mercer, a distant relative of General Mercer of revolutionary fame In 1790 he moved to Westmoreland county, near Everson, where he died January 1, 1812 By his will recorded at Uniontown, Pennsylvania (Will book No 1, page 140) he left his widow well provided for, and the following children Christian, a minister of the Mennonite church, always lived in Fayette county, Peter, located in Wayne county, Ohio, Jacob, of whom further, Henry, removed prior to 1845 to Missouri, where he died, Joseph, born 1787, a farmer of East Huntington township Westmoreland county, married Barbara Beitter, and left a large family, Mary, married Abraham Stoner, Katherine, died unmarried, Henry, Ruth, Susan, married Christian Frink Anna, the mother of these children, died aged eighty-four years, three months and eleven days In this generation the family name became Sherrick

(III) Jacob Sherrick, son of Joseph Sherg, was born in Lancaster, Pennsylvania, about 1780 He was reared in Fayette and Westmoreland counties, and grew up a farmer After attaining his majority he located in Fayette county, where he continued engaged in agriculture all his active life He married and became the father of the following children Mattie married a Mr Myers, daughter, married a Mr Kintiset, John, Abraham, Martin

(IV) Abraham son of Jacob Sherrick was born in Fayette county, Pennsylvania, about 1810, but in youthful manhood moved to Westmoreland county, settling near Mount Pleasant He followed agriculture all his active life, his farm lying at the head of the hollow just above the Alice Mines in Westmoreland county, Pennsylvania He was a member of the Church of God He married Anna Overholt a descendant of Martin Oberholtzer, born near Frankfort, Germany, 1709, died in Bucks county, Pennsylvania, April 5, 1744, and of Henry, his son, who founded the family in Westmoreland county Children of Abraham Sherrick Jacob, Abraham H, of whom further, John, Anna, died young, Betsey, married Joseph Walters, Susan, married Jacob Stover, Martin O, married (first) Margaret Nicely, (second) Caroline Gongawere

(V) Abraham H, son of Abraham and Anna (Overholt) Sherrick, was born in Westmoreland county, Pennsylvania, March 3, 1832, died February 28, 1892 He was a man of good education and for several years taught in the public schools of his native county After completing his studies at Mount Pleasant Institute he worked on the farm in the summer time, worked in his uncle's store and taught in the winter In 1854 he joined a party of 'gold seekers" and spent three years in California, in search of the precious metal Returning to his native county he worked for a time in the distillery owned by Dillinger & Sons and was otherwise engaged until 1862 when he purchased a farm of eighty acres in Bullskin township, Fayette county, Pennsylvania He improved his property by the erection of needed buildings, and as he prospered added additional acres until he had an estate of three hundred acres He was a breeder of fine horses, making a specialty of Clydesdales, also raising many lighter horses In 1872 he began the erection of coke ovens upon his farm and for many years was a successful coke manufacturer, carrying on this branch of business as Dillinger & Sherrick He was a good business man, active and energetic, consequently prospered abundantly He continued actively engaged in both farming and coke-making until his death He was a Democrat in politics and served in both township and county offices, principally on educational boards, as he was always a firm friend of the public schools His tastes were for the quiet of home, however, and he never sought public office He was held in high esteem in his community and lived a consistent Christian life

He married, in 1852, Mary Dillinger born in Westmoreland county, Pennsylvania, July 9, 1834, daughter of Samuel and Sarah (Louck) Dillinger, and granddaughter of Daniel and Mary Dillinger, who came to Westmoreland county from Bucks county, Pennsylvania, before their marriage Daniel Dillinger was a well-to-do farmer. His children Samuel, father of Mrs Abraham H Sherrick, Elizabeth, Jacob, Joseph, Mary, Sarah, Daniel (2), Abraham, Nancy, died in infancy, Christian, Margaret Samuel Dillinger was born in Westmoreland county, Pennsylvania, October 10, 1810, died August 25, 1889 After his marriage in Fayette county to Sarah Louck, he settled on his farm in East Huntington township, Westmoreland county, where he ever afterward lived He was engaged in other business enterprises of importance and became one of the prominent men of his town Both he and his wife were members of the Church of God Sarah his wife, was a daughter of Peter and Annie (Overholt) Louck, a Mennonite family from Bucks county, Pennsylvania Sarah Dillinger died November, 1898, nine years after her husband's death She was fifth of a family of seven Martin, Jacob, Peter, Henry, Sarah, Catherine and Mary Children of Samuel and Sarah (Louck) Dillinger 1 Annie, married Joseph Hixon a farmer of East Huntington township, where both died 2 Mary (of previous mention) She survives her husband, Abraham H Sherrick, and resides in Pennsville, Pennsylvania, now (1912) aged seventy-eight years, but a most capable and well preserved lady 3 Catherine, married Moses Hixon, a farmer of East Huntington, where both died 4 Sarah married Jacob Fouck, of Greensburg, Pennsylvania, both deceased 5 John a resident of the state of California 6 Elizabeth married Cyrus Hanna and lived in Philadelphia, Pennsylvania, both deceased 7 Eliza, married Albert Hasson, both living, residents of Wilkinsburg, Pennsylvania 8 Daniel now living in Greensburg Pennsylvania 9 Samuel, now living in Baltimore, Maryland Children of Abraham H and Mary (Dillinger) Sherrick 1 Franklin, died aged seven years 2 Samuel, born October 10, 1854, now living at Hendricks, West Virginia, a coke manufacturer, married Sarah Yeutsey, child Ralph D 3 Burton T, of whom further 4 John D, of whom further 5 Sarah Luella, married Edgar J Enos, of Connellsville 6 Carrie, married Charles B Woods, and resides in Philadelphia 7 Charles, deceased 8 Nora, deceased 9 Eliza 10 Mollie, deceased 11 Edwin L, residing in Memphis, Tennessee

(VI) Burton T, third son of Abraham H and Mary (Dillinger) Sherrick, was born near Bethany, Westmoreland county, Pennsylvania, April 27, 1858 He was four years of age when his father settled in Fayette county at Pennsville, where he was educated in the public schools When a boy he worked around the coke works with his father and later learned every feature of the business After the death of his father in 1892 he took charge of the works at Pennsville and managed them until 1907 He associated with his brothers, John D and Samuel Sherrick, in organizing the Keystone Planing Mill Company In 1907 he moved to Connellsville and in 1908 with A A Straub became proprietors and managers of the Smith House and so continues He retains his ownership of the Coke Works, has three hundred and seventy-five acres of undeveloped coal land in West Virginia, is interested in the lumber business in that state and owns the home farm in Fayette county He is an active and capable business man and always on the alert for business opportunity He is a Democrat and for eleven years served as school director at Pennsville His fraternal order is Junior Order of American Mechanics He married (first) October 15 1880, Clara Bell Burkhart, born in Somerset county, Pennsylvania, died 1901 daughter of Jacob and Maria Burkhart He married (second) April 6, 1905, Catherine Stevens, born in Orangeville Wyoming county, New York, daughter of Daniel and Mary Elizabeth (Duscham) Stevens Children of Burton T Sherrick by first wife 1 Laura, (or Lola May) born June 7, 1882, married G P Felty, of Connellsville 2 Earl Cleveland, of whom further 3 Ernest Harrison twin of Earl Cleveland, born July 7, 1884, died aged seven years 4 Mary Bell, born November 7, 1898.

(VI) John D, son of Abraham H and Mary (Dillinger) Sherrick, was born at Old Bethany, Westmoreland county, Pennsylvania, April 19, 1860 He was educated in the public schools, and in early life worked on the farm Later he began working with his father at the coke ovens He became an expert at coke manufacture and continued in that business most successfully until 1908, with his brothers owning and operating Pennsville Coke Works He then went in partnership with his brothers Samuel and Burton T organizing the Keystone Planing Mill Company, of which company he is vice-president In addition to manufacturing the regular lines of planing mill products, the company are general contractors and builders He is also interested in the Pittsburgh Safe Company, and other enterprises of a minor nature He is a Democrat in politics, and a member of the Universalist church

He married, in 1880, Emma Jane, born in Westmoreland county, daughter of Jacob Noel, of Allegheny county, Pennsylvania, of German descent Children Dick, William, Pearl, Homer, Eva, Mabel

(VII) Di Earl Cleveland Sherrick, eldest son of Burton T and Clara Bell (Burkhart) Sherrick, was born in Bullskin township, Fayette county, Pennsylvania, July 7, 1884 He attended the Pennsville public school and then entered Connellsville high school, whence he was graduated, class of 1903 After a course at business college in Connellsville he entered Jefferson Medical College, Philadelphia, whence he was graduated M D, class of 1908 He then served seven months as interne at St Timothy's Hospital, Philadelphia, then for ten months at Jefferson Medical Hospital In 1909 he returned to Connellsville and in 1910 began practice and so continued very successfully While at Jefferson he was a member of the W W Keen Medical Society, and from 1906 to 1908 of Jefferson Medical Research Society

He is a member of the American, Pennsylvania State and Fayette County Medical societies, and of the Yough Medico Social Club of Connellsville

SHERRICK A brother of Abraham Sherrick, grandfather of Franklin N Sherrick of Connellsville was John Sherrick, who on the death of his father Jacob came into possession of the old Sherrick farm at Sherrick's Station and there built the first coke ovens in that region, the coal used being taken from the old Eagle Pit Sherrick's Station was so named from the large coke and coal interests the family owned at that point John Sherrick became a leading merchant and banker of Mt Pleasant Westmoreland county

(V) Martin O, grandson of Jacob and son of Abraham Sherrick, was born near Mt Pleasant, Westmoreland county, Pennsylvania, February, 1840 He attended the public schools and became a farmer About 1868 he went to Kansas, where he remained four years On his return to Pennsylvania he located at Tarr Station, in Westmoreland county, where he is yet engaged in farming and teaming, and yet resides there He is a Republican, and a member of the Church of God He married (first) Margaret Nicely, born in the Ligonier Valley, Pennsylvania, near Four Mile Run, in 1844, died 1884 When she was eight months old her father was killed by a falling timber at a barn raising He married (second) Caroline Gongawere Children of Martin O Sherrick and his first wife 1 Curtis Abraham, now living at Carnegie, Pennsylvania 2 Franklin N, of whom further 3 Harry, died February, 1911

(VI) Franklin N, second son of Martin O and Margaret (Nicely) Sherrick, was born near Mt Pleasant, Westmoreland county, Pennsylvania, November 4, 1865 He was three years of age when his parents moved to Kansas, and seven when they returned to Tarr Station, Pennsylvania He attended the old Bethany public school, and while yet a growing boy worked around the coke ovens Afterward he worked while a youth driving a mule in the coal mines attending school during the winter months In 1883, 1884 and 1885 he attended Mt Pleasant Academy In the spring of 1885 he entered Duff's Business College in Pittsburgh, taking a full course and graduating His mother died in 1884 and the home was broken up After leaving business college he went to Maryland, working in a lumber camp In the winter of 1886 he again worked in the mines, but a strike was called and he was one of the strikers He then went to Toronto, Canada, and took a two years course in Ontario Veterinary College, whence he was graduated in 1888 On January 1, 1889, he came to Connellsville and began veterinary practice He has established a good business and has been continuously in practice among the stock and horse owners of the county In the winter of 1903 he took a post-graduate course at Chicago Veterinary College He is a reliable practitioner, understands the horse and his deseases, and has the confidence of the owners who keep him constantly engaged He is a Republican in politics but takes little interest in public affairs beyond exercising his duties as a good citizen

He married, May 3, 1894, a widow, Mrs Mary E (Shaw) Turley, born in Connellsville daughter of George Washington and Ellen (Cunningham) Shaw, of Connellsville Children Ellen, born December 21, 1894, George Dewey, August 2, 1897

The Pierce family is of ancient PIERCE English origin, and the name is spelled in various ways The first, Thomas of Charlestown, spelled his name Pierce, Peirce and Perice Older spellings included Pers, Perss, Parrs and many other forms The arms of the family are Three ravens rising sable, fesse, numette, crest, dove with olive branch in beak, motto, Dirit et Fecit

(I) Thomas Pierce, the immigrant ancestor, was born in England in 1583-4 died October 7, 1666 He came to New England in 1634 with his wife Elizabeth, who was born in England in 1595-6 and settled in Charlestown, Massachusetts He was admitted a freeman May 6, 1635, was one of the twenty-one commissioners appointed September 27, 1642, 'to see that salt peter heaps were made by farmers of the colony" He moved to Woburn and was a proprietor there in 1643, and elected to town offices He made his will November 7, 1665, when aged about eighty-two years, bequeathing to wife Elizabeth, grandchildren Mary

Bridge and Elizabeth Tufts, "now dwelling with him", to all grandchildren, to Harvard College The widow deposed to inventory March 22, 1666-7, aged seventy-one years Children John, mariner, admitted to church at Charlestown, 1652, Samuel, married Mary ——, Thomas, mentioned below, Robert, married February 18, 1657, Sarah Ayre, Mary, married Peter Tufts, Elizabeth, married (first) —— Randall, (second) —— Nicholls, Persis, married (first) William Bridge, (second) John Harrison, Abigail, born June 17, 1639

(II) Thomas (2), son of Thomas (1) Pierce, was born in England in 1608 He lived in Charlestown, in the part now Woburn, and was called sergeant in the records He was the progenitor of President Franklin Pierce Sergeant Thomas Pierce was admitted to the Charlestown church, February 21, 1634 He was an inhabitant of Woburn as early as 1643 In 1660 he was selectman, and served on the committee to divide common lands He was one of the "Right Proprietors" elected March 28, 1667, and also on the committee appointed by the general court in 1668 to divide lands, etc He married, May 6, 1635, Elizabeth Cole, who died March 5, 1688 He died November 6 1683 Children Abigail, born August 17, 1639, John, born March 7, 1643, Thomas, mentioned below, Elizabeth, December 25, 1646, Joseph, September 22, 1648, died February 27, 1649, Stephen, July 16 1651, Samuel, February 20, 1654, died October 27, 1655, Samuel, April 7, 1656, William, March 20, 1658, James, May 7, 1659, Abigail, November 20, 1660, Benjamin, married Mary Reed

(III) Thomas (3), son of Sergeant Thomas (2) Pierce, was born June 21, 1645, died December 8, 1717 He lived in Woburn His will was dated November 26, 1717, and in it he mentioned his children, Timothy, Rachel and Abigail, and children of his son Thomas He married (first) Eliza ——, (second) March 24, 1680, Rachel Bacon, who was born June 4, 1652 Children, born in Woburn Thomas, born February 12, 1670, Timothy, mentioned below, Elizabeth, born January 5, 1676, died February 15, 1699, Rachel, July 24 1681, Abigail, April 14, 1685, Isaac, December 23, 1686, died December 28, 1686, Ebenezer, December 10, 1687, died May 25, 1688, Phebe, February 13, 1689, died July 12, 1707

(IV) Timothy, son of Thomas (3) Pierce, was born at Woburn, January 25, 1673, and died May 25, 1748 He lived at Plainfield, Connecticut His will was dated April 12, 1748 He was one of the most prominent men in Plainfield, and served as judge of probate, colonel of the militia, and member of the governor's council In his will he mentioned Mary Pierce, his daughter-in-law, his grandchildren, sons of his son Timothy, his son Nathaniel, daughter Phebe Smith, the two children of his granddaughter Lydia Cortland, son Ezekiel, who was executor He had a negro girl Dinah whom he left to daughter Phebe Smith He married (first), May 27, 1696, Lydia Spaulding, who died March 23, 1705 (second), October 12, 1709, Hannah Bradhurst, born December 14, 1682, died April 2, 1747 Children Timothy Jr, mentioned below, Nathaniel, born June 3, 1701, Jedediah, February 23, 1703, died February 21, 1746, Lydia, March 10, 1705, Benjamin, June 7, 1710, Ezekiel, January 8, 1712, Phebe, February 19, 1714, Hannah, May 8, 1717, died September 3 1727, Abel, June 17, 1720, died September 4, 1736, Jabez, married Susanna Sheppard

(V) Timothy (2), son of Timothy (1) Pierce, was born October 7, 1698 He lived in Plainfield, Connecticut, and died before 1761 He married, June 12, 1723, Mary Wheeler Children Lydia, born November 1, 1724, Mary, November 15, 1728, Hannah, September 8, 1730, Phebe, May 27, 1732, Timothy (3), May 22, 1734, Azel, Josiah, mentioned below, Sarah, married, December 26, 1768, Squire Sheppard

(VI) Josiah, son of Timothy (2) Pierce, was born in 1745 died August 1, 1805 He married Lydia Sheppard Children Job, mentioned below, Azel, June 26, 1773, Polly, April 1, 1775 Josiah, July 21, 1777, Sheppard, April 29 1780, Lydia, July 23, 1782, Chester, November 25, 1785, died 1799, Dolly, March, 1788, Augustus, September, 1790

(VII) Job, son of Josiah Pierce, was born March 22 1770, and died in 1827 He lived in Caledonia, New York He married (first)

Jerusha Mery, who was born in April, 1780, died May 6, 1802, (second) Mercy Stevens Children, probably not in order of birth Sheppard, married Mary E Pitkin, Dolly, William, mentioned below, Joseph S, born April 22, 1802, Richard, Edward James, Job C Caroline, married —— Moss

(VIII) William, son of Job Pierce, was born about 1800, probably at Caledonia, New York He settled in Jefferson county, Pennsylvania Children James, mentioned below, Joshua, a farmer in the Pierce settlement on the border of Jefferson and Indiana counties, Pennsylvania, daughter, married William Odell and lives at Mahaffey's Station, Clearfield county, Pennsylvania

(IX) James, son of William Pierce was born probably in Jefferson county, Pennsylvania He married Sarah Ann, born about 1834, died in 1900, daughter of Philip Harold, a farmer of German ancestry, of Jefferson county Children of Philip Harold John, lived near the old homestead in Jefferson county and followed farming, Sarah Ann, mentioned above, Mary (Harold) Blystone, lived at Green Oak, Indiana county, Pennsylvania, Lavinia lives in Indiana county, Lizzie, married John R Smith, a farmer, and lives near Marion, Indiana county, Philip, lives on the homestead in Jefferson county James Pierce was a salesman, and died in 1865 His children 1 Mary Elizabeth, died young 2 John H, living in Indiana county, a leading lawyer, married Martha Josephine Moore 3 Mary Jane, died unmarried, aged thirty 4 Elliot C, mentioned below 5 Emma Catherine, married William Nepshild, they live at Cochran's Mills, Armstrong county, he is a farmer 6 James R, married Mary Workman, he lives in Ohio, she is deceased

(X) Elliot C, son of James Pierce, was born in Troutville, Clearfield county. Pennsylvania He was bereft by the death of his father when he was but four years old He attended the district schools in Jefferson and Armstrong counties, Pennsylvania, beginning to work at the age of eleven years Two years later he moved to Larwill, Indiana, where he learned the trade of upholsterer When he returned home after three years and a half, he had acquired a trade, contrary to the predictions of the neighbors, who had not expected a thirteen-year-old boy to support himself and make good He took a unique way of learning his trade, starting in business and hiring an upholsterer to work for him, and learning his trade not from an employer but from an employee He worked for a time at Fort Wayne, Indiana, and when he was seventeen returned to Armstrong county, Pennsylvania, where his mother then lived Thence he went to Clearfield, in the same state, and engaged in business on his own account as an upholsterer, traveling from house to house and working in the homes of his customers In 1880 he moved to Lewiston Pennsylvania He was then married and had one child and no capital He entered the employ of McClintock Brothers, dealers in furniture, for a few months, then moved to Sunbury, Pennsylvania, to work at his trade in the furniture store of Mrs Greenough After a few months he had to leave this position on account of an attack of malarial fever and went to Enterton on a visit When able to work he took a position as brakeman on the Pennsylvania Railroad and worked six weeks

In 1881 he moved to Greensburg, Pennsylvania where he started in business with an upholstery shop At that time Brown's drug store was the only store in that town possessing an awning He devoted his attention to making awnings and in 1899 when he left the town he had made more than 1 300 awnings He came to Connellsville and opened an upholstery and awning shop on West Main street in what was then New Haven In 1905 his business had increased to such an extent that he erected a building for his own use In politics he is a Republican He was a councilman of East Greensburg after it was incorporated as a borough He and his wife are members of the Methodist Episcopal church He is a member of the Royal Arcanum and of the Modern Woodmen of America

He married (first) November 12, 1879, Alberta L Smith, who was born in Clearfield county, Pennsylvania daughter of John and Martha Smith, of Clearfield She died February 28, 1890 He married (second) August 14, 1891, Agnes B Zim-

merman, who was born at Greensburg, Pennsylvania, daughter of Samuel Zimmerman Her father was a contractor and builder in Greensburg Child by first wife 1 Thomas V, born April 19, 1881, married, February 1, 1912, Sarah Cooley, they reside at Wilmerding, Pennsylvania, he is in the employ of the Westinghouse Company Children by second wife 2 Martha E, born March 22, 1892 3 John S, October 18, 1893 4 Anna Rebecca, September 24, 1895 5 Grace Ethel, November 23, 1898 6 Robert C, January 3, 1900 7 Harold Francis January 29, 1902 8 Muriel Ellis, March 28, 1904

The Work family, originally of
WORK   England, settled first in Lancaster county, Pennsylvania, after coming to this country The first of whom we have record is Samuel Work, born July 17, 1749, died in 1833 He settled in Fayette county in 1766 and became a landowner of Dunbar township, where in 1799 he was taxed for three hundred and eighty-two acres of land, four horses, four cows and one slave He married and had sons John, born 1787, married in 1814, Nancy Rogers, Andrew, of whom further, and others

(II) Andrew, son of Samuel Work, was born in Dunbar township, Fayette county, Pennsylvania, about 1780, and became a wealthy farmer, owning one thousand acres of land He was a Whig in politics, and a member of Laurel Hill Presbyterian Church, of which his wife and family were also members He married Rebecca Harris Children Joseph, Andrew (2), Oliphant, Jane, Rebecca, Eliza, Samuel, Jacob H, of whom further, Harriet, Nancy, and two who died in infancy

(III) Jacob Harris, son of Andrew and Rebecca (Harris) Work, was born in Dunbar township, Fayette county, Pennsylvania, where he died in 1905, aged eighty-two years He attended the public school and grew to manhood on the home farm Later he inherited a part of the Work estate and continued its cultivation all his life, then passing title to his son Daniel C Work He was a quiet retiring man and took little active part in public affairs He was a

Whig, later a Republican, and was an attendant of the Cumberland Presbyterian Church, of which his wife was a member. He married Sarah Craft, born near Brownsville, Pennsylvania, daughter of 'Daniel and Mary (Radcliff) Craft, a leading Brownsville family. Daniel Craft was a farmer and a landowner, a Whig in politics, and a member of the Cumberland Presbyterian Church. His children: Altheis, Isaiah, Daniel, Mary, Sarah, of previous mention, Caroline, Harriet, and others. Children of Jacob H. and Sarah Work: 1. Daniel C., of whom further. 2. Andrew, now living in Connellsville, a carpenter. 3. Isaiah, died leaving a daughter, Phoebe. 4. Joseph, died without issue. 5. Samuel, lives near Adelaide, Fayette county, a farmer. 6. George, a farmer of Franklin township. 7. An infant, died unnamed. 8. Jacob, resides in Kansas. 9. Alexander, resides with his brother George, unmarried. 10. Caroline, died unmarried. 11. Emily, died unmarried. 12. Sarah Jane, died aged twelve years. 13. Davis, a farmer of Dunbar township.

(IV) Daniel C., eldest son of Jacob Harris and Sarah (Craft) Work, was born April 3, 1841, on the home farm in Dunbar township, on the hill overlooking Leisenring No. 1, in the same house that is now his home. With the exception of three years spent in Franklin township, this farm has always been his home. He was educated in the public school, grew up his father's assistant, later became manager. After his marriage he farmed in Franklin township for three years, then when his father also moved to Franklin he returned to the home farm, and after the death of the father purchased the interest of the other heirs and became sole owner. He yet retains ninety-six acres of the old farm on which he resides and conducts a general farming business. He is a Democrat in politics and has served as tax collector and road supervisor. He is a Knight of Pythias, and an attendant of the Methodist Episcopal church, his wife being a member.

He married (first), in 1865, Sarah Jane Fleming, born in Ohio, died in 1892. He married (second) Mrs. Melvina Barnhart, daughter of Alexander and Margaret Hager. Children of first wife: 1. Ewing, married

Flora Aspinwall, died and left six children. 2. Albert, married Nancy McIlvaine. 3. Orton, resides in Kansas, unmarried. 4. William, resides in Columbus, Ohio, with wife and two children. 5. Daniel, now residing at home unmarried.

RALSTON

This family, represented in Masontown by Patrick H. Ralston, came to Fayette county from Canada, where original settlement was made by Hugh Ralston, born in Scotland. The grand sire, Hugh Ralston, was a farmer near Edinburgh, his native city. He married and left male issue.

(II) Hugh (2), son of Hugh (1) Ralston, was born in Edinburgh, Scotland, one of six children. He was educated in the common schools, continuing his studies until he was fourteen years of age. He then came with a party of his countrymen to Canada, settling at Bristol. He there drifted into railroad employ and became a well-known division superintendent of the New York Central railroad. He died in Bristol, aged eighty-four years. He was a conservative in Canadian politics, and a member of the Presbyterian church. He married Margaret Fitzsimmons, born in county Cavan, Ireland, died in Bristol, Canada, aged seventy-eight years, daughter of Patrick Fitzsimmons, a farmer of Bristol, Canada. Children: Hugh (3), married Ellen Tulahan, and lives in Bristol, Canada; John W., married Fanny McGrath, and lives in Connellsville, Pennsylvania; Rachel, married John Ray, and lives in Bristol; Mary Jane, married James A. McLean, and resides in Toronto, Canada; Patrick H., of whom further.

(III) Patrick H., son of Hugh (2) and Margaret (Fitzsimmons) Ralston, was born in Bristol, Province of Ontario, Canada, June 5, 1868. He was educated in the public schools of Hudson, New York, and began business life as a clerk in a mercantile house in Hudson, later he came to Fayette county, Pennsylvania, entering the employ of the H. C. Frick Coke Company as bookkeeper at their works at Trotter. He was also stationed at the West Leisenring works, continuing in that employ several years. In 1903 he came to Masontown, where he is now secretary and general manager of the

Masontown Brewing Company He is a member of the Roman Catholic church, the C M B A Benevolent Protective Order of Elks, and is past dictator of the Order of Moose He married, in 1894, Mary Evans, born in England, daughter of John Evans, a miller, and his wife, Matilda Stebbins Of their eight children, three sons are now living in England, Mary in Pennsylvania, and four are deceased The sons are John C, Albert and William Children of Patrick H and Mary Ralston, five born in West Leisenring, and three in Masontown, Pennsylvania, Hugh E, born June 6, 1895, Margaret M, July 18, 1897 Angeline, November 1, 1899 Mary K, January 1, 1901, Eleanor E, July 24, 1903, John J May 5, 1906, Edward March 24, 1909, Patrick H (2), December 25, 1911

CROWLEY The family springs from Michael Crolley, born in Londonderry, Ireland one of a family of eight children, whose parents were residents of the North of Ireland One of the seven sons remained in their native land, six sons and a sister coming to the United States and settling in Western Virginia in 1830 Andrew and Hugh became contractors, and were the principal builders of the Northwestern Turnpike Ambrose later was proprietor of a hotel in Cincinnati, Ohio, John and Dennis became farmers

(I) Michael Crolley, one of the brothers, settling near Parkersburg, in now West Virginia, also became a contractor and, with his brothers, Andrew and Hugh, worked for several years constructing the Northwestern Turnpike through West Virginia Later he engaged in mercantile business, having a store in Ritchie and Pleasants counties, West Virginia He came east to Wheeling in 1846, to purchase goods for his store, and it is thought was attacked by robbers and then thrown in the river He married Jane McQuain, born in Gilmore county, West Virginia, of Scotch parents, sister of Katherine, wife of his brother John Crowley Children 1 John, became superintendent of a narrow-gauge railroad, and died at Bellaire, Ohio, in 1907 married Mary Wheatley, and had Dennis, Charles

and Leola 2 Dennis Matthew, of whom further After the tragic death of her husband, his widow Jane survived him twenty years, dying in 1866

(II) Dennis Matthew, youngest son of Michael and Jane (McQuain) Crolley, was born near Parkersburg, West Virginia, January 29, 1845, one year prior to his father's death His mother died when he was eleven years of age, leaving him to the care of his uncle and aunt, Andrew and Mary Crolley, with whom he lived in Pleasants county, West Virginia, until he reached his eighteenth year He served in the government employ two years, 1864 and 1865 He then came to Connellsville, Pennsylvania, where he entered the employ of the Baltimore & Ohio Railroad Company, becoming an expert in constructing telegraph lines The name Crolley became Crowley on the books of the company, and was so often misspelled by others, that he finally gave up opposing the new spelling and Crowley it has always remained Since 1871 he has been foreman of the telegraph lines for the Baltimore & Ohio, with offices and residence in Connellsville In 1911 he was in charge of batteries on the system He is a member of the old-time Telegraphers' Association and is an active Democrat in politics, having served as councilman for seven years He is a Roman Catholic in religious faith, belonging to the Church of the Immaculate Conception He married Susan Cunningham, born in Connellsville, Pennsylvania, July 17, 1855 daughter of John and Caroline (Sechrist) Cunningham The latter was born in Ohio, in 1831, died in 1883 John Cunningham, born in 1827, is still living, at the age of eighty-five years but for the past ten years has been paralyzed He was engaged in teaming and draying in Connellsville for many years having contracts for the hauling of most of the coal and building sand used in Connellsville He retired from business five years before being incapacitated by paralysis, and now lives at his home at No 1330 West Main street He is a veteran of the civil war, having enlisted and served in a Pennsylvania regiment during the last year of the war He is a son of William Cunningham and Sidney Marietta, the latter born March 24, 1806, daughter of George

Marietta, born June 28, 1780, settling in Connellsville in the year 1800 Caroline, wife of John Cunningham, was a daughter of Henry and Elizabeth (Wilhelm) Sechrist, both of whose parents were born in Germany, came to the United States, settling in Ohio, Henry died in Ohio, his widow Elizabeth came to Fayette county with her family, locating in Dunbar township, where the sons engaged in woolen manufacturing Children of John and Caroline (Sechrist) Cunningham 1 Susan (of previous mention), wife of Dennis M Crowley 2 Charles unmarried, conducts the teaming business in Connellsville established by his father with whom he resides 3 Harry, deceased 4 Albert, deceased, married Mollie Sellers 5 Samuel, unmarried, a teamster, residing at home 6 Wade, married John Haddock, chief of the fire department of Connellsville 7 Lucretia, married Frank Blossom Children of Dennis M and Susan Crowley 1 Hugh, now a resident of Cumberland, Maryland, married Anna Lang 2 Leona, married H E Schenck (q v), cashier of Colonial National Bank of Connellsville 3 John A, member of the firm of Horner & Crowley, shoe dealers, Connellsville, married Augusta Herman, of New York 4 Charles A, of whom further 5 Denton 6 Emma Kate 7 Clifton The latter three are living at home

(III) Charles A, fourth child of Dennis Matthew Crowley, was born in Connellsville, Pennsylvania, January 21, 1888 He was educated in the public school, later attending Gettysburg (Pennsylvania) College for one term He left college and in 1903 began clerking in the shoe store of John Irvins, in Connellsville, later was clerk in the shoe department of the Wright-Metzler Company, and filled the same position with Gorman & Company In 1910 the Horner Crowley Shoe Company was formed, a new store secured on North Pittsburgh street, and after being fully stocked, was opened for business with Mr Crowley in full charge He understands every detail of the retail shoe business, and the firm is having splendid support from the public He is a member of the Christian church (Disciples of Christ) and of the Modern Woodmen of America

He married, September 6, 1910, Nellie Bryner, born in Connellsville, June 27, 1889, daughter of William and Lydia Bryner, of Connellsville, the former an accountant Child Irene, born September 20, 1911

ARISON This family name spelled both Arison and Arisen, was brought to America by an emigrant from Germany, who settled in New Jersey, where he married and reared a family

(II) John Arison, son of the emigrant, was born in New Jersey in 1750, died in Loudoun county, Virginia Prior to 1780 he moved to Loudoun county, Virginia, where he became a large landowner and planter He married Ann Davis and left issue Descendants are found in various parts of Virginia and Pennsylvania The first record of the family is of John (2) Arison

(III) John (2), son of John (1) Arison, was born in Loudoun county, Virginia, in 1780, died in Fayette county Pennsylvania, November 1, 1870 He married young and about 1815 came with his wife, and at least one child, to Fayette county, making the journey by wagon and team, bringing with them such household belongings as could be packed and transported in one wagon They settled on a large tract of land which he owned

He was a cooper by trade, working his farm in connection therewith He was a thrifty, energetic man of quiet tastes and habits devoted to his family and business mingling little in public affairs, but holding some of the local offices He served in the war of 1812 from Virginia He was a Whig, later a Democrat in politics, and a member of the Redstone Baptist church in Franklin township He married September 12, 1812, Catherine Day, born in Loudoun county, Virginia, who at the time of her marriage was aged fifteen years They had a large family, including sons Matthew and William, both of whom further

(IV) Matthew, son of John (2) Arison, was born in Loudoun county, Virginia, March 4, 1814, died in 1897 He was well educated, taught school in German and Franklin townships for twenty-two years He was elected justice of the peace for ten consecutive terms of five years each and served forty-seven years in that office After leaving the schoolroom he purchased a farm on which he resided during his later years He was a deacon of the Baptist church and a faithful Christian worker His wife was also a Baptist He married (first) Alice Gettys, of Allegheny county, Pennsylvania Children 1 John Davis, married (first) Anna Hazen married (second) Amanda Allen 2 Samuel G deceased 3 Hickman, deceased 4 William H, now living at Niagara Falls, New York, with the Carborundum Company Matthew Arison married (second) Margaret Foster, born in Franklin township, Fayette county, November 19, 1836, daughter of Henry and Rebecca Foster, both born in Franklin township; he of English descent Children 5 Enoch A, of whom further 6 Charles T, now living in Dawson, Pennsylvania married (first) Alice Pennington, (second) Della Lindsay 7 James Elmore, now store manager at Colebrook Pennsylvania 8 Jennie 9 Rozanna, married Charles Johns, of Dickerson Run, Pennsylvania 10 Minnie at home

(V) Enoch A, son of Matthew Arison and his second wife Margaret Foster, was born in Franklin township, Fayette county Pennsylvania, February 18, 1869 He received his preparatory education in the public schools, later entering the University of Indiana at Valparaiso, whence he was graduated with the class of 1891 For the next seven years, 1891 to 1898, he taught in the schools of Franklin township, Fayette county In 1898 he entered the employ of the Union Supply Company at their Trotter store, continuing there as clerk for seven years In 1901 he was made manager of the Trotter store In 1906, manager of their store at Adelaide and in 1908, manager of the company store at Leisenring No 1, which position he now holds He is an efficient capable man of business, loyal to his company and careful of the interests of the store patrons He is a Republican and a member of the Baptist church His fraternal order is the Modern Woodmen of America He married, October 14, 1897, Rogua, born in Menallen township, Fayette county, Pennsylvania, in 1881, daughter of Joshua W and Rachel (Sickles) Scott, of

New Salem, Fayette county Her father was formerly a merchant of New Salem, now a farmer Child Mozelle, born April 19, 1900

(IV) William Arison, son of
ARISON John (2) Arison (q v) and Catherine (Day) Arison, was born in Franklin township, Fayette county, Pennsylvania December 20, 1820 died in 1889 He attended the public school, and became a prosperous farmer of the township He was always prominently identified with the affairs of his township, serving as tax collector, assessor, school director, and in other offices He was a Democrat in politics, and a member of the Redstone Baptist church He married, October 27, 1842, Susannah Whetsel, born in Franklin township, Fayette county, daughter of George and Eliza (Jordan) Whetsel, born in Fayette county Children of William Arison 1 Mary Ann, born September 18, 1843, married May 25, 1861, Alexander Johnson, she was an invalid eleven years before her death 2 George W, born January 20, 1846, served three years in the civil war, married December 7, 1865, Bell McDougal 3 Catherine, born April 4, 1847 married, September 20, 1866, George Bradman 4 Elizabeth, September 18, 1848, married, September 20, 1864, Silas Russell 5 Amanda, August 19, 1850, died, married, October 7, 1869, George Shanneyfelt 6 Mahala, June 7, 1852, died, married Martin Pickard 7 Matthew, April 4, 1854, married Anna Mills 8 Campbell B, of whom further 9 Sarah Ellen, May 4 1857, married James Low 10 Dellazona June 6, 1859 married James C Lutz

(V) Campbell B, eighth child of William and Susannah (Whetsel) Arison was born in Franklin township, Fayette county, Pennsylvania September 18, 1856 He was educated in the public schools and until 1883 followed the occupation of a farmer He then learned the carpenter's trade, becoming an expert mechanic and is now a successful and well known contractor and builder of Vanderbilt which has been his home for nearly thirty years He is a Democrat in politics, was appointed in 1880, by the board of county commissioners, tax collector for

E. A. Arison.

Franklin township, reappointed to same office in 1883, and in 1884 collector for Dunbar township, and in 1889 was elected assessor for Dunbar township, serving three years. In 1905 Vanderbilt was incorporated a borough, and Mr Arison was elected a member of the first board of school directors, serving three years, re-elected in 1908, and in 1909 was elected chief burgess, to hold until January 1, 1914. In 1911 he was elected justice of the peace for a term of six years. He is a capable efficient official, and carefully administers the trusts committed to him. He is largely interested in private business investments in his town, owning many residence and business properties. He is a member of the First Presbyterian Church of Vanderbilt, the Independent Order of Odd Fellows, the Knights of Pythias and Knights of the Mystic Chain.

He married, December 21, 1876, Carrie Addis, born October 14, 1856, daughter of Robert and Sarah (Crosier) Addis, and granddaughter of Ever Addis, an early settler of Fayette county. Children of Campbell B and Carrie (Addis) Arison 1 Harry Walter, born February 4, 1878, died February 14, 1880 2 William Robinson, born September 25, 1879, now with Union Supply Company, at Hecla, Pennsylvania, married (first) Mary, daughter of Henry Hoop, children Harold J, Lorna, deceased, and Carrie (After the death of their mother, Harold and Carrie were taken by their grandparents Arison, by whom they were carefully reared and educated) He married (second) Lorna Campbell 3 Grace C, born May 18, 1882, married June 6, 1904, H L Miller child, Lorna Fay 4 Jessie S, born January 28, 1884 5 Clyde Samuel, born August 31, 1886, killed in a railroad accident, January 6, 1907 6 Della May, born March 4, 1890, died April 9, 1891 7 Ray Olin, born December 2, 1893

MORGAN The Morgans of this narrative are of Welsh descent. The founder of the family in Fayette county, David Morgan, was the first of the line to come to America. He was born in Wales, where he grew to manhood, married, and had issue. He became one of the earliest settlers in southwestern Fayette county, and there fought with the forest, the beast and the savage, for the right to exist. He won his fight, saw civilization follow, and ended his days on his cultivated farm surrounded by neighbors and within sound of the church bell. He was a religious man, and one of the founders of Mount Moriah Baptist Church. He died in 1798, aged fifty-four years. Seven or perhaps eight of his ten children were born in Fayette county

(II) Colonel John Morgan, seventh child of David Morgan, the pioneer, was born in Springfield township, Fayette county, Pennsylvania, August 8, 1790. He assisted his father at the farm until as a young man he became an apprentice to the blacksmith's trade, a fellow apprentice with Hon Andrew Stewart. He only followed his trade a few years, then for three or four years became a riverman, flat boating on the Monongahela and Ohio rivers. He then returned to the old homestead, where he remained in the quiet pursuit of agriculture until his death. He served as a private in the war of 1812, but gained his military title of colonel through service in the Pennsylvania militia, being commissioned by Governor William Snyder. When discharged from the army in 1814, he walked one hundred miles to his home, covering the distance in twenty-four hours. He was a Democrat in politics, and in 1843 was elected a member of the house of assembly, serving with such honor that he was re-elected in 1844 and 1845. He was a warm friend of the cause of education, strongly advocating the establishment of public schools, was one of the first school directors elected in Springhill, and held other township offices. He owned a great deal of land, was strong of body, possessed of great powers of endurance, with an abundance of good hard common sense. He was held in high esteem, and was one of those rare characters that leave a deep impress on their day and generation. He married, March 12, 1817, Elizabeth Lyons, of Springhill township. Children 1 William, a farmer, married Sarah Ann Stautz 2 Frank, a farmer, married Amanda Shuff 3 Jackson, a farmer, died unmarried 4 David, of whom further. 5 Lavina, married William

James, a farmer 6 Nancy, married George Beatty, a farmer, now living in Nicholson township 7 Polly, married Daniel Humbert, a farmer

(III) David, son of Colonel John and Elizabeth (Lyons) Morgan, was born in Springhill township, Fayette county, Pennsylvania, in 1825, died there August 1, 1890 He was educated in the public schools, and grew to manhood at the Morgan homestead farm, which he inherited at his father's death By successive purchases he became the owner of nine hundred acres of valuable coal and farm land This he sold, with the exception of two hundred acres which he retained for a home farm He was a Democrat in politics, and held the offices of poor director and justice of the peace He married Caroline Stewart, born in Springhill township, Fayette county, lives in Uniontown (1912) aged eighty years, a daughter of William Stewart, a farmer, died in Springhill township, who married Linnie Johns Children of William Stewart 1 Jackson (deceased), married ———— 2 Alfred married Mary Morris 3 Frank, married Margaret Hall 4 Owen, lives in Smithfield, retired, married Elizabeth Conn 5 Milton, a dentist of New York, married Margaret Abraham 6 Elizabeth (deceased), married William Brown 7 Jennie, married Jacob High 8 Caroline (of previous mention) Children of David and Caroline (Stewart) Morgan 1 Elizabeth, married Robert Higginbotham, a farmer, and lives near Masontown, Pennsylvania, children Linnie, married Howard Berchanal, Catherine, married William Gans, Morgan, a bank clerk in Uniontown 2 Frank, a farmer, married Mollie A Goodwin, and lives in Springhill township, children David, deceased, Benjamin, married Lulu Miller, Thomas, Frank, Emma, married Edward Sisily 3 Lewis, a farmer, married Addie Brown and lives in Smithfield, children Lucy, married ———— Berchanal Charles, Maria, married ———— Hall, Edna, Carrie, Walter, Harry 4 Emma, married George Brown, a farmer, and lives in Uniontown, children Nora, Abraham, George Sally, married William Gans, Catherine 5 E A, of whom further 6 Pleasant

(IV) E A Morgan, son of David and Caroline (Stewart) Morgan, was born in Springhill township, Fayette county, Pennsylvania, October 17, 1865 He was educated in the public schools of the township of his birth, and until attaining his majority was his father's assistant on the farm He later rented the farm and at his father's death inherited it He has since purchased one hundred and nine acres and owns at the present time two hundred and thirty-four acres of the best farming land in that section He is a Democrat in politics

He married, April 17, 1890, Ella Ramsey, born in Nicholson township, Fayette county, Pennsylvania, August 23, 1870, only child of L Dow and Anna (Lyons) Ramsey L Dow Ramsey married (second) Elizabeth Griffith, and lives in Nicholson township Children of L Dow Ramsey Walter, Frank Alice, Dow Children of E A and Ella (Ramsey) Morgan, all living at home George, born May 12, 1892, Earl, April 10, 1894, Helen, August 30, 1895, Anna, July 8, 1897, Andrew, May 23, 1902

HARRIS This branch of the Harris family descends from Scotch, Welsh and French settlement in the United States The Harris family has long been seated in Scotland, and the maternal line, Bolm, is an ancient family of Wales The emigrant ancestor, Joshua Nunn Harris was born in Scotland and grew to manhood in his native land He married there Nancy Bolm, born in Wales and remained in Scotland until 1862, when he came to the United States with his wife and family He settled first in Illinois, where he owned and operated several mill mills He was himself a practical mill sawyer and ran his own mills Later in life he moved to near Logansport, Indiana, where he died Children 1 Winfield, of whom further 2 Louis 3 Joshua Nunn (2), served in the American army during the Spanish war 4 Mary, married John M McLaughlin, and resides in Lafayette, Indiana 5 Anna, married Abraham Harshberger, and resides in Crawfordsville, Indiana 6 Huldah, married Jacob Milligan

(II) Winfield, eldest son of Joshua Nunn and Nancy (Bolm) Harris, was born in

Scotland, June 23 1857 He was five years of age when the family came to the United States, where he was educated in the public schools He learned the carpenter's trade, to which he added that of millwright He worked at his trades as a journeyman for several years, then became a contractor, building many grain elevators and mills in Illinois Later he moved to Indiana, locating at Oxford, where he is now engaged in business He is a Republican in politics, and a member of the Christian church (Disciples of Christ) He married Mary Elizabeth Temple, born in Marseilles, France, January 22 1859, daughter of John and Catherine (Davis) Temple, both born in France but of English descent, their fathers both being engaged in commerce as shipping merchants or exporters of French made goods of various kinds The father of John Temple made several business voyages to the United States and finally died in Ohio Shortly after their marriage John and Catherine Temple came to the United States, bringing their daughter Mary Elizabeth, then an infant of five weeks They came in a sailing vessel and were thirteen weeks on the voyage They settled on a farm near Piqua, Ohio, where John remained several years Later they moved to Indiana, where John Temple owned two farms, one in Cass the other in Carroll county He died in Indiana His widow still survives (1912) aged ninety-nine years Children of John and Catherine Temple Mary Elizabeth (of previous mention), married Winfield Harris, Louis D, Luther C Harriet, married a Mr Loveland, Ella, deceased, married Thomas Byers and lived at Rockfield, Laura, unmarried, resides at the Temple home, and has the care of her very aged mother Children of Winfield and Mary E Harris 1 Minnie, married Joseph Goarnall, a farmer and resides at Oxford, Indiana 2 Harley A, died in infancy 3 Burley Milroy, of whom further 4 Ada Alice, married Elza McVey, a farmer, and resides at Idaville, Indiana 5 Nellie Pearl, married Edward Aldrich, a farmer, now resides at the village of Burnetts Creek, Indiana 6 Daniel Arthur, died aged thirteen years 7 Larry, a hotel proprietor 8 Chloe Irene, married George Blessing, a

farmer, and resides at Otterbien, Indiana 9 Temple died in infancy 10 Alta unmarried

(III) Burley Milroy third child of Winfield and Mary E (Temple) Harris was born in Logansport, Indiana, August 28, 1881 His primary and preparatory education was obtained in the public schools and later entered the University of Indiana, at Valparaiso, whence he was graduated, class of 1902 During the years spent securing his university education, he also taught school in Carroll county, Indiana He was but eleven years of age when he entered the high school fifteen years of age when he was graduated therefrom, and at that same age began teaching school During his senior year at the university he taught classes in psychology and physiology in that institution, being then only twenty years of age The funds for his university course were all provided by himself In 1903 he came to Connellsville, Pennsylvania, where he entered the employ of the Baltimore & Ohio railroad in an humble position in their shops In 1904 was appointed airbrake inspector, then entered the train service as brakeman, continuing until 1908 In that year he entered the service of the Penn Power Company, in the machine department, remaining thirteen months He next joined a bridge building gang working for the Pennsylvania railroad, but after three months began canvassing for the International Correspondence School of Scranton, Pennsylvania, continuing as their representative for nine months In 1910 he entered the employ of the Pittsburgh & Lake Erie railroad as fireman, and in December of that year was appointed night foreman at Dickerson Run, where he still continues He is a Republican in politics

He married, March 12, 1903, Dora Charlotte daughter of Robert and Rebecca Jane (Nicklow) McNeal, of Somerset county, Pennsylvania She was a student at Valparaiso University, where they first met Her only sister Margaret was a school teacher, but is now deceased Her only brother, Robert L McNeal, is a farmer on the old McNeal homestead in Lower Turkeyfoot township, Somerset county The Nicklows and McNeals are old Somerset county families, Rebecca Jane Nicklow being a first cousin of Norman B Ream, the well-known capitalist of Chicago and New York Children of Burley Milroy Harris 1 An infant, died unnamed 2 Burley Milroy (2), born March 27, 1906 3 Dora C, November 5 1908 4 Mary Jennie, September 26, 1911 The family home is at the corner of Snyder and Locust streets, Connellsville, Pennsylvania

This family originally from HERTZOG Germany first settled in Eastern Pennsylvania The first of whom we have record is Andrew Hertzog The family is a prominent one of Fayette county, Pennsylvania

(I) Andrew Hertzog, first of the family to settle in Fayette county, came from Eastern Pennsylvania about 1786 He lived for a time in Lancaster county, where some of his children were born Later he moved to Springhill township Fayette county, where he was a farmer until death

(II) George, son of Andrew Hertzog, was born in Lancaster county, Pennsylvania, February 20, 1776, died in Springhill township, Fayette county, and is buried in the cemetery at Smithfield His early childhood was spent in Lancaster county, his boyhood and mature years in Fayette county He followed his father's trade of gunsmith, and after the death of the latter succeeded to a well established business in Springhill township In that day Indians were numerous and troublesome, every male in the community carrying a weapon, and even the women were taught to shoot with deadly intent He was a man of importance in his section, and a devoted member of Mount Moriah Baptist Church of Smithfield He married and left issue 1 Annie, born June 2, 1798, died August 13, 1839, married Jacob Lyons 2 David, born December 7, 1799, died February 13, 1835, unmarried 3 Catherine, born April 6 1802, died June 15, 1802 4 Andrew, born March 7, 1804, died November 18, 1839 5 John, of whom further

(III) John, son of George Hertzog, was born in Springhill township, Fayette county, Pennsylvania February 11, 1806, died July 24, 1870 He was educated in the public school of Springhill township, continuing at home until he was eighteen years of age, then went to Virginia, where he began learning the tanner's trade He returned to Fayette county after one year, locating in Uniontown, where he served a full apprenticeship of three years, later returning to the old homestead The old log cabin in which he was born was later torn down, and in its stead he erected a more modern home which was known as the Hertzog Home He also built a stone tannery which he operated for ten years, then retired from that business, devoting himself entirely to agriculture He became one of the substantial farmers of his township, and at his death left an estate of two hundred acres that has since been managed by his sons, John A and George He was a member of Mount Moriah Baptist Church, and a Democrat in politics, serving as school director and supervisor He married, March 23, 1843, Margaret Hertzog, born in German township, Fayette county, December 4, 1812, died 1901, daughter of Jacob Hertzog, who was born in German township near the Nicholson township line, and married a Miss Baker His children 1 Andrew, married (first) —— West, (second) Elizabeth Lyons 2 Elizabeth, married Michael Coffman 3 Margaret (of previous mention), married John Hertzog Children of John and Margaret Hertzog 1 Elizabeth, born December 23, 1843 died unmarried 2 George of whom further, 3 John Andrew, born May 14, 1849, in Springhill township, Fayette county, educated in the public schools, now a farmer and stock dealer of his native township He is a Democrat in politics, has served for many years as school director, and is now justice of the peace He married, September 17, 1896, Lucy, daughter of Altha and Mary (Lyons) Gans Their daughter, Lucy Margaret, born March 28, 1904, is the only living grandchild of John and Margaret Hertzog 4 David Morgan, born March 30, 1852 (see sketch) 5 Margaret, died November 10, 1860, aged six years

(IV) George, eldest son of John and Margaret Hertzog, was born in Springhill township, Fayette county, Pennsylvania, October 25, 1846 He was educated in the public schools, and spent his years of minority as his father's assistant in farming, chopping and hauling wood Later he established on his own farm in the same township, and is engaged in dairy farming principally His market is Uniontown, where he disposes of his cream only to the creamery He is a Democrat in politics, has served as school director, and is a member of the Baptist church, his wife of the Christian church (Disciples of Christ)

He married, January 7, 1882, Emma Lyons, born at Morris Cross Roads, Springhill township, March 24, 1853, daughter of John and Clarinda (Litman) Lyons John Lyons was born in Springhill township in the same house in which his father and grandfather were born, and died there January 18, 1890 Clarinda (Litman) Lyons was born in Frogtown in the same township Their children 1 Maria, married Michael Baker, both deceased, children Louisa, John, Lizzie married Thomas Miller, Minnie, Edwin, deceased, Laura Rebecca, married Robert Grove Jesse, Bertha, Helen, and another, died aged two years 2 Rebecca, married Judson Morgan, a farmer, and lives near Gans Station 3 Ann, married Martin Van Buren Scott and resides in Dunbar, Pennsylvania, where he is a blacksmith, children Boyd married Louisa Ache Nellie, married Rev Wilson Winbigler, Ned, married Cora Bear James, married Edna Duncan, John and Lelah 4 Harriet, married Newton Miller, now a farmer of Grundy, Iowa, children Walter and Etta 5 Emma (previous mention), wife of George Hertzog, no issue The mother of these children, Clarinda (Litman) Lyons died at the home farm in Springhill township, aged sixty-three years

HANNAM This family descends from English ancestors on the paternal side and from German forbears on the maternal The English ancestor was born and died in England but lived in America many years founding the family in Baltimore, Maryland

(I) George Hannam born in England, came to the United States at the age of seven years The family settled in Baltimore In later years George Hannam returned to England to claim his inheritance and settle up the English estate He was taken sick and died there about 1838 His wife was of German parentage

(II) William John, son of George Hannam, was born in Baltimore, Maryland, January 27, 1827, died June 9 1883 He was educated in the public schools, and learned the trade of boilermaker and blacksmith He lived in Lancaster Pennsylvania, later in Connellsville, where he was in charge of the Baltimore & Ohio shops from 1866 until 1883, being foreman of both the blacksmith and boilermaking departments He was a Democrat in politics and served as member of the city council of Connellsville He was a member of the English Lutheran church in early life and later became an Episcopalian He was a man of great public spirit and aided materially in the upbuilding of his town He married at Reading, Pennsylvania, in 1854, Matilda Catherine Reinhart of German parentage who died July 12, 1890 They were the parents of eleven children, five of whom are now living (1912) 1 William John (2), now superintendent of the City Iron Works at Erie, Pennsylvania 2 George B, chief boilermaker at the Cleveland, Ohio, shops of the Lake Shore & Michigan Central railroad 3 Mary Belle married J E Miller, of Connellsville 4 Robert Lee of whom further 5 Maud A, married Quincy Sanborn of Cleveland, Ohio

(III) Robert Lee, son of John Hannam was born in Connellsville, Pennsylvania, April 28, 1870 He was educated in the public schools, and when but a boy fourteen years of age began learning the carpenter's trade in the Baltimore & Ohio shops He began working there April 1 1884, and continued until January 1, 1897, then entered the employ of the Connellsville Planing Mill Company where he remained until February 1905 In the latter year he was one of the organizers of the Keystone Planing Mill Company, of which he has been secretary and manager since its incorporation He is a Republican in politics and a member of the Lutheran church He married, October 20, 1891, Mary Ada daughter of William A Artis, who was born in 1846, enlisted in the civil war, serving in Company H One

Hundred and Forty-second Regiment Pennsylvania Volunteer Infantry, receiving a severe wound at the battle of Gettysburg, he married Theresa Sampsell, of Uniontown, Pennsylvania Children of Robert Lee and Mary Ada Hannam Ida Mae, born November 25, 1892, Robert William, born September 5, 1901

GIBSON Daniel Phillips Gibson was a prominent banker and real estate owner of Uniontown He was born on a farm in Fayette county, Pennsylvania, April 20, 1827, and died May, 1910, in Uniontown He attended the common schools, but also was indefatigable in his efforts to acquire knowledge by extra study during his hours at home At the age of sixteen years he apprenticed himself to learn the harness and saddlery trade at Petersburg, Somerset county, Pennsylvania, with John Morrow, with whom he remained a little over five years On attaining his majority he located at Upper Middletown, and was engaged in the harness and saddlery business from 1848 to 1876, a period of twenty-eight years In this town he was very successful, building up a large business, and acquiring the reputation which he justly deserved of an honest and reliable business man He removed to Uniontown in 1876, choosing it as the center for a wider field of operations, and his subsequent career attested the wisdom of his selection Besides his regular line of work, he began in 1876 to handle buggies, and visited the factories, inspected the materials, and examined the process of construction from its earliest stages, thus securing himself and his customers from imposition in the quality of the goods which he put upon the market Mr Gibson also engaged in farming and was in the general mercantile business, and beginning about 1862, for seventeen years he conducted two general stores, one at Upper Middletown the other at Searights After establishing himself at Uniontown he started also a grocery and hardware store but on account of his ill health this was sold in 1881 In every field, success marked his ventures, and the wealth thus acquired was applied in the purchase of valuable property in Osceola, Clark county, Iowa, as well as a large amount of improved real estate in Uniontown in the shape of houses and city lots that returned a handsome rental Mr Gibson was noted for his good judgment, and plain, shrewd conduct of business affairs He lost no chances, missed no opportunities, made no rash ventures or wild speculations, and was satisfied with small but certain profits He is spoken of truly as one of Fayette county's most successful business men He was a valued member of the Independent Order of Odd Fellows, the Masonic order, and of the Great Bethel Baptist Church, of which he was a trustee for many years He was also one of the oldest directors of the First National Bank of Uniontown, being one of the original stockholders and founders

The parents of Daniel Phillips Gibson were Joseph and Rachel (Phillips) Gibson Joseph Gibson was born in Fayette county, Pennsylvania, about 1780, son of John Gibson, a native of Ireland He spent his life as a farmer, and died in 1830, aged fifty years Rachel Phillips was a daughter of Benjamin Phillips, a farmer of New Jersey, where his daughter was born, who moved to Pennsylvania when she was quite young Daniel Phillips Gibson, in 1874, married Hannah Jane, daughter of William Brown, a well known and prominent Fayette county farmer Their only child was Della Pearl, who married Frank Eugene Merts, on November 1, 1905 Born to them, August 30, 1908, a daughter, named Donna Gibson Merts, the only grandchild of Daniel Phillip Gibson

GALIARDI The first of this family to leave their own beautiful Italy and come to the United States was Rimonti Galiardi, born in Northern Italy He is a grandson of Rimonti (whose name he bears), Reijina Galiardi, whose lives were spent in their native land Their son Philip was born in 1825 In 1848 he was a soldier of Italy Residing in the north where timber was plentiful, he followed the occupation of wood chopper and from his earnings supported wife and children, four of whom lived and died in Italy three coming to the United States, one Gudita, after coming, returned to her

D. P. Gibson

native Italy The other two, Rimonti (2) and Constantine, died in the United States Philip Galiardi died in Italy in 1889 His wife, Louise Galiardi (a relative before marriage), born 1831, died in the land of her birth in 1904 The family were all devout members of the Roman Catholic church

(III) Rimonti (2), son of Philip and Louise Galiardi, was born in Northern Italy, March 5, 1853 He was educated in the local schools, early began working at that trade at which the Italian excels, stone cutting He served two months in the Italian army, but was not engaged in actual warfare In 1878 he married, and in 1882, lured by the knowledge of better conditions across the seas, left the home of his ancestors to begin a new life in a new world He arrived in New York City, April 17, 1882, was for a time in Buffalo finally locating in Punxsutawney, Jefferson county, where he worked at his trade with little intermission until the winter of 1886, when he returned to Italy He had so prospered in the United States that he determined to settle permanently and become a citizen Accordingly he settled all his affairs in Italy, and with his wife and son Philip came again to Punxsutawney, where he resumed work at his trade, continuing until 1889, when he made permanent settlement at Connellsville, Pennsylvania, his present residence He secured employment at his trade as a journeyman stonemason, but in 1893 began taking contracts He has been very successful in his building operations, has done a great deal of coke oven work for the H C Frick Coke Company, and a great deal of concrete work, etc He made a second return to his native land in 1900 visiting friends and relatives In 1891 he became a naturalized citizen of the United States, and has exercised the franchise thus acquired in support of the Republican party He is a member of the Roman Catholic church of Connellsville, and of the Columbus Independent Italian Club

He married, January 8, 1878, Rosa Caretti, whose parents, Joseph and Theresa (Battacecti) Caretti, lived and died in Italy In 1906 Mr Galiardi erected a modern comfortable residence at No 279 Fairview street, where he now lives Children 1

Philip, born in Italy, November 1, 1881, now associated in business with his father, he married his second cousin, Rosa Galiardi, and has Lorretta, born June 28, 1908, Magdalena, born September 21, 1910 2 Joseph, born in Punxsutawney, Pennsylvania, September 15, 1887, now working with his father 3 Louis, born in Connellsville, Pennsylvania, February 17, 1892 Two other children died in infancy

---

Samuel Angle born in Somerset county Pennsylvania, of German parents, settled when a young man in Morgan county, Ohio He followed agriculture as a business all his life, married, and left issue

(II) Henry C, son of Samuel Angle, was born in Morgan county, Ohio, July 13, 1851 He was educated in the public school, grew to manhood on the farm, and is now a prosperous merchant of Glouster, Ohio He is a Republican, and a member of the Christian church (Disciples of Christ) He married (first) Mary Kasler, born in Morgan county, Ohio, died 1888, daughter of Abraham and Mary Kasler, born in Morgan county, of German parentage He married (second) Mary C Leffler Children of Henry C Angle, by his first wife 1 Ida, married L C Vest, of Bishopville, Ohio 2 Dora, deceased 3 Clara, married Elza Morris, of Glouster Ohio 4 John, now living at Johnstown Pennsylvania 5 Joseph E, of whom further 6 Burt R, now living in Glouster, Ohio 7 Mont, now living in Glouster, Ohio 8 Frank, now living in Corning, Ohio

(III) Joseph E, son of Henry C Angle, was born at Glouster Ohio January 23, 1882 His mother died when he was six years old, and from then until he was thirteen years of age he attended the public schools He then began working for a plumber and gas fitter, with whom he learned a great deal of the business After two and a half years with his first employer he entered the employ of the Corning (Ohio) Natural Gas Company, being but a boy he was made tool carrier at first, and gradually advanced He remained at Corning until 1901 then came to Connellsville, where he entered the employ of the Fayette

County Gas Company as meter reader and in charge of portions of the line work, but was soon promoted foreman of the Connellsville division In 1907 he was transferred to Johnstown, Pennsylvania, to the employ of the Johnstown Fuel and Supply Company (a subsidiary company) and was made superintendent of construction of a new plant being erected in Johnstown There were changes of ownership which resulted in Mr Angle's appointment as superintendent of the artificial and natural gas departments of the Johnstown plant On February 1, 1911, he returned to the Fayette Gas Company as assistant superintendent at Connellsville, and is now (1912) superintendent of the entire system, which conveys gas in sixteen cities in Fayette, Green and Westmoreland counties He is eminently qualified for his position having learned the business from the very bottom as a boy, and has made gas his life study He is a member of the Progressive Brethren Church the Independent Order of Odd Fellows of Johnstown, Pennsylvania, Knights of the Maccabees of Connellsville, and affiliates with the Democratic party

He married, July 3, 1903, Margaret J Bittner born in Fayette county, daughter of Annanias and Barbara Bittner, of Bullskin township Annanias Bittner is a veteran of the civil war, serving in a Pittsburgh company and regiment Children of Joseph E and Margaret Angle Frank B, born April 8 1904, Belford, October 27, 1905, Margaret, March 30, 1911

The Kerchners descend
KERCHNER from German ancestors who on coming to Pennsylvania settled in Berks county The first of record was William Kerchner, a farmer of Berks county, son of the emigrant from Germany, and a native born son of Berks He married Mary Lint also born in Berks county and of German parentage

(II) James W, son of William Kerchner, was born in Berks county, Pennsylvania, in 1855 He was educated in the public schools and learned the painting trade He located in Reading, Pennsylvania about 1887, where he is engaged in contracting, painting, paper hanging and interior decorating He is a Democrat in politics, and a member of the

Lutheran church He married Emma, born in Berks county, in 1855, daughter of William Sollenberger, born in Pennsylvania, of German parentage He was a teacher in the public schools, married Sarah —— also of German parentage, but born in Pennsylvania Children of James W and Emma Kerchner 1 Warren B, died in infancy 2 Morris B, now living in Reading, Pennsylvania, a linotype operator 3 Lenus Sollenberger, of whom further 4 Mahlon S, a linotype operator, of Reading, Pennsylvania 5 William J, clerk in the Pennsylvania Railroad office at Reading 6 Robert, a student 7 Mary S, a bookkeeper, living at home 8 Lizzie, residing at home

(III) Lenus Sollenberger son of James W Kerchner, was born in Berks county, Pennsylvania, August 27, 1880 He was about six years of age when his parents moved to Reading, where he was educated in the public school After completing his school years he began business life as an employee of the Reading Iron Company, in their laboratory, continuing there two years In 1899 he came to Dunbar, Fayette county, as assistant chemist with the Dunbar Furnace Company In 1901 he was advanced to the position of chief chemist, continuing five years In 1906 he was appointed assistant superintendent which position he now holds He has private business interests, including a directorship of the Dunbar Coal Company He is a member of the Masonic order belonging to Lodge Chapter and Commandery, also a member of the Modern Woodmen of America In religious faith he is a Lutheran, and in politics is a Republican

He married, September 11, 1902, Teresa May born at Dunbar, Pennsylvania, June 21, 1882 daughter of Louis and Josephine Baer, of Dunbar, the former now living retired Children James Harold, born June 16, 1903, Lenus (2), born May 6, 1907, died December 4, 1907

The Titus family originally set-
TITUS tled in Greene county, Pennsylvania, where Benjamin F Titus was born and grew to manhood In 1873 he moved to the state of Texas, where he followed his profession of civil engineer in the employ of a southern railroad, he mak-

ing his home at San Antonio In 1887 he returned north and is residing at Point Marion, Pennsylvania He is a Democrat in politics, has always been locally active in public affairs, filling many of the town offices He is a member of the Masonic Order, and a member of the Disciples of Christ Church, as is his wife He married Jennie M Sadler, born in Fayette county, Pennsylvania Children 1 Moses F, a resident of Point Marion, Pennsylvania 2 Charles L, of whom further 3 Montie Lee, secretary of the Morris Glass Company of Point Marion 4 Binnie Leo, a master plumber of Point Marion 5 Garrett Sadler, a master plumber of Point Marion 6 Bertie Cotulla, married Thomas Richmond 7 Delphus Denver, a master plumber of Point Marion

(II) Charles L son of Benjamin F and Jennie M (Sadler) Titus, was born in Wiley, Greene county, Pennsylvania, April 9, 1871 He was educated in the public schools of San Antonio, Texas, and of Point Marion, Pennsylvania He later completed a course in plumbing, heating and ventilation with the Scranton School of Correspondence, after learning the trade practically he established a plumbing business in Uniontown, in 1897 He has been very successful and still continues in active business, being also interested in other enterprises of profit He is a member of the State Plumbers' Association of Pennsylvania and in 1909-10 was president of that body, now (1912) state vice-president of the National Association of Master Plumbers, and a member of the board of directors He organized the Southwestern Plumbers' Association, comprising the territory of Southwestern Pennsylvania, a portion of Maryland and Western West Virginia, serving the latter organization as secretary He has been identified with the Uniontown fire department for many years, president of the Hook and Ladder Company since its organization in 1901, and is assistant chief of the present fire department He was a promoter of the newsboys' annual supper in 1909, which has become a permanent feature of city philanthropic work He is president of the Uniontown committee of safety, and a Democrat, always actively interested in city affairs He is a member of the Ma-

sonic Order, belonging to Uniontown Lodge of Perfection, fourteenth degree, and Pittsburgh Consistory, thirty-second degree, Ancient Accepted Scottish Rite He is past grand of Uniontown Lodge Independent Order of Odd Fellows, and member of the State Grand Lodge In religious faith he is a member of the Central Christian Church, and with his family active in church and Sunday school work

He married, December 25 1896 Birdie, daughter of Elisha and Bessie (Franks) Snider, of Point Marion, Pennsylvania Child Harry Ward, born in Uniontown, January 18, 1899

The Hibbs family, originally HIBBS from England, settled in Fayette county, Pennsylvania, at an early day The earliest record found is of David Hibbs, whose line follows

(I) David Hibbs was born July 18, 1809, on the old homestead near New Salem, Menallen township, Fayette county, Pennsylvania, died May 18, 1868 He here engaged in general farming and did an extensive business in live stock, which he raised and sold, and if the opportunity offered when he could do so to advantage, he bought He was an elder of the German Baptist church, and in politics a Democrat He married, April 18, 1839, Hannah Walters, born in Masontown, daughter of Ephraim Walters Children 1 Jefferson Walters, of whom further 2 Mary, married Joseph Antram and lives in Uniontown, Pennsylvania 3 Harriet, married John Hess and lives in Uniontown, Pennsylvania 4 Lucetta, married Douglas Ammoris and lives in Waynesburg, Pennsylvania 5 George L died 1907 6 John Gibson, lives in Uniontown, Pennsylvania

(II) Jefferson Walters, son of David and Hannah (Walters) Hibbs, was born on the old homestead near New Salem, Menallen township Fayette county, Pennsylvania, January 1, 1837, died 1907 He attended the local schools, finishing his education at Dunlap Creek Academy He was a farmer all his life and owned two hundred acres of land in Luzerne township, one hundred and seven acres in Redstone township on which he engaged in general farming and raised much live stock and cattle, specializing in the production of wool and succeeding in obtaining a very fine grade He was a Democrat in politics and held several township offices, among them those of school director and township auditor He was a member of the Dunlap Creek Presbyterian Church He married, in 1867, Ellen Abigail, daughter of Theodore Vankirk Children Lula Edna, married Chads Chalfant and lives in Uniontown, Pennsylvania 2 Theodore Vankirk, of whom further

(III) Theodore Vankirk, son of Jefferson Walters and Ellen Abigail (Vankirk) Hibbs, was born at the home of his fathers in Redstone township, Fayette county, Pennsylvania December 12, 1873 His education was obtained in the public schools of Luzerne township where his parents moved when he was young, in the Brownsville public schools and at the Streter high school, Illinois, where he was graduated from the commercial department, class of 1892 He was engaged in farming with his father until the latter's death, when he inherited the home farm on which he now conducts general farming, sheep and cattle raising He is financially although not actively interested in coal lands in various portions of the state A very successful venture, which he has lately inaugurated, is the raising of fruit in Florida He spends his winters in the south and gives his orchards his personal attention growing some of the best oranges and grape fruit produced in that wonderfully rich and fertile section These he ships to Pittsburgh and the other northern markets, where during our cold season they are sold for almost fabulous prices He is a member of the Dunlap Creek Presbyterian Church, and a Democrat in politics

He married in 1899, Mary B English, born in Jefferson township, December 1, 1873, daughter of Di English, a prominent physician of Jefferson township

---

JACKSON-CURRY These families joined by marriage spring one from an English the other from an Irish ancestor The Jackson progenitor came from Ireland and settled in Fulton county, Pennsyl-

vania, where he died leaving a widow and son

(II) Mark Jeremiah Jackson, son of the emigrant from Ireland, was born in Fulton county, Pennsylvania, December 26, 1835, died in Bedford county November 3, 1893 His mother survived his father, married a second husband, and went west, never again returning The lad was then left to his own resources at quite an early age He was bound out to a miller at Ackersville, in Fulton county, who taught him the miller's trade, an occupation he followed all his life with the exception of the three years spent in the Union army during the civil war, serving in the cavalry under General Phil Sheridan After the war he returned to Fulton county, later moving with his family to Bedford county, where he settled at what was known as Jackson's Mills He erected a mill which he operated until his death in 1893 He was a well-known influential man, a Republican, and once the candidate of the party for the state legislature He was a member of the Methodist Episcopal church, the Independent Order of Odd Fellows, and the Grand Army of the Republic

He married Emily Jane Hickson, died at Connellsville, Pennsylvania, January 12, 1909, daughter of Ephraim and Cecil Hickson both born in Fulton county, Pennsylvania Ephraim Hickson was a farmer and a blacksmith His children Emily Jane, of previous mention, Mary, Matilda, Nancy, Joshua, Caleb, Nathan, Jared, Amos, all are deceased except Mary, Nancy and Jared Children of Mark J and Emily J Jackson 1 Edward Vincent, born March 11, 1858, died 1887, unmarried, always remained at home 2 John Upton, born August 9, 1859, now of Everett, Pennsylvania 3 Laura, born April 24 1861, deceased, married William B Cairns 4 Minnie, born November 1 1862, married Charles M Leisinger 5 Harry Sheridan, born July 11 1866 6 Cora, born February 9, 1870, deceased married B F Swartzwelder 7 Matilda (Tillie), born July 15, 1872, died in infancy 8 Charles W, born December 25, 1874 9 George Chester, born October 14, 1878, deceased 10 Frank Stanley, twin of George C

(III) Frank Stanley, son of Mark Jeremiah Jackson, was born at Jackson's Mills, Bedford county, Pennsylvania, October 14, 1878 He educated in the public school, and attended Dickinson Seminary at Williamsport, Pennsylvania, for one and a half years He was taught the miller's trade under the direction of his father, with whom he worked until the latter s death in 1893 He continued milling until 1900, when he moved to Connellsville, Pennsylvania, entering the employ of the Connellsville Grocery Company, remaining five years He then engaged for several years as commercial traveler until October, 1911, when he was appointed manager of the newly established grocery department of Wright-Metzler Company, of Connellsville, a position he now holds He is a Republican, a member of the Methodist Episcopal church, and of the Free and Accepted Masons He married, July 18, 1905, Anna M Curry, who died July 31, 1911 (see Curry)

(The Curry Line)

(I) The paternal great-grandfather of Anna M (Curry) Jackson was Samuel Curry, a farmer of England, who lived and died in his native land He and wife Betsey were members of the Church of England Their five children all died in England Samuel, of whom further, John, Mary, Jens (?), and another died in infancy

(II) Samuel (2), son of Samuel (1) and Betsey Curry, was born at Coal Borns England, where he followed farming all his life, renting land from large estates held by the English gentry He died in 1858 He married, in 1844, a daughter of William and Sarah Fallows who survived and married a second husband William Fallows was a miner His children William, John, Thomas, Peter, Sarah, Helen, Alice and Janis, are all deceased except Sarah and Peter Children of Samuel (2) Curry John, of whom further, James, died in England, Samuel, William, Ralph, died in infancy, Thomas, Ralph, of Mount Pleasant, Westmoreland county, Pennsylvania Three of these are living in England, William, Thomas and Samuel

(III) John eldest son of Samuel (2) Curry, was born in Priestfield county, Durham, England, in October, 1845 He was given little opportunity to obtain an education, only being allowed four terms of three months each He was hired out when but a small boy to neighboring farmers, sometimes for six months or more On the death of his father in 1858 he was thrown entirely upon his own resources, being then a lad of thirteen years He worked among the farmers for a few years, then employed with a cattle dealer and butcher who taught him that trade He continued working at the butcher business until after his marriage several years, having in the meantime established in business for himself In 1877 he became manager of a farm, and in June, 1879, came to America with wife and five children He first settled in the province of Ontario, Canada, nine miles north of Toronto, hiring out to a farmer in summer, and in winter moving to Toronto and working at whatever employment he could secure Two years later he came to Pennsylvania, settling at Mount Pleasant, Westmoreland county, where he worked in the coal mines for a short time He was badly burned in a gas explosion and was obliged to abandon mining He worked for two years at the coke ovens in Bridgeport, then purchased a farm of three hundred and eighty-nine acres near Indian Creek, Fayette county, which he cultivated and greatly improved He continued there for eight years He had considerable timber on his tract which he converted into lumber, and after losing an arm gradually abandoned agriculture and devoted himself entirely to the lumber business He moved to Hammondville, built a residence, and for three years engaged in the lumber trade, thence came to Connellsville and continued there in the same business until 1905, when he organized the Curry and Bittner Lumber Company, of which he is yet secretary and treasurer In 1910, in association with his son, John C Curry, he formed the lumber firm of John Curry & Son, which is one of the successful firms of Connellsville In political faith Mr Curry is a third party Prohibitionist, and in religious faith a member of the Methodist Episcopal church

He married, May 23, 1867, Isabella Corn born in England, daughter of —— and Sarah (Corn) Corn Children of John and Isabella Curry first six born in England

1 Sarah Ann, born July 23, 1868, died November, 1878 2 Mary Isabella, born June 4, 1870, married James D Bigan 3 Elizabeth, born July 12, 1872, married James Williams, of Uniontown Pennsylvania 4 Samuel, born May 15 1874 died in infancy 5 Jane born May 29 1875 died 6 Hannah, born October 8 1877 married F C Bishop of Morgantown West Virginia 7 John C, born in Toronto, Canada February 14, 1880 now a partner of John Curry & Son, Connellsville, married Cora Slonecker 8 Anna M, born in Pennsylvania, February 17, 1883, died July 31, 1911, married Frank Stanley Jackson (see Jackson) 9 Ruth Naomi, born January 17, 1886, died in infancy

FOUST During the earlier years of the nineteenth century, Henry Foust, born and reared in the Valley of the Rhine, Germany, came to the United States with his wife, finally locating in Somerset county, Pennsylvania Among his children he had a son Henry (2), who lived until maturity in Somerset county, Pennsylvania, he married in Fayette county, —— Miller, and among his children was a son George W

(III) George W, son of Henry (2) Foust, was born near Indian Head, Salt Lick township, in 1816 He grew to manhood on the home farm at Salt Lick, was a farmer in his earlier years, and served as constable Later he removed to a point east of Connellsville, where he was proprietor of the Drove House, a regular stopping place for the drovers, who previous to the coming of the railroads drove their cattle on foot to Philadelphia and eastern markets With the advent of the railroads all this was changed, and business at the Drove House languished He next became proprietor of the Yough House, in Connellsville, later of the Page House a large stone hotel on east Main street He was a Democrat in politics, always prominent in local politics, and served as constable for several terms, but was defeated for the nomination of sheriff He was a member of the Dunkard church He died in Texas, at the time of visiting with his son William, in 1902 He married (first) Margaret Hostettler, born in Salt Lick township, died 1854, daughter of Gideon and Margaret (Austin) Hostettler Her father a farmer of Salt Lick township, was born in Germany He married (second) Mrs Rachel (Godby) Swearengen, of Uniontown Children by first wife Priscilla, born 1842, died 1844, William, born 1844, now a ranchman of Texas, Samuel M, of whom further Susan, born 1849 died 1850, Thaddeus A, born 1851

(IV) Samuel M, third child of George W and Margaret (Hostettler) Foust, was born in Westmoreland county, Pennsylvania, September 8, 1846 His mother died when he was eight years of age, and until he was sixteen years of age he lived with his grandfather Hostettler, receiving a good education in the public schools In 1862, he joined his father who was then proprietor of the Yough House in Connellsville, remaining until 1868, assisting in the management of the hotel From 1868 until 1871 he was employed on the construction of the Baltimore & Ohio railroad with the engineering gang as axeman and in other capacities After this division was completed and until 1874 he was engaged on the preliminary survey of projected railroad from New Florence to Indian Head, Pennsylvania, now in part occupied by the Indian Creek Valley railway From 1872 until 1880 he was engineer for the borough of Connellsville In 1880 he was in charge of the construction of ten miles of the Shenandoah Valley railroad in Rockbridge county, Virginia His next work was the building of Breakneck reservoir for the Connellsville Water Company He was next employed for six months at Morgantown, West Virginia, as chief of construction of the Black Bottle railroad, but on the failure of the company he returned to Connellsville For the next two or three years he was engaged as civil engineer by the Dunbar Furnace Company, opening mines, and in other work of a constructive character In 1882 he was again elected borough engineer of Connellsville, serving until 1895, with the exception of three terms In 1892 he was elected surveyor of Fayette county, served three years, and in 1898 was again elected for a term of three years In this election, on the first returns from the county, Mr Foust was defeated by his opponent by 12 votes. The two militia companies from Connellsville and Uniontown, on their way to the Philippines two days after leaving Hawaii, on the day of election cast their votes, and this changed the result, giving Mr Foust a majority of 8 votes

In addition to the operations mentioned, Mr Foust has made extensive surveys in Southern Fayette county, locating coal lands and establishing bounderies He is also chief engineer of the Union Creek Valley Railroad Company He resides on East Main street, Connellsville, in a frame house which he erected in 1898 In politics he is a Democrat He married July 4, 1869, Eliza Jane Marietta, born in Connellsville, daughter of Josiah Marietta, a leading citizen of Fayette county, in his day Children Nina, born 1870, died 1890, May Bell, born June 20, 1871, married, W H Billhartz, of Knoxville, Pennsylvania, Margaret, born August 31, 1874, married Professor W G Gans, of Uniontown, Pennsylvania

COLDREN John Coldren (sometimes spelled Coldron) was a farmer of Pennsylvania, married and had issue Ellis, son of John Coldren, was born in German township, Fayette county, Pennsylvania, where he learned the shoemaker s trade, and in connection with farming made it his lifelong business in Fayette county He was a man of great industry and quiet retiring habits, much respected by the neighbors His wife, Elizabeth Smith, was born in Georges township Fayette county They left issue

(III) John S son of Ellis and Elizabeth Coldren, was born January 1 1848, and is now living a retired life at Uniontown, Pennsylvania He attended the public schools, and early in life learned the carpenter's trade which he followed all his active years as journeyman and contractor He is a Republican in politics, but never sought public office In religious faith, both Mr and Mrs Coldren are Presbyterians He married Margaret J Black born September 26 1844, daughter of Andrew and Rose Ann Black, who died on their farm in middle life, leaving seven children Children of John and Margaret Coldren 1 Violet

J, deceased 2 Ira W, of whom further 3 Raymond I, now living at home, a light foreman with the West Penn Company 4 Emerson A, an electrician, living at home

(IV) Ira W, eldest son of John S and Margaret J (Black) Coldren was born in German township, Fayette county, Pennsylvania October 21, 1871 He was educated in the public schools, finishing his studies in the local normal school and receiving a teacher's certificate He taught for twelve terms in Fayette county common and normal schools, then abandoned teaching for a business career He worked for a short time in a store, then on June 22 1903, entered the employ of the *Evening Genius* at Uniontown as bookkeeper, continuing eighteen months, then became circulation manager a position he now occupies with the three papers printed by the same press—the *Evening Genius, Morning Herald* and *Genius of Liberty* In politics Mr Coldren is a Republican

He married, June 3 1899, Margaret E, daughter of John H and Fanny Newcomer, of an old county family Children J Arlington, born March 2, 1900, I Burdette, March 11, 1902, Raymond W, April 13, 1907

HORTON The Hortons of Connellsville, Pennsylvania, herein recorded, descend from Josiah Horton, born in Ireland, came to the United States and settled at Eagle Foundry, Huntington county, Pennsylvania where he lived and died a farmer He married Ruhama Griffith, also a native of Ireland They had issue including a son William T

(II) William T, son of Josiah Horton, was born in Huntington county Pennsylvania, 1854 died 1902 He engaged in the lumber business in Somerset and Fayette counties and had his residence at Ohiopyle, in the former county where he died He organized and was heavily interested in the Somerset Lumber Company for many years He was a Republican and served for several years as justice of the peace He was a member of the Methodist Episcopal church, as was his wife He married, in 1876, Elizabeth Stewart, born in Fulton county, Pennsylvania, 1852, died in 1903, daughter of

James A and Rebecca (Gibson) Stewart, both born in Scotland, and early settlers at Wells Tannery, Fulton county, Pennsylvania James Stewart was a blacksmith, and followed that occupation until his death Children of William T and Elizabeth Horton David H, of whom further, Nora A, deceased, Susan L and Reuben J

(III) David H, son of William T and Elizabeth (Stewart) Horton was born in Huntington county, Pennsylvania, October 16, 1878 He was educated in the public schools of Somerset and Fayette counties, and Duff's Business College, from whence he was graduated in 1897 He was for six years bookkeeper for a large lumber company in Maryland Later he became manager of the Kendall Lumber Company, and since 1909 has resided in Connellsville He is also interested in the Ohiopyle Company, of which J L Kendall of Pittsburgh is president, David H Horton, secretary and treasurer He is also secretary of the Huston Lumber Company Mr Horton is a man of fine business qualities, and is highly regarded in business circles He is a Republican in politics, and prominent in the Masonic Order, belonging to Meyersdale Lodge Free and Accepted Masons, and Harrisburg Consistory, Ancient Accepted Scottish Rite

He married, November 9 1898, Elizabeth M Stewart, born in Fayette county daughter of George W and Jennie (Corristan) Stewart of an old Pennsylvania family Children of David H and Elizabeth Horton Helen Marie, born August 13, 1899, Walter Harrison, August 27, 1906, Harry Kendall, May 12, 1909

The progenitor of the Guihers GUIHER of Smithfield Pennsylvania, is Emmanuel Guiher, who came to Pennsylvania at an early day settling in Lancaster county He was a Moravian and lived according to the strict faith of the Mennonites He was buried in the Moravian cemetery at Lititz. Lancaster county, Pennsylvania in 1727

(I) A descendant, Andrew Guiher, probably born in Dauphin county, Pennsylvania, lived in Mifflin and Armstrong counties, Pennsylvania

(II) Dr James Guiher, son of Andrew Guiher, was born in Lewiston, Mifflin county, Pennsylvania, in 1820, died in 1869 He was eight years old when his parents moved to Bradys Bend, Armstrong county, Pennsylvania, where he received his preparatory education and lived until manhood He also attended school at Meadville, Pennsylvania, and at Allegheny College He prepared for the profession of medicine and after obtaining his degree located in Waynesburg, Pennsylvania, and in 1845 began the practice of medicine there He became a well-known and skillful physician and a prominent man of Greene county, interested in many business enterprises He married, in 1857, Rebecca Throckmorton Children 1 J A, born 1858, now a lawyer of Winterset, Iowa 2 F T, born 1860, now a machinist of Waynesburg, Pennsylvania 3 Horace B, of whom further 4 W T, born 1865, now a lawyer of Iowa 5 N A, born 1869, now living in Waynesburg

(III) Dr Horace B Guiher, son of Dr James and Rebecca (Throckmorton) Guiher, was born in Waynesburg, Greene county, Pennsylvania, August 14, 1862 He was educated in the public school and Waynesburg College Choosing medicine as his profession he entered Jefferson Medical College, Philadelphia, whence he was graduated in the class of 1887 In the same year he located in Smithfield, Fayette county, Pennsylvania, where he has since been continuously in successful practice Dr Guiher is not only a skillful practitioner and highly esteemed as a man, but is also a leading financier and business man of Smithfield He has taken active part in public affairs and with deep earnestness labored in the cause of public health, education and good government He was one of the principal organizers of the First National Bank of Smithfield and was its first president, serving in that high position for eight years He was also one of the original stockholders of the Crystal Coke Company, the Crystal Supply Company and of several other coal and coke companies of Fayette county

He was a member of the school board of Georges township before the incorporation of Smithfield as a borough, and has been

R. T. Gribble

for ten years a member of the borough council He was the first president of the borough board of health and has been for several years borough physician He is independent in political action, and a member of the Methodist Episcopal church of Smithfield and president of the board of trustees of that church He is a member since 1894, and an ex-president of the Fayette County Medical Society, a member of Pennsylvania State Medical Society since 1895, and since 1896 a member of the American Medical Association He also holds membership in scientific and other national societies including The American Association of Advancement of Science, The National Geographical Society and The American Society for the Judicial Settlement of International Disputes He has been trustee of Gallatin Lodge, Independent Order of Odd Fellows, of Smithfield, since 1895 Whether as physician, business man, citizen or neighbor Dr Gruher meets every requirement and enjoys the fullest confidence and respect of his community

He married, November, 1892, Maud, daughter of John and Melissa (William) Brownfield Children James M, born January 20, 1897, Mary M, July 7, 1901, Edith R, July 12, 1908

GRIBBLE The first of this family to settle in Fayette county, Pennsylvania, was John Gribble, born in Preston county, West Virginia, (then Virginia) April 29, 1790 He grew to manhood on the home farm, and began his business career as a teamster on the old Cumberland Pike at the age of eighteen years He was so employed continuously from 1808 until 1837, when he became proprietor of the old historical "Red Tavern," located three miles from Brownsville He was one of the characters of his day and filled well his position in life He married Ann Welch Children Louis, John, James, Welch T, of whom further, Lydia, Harriet, Margaret, Ann, Louisa, Mary

(II) Welch T, son of John Gribble, was born in Fayette county, Pennsylvania, April 29, 1836 He was educated in the public schools, and became a farmer of that county, also a well-known stock raiser and dealer After a life of great activity he is now living a retired life with his son Dr Gribble, of Fairchance, Pennsylvania He is a Democrat in politics He married Lucy C Frost, born in Red Stone township, February 6, 1836, died February 14, 1910, daughter of Jesse L Frost, of Fayette county Children Russell T, of whom further, Annie, Ellis, John, Margery, Lydia, Newton, Lewis, Ida, Jesse, the last three are deceased

(III) Dr Russell T Gribble, son of Welch T and Lucy C (Frost) Gribble, was born in Redstone township, Fayette county, Pennsylvania, July 8, 1861 He obtained his early and preparatory education in the public schools, then deciding upon the medical profession, entered the University of the City of New York, whence he was graduated M D class of 1885 He began practice in Tippecanoe, Fayette county, in 1885, continuing there eighteen months He then located in Fairchance, Pennsylvania, where he is successfully engaged in the practice of his profession Dr Gribble stands high in his community both as physician and citizen He is a member of the Methodist church, and a Democrat in politics He is a member of Pine Knob Lodge No 559, Independent Order of Odd Fellows, Fairchance Lodge No 195, Knights of Pythias, Washington Camp No 138, Patriotic Order Sons of America, Modern Woodmen of America and Royal Arcanum

He married, December 31, 1887 Luella Martin, born in Morris Illinois June 21, 1866, daughter of Frank H Martin Children Mary R, born September 30, 1888, Justin L, January 26, 1891 Frank, August 12, 1892, died in infancy, John R, August 16, 1893, Clara August 14, 1895, died November 20, 1897, Joanna F, December 20, 1897, Lloyd L, September 7, 1906, Charles W, October 11, 1907, Luella M, March 1, 1910

GILMORE The Gilmores of Connellsville, Pennsylvania, trace on both paternal and maternal lines to the empire of Germany The original name was Kilmer, but in the transition from the fatherland to America this family name was lost, and Gilmore took its place in this branch in America. The earliest ancestor known to this family is Michael Gilmore, who came to the American colonies about the revolutionary period, found his way to Western Pennsylvania, making settlement at Connellsville, where he was in trade until his death about 1844. He married in Connellsville, Elizabeth, daughter of Daniel Colestock, who was born in Germany, came to Connellsville and started a blacksmith shop, when that city was hardly yet a village. Several of the Colestock family served in the revolution. Elizabeth Gilmore survived her husband until 1880, being then in her ninety-second year.

(II) Isaac Thomas, son of Michael and Elizabeth (Colestock) Gilmore, was born at Connellsville, May 8, 1814, died there November 18, 1888. He learned the carpenter's trade, and carried on a general building business, including dwellings, barns, grist mills, all built in the strongest fashion, mortise and tendon style. He was well-known throughout the county, and was highly regarded as a man. He was a steadfast Whig, later a Republican and held many of the local offices, including justice of the peace, school director and councilman, after Connellsville became so far advanced as to take on the dignity of a city. He was a faithful member of the Christian church, as was his wife. He married Rachel Shaw, born at Connellsville November 6, 1814, died January 10, 1899, daughter of Nathan and Katherine (Vance) Shaw, and granddaughter of James Shaw, who came to Connellsville at an early day, being a contemporary of Michael Gilmore. Nathan Shaw was born in Connellsville, was a mill sawyer, and helped to work into lumber a great deal of the timber with which the section abounded in that early day. He was a Whig, later a Republican. He died in 1873, aged eighty-two years. He married Katherine Vance, born in Connellsville, daughter of Crawford Vance an early settler and soldier of the revolution as were others of the Vance family. Nathan and Katherine Shaw had five sons. Solomon, James and David, who all served in the war with Mexico, David being killed at Vera Cruz, George

and Isaac, serving in the civil war. The house in which Isaac Gilmore and Rachel Shaw were married is still standing north of the present city. She was the widow of —— McCoy at the time of her marriage to Isaac Gilmore, and had a daughter Margaret, who married Amos Hutton, a minister of the Christian church. Children of Isaac T. and Rachel (Shaw) Gilmore: 1 Joseph, born March 26, 1836, died September 9, 1836. 2 Elizabeth A., born October 21, 1837, married Joseph Hutton, a farmer of Indiana county, Pennsylvania, both deceased. 3 Vance Cyrus, born May 11, 1839, died February 1905, a veteran of the civil war, he married Vina Robinson, and resided in Connellsville. 4 George Washington, born March 17, 1841, married Sadie Woods, and was killed, eleven days after their marriage in 1878, by an explosion of his own engine on the Pittsburgh & Connellsville railroad, he was a cavalryman of the civil war. 5 Sidney C., born October 8, 1842, died 1876, married Albert Bradman, who died 1878. 6 Catherine Charlotte, born May 6, 1844, married C. B. Scott, they reside in Cleveland, Ohio, he is a retired merchant. 7 Nathan T., born November 15, 1845, died March 17, 1906, he married Margaret Poundstill, and resided in Connellsville. 8 David Shaw, born August 27, 1847, died 1882, married Mary White, he was a machinist of Connellsville. 9 Alfred Cooper, of whom further. 10 John Lester, born December 5, 1850, (q. v.). 11 Joseph Winfield, born January 4, 1853, married Harriet Hitchman, he is a physician of New Stanton, Pennsylvania. 12 Anna Mary, born March 25, 1854, married J. W. Stillwagon, a painter of Connellsville. 13 Robert Goble, born January 21, 1856, married Nannie Orbin, resides at Duke Center, Pennsylvania, where he is foreman of an oil company. 14 Harriet Clera, born September 2, 1858, died 1884, married Mark W. Marsden of Camden, New Jersey.

(III) Alfred Cooper, ninth child of Isaac T. and Rachel (Shaw) Gilmore, was born in Connellsville, Pennsylvania, February 14, 1849. He was educated in the public schools, and learned the carpenter's trade under the instruction of his father. He spent fourteen years in the Pennsylvania oil fields, but the balance of his life has been spent in Connellsville While in the oil fields he was engaged in erecting derricks, etc For the past thirty years, or since 1882, he has been in the employ of the Baltimore & Ohio Railroad Company, in their carpenter shops When a lad of thirteen years, he ran away from home to enlist, but went no further than Pittsburgh, as his youth was so apparent that the recruiting officers would not listen to his earnest plea to be allowed to enlist In 1880 he erected his present home on Fairview avenue He is a Republican, and with his wife a member of the Christian church He also belongs to General Worth Lodge, Independent Order of Odd Fellows, and to the Royal Arcanum

He married, December 19, 1872, Anna Wharf, born in Belmont, Ohio, daughter of William (2) and Elizabeth (Tiernan) Wharf, and granddaughter of William (1) and Elizabeth Wharf of England William (1) Wharf landed first, and remained for a time in Philadelphia, Pennsylvania, then came to Pittsburgh, making the journey westward over the mountains by wagon He was a stonemason and contractor of bridges, culverts, etc He and wife are both buried at Brownsville, Pennsylvania He had children William (2), James, Margaret and Elizabeth, all deceased William (2) Wharf was a lad of eight years when his parents came to Pennsylvania He became a minister of the early Methodist church, and after his first marriage went to Ohio, where his wife died in 1853 He also died in Ohio in 1897 He married (first) Elizabeth Tiernan, (second) Martha James, having issue by both Elizabeth Tiernan, his first wife, was of Irish descent daughter of John and Eliza (Newbold) Tiernan John Tiernan was an early settler of Fayette county, a strong Democrat, and for several years treasurer of Fayette county He and his wife, Eliza Newbold, are both buried at Fayette City, Pennsylvania

Children of William (2) Wharf and his first wife Elizabeth Tiernan Mary Eliza, married Thornton Krepps, John T, deceased, William C, Anna, married Alfred Cooper Gilmore, of previous mention Children of William (2) Wharf and his second wife, Martha James Elizabeth, James, died

in infancy, Thomas, now living in California, Isaac, now living in Ohio, Alsman Baker, deceased, Ella, married Jasper Ansell, Jennie, Grant, now living in Ohio, Dora Children of Alfred Cooper and Anna (Wharf) Gilmore, 1 George William, born November 31, 1873, was educated in the public schools and at Bethany College, West Virginia, whence he was graduated in 1896 He embraced the profession of teacher, and since 1902 has been principal of the high school at Washington, Pennsylvania He married Rose Curtis of Bethany West Virginia, and has children Milton Alfred, and Frances Ann 2 Isaac Tiernan, born September 5, 1875, a graduate of Connellsville High School, now in the employ of the United Fuel Company, and resides at Hazlewood, Pennsylvania He married Addah Henry, and has children Alfred E, Helen Beatrice, and Charles Henry

(III) John Lester Gilmore, GILMORE tenth child of Isaac Thomas Gilmore (q v) and Rachel (Shaw) Gilmore, was born in Connellsville Pennsylvania on December 25, 1850 He attended the public schools of Connellsville, and after completing his studies worked at the machine shops of Boyts, Porter & Company and for four years was their stationary engineer He then served an apprenticeship of over three years at the carpenter trade, under the instruction of Edward Clyde, a builder of Connellsville When oil was discovered in Butler county he went to Petrolia, where he erected a building and opened a grocery store which he conducted for seven years all through the oil excitement He then returned to Connellsville, where he has since been engaged in building and contracting, having established an honorable reputation for reliability and promptness He is an active Republican, and always interested in local political affairs He is a member of the Christian church (Disciples of Christ), his wife also being a member of that denomination He also belongs to the Royal Arcanum

He married, September 25, 1873, Alice M Scott, born December 24, 1854, daughter of Wilson and Ann (Woodward) Scott, and

a great-granddaughter of Crawford (1)
Scott Children of John L Gilmore 1 An
infant, died May 14, 1874 2 Cora Iola, born
April 22, 1875, died October 14, 1880 3 John
Scott, born December 27, 1879, married Margaret Gilliland, he is train despatcher at
Smithfield, Pennsylvania 4 Beulah L,
born October 1, 1882 5 Rachel Ann, born
March 27, 1886 died September 25, 1899 6
Kate Maydell, born July 25, 1888, married
Guy Reed of Beaver, Pennsylvania, cashier
of the Farmers' Bank of Pittsburgh, Pennsylvania 7 Mary May, born May 8, 1891

Crawford (1) Scott was born in the village
of Naria parish of Inniskeel, county Donegal,
Ireland He died in Ireland, but his widow
came to the United States in 1788 Their children, all of whom but Frank came to the
United States September 30, 1788 1 Frank
died in Ireland about 1833 married and had
three children Thomas, Anne, died in Ireland, married, and had a son, Alexander Brandon, now living in Ohio, John came to
America in 1788 2 Thomas, settled in Virginia 3 John, settled near Wheeling, now
West Virginia 4 William, settled in Carroll county, Ohio, died May 12, 1849, aged
eighty-seven years, his wife, Susanna, died
May 12, 1861, at the great age of ninety-six
years, children all deceased Thomas,
Mary, John, Susan, Jane, William 5 Crawford (2) of whom further 6 Rebecca, died
1823, married Charles Scott, their only living child, Thomas resides at Tabor, Ohio
Crawford (2) Scott was born in Ireland,
1767 came to the United States with his
family September 30, 1788, settled at Tabor,
Ohio, died September 6, 1844, and is buried
there He married, 1792, Mary Barnes, born
1775, died May 12, 1845 Children 1
Thomas born October 5 1793 died January
22, 1840, in German township, Fayette county Pennsylvania 2 Robert, born September 24, 1795 moved to Wayne county Ohio,
1832, died October 25 1836 3 Elizabeth,
born January 22, 1798, married Cunningham
Huston, about 1820, moved to Wayne county, Ohio, died May 25, 1865, in Millersburg,
Ohio 4 John, born April 25, 1800, moved
to Wayne county, Ohio, thence to Carroll,
died October 19, 1858 5 Rebecca, born August 12 1802, married Jacob Arford moved
to Wayne county, Ohio, died July 7, 1841

6 James, born October 12, 1804, in German
township, died there April 27, 1876 7
Ruth, born September 2, 1806, died October
16, 1885, married William Scott, in Carroll
county, Ohio 8 Wilson, of whom further
9 Anna, born January 9, 1811, married Daniel Arford, in Ohio, moved to Napa, California 10 William, born August 6 1813,
moved to Mount Pleasant, Iowa, lost with
baggage train en route to Kansas during
the civil war 11 Crawford (3), born October 6 1815, died May 14, 1892, lived in
Carroll county, Ohio 12 Mary, born January 16, 1819, died October 7, 1892, married,
January 16, 1843, William C Scott, born November 23, 1817, lived in Carroll county,
Ohio 13 Barnes born January 16, 1821,
lived in Tabor, Ohio Wilson, eighth child
of Crawford (2) Scott, was born September
30, 1808, died March 13, 1891, married, August 6, 1831 Ann Woodward, born October 26, 1813, died May 5, 1879, daughter of
Joshua and Sarah (Daniels) Woodward, and
granddaughter of Richard Woodward, who
moved from Chester county to Fayette county, Pennsylvania, in 1789 Wilson Scott
was a prominent citizen of Connellsville,
where his death occurred Among his children was Alice M, previously mentioned

FLEMING Alexander Fleming of Uniontown, a prominent manufacturer and metallurgical
chemist, is a grandson of Alexander Fleming who was born June 5, 1822, in the parish
of Inverskeithing Fifeshire Scotland, died
at Newmains May 27, 1888 He married,
January 12, 1844, Isabella Nisbet, born February 28 1824 at Bedyeats, Perthshire died
November 27, 1896 They had the following children 1 Margaret born December
2, 1844 2 John mentioned below 3 Graham, born November 19, 1855 4 Isabella,
born September 1 1859 5 Alexander born
June 4 1862 6 James, born November
4, 1864, married Maggie Stewart, at Dykeshead August 28 1885, she was born April
2 1859 children Christina, born December 6, 1886 Maggie H, October 13 1888,
Alexander, August 25, 1890, Andrew S,
January 8, 1893, James Fleming, October
10 1891, William July 20, 1899

(II) John Fleming, son of Alexander and

Isabella (Nisbet) Fleming, was born August 6, 1847 He came to this country in 1870 and located at Port Washington Ohio, where he obtained employment as a superintendent of blast furnaces After this he became superintendent of other furnaces in Ohio Later he removed to Pennsylvania, settling first, about 1881, in Mifflin county, and later in Huntingdon county where he had charge of a furnace, going from thence to Wampum Lawrence county, and latterly returned in 1884 to Ohio He soon came back to Pennsylvania and spent four years at Pennsylvania Furnace, going from thence to Bellefonte and operating the furnace there for two years He was then engaged by the Cameron Coal & Iron Company as superintendent Mr Fleming has now retired from active business and resides at McKeesport, Pennsylvania He married Elizabeth Cunningham, and they had the following children Isabella wife of J A Little of McKeesport, Grahmey wife of James Bryce, of Homestead Pennsylvania, David, deceased, Magdaline, wife of J C Neth, of West Newton, Pennsylvania, Harry of whom further Alexander, of whom further

(III) Alexander Fleming, son of John and Elizabeth (Cunningham) Fleming was born at Airdry Scotland October 27 1872, and was brought to this country with his father's family when two years of age He early evinced the strong scientific bent that characterized the family ability He went to the Carnegie night school, after which he took a special course in Lafayette College, Easton, Pennsylvania The theoretical knowledge acquired at school he supplemented by shop work in the laboratories of the Bellefonte Furnace Company the Cameron Iron & Coal Company, the Joseph E Thropp Company, Everett, Pennsylvania, and the Monongahela Furnace, McKeesport, Pennsylvania He was then offered a position with the Carnegie Steel Company working in their various plants in and near Pittsburgh Pennsylvania In 1897 he settled at Scottdale, being engaged by the H C Frick Coke Company as chief chemist In this position he continued for seven years, leaving it in 1904 to enter business as an independent chemist opening the laboratory

in Uniontown where he was extremely successful the business having doubled in volume since its establishment He has made a specialty of water analysis and is an expert in firebrick manufacture in addition to the analysis of all kinds of ore, minerals, coal, coke etc He receives commissions from all parts of the United States, and does the work for most of the independent firms in the coke regions He has had to obtain assistance in handling the great volume of work that pours in upon him He was one of the incorporators and at one time one of the stockholders of the Savage Hill Firebrick Company of Fairhope, Pennsylvania He was also vice-president of the West Virginia Fire Clay Company, Thornton, West Virginia, during its existence, and it was through his experiments and investigations that the coke-oven brick has been raised to its present efficiency Formerly the life of a firebrick in the ovens was from thirty days to one year but through the untiring efforts of Mr Fleming the life of a firebrick has been prolonged to from ten to twelve years He stands at the head of his profession and has contributed valuable facts in the metallurgical industry by various investigations which he has conducted He is a member of the American Chemical Society, also of Marion Lodge, No 562, Free and Accepted Masons, of Scottdale Connellsville Chapter, No 283, Royal Arch Masons Uniontown Commandery, No 49, Knights Templar, Syria Temple Ancient Arabic Order Nobles of the Mystic Shrine, at Pittsburgh Mr Fleming is in political belief a Republican, but he has never been willing to accept public office

He married, September 26, 1895, Josephine F Gogley, daughter of Jacob and Elizabeth (Amick) Gogley, of Bedford county Pennsylvania They have four children Ruth Elizabeth, Marion and Frank Alexander Mr and Mrs Fleming are members of the Methodist Episcopal church, Mr Fleming being also a member of the choir

(III) Harry Fleming, son of John and Elizabeth (Cunningham) Fleming, was born at Pennsylvania Furnace, Centre county, Pennsylvania, August 9, 1884 He was educated in the McKeesport public schools, showing at a very early age the mechanical and scientific turn of mind that distinguished his father, after leaving school he was for two years assistant chemist for the H C Frick Coke Company at Scottdale He spent some time in different laboratories near McKeesport, and has for the past four years been assistant in the Uniontown Testing Laboratory, and is an important factor in its success

FLEMING The surname of this illustrous Scotch family was at first assumed from a person of distinction who in the days of King David I (1124) a Fleming by birth, came into Scotland and took the surname Flanderensis, or Le Fleming, from the country of his origin The statue of the armed knight to be seen in Furness Abbey, Lancashire, England, an ancient burial place of the Fleming family, was placed there generations ago in memory of Sir John Le Fleming, a crusader Robert Le Fleming was one of the great barons of Scotland who fought and seated Robert Bruce on his rightful throne A descendant Malcolm, Earl of Wigton, married Janet, daughter of King James IV Sir Thomas Fleming, son of an Earl of Wigton, emigrated to Virginia in 1616, many of the family followed him to the same colony, one of whom was Colonel William Fleming Another was the father of James Fleming, born in North Carolina, 1762, afterward removed to Ohio, where he died 1832 A branch of the family was founded in New Jersey by sons Malcolm Fleming, of Ireland This branch founded Flemington, the county seat of Hunterdon county, New Jersey Thomas is a persistent name in this branch and collateral evidence would indicate that Thomas Fleming descended from the New Jersey family rather than from the Virginia branch of which Governor Fleming was a conspicuous member

(I) The first record we have of the Connellsville family is of Thomas Fleming a farmer of Westmoreland and Fayette counties, owning a good farm In the latter county he was a man of industry and thrift, rearing a family that are yet living in the county Two of his brothers, Robert and Abraham are yet living near Scottdale, Pennsylvania

(II) Thomas Jackson, son of Thomas Fleming, was born in Fayette county, Pennsylvania, died 1890 or 1891, at Uniontown, Pennsylvania He was a farmer until a few years before his death, when he retired and resided in Uniontown His farm was located in Dunbar township, where his children were born Both Thomas J and his wife were members of the Cumberland Presbyterian church He married Mary Ann Smiley, born in Fayette county, died 1879, leaving sons and daughters A son, Charles M Fleming, born March 20, 1854, established in the grocery business in Uniontown in 1888 This record deals with a second son, Christian L

(III) Christian L, son of Thomas Jackson Fleming, was born in Dunbar township, Fayette county Pennsylvania, November 7, 1861 He was educated in the public schools and grew to youthful manhood on the farm He began business life in Uniontown, Pennsylvania, forming a partnership with his brother, Charles M Fleming, and for three years operating a grocery He then entered the employ of the W J Rainey Coke Company and still continues with that company He has been manager of company stores at Acme, Revere and Mount Braddock where he is now in charge His residence since 1893 has been in Connellsville, No 615 North Pittsburgh street He is a Republican in politics

He married, January 29, 1888, Hannah, daughter of Samuel N and Jemima (Humbert) Long, granddaughter of Robert Long, born 1787, a settler of Lancaster county, Pennsylvania, coming from there to Fayette county He was a blacksmith and had a shop at the corner of Main and Meadow streets, Connellsville He was one of the early and strenuous advocates of temperance and one of the organizers of the first temperance societies in Fayette county He married Catherine Foster Samuel N Long was born in Connellsville in 1821 He was a farmer, a Democrat and a strict Presbyterian His first wife, Jemima Humbert, died quite young Her children Humbert, of Scottdale, Catherine, married P S Morrow, of Uniontown Hannah, married Christian L Fleming (of previous mention) He married a second wife who bore him Robert, deceased George R, residing in Connellsville, James C, deceased Two children ot Christian L Fleming died in infancy

Mrs Jemima (Humbert) Long, mother of Mrs Fleming had brothers and sisters, Lydia, married Joseph Beatty, of Uniontown, Rebecca, deceased, married Robert Husted, Eliza, married Robert Parkhill, both deceased, William, deceased, Robert deceased Jacob deceased

---

FLEMING The paternal grandfather of James A Fleming of Connellsville, Pennsylvania, was born in Scotland He was a lumberman, and met his death by drowning in the Juniata river, while following his occupation, when his son, John J Fleming, was but two months old, and his name is therefore not preserved He married, and left issue

(II) John J Fleming was born about 1838 in Central Pennsylvania, died March, 1908 He was a millwright and carpenter He enlisted in Company D, One Hundred and Forty-eighth Regiment Pennsylvania Volunteer infantry, and served four years, attaining the rank of orderly sergeant He was engaged in many battles, including Chancellorsville where he was wounded, Fredericksburg, and Petersburg He settled in Connellsville in 1880 continuing there until his death He was a Republican in politics, was always active in public affairs, and held several offices in the township and in-the, then, borough of New Haven At the time of his death he was employed in the United States Internal Revenue Service as store keeper and gauger, at Johnstown, Pennsylvania He slipped and fell on a pavement in that city, broke his hip, and died in the hospital a short time afterwards, aged seventy years He was a member of the Presbyterian church, the Grand Army of the Republic and the Union Veteran Legion He married Mary C Sample, born in Center county, Pennsylvania, daughter of Alexander and Margaret (Furey) Sample, of Center county Mrs Fleming survives her husband, a resident of Connellsville Children of John J and Mary C Fleming Gertrude, married F W Cunningham of Charleroi, Margaret, deceased, James A, of whom further, Frederick, deceased, Virgil, deceased, Mary, deceased

(III) James A, son of John J Fleming, was born at Bellefonte, Pennsylvania, January 1, 1876 He was educated in the public schools, and at the age of eighteen years entered the employ of the Baltimore & Ohio railroad as a clerk in the office of the machinery department He received several promotions, and on October 15, 1911, was appointed freight agent at Connellsville, a position he most capably fills He is a member of the Presbyterian church, as is his wife, and belongs to the Baltimore and Ohio League, and the Knights of the Maccabees He is a Republican in politics He married, September 8, 1899, Emma, daughter of Samuel McCabe, of Pittsburgh, deceased Their only child died in infancy

---

HART The immigrant ancestor of the Hart family came with the influx of Scotch-Irish to New England before the revolutionary war Thence he drifted to Pennsylvania with the Connecticut pioneers In 1777 the family crossed over the mountains in Pennsylvania

(I) John Hart was born in Westmoreland county, Pennsylvania and married Eliza Barr, who was a native of Allegheny county He established a pottery at Washington, Pennsylvania, the first pottery in that town, and also conducted potteries at Pittsburgh, Pennsylvania, and Birmingham

(II) William, son of John Hart, was born in Allegheny county, Pennsylvania, November 23, 1818 He spent his early years and attended the public schools in Washington, Pennsylvania He was associated in business with his father and continued in the pottery business He enlisted in the Eighth Pennsylvania Regiment of Reserves during the civil war for three months, and re-enlisted for three years On account of illness he was sent home and assigned to duty as provost-marshal in Washington county In later years he had a position in the United States internal revenue service He was a communicant of the Presbyterian church In politics he was a Republican, and he was a delegate to the first Republican convention ever held in Pittsburgh He died April 21, 1891 He married Elizabeth Oliver, born January 15, 1822 at Washington, Pennsylvania, died October 26, 1904, daughter of

William and Eliza (Houston) Oliver Her father was born in 1799 and her mother in 1802 both in Washington county, Pennsylvania Her father was a hatter by trade and manufactured hats, making a specialty of fur hats and caps in Philadelphia William Houston the first white settler in Washington county, father of Eliza, was a native of Scotland, a soldier in the revolution in the American army William Oliver's father was a loyalist His home was in Trenton, New Jersey, but he had grants of land elsewhere in New Jersey and in Washington county, Pennsylvania, where he removed immediately after the revolution William Houston built the first hotel in Washington, Pennsylvania, called the Houston Inn, built of stone, and it was in use until it was taken down about 1897 An heirloom of the Oliver family in the possession of Alexander Wilson Hart is an old checker-board given to his great-great-grandmother by Lord Loveridge, in the old country Children of William Hart 1 Oliver L, living in a western state, served in the rebellion in the War Department at Washington 2 Jennie 3 John C, of Newcastle, Pennsylvania, is in the marble and stone business 4 Eliza O, a school teacher for twenty-five years in Washington Seminary, now retired 5 Alexander Wilson, mentioned below

(III) Alexander Wilson Hart son of William Hart, was born in Washington county, Pennsylvania, June 17, 1858 He attended the public schools of Washington, and for three years was a student at Washington and Jefferson College He then engaged in the marble and stone business in partnership with his brother John C Hart, and afterward alone at Newcastle, Pennsylvania After his father died in 1891 he moved to Washington, Pennsylvania, where he conducted a grocery business He came to Connellsville, Pennsylvania, May 12, 1900, and established a marble and tombstone business, with office and shops on South Eighth street, on the west side of Connellsville He deals extensively in granite, marble and other stones for monumental and other purposes He is a prominent and highly successful business man In politics he is a Republican, he and all of the family

are members of the Presbyterian church He is a citizen of public-spirit, an upright, able and successful business man, kindly, popular and beloved, especially in his home, to which he is devoted

He married, July 27, 1880 Florence Leslie, born at Newcastle, Pennsylvania a daughter of George and Mary McMiller Leslie Her father and mother were of Scotch-Irish descent Their parents were among the pioneer settlers of the country Children Mary Leslie, born May 22, 1884, George Edward, March 14, 1886

MARSHALL
The Marshalls of Broad Ford, Fayette county, Pennsylvania, herein recorded, descend from Henry Marshall, born in Ireland, where he learned the art of weaving He came to this country about 1785 and settled in Eastern Pennsylvania He was then a single man, but soon married an Irish lass, Rebecca Crane who had preceded him to this country During the whiskey insurrection he came to Western Pennsylvania with the United States troops to suppress the rebellion, and liked the country so well that on his return home he sold out all but what could be carried by his wagon and team In 1811 he crossed the mountains with his household goods and wife, finally reached a desired location in Fayette county, on Possum creek, in Dunbar township Here he purchased forty acres of John Strickler, and lived all his after life He set up a loom in his home and in addition to working his forty acres did weaving He prospered and added to his farm acreage He was a Methodist in religion, and an industrious upright man Children John B, of whom further, Samuel, was a major of militia, a title he always retained in Dayton, Ohio, where he died, Phoebe, married Elisha Castle and moved to Illinois

(II) John B son of Henry and Rebecca (Crane) Marshall was born in Eastern Pennsylvania, September 10, 1809 died September 1880 He was two years of age when his parents came to Fayette county, where he was educated and grew to manhood He cultivated his father's farm, then rented and worked other farms, but always was a farmer and always lived in Dunbar township He married (first) Priscilla Wilhelm, born near

Breakneck in Fayette county, in 1814, died in 1850, with four of her children—Mary, Jane, James, John and George—during an epidemic of typhoid fever, one son survived, Joseph Crawford, of whom further He married (second) Cynthia Garven, who bore him several children, now all deceased

(III) Joseph Crawford, son of John B and Priscilla (Wilhelm) Marshall, was born in Dunbar township, Fayette county, Pennsylvania, November 30, 1843 He attended school in his early years but at ten years of age left home to make his own way in the world He worked among the farmers, doing such work as a young boy was fitted for, but as he grew stronger and experienced he found ready employment, finally making a permanent home with Alexander Murphy, a farmer near Broad Ford He remained with Mr Murphy until May 30, 1861, the date of his enlistment in Company F, 11th Regiment Pennsylvania Reserve Infantry, to serve three years He fought at Fredericksburg, where he was wounded in the left thigh, at Gettysburg he was one of the defenders of Little Round Top, and during his three years saw much active service and hard fighting with the Army of the Potomac On May 30, 1864, his last day of service he was captured at City Church, near Cold Harbor, Virginia, and sent to Andersonville Prison, where he was confined most of the time until the war between the states was brought to a close at Appomattox, when he was released and returned to Fayette county There are now (1912) but five men in that county that were confined in Andersonville After a short time in Fayette county he moved to Allegheny county, Pennsylvania, where he was employed in the mines digging coal for three years In 1869 he located at Broad Ford Fayette county, worked in the coal mines, followed carpentry, finally opening a general store, which he has conducted for the past sixteen years He has served as justice of the peace, constable school director, and ten years as tax collector He is independent in politics is in favor of prohibition but is in sympathy with the principles of the Democratic party on national issues He is a member of the Methodist Protestant church the Independent Order of Odd Fellows, and the Grand Army of the Republic He married, January 30, 1869, Mary B Holliday, born in

Dunbar township, Fayette county, December 20, 1846, daughter of Ebenezer, died 1852, and Elizabeth Holliday, of Connellsville Mrs Marshall was also a member of the Methodist Protestant church She died May 14, 1892 Children 1 Elizabeth, born December 17 1869, married Walter Menefee, living at Connellsville, west side 2 Josephine, resides at Broad Ford, her father's homekeeper since the death of his wife 3 Mary Jane, born 1875, married John Hawthorne, resides at Scottdale, Pennsylvania 4 John Burt, of whom further 5 George, born August 1, 1878, now a practicing physician located at West Leisenring, Pennsylvania, married Maude Lint, of Vanderbilt, Pennsylvania 6 Winifred, born 1883 died 1896

Mr Marshall resides at Broad Ford his home for the past forty-three years He has fought well the battle of life, was a good soldier in actual wartare, and is a good citizen of the land he helped defend He is held in highest esteem, and is one of the most reputable business men of his village

(IV) John Burt ("Burt"), eldest son and fourth child of Joseph C and Mary B (Holliday) Marshal, was in Broad Ford, Fayette county, Pennsylvania May 17, 1876 He attended the public schools, and after finishing his studies became clerk in his father's store In 1899 he purchased a lot in South Connellsville, erected a suitable building and established and opened a general store He has prospered and expanded until he is the leading merchant of that part of the city In 1904 he was appointed postmaster of South Connellsville, and has held that office continually until the present date (1912) He is a Republican in politics, active in the party, and interested in all that pertains to South Side development

He married September 7, 1904 Lily May, born at Dickerson Run, Fayette county, daughter of Benjamin and Martha Ann Orbin, both born in Fayette county Children Edwin Orbin, born August 13, 1905, Martha Frances, April 19 1908, Lily May May 9, 1910

FRANKS The name Frank[s] German Fraunk, means free (free born) The Franks claim their descent from one of the German tribes inhabiting Franconia, who in the fifth century under their leader and King, Clovis (Lewis) overran and conquered Gaul and gave it the name of France (or Franc) This may account for the claim of some that they are of French blood Prior to, and on down from the great religious Reformation under Martin Luther, we find them well established along the Rhine and throughout that region of Germany Many of them seemed to have imbibed the spirit and teachings of the Great Reformer

The more immediate ancestors of the Franks families in this country it is claimed, came from some of the Free cities along the Rhine and settled in Alsace-Lorraine (a German possession), and probably in Lorraine

It was from this country that Michael Franks came with his three children, Jacob Michael (2) and a daughter Elizabeth They landed at Baltimore, Maryland about the year 1748 The father seems to have been in very poor health The writer has failed to find any proof that he and his daughter ever came to the High House settlement He probably died shortly after arrival, and the daughter probably married But the two brothers, Jacob and Michael (2) became the progenitors of two great lines of families in this country, whose descendants have multiplied into thousands, and are scattered over perhaps all parts of the United States westward of the Alleghenies to the Pacific Coast Jacob, the older, was born in 1732

They decided to go westward and to carve out a home in the wilderness It is claimed Jacob came over first to "spy out the land" He returned to Baltimore and married Barbary Brandeberry, a German emigrant girl A little later Michael married a Miss Livengood also a German girl, whose parents had come from Germany Neither of the brothers had attained his majority when he married With their little families (Jacob now had one child) they set out together on their somewhat dangerous journey The women rode horses, with blankets thrown across, tent canvas and a light outfit of cooking utensils attached The men walked carrying their guns and an ax When night came on they would pitch can p In order to protect themselves against the more dangerous wild animals, they built log fires, and when the wolves, bears and panthers came prowling around, they pulled

out burning firebrands, and by swinging them about kept the savage beast at bay or until a lucky shot from the trusty rifle brought down the furtive beast and made it harmless

But it is not known that they were molested by the Indians at any time coming over Several times they missed their course and wandered about for days in circles without making any real progress At last they struck an Indian trail which they followed the rest of the way across the mountains

At one of their camping places in the mountains on the Yough river, a son was born to Michael and his wife They called him Henry This event occurred June 11 1753 This Henry in a sense, was a child of destiny This event is also very important as it fixes the time closely as to their arrival at what was later known as High House, Fayette county, Pennsylvania

Each of the brothers took up by 'Tomahawk" right two large tracts of land lying in its primitive state, covered with majestic forests of oak Jacob s claim included the more northerly and northwesterly tract and extending to if not across, Brown's Run, while Michael's claim lay on the southwest side

At this time this whole region was supposed to be in Virginia, and was so claimed by Virginia Afterwards when this dispute had been settled and the line established, the rights of these "Tomahawk" claims by the settlers were respected by Pennsylvania Patents for these lands were granted in 1789 and 1790, based on warrants issued in 1784 or 1785 and signed by Thomas Mifflin as president of the council By this time quite a community of Franks had developed, and the settlement was called Frankston, and patents and other early conveyances were given under the name of Frankton As before stated, Jacob and his brother Michael, with their little families, arrived in June, 1753 They were among the very first permanent pioneer settlers in this region, west of the Allegheny Mountains A few others came about the same time or a little later Of these Frederick Walser (Waltzer) was among the more prominent ones Also a Mr Wendel Brown and two sons, came from eastern Virginia, following the Potomac river to near its source, crossed over and went westward, it is said, as far as to the mouth of Dunkard Creek, Greene county, Pennsylvania Wendel Brown made friends of the Indians here They told him of some rich lands lying northeast across the Monongahela river and offered to take him to them He at once accepted their kindly offer When he saw the rich limestone hills and rich little valleys, covered with fine timber of oak, sugar maple and walnut, he was delighted with it and resolved to secure some of it A few years later he carried out this purpose and secured a large tract of this valuable land This formed the nucleus of what became known as the Brown Settlement, located a few miles west of Uniontown A part of this Wendel Brown tract later was owned by Christopher Brown better known as "Stuffle Brown" A spring at the house of this farm is the head of Brown's run

The Walsers, Browns and others of the High House settlement married and intermarried with the Franks

But little can we know of the hardships to which these first settlers were exposed The country at first was almost an unbroken wilderness Aside from the troublesome wild animals and poisonous snakes, there was the far more dangerous and treacherous redskins And in order to protect themselves against the murderous tomahawk and scalping knife they erected a strong fort

Every community had its fort Every one was on the qui vive, and often a swift courier would suddenly arrive and give the alarm that the Indians were murdering some of the whites of a neighboring community, and the cry "Flee to the fort!" was heard It was from this fact the little town afterward and still is to-day called Flee Town The men carried their rifles wherever they went, whether to work, to worship God at their religious meetings or what not

The lands of Jacob have been divided and sub-divided into many small tracts and are still held mostly by some of his numerous descendants, while that of Michael has long ago passed into other hands It is Michael's family which we are mainly considering Some of Michael's children went to Wayne county, Ohio, and became pioneer settlers there, and later others of the family followed them A portion of the old homestead was later purchased by Colonel Henry Core The same, or a part, is now owned by Charles Jones

The children of Michael (2) were 1 Henry, of Indian captivity, of whom further 2 Charlotte, who became the third wife of Jacob First (German, Furst) 3 Abraham, who settled in Luzerne township, Fayette county, Pennsylvania 4 John went to Ohio Also the following sisters with their husbands and children followed and settled in Ohio, viz Mary, married Nicholas Helmic, Elizabeth married Phineas Flaherty, Dorothy, married Jacob Miller, Catharine, married Jacob Hatfield George settled in the upper part of Greene county, Pennsylvania near to Blacksville John also went to Ohio Charlotte First and her brother Michael remained here, the latter settling in Nicholson township, near New Geneva

Much confusion has already arisen among the later posterity of the Franks families in Fayette county Some cannot tell whether they are descended from Jacob or Michael, or of what Jacob and what Michael There were so many of these two names, especially the latter To make more simple and for convenience the chronicler of the Michael branch has designated the Michaels as Michael 1st, 2d, 3d, etc To add to this confusion another Michael who had two sons, a Jacob and a Michael, came here from Germany some years later This later Michael was a cousin of Jacob and Michael 2d, the first arrivals The cousin and his two sons settled on lands in German township, a short distance northeast of Germantown, now Masontown

It was an extensive tract of land, involving what is now embraced in the St. Jacob's Lutheran church grounds, with its farm and lands later held by the Haydens and the Davids eastward to the road leading from High House to Old Frame Cross Roads in Nicholson The father two sons and a daughter Catharine, who married a man by the name of Baccus, not mentioned above, were all Lutherans The two sons, Jacob and Michael were very zealous and agreed to donate the land and build a church, others of like faith in the neighborhood to assist in building Although brothers, Michael was a member of the English Lutheran and Jacob a member of the German Lutheran The church was built and dedicated as the St Jacob's Lutheran Church, named in honor of its principal founder It was and is still known as the Dutch Meeting House

At his father s death Jacob came into possession of the eastern section on which there is a noted spring which is the head of Jacob s creek and which took its name from the owner, Jacob Franks This part of the write-up is a digression, mainly for the purpose of clarifying much of the Franks history in Fayette county

THE GRAVE OF THE PROUD FARMER
BY NICHOLAS VACHEL LINDSAY
Into the acres of the newborn state
He poured his strength and plowed his ancient
    name,
And, when the traders followed him, he stood
Towering above their furtive souls and tame

That brow without a stain, that fearless eye
Oft left the passing stranger wondering
To find such knighthood in the sprawling land,
To see a Democrat well-nigh a king

He lived with liberal hand, with guests from far,
With talk and joke and fellowship to spare—
Watching the wide world s life from sun to sun,
Lining his walls with books from everywhere

He read by night, he built his world by day
The farm and house of God to him were one
For forty years he preached and plowed and
    wrought—
A statesman in the fields, who bent to none

His plowmen-neighbors were as lords to him
His was an ironside, democratic pride
He served a rigid Christ, but served him well—
And for a lifetime saved the countryside

Here lie the dead who gave the Church their best
Under his fiery preaching of the word
They sleep with him beneath the ragged
    grass
The village withers, by his voice unstired

And though his tribe be scattered to the wind
From the Atlantic to the China Sea,
Yet do they think of that bright lamp he burned
Of family worth and proud integrity

And many a sturdy grandchild hears ,his name
In reverence spoken till he feels akin
To all the lion-eyed who built the world—
And lion-dreams begin to burn within

Henry eldest child of Michael (2) Franks, was born June 11, 1753 at a camp in the mountains as before noted He was a powerfully built muscular fellow very active and fleet-footed As a frontiersman much of his life was wild and romantic, a rugged and hard life from his youth onward But he was a born fighter and gloried in it Both he and his father were in the colonial and revolutionary wars Henry was also in the war of 1812 At one time he was engaged in a desperate battle with the Indians near Sandusky, Ohio Here with a number of others, he was taken a prisoner As to the length of time he was held a prisoner there has been some difference in the traditional statements

This battle was probably the one fought by Colonel Crawford in 1782 The warring Wyandottes had been giving much trouble in northwestern Ohio, and Colonel Crawford had been commissioned by Washington to go and quell them But Crawford s little army was defeated by the savages who many times outnumbered them The Colonel with a number of his men (many were killed in the battle) were taken prisoners Crawford was put to a cruel death by burning at the stake As stated Henry was one of the prisoners, and he was tested for Indian citizenship by causing him to run the gauntlet between two lines of redskins armed with withes to lacerate his bared back and shoulders If he reached the goal (wigwam) at the end of the race for life, or that is what it was, without succumbing to pain or fear his life would be spared and his prowess revered If not a cruel death would follow Suffice it to say, he performed so well, even to the knocking down with his hatchet and almost killing an Indian who tried to block his way in running that a great savage war whoop of admiration rang out

Although in this mighty test of valor he received a knife wound at the hands of the Indian he had struck down with his hatchet, yet his stoicism and valor made them his friends They nursed him and doctored him (Indian fashion) until he had entirely recovered He soon learned their habits of life and skillfully adapted himself to them, thus strengthening their confidence, so that in time they allowed him to go away by himself for several days at a time, but he never broke his word with them until the time of his escape

They roamed together over the very lands on which he afterward settled with his family, though his oldest son John seems to have settled on land in Wayne county, Ohio, before his father Henry's wife Christina (Van Buskirk) Franks, died August 16, 1842, aged seventy-seven years

The account of the escape of Henry Franks back to civilization and finally to his friends in Fayette county, Pennsylvania, is the one given the writer by Isaac Franks as he remembered his father, Michael brother of Henry, tell it. The account as given in the history of Wayne county, Ohio, says he made his escape by reaching the lake coast, boarding an English vessel bound for Montreal, Canada, thence crossing to the American side and walking to Philadelphia, thence to Pittsburgh, and from there back to his family in the Franks settlement at High House, Fayette county, Pennsylvania. This account also differs as to the length of time Henry was in captivity, having the time as much as four or five years. As to the fact of his being in the Indian wars and his capture at a battle near Sandusky, Ohio, there can be no doubt.

Henry Franks died May 5, 1836. His body has been reinterred and now rests in Chestnut Hill cemetery at Doylestown, Ohio. A few years after his return home to High House settlement he moved with his family and old mother to Ohio and settled on Chippewa creek, Wayne county. His mother lived to a great age.

The names of Henry's children are as follows: Sons, John, Michael, Henry, Uriah and Abraham. Daughters, Abigail Huffman, Betsy Higgins, Christina Collins, Sallie Roatson, Phoebe and Katie not married. Abigail, born 1802, died September 22, 1841. John, oldest child of Henry, who settled in Wayne county before his father, is buried in the Huffman lot at Doylestown. Mrs. Mary Elliot, a widow, and a daughter of John, is still living (1912) at Doylestown, Ohio, at the advanced age of eighty-three years. Also a Mrs. Bowlby, of Canon City, Colorado. Data of the rest of John's children not known.

Michael (3), son of Michael (2) Franks, was born in German township, Fayette county, Pennsylvania, at the High House settlement, about the year 1773, perhaps the early part of that year. At the age of about twenty-three he married Amy Furst (German Furst), who at the time was less than sixteen years old. She was a daughter of Jacob Furst, who came from Germany. Amy was a daughter by his first wife, his third and last wife being Charlotte Franks (see Charlotte). The Firsts, or Fursts, were among the early settlers. Shortly after marriage Michael and his wife settled in Nicholson township, a few

miles northeast of New Geneva. He was a man of great energy and physical endurance. He was a muscular man, standing six feet high, rather dark complexion and weighed about 180 pounds. His wife was short and small, but later became stout, in complexion fair, with a sweet face and placid and even disposition, and matched her husband as a worker and manager. Constitutionally she was a remarkably good woman. In his life Michael was a man of correct and regular habits and of uncommon industry. When they set up housekeeping they did not have much, but they toiled and saved and constantly added to their savings. Of course he was a farmer, one of the best and most thrifty in the country. Michael became the largest land owner in the township, owning nine excellent farms. He raised large crops of grain, especially corn. He raised and fed many hogs. He also raised many good horses. He was one of the first to mine and haul coal to New Geneva. Strange to say, it was then little used as a fuel. He also hauled stone for Albert Gallatin to build a house on the historic Friendship Hill farm, above New Geneva. It is said he was listed for the war of 1812, and was to hold himself in readiness for one year and a day. He was not notified until a day after the time had expired, and therefore could not be held. Michael and his wife were at first Lutherans, but shortly after marriage their religious views underwent a change, and they united with the Mount Moriah Baptist Church at Smithfield, Pennsylvania, in which fellowship they remained until death. He was a deacon thirty-seven years, a man of strong personality and a forceful citizen. He neither had time nor inclination for public office, but was alert for the public good. His influence, with his sons, was always a potent factor, especially in county and township politics. He and his sons were of the old 'Hickory Jackson' mold. His home was a Mecca for Baptist ministers, and the poor and worthy were never turned away empty. He died in 1857 at the age of seventy-eight years. His wife died in 1872 in the ninety-first year of her age. They rest in the old Baptist cemetery at Smithfield.

Jacob, first child of Michael (3) and Amy (Furst) Franks, was born February 20, 1798. By occupation he was a farmer. He married

Rebecca Rose (date of which cannot now be found) In early life he bought a farm in Monongalia county, Virginia, now West Virginia, near Easton Later in life he sold out there and moved to his father's old home in Nicholson township, Fayette county, Pennsylvania, to care for his aged mother, then a widow He died a little over seventy-five years of age His wife survived him for some years and died at the advanced age of eighty-seven years They were good people and given to hospitality and most highly respected by all who knew them Having both united with the Baptist church at an early age, they were faithful unto death In politics he was a Democrat They had eleven children, but for lack of data only a few notes can be given Children Michael, the oldest, served in the Union army throughout most of the civil war He was a farmer by occupation, and for many years to the time of death was located in Tyler county, West Virginia He married and raised a highly respected family He was a faithful and influential member of the Baptist church, and was also his noble wife He was an influential, leading citizen in his county He died a few years ago at an advanced age

Of the large and respectable family of Jacob and Rebecca the only one now living (1912) is Mrs Rebecca A, wife of H T Jaco (insurance) of Uniontown, Pennsylvania By this union she is the mother of five children J W, a fine dentist, owns and has his office in the Flatiron, at the water fountain, on Morgantown street, Uniontown, and lives in a fine brick residence on Beeson avenue He is a member of the Great Bethel Baptist Church Another son, Charles H, also a dental doctor, located in Philadelphia, Pennsylvania, and is demonstrator and lecturer in the Pennsylvania Dental College the school from which he graduated in 1906 He is still single Frank R youngest child, is a jeweler and has charge of the watchmaking department of the George Bennett Company, a wholesale house in Pittsburgh, Pennsylvania He is married Mrs Dora Moore (widow) has been for a number of years one of the leading clerks in the Wright-Metzler Department Store in Uniontown, Pennsylvania, successors to Captain James M Hustead and I W Semans, with whom she was employed

At present she has charge of the ladies' suit department She is considered an expert in her line of work Miss Anna is still at home W Thomas Miller a grandson of Jacob and Rebecca Franks, living on a cozy little farm in Nicholson township, near Smithfield, has been a justice of the peace for many years, and is uncommonly well posted as to the duties of the office, and frequently uses his influence for a peaceful settlement of difficulties without going to law in the courts, where the public welfare is not involved, and has the full confidence of the people in his integrity, good judgment and safe counsel For some years after the First National Bank of Smithfield was organized he was bookkeeper and treasurer, and thoroughly demonstrated his fitness as a banker

He has strong moral and religious convictions He is an active church and Sunday school man and deacon in the Oak Hill Baptist Church at Old Frame of which his good wife is also a member He has one daughter, Lenora, at home Also three sons, of which Jacob F is a Baptist minister The other two, John and Charles, are well equipped by education and training for success in life Rev Ellsworth Hare another grandson of Jacob and Rebecca Franks, is now pastor of a Baptist church at McKeesport, Pennsylvania

Elizabeth, second child of Michael (3) and Amy (Furst) Franks, married, May 13, 1819, Jonathan Higgins, a successful farmer Elizabeth died at the age of thirty-six years, he later married her sister Amy, November 19, 1837 In 1839 he moved from near New Geneva to Adams county, Ohio, and lived there until the time of their deaths

Mary (Polly), third child of Michael (3) and Amy (Furst) Franks, was born March 29, 1801, and was married to Andrew Kramer in 1829 Andrew Kramer at the age of sixteen years took up the trade of glass blowing and was one of the pioneer glass manufacturers of the Monongahela valley Later he operated a glass factory below Greensboro, Greene county, Pennsylvania, in partnership with Philip Reitz, below New Geneva, but on the opposite side of the river It is worthy of note that the first glass made west of the Alleghany mountains was at or just above New Geneva, on Georges creek, promoted by

Albert Gallatin, of national fame, and who lived at the now historic place called Friendship Hill, at present owned by J V Thompson, the noted banker and coal king Gallatin founded New Geneva in 1797

Andrew Kramer moved to Linn county, Iowa, in 1839, and for years endured the hardships incident to a pioneer life He finally conquered and made good—raised a large family—some of them filling important positions in life One, Isaac N, now at the age of eighty years (1912), with a son, has two extensive floral and greenhouse establishments, one at Marion and the other at Cedar Rapids, Iowa Another son, Michael, aged eighty-two, is living at Denver City, Col, who in turn has a son who is a physician In politics Andrew Kramer was a Whig Both he and his wife were Baptists He died September 1, 1872, in his eighty-third year His wife died August 25, 1877

Michael (4), fourth child of Michael (3) and Amy (Furst) Franks was born October 29, 1803 He lived all his life in Nicholson township, Fayette county, Pennsylvania He was a short, compactly built man of fair complexion, fine auburn hair and very regular features, and weighed about 150 pounds He had a genial, happy temperament, was a pleasing conversationalist, and his company was always a pleasure He was a progressive farmer, and, like his brothers, who were true to their instinct and training, abhorred bad fences and dirty fence corners During his life he became possessed of several hundred acres of well-improved land, but in different farms The last farm he bought was the James W Nicholson farm in the early fifties

The fine brick mansion (for that day) was on the top of a high hill one-half of a mile above Geneva, commanding a beautiful view of the winding silvery band of the Monongahela river, Greensboro and its neighborhood section of the valley To this farm he moved and spent the remainder of his days with his excellent wife Michael Franks was a Democrat Both he and his wife were Baptists Both died at a good age, their deaths being only a few days apart, and they were buried in Cedar Grove cemetery, New Geneva On November 13, 1828, he married Charity Kendall, sister of Rev Samuel Kendall, an old-

time Baptist preacher To this union were born 1 Isaac K, born January 4, 1830, married Mary Eberhart, of New Geneva, a daughter of Martin Eberhart, a glass manufacturer He was a farmer and mill owner, etc Later in life he moved to Kansas and died some years ago, aged seventy-six years His widow is still living with a son in Oklahoma, a large land owner and wealthy She is now (1912) enjoying good health at the age of eighty-one years 2 Michael W, born April 29, 1832, was much like his father in looks, size, build, and complexion, except that his hair was darker colored and inclined to baldness He was a farmer, but often in township offices, and in November, 1878, was elected county treasurer for three years Also he was later made cashier of Internal Revenue of the Twenty-third District In political faith he was a Democrat He was a courteous, pleasing gentleman and made and held friends wherever he went On May 17, 1864, he married Martha J, daughter of John Bell, of Greene county, Pennsylvania, a wealthy and well known farmer He died at his home near New Geneva, December 14, 1899, in his sixty-eighth year His wife died March 23, 1904, aged about sixty-seven years He and his wife were buried in Cedar Grove cemetery He left children Charles Boyle, a sketch of whom follows, Emma married (first) James C Long, (second) Jesse Dills, they own and cultivate the old Franks homestead 3 Estella, married Allen Fast, a teacher and clerk, and resides in Masontown 4 Frances A, born October 28, 1842, married John Morris, a farmer Both are dead and survived by four sons 5 Amedee M, born January 18 1848, a powerfully built man of great physical strength; in the prime of life was a farmer and carpenter He was a good, useful and upright citizen, a Democrat, and he served as county commissioner with credit to himself and to the county He was a man of good business judgment and always stood squarely for the right Both he and his wife were Baptists On March 3, 1866, he married Nancy Longanecker He died at his home in Uniontown, March 3, 1906, and was buried in Cedar Grove cemetery He left a family Holly W, of the J S Douglass agency, is his son His widow also survives him 6 Alice R, born May 21, 1851, married James

K Dills, a farmer of Nicholson township, has a family of grown-up children Several others died in infancy

James, fifth child of Michael (3) and Amy (Furst) Franks, married Maria Chick, a cousin of William Chick, of Uniontown He was a successful farmer and lived on the farm where William Trader resided until the time of his death, and now owned by his son, William H Trader, Jr In about the year 1847 he moved to Wayne county, Ohio, and settled on a fine farm a few miles from Doylestown They raised a large family. He died at the age of seventy-six years His wife lived to a good old age Their children that are living are well settled in life, mostly on large, well tilled farms, prosperous and favorably known in Fayette county In religion Baptists, in politics Democrats

Samuel, sixth child of Michael (3) and Amy (Furst) Franks, died in infancy

Samuel, seventh child of Michael (3) and Amy (Furst) Franks, was born in Nicholson township, Fayette county, Pennsylvania He married Susan Trader (sister of the late William H Trader Sr) He died August 12, 1894 in the eighty-eighth year of his age His wife died April 24 1865, in her fifty-ninth year

Like his brothers (except Abraham), a farmer, and pursued farming throughout his long life He inherited the strong traits of both parents, some of which were honesty, amiableness of temper, with a kindly disposition toward all He possessed a modest appreciation of the humorous side of life Consequently he had many friends and but few if any enemies, but was firm in his convictions as to right and wrong He was always cheerful, happy and contented, never moody or fretful After this simple analysis of the man it would scarcely seem necessary to add that he was a model citizen, father and husband At an early age he united with the Mount Moriah Baptist Church at Smithfield, Pennsylvania, under the pastorate of Rev John Patton His wife, Susan, was noted for her kindness and sweet disposition She was a Presbyterian and died in that faith Her pastor was Rev Ashabel Fairchild, widely known as a theological writer In politics he was a Democrat The children that grew up and married are the following Sarah A,

born 1836, wife of the late John Whetstone Elizabeth, married John Jaco, who enlisted as a private in the civil war in the Sixty-third Pennsylvania Regiment He was wounded in one of the Seven Days battles of the Wilderness Was taken to the hospital at Washington City, D C, and died at the age of about thirty years The wife is now dead William H, a physician, read medicine with the late Dr F C Robinson, of Uniontown, and took a full course in Jefferson Medical College, Philadelphia graduating some time in the early sixties Shortly after he went to Brimfield, Noble county, Indiana, where he began the practice of his chosen profession Being an ardent student, of good judgment, patient and sympathetic, he rose rapidly in favor with the people He married May Gibson, of near that place Later he moved to Ligonier, in the same county, where he now lives as a retired physician Mary (Mollie), married Luther Wheeler and lives at Deer Park, Maryland Amanda married Harry Zimmerman, who for many years has held a responsible and lucrative position with the Baltimore & Ohio Railroad Company at Cameron, West Virginia where they reside Eliza J, married Charles Griffin, son of the late W P Griffin, of Nicholson township They live at Chanute, Kansas, and are well fixed in life

Abraham, eighth child of Michael (3) and Amy (Furst) Franks, was born in Nicholson township, Fayette county, Pennsylvania, October 29, 1806, where he grew to manhood His early education was limited to the meager advantages of the subscription schools of that day, but by severe application of mind to the pursuit of knowledge he succeeded in storing his mind with a degree of education far beyond the average teacher of the day in the community

For a few years he taught school in his own neighborhood and also in the High House settlement He then engaged in the mercantile business at New Geneva At the age of twenty-eight years he sold his store at New Geneva and went westward, expecting to go to Chicago, Illinois Chicago at that time, 1834, was merely a trading post. Going by the way of Wayne county, Ohio, he concluded to stop off at Doylestown and visit some of the Franks living in that section While visiting Abraham Franks, a son of one of the former settlers of the Franks region at High House, Pennsylvania, this Abraham was persuaded to remain and go into business with him To this he agreed, and they conducted successfully for years a general store business at Doylestown under the firm name of Abraham Franks, Sr, and Abraham Franks, Jr He married September 9, 1848, Amanda, daughter of Abraham Franks, Sr, and Lydia (Blocker) Franks Soon after his marriage he was elected to the state legislature on the Democratic ticket He was re-elected and served with credit to himself and the people of his district On leaving the legislature he returned to Doylestown and engaged in the hotel business (no bar or liquor sold) for several years Tiring of this, he moved to his farm and for a number of years engaged in farming In 1861 he again returned to Doylestown and again engaged in the mercantile business, and so continued until 1878, when he retired from active business life on account of age On December 3, 1887, his wife died at the age of fifty-eight years He was among the early settlers of Wayne county, Ohio, and aside from his more public life, as already stated, was one of the prominent citizens of the county, and was for many years a justice of the peace

He was an able and intelligent man and wrote much for the papers However, he lacked the oratorical gift of expressing himself orally, which proved somewhat of a bar to his public advancement* At an early age he united with the Baptist church at Smithfield, Pennsylvania, and throughout his long life was a consistent and upright follower of his Lord and Master He was an everyday Christian, and this was the testimony of those who knew him best He died January 26, 1890, at the age of eighty-three years, two months and twenty-seven days He was a model husband and father Constitutionally kind and sympathetic, he was an example worthy of imitation by all

Amanda, wife of Abraham Franks Jr, was born at Chippewa, Wayne county, Ohio, August 1, 1829 She united with the Baptist church at an early age She was a woman of strong Christian character and her faith and trust in her Saviour seemed to increase as the years passed by In her last sickness she was a great sufferer for many months But her patience and fortitude were said to be beautiful and sublime As before noted, she passed through the pearly gates ajar" to rest in the heavenly Beulah land on December 3, 1887

To this union were born two children Jennie, born at Doylestown, Ohio, May 17, 1850, and Louis Kossuth, born in Chippewa, Wayne county Ohio, November 29 1854 Jennie was given the advantages of the best schools the town afforded, and displayed quite a talent for music, for the development of which she had training under the best instructors the town afforded, also a course at Wooster, Ohio She was bright and well equipped to maintain a high standard of usefulness and social distinction While in Wooster she met Rev J W Lowe, minister of the Disciple church This mutual acquaintance ripened into love They were married in May 1872 At the date of this information (1894) they had one daughter, Lucy Virginia, a young woman of twenty-one years, an accomplished musician

Louis K was born in Chippewa, Wayne county, Ohio, November 29, 1854, as before noted, he was given the advantages of the common schools and also started in a college course, but owing to the advanced age and consequent infirmities of his father, was prevented from completing his college course The practical part of his education was received at an early age and in his father's store, the latter proving of great advantage in all the succeeding years of his life At the age of twenty-five years he engaged as a partner in the drug business, and was thus engaged for three years, making of it a financial success On August 1, 1883, he married Linda Wharton, of Ashland county, Ohio Since his marriage he has pursued various callings, serving as deputy county treasurer of his native county for two years In June, 1912, the writer found him a farmer, cultivating a fine farm a few miles from Doylestown, where he was enjoying the comforts of a good home He drives to and from his farm and greatly enjoys the blending of country and town life He possesses strong physical and mental vigor, is kindly and hospitable in disposition, but has a high standard of positive convictions in morals, religion and politics

He is a man of strong personal influence in the community where he lives, and is most highly respected His politics, like his father's, were cast in the mold of the old Jeffersonian Democracy His wife is a befitting helpmeet and at once a loving companion and mother and a practical and thorough housekeeper and homemaker Their children are Metta C, a teacher, at home, Kent Wharton, in Ohio University, veterinary department, Carrie, at home

George, ninth child of Michael (3) and Amy (Furst) Franks, died at the age of twenty

John, tenth child of Michael (3) and Amy (Furst) Franks also the seventh son born consecutively was born in Nicholson township in the early part of 1811 His education was that of the average country boy of his day — reading, writing, spelling and some arithmetic Like his father and the remainder of the family, he possessed strong instinct to stick close to the bosom of mother earth Here it may be stated that while a youth he learned the trade or art of weaving, and in addition to the more ordinary products of the loom that were used in those days largely for home clothing and other household purposes, he made the heavy bedspreads (or coverlets) with their beautiful inwoven figures, very popular in those days But he soon quit weaving and from that time on was a farmer

On April 10, 1837, he married Mary, daughter of Peter and Ann (Fuller) Hess The marriage took place at the home of the bride, a few miles northwest of McClellandtown, the officiating minister being Rev William Wood, a noted Baptist preacher and evangelist, and who in turn was the father of the late Rev W S Wood, of Mount Pleasant Pennsylvania, a noted theologian and preacher They set up housekeeping, and for a short time lived on William Greenlee's farm, near what is now Ruble, in Georges township

In the year 1838 Peter Hess sold out and moved to Fayette county, Ohio, which was then a new country, beginning to settle up Peter Hess wished to have all his children settle near him In a short time thereafter John Franks, with his wife, followed and settled on a farm on Compton creek, in Fayette county, Ohio, four or five miles from Washington Court House Here John contracted malaria so badly is to make life miserable,

and they remained there only a little over two years, when they returned to Fayette county, Pennsylvania It was while in Ohio that Peter Hess, the oldest child, was born, the birth occurring December 18, 1839, of whom more hereafter A second child born in Ohio died in infancy As before stated, John returned to Fayette county, Pennsylvania, and settled on the farm in Nicholson township, on which his brother-in-law, Andrew Kramer, had lived In 1847 he moved to the farm lying close to New Geneva, where he remained to the time of his death, which occurred October 16, 1858

John Franks early united with the Mt Moriah Baptist Church at Smithfield Later in life he was made a deacon He was a man of strictest moral integrity, never broke his word though he might suffer loss thereby His word was considered as good as his bond This was certified by all who knew him most intimately in life He never sought public office, but nevertheless was a forceful personality as a citizen and in every sphere of his life

At the time of his death (at forty-eight) he was the owner of two valuable farms in Nicholson township The home on which he erected a good brick house in 1855-56 contained about one hundred and sixty acres of productive land, with coal and other valuable minerals, and another farm of about one hundred and twenty-one acres In politics he was a Democrat His wife survived him many years She was a Baptist Both were buried in Mt Moriah cemetery, Smithfield, Pennsylvania

Children of John and Mary Franks 1 Peter Hess, whose sketch follows

2 An infant daughter, Amy Ann, named for its two grandmothers, was born and died in 1841 while in Ohio

3 John Irvin born July 3, 1843 died October 21, 1858 He was a promising boy

4 David Jackson born April 13, 1846, married Fannie, daughter of James and Sarah Daugherty, of New Geneva First a farmer, but for years conducted successfully a large hotel at Greensboro, Greene county, opposite New Geneva Later he added to the hotel business a grocery store with Mr Lee Burns as partner The latter business so increased in volume that another storeroom on the op-

posite side of the street is also occupied They have no children In politics he has always been a Democrat

5 Margaret Caroline, born August 28, 1847, married James Hare, a farmer, and by trade a blacksmith They live in Springhill township They have a large family of grown children, some are married He is a Democrat

6 William W F, born May 9, 1849, died September 25, 1858

7 Mahala, born November 20, 1852, she married Asbury La Poe, once a prosperous farmer and business man, but now in poor health They have one child living, James Lindsay, born in 1896 He has a fine, practical mind with a good foundation in education already laid, promises a life of great usefulness Their home is in Greene county, Pennsylvania, near Crow's Ferry

8 Elizabeth Harriet, born February 23, 1855, died March 25, 1859

9 Charles Spurgeon, born May 5, 1858, while a young man he learned the art of photography and practiced it for some time at Carmichaels, Greene county, Pennsylvania He married Melissa Stull, of Washington county, Pennsylvania He then bought a small farm in Dunkard township Greene county, Pa In a few years sold out and moved to Rehway, Iowa county, Wisconsin, where he is still living They have two children a son, and a daughter, Pearl, at home They are graduates of the high school of Rehway

Mary (Hess) Franks, wife of John and mother of Peter H Franks, as already noted, was the daughter of Peter and Ann (Fuller) Hess Peter Hess was a son of Peter and Susanna Hess, who came from Germany to Lancaster county, Pennsylvania, thence to Fayette county, Pennsylvania They were among the very early settlers west of the Alleghany mountains Peter, the second, was born near New Salem, on Dunlap's creek, about the year 1787 He was a very thrifty business man, owning large and valuable farms in German township He dealt largely in stock and was known as a drover, driving large numbers of cattle and hogs to the eastern markets He imported from England and introduced the first pure blood Durham cattle into the Dunlap's creek valley When he moved to Ohio he bought a large tract of rich

land not far from the town of Bloomingburgh, Fayette county, Ohio This he improved into a fine home, and at death left a large estate

His wife, Ann Fuller was the daughter of Daniel Fuller, who was born in Ireland about the year 1777, and came at the age of fifteen years first to a Quaker settlement and soon after came over the Alleghany mountains and settled not far from Connellsville, Fayette county, Pennsylvania Her brothers and sisters were James, father of Dr James Fuller, deceased John a member of the legislature three terms and father of the late Dr Smith Fuller Sr of Uniontown, James, of Perryopolis, and Daniel, of near Newtown, Greene county, Pennsylvania, a very wealthy farmer and stock man Mary (Polly) married George Hess, a brother of Peter Hess, and Elizabeth (Betsy) married David Jackson a wealthy farmer and banker They have all been dead many years

The children of Peter and Ann Hess were Fuller, married Mary A Stevens, of Uniontown, Pennsylvania, he became a wealthy farmer and lived not far from Washington, Fayette county, Ohio, a son, Bowman, at the latter place, still survives Ann married Samuel Greenlee, Caroline married "Gus' Parrott, Elizabeth, never married, Margaret, married Thomas Porter Greenlee, brother of Samuel, they were sons of William Greenlee, of Georges township, Fayette county, Pennsylvania, Irvin, who came into possession of his father's homestead, well improved and having about eight hundred acres of very rich land These children of Peter and Ann (Fuller) Hess were all born in Fayette county, Pennsylvania, but as noted, all settled and died in Fayette county, Ohio

Children of Peter Hess and his first wife, Eliza (Poundstone) Franks are as follows 1 Mary Elizabeth born in Nicholson township, May 11 1862 died January 28 1887 2 Sarah M born in san e township October 17, 1863 she married Walter G Rea, December 25, 1890, a son of Major J Harvey Rea, of Carmichaels, Pennsylvania, she died at her home in Albuquerque New Mexico, January 25, 1909 To them two children were born, Anna Ethel, March 18, 1892, died May 26, 1896 and Nellie, May 9 1896, now (1912) at Pittsburgh Pennsylvania 3 Anna B, born April 12, 1865 later went to Pittsburgh, and took a graduating course in M Garnier's school of ladies' tailoring and dressmaking Returned to Uniontown, established herself in that business on Morgantown street, opposite the Messmore block In a few years she changed into a millinery business, sold out and went west in 1898 with her sister, Mis Rea and settled in business at Pueblo, Colorado On April 30 1899, she married John J Ryan a business man For some years conducted the St Remi Hotel in that city In 1910 quit the hotel and established themselves in other business She is a woman of great business energy She is a Baptist They have two interesting children, William J and Martha, who recently at the age of six years gave readings from Shakespeare, Burns and others, that excited the admiration and astonishment of all who heard them 4 John Fuller born April 26 1867 at McClellandtown Fayette county, Pennsylvania, is an able and efficient Baptist minister He is now pastor of the First Baptist church at Alice, Texas He received his education in the public schools, at Waynesburg College, Denison University Ohio, Louisville, Kentucky and the Western Pennsylvania Classical and Scientific institute, Mount Pleasant Pennsylvania On June 27, 1895 he married Ida Bell daughter of the late Benjamin and Caroline (Fulton) Phillips, of Redstone township, Fayette county Pennsylvania They have three children living Carolyn, now a young woman, Mary and Fulton A son Charles died in infancy 5 William Passavant born January 22, 1871, was educated in the public schools of Nicholson township at University of West Virginia one term, at Mount Pleasant Classical institute and California Normal He then taught eight terms in the public schools For some years he has been in the real estate business December 21, 1899 he married Hester A, daughter of James and Lucinda (Hogsett) Hankins, of Uniontown To them have been born seven children Three are dead, the living are Raymond H Wilbur, Mildred and an infant son 6 Hester A born October 19, 1872 in Nicholson township for some years a nurse in East End Pittsburgh married August 16 1911 John J Gallagher, a well-to-do farmer of Beaver county, Pennsylvania A grandson, E H Trader, born October 25, 1884, is the efficient city agent for the American Express Company at Akron, Ohio He started at the bottom as driver for the Adams

Express in Uniontown, when sixteen years old and rose rapidly through all the routine of grades in the business to his present remunerative but responsible position In 1905 he married Sara Ullery, of Brownsville, Pennsylvania They have one child, Peter Hess Franks Trader, born July 6, 1906

Amy the eleventh child of Michael (3) and Amy (Furst) Franks became the second wife of Jonathan Higgins, who married for his first wife her older sister Elizabeth

Charlotte, twelfth child of Michael (3) and Amy (Furst) Franks, was born October 16, 1816, died January 1, 1898 In March, 1840 she married William H Trader, born January 15, 1816 died June 1 1889 Both were buried in St Jacob's Lutheran church cemetery They were members of Mt Moriah Baptist church, Smithfield Pennsylvania She united with the church in 1832 In disposition she was naturally quiet and retiring, ever true to her religious convictions She was a modest but faithful follower of her Lord and Master, and when the end came it was serenely sweet and peaceful After her husband s death she moved in 1890 to her new home on Fayette street, Uniontown Pennsylvania, near the Great Bethel Baptist church, with which she then united

Her husband was a man of uncommon business energy, and though starting life at the bottom of the ladder, with the assistance of his wife, became a rich man for his time He owned and lived on a large and valuable farm in Georges township, near Walnut Hill He was also the owner of other tracts He was a fine judge of stock especially horses and made much of his wealth in that way He was a director of the People's Bank of Uniontown, Fayette county, Pennsylvania, and as such was a safe counsellor and his advice in business was much sought by the community

He left an estate that gave to each of his ten children about $10 000 or its equivalent His widow was left amply provided for The names of his children in order of age are Sarah Ann Amy Mary, John, Eliza, Amedee M Mahala, William H Jr, Charlotte and Minnie Sarah Ann the oldest married Nicholas Poundstone for years a renter, but by hard work and good management by him and his wife, continually added to their savings They then moved to a farm in Marion county, West Virginia, near Farmington This was a farm of about two hundred and thirty acres and was equally divided between her and her brother, Amedee M Trader, a lift from their father William H Trader Sr. They afterward sold these farms Poundstone and his wife moved to Washington county Pennsylvania and purchased a good farm six or seven miles north of Claysville. The wife (Sarah Ann) died January 3 1903, aged about sixtyone years She was buried at Claysville, services conducted by Rev J Fuller Franks now of Alice Texas Her husband survives with several children Both husband and wife were Baptists Amy married Samuel Deffenbaugh and lives on a farm in the Walnut Hill neighborhood Mary married A S Richey and lives in Uniontown Has a good home with a liberal supply of means They have a large, well-to-do family John lives in Ashtabula county Ohio, and is a farmer Eliza married Nicholas Honsaker and is dead Amedee M moved west and bought a farm in Vernon county, Missouri. Sold this and moved to Mountain Park, Oklahoma, where he still lives He is worth over $100 000, mostly made out of coal lands sold in West Virginia He married Virginia Freemen, of Walnut Hill Georges township Mahala married James Sesler, now dead His widow resides in Uniontown William H Jr, is now owner of and lives on the old homestead farm formerly owned by his father He married Nancy Newcomer He is a good business man, prosperous and a highly respected and a useful citizen A member of the Great Bethel Baptist church His wife is a splendid woman and is well known as an active leader and organizer in Sunday school work Charlotte twice married, her first husband being dead Her present husband is J C Parker, who owns and conducts a very successful general store business at Scottdale, Pennsylvania Minnie, the youngest, married Dr J W Higgins, said to be a very skillful doctor and surgeon They live in Denver City, Colorado

Christina thirteenth child of Michael (3) and Amy (Furst) Franks, was born about the year 1816, died July 20, 1894 She was married to James Hess when about thirty-three years of age He preceded her in death by some years He was a thrifty farmer, living near New Geneva They amassed considerable wealth during life Both were members of the Mt Moriah Baptist church Smithfield,

Pennsylvania, at which place they were buried In politics he was a Republican They had five children Margaret married Newton Griffin, son of the late W P Griffin, of Nicholson township Shortly after their marriage they moved to Fayette county Ohio, where they purchased a farm near Washington, where they now live They have two sons who are Baptist preachers John J the only son, is a retired and wealthy farmer now living in a fine home near Uniontown Is now in poor health He is father of Dr Frank Hess (dentist) of Uniontown Also of several other children Frances, married Ezekiel Zimmerman and is living in Wayne county, Ohio Harriet married Jacob Galley, now lives at Mechanicsburg Pennsylvania Alsa C, wife of Ira W Ross living at Masontown, Fayette county Pennsylvania

Henry fourteenth child of Michael (3) and Amy (Furst) Franks was born November 12, 1818 He married Sarah, daughter of Henry and Louisa (Showalter) Hughn January 30, 1844, ceremony performed by Rev Dr Fairchild, the bride's pastor Henry like most of his family, was a successful farmer and kept his farm in first class order His wife was a good manager They spent most of their life on the farm near New Geneva once owned and occupied by Andrew Kramer his brother-in-law (noted elsewhere) The farm with its substantial buildings fine orchard and luscious fruits general trimness and neatness of the whole, were the attractive features which at once stamped it as a first class home in the best sense of the word, and the owner and his family as thrifty and contented He died December 5, 1892 His wife died October 11, 1905 They were both Presbyterians and their bodies now rest in the Old Frame cemetery in Nicholson township To this union were born these children, all living Amy, married Joseph Burwell a farmer They have two sons and two daughters Harry an expert accountant and bookkeeper, married and lives in Uniontown Frank, single, in the employ of the Bell Telephone Company at Charleroi Pennsylvania, Louis at home, and Gertrude married Abraham H born May 6, 1847, married Sadie, daughter of Jacob and Matilda (Hall) Cover At this time, 1912, he owns four hundred and twenty acres of well improved land and is now a man of considerable wealth   He has a large and respected family of children

Charles Newell, not married formerly a successful farmer, but now retired, having plenty of means, he can well afford to enjoy the fruits of his labor and good business judgment   When not traveling he makes his home with his sister, Mrs Lucetta A   wife of Frank P Goodwin, of Fairchance   She is the youngest living grandchild of Michael and Amy (Furst) Franks   Her husband is a successful business man, conducting a slaughter house meat store and grocery   Both Mrs Goodwin and her brother, Charles Newell, are Presbyterians   He is from principle a strong advocate of temperance and always casts his vote accordingly

Isaac, fifteenth child of Michael (3) and Amy (Furst) Franks was born in Nicholson township, August 15 1820, on his father's farm where he was reared   A large part of his earlier life was devoted to farming   In 1844 he married Nancy, daughter of Philemon and Lydia Morgan   He had a vigorous constitution and possessed uncommon energy and determination of purpose   And the motto, "Labor Conquers All Things," was practically demonstrated by him throughout his long life   As said, he was first a farmer, then a merchant from 1857 to 1859 at Smithfield

He then engaged in the foundry business and continued it from 1859 to about 1868   At this time he owned and lived in a house on Main street, Smithfield, the home of the late Alfred Core, J P   and oposite the intersection of Water street, the foundry was on the adjacent ground eastward   Here his products were stoves grates and plow points   Later he moved his business into his new building on East Main street, opposite Henry Kyle's   This consisted of a large molding room, engine house, etc   He manufactured cane crushers and fixtures   He took into partnership John E Patton and John McCurdy   In 1868 the partnership was dissolved and he quit the business

He then went into the mail service   He carried the mail between Smithfield and Morgantown, West Virginia   In 1874 he moved to Morgantown and continued in the mail service, in all about fifteen years   He made a good and faithful servant for 'Uncle Sam"   There were but very few days in all that time when he failed to deliver the mail   Often the

treacherous Cheat river was in so dangerous a condition from its winter gorges breaking up with heavy floods that to attempt crossing it would seem like almost certain destruction and would have filled with fear and deterred a less courageous spirit   he would sometimes make a detour up or down the river for miles seeking a possible point of passage, and would only desist when the risk would be almost certain destruction   While in Morgantown he suffered a severe loss in the death of his beloved wife, which occurred February 21, 1886   She was buried at Smithfield in the Baptist cemetery, where her husband was later buried

On April 3, 1890, he married (second) Annie H, daughter of Thomas and Sarah Kefover, of Nicholson township   He had purchased a part of the old Colonel Henry Core farm, with the old stone mansion and beautiful in itself and surroundings in former years   Its location is near Old Frame, in Nicholson township   And now for the first time in several generations it passed out of the Core name, a marked historic family in the early and later history of Fayette county

Here he again established himself as a farmer, and although well past "three-score and ten," he personally took up the hard labor of plowing, planting and gathering the ordinary crops, as well as stock raising, improving his farm and tearing away the old frame part of the house and rebuilding it, etc   He was a living dynamo of energy   From youth he had been a member of the Baptist church   In politics a Democrat   He was a good citizen and his influence and personality were felt wherever he went   He died October 12, 1902   His second wife still survives, no children were born to this union

Children of Isaac and Nancy Franks Lydia Ann and Michael Skiles Franks   Lydia Ann married John, a son of Rev Benjamin F and Mariah (Lyons) Brown, of Woodbridgetown, Springhill township   By this union five children were born Ewing Charles Mattie, Frank and Lolo   All are dead except Mattie, who married Humphrey Humphreys a merchant of Fairchance, and Charles single   Mrs Brown has been proprietor of the well-known Fairchance House for many years   Her cuisine and table enjoy an enviable reputation from Pittsburgh south to Fairmont, West Virginia   For some years Mrs Brown was pro-

Peter H. Franks.

prietor of the noted Glenmoor, a summer resort on Cheat river, a short distance above Ice's Ferry

Michael Skiles was born March 22 1849, in Nicholson township, Fayette county Pennsylvania, as was also his sister just noted Mrs Lydia A Brown He attended the public schools and Georges Creek academy at Smithfield For fifteen years he taught schools in West Virginia and Pennsylvania In May, 1883, he married Ella J, daughter of William and Mariah (West) Conn of Smithfield In 1884 he engaged successfully in the drug business at Fairchance He was a regular registered pharmacist and his drug store was first class in every respect He was elected justice of the peace in February, 1889, and held the office for several terms

He has been a suffering cripple from a boy, the result of bone erysipelas necessitating the use of crutches but his great perseverance and will power broke down all opposing obstacles and won the commendation and respect of all He has three children, all grown into man and womanhood Their names are William C Annie and Edgar C Michael S with his family, is now a resident of Warren, Ohio, and has a good position in business there

Phineas, sixteenth and youngest child of Michael (3) and Amy (Furst) Franks, was born about 1824 in Nicholson township He grew up and worked on the farm He had a thirst for knowledge and used the advantages of the books he had and of the inadequate schools in the neighborhood at the time He attended Denison University Ohio, a few terms, and at this time thought of preparing himself for the ministry, but for some reason he never carried out this laudable ambition

At the age of twenty-eight or thirty he married Nancy Buttermore of near Connellsville, Fayette county, Pennsylvania, a sister of the late Dr Smith Buttermore She was an intelligent Christian lady, having a most amiable disposition After his marriage he first moved in with his parents and engaged in farming A few years after this he moved to a good farm near Brimfield, Noble county, Indiana He was there for a number of years He then sold out and moved to Vernon county, Missouri where he purchased a farm and continued the business of farming until 1874, when the light of his home went out in the

death of his beloved wife From this time on we find him a disconsolate wanderer He was in Iowa Kansas Nebraska Idaho Montana, Wyoming back to Missouri and finally back to Kendallville Indiana where he spent the remainder of his days with his son, Charles Spurgeon Franks The manner of his death was sad and pathetic and though he was seventy-nine years old at the time of his death, yet he was still strong in body and mind He went out one morning to clear off some land of its timber and brush Not returning at the noon hour for his dinner, the family became uneasy and went to the clearing in search for him They found his body crushed by the body of a large tree which he had chopped down and evidently had fallen in an unexpected direction He was a good man with a very generous disposition and most highly respected by all who knew him He was very religious and maintained his Christian integrity to the last He was a lifelong Democrat

The children of Phineas and Nancy Franks were George, living at White Hall, near Butte Montana, where he owns a large stock ranch and also a dairy business He raises large numbers of horses cattle and hogs He is said to be very rich

One daughter Mollie married Henry McCullough, a well-to-do farmer They live in Vernon county Missouri, and have a small family Spurgeon the youngest, was a very successful business man married and lived in Kendallville Indiana He conducted a very successful loan and real estate business He died a few years after his father

Peter Hess Franks, son of John Franks, was born in Fayette county, Ohio, December 18, 1839 During his infantile years he was a very delicate child, and it was not thought possible for him to live to manhood This sickly condition continued until he was about five years old, at which time his parents, with him and a younger brother, were returning homeward from a visit to the Hesses in Ohio They stopped over night at Wheeling, Virginia (now West Virginia) There the two children contracted what was called the black smallpox After recovery the sickly child grew healthy As a child he seemed to have a lively imagination a good memory, and can now relate a number of little incidents which happened to his experi-

once when but little past two years old When his parents moved to Geneva in 1847, as before stated, he had as yet never attended school, but his mother had taught him the alphabet, the spell-easy words, and he could read a few simple sentences In the summer of 1858 Rev Elias Green taught a subscription school at New Geneva and boarded with the child's parents He was a very kind man, with a great love for children He soon overcame the boy's timidity and induced him to go to school McGufiey's Second Reader and Cobb's Spelling Book and later a simple child's geography and writing were added Before the term of five months had closed he could read and spell quite glibly, and knew much of the reader by heart

A few years after this his parents moved from the suburbs of the town to another house on the hill, on the road leading to Crow's Mill and Morris X Roads When he was about fourteen or fifteen years old John G Hertig bought and moved on to a small farm in Nicholson township about a mile distant Hertig was a Frenchman, who graduated in Switzerland at the age of fifteen, and came to Fayette county, Pennsylvania, when about nineteen years old He was well known in Fayette county as a teacher and as a man of vigorous intellect, with a most tenacious memory He was a fine scholar and perhaps the greatest mathematician who has ever lived in Fayette county Mr Hertig taught the Pleasant Hill winter school for a number of years, and Peter H was fortunate to become one of his pupils Under the instruction of this master mind he laid a thorough foundation in the branches then required in the public schools, especially in grammar and arithmetic He afterward attended Georges Creek Academy at Smithfield, under the class instruction of Professors Gilbert and Ross It should be said that he was one of the victims of that most malignant typhoid fever in the fall of 1858, causing the death of his father and two brothers His recovery was in doubt for many weeks and his memory was somewhat impaired thereby

He married, March 31, 1861, Eliza, daughter of Jesse and Elizabeth (Case) Poundstone Her grandparents Nicholas and Elizabeth (Everly) Poundstone, were among the early settlers in Nicholson township

After marriage they first moved in with his mother (then a widow) and managed the homestead for one year, then moved to another farm, a part of his father's estate, which he purchased In the winter of 1860-61 he taught the Pleasant Hill school, where he had been a pupil under John G Hertig He was examined by Joshua V Gibbons, the first county superintendent of Fayette county, but at this time he had no idea of following teaching

Being raised on a farm and always loving the free, outdoor life with nature, he expected to confine his life work to that sphere But a mere and common incident changed somewhat the after current of his life In a few years after his marriage he sold his farm in Nicholson township and bought a farm in German township, near Middle Run, to which he moved When the time for the employment of teachers came the teacher for the Middle Run school had not been supplied Some of the directors and citizens persuaded him to teach the school From this time forward his services as a teacher were in demand, and thus it was he became a confirmed pedagogue, but except for a short time when he lived at McClellandtown, he taught subscription school as well as the regular winter term

In the spring of 1868, having sold his Middle Run farm, he purchased a farm in Nicholson township on Jacob's creek, to which he moved, and he continued teaching with farming For a number of years he was principal of the Geneva schools In 1891 he taught his last school and retired from the profession, somewhat broken in health His teaching covered thirty years His most excellent Christian wife died November 6, 1892 She was a faithful and devout member of the Greensboro Baptist church She was buried in Cedar Grove cemetery, near New Geneva In the following spring, most of his children having grown and gone, he sold his farm, stock and implements and moved to Mount Pleasant Westmoreland county, Pennsylvania, where he lived one year, going thence to Uniontown, where he has since resided

In February, 1896 he took up a valuable field of coal lands in Redstone township, on Dunlap's creek and held by renewals until it was sold Since February, 1902, he has been secretary and treasurer of the Short Line

Fuel Company, a West Virginia corporation, and chartered (it is simply a large holding, not an operating company) In the spring of 1911 he moved into his new home, a fine brick house, on Woodlawn avenue In 1855 Mr Franks united with the Mount Moriah Baptist church at Smithfield, under the pastorate of Jesse M Purinton, D D, the father of Dr D B Purinton, a former president of West Virginia University, and remains steadfast in the faith of his fathers For many years a Democrat, but later independent, voting for McKinley and Roosevelt, but utterly opposed to the saloon business and a strong advocate of temperance

On January 3 1900, he married (second) Elizabeth S, daughter of Alexander and Harriet (Campbell) Conn, of Steubenville, Ohio Her father was a most highly respected and influential citizen of that city He was a personal friend of Edwin M Stanton, the great war secretary under Lincoln, and was appointed to a position in the commissary department The Campbells have been prominent in the early and later history of Uniontown

Charles Boyd Franks, only son of Michael W Franks, was born near New Geneva, Nicholson township Fayette county, Pennsylvania, July 29, 1867 He obtained his primary education at the Pleasant Hill school in Nicholson township, then entered the Institute at Mount Pleasant, Pennsylvania, whence he was graduated, class of 1887 He returned to the home farm one year, then having attained his majority began business life working for the Union Supply Company at Valley Works, as clerk in the retail store remaining until July 1, 1890 when he entered the employ of the H C Frick Coke Company, at Mammoth Westmoreland county, as shipping clerk On February 1, 1891, he was promoted to assistant superintendent at Mammoth under Superintendent Fred C Keithly On October 1 1891 his chief resigned, and Mr Franks was appointed superintendent of the Mammoth plant He continued there until February, 1900, as superintendent, then was transferred to Leisenring No 1 as superintendent of the coke works and coal mines there belonging to the H C Frick Coke Company, and still continues in that position He is, as all the Franks have always been, a strong Democrat, and has for the past ten

years served continuously as school director In 1909 he represented Fayette county at the State School Directors Convention held in Harrisburg It was through his influence and effort that the first township high school in Fayette county was established at Leisenring No 1 in 1907 Outside his business, there is nothing in which Mr Franks is more deeply interested than in providing adequate facilities for the education of the youth of his county He is a member of the Baptist church, as is his wife

In May, 1912, he represented his party at the Democratic State Convention at Harrisburg His private business interests are in undeveloped coal lands, and he is a director of the Union National Bank of Connellsville

He married, October 11, 1895, Sarah Elizabeth Pollins, born in Westmoreland county, Pennsylvania, July 30 1871 daughter of Jesse Pollins, a farmer and native of Westmoreland county Child Jesse Pollins Franks, born April 29, 1897

PERSHING The Pershings of Mount Pleasant, Pennsylvania, descend from Frederick Pioersching, born in 1724 in Alsace, France (now Germany), three-fourths of a mile from the river Rhine The name in French means milk, in Germany, peach, which is also the Anglo-Saxon word After the arrival in America the name was anglicized to Pershin, and in 1838 Isaac Pershin added the final g, as now used—Pershing

(I) Frederick Pershing learned the weaver's art, making coverlets of all grades, from the lightest to the heaviest weaves He also understood the making of saltpetre and gunpowder He was ambitious, and, foreseeing the greater possibilities of the new world, also being subject to persecution for his religion he came to America He took passage at Amsterdam in May, 1749, coming via Liverpool, England, in the sailship "Jacob," commanded by Captain Adolph De Grove, and after a stormy voyage of five months arrived at Baltimore, Maryland (Penn Archives, 2d series, vol xvii, p 300) He had taken passage as a 'redemptioner" as did a large majority of the emigrants of that period After landing at Baltimore he entered into a contract with Captain De Grove and a Baltimore merchant whereby he was to work three years to pay for his passage, the term of service in such cases being determined by the length of time consumed on the voyage, the cost of living and the value of the passenger's services to his employer On account of the faithful performance of his contract and his valuable service the merchant considered he had been sufficiently compensated for the money advanced Captain De Grove, and released Frederick Pershing at the end of twenty-one months, when he could have exacted the full three years' service He then began working at his trade, and prospered so abundantly that in a few years he purchased a small farm in Frederick county, Maryland About this time he married a German lady of Baltimore, Elizabeth Wyant (German, Weyand) They lived on the Frederick county farm until 1773, during which period their five sons and three daughters were born In 1773, being ambitious for greater possessions to supply the needs of his large family, and in advance of the first Gospel messenger that crossed the Alleghanies and only four years after Penn s treaty with the Indians and purchase of land from the Iroquois, he started westward He traveled on foot, carrying a knapsack over the Alleghany mountains and through the dense forests filled with wild beasts that lurked everywhere to do him harm In fourteen days he reached the headwaters of Nine Mile Run, so called because the mouth of the run is nine miles from Fort Ligonier, in what is now Unity township, Westmoreland county, Pennsylvania There, amid the finest of oak timber, he took "tomahawk" possession of two hundred and sixty-nine acres of land There was no county court, no court officers, no assessors or tax collectors, until Hannastown, ten miles away, was established It was not until after the revolution and Pennsylvania became a commonwealth that he received a patent for his land, as recorded in patent book 17, p 107 "Commonwealth of Pennsylvania to Frederick Pershing, September 21, 1789, for tomahawk possession, a tract of land called Coventry, on the Nine Mile Run, containing two hundred and sixty-nine acres, more or less." This tract of land was for several generations conveyed from father to son The county records show that for one hundred and twenty years it was the only farm in the county that was never in

orphans' court or sheriff's hands, nor were any of the owners of said land in any litigation or lawsuit Here he built a round log cabin of one large room, with stick" chimney, clapboard roof poled on with hickory withes, a "puncheon" floor, hewed door with wooden hinges, not a nail used in the construction, and without glass windows The cabin being finished, he began clearing out the undergrowth and "ringing" the trees over five acres of his tract He then sowed it in rye and returned to Maryland In the spring of 1774 he came again to the home in the wilderness, bringing his family During the winter the deer had eaten every stalk of the rye but the forest abounded in game, furnishing meat for the family, while the pelts were exchanged for corn and rye meal, so that hunting and trapping the wild animals was not only sport for the father and sons, but also profitable On one ocasion Mr Pershing came near losing his life in an encounter with a bear His rifle yet preserved in the family, plainly shows the marks of the bear's teeth Fort Ligonier was fourteen miles away, and the nearest cabin was three miles distant Indians were plentiful, although the Pershings were never molested, as their home was somewhat secluded and at the greatest distance from the usual camping places of the Indians along the Conemaugh river on the east and the Youghiogheny on the west The work of clearing the farm rapidly progressed, crops were grown, herds of cattle appeared, among which deer were often found and easily killed, furnishing, with other game, an abundant table The work was laborious, the hardships many, and in 1778 the father, who was never known to have had a days sickness in his life, broke beneath the strain, was stricken with fever and in a few days died There was no physician to be had, as at that period they were found only in the more thickly settled communities He was in his fifty-fourth year, and is described as of large, stout build, broad shoulders, ruddy complexion, face of large French type, large nose and a heavy head of hair inclined to be curly His four sons and a neighbor made his coffin from a split white oak log the larger half hollowed out, the smaller half forming the lid He was buried in the Smith graveyard, one mile west of the old Pershing home There, forty-six years later, in 1824, his wife, Elizabeth, who ever remained his widow, was laid by his side, aged ninety-six years, having been born in Germany in 1728 Both were baptized members of the Lutheran church, and lived consistent Christian lives Elizabeth came to America the same year as her husband, but by another ship Their youngest son, Abraham, died in Maryland, aged two years Christian, the eldest son, remained on the farm, which he inherited and which passed to his son, Henry J Pershing Two others of the sons of the emigrant, Revs Conrad and Daniel Pershing, entered the ministry

Rev Conrad, the third son, was a minister of the United Brethren church, but before his death changed to the Methodist faith He was in Captain Campbell's company in 1792 at the time of his last expedition against the Indians They found an Indian camp and formed a plan to attack it at 3 o'clock in the morning, and slay them before they could awake and defend themselves Rev Conrad did not like this plan as it seemed too much like murder He asked Captain Campbell to allow him to lead in prayer for Divine direction After some parleying they all knelt upon the ground, and Rev Pershing began his prayer slowly and quietly, but soon became so earnest that his voice was raised to so loud a pitch that Captain Campbell interfered, fearing the Indians might be aroused He quieted somewhat, but soon became louder than ever in his supplications, when he was peremptorily ordered to cease praying When the attack was made later, to his glad surprise, the camp was deserted Whether a spy from the Indian camp or the loud praying had given the alarm is not known, however, they had flown, leaving their camp equipage, and never again molested that neighborhood Of the second son nor the daughters of Frederick Pershing have we any record

(II) Rev Daniel Pershing, fourth son of Frederick and Elizabeth (Wyant) Pershing, was born in Frederick county, Maryland, June 4, 1764, died in Derry township, Westmoreland county, Pennsylvania, September 28, 1838 He was ten years of age when brought by his parents to the forest home in (now) Unity township, Westmoreland county, and fourteen years of age when his father died, consequently his early life was one of

toil, privation and adventure He never attended other than nature's school, but received his only education in his own home with his brothers and sisters, taught by a pious, educated mother in the German language After their father's death the sons nobly remained with their mother The farm not yet being sufficiently clear to support the family of eight, the sons erected a saw mill, run by water power, flaxseed oil mill and later a home-made "burr' flouring mill When Daniel was twenty-one years of age Pittsburgh, Pennsylvania, was a hamlet of ten to twelve houses In 1796, at the age of twenty-two years he married, and in 1801, with his family of three children, moved to Derry the adjoining township All his belongings, wife and youngest child, Isaac, were taken in a one-horse wagon, the road being through deep woods all the way He was a carpenter, stonemason, plasterer and weaver having been taught the latter art in early life by his father and brother In their Derry home economy was the watchword The simplest food, pork, with an occasional saddle of venison, being the only meat Their farm supplied the corn and rye used in the bread and pone The girls wore homespun and linsey woolseys, the boys buckskin breeches, linen shirts, home-made wamuses and hunting jackets, for the summer, homemade straw hats, for the winter, coonskin caps Frequently the father and sons would arise in the night and with their guns drive wolves from the sheep fold

Daniel Pershing was always deeply religious, and had a deep desire to preach the Gospel He made such preparations as he could, and on August 13, 1816, at Mount Pleasant Quarterly Conference of the Methodist Episcopal church, was licensed to preach His authority is signed "Christopher Fox, presiding elder This license was renewed January 24, 1818, by Asa Shinn, presiding elder On March 27 1818 he was elected and ordained to deacon's orders by the Baltimore Annual Conference, his papers being signed by Bishop Benjamin Waugh On September 6 1819, he was ordained to elder's orders at Baltimore, signed by Bishop R R Roberts His family record ministerial record, book of sermons, licenses, library, arm chair and writing desk are preserved in the family of Professor A N Pershing, at Greensburg, Pennsylvania

He was a good penman, and his writings show that he acquired a fair degree of scholarship The following words copied from the first page of his 'Ministerial Record' were written by him January 26, 1836, not long before his death In the year of our Lord 1799, in the month of February, I attached myself to the Methodist Episcopal church, and on December 29, 1799, as an humble penitent, I sought the Lord with my whole heart, God spake peace to my soul and put me in evidence of pardon through the merits of Jesus Christ " He wrote both in German and English, and preached in both languages, better in German than in English He traveled and preached as far south as Uniontown, as far north as there were people to listen, east to the Alleghanies and west to the Ohio line His salary was as low as thirty-six dollars yearly, and never exceeded two hundred, paid in pounds, shillings and pence He always traveled on horseback, with saddle bags in which he carried religious books for sale, and always carried a rifle, that being as much a part of these itinerant circuit riding ministerial heroes as their Bibles He was absent from home for months at a time, where he is remembered as being very methodical in his ways, strictly pious in his family exacting in little things, even forbidding whistling on the Sabbath Day After more than a score of years in the ministry of the Gospel, traveling thousands of miles through sunshine and storm, he pillowed his weary head in death, surrounded by his family, leaving sweet benediction upon all in his last moments Tired and weary with the march of life, he sleeps, but not forever, 'on the hill' that overlooks the surrounding country for many miles Three acres of ground now constitute a beautiful burying ground, one acre of which was given by him in his will In 1880 it was chartered by the legislature of Pennsylvania as the Pershing Cemetery He was somewhat averse to having a monument placed over his remains, his spirit being of the humblest kind A few moments before he died he said "The Lord buried Moses, and did not dig his grave, yet the Lord knows where his grave is, and in like manner he will know where my grave is " Nevertheless a suitable monument, beautiful-

ly inscribed marks the resting place of one of the heralders of the coming "Resurrection Morning," when every generation of Adam's race will meet in reunion of thanksgiving and overarch the Great White Throne in anthems of praise A description of Rev Daniel Pershing says Mostly a 'shadbelly' coat and broad-brimmed hat of the Quaker style and a stuffed 'stock' for a necktie He always went clean shaven, and neither parted his hair in the middle or elsewhere His face was more lengthy than round, very high forehead, with a large mole on the side of his nose "

He married, January 26, 1796, Christena Milhron, born in Indiana county, Pennsylvania, February 2, 1777, died January 21, 1863, surviving her husband twenty-five years

(III) Abraham eldest son of Rev Daniel and Christena (Milhron) Pershing, was born near Lycippus, Westmoreland county, Pennsylvania, November 2, 1796 His birthplace was the original 'tomahawk' claim taken up by his grandfather, Frederick Pershing in 1773 He was five years of age when his parents moved to Derry township, where he grew to manhood In 1820 he received from his wife s father eighty acres of land near the iron bridge on Jacob's creek, and in 1828 he purchased the farm nearby on which he afterward lived and died His first home was a log house in which he lived until 1845, then replaced it with a commodious brick residence He served as justice of the peace four terms of five years each and so just and legally correct were his decisions that he was never reversed He was more of a peacemaker than a justice, and many were the reconciliations he effected between would-be litigants He was an authority on land titles, and was frequently summoned to attend at the county seat as a witness in the proceedings necessary to settle estates His testimony was rendered very valuable by his knowledge of dates, and agreements of boundaries of days long past In 1823 he was a member of the Mount Pleasant Rifles, the first uniform militia company in Westmoreland or Fayette counties, his brother, Isaac Pershing being captain He was a member of the United Brethren church for sixty years and for fifty years superintendent of the Sunday school In politics he was a Democrat, but never held other office than justice of the peace

He married, in 1820, Barbara daughter of John Troxell, at Iron Bridge, on Jacob's creek. Isaac Pershing, brother of Abraham, married Frances, a sister of Barbara Troxell. In 1823, Abraham and wife were housekeeping above the Iron Bridge across Greenlick creek, which flows into Jacob's creek just a few rods above the Iron Bridge in Bullskin township, Fayette county where they resided until 1828, then moved to their farm at Hammondville. Children 1 Ann Crider, married Jacob Myers, at her marriage her father gave her forty acres of land on which the village of Bradenville now stands in part. this forty acres was part of the division of land made by Isaac Pershing, brother of Abraham, after the death of their father, Rev Daniel Pershing 2 John, married Elizabeth Hammond, their son, James H Pershing resides in Denver, Colorado. John Pershing was third sergeant and served five years with the Mount Pleasant cavalry company, the first and only uniformed cavalry company of Westmoreland or Fayette counties. It had its existence from 1855 to 1860 and was recruited in both Fayette and Westmoreland counties. His father and Uncle Isaac Pershing were members of the Mount Pleasant Rifles, a foot company, Isaac being the captain 3 Daniel H, of whom further 4 Isaac went west to the "gold country" in 1859, died unmarried in 1895, having only once returned to visit his family and the scenes of his childhood Abraham Pershing, the father of these children, died in 1879, his wife, Barbara, in 1856 stricken by apoplexy while passing from the spring house to the dining room with the butter and cream for the dinner table

(IV) Daniel H, second son of Abraham and Barbara (Troxell) Pershing, was born in a log house (still standing) at Hammondville Westmoreland county, Pennsylvania, in May, 1832, died April 5, 1905 He grew to manhood on the home farm, received a good education and for several years taught school He also was a surveyor and engineer, having taken these branches up and acquired proficiency through a regular course of study He prospered in business, and lived upon his farm of one hundred and fifty acres, also owning two hundred acres elsewhere

He was a Democrat in politics, later in life becoming a Republican He held many local offices, and was a man of much influence in his locality He married, in Lebanon county, Pennsylvania, Amanda Miller, born in Lebanon county, March 8, 1838, died March 5, 1912 She met her husband in Westmoreland county, but was married at her home in Lebanon Her mother, Leah Stewart, was daughter of an English emigrant, she married —— Miller, of German descent, who died in Lebanon county Children 1 Isaac, died aged twenty-two years 2 Nevada, married Jacob Atkinson, of Williamsport, Pennsylvania 3 Louisiana, married John H Seaman, and lives at Sheridan, Pennsylvania 4 Minnesota, married David M Steyer, and lives at Dos Polos, California 5 Idaho, married Burton Jackson 6 Missouri, married John H Brader, lives in Hugo, Indiana 7 Abiaham, married Laura Weber, lives in Mount Pleasant Pennsylvania 8 Stuart (or Stewart), resides in Chicago, Illinois, he married Etta Steyer, deceased 9 Ira S, of whom further 10 Emerson, born May 1, 1879, now an engineer at Stauffer, Pennsylvania, married Irma McClov Also Alva E and Noble both deceased

(V) Ira Sankey, son of Daniel H and Amanda (Miller) Pershing, was born in Bullskin township, Fayette county, Pennsylvania, March 1, 1877 He was educated in the public schools of Bridgeport, Pennsylvania, and spent his early life upon the farm He was his father's assistant for several years working the home farm, but later entered the employ of the H C Frick Company and is now foreman at the Buckeye works near Hammondville He is a Republican in politics and a member of the United Brethren church, as is his wife

He married December 31 1896 Edna V Carson, born at Perryopolis, Fayette county, June 28, 1879, daughter of A C and Elmira J Carson Children Erda Pearl born November 14, 1897, Beatrice Naomi, October 29, 1899 Olaf Carson, September 18, 1901, Delmar Homer born September 16 1905, Samuel Allen November 7 1907 Frederick Ellsworth, September 7 1909 The family home is at Hammondville, Fayette county, Pennsylvania

LYONS Jonathan Lyons was an early settler of Somerset county Pennsylvania, where he grew to mannood, but in early married life moved to Salt Lick township, Fayette county, where he was the owner of three hundred acres of land on which he lived until his death He was a staunch Republican and a man of influence in his township He married, early in life, Sarah Boucher, who bore him five children 1 Hannah, married Irving Brooks a farmer of Salt Lick township Fayette county, Pennsylvania, where both died 2 John B of whom further 3 Eliza, married William Miller, a farmer of Salt Lick township where both now reside 4 Margaret, married James Miller a miller, who died in Pittsburgh, Pennsylvania, where his widow now resides 5 Rebecca residing in Fayette county, unmarried

Sarah Boucher was a daughter of Henry (2) Boucher, youngest son of Henry (1) Boacher, the founder of the family in America He was no doubt a Frenchman from one of the provinces bordering Germany, as he spoke the German language He came in the ship "President," it is said, and in the old Boucher family Bible it is written in his own hand that he landed in Philadelphia, June 20, 1755 with wife and children He settled in Berks county, Pennsylvania, where he purchased land in Albany township and followed farming He was a member of the German Reformed church and chiefly instrumental in erecting the church edifice known as "Bethel" near his home It has been rebuilt three times, but still retains the name given it by its pioneer founder It is further known of him that he lost heavily by the revolution, that he died early in the nineteenth century and is buried in the churchyard near the church which he built He had sons Peter, William Philip Jacob and Henry Peter died without issue William settled in Ross county, Ohio, in 1801 Philip remained with his father and inherited the estate much of which is yet owned by descendants, Jacob settled in Schuylkill county, Henry, the youngest son was born in Berks county Pennsylvania March 10, 1759 He married Mary Shoemaker, and moved to Hamburg, Pennsylvania, where he farmed and followed his trade of shoemaker In 1801 he started west on horseback with a neighbor, Jacob Will, intending to purchase lands there and settle He proceeded as far as the Miami valley, in Ohio, where the prevalence of fever and ague so alarmed him that they returned

east On reaching Somerset county, Pennsylvania, they bought lands to which they moved their families in the spring of 1802 The lands bought by Henry Boucher lay about three miles from Glade, and consisted of four hundred and fifty acres He spent the remainder of his days there as a farmer and died January 22, 1834 His wife, Mary Shoemaker, born January 22, 1762, died May 12, 1840 They are both buried at Glade, Somerset county Children Jacob, Henry, Christian, David, Solomon, John, Elizabeth, Magdalhne, Mary, Rebecca, Catherine, Sarah (of previous mention), married Jonathan Lyons, and Hannah

A great-grandson of Henry Boucher is John Newton Boucher, the well-known attorney of Greensburg, Pennsylvania, and author of a standard history of Westmoreland county, published by the Lewis Publishing Company of New York in 1906

(II) John B, eldest son of Jonathan and Sarah (Boucher) Lyons, was born in Salt Lick township, Fayette county, Pennsylvania, in 1838 He attended the public school and grew to manhood on the home farm of three hundred acres, which he afterward bought and on which he still resides, although he has reduced the acreage by sale He is an ardent Democrat, and has held several township offices, including school director and register He was drafted for army service during the civil war, but furnished a substitute, and was released from military duty

He married Ann Resler, born in Springfield township Fayette county only child of Daniel and Esther (Brooks) Resler, both born in Somerset county, Pennsylvania but early in their married life settled in Springfield township, where their only child Ann was born and early left an orphan Daniel Resler married (second) Tina Dull Their children Peter, now living in North Dakota, and Mary, who married Martin King, both deceased. Mrs Ann Lyons has been a member of the United Brethren church since girlhood Children of John B and Ann Lyons 1 Norman Resler, of whom further, 2 Sarah, married Warren Christner, who survives her 3 Eliza, married William Snyder, who survives her 4 James, a farmer, married Lizzie Ritenour 5 Mary, married Robinson Berg, resides in Hammondville, Fayette county 6.

Laura, deceased married John Ritenour 7 Samuel, a farmer of Fayette county, married Rosa Newman 8 Emma, died aged eleven years 9 Gertrude, died aged twenty years 10 Infant died unnamed

(III) Norman Resler, eldest child of John B and Ann (Resler) Lyons, was born in Salt Lick township Fayette county, Pennsylvania, March 14 1862 He was educated in public and normal schools and remained on the home farm, his father's assistant, until he was of legal age

At the age of twenty-one years he began teaching, and for twenty-seven years was a most successful instructor of youth, continuing until 1911 He passed all required teachers' examinations, and in 1896 was granted a permanent teacher's certificate During most of these years he owned a farm of seventy acres in Bullskin township, which he cultivated during the vacation periods, gaining considerable fame as a breeder of fine Berkshire and O I C hogs

In politics he is a Prohibitionist, and has held several town offices He is a member of the local grange, Patrons of Husbandry, and with his wife belongs to the Evangelical association He married, July 29 1886, Kate Bailey, born in Springfield township Fayette county daughter of James and Sarah Bailey

James Bailey was a soldier of the civil war, was taken prisoner and died in Libby prison He was a son of William Bailey and a grandson of John Bailey, who died in Springfield township, leaving William Riley, Fanny, Michael, Rebecca and Margaret William Bailey was a farmer of Stewart township, Fayette county, where he owned several hundred acres of land He and wife Mahala, were the parents of fifteen children James (of previous mention) father of Kate Bailey Lyons, John, died in infancy, as did George and Catherine, David, now living at West Newton, Rebecca, married (first) Thomas Mitchell, (second) William Dull and is now living at Confluence, Pennsylvania, Ann, married James Rush and lives in Iowa, Ellen, died aged twenty years, Hiram, married Rena Mitchell, and lives at Ohiopyle, Pennsylvania, Thomas married Alice Immel and lives on the old Bailey homestead Clara married E S Jackson, and lives at Ohiopyle, Amanda, married George Moon, and lives at McKeesport, Pennsylvania, William, a farmer of Nebraska,

married Miss Immel, Cramer married Mary Dal and lives at Confluence, Irwin married Mattie Seybert, and lives at Ohiopyle, James Bailey, father of Kate Bailey Lyons, married Sarah daughter of Joshua and Susan (Mariette) Kern both of Fayette county Joshua Kern was a farmer and small land owner, also a soldier of the war of 1812 He died aged eighty-six years His children 1 John, killed in the civil war 2 William, now living in Springfield township 3 George a farmer of Springfield township 4 Mary, died young 5 Sarah (of previous mention) married James Bailey 6 James, killed in the civil war 7 Margaret, married Silas Prinkey, and lives in Springfield township James Bailey was born in Springfield township October 18, 1837 He married in 1858, later served four years in the Union army nine months of which he spent in Libby prison He died at Hilton Head, South Carolina on his way home He was a private of Company K Eighty-fifth Regiment, Pennsylvania Infantry His widow never remarried Their children 1 Joshua now living at Coal Brook, Fayette county 2 Kate, married Norman Resler Lyons; their children Randall Bailey, born October 16, 1890, now employed with the Crystal Ice Company of Connellsville, Pennsylvania, Maude Esther born October 19, 1892, now a student of the Pennsylvania State Normal school at California, class of 1913

POORBAUGH The earliest record found of this family is of Philip Poorbaugh, born in Germany, who came to Somerset county, Pennsylvania, shortly after the revolutionary war He was a pioneer settler in Northampton township, part of Somerset county, lying east of the Alleghanies He became the owner of a goodly number of acres of this mountain land, not the best suited for agricultural purposes, but heavily timbered When he first settled there he had to go as far as Chambersburg for flour and salt Under such conditions many of the early settlers became discouraged and abandoned their improvements, but Philip Poorbaugh had come to stay, and stay he did He engaged chiefly in lumbering, but soon had part of his acres under cultivation He prospered, and many of his descendants are yet found in Northampton and part of the original land taken up from the government by Philip Poorbaugh is yet in the family name Prior to the coming of Philip Poorbaugh to Somerset county he had lived in York county, Pennsylvania In 1793 he obtained his warrant for seven hundred and ten acres of land His children were Henry, who moved to the state of Indiana in 1848, Philip, lived and died in Northampton, John J, of whom further, George, lived and died in Northampton

(II) John J, son of Philip Poorbaugh, was born in Northampton township, Somerset county, Pennsylvania in 1795, and lived near his birthplace until his death in 1862 He was a farmer and lumberman all his life, and well to do, as the times then considered wealth He was a Whig in politics, later a Democrat, and active in local affairs The first election in the township was held at his house He married Elizabeth Gerry, who died in 1876 Children 1 Jacob, died January 1, 1911 aged eighty-four years, he lived on a part of the original homestead and served many years as justice of the peace 2 Samuel, died 1905, a farmer of Northampton, living at Glencoe, where his son was a merchant, married a Miss Rengler 3 John J, of whom further 4 Mathias, died 1907, a farmer of Northampton 5 Gideon, moved to Illinois, served three years during the civil war, settled in Nebraska, where for thirty years he has been a farmer 6 Herman, a soldier of the civil war, was wounded in battle and died a year later from the effects Ellen, the only daughter, was the first born child

(III) John J, son of John J and Elizabeth (Gerry) Poorbaugh, was born in Northampton township, Somerset county, Pennsylvania, 1830, died there May 15, 1912 He was a farmer all his life, first for his father, and later purchasing the home farm, on which he resided until death He was drafted during the civil war, but for some unknown reason was never called into active service He was a lifelong Democrat and served in many township offices In religious faith he adhered to the German Reformed church He married (first) Mary Elizabeth Weisel, born in Somerset county, Pennsylvania, February 20, 1835, died March 16 1868 daughter of David and Mary (Polly) (Sellers) Weisel David

Weisel was born in Bedford county, Pennsylvania, his wife in Hagerstown, Maryland, but her parents died when Mary was young and she was reared under the guidance of an older sister, Mrs Rock, of Bedford county, where she met and married David Weisel He was a millwright and miller, building and operating many of the early mills of Somerset county He also owned seventeen hundred acres of timber, some of which he cleared and farmed He was an ardent Whig, and with his wife belonged to the German Reformed church He was a natural mechanic, and in addition to his milling and farming made coffins for his neighbors when needed, and was a generally "handy man" He was born September 9, 1795, married March 23, 1820, died August 13, 1853 His wife, Polly Sellers, was born February 7, 1797, died May 18, 1879 Their children 1 John, born February 26, 1821, died unmarried, January 23, 1859 2 George W, born September 13, 1823, died April 17, 1857, married Susan, sister of Dennis Comp, mentioned especially in this work 3 Philip, born December 25, 1825, died March or April, 1900, married Eliza Miller and lived on the home farm 4 Sarah Anne, born December 30, 1827, died February 7, 1864, married Hezekiah Fair, who survived her, and again married 5 Henry, born May 30, 1830, died unmarried, September 9, 1861 6 David, born January 12, 1833, died December 30, 1838 7 Mary Elizabeth, born February 20, 1835, died March 16, 1868, married John J Poorbaugh of previous mention 8 Emeline, born August 20, 1837, now living in Scottdale, Pennsylvania married (first) Henry Suder, (second) Henry D Bole a soldier of the civil war, serving in the Pennsylvania Regiment, Pennsylvania Heavy Artillery, commanded by Colonel Gallup, they are now living in Scottdale, Pennsylvania 9 Samuel, born September 27, 1841, died September 24, 1882, married Charlotte Dively John J Poorbaugh, married (second) Mrs Mary Sumpstine, widow of William Sumpstine She bore him three children Wilson, of Meyersdale, Pennsylvania, Jacob Franklin, of Nebraska, Elam, of Mount Pleasant, Pennsylvania He married (third) at the age of sixty-seven years a widow, Mrs Martha Hamilton, aged forty years, who bore him Helen and

Marshall   Children of John J Poorbaugh and his first wife, Elizabeth Weisel   1 Henry A, of whom further   2 Silas, died in infancy   3 Herman, an invalid, now residing in Mount Pleasant, Pennsylvania.   4 Nelson, a farmer and dairyman, near Mount Pleasant   5 John died aged ten years, his mother giving up her life at his birth

(IV) Henry A, eldest son of John J and Elizabeth (Weisel) Poorbaugh, was born in Northampton township, Somerset county, Pennsylvania, May 26, 1859   He attended the public schools and grew to manhood on the home farm, continuing his father's assistant until his marriage in 1886   He then rented a farm, on which he lived until 1899, then moved to Bullskin township, Fayette county, and bought a farm of fifty acres   Later he sold that property and bought his present farm of seventy acres, on which he lives and conducts general farming operations and stock raising and dairying   He is a Democrat in politics, has served in several township offices and as member of the Democratic county committee   He is a member of the local grange, Patrons of Husbandry   Both Mr Poorbaugh and wife are members of the Reformed church

He married, in Meyersdale, Pennsylvania, September 26, 1886, Sarah Baumaster, born in Somerset county, Pennsylvania, daughter of Elias and Elizabeth (Harshberger) Baumaster, of German parents, she died December 7, 1903   He married (second) June 24, 1908, Mary, daughter of John and Tina (Hoover) Long, both living in Somerset county, Pennsylvania   Children of Henry A Poorbaugh and his first wife   1 Edward, born September 15, 1888, now a teamster and farmer living in Bullskin township, married Katherine Hinkle   2 John, born May 1892, died December 21, 1897   3 Raymond born January 13, 1899.   4 Elizabeth, born June 7, 1902   Children of second wife   5 Lucy Emeline, born May 12, 1910   6 Joseph Glenn May 13, 1912

PISULA   This is an ancient Polish family transplanted from the land of their birth to the United States in recent years comparatively   The grandfather Martin Pisula, was born in Poland, and worked a farm near the city of Posen   He was born in 1826, was educated in the state schools and followed the occupation of farming until 1885, when he came to Mount Pleasant, Pennsylvania, joining his son, who had preceded him a few years   He found employment about the coke ovens near Mount Pleasant, continuing until his death in 1902, aged seventy-six years   His wife, Mary Pisula, still survives him   They were members of the Catholic church   Children John, of whom further, George, a hotelkeeper of Everson, Fayette county, Pennsylvania, Philip, now a mine fire boss in West Virginia, Jacob, deceased   Several children died in infancy

(II) John, son of Martin and Mary Pisula, was born near Posen Poland, in 1859, died 1907   He attended the state schools, grew up on the farm, and on arriving at suitable age began learning the stonemason's trade He married in 1879 and in 1880 emigrated to the United States, settling at Mount Pleasant, Pennsylvania   He found employment at the coke ovens, working as a coke drawer for a few years   He was economical, and in 1885 moved to Everson, where for several years he worked for the Scottdale Brewing Company   In 1899 his capital was sufficiently large to purchase the Everson House in Everson, Pennsylvania, continuing proprietor until his death in 1907   He was a Roman Catholic in religious faith   He married Josephine Jozviak, born in Poland, 1865 died in Everson, Pennsylvania 1899, daughter of Martin and Catherine Jozviak, both born in the same Polish village, came to Mount Pleasant, Pennsylvania, about 1848, where he worked at coke burning until his death in 1910   His wife Catherine died 1912   Their children   1 Josephine, wife of John Pisula 2 Margaret, married Lawrence Koscielniak, now living at Alice Mines, Fayette county   3 Mary, married John Raczunski, and lives at Morgan, Fayette county 4 Andrew, now living in New Salem, Fayette county   Children of John and Josephine Pisula   Vincent Paul, of whom further, Josephine student at Eastman's Business College, Harry Alexander, Leo and Anna, all attending school

(III) Vincent Paul, eldest son of John and Josephine (Jozviak) Pisula, was born at Mount Pleasant Pennsylvania, July 7 1888 His parents moved to Everson, Fayette county, when he was quite young and there his first ten school years were spent in the parochial school. In 1901 he entered St. Mary's Seminary at Detroit, Michigan, where he was graduated, class of 1905. He chose medicine as his profession, entered the Medico Chirurgical College, Philadelphia, whence he was graduated M. D., class of 1909. He served one year as interne at Uniontown Hospital, then, in July, 1910, located in Everson, where he is securing a good practice. He is highly respected among his professional brethren. He is a member of the state and Fayette county medical societies. He is deeply immersed in professional work, study and investigation, constantly fitting himself for greater usefulness in the future. He is a member of the Roman Catholic church, the Knights of Columbus, and in politics a Democrat.

He married, September 7, 1911, Anna Stackowiak, born at Everson, July 22, 1889, daughter of Andrew and Margaret Stackowiak, both born in Poland and now living in Everson.

CROW This family is of either Dutch or German origin, the founder in Fayette county being Michael Crow, whom authorities differ in assigning a birthplace, giving both Maryland and Holland as the place of his nativity. The greater probability is that he was born in Maryland, as he came to Fayette county when a boy of eighteen years with a party from Maryland, settling in Springhill township. Later he married a daughter of one of his old Maryland neighbors. She lived to be very old and was known for many years as "Granny Crow." Michael Crow built a grist mill on Georges creek, in Springhill township, which he operated until his death, aged nearly one hundred years. It was a burr mill, operated by water power. Children of Michael and "Granny Crow": 1. John, lived at Crow's Ferry, on the Monongahela river, and operated the ferry there for many years; also owning a farm on which he lived. 2. Isaac, of whom further. 3. Michael, a farmer of Springhill township; married Sallie Cover. 4. Alexander, lived at Geneva, Pennsylvania, and for two terms was associate judge of Fayette county; married Sarah Hustead. 5. Nathaniel, a miller, and with his brother Isaac, ran the Georges creek grist mill after

the death of Michael Crow; he married Elizabeth Brown. 6. Jacob, lived near Crow's Mill and cultivated the old homestead farm; he served a term as treasurer of Fayette county; he married a Miss Gans. 7. Elizabeth, married A. Neal, and lived on a farm near Geneva, Pennsylvania. 8. Kate, married Alexander Dunham, a farmer of Springhill township. 9. Mary, died unmarried.

(II) Isaac, second son of Michael Crow, was born at Crow's Mill, German township, Fayette county, Pennsylvania, July 31, 1799, died February 3, 1889. In 1807 he took the management of the mill, his father then being an old man and getting feeble. He continued the operation of the mill for thirty-one years until 1838, when he purchased a farm of one hundred and seventy-six acres, one mile east of McClellandtown, in German township, Fayette county. There he lived the remainder of his days, retaining active control of its operation until old age put an end to his activity. He was a strong Democrat, serving as school director and tax collector. He was always active in town affairs and a man of influence.

He married Nancy Kendall, born in Springhill township in 1800, died June 6, 1872. Her father died a young man and her mother married (second) a Mr. Schnatterley, by whom she had a son, Henry. Nancy Kendall was the second child of her parents and had an elder brother, Samuel, a Baptist minister of Greenlee, Pennsylvania. She had three younger sisters: Peggy, married Samuel Hall, a farmer of Springhill township; Charlotte, married Michael Franks, of Springhill township; Malinda, married A. Schnatterley. Children of Isaac and Nancy (Kendall) Crow: 1. Eliza Ann, born January 12, 1823; married Vincent Parshall, of German township, later moved to Carroll county, Virginia. 2. Hannah, born August 24, 1824, married Samuel Antrim, of German township; later moved to La Salle county, Illinois, where she died. 3. Eugene, born August 20, 1826, died unmarried, aged twenty-five years. 4. Elizabeth, married Evans McWilliams, whom she survives, a resident of German township. 5. Michael, born September 6, 1830, moved to Ohio, where he married (first) Sally Kendall, (second) in Virginia, Susan Bushhorn. 6. Margaret, born October 7, 1832, died March 11, 1833. 7. Mary Ann, born January 2, 1834, married Evans Finley, a farmer, and moved

to Grand Ridge La Salle county, Illinois 8 Harvey, born June 16 1836, died March 11, 1837 9 Josephus Melanchthon born November 9 1839, married Sarah Parshall and moved to Grand Ridge, La Salle county, Illinois, where he died she now resides in Uniontown 10 Josiah Brown, of whom further

(III) Josiah Brown youngest child of Isaac Crow, was born at Crow's Mill German township, Fayette county Pennsylvania October 10, 1841 He attended the public school of McClellandtown and as the youngest son remained on the farm with his parents After his father's death he purchased the homestead which he still owns He continued actively engaged in the cultivation of his farm until 1905, when he moved to Uniontown, built a modern home on Ben Lamond avenue, where he now lives a retired life after one of successful effort He was a Democrat in earlier life, but is now a supporter of the Republican party He has been a member of the Presbyterian church, with his wife, for forty-five years

He married, February 8, 1866, Elizabeth McCombs born in German township, Fayette county, near New Salem December 29, 1841 daughter of John McCombs, born March 1, 1809 in German township died 1884, son of William and Margery (Moss) McCombs, of German township The latter died and William McCombs married a second wife and moved to Ohio John McCombs was reared by an uncle Jacob Moss, and became a prominent well-to-do farmer of German township He attended the Presbyterian church and his wife was a member of that church He married Mary Jane Gallaher, born September 30 1818 died September 9 1861 daughter of George and Hannah (Baird) Gallaher, of Scotch-Irish descent Children of John and Mary Jane McCombs 1 Eliza married a Mr Brown and lived in Luzerne township 2 Lydia, married John Miller and moved to the state of Indiana 3 Elizabeth (of previous mention) 4 William, a farmer of Redstone township, Fayette county 5 Johnson Gallaher, moved to Illinois

Children of Josiah B and Elizabeth Crow 1 Mary Alice, born November 16 1866, died May 17, 1867 2 Eliza Ann born August 4 1868 married John Blaney and lives in Franklin township children William Harold and Ralph Crow 3 William Evans, born March

10 1870 (of whom further) 4 John M, born April 29 1872, married Alice Riffle and lives on the home farm in German township, child Caroline E 5 Frank R, born June 1, 1874, married (first) Emily Parshall, (second) Florence Brumbaugh children Martha, Frank and Geraldine 6 Arthur E born April 22, 1878 (of whom further) 7 Elizabeth born February 11 1880 married Charles Hubbard, child Charles 8 Josiah Benton, born March 30, 1884, married Maude Rush and lives in Uniontown

(IV) William F eldest son of Josiah B and Elizabeth (McCombs) Crow was born in German township Fayette county, Pennsylvania, March 10 1870 He began his studies in the district public school, later entering Pennsylvania State Normal school at California whence he was graduated He taught school two terms in German township, but resigned that profession in favor of journalism and was reporter on Pittsburgh papers for three years, 1891 to 1894 He continued his journalistic career as local editor of the Uniontown Standard, and when that paper was merged with The News became local editor of the consolidated News-Standard He had previously studied law with Boyd & Umbel, of Uniontown, and in December, 1895, was admitted to the Fayette county bar One month later he was appointed assistant district attorney of Fayette county under Ira E Partridge, the then district attorney In November 1898, he was elected district attorney, serving most efficiently for three years After retiring from office he resumed private practice, and has so continued until the present time having a large practice in state and federal courts He has given much time to the public service and is an active influential member of the Republican party In 1895 he became secretary of the county central committee, and in 1899 was elected chairman, serving three years as the directing head of the committee In 1902 he was the candidate of his party for the state senate, but through an unfortunate rupture in the party was defeated In 1906 he was again the candidate for the senate and elected He served with distinction and in 1910 was again elected and served as president pro tempore of the senate during the session of 1911 He has frequently represented his district at the county and state conventions of his party, and was chairman of the Republican state conventions of 1909 and 1910. He has served in every position with fidelity and distinction, and is one of the influential party leaders of western Pennsylvania. His practice of the law has been continuous, and his position at the bar is an honored one. His offices are in the First National Bank building; the family home at No. 127 North Gallatin avenue. He is a member of the Masonic order, being a thirty-second degree Mason of the Ancient Accepted Scottish Rite. He also belongs to the Benevolent Protective Order of Elks. His clubs are the Uniontown Country, the Duquesne, the Young Men's Tariff and the Athletic, the latter three of Pittsburgh. In religious preference he is a Presbyterian.

He married, March 24, 1897, Adelaide, daughter of James P. Curry, of North, Union township. Children: William J., January 22, 1902; Evan Curry, April 19, 1908; W. E., Jr., September 25, 1911.

(IV) Arthur E., fifth child of Josiah B. Crow, was born in German township, Fayette township, Pennsylvania, near McClellandstown, April 22, 1878. He attended the public schools, and became later a student at Knox College, Galesburg, Illinois. He had, however, decided upon a profession, and leaving Knox entered Jefferson Medical College at Philadelphia, 1899, from whence he was graduated M. D. in 1903. For one year he was resident physician at Jefferson Hospital, and in September, 1904, located at Uniontown, Pennsylvania, where he is now well established as a skillful physician and surgeon. He is a member of the Pennsylvania State and Fayette county medical societies; Laurel Lodge, Free and Accepted Masons; the Order of Moose; Phi Beta medical fraternity and Alpha Omega Alpha. He is a Republican in politics, and a member of the Presbyterian church. He married, October 12, 1909, Edith M. Abraham, daughter of Enoch H. and Belle R. Abraham, old residents of Fayette county. One child, Arthur E., Jr., born February 18, 1912.

ENGLISH   This name is said to be an additional name, applied for distinction's sake in Great Britain in early Norman times, to such persons as were permitted to retain their lands. Of the American families of this name, the longest settled in this country is probably the New Haven (Connecticut) family, which is still prominent in that city. The best known American of this name was William H. English, of Indianapolis, Indiana, a Democratic nominee for vice-president of the United States.

(I) —— English, the first member of this family about whom we have definite information, is said to have come from England to America, with three sons, one of these being Henry, of whom further.

(II) Henry, son of —— English, was born in England, and died in Alabama. In that state he lived, a farmer and slave owner. He was a Whig, and both he and his wife were Presbyterians. He married —— McCracken. Children: 1. Henry; he was a surveyor in Alabama, and went to South America, after which knowledge of him was lost. 2. Elbert; a lawyer, and for twenty-two years chief justice of Arkansas. 3. Alfred, died in Jefferson county, Arkansas, in young manhood; he was a farmer. 4. Noah D., of whom further. 5. Cyrus, died in Little Rock, Arkansas, at the age of nineteen. 6. William, a lawyer in Arkansas, died in Texas. 7-8. Died young.

(III) Noah D., son of Henry and —— (McCracken) English, was born in October, 1821, and died in Jefferson county, Arkansas, in February, 1869. He was raised in Athens, Alabama, and settled in Jefferson county, Arkansas, where he owned 1120 acres of land and many slaves, and was a great cotton planter. For many years he was county judge, and he served in the legislature at the outbreak of the civil war. Although he was a Whig, he was strongly opposed to secession, and made many speeches against the attempt to secede. He married, about 1847, Anna Eliza, daughter of James and Mary (Caldwell) Cox, who was born in Saline county, Arkansas, about 1829, and died in Jefferson county, Arkansas, in October, 1867. Her father was a native of Kentucky, born and married in Kentucky; thence he went to Benton, Saline county, Arkansas, where he died. At that place he was a merchant. His widow lived afterward with their son-in-law, Noah D. English, and died in Jefferson county, Arkansas, about 1846. He was a Whig and a slave owner, yet he is said to have been a Quaker. Mrs. Cox was a Presbyterian.

H J English Mo

Their daughter, Anna Eliza, was brought up in Saline county their only child who lived to maturity, a brother, James died in young boyhood Mrs English was an Episcopalian Children of Noah D and Anna Eliza (Cox) English 1 Henry J, of whom further 2 Mary Leona born 1851 died about 1868 3 A daughter, died young 4 Elbert T, born 1854, died at Benton, young, married Mary Wright, he was a clerk 5 William, died when three years old 6 Elizabeth, d ed when one year old 7 Stonewall Jackson, born 1863 died in Cincinnati, Ohio, about 1884 8 Blonde born 1865, married Silas Hayes, they now live in Little Rock, where he is a printer

(IV) Henry J son of Noah D and Anna Eliza (Cox) English was born in Jefferson county, Arkansas, February 5, 1849 After attending private school he finished at S John's College, Little Rock, Arkansas, taking there a three years' course Then he went to Jefferson Medical College, Philadelphia, Pennsylvania, where he studied for two years, and graduated in 1873 with the degree of Doctor of Medicine For five years he practiced in Little Rock In 1878 Dr English came to Fayette county, Pennsylvania and bought a farm of one hundred and fifteen acres known as the William G Patterson farm, near Grindstone Here he has lived continuously from that time Until 1910 he practiced medicine, he has now retired from practice, and is engaged solely in general farming and stock raising Besides his farm he owns three cottages and a business block at Manatee, Florida on the banks of the Manatee river, near Tampa bay He is a Republican, he has been school director for twenty-one years, but has never aspired to county office Dr English married (first), in Pennsylvania, in April, 1873, Mary L, daughter of Eli J and Mary (Cox) Bailey, who died in 1905 Her father was a grist and saw mill manager and general farmer, living at Albany, Pennsylvania He married (second), in September, 1908, Jessie F, daughter of James and Caroline Craft Her father was a farmer and land owner in Redstone township Fayette county, Pennsylvania Children, all by first marriage 1 Bailey J, born February 1876 he was a physician practicing at Perryopolis, Fayette county, Pennsylvania and died in March 1908 2 Mary B born December

1874, married T V Hibbs, he is a farmer in Fayette county, Pennsylvania, no children 3 Josephine, married Stewart Anderson, he is a farmer living near Brownsville, Fayette county, Pennsylvania 4 Henrietta, married C C Carter, he is an attorney, and lives at Brownsville Children Ross and Louisa 5 Noah D, lives in Pittsburgh and is a railroad passenger brakeman 6 Rufus M, born 1887, died January, 1912, unmarried 7 Ethel married Duncan Porter, he is a plumber at Brownsville no children

BERKEY The ancestors of Charles R Berkey, of Connellsville were among the earliest settlers of Somerset county, coming from Germany There was a Jacob Berkey came from Germany in 1775 and settled in Berlin, Somerset county where he died in 1820 He had nineteen children, and from them spring most of the Somerset county families Of these are many influential and prominent in public and business life, including John Albert Berkey, a prominent political leader of Somerset county, appointed in 1905 by Governor Pennypacker, banking commissioner of the State of Pennsylvania Other early settlers were two brothers, John and Christopher Berkey, who settled in the southern part of the county about 1760 and became large land owners in Meyersdale and vicinity From one of these brothers the family herein recorded descend

(III) Adam Berkey, grandson of the emigrant, was born in Meyersdale, Pennsylvania, about 1780 He moved with his father to the foot of Laurel Hill, where he lived and worked at the carpenter's trade until his death, also engaged in farming He married Susan Miller, and left issue

(IV) Henry, son of Adam and Susan (Miller) Berkey, was born about 1812, in Somerset county, his life long home He grew up on the home farm and learned his father's trade of carpenter, following these occupations many years He was a member of the Evangelical Lutheran church, and was a preacher of that denomination, officiating in the early churches of the county He married Louise Philson, daughter of William and Faith Philson, and granddaughter of Robert Philson, born in County Tyrone, Ireland, in 1759, came to the United States, settling in Berlin, Somerset county, Pennsylvania, in

1785 He became a prosperous merchant of Berlin, and founded a business yet carried on by descendants He was associate judge of the district for twenty years, was a member of the state legislature, and in 1819 elected to Congress from the 16th Pennsylvania Congressional District, a serious accident compelling his resignation before the completion of his term of office He married Julia, daughter of John Lowry, who bore him eleven children He died July 25, 1831 Descendants of Robert Philson have ever been prominent in banking and business in Somerset county The Philson National Bank of Berlin and the Citizens Bank of Meyersdale were founded by his son, Samuel Philson, and are now presided over by grandsons of the pioneer Henry and Louise (Philson) Berkey were the parents of thirteen children, ten of whom reached years of maturity

(V) Annanias, son of Henry and Louise Berkey, was born in Somerset county, Pennsylvania, December 14, 1833 He attended the public school, and worked on the farm until reaching a suitable age, then began learning the carpenter's trade, always a favorite one in the family He also owned teams and did a general hauling business He enlisted as a volunteer in Company E, 133rd Regiment, Pennsylvania Infantry, in August 1862, serving nine months, and seeing hard service, including the battles of Fredericksburg and Chancellorsville, returning home with an honorable discharge He was drafted in 1865 and served four months in the 91st Pennsylvania Regiment, but was not called into active service He was a member of the Evangelical Lutheran church, his wife also being a communicant He married Mary Atchison, who died May 24, 1880, daughter of James and Mary (Pritz) Atchison of English and German descent, both born in Somerset county, where they died James Atchison was a good carpenter, and owned a farm They were parents of seven children, one son, Henry Atchison, serving in the civil war Children of Annanias and Mary (Atchison) Berkey, all born in Somerset county, and all deceased except William, Charles R and Samuel (in order of birth): Sarah, James Henry, Elizabeth, Louisa, Ida, William, Charles R (of whom further), Emma and Samuel

(VI) Charles R, son of Annanias Berkey,

was born in Somerset county, Pennsylvania, March 15, 1873 He was educated in the public schools of Garret, Somerset county, and began business life as a worker in the saw mills so plentiful in that region at one time January 1, 1895, he entered the employ of the Baltimore & Ohio Railroad Company as brakeman, taking up his residence at Connellsville He was promoted conductor December 12, 1900, and is still holding that responsible position He is a member of the Knights of Malta and the Order of Railway Conductors, in politics a Republican

He married, June 2, 1895, Ella B, daughter of George and Jane Kyle (Wolheter) Langford Children Leroy F, born July 5, 1896, Victor Herbert, February 5, 1899, died in infancy, Paul F, born July 30, 1900, Charles, February 20, 1904, Nellie Veritas, July 25, 1908

ALBRECHT This family descend from George Gustavus Albrecht, born in Hamburg, Germany He was a man of excellent family and education, and for many years a teacher in the Hamburg schools He married Louisa ————, of the same city, where both died Children Gustave, died in Australia, Louisa, died in South America, George A (of whom further) and two who died in Germany

(II) George Alphonse son of George G. and Louisa Albrecht, was born in Hamburg, Germany, April 16, 1827, died at Indianapolis Indiana May 20, 1911 He was educated in his native city, and became a sailor, following the sea until on one of his voyages he met his future wife, whom he married on arriving in the United States, abandoned the sea and with her settled at Lawrenceville, Indiana He became a furniture maker, and after a few years moved to Indianapolis, where he started a furniture factory of his own which he operated successfully until his retirement from business He was a capable man of business and stood high in the estimation of his fellows He was a member of the German Methodist Church of Indianapolis, took no part in politics beyond voting with the Republican party He was a member of the Independent Order of Odd Fellows and the Red Men He married (first) Kate Seekamp, born in Germany October 9, 1833, died in Indianapolis, April, 1869 He married (second) Louisa Leader, born in England Children of first marriage Wesley, deceased, Matilda, now a resident of Berea, Ohio, Delia, deceased, Anna, deceased, George Edward, (of whom further) Children by second marriage Ella, deceased, Charles Alphonse, now residing in Indianapolis, Rudolph, deceased, Gertrude, married Arthur Conn, of Point Marion, Fayette county, Pennsylvania

The parents of Kate (Seekamp) Albrecht were both born in Germany, where her mother also died Her father later came to the United States, where he lived a retired life until death Their children 1 Kate (of previous mention) 2 Margaret, married Eugene Engus, came to the United States, settled in Indianapolis until 1885, when they moved to Kansas City, where they died 3 Richard, died in Indianapolis, in 1903 4 John, died at Lafayette, Indiana

(III) George Edward, youngest child of George A Albrecht and his first wife, Kate Seekamp, were born in Indianapolis, Indiana, December 1, 1865 He was educated in the public school of that city, finishing his studies at Kerner's Business College He began business life as clerk in the retail store of H P Wasson, continuing five years, then for fourteen years was in the employ of the Van Camp Packing Company both Indianapolis concerns In September 1906, he came to Connellsville and became a traveling salesman for the Westmoreland Grocery Company, a position he still most capably fills He has acquired mining interests, being interested in mines in Spring Hill township, Fayette county He is a Republican, and has served on the election board in his ward He is a member, with his wife, of the First Presbyterian church, and belongs to the Travelers Protective Association of Indianapolis also to the Masonic lodge of Connellsville, Pennsylvania He married May 30, 1904, Lulu Belle McGough, born in Parkersburg, West Virginia, daughter of Captain James McGough, an old river captain Child Sarah Phyllis, born January 1, 1906

Mrs George Edwards Albrecht is daughter of Captain James and Sarah Jane McGough, born in Cambria County, Pennsylvania, whose other children were Mrs W G Conn or Point Marion, Pennsylvania, and Mrs H N Bergmann of Monongahela, Pennsylvania, both born in Parkersburg, West Virginia

---

COLLIER The Colliers of Fayette county, Pennsylvania, descend from Irish ancestry A John Collier settled in Surrey county before 1668, and left numerous descendants William Collier, a citizen and weaver" of London, England settled in New Kent county, Virginia, and in 1675 was lieutenant-colonel He was the father of Charles Collier, father of John Collier who married a Miss Ironmonger There is preserved in Hanover county a will of John Collier, Jr, dated September 22, 1749, which names a son John

(I) John Collier the first of whom we have definite record in this line, was born in Virginia or Somerset county, Pennsylvania, about 1770 He was the original owner or proprietor of the old tavern at Mount Augusta, 1805, on the National Pike, continuing as proprietor until his death He was also a farmer of Addison township, Somerset county where he owned a good farm He married and had issue Joseph, died in Virginia, Daniel, of whom further John, a retired farmer, died at McKeesport, Pennsylvania Thomas, died a young man Perry, died at the homestead farm, which he owned, also three daughters

(II) Daniel, son of John Collier, was born in Addison township, Somerset county Pennsylvania, May 9 1799, died January 24 1877 He grew to manhood on the homestead farm, and when a young man was proprietor of a hotel on the National Pike at Mount Augusta, continuing fifteen years This tavern originally owned by his father, was of brick and one of the largest and most commodious houses on the Pike and in the palmy days of the National Road did a large business Daniel Collier continued its proprietor for a number of years, then sold out to Thomas Brownfield It was finally destroyed by fire and was never rebuilt In 1836 he moved to Georges township, Fayette county where he purchased a farm and prospered to such an extent that he finally owned seven hundred acres of good land and a great deal of other property He dealt largely in live stock, buying, feeding and driving to the eastern markets, having a partner in Loudoun county, Virginia He was a Whig in politics, and a member of the Presbyterian church He married Susan Seaton born December 10, 1805, in Uniontown, died June 11, 1879 daughter of James Carmichaels and Elizabeth (Swan) Seaton, who came from Eastern Pennsylvania to Uniontown among the first settlers, and ran the Seaton House a popular place of entertainment during the life of the National Pike They were of Scotch descent and left numerous posterity Their children 1 Hiram, born October 7, 1801 married Sarah Vorhees 2 Frances, born 1803, died September 25 1826 3 Susan (of previous mention), married Daniel Collier 4 Sarah, married William Crawford a saddler and harness maker, of Uniontown 5 Mary, born June 23, 1810, married William Ingram, and lived in Waynesburg, Pennsylvania 6 Rebecca, born July 18 1812 married George Martin, merchant of Uniontown 7 Marchant, born September 21 1814, died young 8 Juliet, born March 31, 1817, married Robert Barry, a merchant of Uniontown 9 James Carmichaels (2), born August 3, 1819, died 1851, unmarried 10 John S born September 12, 1823 a merchant of Baltimore, Maryland and veteran of the civil war, married Mary Ellen Rose Children of Daniel and Susan Collier 1 Frances, born February 5, 1830 married Allen Johnson both deceased 2 Elvira, born August 4, 1831, married (first) Samuel Griffith (second) Amos Boggs, all deceased 3 John James, born April 15 1833, died May 23, 1890, cultivated the home farm in Georges township, married Agnes Laidley both deceased 4 Marchant, born September 3 1835, married Harriet Hustead, both living on their farm in Georges township (1912) 5 William Crawford, of whom further 6 Elizabeth, born April 14 1840, died September 22 1841 7 Thomas born May 1, 1842 he was engaged in farming in Georges township until 1893, when he retired to his present residence in Uniontown married Harriet Ann Cocklan (or Cochran) 8 Daniel (2) born January 30, 1845 a farmer married Louisa Sturman, and died aged twenty-seven years 9 James Seaton born August 1, 1849 now a retired farmer of Uniontown, married Cornelia Brown

(III) William Crawford son of Daniel and Susan (Seaton) Collier was born in Georges township, Fayette county, Pennsylvania April 13, 1837 died June 14, 1901 He was educated in the public school, and passed almost his entire life on the homestead farm only moving a few years before his death to Fairchance, Pennsylvania, where he died His farm was a part of the original Collier homestead and there he conducted farming operations until his retirement from active labor He was a Republican in politics and a member of the Presbyterian church, his wife also being of that faith He married Mary Ann Longnecker, born 1843, died aged forty-four years and eleven days, she was the only daughter of Matilda and Jacob (Moser) Longnecker both born in Fayette county and members of the United Brethren church Jacob Longnecker was a farmer of Georges township a Republican in politics and died at a good old age in 1894 His wife still survives him, aged ninety-one years (1912), residing in Pittsburgh, with her son Their children 1 Dr William A a practicing physician, Pittsburgh, East End 2 Mary Ann (of previous mention), married William Crawford Collier Their children 1 Nellie, married (first) Walter Sterling (second) Frank Goosman, a lumber merchant of New Salem Fayette county 2 Lula, married William Defenbaugh, a tinsmith, of Fairchance, Pennsylvania 3 Ewing, a graduate M D of Baltimore Medical College, now practicing at Roscoe Pennsylvania, married Lillian Dorman 4 Elizabeth married Leslie Johnson 5 Harry, deceased, married Mary Shoals 6 Charles William, of whom further

(IV) Charles William, youngest son of William Crawford and Mary Ann (Longnecker) Collier, was born in Georges township, Fayette county Pennsylvania, October 23, 1877 He was educated in the De Armon public school and at Fairchance, Pennsylvania He began business life as a grocer's clerk for Humphrey Humphrey, going thence with the Union Supply Company at their Fairchance store, thence to their store at Adelaide, Fayette county, thence to their store at Leisenring No 2 He was then transferred to their Fairchance store and in 1903 to their McClure store as manager After six months he was transferred to the Baggaley store as manager, remaining two years. He then left the employ of the Union Supply Company, going to Pittsburgh, where he purchased a grocery store at the corner of Climax and Estella streets. He transacted a large and profitable business there for four years, then sold out and returned to the Union Supply Company as manager of their store at Dearth, Fayette county. He continued in that position from July, 1909, until March, 1911; then served two months as clerk in their Leith store, until August 21, 1911, when he was appointed manager of the company store at Bitner, Fayette county, a position he now most capably and satisfactorily fills. He is a member of Fayette Lodge No. 288, Free and Accepted Masons, and Uniontown Lodge of Perfection. In politics he is a Republican, and in religious faith a Presbyterian.

He married, October 23, 1900, Mary Taylor, born in England, January 13, 1882, died July 21, 1911, daughter of Joshua and Dorothy Taylor both now living at Mount Oliver—he a mine foreman. Child: Charles Ewing, born July 19, 1909.

The Lauffers are of German
LAUFFER origin, and first settled in Pennsylvania, "east of the mountains," later coming to Western Pennsylvania, in Westmoreland county, where they have ever occupied honorable position.

(I) Christian Lauffer, born 1730, died about 1800. He came to Westmoreland county, Pennsylvania, from Northampton county, bringing his entire family except Peter. He was a land owner, and had a family of eleven children. He is buried in the old Bash cemetery, but no tombstone marks the spot. Children: Barlot, Christian, Henry, John, Peter, Adam, Elizabeth, Susanna, Catherine, Mary, Magdalene.

(II) Henry, son of Christian Lauffer, was born in Northampton county, died in Westmoreland county, Pennsylvania, in February, 1821, aged sixty-seven years. He is buried in the Bash cemetery, with his father Christian. He came to Westmoreland county when a young man with his father and family, settling near Pleasant Unity, where he followed farming all his after life. He married Barbara Allison. Children: Henry (2) of

whom further: John, Susanna, Mary, (Polly), and Elizabeth.

(III) Henry (2), son of Henry and Barbara (Allison) Lauffer, was born in Westmoreland county, Pennsylvania, December 27, 1793, died April, 1873. He remained on the home farm as his father's assistant until the death of the latter, then moved to a farm west of Greensburg, Pennsylvania. He became quite wealthy, owning lands and a fulling mill in Manor Valley. He married Anna Mary Gress, born September 3, 1795, died April 24, 1870. Children: 1. Hannah, born January 12, 1815, died November 5, 1904, married Isaac Baer. 2. Daughter, born 1817, died unnamed. 3. Mary Ann, born March 11, 1820, died September 30, 1905; married March 23, 1837, Peter Waugeman; eleven children. 4. John, died aged eighteen years. 5. Jacob F., born March 24, 1822, died October 22, 1891; married, 1845, Susanna Scribs, ten children. 6. Henry, born March 25, 1824, died November 15, 1833. 7. Samuel, born September 28, 1826, died in 1890; married Eliza Ellen Buchanan; left son John, soldier of the civil war. 8. William Paul, born April 22, 1828, died September 13, 1839. 9. Isaac, of whom further. 10. Paul, born October 23, 1832, died September 21, 1840. 11. Simon Peter, born August 4, 1837, died 1902; he was a soldier of the civil war.

(IV) Isaac, ninth child of Henry (2) and Anna Mary (Gress) Lauffer, was born in Westmoreland county, Pennsylvania, May 12, 1830. He was educated in the public schools, and spent his early life on the home farm. After his marriage in 1853 he bought a farm of one hundred and eighty acres in Manor Valley, which he increased later by purchase and trade to two hundred and twenty acres. He conducted general farming operations, was active, energetic and capable, prospering to such an extent that he acquired an estate of five farms aggregating seven hundred seventy acres, also Greensburg real estate, consisting of dwellings and unimproved city lots. As years came on he diminished his holdings by sale, now only retaining about forty acres. He is a Republican in politics, but never sought public office. He is a member of the Second Reformed church of Greensburg, of which his wife was also a member. He married, March 10, 1853, Lydia Fox, who died March 8, 1906, daughter of Henry and Polly (Mary) Fox, both born in Fayette county. Children.

1. Cyrus Markle, who was born January 25, 1854, died April 10, 1855. 2. Anna Mary, born July 12, 1855; married, June 1, 1876, James S. McKeever; resides in Jeanette, Pennsyivania. 3. William D., born August 30, 1856; married, February 2, 1882, Annie E. Klingensmith; resides at Jeanette. 4. Alice Rebecca, born January 15, 1858; married, January 13, 1881, Moses McIlvain; resides near Bouquet, Pennsylvania. 5. Franklin Edward, born August 7, 1859, died April 5, 1912; married, September 15, 1896, Emma E. Klingeman. 6. Henry John, born December 31, 1860; married, February 22, 1882, Nannie J. Russell; resides near Irwin, Pennsylvania. 7. Infant, born September 16, 1862, died November 12, 1862. 8. Elmer E., of whom further. 9. Elizabeth Florence, born February 26, 1867, died April 7, 1877.

(V) Elmer E., eighth child of Isaac and Lydia (Fox) Lauffer, was born in Westmoreland county, November 10, 1863. He was educated in the public schools of Manor Valley (Old Manor Church) and remained on the home farm until sixteen years of age. After his marriage in 1889, he located on one of his father's farms near Trogger, where he remained seven years. In 1908 he moved to Bullskin township, Fayette county, where he purchased a farm of one hundred and nine acres where he conducts general farming operations.

In politics Mr. Lauffer is a Republican, and in religion a Lutheran, his wife also belonging to that faith.

He married Anna Elizabeth, daughter of Elias and Mary Ann (Salvis) Fink, both born in Indiana county, Pennsylvania, but moved to Westmoreland county after the birth of their daughters Ida and Mary Ann. Mrs. Mary Ann Fink died May 24, 1880. Elias Fink married (second) Elizabeth Kepple. Children of Elmer E. and Anna Elizabeth Lauffer.

Olive, born March 29, 1890; Fink, November 14, 1891; Lydia, October 16, 1893; Edgar, September 9, 1895; Clarence, March 17, 1898; Elkins, July 20, 1900; Mabel, February 13, 1902; Kenneth, December 24, 1904; Wayne, December 9, 1908; Catherine, June 27, 1911.

SNIDER This family is of German descent, and first made an American settlement in the colony of Virginia. The name is spelled with many variations, usually Snyder or Snider, the latter a form that has prevailed in this branch for several generations. The first of record in this branch is John Snider, who was of the second generation in America. His parents settled in Virginia, where the boy John was born. At the age of ten years he was carried awy by a band of Indians with whom he lived until a full grown man. He then settled among the whites in West Virginia, owning a farm which he cultivated, mostly with the labor of others. He had acquired the Indian mode of living, and was more of a hunter and woodsman than a farmer. He married and left issue.

(III) Elisha, son of John Snider, was born in Monongalia county, West Virginia, where he lived his entire life. He owned a large farm near Rosedale on the south, and was a prosperous influential man. He married Edith Britton.

(IV) Colonel Joseph Snider, only child of Elisha and Edith (Britton) Snider, was born on the home farm near the state line at Rosedale, Monongalia county, West Virginia, February 14, 1827, died at Point Marion, Fayette county, Pennsylvania, January 9, 1904. He was educated in the common school, and lived on the home farm until his father's death. He inherited the homestead, but soon after coming into possession sold it and moved to Wheeling, West Virginia, where he was in the hotel business for several years. He then disposed of his interests and returned to agriculture, on a farm near Morgantown, West Virginia, where he remained all his remaining years of activity. After his retirement from the farm he made his home with his son, Elisha M. Snider, at Point Marion, Fayette county, Pennsylvania. He served three years in the war between the states in the 7th Regiment, West Virginia Volunteers, attaining the rank of colonel. He led his regiment in the battles of Antietam, Fredericksburg, and Chancellorsville, being wounded once seriously in the head and twice less seriously in the body. He was a member of the constitutional convention that arranged the details of the division of the state of Virginia and formed the constitution of the new state of West Virginia He was a member of the Grand Army of the Republic and always a strong and active Republican He served two terms in the lower house of the West Virginia legislature and two terms in the state senate As long as he remained in West Virginia he was active and influential in state politics In religious faith he was a member of the Disciples of Christ, better known as the Christian church

He married, in 1844, Margaretta Miller, born in Greene county, Pennsylvania, in 1824, died July 7 1878 daughter of Jacob and Mary (Gans) Miller Jacob Miller was of German parentage but born in Greene county, where he grew to manhood, later he moved to Monongalia county, West Virginia, where he owned and conducted a farm near Morgantown Mary Gans was born in Fayette county, Pennsylvania, one of a large family who are of further mention in this work Children of Jacob Miller 1 Dr Benjamin F a physician of Cincinnati, Ohio 2 Dr Jonathan (deceased), was a physician of Fort Scott, Kansas 3 Esther (deceased), married Nicholas Vandervoort a farmer near Morgantown, West Virginia 4 Rev Oliver W (deceased), a minister of the Christian church, and in early life a professor of learning 5 Susannah (deceased) married Berry Baker a lawyer of Kingwood, West Virginia 6 Laura, resides in Morgantown, West Virginia Children of Colonel Joseph Snider 1 Ollie, died aged six years 2 Edith M, died at age of twenty-two years 3 Elisha M, a prominent citizen of Point Marion Fayette county Pennsylvania, president of the Bank of Point Marion, and manager of the Jeannette Glass Company, married Bessie Franks 4 Frank, of whom further

(V) Frank, youngest child of Colonel Joseph and Margaretta (Miller) Snider was born February 26 1863 at Rosedale, just a few yards across the line in West Virginia, but near the town limits of Rosedale, Pennsylvania His early education was attained in the public schools near Easton West Virginia, and later entered the University of West Virginia whence he was graduated A B in class of 1888 During his university term he taught two years in the public schools of Monongalia county West Virginia, then returning and finishing his course After graduation he was principal of the high schools of Parkersburg and Morgantown, West Virginia and for four years principal of Blackburn College for girls at Senatobia, Mississippi In 1895 he came to Uniontown, Pennsylvania and while waiting for favorable opportunity to engage in business, taught in the public schools for one year In 1897 he became associated with W F Frederick as bookkeeper in his piano establishment When the W F Frederick Piano Company was incorporated in 1907, he was elected treasurer, an office he yet holds This is a prosperous company, maintaining stores for the sale of musical instruments in Washington D C Altoona, Pittsburgh, McKeesport and Uniontown, Pennsylvania, Cumberland, Maryland Canton and Cleveland, Ohio The main office is at Uniontown, where the records, involving an annual business of one and a half millions of dollars, are all kept Mr Snider is also a director in the Davis, Burkham and Tyler Company of Wheeling West Virginia also a piano company He is a Republican in politics and an active member of the Central Christian church He is interested in work among the young, and has been for sixteen years superintendent of the Sunday school of the Central Christian church

He married September 3 1890, Hannah Matilda (Happie) Lyons, born in Fayette county Pennsylvania near Morris Cross Roads, daughter of Thomas W and Mary Parshall Lyons Children 1 Joseph L, born August 25, 1894 now a student at Amherst College, Amherst Massachusetts 2 Mary L, born December 20, 1895 3 Marguerite L, born December 20 1895 4 Thomas W L, born June 13, 1897 died July 24, 1898 5 Frank L (2), born August 30, 1898

SNIDER The various Snyder, Snider and Sneider families of the United States spring from the German family of "Schneider (the word meaning in German tailor") The ancestor of this branch was born near Berlin, Prussia and in 1770 came to America settling in York county, Pennsylvania He enlisted in the revolutionary army, serving under General Washington from Long Island to Yorktown He survived all the danger and hardships of that war, then retired to the peaceful life of his trade But when war was declared a second time against Great Britain in 1812, he enlisted and served during that war He was a wagon maker, and carried on that business in York county until after 1814, then moved to Washington county, Pennsylvania, where he died leaving issue The supposition is strong that his name was Andrew

(II) Andrew (2), son of Andrew (1) Snider, was born in York county, Pennsylvania, January 6 1792 died in Maryland, July 5 1865 He grew to manhood in Washington county, Maryland, and become a wealthy land owner and planter, but did not own slaves, cultivating his farms with free, paid labor He married Rachel McCoy, born in Washington county, Maryland, in 1797 daughter of Andrew McCoy who came to Washington county from his native land Ireland He married Mary Mountz born in Scotland Children of Andrew Snider Jacob, James John, Henry and several sisters

(III) John, son of Andrew (2) and Rachel (McCoy) Snider was born in Washington county Maryland, January 14, 1819 died December 30, 1889 He grew to manhood on the home farm and became a teamster on the old National Road, owning two freighting lines running between Cumberland Maryland, and Wheeling, West Virginia He drove a six-horse team on the road for twenty years, and became a rich man He is described as 'a clear headed intelligent, sober, discreet and observing man, whose statements could be relied on as accurate ' In 1852 when the railroad sounded the death knell of the Old Pike' he retired to Hopwood Fayette county, Pennsylvania and thereafter was engaged in railroad construction iron manufacturing and farming He built during 1872-1873 a section of the Pennsylvania railroad between Greensburg and Connellsville, Pennsylvania, and in 1874 to 1876 the section between Connellsville and Uniontown He had previously in 1871 built a line from Uniontown to Fairchance In 1878 he built the 'June Bug' branch line in Westmoreland county, Pennsylvania, for the H C Frick Coke Company In 1864 he bought a farm in South Union township on which he moved in 1867 continuing his residence there until his death He also engaged in coal mining, opening the Snider coal bank in 1867, which for many years was the source of Uniontown's local coal supply His farm of two hundred and

forty acres was well located and yielded abundantly As an iron manufacturer he operated the Redstone Iron Furnace until 1866 He was a good business man and successful in all his undertakings He was a Democrat, very public spirited, never sought office, but took an active interest in public affairs He married Margaret Pence born in Somerset county, Pennsylvania, in 1821 died June, 1895, eldest child of William and Mary (Shirei) Pence Her father, William Pence, born in Eastern Pennsylvania, located in Somerset county, later at Cook's Mills, now Tippecanoe, in Fayette county, where he died in 1858, but most of his life was spent as a farmer in Somerset county, of which county his wife Mary was a native Children of John Snider 1 Andrew, died in infancy 2 Mary, unmarried, now living in Uniontown 3 Henry, died in infancy 4 William, died February 16, 1889, was engaged for many years with his father in railroad construction, married Olive Morris 5 Elizabeth, married L F Patterson, and resides in Uniontown 6 John (2), now living on the old Snider farm in South Union township married Belle Sample 7 Josephine, married Thomas Rockwell, now a farmer of Nebraska 8 Lydia, married John N Dixon a farmer of South Union township 9 Edward, of whom further

(IV) Edward, fifth son and youngest child of John and Margaret Pence, was born at Hopwood, Fayette county Pennsylvania, February 17, 1865 He grew to manhood on the farm in South Union township his parents locating thereon in 1867 He attended the Poplar Lane public school, and worked on the home farm until he was twenty-two years of age He then was appointed manager of the company store at Oliphant Pennsylvania, remaining four years After his father s death in 1899 he leased the Snider coal bank of the other heirs continuing its operation for several years When his lease expired he associated with two others and bought a coal and coke plant at Beechwood, Monongalia county West Virginia He was in charge of this plant 1898-1901 then it was sold to the Fairmount Coal Company From 1901 to 1905, Mr Snider was manager of the company store of Hustead & Seamans at Dunbar Pennsylvania In the latter year he purchased the brick manufacturing plant of Leo-

naid & Colley, on Coal Lick Run, near Uniontown. He is also interested in coal lands, and
has lumber manufacturing interests in
Georges township, Fayette county, Pennsylvania. He is an active Democrat, but never
an aspirant for public office. His residence
is a cream brick structure erected in 1907 and
1908 at the corner of Nassau and Stockton
streets, one of the fine residence sections of
Uniontown.

He married, March 31, 1885, Josephine
Hustead, born in Georges township Fayette
county Pennsylvania, daughter of Captain J
M Hustead (see Hustead). Children 1
Paul Hustead, graduate of Washington and
Jefferson College, class of 1910 now taking
a post-graduate course in forestry at Colorado
College of Forestry, Colorado Springs, Colo-
rado 2 Julia graduate of Washington Sem-
inary, class of 1909 Washington, Pennsyl-
vania, and attended the State Normal College,
Indiana, Pennsylvania 3 Edwina

DAWSON

The Dawsons came to Fay-
ette county from Maryland in
1768 and have ever been
prominent in the civil and professional life
of the county. Their first settlement was in
North Union township—that and Uniontown
being the principal family seats

(I) John Dawson came to the American
colonies prior to the revolution, sailing from
Whitehaven, England. He settled in Prince
George now Montgomery county, Maryland,
where he died. He married Rebecca Doyne,
also born in England daughter of John
Doyne. They had issue including a son
George

(II) George, son of John and Rebecca
(Doyne) Dawson, was the founder of the family in Fayette county. He was a farmer of
Montgomery county, Maryland, and in 1768
settled at Bethelboro, Fayette county, Pennsylvania. He died prior to 1785 as on December 27 of that year a tract of three hundred and twelve acres was surveyed to Eleanor, widow of George Dawson, under authority of a certificate from a surveyor in Virginia,
dated March 18, 1785 His wife was Eleanor
Lowe, whom he married in Maryland. They
left issue including a son Nicholas

(III) Nicholas, son of George and Eleanor
(Lowe) Dawson was born in Montgomery
county, Maryland, April 3, 1745, died in Han-

cock county, Virginia, May 31, 1789 He
was with Washington in the Indian warfare
of 1764 and served under him in the revolution. He was with Colonel Crawford on his
last expedition and narrowly escaped capture.
In 1783 he removed to the 'Pan Handle' of
Virginia, now West Virginia, where he died
May 31, 1789 He married Violette Littleton,
born January 30, 1759, near Bull Run, Virginia, of historic fame. She died in Springfield, Ohio, September 19, 1842, aged eighty-
three years. Both Mr and Mrs Dawson
were members of the Church of England
(Episcopal) Children 1 Eleanor married
William Moore, Harrison county, Kentucky
2 George married Sarah Kennedy, of
Brownsville, Pennsylvania, and they were the
parents of Hon John Littleton Dawson, a
distinguished member of the Fayette county
bar, who served four terms in congress and is
known as the father of the 'Homestead Act"
3 Nancy, married Micajah Phillips 4 John,
of whom further

(IV) Judge John (2) Dawson, son of Nicholas and Violette (Littleton) Dawson, was
born near Georgetown, Hancock county, Virginia, July 13, 1788 died in Uniontown, Pennsylvania, January 16, 1875, aged eighty-six
years. He was reared in Harrison county
Kentucky obtained a good English education in private schools, and when twenty years
of age moved to Uniontown, Pennsylvania
where he studied law in the offices of General Thomas Meason and Judge John Kennedy. He was admitted to the Fayette county bar, August 17 1813, and successfully
practiced for more than thirty years in Fayette county. In 1851 he was appointed associate judge of Fayette county by Governor
William F Johnston, and served in that capacity until the office was made elective by the
new state constitution. He retired from the
bench to his farm which he superintended
until about 1865 after which he made his
home with children in Uniontown. For several years prior to his death his sight failed,
leaving him at times in total blindness. He
was a Whig and Republican in politics. The
tribute paid to his memory by his brethren of
the Fayette bar recites. "No tribute to his
memory can speak too warmly of the manner
in which he discharged the duties of every
relation in life" He was a man of sterling
character and held in highest esteem. He

was an Episcopalian, his wife a Presbyterian.

He married, in 1820, Ann Gregg, born in Uniontown, Pennsylvania, September 8, 1799, died there May 6, 1859, only child of Ellis Baily, who for forty years was a merchant of Uniontown until his death, November 10, 1853. His wife, Ruth (Gregg) Baily, was of the Loudoun county, Virginia, family of Greggs. Children of Mr. and Mrs. Dawson: 1. Ellis Baily, of whom further. 2. Mary Ann, died in early life. 3. Eliza, died young. 4. Ellen Moore, married A. Ruby. 5. Emily Violette, married Dr. W. H. Sturgeon. 6. George Littleton, died in infancy. 7. Maria, married Henry Baldwin. 8. Henry Clay, married Mary A. McCloskey. 9. Ruth Elizabeth, married A. K. Johnson, now living at Hillsboro, Ohio. 10. Louisa Cass, married John M. Berry; now living at Lexington, Kentucky. 11. An infant, died unnamed. 12. John Nicholas, of whom further. 13. Richard Williams, died February 1, 1865.

(V) Ellis Baily, eldest son of Judge John (2) and Ann Gregg (Baily) Dawson, was born in Uniontown, Pennsylvania, August 29, 1820; died October 30, 1900. He received his early education at Madison College, Uniontown, and was graduated from Washington College in the class of 1839. After his graduation he began to read law with his father and was admitted to the Fayette county bar June 6, 1843, and to the supreme court of Pennsylvania in 1846. He was largely interested in private business affairs, the multiplicity of which compelled him to abandon his legal career after a few years of active and successful practice. He held but one political office, that of "commissioner of the draft," to which he was appointed by Governor Curtin in 1862. This trust he fulfilled with strict impartiality and in a short time Fayette county's twenty-five hundred men were at the disposal of the national government. He was always known as a public spirited man, ready and anxious to advance the best interests of Uniontown. He served for several years on the town council of Uniontown and was one of the first stockholders and for twenty years a director of the National Bank of Fayette county. He was a Republican in politics and an attendant of the Cumberland Presbyterian church, his wife being a member.

He married, May 24, 1888, Elizabeth Jane McGregor, born in Allegheny county, Pennsylvania, November 1, 1856, daughter of Matthew G. McGregor, born in Allegheny county, died in 1885, aged about fifty years. He was a resident of the vicinity of Pittsburgh for many years, then moved to Fayette county where he resided several years and there died. He married Margaret Wallace, also born in Allegheny county. Their children were: 1. Robert Wallace, died in 1900, aged fifty-two years, married (first) Mary V. Richmond; married (second) Barbara E. Slack. 2. James, killed in a Colorado Gold Mine, in 1882. 3. Matthew Walker, died young. 4. Joseph Greer, married Sarah Welch and lives at Cool Spring, North Union township, Fayette county, where he is engaged in farming. 5. Elizabeth Jane, of previous mention, married Ellis Baily Dawson, and survives him a resident of Uniontown. 6. Mary Ann, married (first) Jacob Beeson, (second) William Davis, also deceased. 7. William Craig, married Mollie Jacobs, both deceased.

The only child of Ellis Baily and Elizabeth Jane (McGregor) Dawson, John Baily Dawson, born July 23, 1889, is now a student in a New York City business college.

(V) John Nicholas, son of Judge John (2) Dawson, was born in Uniontown, Pennsylvania, December 6, 1839. He was educated at Madison College, Uniontown, and Washington College, now Washington and Jefferson, Washington, Pennsylvania, whence he was graduated in 1861. He chose farming as his occupation and owned a farm at Oak Hill, which he cultivated until 1870, when he came to Uniontown and leased the plant of the Union Woollen Mill. Shortly afterward he purchased the mill and successfully operated it until May 8, 1879, when it was entirely destroyed by fire. He did not rebuild but at once established a general store in Uniontown, which he continued until 1888, when he was elected justice of the peace and gradually retired from other business. He has held the office of justice continuously by successive re-elections for twenty years. He is a member of the Episcopal church, which he has served as senior warden for many years. In politics he is a Republican.

He married, September 9, 1863, Lucy Strother, born at Morgantown, Virginia, January 11, 1844, daughter of Colonel James and Delia Elizabeth (Ray) Evans, of Morgan-

Ellis B. Dawson

town, West Virginia, the former born there, was a farmer, died there November 23 1888 aged seventy-eight years Mrs Evans was also a native of Morgantown, died September 19, 1898 Children of John N and Lucy S (Evans) Dawson 1 James Evans born September 18, 1864, graduate of the University of West Virginia, class of 1889, studied law, was admitted to the bar in 1892, and is now manager of the Trotter Water Company and of the Oliver Coke & Furnace Company he married Eleanor, daughter of F C Van Dusen, child Lucy Evans, born April 26, 1911 2 Richard W (see below) 3 Anne Baily, of Uniontown, single 4 John Littleton, employed by Oliver Coke & Furnace Company, single 5 Harvie Ray, daughter, single 6 George Ray died in infancy

(VI) Richard William, son of John Nicholas Dawson, was born in Union township, Fayette county, Pennsylvania, April 2, 1866 When four years of age his parents moved to Uniontown, where his early education was obtained in the public school He then entered the University of West Virginia, at Morgantown, whence he was graduated A B class of 1886 He then took a law course in the same university and was graduated B L in 1887 On September 10, 1888, he was admitted to the Fayette county bar, and at once began the practice of law in Uniontown, where he continues well established and successful He has important business interests outside of his profession and is a director of the Citizens' Title & Trust Company He is a member of the bar association of the county, and possesses the confidence of his clients as well the respect of his professional brethren He is a Democrat in politics, has been an active party man but never held any public office He has always taken a deep interest in public affairs from the standpoint of the citizen, not as the partisan His influence is solely for the public good, and all that is best in our public life He is a member of the Protestant Episcopal church of Uniontown, his family being communicants of the same faith

He married October 2, 1890, Nettie Winfield, daughter of Adam L Nye, of Morgantown, West Virginia Children 1 George Littleton, born January 12, 1892, educated in the Uniontown public schools, Washington and Jefferson Academy at Washington, Pennsylvania, passed his freshman year at Wash-

ington and Jefferson College, entered Amherst College as a sophomore, and was graduated B A in class of 1912 He is now a law student under the preceptorship of his father 2 Mary Wallace, born January 5 1896 now a student in Bradford Academy, Bradford Massachusetts (1912) The family home is on Ben Lomond street, Uniontown

DAWSON (V) William H Dawson, son of John Dawson was born in Fayette county Pennsylvania He was educated in the public schools and grew to manhood on the farm He choose agriculture for his business, and followed it all his life He was a member of the Baptist church, his wife also being a communicant He was a Republican in politics, and filled nearly all township offices He married Cerice Nixon Children 1 Emma V, married Homer S Lewis, of German township 2 William Newton residing in Morgantown, West Virginia 3 Louisa, married Mack Ingram, of Newton, Kansas 4 Tavlor N of whom further 5 Laura, married Seawright Brown, of Uniontown 6 Erwin M, married, and resides in Uniontown 7 Ella married Kenly E Porter, of Uniontown 8 Russell E, unmarried 9 Robert W, married, resides in Los Angeles California

(VI) Taylor Nixon, fourth child and second son of William H Dawson was born in Georges township, Fayette county Pennsylvania, July 10, 1865 He was educated in the public schools of his district finishing his studies at Uniontown high school He grew to early manhood on the home farm, and began business life as a commercial traveler After leaving the road he began dealing in coal lands a business he still continues He is a capable energetic man of business and a successful operator He is a Republican in politics, but never has sought or held office, excepting as member of his ward election board He is a member of the Methodist Episcopal church his wife also being a member He is active in church and Sunday school work in which he is interested and useful He married (first) Emma P daughter of Ernest E and Anna E Wengle Children Pauline, Elizabeth, Ruth He married (second) December 2 1904 Mary Edith, daughter of Thomas M and Margaret M (Cooper) Gregg

DAWSON Harrison Dawson, father of John W. Dawson, was born in Georges township, Fayette county, Pennsylvania. He was a farmer there, but now resides in Charleroi, Pennsylvania. He married Elizabeth Richey, also born in Fayette county, died April 25, 1912, aged seventy-one years. Children: 1, John William, of whom further. 2. Sarah Margaret, married Clark Lancaster, of Beallsville, Pennsylvania. 3. James, of Charleroi, Pennsylvania. 4. Alice C., married George B. Nolan, of Charleroi, Pennsylvania. 5. Lutellus. 6. George W.

(II) John William, eldest son of Harrison and Elizabeth (Richey) Dawson, was born January 4, 1867, in Georges township, Fayette county, Pennsylvania, in the same house in which his father was born. He grew up on the home farm, attended the public school of his district, continuing his study at Madison Academy, Uniontown, and at Smithfield Academy. He taught in the public schools of Fayette county for nine years, until 1895, then entered the law department of the University of West Virginia at Morgantown, whence he was graduated, receiving the degree of B. A., class of 1896. He located in Marion, Indiana, where he engaged in practice with Judge Joseph L. Custer, a lawyer of that city, formerly a resident of Fayette county, Pennsylvania. After two years in Marion he came to Uniontown, where in 1900 he was admitted to the Fayette county bar. He has since been admitted to practice in all courts of this state and is well established in his profession. He is also interested in the development of coal lands in Fayette county and western Pennsylvania, and director of the Title & Trust Company of Uniontown. He is a Republican in politics, but extremely independent in political action. He is public-spirited and interested in all that concerns the public good. He is an elder and trustee of the Third Presbyterian Church of Uniontown, and superintendent of the Sunday school. He is a member of the Fayette County Sunday School Association and deeply interested in its work, which has for its object the moral and spiritual advancement of the young.

He married, June 21, 1904, Mary Emma, daughter of Isaac and Hettie (Hornbeck) Mills, both deceased, former residents of Fayette county, Pennsylvania. She is also a member of the Third Presbyterian Church. Chil-

dren: Edgar William, born July 25, 1905; Ruth E., December 27, 1907; Paul M., June 23, 1909. The family residence is at No. 204 West Main street, Uniontown, a purely residential section of the city.

COLLINS There are several families bearing this name in Fayette county, Pennsylvania, springing from both Irish and English ancestors. The name has always been an honored one in the county; those bearing it have been important factors in the development of Fayette industries and in the military history of the county. The branch herein traced springs from William Collins, born in England in 1762, who may have been of the same English family as an earlier emigrant, Charles Collins, who came from Bristol, England, about 1734, settled in New Castle county, Delaware; married Sarah Hammond, and had a son, Isaac, founder of the Collins family of Burlington, New Jersey.

(I) William Collins was born in England in 1762, and when a young man came to Kent county, Maryland, where he passed the remainder of his life, engaged in farming. He married a Miss Gail, of the same county. They died leaving issue: William, John, George and James. From the latter springs the Collins branch herein recorded.

(II) James, youngest son of William Collins, the emigrant, was born October 17, 1777, in Kent county, Maryland, where he was educated, grew to manhood and married. In 1822 he came with his family to Fayette county, Pennsylvania, settling on a farm in Dunbar township, known as Fort Hill. He devoted his life to agriculture both in Maryland and Pennsylvania. He was a man of steady, industrious habits, and bore a high character in his neighborhood. He served in the war of 1812, in the commissary department. He married, in Kent county, Maryland, Sarah Dudley, daughter of Nicholas Dudley. Children: 1. William (2), of whom further. 2. James, born April 20, 1810. 3. John D., born April 29, 1813; came to Fayette county with his parents; married Agnes, daughter of Christian Stoner; he was a member of the Cumberland Presbyterian church, trustee, and a man noted for charity and benevolence. 4. Louisa, born May 19, 1816; married William Patterson, who died March

8, 1838 Nicholas Dudley, father of Sarah (Dudley) Collins, was born in England, came to America and settled in Maryland, where he died, leaving children Benjamin, Nicholas (2), Francis, Elizabeth, Mary, Sarah, married James Collins, Samuel, died in Fayette county, May 25, 1889 aged 87 years

(III) William, son of James and Sarah (Dudley) Collins, was born in Kent county, Maryland, in 1807, died October 24 1888 He came with his parents to Dunbar, Fayette county, in 1822, and from that time forward was a resident of that township until 1822, when he moved to Kansas He was reared a farmer, educated in the public schools, and always followed agriculture as a business He was highly respected in his town, was a faithful member of the Cumberland Presbyterian church of East Liberty, and always found on the side of morality and clean living He moved to Kansas in December 1882, where he lived near seven of his ten living children until his death six years later, aged over eighty years He was carried to the grave by his six sons, that having been among his dying requests He married (first), August 28, 1833 Eliza Cox, died July 22, 1851, daughter of Joseph Cox He married, (second) October 1, 1851, Mary B Stone, of Knox county, Ohio Children by first marriage 1 George W, born June 25, 1834, died 1837 2 Joseph R, born April 9, 1836, died young 3 Lutelus L, of whom further 4 James C, August 20, 1840, served in the Union army three years of the civil war, in the Fifteenth Regiment Cavalry 5 William H, born February 13, 1843, also a veteran of the civil war, enlisted as private, rose to the rank of captain, in the Seventh Regiment Pennsylvania Cavalry, served nearly four years, was engaged in numerous battles and was with the troops that captured Jefferson Davis, president of the Confederacy 6 Susan E, born October 21, 1845, married William Parkhill, of Franklin township 7 Sarah, born April 24, 1848, died young 8 Eliza Alice, born October 24, 1849, married Clark Shaw, of Connellsville, Pennsylvania Children of second marriage 9 Mary A, born July 20, 1852, married Henry Ackley, of Kansas 10 John E, born May 26, 1854 11 Alonzo D, May 18, 1857 12 Ida M, July 20, 1858, married John Smith, of Kansas 13 Margaret O, born

August 17 1862 died young 14 Charles E, born December 4, 1864

(IV) Lutelus, son of William Collins and his first wife, Eliza Cox, was born in Dunbar township, Fayette county, Pennsylvania, April 7, 1838 He was educated in the public schools and at Chesterville (Ohio) Seminary He was a lad of thirteen when his mother died, and six years later, in 1857, he migrated to Kansas, where, although yet not a legal voter, he threw all his influence in favor of the Free Soil movement, and in 1858 worked for the election of the first Free Soil state legislature elected in that state He caught the gold fever then raging through the west and crossed the southern plains to California, where he worked for a time in the gold mines of Nevada county He left San Francisco December 5, 1862, on a Pacific mail steamship to the Isthmus, crossed and took passage for New York on the steamer "Aerial" which on the passage was chased by the celebrated Confederate cruiser "Alabama," but escaped In August 1864, he enlisted in the Sixth Regiment Pennsylvania Heavy Artillery for the defense of Washington, was detailed as clerk at headquarters of De Bussey's division, and served in that capacity until mustered out at Washington June 13, 1865 After the war he returned to Fayette county, where he engaged in farming and stock dealing purchasing a farm from his father He is a member of the Cumberland Presbyterian church of East Liberty, holding the office of elder several years He is a member of William Kurtz Post, Grand Army of the Republic, of Connellsville, and a Republican in politics He married, November 5 1863, Anna daughter of Christian and Mary H (Shallenberger) Stoner, she was born June 20, 1845 Children 1 Mary E, born September 21 1864, died May 18, 1882 2 George A, born November 10, 1866, married Elizabeth, daughter of William Leighty, of Ohio 3 John W, born August 18, 1868, married Millie, daughter of John Lint, of Dickerson Run, Pennsylvania 4 Blanche, April 20, 1871, married Ulysses S Thompson, who was killed in a shaft at Trotter Coke Works, August 9 1908 5 Curte C, of whom further 6 Ken H born February 19 1881, married Jennie Bunnell 7 Florence, March 22, 1886, married John Leslie Love, of Pittsburgh, Pennsylvania

(V) Curtie Christian, son of Lutelus Collins, was born in Dunbar township, Fayette county, Pennsylvania, October 26, 1876. He was educated in the township schools and Vanderbilt high school. He grew to manhood on the farm, and in January, 1898, established in the lumber business in Vanderbilt, Pennsylvania and in 1900 became one of the proprietors of the mills, retail lumber yards and contracting business of the firm Ogilvie McClure & Company, a thoroughly well established concern of Vanderbilt. Mr. Collins is a Prohibition Republican in politics, served three years as school director of Dunbar township, and now a member of the town council of Vanderbilt. He is a member of James Cochran Lodge, No. 614, Free and Accepted Masons, Connellsville Chapter, No. 283, Royal Arch Masons, Uniontown Commandery, No. 49, Knights Templar, Uniontown Lodge of Perfection, Ancient Accepted Scottish Rite, in which he has attained the fourteenth degree. He is also a member of Modern Woodmen of America and has been clerk of the Vanderbilt Camp since it was organized thirteen years ago. He is a member of the Presbyterian church at Vanderbilt, in which he has taken an active part for more than fifteen years, is chorister and choir leader and superintendent of the Sunday school, in which capacity he has served about fifteen years.

He married, April 27, 1905, Estella Arison, born in Fayette county, January 30, 1886, daughter of Hickman and Althea (Evans) Arison. Hickman Arison was killed at Star Junction, being crushed between cars on coal tipple. His wife survives him, a resident of Vanderbilt, Pennsylvania. Their children Ethel, Clayton, Estella, Joel E., Arleigh A. and Lela. Children of Curtie C. and Estella Collins: Grace, born March 19, 1906, Clarendon, June 27, 1907, Harold Dudley, June 6, 1908, died August 8, 1908, Ethel May, born May 7, 1909, Harry J., January 29, 1911.

COLLINS   This branch of the Collins family descends from James Collins, born in Ireland, who came to the United States, settling in Somerset county, Pennsylvania. The name of his wife has not been ascertained. He lived to a good old age, was prosperous and respected. One of his sons, William Collins, was associate judge of Somerset county and was noted for his great height, standing six feet five inches, another son Moses, is of further mention.

(II) Moses, son of James Collins, the emigrant, was born in Somerset county about 1820. He was a millwright by trade and superintendent of the woolen mills at New Haven, Pennsylvania, at one time, also superintendent of the Dunbar Furnace Company at Dunbar, Pennsylvania, for many years. When the railway mail was established he was one of the first appointees on the Baltimore & Ohio road, running between Pittsburgh, Pennsylvania, and Cumberland, Maryland. He met his death in the wreck at Bidwell, Pennsylvania October 22, 1871 being caught in his car and literally burned to death. He married Phoebe Scritchfield born in Fayette county, Springfield township, of German parentage. Moses Collins left issue.

(III) James S., son of Moses Collins, was born August 1, 1841, died January 29, 1890. His early education was obtained in the schools of Dunbar township and Connellsville, Pennsylvania, his parents settling in the latter town when he was about eight years of age. He enlisted at the beginning of the civil war in Company C, Eighty-fifth Regiment Pennsylvania Volunteer Infantry, and served during the entire war, enlisting a second time, serving in the latter year as commissary sergeant. He was shot in the thumb and hit by flying pieces of shell, but never received serious injury. After the war he returned to Fayette county, learned the carpenter's trade, and for thirteen years was employed in the Calhoun planing mill at New Haven. He was an invalid during the last six years of his life, but bore his sufferings with Christian fortitude. He was a member of the Baptist church and a faithful, consistent follower of the Master. He married Martha Ann Artis, born near Connellsville, February 28, 1849, daughter of Isaac and Christiana (Murphy) Artis, both born in Springfield township, Fayette county. Isaac Artis was a steel mill worker, Christina Murphy was daughter of John Murphy, of Springfield township, she died in 1881, her husband, Isaac Artis, preceding her to the grave many years. She married (second) John Basenger. Martha Ann Artis made her home from early childhood with Joseph and Mary Kimmel, who reared her as their own Children ot James S and Martha Ann (Artis) Collins Alvin E and Clarence N, of whom see toward Fred and Frank died in infancy, Moses Lawrence, assistant foreman in Kelly and Jones brass manufacturing works at Greensburg, Pennsylvania, Elizabeth, married Fred Yeskey, of Greensburg, Mary died in infancy, Charles C, of whom further The mother of these children survives her husband, and resides with her son, Clarence N Collins, in South Connellsville

(IV) Alvin E, eldest son of James S and Martha Ann (Artis) Collins, was born in Connellsville, Pennsylvania February 10, 1868 He was educated in the public schools of New Haven (Connellsville, West Side), where the family then resided, but at the age of twelve left school and began working in the grocery store ot Woodfield Brothers, at the age of thirteen he began working in the planing mill of Calhoun & Company, running mostly a molding machine At the age of sixteen years he was promoted foreman and manager of the main floor of the mill, at the age of eighteen he began learning the general carpenter s trade, continuing four years more with Calhoun & Company, at the age of twenty-one years he married, and the next year worked for eight months in the Baltimore & Ohio carpenter shops, following with six months with the Connellsville Planing Mill Company, two years with the H C Frick Coke Company as carpenter at their Davidson Works, three years with the City Electric Light Plant as assistant engineer, two years at the Everson Car Shops for the H C Frick Coke Company, one and a half years at their Davidson shops, and two years for the Home Building Society Campbell and Wilson, proprietors In 1902 he entered the employ of the Connellsville Construction Company, with which he still continues He is independent in politics, voting for the best candidates, regardless of party In 1881 he became a communicant of the Baptist church, his wife joining in 1878

He married, March 21 1889, Margaret Bell Hill, born in Connellsville August 23, 1869, daughter of George W and Rosanna (Martin) Hill Her father is a locomotive engineer, living in Scottdale, Pennsylvania, he was born in Ohio, August 12 1840 came to Connells-

ville Pennsylvania in 1869, was pit boss at the Davidson coal mine north ot the city, finally becoming a locomotive engineer on the Baltimore & Ohio railroad Rosanna Miller was born in Ohio May 1846, and married there Children of George W Hill Mary Ellen deceased Mary Ellen, married James A Rajmer, Alice Jane resides in Connellsville, Margaret Bell (of previous mention), Charles Henry, a traveling salesman residing at Point Pleasant, West Virginia married Harriet Reynolds William Ellis, died in infancy, Anna Malinda, married J E Yenney, and lives in Salt Lake City, Utah, Olive Myrtle, married Harry Osterwise a blacksmith ot Scottdale, Pennsylvania, Ida May, now living in Connellsville Edna Pearl, married Lloyd S Hoyle, a railroad man of Uniontown Pennsylvania, Robert Roy, married Leona Province and lives in Scottdale Children of Alvin E and Margaret B (Hill) Collins Wilbur E, born December 20 1889, Charles F, February 10, 1892, George Morgan August 21, 1894, died November 1903, Annabel, born December 19, 1896 Agnes January 29, 1899, Laurence, July 7, 1901, died November, 1903, Francis Valentine, born February 14, 1905, Harold, May 31, 1908, William, September 13 1910

(IV) Clarence N, second son of James S and Martha Ann (Artis) Collins, was born in New Haven Pennsylvania (Connellsville West Side), August 16, 1869 He attended the public schools of New Haven and Connellsville working at all kinds of boy's work outside of school hours, and at the age of fifteen years becoming clerk in a grocery store He continued clerking for two years, then began learning the carpenter s trade He has continued without interruption working at his trade until the present time (1912), sometimes as journeyman and again taking building contracts himself In December, 1900, he moved to South Connellsville, where he erected his present home in 1901 He is a Republican

He married November 19, 1891 Amelia Guard born at Parkersburg West Virginia daughter ot Thomas and Margaret (Hicks) Guard Thomas Guard was born in West Virginia, of German descent died November 16, 1889, aged fifty-six years, he was tailor by trade and during the civil war served in the Confederate army Margaret Hicks was reared in Charlestown, West Virginia, she was burned to death in 1901 Children of Clarence N Collins Mary Elsie, born September 5, 1892, died October 5, 1898, Margaret, born March 29, 1895, Inc, January 28, 1898, Clarence (2), March 22, 1900, Albert, February 3, 1902

(IV) Charles C, youngest son of James S and Martha Ann (Artis) Collins was born in New Haven, Pennsylvania (now Connellsville, West Side), September 7, 1875 He was educated in the public school, and all during his school years worked after and before school hours in a grocery store, delivered papers and took care of Dr S S Stahl's horses He was such an earnest, energetic worker that he always was in demand After leaving school he became clerk in Edward Turner's hardware store on Brimstone Corner, then, until December 4, 1898, was employed in the tinplate mill He then spent a year in Greensburg, learning iron molding, later returning to Connellsville, where he was employed for a time in the J R Balsley lumber yard He was again employed in the tinplate mills (doubling) until the mills shut down, then resumed work at the carpenter trade, begun with Mr Balsley In 1911 he became a stockholder in the South Connellsville Lumber Company, and is now employed at carpentering in that company He is a Republican in politics, and has served as school director

He married, March 14, 1904, Julia Adams, born in Bullskin township, Fayette county, daughter of William Adams, born in Bullskin, May 4, 1827, son of William Adams an immigrant from Ireland William Adams was a farmer and a veteran of the civil war, serving four years in Company D, Eighty-fifth Regiment, Pennsylvania Volunteer Infantry, being twice wounded in battle He married Sarah Easter, born in Fayette county, May 25, 1827 Children of William and Sarah (Easter) Adams Mary Jane, deceased, married Samuel Hughy, Harriet, married Simon Hughy and lives at Breakneck (Connellsville suburb) Sarah Elizabeth, married Weldon Baker, John, lives in Bullskin township, William Calvin died in infancy, Julia (of previous mention), Laura Bell married Henry Richter, of Bullskin township Maria, married George Stillwagon of Connellsville

Mrs Charles C Collins was Julia Adams,

and married (first) Samuel Hawk and had children 1 William L Hawk, born August 27 1880 died December 15, 1906, he was killed at the Southampton Mills by a Baltimore & Ohio railroad train, he was a brakeman, he married Elizabeth Hyde, children Viola, born January 18, 1903, Edith Christiana, born October 14, 1905 2 Lida 3 Daisy 4 Christiana 5 Georgia 6 Emma Pearl 7 Sarah 8 Harry W

The paternal grandfather of KEARNS Thomas Kearns, of Trotter, Fayette county, Pennsylvania, was William Kearns born in Ireland, married Ellen Welsh, and about 1828 came to the United States, leaving his wife and six children in Ireland He remained in this country twelve years, prospered and returned to Ireland with the intention of bringing his family back with him to the United States His intentions were defeated by death, he falling a victim to the plague then raging in Ireland His wife also died in Ireland Children Richard, came to the United States and settled in the south William, died in New York City, Thomas, of whom further, Kate, never married, died in the United States, Ellen, died in Ireland, Mary, now living in St Louis, Missouri

(II) Thomas, son of William and Ellen (Welsh) Kearns was born in Ireland about 1814, died October 9 1889 He was a miller, and followed that occupation in Ireland until his coming to the United States in 1885, then an old man He married Mary O'Bivan and reared a family of eleven children After they had grown up they all drifted away from the old home in Ireland and came to the United States In 1884 the mother followed them, and in 1885 Thomas, the father the last to leave the old sod, closed up his business affairs and joined the family in this country, leaving only a son Matthew, in Ireland He lived a quiet retired life until his death four years later His wife Mary born about 1814, still survives him, now very near the century mark in years Her mother, Joanna (Powers) O'Bryan died in Ireland in her ninety-seventh year Her father Pierce O'Bryan, was a farmer, lived and died in Ireland Children of Thomas and Mary (O'Bryan) Kearns 1 William, died in Westmoreland county, Pennsylvania 2 Richard, now living at Mammoth,

Pennsylvania 3 Thomas (2), of whom further 4 Martin, now living at Mammoth, Pennsylvania 5 Ellen, married Patrick Rowan 6 Mary, married Patrick Powers 7 Michael, now employed at Jamison Coke Works 8 Morris deceased 9 Matthew, remains in Ireland at the old homestead 10 Kate married Michael O'Toole 11 Died unmarried

(III) Thomas (2) third son of Thomas (1) Kearns was born in County Waterford Ireland July 8 1858 He was educated in the schools of his native parish, grew to manhood and married in England In 1884, in company with two of his brothers, he came to the United States landing in New York City April 26 He came to Connellsville soon after and entered the employ of the H C Frick Coke Company, continuing with that concern twenty-two years In May 1905, he bought a small farm of thirty-two acres remodeled the house standing thereon, and has since resided there His intention is to spend his remaining years in gardening and poultry raising He is a Democrat in politics, and has served as road supervisor In religious faith he is a Roman Catholic, the family faith for many generations He is a member also of the Ancient Order of Hibernians

He married, January 6, 1883, in England, Katherine Hennessy, born at Marley Hall, County Dulane England, of Irish parents, Thomas and Mary (Morrison) Hennessy, and granddaughter of William and Katherine Hennessy, the latter both dying in Ireland Of their eight children, Thomas Hennessy was the only one to come to the United States he settled in Fayette county, dying at Leisenring No 1 Mary Morrison his wife, was a daughter of John and Katherine (Powers) Morrison, who also lived and died in Ireland After the death of his first wife Mary Morrison, Thomas Hennessy married (second) Elizabeth Edgar and came to the United States where both died No issue by this marriage Children by his first marriage William now living in Leisenring, Pennsylvania John deceased Katherine wife of Thomas (2) Kearns Ann, married Philip Meegan

Children of Thomas (2) and Katherine Kearns 1 William, born November 21, 1883, married Lena Moore, one child, Catherine, they reside in Washington county 2 Martin,

born October 11, 1885 3 Thomas born July 27, 1887, married Dora Skyles, resides at Connellsville Pennsylvania 4 Matthew, born September 19, 1889 5 Richard, twin of Matthew, both died in infancy 6 Mary, born September 27, 1890, died aged thirteen months 7 Michael, twin of Mary, died in infancy 8 Mary born October 27, 1891, died in infancy 9 Patrick born August 1, 1893, died in infancy 10 Michael Richard, twin of Patrick, died in infancy 11 John, born August 24, 1894 12 Helen, born February 4, 1897 13 Matthew born August 3 1900, died aged two years four months 14 Katherine born October 9, 1903, burned to death in fire from open grate 15 Michael, born November 12, 1904 16 Mary, born May 1, 1906

CONWELL The names Cornwell, Cornwall and Conwell are of frequent occurrence in the early records of Sussex county Delaware, as variant forms of the same family name Francis Conwell was sheriff of the county from 1686 and was made justice of the peace April 9 in that year he died before November 12, 1691 The name is not confined to one of the hundreds of Sussex county, but there were many of this name in Broadkiln hundred in 1785, and the name is found there to or near the present day

There are probably at least four or five families of the name in America A variety of spelling is found in England also the name is probably of local origin from Cornwall, England However, one of these American families is of Dutch origin the name in this case having been originally Cornelise and the American center of this family being at Flatbush, Kings county Long Island If Francis Conwell was not himself an immigrant from England or at least from Great Britain and Ireland it seems probable that the present family is an offshoot of this Dutch stock

(I) Jehu Conwell, the first member of this family about whom we have definite information, was born in Sussex county Delaware in 1749, and died in January 1834 With his brother William he settled in Luzerne township Fayette county, Pennsylvania, in June, 1767 They found James Bredin living in a log cabin on a tomahawk claim he having come in the preceding April For a small consideration they purchased of him his claim, seven hundred acres in extent, with the improvements which he had made. At first the Indians were friendly, but the revolution was drawing near, and there were after a time signs of hostilities, leading to the temporary withdrawal of the Conwells from the country. In August, 1772, Jehu Conwell returned to his old home in Delaware; in October he married, and in November he and his bride set forth on horseback for his Luzerne clearing. They lived in comparative quiet until 1774, when Indian aggressions on the colonial frontiers began in earnest. It was largely due to the Conwell brothers that in 1774 a block house was hastily constructed on the Coleman plantation on the west side of Dunlap's creek, about half a mile below Merrittstown. Assisted and directed by them, the pioneers completed this fort in quick time, and it was occupied in May. It was used by them for safety, but there is no evidence that it was ever attacked nor that the people of this region were ever seriously injured by the Indians. Probably the great battle of Point Pleasant, in northwestern Virginia, insured the safety of the settlements in Fayette county and elsewhere along the frontiers of white civilization. For a time, however, the Fayette county settlers were in great terror of Indian attacks. In 1776 the brothers Conwell entered the continental army, and they fought through the revolutionary war. Jehu Conwell, on account of the distance to which he had had to go in order to have his grain ground, erected a mill of his own, the first in Luzerne township, perhaps the first in the county. It was used simply for pounding corn; a flutter wheel was the motive power for a great sweep, to which the pounder was attached; the mortar was a rock in which an excavation was rudely made. He is said to have constructed this primitive mill the year after his coming into the township. He was a generous man, liberal in his views, conscientious, respected by his neighbors and those who had his acquaintance. His home was headquarters for immigrants westward bound from Delaware. He married, in Delaware, in October, 1772, Elizabeth, daughter of Yates Stokely. Children: Sheppard; Yates Stokely, of whom further; John; George; ———, married William Ewing; ———, married Andrew Porter; ———, married John Arnold.

(II) Yates Stokely, son of Jehu and Elizabeth (Stokely) Conwell, was born in Luzerne township; he died December 25, 1865. He was a farmer, and the founder of the settlement known as Heistersburg, in Fayette county. August 1, 1814, he was commissioned ensign in the Eighth Regiment, Pennsylvania militia. The most of his life he was a Whig, but the latter years a Republican. He married Anna, daughter of David and Anna (Vankirk) Craft; her father lived in Redstone township; she survived her husband by several years. Children: John Stokely, of whom further; David C., born September 8, 1824, married, 1880, Elizabeth (Kelly) Christopher; Jehu B., born June 25, 1820, married Elizabeth Fulton; George; Eliza A., married William Elliott; Margaret, married James E. Davidson; one other son.

(III) John Stokely, son of Yates Stokely and Anna (Craft) Conwell, was born in Luzerne township, June 30, 1815, and died about 1896. He attended the local school. For a while he farmed with his father. He was for several years engaged in mercantile business at Heistersburg, and in 1850 was appointed the first postmaster at that place. In 1861 he left Heistersburg and removed to his farm of two hundred and fifty acres. On this farm he lived for the rest of his life, doing general farming and raising cattle; he gave special attention to sheep raising. He was a Republican, and held several township offices. Among these was the office of township clerk, which he held for many years. He and his wife were members of the Presbyterian church. He married Anna, daughter of John and Orpha (Davidson) McDougal, who was born at Merrittstown, Fayette county, Pennsylvania, about 1816, and died December 15, 1888. Children: James William, of whom further; Albert D., deceased; Mary Eliza, married John W. Foster, they live at Uniontown, Fayette county, Pennsylvania; John, deceased; Walter B., lives in the west; Maria Louisa, died young.

(IV) James William, son of John Stokely and Anna (McDougal) Conwell, was born in Luzerne township, July 1, 1839. He attended the district school near his home, and worked with his father on the farm. He afterward took this farm over on his own account. Until 1899 he lived on this farm, near Heistersburg, and did general farming, also raising live stock. In the spring of 1899 he sold this farm and removed to Merrittstown, where he has one of the finest stone buildings in the township. At the present time he has a few acres of land under cultivation, but is leading a retired life. He is a genial man and enjoys the confidence of his fellow citizens. He is a Republican. Several times he has served on the school board and he has acted in the capacities of president and of treasurer of this board. For a term of three years he was town assessor. His church is the Presbyterian.

He married, November 14, 1867, Mary Maria, daughter of John and Emily (Johnson) Wood, who was born in Luzerne township, July 4, 1847; her father was a prominent farmer. Children: 1. George Jay, born October 25, 1868; lives at Merrittstown. 2. Anna Alberta, born November 13, 1874; married Richard Swan; reside in Bucks county, Pennsylvania; children: William, Richard and Susan. 3. Emma Matilda, born December 18, 1876, died November 10, 1897; married Richard Swan. 4. William Stokely, born December 10, 1879; resides at Brownsville. 5. Mary Idella, born December 16, 1882; married Martin Hess; live at Brownsville. 6. Susan Rebecca, born December 3, 1887; married Edwin Moyer; live at Merrittstown. 7. John Walter, born July 18, 1891, unmarried, living at home.

DAVIDSON This family came to Fayette county from Westmoreland county, Pennsylvania, the founder in the latter county being Jacob Davidson, born in England. He came to the United States when young with his father, who was a minister of the gospel. They settled in Philadelphia, where Jacob was educated. He married Mary Young, of Franklin county, Pennsylvania, and settled in Westmoreland county. In 1837 he moved to Fayette county, settling on the Basil Brown tract near Brownsville. He was a miller by trade and became quite wealthy, owning a large amount of land. He was also connected with the Monongahela Bank of Brownsville for many years as a director. He died April 15, 1856, aged seventy-four years.

(II) Jacob (2), son of Jacob (1) and Mary (Young) Davidson, was born in Westmoreland county, Pennsylvania, in 1806, died in 1858 in Fayette county. He came with the family to Fayette county in 1837 and also settled near Brownsville. He was a miller by trade and also a farmer. He was a leading member of the United Brethren church and a local preacher, noted for his deep piety and the purity of his life. He was a Whig in politics, but took little part in public affairs, his family and the church being the greatest concerns of his life. He owned a good farm and was in comfortable circumstances. He married Hannah Kelley, who died in 1880, daughter of Jacob Kelley, who was born in England, came to the United States when a young man and settled in Westmoreland county, where Hannah was born. Children: 1. Mary, married, November 2, 1855, John Rice. 2. Elizabeth, deceased, married, March 12, 1862, Otto Brashear. 3. Dr. John H., born November 15, 1845, a practicing physician of Perryopolis, Fayette county, and a leading business man; he married (first) December 26, 1871, Cillnissae Torrence Chalfant, (second) Mary E. Chalfant, a sister of his first wife, daughter of Dr. S. B. and Elizabeth Chalfant. 4. Kate, married, January 23, 1867, Benton Bennett. 5. Lou, married, January 3, 1871, James F. Grahle. 6. Haddie, married, July 24, 1873, Jesse Coldren. 7. Anna, married, November 12, 1874, Luther Noble. 8. Amos W., of whom further. 9. Ada, married A. J. Nixon. 10. Child, died in infancy.

(III) Amos W., son of Jacob (2) and Hannah (Kelley) Davidson, was born near Brownsville, Pennsylvania, in 1855. He was educated in the public schools of Redstone, and learned the carpenter's trade. He also was a farmer of Redstone township, and for several years was engaged in mercantile business in Brownsville. He is now living in Redstone township. In politics he is a Republican and has served as both school director and road supervisor. Both he and wife are members of the Presbyterian church. He married, May 29, 1878, Huldah Vernon, born in Luzerne township, February 22, 1858, daughter of Reese Vernon, a farmer of Luzerne township, who died at his farm (now the Allison Works) at the age of eighty years. His wife, Clara (Porter) Vernon, was also born in Luzerne township. Children of Mr. and Mrs. Vernon: 1. Margaret, married Benton Covert, now deceased. 2. William D., married Florence Stevens. 3. John, died aged twenty-one years. 4. Frazier, died aged sixty-five years. 5. Mifflin, died aged fifty-one years.

6. Armstrong, died aged twenty years. 7. Nancy, died aged fourteen years. 8. Huldah, married Amos W. Davidson. Children of Mr. and Mrs. Davidson: 1. Carlton H., of whom further. 2. Grace C., born December 28, 1880; married Jesse Wonsettler, a contractor and builder of Scenery Hill, Washington county, Pennsylvania. 3. Charles L., of whom further. 4. Chester A., born February 8, 1887; married Carrie Randolph; he is now postmaster at New Salem, Pennsylvania. 5. Margaret, born 1893; resides at home. 6. John H., a student. 7. Vernon, a student.

(IV) Carlton H., eldest son of Amos W. and Huldah (Vernon) Davidson, was born near Brownsville, Pennsylvania, March 25, 1879. He attended the public schools and Dunlap Creek Academy, and spent his minority at the home farm. He decided upon the profession of medicine, and in 1903 entered the medical department of Western University of Pennsylvania (now University of Pittsburgh), whence he was graduated M. D., class of 1907. After graduation he was interne at the South Side Hospital, Pittsburgh, then was appointed superintendent of Uniontown Hospital, resigning in March, 1908, and locating in New Salem, where he is now firmly established in the practice of his profession. He is a Republican in politics and is a school director of New Salem, elected in 1910. He is a member of Fayette County Medical and Pennsylvania State Medical societies; Laurel Lodge, Free and Accepted Masons; Modern Woodmen; Knights of Maccabees, and with his wife belongs to the Presbyterian church. Dr. Davidson is a veteran of the Spanish-American war; enlisted in 1898 in the Eleventh Regiment, United States Army, and served in Porto Rico for two and a half years. From 1903 he served in the National Guard of Pennsylvania on hospital service.

He married, December 23, 1905, Lucretia G. Gallatin, born near Dawson, Pennsylvania, January 7, 1884, daughter of John Gallatin, of Uniontown, Pennsylvania, and his wife, Jane (Gault) Gallatin, of Dawson. Other children of Mr. and Mrs. Gallatin: Bruce; Lois, married Charles Snyder; Imogene, married Charles B. Rhodes; Hallie, married John K. Gallatin.

Child of Dr. and Mrs. Davidson: Albert Gallatin, born December 24, 1910. This child bears the name of an illustrious maternal ancestor, Albert Gallatin, the famous statesman and early citizen of Fayette county.

Albert Gallatin was born in Geneva, Switzerland, came to the American colonies in 1780, purchased property in Springhill township, Fayette county, Pennsylvania, which he called "Friendship Hill," and resided there from 1786 to 1827, when he removed to New York City, dying at Astoria, Long Island, August 12, 1849. He was the father of the glass industry in Fayette county, but it was as a public man that he is best known. He was a member of the Pennsylvania legislature, elected to the United States senate, but unseated on account of foreign birth. He was elected to congress in 1794-96-98 and 1800, resigning in 1801 to become secretary of the treasury under Presidents Jefferson and Madison; was commissioner in 1814 with Adams and Bayard to make and sign the treaty of peace with Great Britain; minister to France from 1815 to 1824, refused a seat in the United States senate and a nomination for vice-president; minister to England one year, then withdrew from public life. He married (first) in 1789, Sophia Allegre, of Richmond, Virginia, (second) in 1793, Hannah, daughter of Commodore James Nicholson, United States navy. In 1825 he entertained the Marquis de Lafayette at "Friendship Hill," an occasion that yet lives in the traditions of the neighborhood. He died in the eighty-ninth year of his age, leaving issue.

(IV) Charles Luther, son of Amos Wood and Huldah (Vernon) Davidson, was born at the home farm in Redstone township, Fayette county, Pennsylvania, near Brownsville, March 20, 1883. He was educated in the public school and spent his early years in Redstone township, later attending high school at Bridgeport, Pennsylvania. He began business life as an insurance agent, and is now a law student, also an officer of the Fayette county court. He is a Republican in politics, and with his wife belongs to the Baptist church.

He married, January 5, 1905, Leora E. Armstrong, born in Franklin township, near Perryopolis, Fayette county, July 6, 1880, daughter of James R. Armstrong, born in Jefferson township, Greene county, Pennsylvania, a farmer, now living near Perryopolis; married Mary E. Craft, born in Jefferson township, Greene county, died at the age of

Davidson Family, New Salem, Pa.

sixty-five years; their children: 1. George L., married Ermina Bute, and lives in Connellsville, Pennsylvania. 2. Mary F., married Martin E. Townsend, of Perry township. 3. Harriet, married C. L. V. Bute, and lives in Uniontown; child: Gladys P. 4. Leora E. (of previous mention). The only child of Charles L. and Leora E. Davidson, Charles L. (2), died in infancy.

DAVIDSON This branch of the Davidson family is of comparatively recent settlement in Fayette county. The founder of the family, Thomas Davidson, came from England in 1884. He is a grandson of William and Ellen (Bracket) Davidson, lifelong residents of county Durham, England, although William was born in White Haven, Cumberland. He was a glassworker engaged in bottle making, later a fisherman, following the sea until quite old. He had a brother, George Davidson, who came to the United States. The five sons of William and Ellen Davidson all lived and died in Sunderland, England; Esabel, Thomas, William (2), John, Henry (of further mention). George and James Edward.

(II) Henry, son of William and Ellen (Bracket) Davidson, was born at Sunderland county, Durham, England, March 21. 1837. He began at an early age following the sea as a fisherman, continuing in that occupation all his early life. He died in 1879. He married Mary Downey. born in South Shields, England, in 1836, died in 1902, daughter of William and Ellen Downey, born in Sunderland. Four of their ten children are living in England: James, Hannah, Eleanor and Thomas; another. Tamah. resides near Aberdeen, Scotland, while Jane, Mary. Sarah, Isabel and Eliza are deceased. Children of Henry and Mary Davidson: 1. Henry, born 1857, died 1864. 2. Isabel, married James Snaith, and resides in Scottdale, Pennsylvania. 3. Thomas W., of whom further. 4. George. lives in Scottdale, Pennsylvania. a water tender. 5. John Henry. living in Sunderland, England. 6. James Edward, living in Sunderland, England. Two died in infancy.

(III) Thomas W., second son of Henry and Mary (Downey) Davidson, was born at Sunderland county. Durham. England, March 24. 1861. He was educated in Wesleyan public school, and in early life began working in the mines at Shotton, near Sunderland. In 1884, after his marriage, he came to the United States alone. The following year his wife joined him at Rock Springs, Wyoming, where he first worked at coal mining, later was employed in silver and copper mining, remaining in Wyoming about two years. His wife died at Denver, Colorado. He then worked in New Mexico and Washington mines for two years, finally, in 1889, returning east to Tarr Station, Westmoreland county, Pennsylvania, where he was coal mining for three years, rising by promotion to the position of "fire boss." He then entered the employ of the W. J. Rainey Coal and Coke Company as fire boss at their Paul mine; then for six months was mine foreman at the Mutual mine; later held the same position at the Paul mine at Vanderbilt. He next was in the employ of the Cochran Company at Juniata, continuing until September 1, 1905, when he was appointed mine foreman at Moyer, a position he now most capably fills.

Mr. Davidson fitted himself for the position of mine foreman through a course of study with the International Correspondence School, a technical knowledge that combined with his practical mining experiences thoroughly equips him for so important a position. He has a farm of nearly one hundred acres located in Virginia, which he rents, and has accumulated other property. He is a member of the Methodist Episcopal church of Connellsville, of which his wife is also a member. He holds advanced progressive political views, classing as a Social Democrat.

He married, in 1881, in England, Dorothy Stoker, who died in Denver, Colorado. He married (second) July 23. 1892, Fredonia Flescher, born in West Virginia. Children of first marriage: 1. Henrietta, married John Hipson, and lives in South Shields, England. 2. Fred, a chauffeur, married Rose Herbert and resides at Pittsburgh, Pennsylvania. Children of second marriage. 3. Curtis, born April 6, 1893, died aged five years. 4. Pearl, born December 25, 1894. 5. Beatrice, December 13. 1897, died December 25. 1897. 6. Lily, born April 16, 1900, died February. 1904. 7. Adrian, born March 2, 1903. 8. Paul, December 15. 1905. 9. Louis, August 12, 1909. 10. Eleanor Frances, April 17, 1912.

The family home is on East End avenue, Connellsville, Pennsylvania, where Mr. Davidson erected a residence in 1911.

NORTON This family migrated to Connellsville as early, probably, as the year 1799—certainly prior to 1812—when Lester Leroy Norton, his brother, Daniel S. Norton, and their mother, together with an uncle, came here from Newtown, Connecticut, and began the manufacture of cotton, erecting and operating a four-story stone cotton mill on Baldwin's, or Connell run. This location was the property of Abram Baldwin, another of the ancestors of the present family, who was a native of New England, and came to Connellsville in or about 1806; he was a prominent man in church, politics and business; manufactured the first carding machines ever made in this section of the country. His shop was on Baldwin's run, immediately south of the old burial ground, and his millpond was a famous fishing and skating place for the boys of Connellsville. In 1816 Daniel S. Norton left the rest of his family and removed to Ohio.

Lester L. Norton remained in Connellsville, becoming a prominent manufacturer and the leading man in the town, adjusting matters of importance to the community and arbitrating the affairs of his friends and neighbors. Several years after the erection of the first mill Mr. Norton erected and operated a little further down the stream a factory for the carding, spinning and fulling of wool only, the motive power being water.

With keen business foresight he soon perceived that the making of iron was destined to become one of the leading industries of Western Pennsylvania, so he converted his mill into a foundry, having a cupola large enough to melt three tons of iron ore a day. The blast was produced by connecting the crank from the water wheel to an overhead beam, which in turn worked a piston in an air-tight box or bellows. This system, which Mr. Norton worked out for himself, is identically the same as that employed on a vastly more extensive scale by the million dollar blowing engines of the Homestead furnaces. Mr. Norton also became one of the original coke producers of this place, making, in fact, the first coke ever taken out of Connellsville.

He engaged a Mr. Nichols, from Durham, England, where coke for gas had been made in beehive ovens and pits in the ground, to come over and take charge of the foundry. An oven twelve feet square was designed by Mr. Nichols and built by John Taylor, a mason; and here at Norton's foundry, in the year 1833, the first coke ever made in the Connellsville region was produced, and, in fact, the first successful coke in America. Others soon began to buy from Mr. Norton, who had associated his son Philo with him in the business, and a flourishing industry was established; ricks were made in the ground to produce the coke, which was shipped in boats down the Youghiogheny river. This business has later passed into the ownership of the Davidson interest, having gained for its founder eminence as a citizen and manufacturer.

Mr. Norton was one of the best educated men of his time. Born at Newtown, Connecticut, in 1791 or 1797, his education was completed at Washington and Jefferson College, where he became an excellent scholar in Latin and Greek. At the age of seventy-five years his faculties were so well preserved that he was still able to read from the Bible in the original Greek. He was one of the pillars of the Christian church at Connellsville, which he assisted Alexander Campbell in founding, and his house was considered Mr. Campbell's headquarters in that vicinity. The old house, which was built in 1829, is still occupied by Mr. Norton's descendants. A leading man in every walk in life, upright, progressive and intellectual, he lived to a ripe old age, dying at the age of eighty years. His wife was a Miss Harriet Gibbs, born in Washington county, Pennsylvania, in the year 1798, and dying February 1, 1869, at the age of seventy years and seven months; she was the daughter of Thomas and Harriet (Baldwin) Gibbs, Harriet (Baldwin) Gibbs having been the daughter of Abram and Sarah Baldwin. This is the Abram Baldwin referred to previously as the owner of Baldwin's run, upon which place Mr. Philo Norton, father of Lester L. Norton, erected the first carding machine west of the Alleghany mountains, being associated with Mr. Baldwin. He was a New Englander, coming to Connellsville in about the year 1806, and acquiring prominence in the community as a churchman, politician and business man; he died October 7, 1832, in his seventy-third year. His wife Sarah died September 24, 1836, in her seventy-fith year. Children of Mr. and Mrs. Lester Leroy Norton: 1. Philo, born in Connellsville, Pennsylvania, March 26, 1823 (see further mention). 2. Abraham B., died April 16, 1854, aged nineteen years three months. 3. Lester L. Jr., died June 6, 1855, aged seventeen years seven months. 4. Harriet G., died October 1, 1855, aged fifteen years five months. 5. Margaret C., died October 28, 1850, aged twenty-five years eight months. 6. Dorcas C., died March 20, 1850, aged one year two months. 7. David C., died January 8, 1834, aged one year eight months. 8. D. Baldwin, died July 27, 1822, aged one year. 9. Anna B., died January 7, 1834, aged two years nine months. 10. Olivia, died December 29, 1833, aged two months. 11. Le Roi, born March 25, 1827, died October 31, 1892.

(II) Philo Norton, son of Lester Leroy and Harriet (Gibbs) Norton, was born in Connellsville, March 26, 1823. His father, not being content with the methods of teaching which prevailed in the place at that time, conducted his education personally and made of the son as fine a scholar as the father himself had been. Philo became well versed in mathematics, science and foreign languages, and was especially skilled in the classics, being able even when at the advanced age of eighty years to translate Horace and Virgil with ease. Upon attaining his majority he turned his attention to surveying, and became a civil engineer. As in his earlier studies, he had made a specialty of the geology of his native country, he became convinced of the great value of the coal and iron deposits of Western Pennsylvania, and interested himself in coal, steel and mining industries in connection with Daniel Davidson, J. M. Faber and James Maskimans, at Connellsville. Later he sold out his interests here and removed to Brownsville, in Fayette county, Pennsylvania, also opening a coal mine at Bridgeport. His thorough knowledge of geology stood him in good stead, assuring him of the vast fields of coal deposit then unknown to the general public, whose use of this commodity was then very much less extensive than it is at present. With keen business intuition he secured an option on all the coal lands of the Monongahela valley, now worth

billions of dollars, and proposed to float a company for their development; in his prospectus he prophesied the subsequent wealth of this coal region, stating how iron ore could be brought here cheaply and smelted. All of this has since proved true. He was associated in his business enterprises with a number of other persons, one of whom, Jay Cook, failed in his dealings and brought disaster upon all of the others, causing them to lose all of their possessions. This has indeed often been the misfortune of the pioneer developers of any great product, who clear the field and do the hard work, meeting with many setbacks, only that their successors reap the harvest. The hard luck and disappointment, however, seemed to break Mr. Norton's spirit; he removed to North Carolina, where he remained until his death. He was far from being inactive here, however; recognized by all of the principal geological societies as being one of the highest authorities in mineralogy, he busied himself in making a collection for the New Orleans Exposition of all the different minerals of the state of North Carolina, making a personal tour of the country for that purpose; he was highly successful in this, showing that North Carolina possessed a greater variety of mineral products than any other state in the Union, and received unstinted praise for his excellent work. He was urged to make a similar collection for the Boston Museum, but owing to his advanced age was compelled to decline. Throughout his entire life he manifested a strong interest in education and public matters, serving as a director on the school board and being in his political convictions a member of the Democratic party. He lived to the age of eighty-six years, dying in the year 1908. His wife was a Miss Martha Herbert, who was born in Connellsville, then called New Haven, on June 2, 1824. She was the daughter of Joseph and Barbara (Shallenberger) Herbert, and the granddaughter of John Herbert, all of whom came to Connellsville in the year 1799, being some of the earliest settlers; they were of English descent, coming from Elizabethtown, New Jersey. Joseph Herbert was a shoemaker by trade, becoming postmaster of Connellsville, in which capacity he served for over thirty years. His dwelling house stood on the present site of the First National Bank Building. Mr. and Mrs. Philo

Norton had eight children, six sons and two daughters, as follows 1 Maria, deceased 2 Margaret Cooke 3 Carlos Alonzo who is treasurer and secretary of the Hazelwood Oil Company at Pittsburgh, he is a man of eminent learning 4 Joseph Herbert, of Norfolk, Virginia 5 Abram Baldwin 6 Clarence L, of Mars, Pennsylvania 7 James McIlvaine, who died in 1865, aged eighteen months 8 Eugene Trump, of whom further

(III) Eugene Trump Norton, son of Philo and Martha (Herbert)) Norton, was born in Bridgeport, Fayette county, Pennsylvania, October 10, 1866, being the youngest child of the family At the age of seven years he removed with his parents to Connellsville, where he attended the high school, from which he was graduated in the year 1882, this was the first graduating class of the institution, and Eugene Norton was the only boy in the class Two weeks later he began his business career as a messenger boy in the First National Bank of Connellsville and has worked his way up through the various positions of teller, assistant cashier and cashier until his unsolicited election by the directors as vice-president This post he now occupies, taking an active interest in the management of the bank He is a man of many interests, and is a very prominent person in the community, being an officer or member of seventeen different companies, among these are the Riverside Metal Refining Company, of which he is president and director, the Gurler-Kendall Sand Company, of which he is vice-president and director, the Sligo Iron and Steel Company and the Meyersdale Coal Company, of which he is treasurer and director, the Fayette Securities Company, of which he is secretary and treasurer, and the Connellsville Construction Company the Connellsville News Publishing Company, the Provident Coke and Mining Company and the Wells Creek Supply Company, of which he is a director Besides these he is president of the First National Bank of Vanderbilt, vice-president and director of Connellsville Chamber of Commerce, trustee of Bethany College of West Virginia, first secretary of the Connellsville Clearing House Association, director of Connellsville Y M C A, and trustee of the Christian church, of which he is a member, as all of his family have been He was also made, unsolicited, a director of

the Connellsville Masonic Association, which is very powerful here He is a thirty-second degree Mason, member of King Solomon Lodge at Connellsville, the Lodge of Perfection at Uniontown and the Pennsylvania Consistory at Pittsburgh In his political convictions he is a Democrat, and has served on the city school board, of which he was at one time president

His residence is on the family estate on Mount Pleasant road, just outside the limits of the city of Connellsville, where he has a most delightful home, enjoying the respect and esteem of the entire community, his career has been a credit to the family name of which he is justly proud, for he is a most courteous, business-like and distinguished man Mr Norton has been twice married June 8, 1893, he married Miss Clara Hayes Barge, daughter of John and Rachel Barge, she was born on the 16th of October, 1866, near Newcastle, Pennsylvania, and died January 14, 1895, having one child that died at birth Mr Norton's second marriage was to Mrs Elizabeth (Barge) Porter a sister of his first wife, who was born February 6, 1864, also at Newcastle By this marriage he has two children John Barge Norton, born December 22, 1904, and Virginia Norton, born August 23, 1906

NORTON (III) Abram Baldwin Norton, son of Philo Norton (q v), and Martha (Herbert) Norton, was born in Brownsville, Pennsylvania, February 14, 1858 He grew to maturity in Connellsville and became a jeweler and optician, learning the business under Mr Yates, of that place He afterward removed to Altoona, Pennsylvania, and from there to Minneapolis, Minnesota, where he was employed for a while, but returned to Altoona, where he conducted a store In the year 1907 he finally removed to Ellwood City, Pennsylvania, where he is now an optician and jeweler He is a member of the Methodist Episcopal church, and is a Democrat in his politics Mr Norton was married at the age of twenty-six years to Laura Matilda Ake born in Somerset county, Pennsylvania, April 20, 1859 died May 27, 1906, at Cumberland, Maryland Mr and Mrs Norton had five children Abram Baldwin Jr, of whom further, Charles Wood, deceased, Harold

Orlando, of Pittsburgh; Kenneth White, of Chicago; Martha Herbert Norton, living in Ellwood City, Pennsylvania.

(IV) Abram Baldwin Norton Jr., son of Abram Baldwin and Laura Matilda (Ake) Norton, was born in Minneapolis, Minnesota, March 7, 1885. He attended the public schools of Altoona, Pennsylvania, and Cumberland, Maryland, taking a subsequent commercial course in Cumberland. After this he entered business, becoming a mail clerk on the Pennsylvania railroad at their general offices in Altoona. He then entered the employ of the Westinghouse Electric Company of East Pittsburgh, remaining for six years in their construction department. On February 15, 1908, he came to Connellsville and assumed the management of the Riverside Metal Refining Company, of which his uncle, Eugene T. Norton, is president, and John Gans is secretary and treasurer. This company was organized in 1904 and handles solder, babbitt metals and white metal alloys; it employs about a dozen men and a number of others on the road. Mr. Norton is an enterprising young man and full of energy and progressiveness; he is well known in the community, not only as a capable business man, but as a staunch member of the Republican party, and as a member in good standing of the First Presbyterian Church of Connellsville. On June 1, 1910, he was married to Jennie Mary Reynolds, born in Oil City, Pennsylvania, February 28, 1885, daughter of Ernest Leutellis Reynolds and Mary Elizabeth Reed, both natives of Clarion county, Pennsylvania, where Mr. Reynolds was born in 1855 and his wife the year afterward. Mr. and Mrs. Norton have one child, Abram Baldwin Norton, the third of the name, born August 2, 1911.

NORTON Lester Philo Norton was born in Mount Vernon, Knox county, Ohio, April 27, 1828. His father was Philo L. Norton and his mother was Jane C. Norton, both of whom died when he was quite young. The earlier years of his life were spent in and around Mount Vernon in the employ of his uncle, Daniel S. Norton, who was an extensive real estate owner and who also operated a flour and feed mill and an oil mill. He was also the Mount Vernon agent of the Baltimore & Ohio Railroad Company when the line was first built from Newark, Ohio, to Chicago Junction. After some time in their employ he came to Connellsville, Pennsylvania, where he managed the Philo Norton farm, located east of Connellsville, where he remained for some years, afterward removing to Uniontown, Pennsylvania, entering the commissioner's office as clerk. In 1874 he came to Connellsville again, entering into the public life of the place. Being an intensely public-spirited man and always interested in the betterment of whatever place was his home he immediately became prominently identified with the political life of Connellsville. He served as borough treasurer for a period of nearly twelve years, and was also secretary of the board of education for thirteen consecutive years. As a member of the board of education he bore a material part in the origination of the first graduating class of the Connellsville public schools, which at that time had no high school, and helped to lay the foundation for the building of the present efficient public schools of Connellsville.

During the civil war he was active in the recruiting of troops and delivering them to the nearest railroad station for transportation to military headquarters. Owing to an accident occurring in early youth which crippled his left arm and also his eye, he was prevented from entering the service. He was a Democrat in politics and always an active worker for the interests of the party. He was a member of the Christian church (Disciples of Christ), being the treasurer for a number of years. Mr. Norton died February 24, 1896.

In June, 1871, Mr. Norton married Dorcas French, of Uniontown, Pennsylvania. Henry Clay, named after his uncle, who was a veteran of the Mexican war, the only child, was born at Uniontown, Pennsylvania, July 6, 1872, where he lived until he was two years of age, when his parents moved to Connellsville, Pennsylvania, where he was educated and grew to manhood. Immediately after his graduation from the public schools he entered the First National Bank of Connellsville as clerk, and after serving in that position for some years was advanced to teller, and in 1908 was made assistant cashier. In 1909 he served as a member of the board of education, resigning when he was appointed to fill the unex-

pired term of tax collector. He is a member
of the Christian church and of the Grand Fraternity. On June 20, 1906, he married Mabel,
daughter of Kell and Elizabeth (Curry) Long,
of the West Side, Connellsville, Pennsylvania.

BOYD   The Boyds of Connellsville, Pennsylvania, descended from William
Boyd, of Scotch forbears who
came from Winchester, Virginia, in 1784,
making the journey on packhorses with several slaves, and six negro children were registered as being born of these slaves between
the years 1795 and 1809, viz.: Andrew, Millie,
Ben, Pussie, Samuel and Alexander.

(1) William Boyd selected land on Mount's
creek, Bullskin township, that was surveyed
to him as Springhill, in June, 1786. He did
not bring his family on his first coming, but
after making location started for Virginia to
bring them to the new home in Fayette county. He was taken ill, however, and having no
way of getting word to his wife, was greatly
worried. In the meantime she, having become uneasy at his long absence, mounted
with her two children and started westward;
very fortunately they met upon the road, and
all returned to Fayette county. He was a man
of considerable education, and from 1792
served for many years as justice of the peace.
His farm of three hundred and fifty acres was
well selected and fertile, and there he died
and was buried in 1812. He married and had
sons: 1. Thomas, of whom further. 2. John,
died at Connellsville, in 1857. 3. Robert, one
time associate judge of Fayette county and
grandfather of Albert Darlington Boyd, the
celebrated lawyer of Uniontown. 4. James,
died in Tyrone township. 5. William, moved
to Ohio. 6. Jeremiah, became a physician, and
after living in Louisiana for several years
moved to Washington. The only daughter of
William Boyd married (first) Joseph Barnett,
of Connellsville, (second) Stewart H. Whitehill.

(II) Thomas, eldest son of William Boyd,
was born in the Shenandoah valley of Virginia, near Winchester, died in Fayette county, Pennsylvania, 1856. He inherited the
Bullskin township homestead, and there also
conducted a distillery. He was a very popular man in his community, and was considered
a wealthy man. Both Thomas and wife were
Unitarians in religious faith. He married

Nancy Rice, of Fayette county. Children: 1.
Eliza, never married. 2. William, of whom
elsewhere. 3. John, moved to Illinois, where
he died. 4. Rice, the last survivor. 5. Thomas,
never married. 6. Randolph. 7. Ann, married George Blocker, who died in 1849; children: Clark and Eliza. 8. Richard, of whom
further.

(III) Richard, youngest child of Thomas
and Nancy (Rice) Boyd, was born September 8, 1829, in Bullskin township, Fayette
county, Pennsylvania, died March 27, 1899.
He was a farmer, and owned a fertile field of
three hundred and fifty acres, part of it the
old Springhill farm of his grandfather William
and father Thomas Boyd. He was a Republican in politics, but never sought public office,
and was a member of the Christian church.
He married Maria Strickler, who survives
him, a resident of Scottdale, Pennsylvania.
She is the daughter of Stewart Strickler, a
pioneer coke burner and large land owner at
Jimtown, Fayette county. Later he moved
to Tennessee with three of his daughters. He
married Mary Newcomer. One of their sons
was a soldier in the civil war, and while in
Tennessee saw so much that pleased him that
after the war he settled there and persuaded
his father to also become a resident of Tennessee.

Stewart Strickler, only son of Jacob Strickler, a farmer of Fayette county, was born at
New Salem, near Uniontown, February 17,
1812, and received a common school education. When he was sixteen years old his
mother died, and his father breaking up housekeeping, Stewart and his eight sisters, all
younger than himself, were scattered among
their relatives. In the spring of 1830 Stewart
hired out to John Smiley, a farmer, at six
dollars per month, and stayed with him till
Christmas, after which he began peddling
chickens and eggs, which he carried down
along the Youghiogheny river in a very simply constructed boat made by himself of
boards, giving away the boat when he had sold
his merchandise, and walking back, making
such a trip every few weeks during the year
1831. Early in 1832 he began working about
for different persons at making rails and
washing sand, which was taken to Pittsburgh
to the glass makers. In the latter part of
1832, Jacob Strickler got his children together
again, Stewart, with the rest, joining him on

the old place known as the Jimtown farm, where Stewart remained till 1835 when he married Mary Newcomer, of Tyrone township, and bought a piece of land from his father at Jimtown, built thereon a house and barn and commenced farming In 1837 the great financial panic came and found Stewart badly in debt for his farm He said "times were then so hard that I had to pay fifty cents in shin-plasters' to see a quarter in silver " He struggled on till 1840, when times began to improve, but farming being poor business, he found it necessary to exercise his ingenuity and began to conjure up ways to enable him to pull through and get out of debt At an early day there had been an iron furnace at the mouth of Jacob's creek known as Turnbull Furnace, but then long abandoned and in ruin Near it was a huge pile of cinders containing a great amount of iron unextracted from the ore Mr Strickler conceived the notion of taking the cinders to iron works in Pittsburgh, bought it for fifty cents a ton, built a large flatboat on which he carried the cinders to the city, and there sold it for four dollars and a half a ton, and afterward sold his boat, making something on it This enterprise stimulated him to greater effort, and early in 1842 he bought ten acres of coal land on the Youghiogheny river at the point now called Sterling Coal Works, built six ovens and began making coke, which he shipped by flatboats to Cincinnati, Ohio He carried on this business successfully for several years At the same time there were others engaged in the business, but they were not successful and became discouraged and gave it up About 1855 Mr Strickler bought eighty acres of coal land, known as the John Taylor farm, and began improving it with the intent to carry on the coal business as before, but on a larger scale In 1857 the Pittsburgh & Connellsville railroad was completed, and Mr Strickler put into operation on his farm eighty coke ovens At this time he built a sidetrack from his works to the main line of the railroad for the purpose of shipping coke and coal to the Graff Bennett Company of Pittsburgh keeping their furnace going from 1860 to 1864 with two thousand bushels per day He then sold a third interest in his business to the above named firm for $35 000, a few months afterward selling the balance to Shoenberger & Company for $45,000 Some-

where between 1835 and 1840, Mr Strickler bought all of his father's old farm, paying $30 per acre In the spring of 1864 he sold it to J K Ewing for $200 per acre the latter afterward selling it for over $400 an acre In 1867 he removed with a portion of his family to middle Tennessee, near the Cumberland mountains

Children of Stewart Strickler Caroline, married Alexander Hill, and died in 1879, Maria, married Richard Boyd (of previous mention), Lyman and Dempsey, both lived upon the John Smiley farm upon which their father worked in 1830, Martha, married Bowman Herbert, Harriet, married David Ramsey, of Tennessee, Kate married Dr James Thompson, of Tennessee, Dessie F married Joseph G Wilkinson then of Tennessee, now of Texas, other children Emily Hardy, George and Norman, died young Mr Strickler died aged over seventy years, and notwithstanding his serious labors in life and many dangers encountered, from some of which he barely escaped with his life, he kept his health and full possession of intellectual vigor until the last He was respected by his wide circle of acquaintances as a man of strict integrity and of nobility of heart Not only could he look back upon a life well spent, triumphant over early and great difficulties, but he was also entitled to enjoy the reflection that through his excellent judgment, advice and influence not a few persons in the region where he spent his most active years also were successful, enjoying many of them, the blessings of wealth

Children of Richard and Maria (Strickler) Boyd 1 Charles S, of Dawson, Pennsylvania 2 Edgar L, of whom further 3 Mary Lou, married Robert McCoy, and died in Colorado Springs Colorado 4 Herbert, superintendent of Adelaide plant of H C Frick Coke Company 5 Benton, now residing in Uniontown 6 George, deceased

(IV) Edgar L second son of Richard and Maria (Strickler) Boyd was born in Bullskin township, Fayette county Pennsylvania, October 8, 1863 He was educated in the public schools and at Mount Pleasant Academy He became a farmer and after working the home farm two years bought a farm of eighty acres in Connellsville township, where he yet resides For many years he followed dairy farming, but now is conducting regular farming operations He is a Republican, but very independent in political action He has served in several township offices, and is a member of the Methodist Episcopal church, his wife also being a communicant He married March 10, 1886, Molly E Chalfant, born May 1, 1861, near Johnstown Pennsylvania daughter of Dr William B and Ellen (Fowler) Chalfant

The Chalfants are of English descent early settlers in Pennsylvania, said to have arrived with William Penn William B, a grandson of Chads Chalfant, is said to have been the first Freemason to cross the mountains and settle in Fayette county He settled at Brownsville, and was a charter member of the first Masonic lodge established there He married Margaret McManimee Children Abner, Mordecai Basil James, Robert, Walter (of whom further) and Elizabeth Chads Chalfant was a wheelwright by trade and a circuit riding Methodist preacher He also conducted a farm Walter Chalfant was born in Brownsville Pennsylvania May 8, 1794 He became a farmer and owned the homestead farm He married a Quakeress, Mary Brown, and had issue Eliza, Chads (2), Samuel B a physician James, a farmer, died 1891, Fletcher, a soldier of the civil war Henry, a physician, Margaret, married Frank Wright of Greene county, Charles B, a physician, died 1862 William B, of whom further, Duncan, a veteran of the civil war, died in Nebraska Ann, married Jackson Mulholland This was a long lived family, their average at death being sixty-seven years

Dr William B Chalfant, son of Walter Chalfant, died December 19 1909 He married, June 28 1860 Ellen Fowler who died March 23, 1896 Children Molly E (of previous mention) Anna Belle now living in Scottdale, Pennsylvania Ora, died in infancy, Dr John Fowler died aged twenty-seven years, leaving children Edna and Beulah Carl R, died in infancy Ethel, married Homer Herbert of Seattle Washington, now deceased, Vivian resides in Seattle with her sister Ethel Ellen Fowler, wife of Dr William B Chalfant was a daughter of John and a granddaughter of George Fowler a revolutionary soldier, and a farmer of Bradford county, Pennsylvania He married Sarah Woods John Fowler came from Bedford to Ligonier Westmoreland county Pennsylvania, where he followed his trade of shoe-

maker He married Elizabeth Mickey, daughter of —— and Margaret (Speer) Mickey, both born in Ireland John and Elizabeth Fowler both died on their farm, which he bought after giving up his trade of shoemaker Their children Margaret, died in infancy, George, a shoemaker, died in Kansas, James a farmer, died in Crabtree, Pennsylvania, Sarah, married Samuel Payne, Margaret, married Dr Morrison, and died in Kansas, Ellen (of previous mention), wife of Dr William B Chalfant Alexander, a blacksmith died in Kansas, Mary, married J R Wadsworth and lives in Michigan, John, died young

Children of Edgar L and Molly E (Chalfant) Boyd 1 Earl Richard, born December 22, 1886, died March 18, 1894 2 Carroll, born March 19 1889, married Jennie Youthers, March 10, 1912 3 Ellen, born November 6, 1891 4 Pauline, May 31, 1894 5 Anna Mary, August 20 1899

(III) William Boyd, eldest son of BOYD Thomas Boyd (q v), and Nancy (Rice) Boyd, and grandson of William Boyd, the first settler, was born at the old Boyd homestead, Spring Hill, in Bullskin township, Fayette county, Pennsylvania, about the year 1800 He became a wealthy farmer and lumberman, owning several farms and a saw mill He ran the latter partly as a custom mill, sawing lumber for the neighborhood and doing a large business He married (first) —— Kell, (second) Lydia Ober Children of first wife James L., of whom further, Robert, a farmer of Fayette county, deceased Catherine died unmarried Children of second wife Frank, deceased, Hiram, now living near Erie, Ohio, Elizabeth, married Frank Robbins

(IV) James L eldest son of William Boyd and his first wife was born in Bullskin township, Fayette county, Pennsylvania died June 26, 1900 He was educated in the public school and grew to manhood at the home farm He was engaged a great part of his time on the public works in the county, also owning and cultivating a small farm During his latter life he operated this as a truck and vegetable farm He was a Republican in politics, and a member of the Baptist church He married (first) Eliza Myers born in Westmoreland county, Pennsylvania died Novem-

CPSIA information can be obtained
at www.ICGtesting.com
Printed in the USA
BVHW050846090723
666954BV00009B/581